Nonverbal Communication in Human Interaction

Second Edition

MARK L. KNAPP

Purdue University

Holt, Rinehart and Winston

New York   Chicago   San Francisco   Atlanta   Dallas
Montreal   Toronto   London   Sydney

To Human Body . . .
without whom
this book would never have been written

Consulting Editor: Michael Burgoon

Library of Congress Cataloging in Publication Data

Knapp, Mark L
  Nonverbal communication in human interaction.

  Bibliography: p.
  Includes indexes.
  1. Nonverbal communication. I. Title.
BF637.C45K37 1978   153   77-21262
ISBN 0-03-089962-1

Book and cover design by Arthur Ritter

Acknowledgments
Figure 1.1: From D. M. MacKay, "Formal Analysis of Communicative Processes," in R. Hinde (ed.) *Non-Verbal Communication* (New York: Cambridge University Press) 1972, p. 24.
Figure 1.2: From Nolan, "The Relationship Between Verbal and Nonverbal Communication," from *Communication and Behavior,* by G. J. Hanneman and W. J. McEwen, 1975, Addison-Wesley, Reading, Mass.
Figures 1.3 and 1.4: Reprinted from "Movements with Precise Meanings" by Paul Ekman in the *Journal of Communication* (26:3). Copyright © 1976 by the Annenberg School of Communications. All rights reserved.
Figure 2.9: From P. Ekman, "Cross-Cultural Studies of Facial Expression" in P. Ekman (ed.), *Darwin and Facial Expression* (New York: Academic Press) 1973, p. 206.
Table 3.1: Copyright 1954 by the American Psychological Association. Reprinted by permission.
Figure 3.2: From Figure 4, p. 92, in *Public Places and Private Spaces: The Psychology of Work, Play, and Living Environments,* by Albert Mehrabian. © 1976 by Basic Books, Inc., Publishers, New York.
Figure 4.1: From McCroskey, Larson, Knapp, *An Introduction to Interpersonal Communication,* ® 1971, p. 98. Reprinted by permission of Prentice-Hall, Inc., Englewood Cliffs, New Jersey.
Table 6.3: Adapted from N. M. Henley, *Body Politics: Power, Sex, and Nonverbal Communication* (Englewood Cliffs, N.J.: Prentice-Hall) 1977, p. 181. By permission.
Figure 9.2: From R. V. Exline, J. Thibaut, C. B. Hickey and P. Gumpert, "Visual Interaction in Relation to Machiavellianism and an Unethical Act," in R. Christie and F. L. Geis (Eds.) *Studies in Machiavellianism* (New York: Academic Press) 1970, p. 67.
Figure 10.2: From P. Ladefoged and R. Vanderslice, "The Voiceprint Mystique," Working Papers in Phonetics 7, University of California, Los Angeles (November, 1967) and reprinted in M. H. L. Hecker, "Speaker Recognition: An Interpretive Survey of the Literature," *ASHA Monographs* No. 16 (American Speech and Hearing Assn: Washington, D. C.) 1971, p. 70.
Table 10.4: From K. R. Scherer, "Acoustic concomitants of Emotional Dimensions: Judging Affect from Synthesized Tone Sequences," in S. Weitz (ed.) *Nonverbal Communication: Readings With Commentary* (New York: Oxford University Press) 1974, p. 109.

Preface

Typically, prefaces to second editions of textbooks begin with a statement that "a lot has happened" or "dramatic changes have occurred" since the first edition was published. The magnitude of these assessments may or may not be perceived by others, but they provide a useful *raison d'être* for the second edition. Keeping this in mind, I am still compelled to say that, in my opinion, phrases like "dramatic changes" approach understatement to describe public and scientific activity in the area of nonverbal communication during the last six years. Trade magazines and books provide a steady stream of popularized accounts of the "secrets of body language"; at least ten textbooks which were not available six years ago now compete for the same market served by this book—not to mention numerous specialized volumes which report research efforts in a particular area; there also seem to be an increasing number of college courses devoted exclusively to the study and understanding of nonverbal phenomena and some offerings have been instituted on the secondary and elementary level too; several new scholarly journals with a specific focus on nonverbal behavior have also been undertaken. Fortunately, the information in this area continues to emanate from many sources. Scholars in anthropology, child development and family relations, communication, counseling, education, ethology, linguistics, psychiatry, social psychology, sociology, and speech science contribute to our understanding of nonverbal behavior.

We all derive some obvious and important benefits from this continuing interest in nonverbal communications by both the public at large and researchers in the behavioral sciences. There are also some potential costs. One of these "costs" may be incurred when people see the nonverbal system of communication as an entity distinct and isolated from the total system of human communication. As I said in the preface to the first edition:

> In a sense, it is unfortunate that an entire book should be devoted to only one aspect of the total process of social interaction, because it may be deceiving. To prevent such deception, the reader should be cautioned that nonverbal communication is so inextricably bound up with verbal aspects of the communication process that we can only

separate them artificially. In actual practice such separation does not occur. Such dynamic interaction and dependence not only applies to the verbal and nonverbal systems, but also to the various areas of nonverbal communication treated in each chapter of this book. To leave the impression that you respond to someone's voice, appearance, facial expression, or the distance one stands from you, independently of one another is to leave you with a distorted impression of the process.

Similarly, we must be wary of those who proclaim that an understanding of nonverbal communication is somehow a magic elixir for success in interpersonal relations. There is a certain fascination with behavior which is on the periphery or completely out of our awareness. But understanding "body language" is much like understanding the nuances of persuading, informing, entertaining, expressing emotions, and managing interaction through verbal behavior, that is, it is only a part of understanding the total communication process; only a part of the skill necessary to become an effective communicator. It can be very important in some situations and not very important in others.

I have made a number of changes in this edition, but some things remain the same. For instance, I have tried to maintain a writing style which is scientifically accurate and, at the same time, interesting to read. As in the first edition, I have attempted to provide a thorough synthesis of the major nonverbal studies by behavioral scientists. Extensive bibliographies are again provided for those who desire greater depth in specific areas. This edition is again generally organized around various parts of the body. Throughout, however, the reader is reminded that communicative goals or outcomes are most often the result of many body parts acting together.

The current edition has five more chapters than the previous edition. Some of these chapters are totally new—for example, one chapter covers the development of nonverbal behavior in the species and in the child and another chapter is devoted to an analysis of skills in sending and receiving nonverbal signals. Some of the additional chapters resulted from the division of a single chapter into two chapters. Many new subheadings within the chapters include conversational turn-taking, greeting and goodbye rituals, nonverbal feedback, density and crowding, silence, speaker recognition by voice, the process of systematic observation, speech/body movement interrelationships, among others. Chapter One has an expanded discussion of traditionally "sticky wickets" for human communication theory in general as well as nonverbal communication in particalar—that is, intentionality, coding, classification systems, and definitions. These changes are a direct result of trying to update the material through the inclusion of the latest research and theory available. Additional research has also made much needed visual materials more accessible. As a result, this edition relies more heavily on the visual materials which are so central to the study of nonverbal communication.

Preface

The Instructor's Manual for this text has also been completely revised by Mary Wiemann. Behavioral objectives, participative exercises, test questions, and audio-visual resources can help instructors to more effectively adapt this text to classroom learning experiences.

For me, writing this was an enjoyable and important learning experience. Several people made major contributions to my well-being and enlightenment during the writing of this book. I now want to accentuate my private thank yous with a public acknowledgement. First, I'd like to thank everyone who had a part in making Lillian Davis who she is. She is a constant delight at work and play—and besides, it's nice to find someone who shares my view of sanity. The "Oryx" performed brilliantly as an omnipresent walking library of common and obscure references—not to mention a valuable contributor to the section on nonverbal communication in infancy and childhood. The patient understanding of my students, colleagues, Department Head, and Dean was critical. It allowed me to maintain an almost failsafe method for avoiding disturbances and interruptions while working on this manuscript—and also resulted in my being called the phantom professor. And to the many well-intentioned readers who felt obligated to send me their "interpretation" of the toilet paper photograph on the last page: "No, that's not what I intended!"

Hazel Crest, Illinois   MARK L. KNAPP

Contents

Contents

5
The Effects of Physical Appearance and Dress on Human Communication   152

6
The Effects of Physical Behavior on Human Communication   196

7
The Effects of Touching Behavior on Human Communication   242

8
The Effects of the Face on Human Communication   263

Contents

vii

Contents

viii

1 Nonverbal Communication: Basic Perspectives

Those of us who keep our eyes open can read volumes into what we see going on around us.
E. T. HALL

Herr von Osten purchased a horse in Berlin, Germany, in 1900. When von Osten began training his horse, Hans, to count by tapping his front hoof, he had no idea that Hans was soon to become one of the most celebrated horses in history. Hans was a rapid learner and soon progressed from counting to addition, multiplication, division, subtraction, and eventually the solution of problems involving factors and fractions. As if this were not enough, von Osten exhibited Hans to public audiences, where he counted the number of people in the audience or simply the number wearing eyeglasses. Still responding only with taps, Hans could tell time, use a calendar, display an ability to recall musical pitch, and perform numerous other seemingly fantastic feats. After von Osten taught Hans an alphabet which could be coded into hoofbeats, the horse could answer virtually any question—oral or written. It seemed that Hans, a common horse, had complete comprehension of the German language, the ability to produce the equivalent of words and numerals, and an intelligence beyond that of many human beings.

Even without the promotion of Madison Avenue, the word spread quickly, and soon Hans was known throughout the world. He was soon dubbed Clever Hans. Because of the obviously profound implications for several scientific fields and because some skeptics thought there was a gimmick involved, an investigating committee was established to decide, once and for all, whether there was any deceit involved in Hans' performances. Professors of psychology and physiology, the director of the Berlin Zoological Garden, a director of a circus, veterinarians, and cavalry officers were appointed to this commission of horse experts. An experiment with Hans from which von Osten was absent demonstrated no change in the apparent intelligence of Hans. This was sufficient proof for the commission to announce there was no trickery involved.

The appointment of a second commission was the beginning of the end for Clever Hans. Von Osten was asked to whisper a number into the horse's left ear while another experimenter whispered a number into the horse's right ear. Hans was told to add the two numbers—an answer none of the onlookers, von Osten nor the experimenter knew. Hans failed. And with further tests he continued to fail. The experimenter, Pfungst, discovered on further experimentation that Hans could only answer a question if someone in his visual field knew the answer.[1] When Hans was given the question, the onlookers assumed an expectant posture and increased their body tension. When Hans reached the correct number of taps, the onlookers would relax and make a slight movement of the head—which was Hans' clue to stop tapping.

The story of Clever Hans is frequently used in discussions concerning the capacity of an animal to learn verbal language. It also seems well suited to an introduction to the field of nonverbal communication. Hans' cleverness was not in his abilty to verbalize or understand verbal commands, but in his ability to respond to almost imperceptible and unconscious movements on the part of those surrounding him. It is not unlike that perceptiveness or sensitivity to nonverbal cues exhibited by a Clever Carl, Charles, Frank, or Harold when picking up a woman, closing a business deal, giving an intelligent and industrious image to a professor, knowing when to leave a party, and in a multitude of other common situations. This book is written for the purpose of expanding your conscious awareness of the numerous nonverbal stimuli which confront you in your everyday dialogue. Each chapter will summarize behavioral science research on a specific area of nonverbal communication. First, however, it is necessary to develop a few basic perspectives—a common frame of reference, a lens through which we can view the remaining chapters.

Perspectives on Conceptualizing and on Defining Nonverbal Communication

Conceptually, the term *nonverbal* is subject to a variety of interpretations—just like the term *communication*. The basic issue seems to be whether the events traditionally studied under the heading *nonverbal* are

[1]O. Pfungst, *Clever Hans, The Horse of Mr. Von Osten* (New York: Holt, Rinehart and Winston, 1911).

literally *non*verbal. Ray Birdwhistell, a pioneer in nonverbal research, is reported to have said that studying *nonverbal* communication is like studying *noncardiac* physiology. His point is well taken. It is not easy to dissect human interaction and make one diagnosis which concerns only verbal behavior and another which concerns only nonverbal behavior. The verbal dimension is so intimately woven and so subtly represented in so much of what we have previously labeled *non*verbal that the term does not always adequately describe the behavior under study. Some of the most noteworthy scholars associated with nonverbal study refuse to segregate words from gestures and hence work under the broader terms *communication* or *face to face interaction.*

The theoretical position taken by Dance concerning the whole process of communication goes even further in order to call to our attention that perhaps not everything labeled nonverbal is literally nonverbal. Dance might even argue that there is no such thing as uniquely human communication that is nonverbal. He takes the position that all symbols are verbal and that human communication is defined as the eliciting of a response through verbal symbols. He does not deny the fact that we may engage in nonverbal behaviors, but the instant these behaviors are interpreted by another in terms of words, they become verbal phenomena. In other words, we should be careful not to confuse the label attached to the type of signal *produced* (nonverbal) with the internal code for *interpreting* the signal (frequently verbal). Generally, when people refer to nonverbal behavior they are talking about the signal(s) to which meaning will be attributed—not the process of attributing meaning. Not always, however, as we shall soon see.

In the process of making a useful distinction between the terms *vocal* and *verbal*, we get further insights into Dance's point of view concerning nonverbal communication.

> The confusion of *verbal* and *vocal* in reference to communication exists in a great deal of our literature and dialogue. A verbal symbol can be either vocal or nonvocal. A vocal sound need not always be symbolic. A scream, for instance, may be vocal and nonverbal on the reflex discharge level. On the other hand, a scream, when interpreted by a passerby in terms of circumstances, may be vocal and also may have meaning for the passerby beyond the meaning to the screamer. Thus, the passerby's meaning, being the result of his past actual or vicarious experience, is interpreted by him in terms of words and becomes both vocal and verbal. A traffic signal derives its meaning from the observer's past experiences in learning law and order through words. The traffic signal, then, is nonvocal and verbal. The essential attribute of *verbal* is not the existence of sound in acoustic space, but the representation of abstractions of many specific instances by one sign that then becomes a sign of signs or a symbol.[2]

[2]F. E. X. Dance, "Toward a Theory of Human Communication," in F.E.X. Dance (ed.), *Human Communication Theory* (New York: Holt, Rinehart and Winston, 1967), p. 290.

Nonverbal Communication: Basic Perspectives

3

Dance's comments make it clear that in order to conceptualize and define our area of study, we now have to be concerned about vocal/nonvocal distinctions as well as verbal/nonverbal ones. It is not always a clear distinction to have to make. Consider the following: (1) Not all acoustic phenomena are vocal—for example, knuckle cracking; a gurgling stomach; farting; slapping one's thigh, another's back, or a desk top; snapping one's fingers; and clapping. (2) Not all nonacoustic phenomena are nonverbal—for example, some of the gestures used in American Sign Language used by many deaf people. (3) Not all vocal phenomena are the same—some are respiratory and some are not. A sigh or prespeaking inspiration of breath may be considered vocal and respiratory; a click or "tch, tch!" might be classified as vocal but nonrespiratory. (4) Not all words or "apparent" word strings are clearly or singularly verbal—for example, onomatopoetic words like *buzz* or *murmur* and non-propositional speech used by auctioneers and some aphasics. Neat categorization for each behavior under consideration is often difficult. More realistically, we should recognize the different nature of the behaviors we study, but we should also expect that there will be points of overlap—behaviors which fit some aspects of one category and some aspects of another.

The preceding definitional perspectives focus on the terms used. Another way of looking at this verbal/nonverbal dichotomy is to look at the information processing of the brain. As we said earlier, the common referent for nonverbal signals is the behavior produced; sometimes, however, the manner of interpreting these signals in the brain is the referent.

Nonverbal Information Processing. Although we frequently attach verbal labels to nonverbal behavior, there are times when we just can't verbalize something. There are times when we react to a face or voice without naming our impression first. There are times when we may be unaware of our response and/or what prompted it. There are times when we can only refer to our response as "intuition." Have you ever noticed how easy it is to spot a friend in a group of people and how difficult it may be to explain to another person how to spot that same friend by describing his or her features? The brain, needless to say, is a complex mechanism. Our understanding of how the brain works is still primitive, and we are revising theories and proposing new ones regularly.

Currently, many neurophysiologists believe that the two hemispheres of the brain specialize in very different information processing. It is believed that the left hemisphere processes mainly sequentially ordered, digital, verbal, or linguistic information; the right hemisphere processes mainly nonverbal, analogic, or Gestalt information. The right hemisphere of the brain, then, is credited with processing visual/spatial relationships which compose a large part of what is traditionally treated as nonverbal stimuli. Few argue that either side of the brain deals exclusively with a particular kind of information. In fact, a recent case illustrates how adaptable the brain can be.

Bruce Lipstadt had the left hemisphere of his brain removed when he was 5½ years old.[3] Few people had hope for the development of his verbal ability, and most thought the operation would paralyze part of his body. Twenty-six years later, Bruce has an I.Q. of 126 (better than nine out of ten people), swims, rides, bikes, and got an A in a statistics course. Since his speech is normal, it is assumed that the right side took over many of the functions formerly conducted mainly by the left side. Obviously, this does not always happen as a result of operations of this type. It does suggest that while our right and left hemispheres seem to specialize in processing certain information, they are by no means limited to one type.

Some people, then, would classify nonverbal phenomena as those which are processed by the right hemisphere of the brain; verbal as those which are processed by the left hemisphere. The apparent nonexclusivity of each hemisphere, however, would still subject our classification to a certain margin of error. In the Lipstadt case, the error would have been sizable. Perhaps one of the most important implications of this knowledge of information processing is for our methods of testing nonverbal ability and conducting research. We may, for instance, be paying far too much attention to verbal recall in assessing nonverbal skills or reactions. This issue will be discussed further in Chapter 11.

Another way of defining an area of study is to delimit the kind of behavior to be examined. This, then, raises the question of whether we should consider all unspoken events as nonverbal phenomena (for example, raindrops falling on your head) or whether we should narrow our focus to a particular kind of human exchange. This confronts us with the important matter of intentionality—that is, conscious awareness of signals being sent and/or received for a particular purpose.

Intentionality. Sometimes we design a message very carefully and the other person doesn't get it; sometimes we do things we aren't even aware of and other people respond as if we had deliberately designed the behavior to evoke a particular response.Figure 1.1 illustrates these and other possible patterns.

The distinctions presented in Figure 1.1 may have important implications for defining, investigating, and interpreting this area we are calling nonverbal communication. As MacKay says:

> Situations of these four types may be expected to differ radically both in their dynamics and in the categories of scientific explanation that they will demand in

[3]R. Kotulak, "With Half a Brain, His IQ Is 126, and Doctors Are Dumbfounded," *Chicago Tribune* (November 7, 1976): section 1, p. 6.

Nonverbal Communication: Basic Perspectives

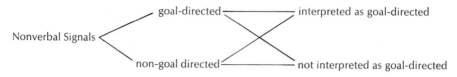

Figure 1.1 MacKay's Model of Intentionality

order to be fully understood. It seems important that experiments on non-verbal 'communication' should be designed as far as possible to distinguish between them.[4]

Perhaps the process of deciding whether an act fits one of two extremes (intentional or goal-directed vs. unintentional or non-goal-directed) forces us to choose an alternative which might best be explained by considering the *degree* of intentionality. We do have experiences which seem to defy this either/or classification of intent. As a sender you may be aware that your behavior caused another person to dislike you, but you can't be sure in your own mind whether your behavior was consciously planned or just seemed to appear spontaneously in response to the unpleasant qualities you saw in the other person. As a receiver, you may feel a person has been rude to you, but it is not clear in your own mind the extent to which the person "didn't know any better" or *wanted* you to feel bad. Determining whether intentionality is more productively thought of in terms of degrees or gradations is only one of several problematic issues in this area.

For instance, the time we choose to assess intentionality may be very important. Your awareness of doing something during the interaction may be very low, but as soon as it is brought to your attention you may feel the need to explain the degree of intent (whether your awareness has changed or not)—for example,

"Did you know you were pounding your fist into the chair during our argument last night?"

"No. If I was, it didn't mean anything."
or
"I wasn't aware of it, but I must have been unconsciously trying to show you how aggressive you made me feel."

Attributions of intention may also vary depending on the nature of the behavior in question. Some people feel spoken words are generally designed with some goal in mind, but what about situations where you "didn't mean to say that" or

[4]D.M. MacKay, "Formal Analysis of Communicative Processes," in R. A. Hinde (ed.) *Non-Verbal Communication* (New York: Cambridge University Press) 1972, p. 24. For those interested in a more detailed schema of the interrelationships of meaning, usage, and intent from both encoder and decoder perspectives, see P. Ekman and W. V. Friesen, "The Repertoire of Nonverbal Behavior: Categories, Origins, Usage and Coding," *Semiotica* 1 (1969) pp. 53-58.

Nonverbal Communication: Basic Perspectives

ritualistic verbal exchanges like: "Hi." "Hi." "How ya doin'?" "Fine." "How 'bout you?" "Fine."? How much conscious intent is represented here? Some people feel that the more easily observed behaviors are subject to greater control—and therefore, are more likely to be intentional. In other instances, we alter our expectations about intentionality based on who we are communicating with—for example, "We've known each other for ten years, Schultz. Don't tell me you didn't know what you were doing." Of course, we are more confident in attributing intentionality to someone if we perceive the same message in several channels.

In some situations, it is important to know why a person is judging another's degree of intention. Is it an experimenter whose subjects have behaved contrary to the hypotheses? Is it a person who must attribute a certain intent to you in order to justify his or her own behavior? And finally, there are certain environments which will cause us to focus or attend to the issue of intention more than others. Take the act of being bumped by another person, for instance. At a crowded football stadium, the question of the person's intent may not even be considered; getting bumped while walking down an uncrowded hallway may be another matter entirely. Needless to say, a full understanding of the nuances of intentionality poses many difficult barriers. Sorting out the intentions based on or attributed to expectations, perceptions, and post hoc analyses is only the beginning. However, we also know the issues facing us are important enough so they cannot be dismissed or ignored. Knowing the extent to which a person's behavior is consciously planned to elicit certain desired responses is important information for any practicing communicator. For the communication scholar, it may be a factor in delimiting the type of behavior studied.

Wiener and his colleagues, for instance, have proposed a research program in nonverbal communication which focuses entirely on those behaviors which are considered to be part of a shared code.[5] A set of behaviors constitutes a code in this conceptualization, if it can be shown that the behaviors have referents and that these referents are known and used by a group of people. Awareness and intent, then, take on a central role. To observe nonverbal communication, according to this schema, we need only observe a person making something public via the nonverbal code and a receiver responding systematically to that code.

The logic behind this conceptualization goes like this: (1) You start with a known code, for example, verbal language. (2) Nonverbal behaviors associated with certain verbal behaviors are then identified. (3) When the verbal channel is eliminated, these nonverbal behaviors will predictably be introduced for

[5]M. Wiener, S. Devoe, S. Rubinow, and J. Geller, "Nonverbal Behavior and Nonverbal Communication," *Psychological Review* 79 (1972): 185–214.

Nonverbal Communication: Basic Perspectives

communicating. (4) If the introduction of the nonverbal behaviors does not significantly change the receiver's understanding of the message, then those nonverbal behaviors are considered a substitute for verbal behavior and therefore components of a nonverbal code.

For clarity, let's look at some of the behaviors Wiener and his research group have hypothesized to be components of this nonverbal code.

First there are pantomimic gestures—formal or improvisational. The formal pantomimic gestures substitute for or add redundancy to the verbal. Waving good-bye or signaling "A-OK" with a circle made from the thumb and index finger are examples of this type. Making a motion as if you were swinging a baseball bat would be considered an improvisational pantomimic gesture. Wiener says these are for emphasizing, concretizing, or focusing on a particular object being discussed verbally.

The second class of gestures co-occur with speech and serve to (1) specify the referent of an ambiguous verbal statement, (2) specify a speaker's relationship to his or her verbal message, and (3) specify the intensity or emphasis for a particular message. Pointing movements, for instance, may help reduce the ambiguity of a verbal referent like "you" by indicating which "you" is being talked about. The positioning of the palms may show very different orientations toward one's own message—for example, (1) palms up for uncertainty ("I think" or "I'm not sure"); (2) palms down for certainty ("clearly" or "absolutely"); or (3) palms out—facing toward the receiver—for assertions ("Let me say this...." or "Don't interrupt."). A slow continuous series of circular movements with the hand and/or arm may suggest nonspecificity—for example, "I mean more than the specific words I've used." There are slow to moderate oscillating movements of the hands which seem to suggest "either/or" or "one or the other" of two components. When we speak of a series of things, we may communicate discreteness by linear, stacatto-like movements of the arm and hand—for example, "We must consider A, B, and C." When we insert one of these chopping gestures after each letter it may suggest a separate consideration of all three letters; a single chop after C might indicate either a consideration of all three (as a group) or just C in particular. There are other rhythmic chopping gestures which are produced similarly, but do not seem to be as closely linked to the verbal content. These seem to imply emphasis. Expansion and contraction gestures—similar to those made by accordian players—help indicate size and extent of the subject being discussed verbally.

On the basis of the preceding hypotheses, Wiener and his colleagues would predict more uncertainty (palms up) and vagueness (circling) gestures when a person was asked to talk about a subject he or she didn't know much about; they would also predict a marked increase in pantomimic gestures when an adult speaks to a child or when a person speaks to a foreigner. This approach to studying nonverbal communication is heavily grounded in the assumption of

Nonverbal Communication: Basic Perspectives

8

code usage—that is, an agreed upon set of rules for determining meanings assigned to certain signals. Some are less optimistic about how fruitful the pursuit of a nonverbal code will be; others feel the pursuit is critical but first there is a need to distinguish the type of code we are likely dealing with when studying nonverbal phenomena.

Nonverbal Codes and Coding. Mehrabian, unlike Wiener, seemed to feel that the identification of a nonverbal code was impractical. Although he recognized the existence of some culture-bound and intercultural nonverbal signals which seem to meet the criteria for a code, he argues:

> Whereas verbal cues are definable by an explicit dictionary and by rules of syntax, there are only vague and informal explanations for the significance of various nonverbal behaviors. Similarly, there are no explicit rules for encoding or decoding paralinguistic phenomena or the more complex combinations of verbal and nonverbal behavior in which the nonverbal elements contribute heavily to the significance of a message.[6]

Instead of trying to classify behavior as either nonverbal or verbal, Mehrabian chose instead to use an "explicit-implicit" dichotomy. In other words, Mehrabian felt that it was the subtlety of a signal which brought it into the nonverbal realm—and subtlety seemed to be directly linked to a lack of explicit rules for coding.

Mehrabian's work has focused primarily on the referents people have for various configurations of nonverbal and/or implicit behavior—that is, the meaning you attach to these behaviors. The results of extensive testing reveal a threefold perspective:[7] (1) Immediacy. Sometimes we react to things by evaluating them—positive or negative, good or bad, like or dislike. (2) Status. Sometimes we enact or perceive behaviors which indicate various aspects of status to us—strong or weak, superior or subordinate. (3) Responsiveness. This third category refers to our perceptions of activity—slow or fast, active or passive. Most of this work, however, is dependent on subjects translating their reactions to an unspoken act into one identified by verbal descriptors. We have already addressed this issue in our discussion of the way the brain processes different pieces of information. Now let's look at it from the standpoint of the type of coding.

[6]A. Mehrabian, *Nonverbal Communication* (Chicago: Aldine-Atherton, 1972), p. 2.

[7]In various verbal and nonverbal studies over the last three decades, dimensions similar to Mehrabian's have been consistently reported by investigators from diverse fields studying diverse phenomena. It is reasonable to conclude, therefore, that these three dimensions seem to be basic responses to our environment and are reflected in the way we assign meaning to both verbal and nonverbal behavior. Cf. A. Mehrabian, "A Semantic Space for Nonverbal Behavior," *Journal of Consulting and Clinical Psychology* 35 (1970): 248–257; and A. Mehrabian, *Silent Messages* (Belmont, Calif.: Wadsworth, 1971).

Nonverbal Communication: Basic Perspectives

Ekman and Friesen have pointed out that verbal and nonverbal signals can be coded in many different ways.[8] Their conceptualization follows a continuum like this:

INTRINSIC _____ ICONIC _____ ARBITRARY
CODING   CODING   CODING

Before we explain these terms, it is important that you remember: (1) We are dealing with a continuum, not discrete categories. You may identify a behavior which seems to fall between two of these points. (2) Although verbal behavior seems primarily suited for the right side of the continuum and nonverbal for the middle and left, there are exceptions. (3) The primary distinguishing feature among these three types of coding is the proximity of the code to its referent.

Arbitrary coding puts the greatest distance between the code used and the referents for the code. Resemblance to the referent is nonexistent. Most words, for instance, are arbitrarily coded with letters which show no resemblance to the things they refer to. Neither the word *cat*, nor any of its letters, look like a cat. Onomatopoetic words, however, like *buzz* and *murmur*, do take on aspects of the sounds they are trying to describe. Some nonverbal signals may also be arbitrarily coded—for example, the motions involved in hand waving during the good-bye ritual do not seem to portray the activity of leaving with much fidelity.

Iconic coding preserves some aspects of the referent—that is, there is a close resemblance of the code to the referent. A three-dimensional life-sized wax figure of yourself would probably be the next best thing to actually seeing you (the referent) if one wanted to get an idea of what you were like. Other portrayals may look less like you—for example, a still photograph or a cartoon figure. Making your hand look like a gun, "slitting" your throat with your finger to indicate you're "finished", or indicating with your hands how close you'd like to be standing to someone (with each hand representing a person) are other examples of iconic coding.

Intrinsic coding puts the least distance between the code used and the referents for the code. At the extreme, we might even say the manner of coding is the referent itself. Pointing, moving closer to someone, or actually hitting the person are examples of behaviors which do not resemble something else—they *are* the something else.

Thus far we've introduced a lot of terms, concepts, and conflicting points of view. It's time to look at what we've learned. We've examined a lot of dichotomies: verbal/nonverbal; vocal/nonvocal; right brain/left brain;

[8]P. Ekman and W. V. Friesen, "The Repertoire of Nonverbal Behavior: Categories, Origins, Usage and Coding," *Semiotica* 1 (1969): 49–98.

Nonverbal Communication: Basic Perspectives

intentional/unintentional; coded/not coded. In each case we found the dichotomy inadequate to describe things which actually occur in varying degrees. Our analysis of the brain helped us understand why the verbalization of some nonverbal phenomena is so difficult sometimes. The way we process information in our brain also suggested the possibility of studying some nonverbal acts by asking subjects to respond nonverbally. Our examination of communicator intent cautioned us to look at sender intent and its relationship to perceived intent by the receiver. We haven't provided complete answers to the problems and questions posed so far, but in seeking the answers, scholars have provided vivid testimony to the complexity of the nonverbal world—and its relationship to the verbal domain. If we want to be precise, we can no longer settle for the simple explanation that if words are not spoken or written, we are dealing with nonverbal behavior.

To further summarize our explorations thus far, examine Figure 1.2. Nolan's model shows us how we can plot various verbal and nonverbal acts according to the channel used, the type of coding, and the degree of intent.[9] For instance, in one situation we might classify the word *buzz* as spoken, iconic,

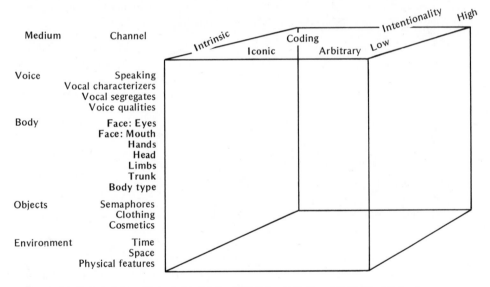

Figure 1.2. Adapted from Nolan's Model For Classifying Verbal and Nonverbal Behavior

[9]M. J. Nolan, "The Relationship Between Verbal and Nonverbal Communication," in G. H. Hanneman and W. J. McEwen (eds.), *Communication and Behavior* (Reading, Mass.: Addison-Wesley, 1975), p. 117.

Nonverbal Communication: Basic Perspectives

and highly intentional. We might classify a belch as a vocal characterizer, intrinsic, and unintentional.

Perspectives on Classifying Nonverbal Behavior

In their early classic, *Nonverbal Communication: Notes on the Visual Perception of Human Relations*, Ruesch and Kees outlined what they considered to be the primary elements in the study of nonverbal communication. This classification system was highly influential in providing a basis for most of the early work done in this field of nonverbal communication.

> In broad terms, nonverbal forms of codification fall into three distinct categories:
> *Sign Language* includes all those forms of codification in which words, numbers, and punctuation signs have been supplanted by gestures; these vary from the "monosyllabic" gesture of the hitchhiker to such complete systems as the language of the deaf.
> *Action Language* embraces all movements that are not used exclusively as signals. Such acts as walking and drinking, for example, have a dual function: on one hand they serve personal needs, and on the other they constitute statements to those who may perceive them.
> *Object Language* comprises all intentional and nonintentional display of material things, such as implements, machines, art objects, architectural structures, and—last but not least—the human body and whatever clothes or covers it. The embodiment of letters as they occur in books and on signs has a material substance, and this aspect of words also has to be considered as object language.[10]

Another classification schema can be derived by examining the nature of the writing and research currently being conducted in which the authors either explicitly or implicitly categorize their own work as subsumable under the label *nonverbal*.

I. BODY MOTION OR KINESIC BEHAVIOR

Body motion, or kinesic behavior, typically includes gestures, movements of the body, limbs, hands, head, feet and legs, facial expressions (smiles), eye behavior (blinking, direction and length of gaze, and pupil dilation) and posture. The furrow of the brow, the slump of a shoulder and the tilt of a head—all are within the purview of kinesics. Obviously, there are different types of nonverbal behavior just as there are different types of verbal behavior. Some

---

[10]J. Ruesch and W. Kees, *Nonverbal Communication: Notes on the Visual Perception of Human Relations* (Berkeley and Los Angeles: University of California Press, 1956), p. 189.

nonverbal cues are very specific; some more general. Some are intended to communicate; some expressive only. Some provide information about emotions; others carry information about personality traits or attitudes. In an effort to sort through the relatively unknown world of nonverbal behavior, Ekman and Friesen[11] developed a system for classifying nonverbal behavioral acts. These categories include:

A. Emblems. These are nonverbal acts which have a direct verbal translation or dictionary definition, usually consisting of a word or two or a phrase.[12] There is high agreement among members of a culture or subculture on the verbal "translation" of these signals. The gestures used to represent "A-OK" or "Peace" (also known as the victory sign) are examples of emblems for a large part of our culture. Mostly, these emblems are culture specific. For example, Figure 1.3 shows variations in suicide emblems depending on the popularity of a method (hanging, shooting, or stabbing) for a particular culture. There are, however, some emblems which portray actions which are common to the human species and seem to transcend a given culture. Eating (bringing hand up to mouth) and sleeping (tilting head in lateral position, almost perpendicular to the body—accompanied sometimes with eye closing and/or a hand or hands below the head like a pillow) are two examples of emblems which Ekman and his colleagues have observed in several cultures. Ekman also found that different cultures also seem to have emblems for similar classes of messages, regardless of the gesture used to portray it—for example, insults, directions (come, go, stop), greetings, departures, certain types of responses (yes, no, I don't know), physical state, and emotion. The number of emblems used within a given culture may vary considerably—from less than 100 (Americans) to more than 250 (Israeli students).

Emblems are often produced with the hands—but not exclusively. A nose-wrinkle may say "I'm disgusted!" or "Phew! It stinks!" To say "I don't know" or "I'm helpless" or "I'm uncertain" one might turn both palms up, shrug the shoulders, or do both simultaneously. Ekman believes that facial emblems probably differ from other facial expressions by being more stylized

---

[11]P. Ekman and W. V. Friesen, "The Repertoire of Nonverbal Behavior: Categories, Origins, Usage, and Coding," *Semiotica* 1 (1969): 49–98. Also see the following for updated reports with specific research foci: P. Ekman and W. V. Friesen, "Hand Movements," *Journal of Communication* 22 (1972): 353–374 and P. Ekman and W. V. Friesen, "Nonverbal Behavior and Psychopathology," in R. J. Friedman and M. M. Katz (eds.), *The Psychology of Depression: Contemporary Theory and Research* (Washington: Winston & Sons, 1974).

[12]One treatment of emblems *per se* can be found in P. Ekman, "Movements with Precise Meanings," *Journal of Communication* 26 (1976): 14–26. Figures 1.3, 1.4 and the research reported in this section are drawn primarily from this work. Additional information on American emblems can be found in Chapter 6.

Nonverbal Communication: Basic Perspectives

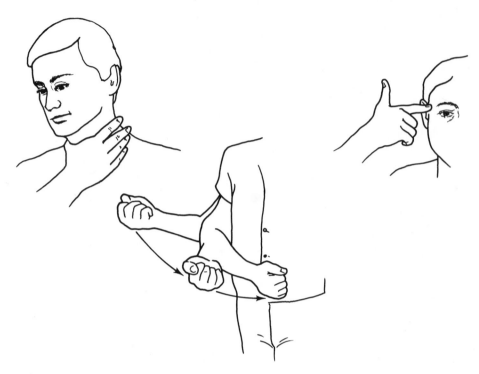

Figure 1.3 Emblems for Suicide (Top left: the South Fore, Papua, New Guinea; Top right: the United States; Bottom: Japan)

and being presented for longer or shorter duration. Facial emblems may also emphasize particular parts of the face—for example, the smile to indicate happiness or surprise shown by mechanically dropping the jaw or dramatically raising the eyebrows.

Emblems are frequently used when verbal channels are blocked (or fail) and are usually used to communicate. Some of the sign language of the deaf, nonverbal gestures used by television production personnel, signals used by two underwater swimmers, or motions made by two people who are too far apart to make audible signals practical—all these are situations ripe for emblem production.

Our own awareness of emblem usage is about the same as our awareness of word choice. Also, like verbal behavior, context can sometimes change the interpretation of the signal—that is, giving someone "the finger" can be either humorous or insulting, depending on the other cues accompanying it. Ekman has also observed "emblematic slips," analogous to slips of the tongue. He gives an example of a woman who was subjected to a stress interview by a person whose status forbade free expressions of dislike. The woman, unknown to herself or the interviewer, displayed "the finger" for several minutes during the interview.

Unlike verbal behavior, however, emblems are not generally strung together like words. There are exceptions. You may be talking on the phone when a visitor enters and you have to indicate "wait a minute," "come in," and "sit down" in succession. Finally, there seem to be some emblems which are specifically adapted to particular subgroups within a given culture. For instance, Figure 1.4 shows two gestures, one which seems to be used primarily when adults are talking to children ("no-no") and one which seems primarily limited to usage by children ("shame on you").

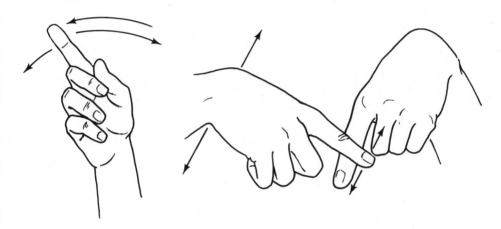

Figure 1.4 Finger Emblems (United States) for "No" (left) and "Shame on You" (right)

B. Illustrators. These are nonverbal acts which are directly tied to, or accompany, speech—serving to illustrate what is being said verbally. These may be movements which accent or emphasize a word or phrase, sketch a path of thought, point to present objects, depict a spatial relationship, depict the rhythm or pacing of an event, draw a picture of the referent, or depict a bodily action, and emblems used to illustrate verbal statements, either repeating or substituting for a word or phrase. Illustrators seem to be within our awareness, but not as explicitly as emblems. They are used intentionally to help communicate, but not as deliberately as emblems. Many factors can alter the frequency of illustrators displayed. We would expect to find more illustrators in face to face communication than when communicating over an intercom;[13] we would expect people who are excited and enthusiastic to display more illustrators than those who are not; and we would expect more illustrators during "difficult" communication situations—for example, not being able to find the right words to express a thought or being confronted by a receiver who either isn't paying attention or isn't comprehending what you're trying to say. Illustrators are probably learned by watching others.

C. Affect Displays.   These are primarily facial configurations which display affective states. Although the face is the primary source of affect, the body can also be read for global judgments of affect—for example, a drooping, sad body. Affect displays can repeat, augment, contradict, or be unrelated to, verbal affective statements. Once the display has occurred, there is usually a high degree of awareness, but it can occur without any awareness. Often, affect displays are not intended to communicate, but they can be intentional.

D. Regulators.   These are nonverbal acts which maintain and regulate the back and forth nature of speaking and listening between two or more interactants. They tell the speaker to continue, repeat, elaborate, hurry up, become more interesting, give the other a chance to talk, and so forth. Some of the behavior associated with greetings and good-byes may be regulators to the extent that they indicate the initiation or termination of face to face communication.

In recent years, the various nonverbal behaviors associated with turn-taking have been the regulators given most attention.[14] Turn-taking refers to the cues we use: to tell another person we want to talk, to keep another person from getting the floor away from us, to give up a speaking turn and ask the other person to continue, and to show we are finished speaking and the other person can take a turn. Generally we don't say these things verbally; they are communicated by many nonverbal behaviors. Probably the most familiar regulators are head nods and eye behavior. If head nods occur frequently in rapid succession, the message may be "hurry up and finish," but if the nods follow points made by the speaker and appear slow, deliberate, and thoughtful they may signal "keep talking" or "I like what you're saying." We found people who

[13]A. A. Cohen and R. Harrison, "Intentionality in the Use of Hand Illustrators in Face-to-Face Communication Situations," *Journal of Personality and Social Psychology* 28 (1973) 276–279. See also A. A. Cohen, "The Functions of Hand Illustrators in Giving Spatial Directions," *Journal of Communication* (in press).

[14]For a summary of these efforts, see J. M. Wiemann and M. L. Knapp, "Turn-Taking in Conversations," *Journal of Communication* 25 (1975): 75–92.

were trying to terminate a conversation severely decreased the amount of eye contact with the other person.[15]

Regulators seem to be on the periphery of our awareness and are generally difficult to inhibit. They are like overlearned habits and are almost involuntary, but we are very much aware of these signals sent by others.

E. Adaptors.   These nonverbal behaviors are perhaps the most difficult to define and involve the most speculation. They are labeled adaptors because they are thought to develop in childhood as adaptive efforts to satisfy needs, perform actions, manage emotions, develop social contacts, or perform a host of other functions. Ekman and Friesen have identified three types of adpators: self-, object-, and alter-directed.

Self-adaptors, as the term implies, refer to manipulations of one's own body—for example, holding, rubbing, squeezing, scratching, pinching, or picking oneself. Often these self-adaptors will increase as a person's anxiety level increases. Picking one's nose can be a self-adaptor; an adult who wipes the corner of his or her eye during times of sadness (as if to brush away tears) may be showing a response which reflects early experiences with sadness. Ekman and his colleagues have found the "eye cover act" to be associated with shame and guilt, and the "scratch-pick act" to be associated with hostility—aggression toward oneself or toward another displaced onto oneself.

Alter-adaptors are learned in conjunction with our early experiences with interpersonal relations—giving and taking from another, attacking or protecting, establishing closeness or withdrawing, and the like. Leg movements may be adaptors, showing residues of kicking aggression, sexual invitation, or flight. Ekman believes that many of the restless movements of the hands and feet which have typically been considered indicators of anxiety may be residues of adaptors necessary for flight from the interaction. An example from the interaction behavior of baboons will help illustrate the nature of these alter-adaptors. When a young baboon is learning the fundamentals of attack and aggression, the mother baboon is watching from close by. The young baboon will enact aggressive behavior, but will also turn the head laterally—to check whether the mother is still there. As an adult, the baboon still performs this lateral head movement in threatening conditions even though the mother is no longer there and no functional purpose seems to be served by this movement.

Object-adaptors involve the manipulation of objects and may be derived

[15]M. L. Knapp, R. P. Hart, G. W. Friedrich, and G. M. Shulman, "The Rhetoric of Goodbye: Verbal and Nonverbal Correlates of Human Leave-Taking," *Speech Monographs* 40 (1973): 182–198. A more complete elaboration of this and related studies dealing with regulators can be found in Chapter 6.

Nonverbal Communication: Basic Perspectives

from the performance of some instrumental task—for example, smoking, writing with a pencil, and so on. Although we are typically unaware of performing these adaptor behaviors, we are probably most aware of the object-adaptors. They are often learned later in life, and there seem to be fewer social taboos associated with them.

Since there do seem to be social constraints on displaying these adaptive behaviors, they are more often seen when a person is alone. At least, we would expect that we would see the full act rather than just a fragment of it. Alone you might pick your nose without inhibition; with other people you may just touch your nose or rub it "casually." If the full act is performed it is probably intrinsically coded; fragments of the act are more likely to be iconically coded. Adaptors are not intended for use in communication, but they may be triggered by verbal behavior in a given situation which is associated with conditions occurring when the adaptive habit was first learned.

II. PHYSICAL CHARACTERISTICS

Whereas the previous section was concerned with movement and motion, this category covers things which remain relatively unchanged during the period of interaction. They are influential nonverbal cues which are not movement-bound. Included are such things as physique or body shape, general attractiveness, body or breath odors, height, weight, hair, and skin color or tone.

III. TOUCHING BEHAVIOR

For some, kinesic study includes touch behavior; for others, however, actual physical contact constitutes a separate class of events. Some researchers are concerned with touching behavior as an important factor in the child's early development; some are concerned with adult touching behavior. Subcategories may include stroking, hitting, greetings and farewells, holding, guiding another's movements, and other, more specific instances.

IV. PARALANGUAGE

Simply put, paralanguage deals with how something is said and not what is said. It deals with the range of nonverbal vocal cues surrounding common speech behavior. Trager felt paralanguage had the following components:[16]

A. Voice Qualities. This includes such things as pitch range, pitch con-

---

[16]G. L. Trager, "Paralanguage: A First Approximation," *Studies in Linguistics* 13 (1958): 1-12.

trol, rhythm control, tempo, articulation control, resonance, glottis control, and vocal lip control.

B. Vocalizations.

1. *Vocal characterizers.* This includes such things as laughing, crying, sighing, yawning, belching, swallowing, heavily marked inhaling or exhaling, coughing, clearing of the throat, hiccupping, moaning, groaning, whining, yelling, whispering, sneezing, snoring, stretching, and the like.

2. *Vocal qualifiers.* This includes intensity (overloud to oversoft), pitch height (overhigh to overlow), and extent (extreme drawl to extreme clipping).

3. *Vocal segregates.* These are such things as "uh-huh," "um," "uh," "ah," and variants thereof.

Related work on such topics as silent pauses (beyond junctures), intruding sounds, speech errors, and latency would probably be included in this category.

V. PROXEMICS

Proxemics is generally considered to be the study of our use and perception of social and personal space. Under this heading, we find a body of work called small group ecology which concerns itself with how people use and respond to spatial relationships in formal and informal group settings. Such studies deal with seating arrangements, and spatial arrangements as related to leadership, communication flow, and the task at hand. The influence of architectural features on residential living units and even on communities is also of concern to those who study human proxemic behavior. On an even broader level, some attention has been given to spatial relationships in crowds and densely populated situations. Our personal space orientation is sometimes studied in the context of conversational distance—and how it varies according to sex, status, roles, cultural orientation, and so forth. The term *territoriality* is also frequently used in the study of proxemics to denote the human tendency to stake out personal territory—or untouchable space—much as wild animals and birds do.

VI. ARTIFACTS

Artifacts include the manipulation of objects in contact with the interacting persons which may act as nonverbal stimuli. These artifacts include perfume, clothes, lipstick, eyeglasses, wigs and other hairpieces, false eyelashes, eyeliners, and the whole repertoire of falsies and "beauty" aids.

Nonverbal Communication: Basic Perspectives

VII. ENVIRONMENTAL FACTORS

Up to this point we have been concerned with the appearance and behavior of the persons involved in communicating. This category concerns those elements which impinge on the human relationship, but which are not directly a part of it. Environmental factors include the furniture, architectural style, interior decorating, lighting conditions, smells, colors, temperature, additional noises or music, and the like, within which the interaction occurs. Variations in arrangements, materials, shapes, or surfaces of objects in the interacting environment can be extremely influential on the outcome of an interpersonal relationship. This category also includes what might be called traces of action. For instance, as you observe cigarette butts, orange peels, and waste paper left by the person you will soon interact with, you are forming an impression which will eventually influence your meeting.

Perspectives on Nonverbal Communication in the Total Communication Process

We are constantly being warned against presenting material out of context. Although this book was written as a supplement to a treatment of verbal behavior, the fact is that the book deals almost exclusively with nonverbal communication. There is a danger that the reader may forget that nonverbal communication cannot be studied in isolation from the total communication process. Verbal and nonverbal communication should be treated as a total and inseparable unit. Birdwhistell makes this point when he says:

> My own research has led me to the point that I am no longer willing to call either linguistic or kinesic systems *communication* systems. All of the emerging data seems to me to support the contention that linguistics and kinesics are *infra-*communicational systems. Only in their interrelationship with each other and with comparable systems from other sensory modalities is the emergent communication system achieved.[17]

Argyle flatly states, "Some of the most important findings in the field of social interaction are about the ways that verbal interaction needs the support of nonverbal communications."[18] What are some of the ways in which verbal and nonverbal systems interrelate?

[17]R. L. Birdwhistell, "Some Body Motion Elements Accompanying Spoken American English," in *Communication: Concepts and Perspectives*, ed. I. Thayer (Washington, D.C.: Spartan Books, 1967), p. 71
[18]M. Argyle, *Social Interaction* (New York: Atherton Press, 1969), p. 70-71.

Nonverbal Communication: Basic Perspectives

Before we outline some of the verbal/nonverbal interrelationships, we should recall that there may be nonverbal interrelationships as well—that is, one nonverbal channel interacting with another. An example of this would be a loud "Well!" preceding a handshake, which makes you anticipate a firm handshake. Odors can shorten or lengthen interaction distance, interaction distance can affect vocal loudness, and so on. Argyle has identified the primary uses of nonverbal behavior in human communication as: (1) expressing emotion, (2) conveying interpersonal attitudes (like/dislike, dominance/submission, and the like), (3) presenting one's personality to others, and (4) accompanying speech for the purposes of managing turn-taking, feedback, attention, and the like.[19] Notice that none of these functions of nonverbal behavior are limited to nonverbal behavior alone—that is, we can express emotions, attitudes, ourselves and manage the interaction verbally too. In some cases, however, you will find that we rely more heavily on the verbal for some purposes and the nonverbal for others. Like words and phrases, nonverbal signals can have multiple meanings and multiple uses—for example, a smile can be part of an emotional expression, an attitudinal message, part of a self-presentation, or a listener response to manage the interaction. Nonverbal behavior can repeat, contradict, substitute for, complement, accent, or regulate verbal behavior.[20]

Repeating.   Nonverbal communication can simply repeat what was said verbally. For instance, if you told a person he had to go north to find a newspaper stand and then pointed in the proper direction, this would be considered repetition.

Contradicting.   Nonverbal behavior can contradict verbal behavior.[21] A classic example is the parent who yells to his or her child in an angry voice, "Of course I love you!" Or the not-so-confident person about to make a public speech who, despite trembling hands and knees and beads of perspiration on the brow, says, "I'm not nervous." If there is no reason to suspect conflicting cues might be present, we probably rely mainly on verbal messages. It has been said that when we receive contradictory messages on the verbal and nonverbal

[19]M. Argyle, *Bodily Communication* (New York: International Universities Press, 1975).

[20]Cf. P. Ekman, "Communication Through Nonverbal Behavior: A Source of Information About an Interpersonal Relationship," in *Affect, Cognition and Personality*, edited by S. S. Tomkins and C. E. Izard (New York: Springer, 1965).

[21]A sometimes subtle inconsistency can also be perceived within verbal communication. When you are trying to express an idea that you basically disagree with, the linguistic choices may reflect differences in directness—for example, "John has done good work" is less direct than "John does good work." Cf. M. Wiener and A. Mehrabian, *Language Within Language* (New York: Appleton-Century-Crofts, 1968).

Nonverbal Communication: Basic Perspectives

21

levels, we are more likely to trust and believe in the nonverbal message.[22] It is assumed that nonverbal signals are more spontaneous, harder to fake, and less apt to be manipulated. It is probably more accurate to say, however, that some nonverbal behaviors are more spontaneous and harder to fake than others— and that some people are more proficient than others at nonverbal deception.[23] With two contradictory cues—both of which are nonverbal—again we predictably place our reliance on the cues we consider harder to fake. Sometimes we choose to be more direct with nonverbal cues because we know they will be perceived as less direct.

Interestingly, young children seem to give less credence to certain nonverbal cues than do adults when confronted with conflicting verbal and nonverbal messages.[24] Conflicting messages in which the speaker smiled while making a critical statement were interpreted more negatively by children than adults. This was particularly true when the speaker was a woman. Other work casts a further shadow on the "reliance on nonverbal cues in contradictory situations" theory.[25] Shapiro found student judges to be extremely consistent in their reliance on either linguistic or facial cues when asked to select the affect being communicated from a list of incongruent faces (sketched) and written messages. Vande Creek and Watkins extended Shapiro's work by using real voices and moving pictures. The stimulus persons were portraying inconsistencies in the degree of stress in verbal and nonverbal channels. Again they found some respondants tended to rely primarily on verbal cues; some on nonverbal cues; and some responded to the degree of stress in general—regardless of the channels manifesting it. The cross-cultural research of Soloman and Ali suggests that familiarity with the verbal language may affect the reliance one has on verbal or nonverbal cues. They found, for instance, that persons who were not as familiar with the language used to construct the contradictory message would

[22]Some evidence to support this notion is found in the following two sources: E. Tabor, "Decoding of Consistent and Inconsistent Attitudes in Communication," (Ph.D. diss., Illinois Institute of Technology, 1970); and A. Mehrabian, "Inconsistent Messages and Sarcasm," in A. Mehrabian, *Nonverbal Communication* (Chicago: Aldine-Atherton, 1972), pp. 104–132. For an understanding of the cognitive processes used in interpreting inconsistent messages, see: D. E. Bugental, "Interpretations of Naturally Occurring Discrepancies Between Words and Intonation: Modes of Inconsistency Resolution," *Journal of Personality and Social Psychology* 30 (1974): 125–133.

[23]See pages 12–20 for a discussion of our level of awareness of various nonverbal behaviors.

[24]D. E. Bugental, J. W. Kaswan, L. R. Love, and M. N. Fox, "Child Versus Adult Perception of Evaluative Messages in Verbal, Vocal, and Visual Channels," *Developmental Psychology* 2 (1970): 367–375. Also see D. E. Bugental, L. R. Love, and R. M. Gianette, "Perfidious Feminine Faces," *Journal of Personality and Social Psychology* 17 (1971): 314–318.

[25]J. G. Shapiro, "Responsivity to Facial and Linguistic Cues," *Journal of Communication* 18 (1968): 11-17; L. Vande Creek and J. T. Watkins "Responses to Incongruent Verbal and Nonverbal Emotional Cues," *Journal of Communication* 22 (1972) 311–316; and D. Solomon and F. A. Ali, "Influence of Verbal Content and Intonation on Meaning Attributions of First-And-Second-Language Speakers," *Journal of Social Psychology* 95 (1975) 3-8.

Nonverbal Communication: Basic Perspectives

rely on the content for judgments of affective meaning. Those who knew the language well were more apt to rely on the vocal intonation for the affective meaning. So, it appears some people will rely more heavily on the verbal message while others will rely on the nonverbal. We don't know all the conditions which would affect these preferences. Although one source of our preferences for verbal or nonverbal cues may be learned experiences, others believe there may also be an even more basic genesis—such as right-left brain dominance.

Although there are times when inconsistent messages are produced to achieve a particular effect, such as sarcasm, there are some who feel a constant barrage of inconsistent messages can contribute to a psychopathology for the receiver. This may be particularly true when people have a close relationship and the receiver has no other people he or she can turn to for discussion and possible clarification of the confusion. Some research finds that parents of disturbed children produce more messages with conflicting cues;[26] other work suggests that the differences are not in conflicting cues, but in negative messages—that is, parents with disturbed children sent more negative messages.[27] Either situation is no doubt undesirable and the combination of negativity, confusion, and punishment can be very harmful.

Substituting.   Nonverbal behavior can substitute for verbal messages. When a dejected and downtrodden executive (or janitor) walks into his or her house after work, a facial expression substitutes for the statement, "I've had a rotten day." With a little practice, people soon learn to identify a wide range of these substitute nonverbal displays—all the way from "It's been a fantastic, great day!" to "Oh, God, am I miserable!" We do not need to ask for verbal confirmation of our perception. Sometimes, when substitute nonverbal behavior fails, the communicator resorts back to the verbal level. Consider the woman who wants her date to stop "making out" with her. She may stiffen, stare straight ahead, act unresponsive and cool. If the suitor still comes on heavy, she is apt to say something like, "Look Larry, please don't ruin a nice friendship," and so on.

Complementing.   Nonverbal behavior can modify, or elaborate on, verbal messages. A student may reflect an attitude of embarrassment when talking to a professor about a poor performance in class assignments. Further, nonverbal behavior may reflect changes in the relationship between the student and the professor. When a student's slow, quiet verbalizations and relaxed

[26]D. E. Bugental, L. R. Love, J. W. Kaswan and C. April, "Verbal-Nonverbal Conflict in Parental Messages to Normal and Disturbed Children," *Journal of Abnormal Psychology* 77 (1971): 6–10.
[27]N. G. Beakel and A. Mehrabian, "Inconsistent Communications and Psychopathology," *Journal of Abnormal Psychology* 74 (1969): 126–130.

posture change—when posture stiffens and the emotional level of the verbalized statements increases—this may signal changes in the overall relationship between the interactants. Complementary functions of nonverbal communication serve to signal one's attitudes and intentions toward another person.

Accenting. Nonverbal behavior may accent parts of the verbal message much as underlining written words, or *italicizing* them, serves to emphasize them. Movements of the head and hands are frequently used to accent the verbal message. When a father scolds his son about staying out too late at night, he may accent a particular phrase with a firm grip on the son's shoulder and an accompanying frown on his face. In some instances, one set of nonverbal cues can accent other nonverbal cues. Ekman, for instance, found that emotions are primarily exhibited by facial expressions, but that the body carries the most accurate indicators regarding the *level* of arousal.[28]

Regulating. Nonverbal behaviors are also used to regulate the communicative flow between the interactants. The way one person stops talking and another starts in a smooth, synchronized manner may be as important to a satisfactory interaction as the verbal content exchanged. After all, we do make judgments about people based on their regulatory skills—for example, "talking to him is like talking to a wall" or "you can't get a word in edgewise with her." When another person frequently interrupts or is inattentive we may feel this is a statement about the relationship—perhaps one of disrespect. There are rules for regulating conversations, but they are generally implicit. It isn't written down, but we seem to "know" that two people shouldn't talk at the same time, that each person should get an equal number of turns at talking if he or she desires it, that a question should be answered, and so forth. Wiemann's research, for instance, found that relatively minute changes in these regulatory behaviors (interruptions, pauses longer than three seconds, unilateral topic changes, and the like) resulted in sizable variations in how competent a communicator a person was.[29] As listeners, then, we are apparently attending to and evaluting a host of fleeting, subtle, and habitual features of another's conversational behavior. There are probably differences in the actual behaviors used to manage conversational flow across cultures or with certain subcultural groups. We know that as children are first learning these rules they use less subtle cues—for

[28]P. Ekman, "Body Position, Facial Expression and Verbal Behavior During Interviews," *Journal of Abnormal and Social Psychology* 68 (1964): 194–301. Also P. Ekman and W. V. Friesen, "Head and Body Cues in the Judgement of Emotion: A Reformulation," *Perceptual and Motor Skills* 24 (1967): 711–724.
[29]J. M. Wiemann, "An Exploration of Communicative Competence in Initial Interactions: An Experimental Study," Unpublished PhD dissertation, Purdue University, 1975.

Nonverbal Communication: Basic Perspectives

example, tugging on clothing, raising a hand, and the like. Some of the behaviors used to facilitate this conversational regulation follow.[30]

When we want to indicate we are finished speaking and the other person can start, we may increase our eye contact with the other person. This is often accompanied by the vocal cues associated with ending declarative or interrogative statements. If the other person still doesn't pick up the conversational "ball" we might extend silence or interject a "trailer"—for example, "you know..." or "so, ah..." Keeping another from getting in means we have to keep long pauses from occurring, decrease eye contact, and perhaps raise the volume if the other tries to "get in." When we don't want to take a speaking turn we might give the other some reinforcing head nods and maintain attentive eye contact—and, of course, keep from speaking when the other begins to yield. When we do want the floor we might raise our index finger, enact an audible inspiration of breath with a straightening of the posture as if we were "ready" to take over. Rapid nodding may signal the other to hurry up and finish, but if we have trouble getting in we may have to talk simultaneously for a few words or engage in "stutter starts" which, hopefully, will be more easily observed cues to exemplify our desire.

Conversational beginnings and endings also act as regulatory points. When greeting others, eye contact signals that the channels are open. A slight head movement and an "eyebrow flash" (a barely detectable but distinct up and down movement of the eyebrows) may be present. The hands are also used in greetings for salutes, waves, handshakes, handslaps, emblematic signals like the peace or victory sign, a raised fist, or thumbs up. Hands may also perform grooming activities (putting fingers through one's hair) or be involved in various touching activities like kissing, embracing, or hitting another on the arm. The mouth may form a smile or an oval shape—as if one were ready to start talking.[31]

Saying goodbye in semiformal interviews brought forth many nonverbal behaviors, but the most common included the breaking of eye contact more often and for longer periods of time, positioning one's body toward an exit, leaning forward and nodding. Less frequent, but very noticeable were accenting behaviors—for example, "This is the termination of our conversation and I don't want you to miss it!" These accenters included what we called explosive

[30]Vocal cues involved in the turn-taking mechanism are treated in Chapter 10. For further reading in this area, see S. Duncan, "Some Signals and Rules for Taking Turns in Conversations," *Journal of Personality and Social Psychology* 23 (1972): 283–292; S. Duncan, "Toward a Grammar for Dyadic Conversation," *Semiotica* 9 (1973): 29–46; and J. M. Wiemann, "An Exploratory Study of Turn-Taking in Conversations: Verbal and Nonverbal Behavior," unpublished M.S. thesis, Purdue University, 1973.

[31]P. D. Krivonos and M. L. Knapp, "Initiating Communication: What Do You Say When You Say Hello?" *Central States Speech Journal* 26 (1975): 115–125.

Nonverbal Communication: Basic Perspectives

hand and foot movements—raising the hands and/or feet and bringing them down with enough force to make an audible slap while simultaneously using the hands and feet as leverage to catapult out of your seat. A less direct manifestation of this is to place your hands on your thighs or knees in a "leveraging" position (as if you were soon to catapult) and hope that the other person picks up the good-bye cue.[32]

Like the preceding studies of greetings and farewells, the future of research in human communication will also require an analysis of verbal and nonverbal behavior as an inseparable unit. Some efforts in this direction have already been made and they are reported in Chapter 6. Harrison[33] and Buehler and Richmond[34] have outlined basic frameworks for the analysis of verbal and nonverbal behavior in two-person settings. Reece and Whitman,[35] among others, are trying to isolate the verbal and nonverbal components which convey interpersonal "warmth." Exline[36] is trying to relate eye behavior to various kinds of verbal material. Agulera[37] found touch gestures by nurses changed the nature of their verbal interaction with patients. Goldman-Eisler[38] is studying the predictabilty of verbal content following pauses of various types and lengths.

Birdwhistell feels that the whole system of body motion is comparable to spoken language. He reports the existence of kinemes and various types of kinemorphs which combine to form higher level syntactic structures. These kinesic units are comparable to the phoneme, morpheme, and other syntactic units used to analyze spoken language. He even goes so far as to state that a well-trained "linguistic-kinesiologist" should be able to tell what movements a man is making simply by listening to his voice. In like manner, he claims to be able to tell what language the late New York mayor, Fiorello LaGuardia, was speaking simply by watching his gestures. LaGuardia spoke Italian, Yiddish, and English.

[32]M. L. Knapp, R. P. Hart, G. W. Friedrich, and G. M. Shulman, "The Rhetoric of Goodbye: Verbal and Nonverbal Correlates of Human Leave-Taking," *Speech Monographs* 40 (1975): 182–198.

[33]R. Harrison, "Verbal-Nonverbal Interaction Analysis: The Substructure of an Interview" (paper presented to the Association for Education in Journalism, Berkeley, Calif., August, 1969).

[34]R. E. Buehler and J. F. Richmond, "Interpersonal Communication Behavior Analysis: A Research Method," *Journal of Communication* 13 (1963): 146–155.

[35]M. Reece and R. Whitman, "Expressive Movements, Warmth, and Verbal Reinforcement," *Journal of Abnormal and Social Psychology* 64 (1962): 234–236.

[36]R. V. Exline et al., "Visual Interaction in Relation to Machiavellianism and an Unethical Act," *American Psychologist* 16 (1961): 396. Also see R. V. Exline, D. Gray, and D. Schuette, "Visual Behavior in a Dyad as Affected by Interview Content and Sex of Respondent," *Journal of Personality and Social Psychology* 1 (1965): 201–209.

[37]D. C. Agulera, "Relationship Between Physical Contact and Verbal Interaction Between Nurses and Patients," *Journal of Psychiatric Nursing and Mental Health Services* 5 (1967): 5–21.

[38]F. Goldman-Eisler, *Psycholinguistics: Experiments in Spontaneous Speech* (New York: Academic Press, 1968).

Nonverbal Communication: Basic Perspectives

Historical Perspectives

The scientific study of nonverbal communication is primarily a post–World War II activity. This, of course, does not mean we can't find important early tributaries of knowledge; even ancient Greek scholars are said to have commented on what we would today call nonverbal behavior. If we traced the history of fields like psychiatry, dance, psychology, anthropology, philosophy, linguistics, sociology, speech, and animal behavior we would no doubt find important antecedents for today's work. Nonverbal studies have never been the province of any particular discipline. In the last half of the nineteenth century Delsarte (among others) attempted to codify and set forth rules for managing both "voice culture" and body movements/gestures. Although Delsarte's "science of applied esthetics" and the elocutionary movement gave way to a less formal, less stylized twentieth century, they represent one of several early attempts to identify and manage bodily expressions. Perhaps the most influential pre–twentieth century work was Darwin's *The Expression of the Emotions in Man and Animals* in 1872. This work spawned the modern study of facial expressions and many of his observations and ideas are now being validated by other researchers.[39]

During the first half of the twentieth century there were isolated studies of the voice, physical appearance and dress, and the face. An unsystematic look at the publications during this period suggests that studies of proxemics, the environment, and kinesics received even less attention, while the least attention was given to the investigation of eye behavior and touching. At least two influential works appeared during this period. The study of body types was given increased attention by Kretschmer's *Physique and Character* in 1925 and Sheldon's *The Variations of Human Physique* in 1940. Efron's 1941 classic, *Gesture and Environment*, introduced innovative ways of studying body language, set forth the important role of culture in shaping many of our gestures, and constructed a framework for classifying nonverbal behaviors which influences researchers today.[40]

The 1950s show a significant increase in the sheer number of nonverbal research efforts. Some of the milestones of this decade include the following. (1) Birdwhistell's *Introduction to Kinesics* in 1952 and Hall's *Silent Language* in 1959. These anthropologists were responsible for taking some of the principles of linguistics and applying them to nonverbal phenomena, providing new labels for the study of body movement (kinesics) and space (proxemics) and launching a program of research in each area. (2) The precision with which we

[39]A centennial tribute to Darwin's work is found in P. Ekman (ed.), *Darwin and Facial Expression: A Century of Research in Review* (New York: Academic Press, 1973).

[40]A tribute to the lasting influence of Efron's work is the republication of his work—thirty years after it was first published. Cf. D. Efron, *Gesture, Race and Culture* (The Hague: Mouton) 1972.

Nonverbal Communication: Basic Perspectives

classify and study vocal cues was greatly enhanced during this period by Trager's 1958 delineation of the components of paralanguage (Cf. pp. 18–19). (3) The concern of therapists for nonverbal cues had been evident for a long time (at least since Freud), but psychiatrist Jurgen Ruesch and photographer Weldon Kees combined their efforts to produce a most popular book entitled *Nonverbal Communication: Notes on the Visual Perception of Human Relations* in 1956. This was probably the first book to use the term *nonverbal communication* in its title. It provided additional theoretical insights into the origins, usage, and coding of nonverbal behavior and provided extensive visual documentation for the communicative role of environments. It was also in 1956 that Maslow's and Mintz's study of the environmental effects of a "beautiful" and "ugly" room was published—an oft-cited study which would certainly be a "highlight" in the history of environmental forces impinging on human communication. (4) Although the study of touching behavior had been the subject of little systematic research until this decade, Frank's comprehensive article, "Tactile Communication" appeared in 1957 and suggested a number of testable hypotheses.

If the 1950s produced an explosion in the quantity of nonverbal studies, the 1960s must be classified as a nuclear eruption. Specific areas of the body were the subject of extensive programs of research—for example, Exline's work on eye behavior; the Davitz work on vocal expressions of emotion which culminated in the book *The Communication of Emotional Meaning* in 1964; Hess' work on pupil dilation; Sommer's continued exploration of personal space and design (*Personal Space*, 1969); Goldman-Eisler's study of pauses and hesitations in spontaneous speech; and the study of a wide range of body activity by Dittman, Argyle, Kendon, Scheflen, and Mehrabian. It was also during this time period that psychologist Robert Rosenthal brought vividly to our attention the potential impact of these nonverbal subtleties when he showed how experimenters can affect the outcome of experiments and teachers can affect the growth of their students through nonverbal behavior (*Experimenter Effects in Behavioral Research*, 1966, and *Pygmalion in the Classroom*, 1968). Perhaps the classic theoretical piece of the 1960s was Ekman's and Friesen's article on the origins, usage, and coding of nonverbal behavior. This article, as we have previously noted, distinguished five areas of nonverbal study which compose a major part of Ekman's and Friesen's current research—that is, emblems, illustrators, affect displays, regulators, and adaptors.

The 1970s began with a journalist's account of nonverbal study from the perspective of a handful of researchers (Fast's *Body Language*, 1970). This best-selling volume was followed by a steady stream of books which attempted to make nonverbal findings understandable and usable to the American public. These books, in the interest of simplification and readability, often misrepresented findings when recounting how to make a sale, detect deception, assert one's dominance, obtain a partner for sex, and the like.

Nonverbal Communication: Basic Perspectives

The 1970s are also a time of summarizing and synthesizing. Ekman's research on the human face (*Emotion in the Human Face*, 1972, with W. V. Friesen and P. Ellsworth); Mehrabian's research on the meaning of nonverbal cues of immediacy, status, and responsiveness (*Nonverbal Communication*, 1972); Scheflen's kinesic research in the framework of general systems theory (*Body Language and Social Order*, 1972); Hess' study of pupillometrics (*The Tell-Tale Eye*, 1975); Argyle's study of body movement and eye behavior (*Bodily Communication*, 1975, and *Gaze and Mutual Gaze*, with M. Cook, 1975); Montagu's *Touching* (1971); and Birdwhistell's *Kinesics and Context,* 1970, are all attempts to bring together lengthy research programs with specific foci in a single volume.

Although such books were able to arouse the public's interest in this research, they had, as expected, additional fallout.[41] Readers of the popular literature were too often left with the idea that reading nonverbal cues was *the* key to success in any human encounter; some of these books left implied that single cues (legs apart) represent single meanings (sexual invitation). Not only is it important to look at nonverbal *clusters* of behavior, but also to recognize that nonverbal meaning, like verbal, is rarely limited to a single denotative meaning. Some of these popularized accounts do not sufficiently remind us that the meaning of a particular behavior is often understood by looking at the context in which the behavior occurs—for example, looking into someone's eyes may reflect affection in one situation and aggression in another.

Another common reaction to such books was the concern that once the nonverbal code was "broken" we would be totally transparent—people would know everything about us because we couldn't control these nonverbal signals. As you'll learn from this book, we have varying degrees of control over our nonverbal behavior. Some behavior is very much under our control; other behavior is not (but may be once awareness is increased). Further, it is not at all unlikely that, as soon as someone feels he has an understanding of your body language, you'll modify it and make adaptations. We've been studying verbal behavior for over two thousand years, and we know a lot about the impact of certain verbal strategies—but we're still a long way from understanding the totality of verbal behavior.

Currently we are also experiencing further specialization—for example, books devoted to territoriality or environmental factors. Some fusion is also beginning to take place as researchers combine many nonverbal and verbal variables for studying a given phenomenon. We're also beginning to look carefully at methods of testing one's ability to send and receive nonverbal cues. And a number of scientists who formerly specialized in animal studies are now

[41]J. H. Koivumaki, "Body Language Taught Here," *Journal of Communication* 25 (1975): 26–30. Also see R. Harrison, "Body Language Revisited," *Journal of Communication* 25 (1975): 223–224.

Nonverbal Communication: Basic Perspectives

applying similar methods and hypotheses to the study of human behavior—an approach called human ethology. Such a brief historical tour inevitably leaves out many important contributions. The preceding purports to be nothing but a personal attempt to highlight some important developments and depict a general background for current perspectives.

Current Perspectives: Nonverbal Communication and American Society

The importance of nonverbal communication would be undeniable if sheer quantity were the only measure. Birdwhistell, generally agreed to be a noted authority on nonverbal behavior, makes some rather astounding estimates of the amount of nonverbal communication taking place. He estimates that the average person actually speaks words for a total of only 10 to 11 minutes daily—the standard spoken sentence taking only about 2.5 seconds. He goes on to say that in a normal two-person conversation, the verbal components carry less than 35% of the social meaning of the situation; more than 65% is carried on the nonverbal band.

Another way of looking at the quantity of nonverbal messages is to note the various systems humans use to communicate. Hall outlines ten separate kinds of human activity which he calls "primary message systems."[42] He suggests that only one involves language. Ruesch and Kees discuss at least seven different systems—personal appearance and dress, gestures or deliberate movements, random action, traces of action, vocal sounds, spoken words, and written words. Only two of the seven involve the overt use of words.[43]

It is not my purpose here to argue the importance of the various human message systems, but to put the nonverbal world in perspective. It is safe to say that the study of human communication has for too long ignored a significant part of the process.

Further testimony to the prevalence and importance of nonverbal communication is available if we scrutinize specific facets of our society. For example, consider the role of nonverbal signals in therapeutic situations; an understanding of "disturbed" nonverbal behavior would certainly help in diagnosis and treatment. Nonverbal cues are also important in certain situations where verbal communication is constrained—for example, doctor-nurse interaction during an operation. The significance of nonverbal cues in the arts is obvious—dancing, theatrical performances, music, pictures, and so on. It is

[42]E. T. Hall, *The Silent Language* (Garden City, N.Y.: Doubleday, 1959).
[43]Ruesch and Kees, *Nonverbal Communication*.

Nonverbal Communication: Basic Perspectives

the nonverbal symbolism of various ceremonies and rituals which creates important and necessary responses in the participants—for example, the trappings of the marriage ceremony, the Christmas decorations, religious rituals, funerals, and the like. We can also see how an understanding of nonverbal cues would better prepare us for communicating across cultures, classes, or age groups—and with different ethnic groups within our culture. Teaching and understanding the blind and deaf is largely a matter of developing a sophistication with nonverbal signals. Everyday matters like forming impressions of people you meet, getting through a job interview, understanding advertising or the audience/speaker relationship in a public speech are all heavily laden with nonverbal behavior. Nonverbal cues are also being analyzed in the hope of predicting future behavior of people.[44] One expert, for instance, claims to have analyzed hand gestures of prospective jurors in eleven major trials in 1975, hoping to predict how they would vote on the defendant. A list of situations where nonverbal communication is critical is interminable so we'll briefly describe only four areas: televised politics, classroom behavior, behavioral research, and courtship behavior.

Televised Politics. The tired, overweight, physically unappealing political boss is slowly being replaced by the young, good-looking, vigorous candidate who can capture the public's vote with an assist from his nonverbal attraction. We currently watch between thirty and forty hours of television each week. Television has certainly helped to structure some of our nonverbal perceptions, and more and more political candidates recognize the tremendous influence these perceptions may have on the eventual election outcome. Perhaps the most frightening and vivid example of the role of nonverbal communication in televised politics is found in McGinniss' book, *The Selling of the President 1968:*

> Television seems particularly useful to the politician who can be charming but lacks ideas.... On television it matters less that he does not have ideas. His personality is what the viewers want to share. He need be neither statesman nor crusader; he must only show up on time. Success and failure are easily measured: how often is he invited back? Often enough and he reaches his goal—to advance from "politician" to "celebrity," a status jump bestowed by grateful viewers who feel that finally they have been given basis for making a choice.
>
> The TV candidate, then, is measured not against his predecessors—not against a

[44]M. J. Saks, "Social Scientists Can't Rig Juries," *Psychology Today* 9 (1976): 48–50, 55–57. Also see R. T. Stein, "Identifying Emergent Leaders from Verbal and Nonverbal Communications," *Journal of Personality and Social Psychology* 32 (1975): 125–135; and P. Ekman, R. M. Liebert, W. V. Friesen, R. Harrison, C. Zlatchin, E. J. Malmstrom, and R. A. Baron, "Facial Expressions of Emotion While Watching Televised Violence as Predictors of Subsequent Aggression" (report to the Surgeon General's Scientific Advisory Committee on Television and Social Behavior, June 1971).

Nonverbal Communication: Basic Perspectives

standard of performance established by two centuries of democracy—but against Mike Douglas. How well does he handle himself. Does he mumble, does he twitch, does he make me laugh? Do I feel warm inside?

Style becomes substance. The medium is the massage and the masseur gets the votes....[p. 29–30]

The words would be the same ones Nixon always used—the words of the acceptance speech. But they would all seem fresh and lively because a series of still pictures would flash on the screen while Nixon spoke. If it were done right, it would permit Treleaven to create a Nixon image that was entirely independent of the words. Nixon would say his same old tiresome things but no one would have to listen. The words would become Muzak. Something pleasant and lulling in the background. The flashing pictures would be carefully selected to create the impression that somehow Nixon represented competence, respect for tradition, serenity, faith that the American people were better than people anywhere else, and that all these problems others shouted about meant nothing in a land blessed with the tallest building, strongest armies, biggest factories, cutest children, and rosiest sunsets in the world. Even better: through association with these pictures, Richard Nixon could become these very things....[p. 85]

"You know," Sage said, "what we're really seeing here is a genesis. We're moving into a period where a man is going to be merchandised on television more and more. It upsets you and me, maybe, but we're not typical Americans. The public sits home and watches Gunsmoke and when they're fed this pap about Nixon they think they're getting something worthwhile...." [p. 114–115][45]

It does not surprise us, then, to note Ron Nesson, President Ford's press secretary, hosting the satirical "Saturday Night Live"; to recall former mayor of New York, John Lindsay, making frequent visits to the "Johnny Carson Show"; to see Robert Finch, presidential advisor, appearing on an antidrug episode of "The Name of the Game"; to find former Vice President Spiro T. Agnew introducing the 1970 fall season of the "Red Skelton Show." Fortunately, the media experts do not control all the variables. The batting average for the top public relations and media experts in 1970 for both Democrats and Republicans was only about .500—sufficiently low to jeopardize their major-league status. We don't have a full accounting of the 1976 presidential debates, but a former movie star was unable to take the nomination from the incumbent president. Currently newscasts are under similar scrutiny—that is, the extent to which news programs are guided by "entertainment" considerations.

Nonverbal symbols have long been important in political behavior—before television marketing became popular. Picketing, parades, music, flags, uniforms, torches, hair styles, sit-ins, demonstrations with a large number of

---

[45]J. McGinniss, *The Selling of the President 1968.* © 1969 by Joemac, Incorporated. Reprinted by permission of Trident Press, division of Simon & Schuster, Inc.

Nonverbal Communication: Basic Perspectives

people marching with linked arms—all these and more have been a part of our nonverbal political heritage.

Classroom Behavior.   The classroom is a veritable gold mine of non-verbal behavior which has been relatively untapped by scientific probes. Acceptance and understanding of ideas and feelings on the part of both teacher and student, encouraging and criticizing, silence, questioning, and the like—all involve nonverbal elements. Consider the following instances as representative of the variety of classroom nonverbal cues: (1) the frantic hand waver who is sure he has the correct answer; (2) the student who is sure she does not know the answer and tries to avoid any eye contact with the teacher; (3) the effects of student dress and hair length on teacher-student interaction; (4) facial expressions—threatening gestures, and tone of voice are frequently used for discipline in elementary schools; (5) the teacher who requests student questioning and criticism, but whose nonverbal actions make it clear he or she will not be receptive; (6) absence from class communicates; (7) a teacher's trust of students is sometimes indicated by arrangement of seating and monitoring behavior during examinations; (8) the variety of techniques used by students to make sleeping appear to be studying or listening; (9) the professor who announces he or she has plenty of time for student conferences, but whose fidgeting and glancing at a watch suggest otherwise; (10) teachers who try to assess visual feedback to determine student comprehension;[46] (11) even classroom design (wall colors, space between seats, windows) has an influence on student participation in the classroom.

The subtle nonverbal influences in the classroom can sometimes have dramatic results, as Rosenthal and Jacobson found out.[47] Briefly, here is what happened: Rosenthal and Jacobson gave I.Q. tests to elementary school pupils prior to their entering for the fall term. *Randomly* (not according to scores) some students were labeled as high scorers on an "intellectual blooming test" which indicated they would show unusual intellectual development in the following year. Teachers were given this information. These students showed a sharp rise on I.Q. tests given at the end of the year. The experimenters attribute this to teacher expectations and to the way these "special" students were treated.

To summarize our speculations, we may say that by what she said, by how and when she said it, by her facial expressions, postures, and perhaps by her touch, the

[46]At least one study suggests even experienced teachers are not very successful at this. Cf. J. Jecker, N. Maccoby, M. Breitrose, and E. Rose, "Teacher Accuracy in Assessing Cognitive Visual Feedback from Students," *Journal of Applied Psychology* 48 (1964): 393–397.

[47]R. Rosenthal and L. Jacobson, *Pygmalion in the Classroom* (New York: Holt, Rinehart and Winston, 1968).

Nonverbal Communication: Basic Perspectives

teacher may have communicated to the children of the experimental group that she expected improved intellectual performance. Such communications together with possible changes in teaching techniques may have helped the child learn by changing his self-concept, his expectations of his own behavior, and his motivation, as well as his cognitive style and skills.[48]

Behavioral Research. Closely related to Rosenthal's work on nonverbal classroom behavior is his exposé of how nonverbal cues in behavioral science experiments often influence the experimental results. This concept is sometimes called "experimenter bias."

Rosenthal once asked, "Covert communications occur routinely in all other dyadic interactions; why then, should they not occur in the dyad composed of the experimenter and his subject?"[49] With this as a guiding premise, he has thoroughly explored the nonverbal dimensions of what happens when experimenter and subject get together.[50] A few findings from his work will illustrate: (1) Considerable evidence is available to show that male and female experimenters sometimes obtain significantly different data from subjects. It has been noted that male experimenters may behave in an "interested" manner toward female subjects—spending more time in preparation behavior, leaning much closer. Female subjects are sometimes more protectively treated during investigations involving tension and stress. Female subjects may gain more attention and consideration than males. (2) In some instances, black experimenters have been able to obtain different responses on questionnaires and GSR equipment than white experimenters. (3) Changes in the appearance of an interviewer, designed to make her more or less "Jewish," changed the responses to a public survey containing anti-Semitic items. (4) Experimenters perceived as high-status sometimes obtain different responses than low-status ones. (5) The experimenter's need for approval, dominance, authoritarianism, warmth or coldness; prior contact with the subjects; and amount of research experience will frequently influence the dyadic relationship and hence, the results of the experiment. (6) Sometimes the subjects will act as a source of behaviors later manifested by the experimenter. Take, for instance, the particularly obnoxious subject who affects an experimenter's entire day of testing—making him or her hostile and moody.

[48]Another experiment was designed in which different experimenters were told that their rats (though from the same population) were either "Maze-Bright" or "Maze-Dull" in relation to their ability to learn a maze. Those experimenters expecting better performance of the rats obtained it. Cf. R. Rosenthal and K. Fode, "Psychology of the Scientist: V. Three Experiments in Experimenter Bias," *Psychological Reports* 12 (1963): 491–511.

[49]R. Rosenthal, "Covert Communication in the Psychological Experiment," *Psychological Bulletin* 67 (1967): 357.

[50]R. Rosenthal, *Experimenter Effects in Behavioral Research* (New York: Appleton-Century-Crofts, 1966).

Nonverbal Communication: Basic Perspectives

The particular cues given by experimenters cover a wide range of visual and acoustic cues.[51] If the subject and experimenter have to interact it may be a matter of "approving" a response with an "uh-huh," a smile, a glance, or some combination of these behaviors. Explicit interaction is not necessary, however. The experimenters can set the mood and convey their expectancies by the way they read instructions—stressing certain words, reading at certain speeds, and so on. We might also see the tension release and head movement discussed earlier in the case of Clever Hans. One experiment revealed that when Japanese experimenters were given different expectations for subject responses, observers could note differences in their vocal tone—even though they couldn't understand the Japanese language![52] In another effort to identify the cues associated with experimenter bias, people were asked to tutor a twelve-year-old boy.[53] The boy was described as either bright or dull to some, and a third group was given no information about the boy's intelligence. A five-minute videotape of the tutoring was analyzed for behaviors indicating liking and approval. Tutors of the so-called bright boy smiled more, had more direct eye contact, leaned forward more, and nodded more than either of the other two groups.

Courtship Behavior.   One commentary on nonverbal courtship behavior is found in the following excerpts from the Beatles' song "Something" (copyright © 1969 Harrisongs Ltd. Written by George Harrison. Used by permission. All rights reserved, International copyright secured.):

Something in the way she moves
Attracts me like no other lover
Something in the way she woos me...

Something in her smile she knows
That I don't need no other lover
Something in her style that shows me...

You're asking me will my love grow...

You stick around, now
It may show...

[51]Cf. E. Timaeus, "Some Non-verbal and Paralinguistic Cues as Mediators of Experimenter Expectancy Effects," in M. von Cranach and I. Vine (eds.), *Social Communication and Movement* (New York: Academic Press, 1973), pp. 445–464; and J. C. Finkelstein, "Experimenter Expectancy Effects," *Journal of Communication* 26 (1976): 31–38.

[52]K. B. Scherer, H. Uno, and R. Rosenthal, "A Cross-Cultural Analysis of Vocal Behavior as a Determinant of Experimenter Expectancy Effects: A Japanese Case," *International Journal of Psychology* 1 (1972): 109–117.

[53]A. L. Chaikin, E. Sigler, and V. J. Derlega, "Nonverbal Mediators of Teacher Expectancy Effects," *Journal of Personality and Social Psychology* 30 (1974): 144–149.

Nonverbal Communication: Basic Perspectives

As the song suggests, we know there is "something" which is highly influential in our nonverbal courtship behavior. Like other areas of nonverbal study, however, we are still at a very early stage in quantifying these patterns of behavior. On a purely intuitive level, we know that there are some men and some women who can exude such messges as "I'm available," "I'm knowledgeable," or "I want you" without saying a word. For the male, it may be such things as his clothes, sideburns, length of hair, an arrogant grace, a thrust of his hips, touch gestures, extra long eye contact, carefully looking at the woman's figure, open gestures and movements to offset closed ones exhibited by the woman, gaining close proximity, a subtleness which will allow both parties to deny that either had committed themselves to a courtship ritual, making the woman feel secure, wanted, "like a woman," or showing excitement and desire in fleeting facial expressions. For the woman, it may be such things as sitting with her legs symbolically open, crossing her legs to expose a thigh, engaging in flirtatious glances, stroking her thighs, protruding breasts, using appealing perfume, showing the "pouting mouth" in her facial expressions, opening her palm to the male, using a tone of voice which has an "invitation behind the words," or any of a multitude of other cues and rituals—some of which vary with status, subculture, region of the country, and the like. A study by some students in Milwaukee of a number of singles' bars suggested that a cigar was taboo for any male wishing to pick up a female in these places. Other particularly important behaviors for males operating in this context seemed to be looking the female in the eyes often; dressing slightly on the "mod" side, but generally avoiding extremes in dress; and staying with one girl for the entire evening.

Another group of Milwaukee undergraduate students focused on nonverbal courtship behavior of homosexuals and found many similarities to heterosexual courtship rituals. Homosexuals were found to lavishly decorate their living quarters to impress their partners, use clothing for attraction and identification, and use eye behavior to communicate intentions. Scheflen has outlined four categories of heterosexual nonverbal courtship behavior—courtship readiness, preening behavior, positional cues, and actions of appeal or invitation.[54] The Milwaukee students found these to be useful categories in analyzing homosexual nonverbal courtship behavior too. Contrary to the popular stereotype, most homosexuals do not have effeminate and lisping characteristics. This raises the interesting question of what cues are used for identification purposes between two homosexuals. Certainly the environmental context may be very influential (gay bars), but other cues are also used. For instance, slang terms, brief bodily

[54]A. E. Scheflen, "Quasi-Courtship Behavior in Psychotherapy," *Psychiatry* 28 (1965): 245–257.

Nonverbal Communication: Basic Perspectives

contact (leg to leg), and other body movements such as certain lilts of the head or hands have been reported. In public places, however, the most common and effective signals are extended eye glances. Uninterested males will most likely avoid these long, lingering glances while those who maintain such eye contact suggest they are open for further interaction.

Nielsen, citing Birdwhistell, has described the "courtship dance" of the American adolescent.[55] He claims to have identified twenty-four steps between the "initial contact between the young male and female and the coitional act." He explains that these steps have an order to them. By this he means that when a boy begins holding a girl's hand, he must wait until she presses his hand (signaling a go-ahead) before he can take the next step of allowing his fingers to intertwine with hers. Girls and boys are labeled "fast" or "slow" according to whether they follow the order of the steps. If a step is skipped or reversed in the order, the person who does so is labeled "fast." If a person ignores the signal to move on to the next step, or takes actions to prevent the next step, he or she is considered "slow." This ordering would suggest that only after the initial kiss may the male attempt to approach the female's breast. She will probably block his approach with her upper arm against her side since protocol forbids approaching the breast from the front. The male really does not expect to reach the breast until after a considerable amount of additional kissing.

Up to this point, we have concentrated on the nonverbal courtship behavior of unmarried men and women. Certainly there are additional volumes to be written on marital nonverbal courtship behavior patterns. The whole repertoire of messages for inviting or avoiding sexual intercourse is largely nonverbal. Some observers, for instance, have noted that "staying up to watch the late show" is a common method of saying "not tonight."

Morris believes that heterosexual couples in Western culture normally go through a sequence of steps—like courtship patterns of other animals—on the road to sexual intimacy.[56] Notice the predominant nonverbal theme: (1) eye to body, (2) eye to eye, (3) voice to voice, (4) hand to hand, (5) arm to shoulder, (6) arm to waist, (7) mouth to mouth, (8) hand to head, (9) hand to body, (10) mouth to breast, (11) hand to genitals, (12) genitals to genitals and/or mouth to genitals. Morris, like Nielson, believes these steps generally follow the same order although he admits there are variations. One form of skipping steps or moving to a level of intimacy beyond what would be expected is found in socially formalized types of bodily contact—for example, a good-night kiss or a hand-to-hand introduction.

[55]G. Nielsen, *Studies in Self-Confrontation* (Copenhagen: Munksgaard; Cleveland: Howard Allen, 1962), p. 70–71.

[56]D. Morris, *Intimate Behavior* (New York: Random House, 1971), pp. 71–101.

Nonverbal Communication: Basic Perspectives

Summary

The term *nonverbal* is commonly used to describe all human communication events which transcend spoken or written words. At the same time we should realize that these nonverbal events and behaviors can be interpreted through verbal symbols. When we consider a classification schema of vocal/nonvocal, verbal/nonverbal, acoustic/nonacoustic, respiratory/nonrespiratory we learn to expect something less than discrete category placement of variables for study. Instead we might more appropriately put these behaviors on continua with some behaviors overlapping two continua.

Although the right hemisphere of the brain is credited with processing much nonverbal information, it seems that again we have considerable overlapping of functions between right and left hemispheres—especially if one side has to compensate for surgery on another hemisphere. To fully understand any communication act (in this case, nonverbal) we need to consider the intent of the sender and the perceived intent by the receiver. One reason these conceptualizations of intent are so critical is that they may set the boundaries for what is considered nonverbal communication. In one case researchers felt they could only call behaviors which were part of a shared code between sender and receiver signals in nonverbal communication. These same behaviors would only be a part of another schema—for example, primarily emblems and illustrators. Verbal and nonverbal signals can be coded in different ways. We reviewed a continuum of coding behavior—ranging from intrinsic (the referent) to iconic (some aspects of the referent preserved) to arbitrary (none or little of the referent preserved).

The theoretical writings and research on nonverbal communication can be broken down into the following seven areas: (1) body motion or kinesics (emblems, illustrators, affect displays, regulators, and adaptors), (2) physical characteristics, (3) touching behavior, (4) paralanguage (vocal qualities and vocalizations), (5) proxemics, (6) artifacts, (7) environment. Nonverbal communication should not be studied as an isolated unit, but as an inseparable part of the total communication process. Nonverbal communication may serve to repeat, contradict, substitute, complement, accent, or regulate verbal communication. Nonverbal communication is important because of the role it plays in the total communication system, the tremendous quantity of informational cues it gives in any particular situation, and because of its use in fundamental areas of our daily life.

This chapter also reviewed some of the historical highlights—noting the current influence of the works of Darwin, Efron, Birdwhistell, Hall, Ruesch and Kees, Mehrabian, Rosenthal, and others. The current theoretical framework by Ekman and Friesen was identified as a current highlight—a framework which should provide guidelines for current researchers. The popular literature—its important role and shortcomings—was reviewed. The chapter concluded with an account of the prevalence and importance of nonverbal signals in our daily life. We particularly emphasized nonverbal manifestations in televised politics, classroom behavior, behavioral research, and courtship behavior.

SELECTED BIBLIOGRAPHY

The following references were selected with the same criteria as the material in Chapter 1—to provide an introductory, broad-based perspective for understanding nonverbal communication.

Theories, Summaries, and Overviews

Benthall, J., and Polhemus, T. (eds.), *The Body as a Medium of Expression*. New York: E. P. Dutton, 1975.

Duncan, S. "Nonverbal Communication." *Psychological Bulletin* 72 (1969): 118–137.

Duncan, S., Jr., and Fiske, D. W. *Face-to-Face Interaction: Research, Methods, and Theory*. Hillsdale, N.J.: Lawrence Erlbaum Associates, 1977.

Ekman, P. "What's in a Name?" *Journal of Communication* 27 (1977): 237–239.

Ekman, P., and Friesen, W. V. "The Repertoire of Nonverbal Behavior: Categories, Origins, Usage, and Coding." *Semiotica* 1 (1969): 49–98.

Goffman, E. *Relations in Public*. New York: Basic Books, 1971.

Harrison, R. P. "Nonverbal Behavior: An Approach to Human Communication." In R. W. Budd and B. D. Ruben (eds.), *Approaches to Human Communication*. New York: Spartan Books, 1972. Pp. 253–268.

Harrison, R. P. "Nonverbal Communication." In I. deSola Pool, W. Schramm, F. W. Frey, N. Maccoby, and E. B. Parker (eds.), *Handbook of Communication*. Chicago: Rand McNally, 1973. Pp. 93–115.

Harrison, R. P., and Crouch, W. W. "Nonverbal Communication: Theory and Research." In G. J. Hanneman and W. J. McEwen (eds.), *Communication and Behavior*. Reading, Mass.: Addison-Wesley, 1975. Pp. 76–97.

Harrison, R. P., and Knapp, M. L. "Toward an Understanding of Nonverbal Communication Systems." *Journal of Communication* 22 (1972): 339–352.

Henley, N. M. *Body Politics: Power, Sex, and Nonverbal Communication*. Englewood Cliffs, N.J.: Prentice-Hall, 1977.

Koneya, M. "Nonverbal Movements or Verbal Surrogates?" *Journal of Communication* 27 (1977): 235–237.

McMahan, E. M. "Nonverbal Communication as a Function of Attribution in Impression Formation." *Communication Monographs* 43 (1976): 287–294.

Mehrabian, A. *Nonverbal Communication*. Chicago: Aldine-Atherton, 1972.

Melbin, M. "Some Issues in Nonverbal Communication," *Semiotica* 10 (1974): 293–304.

Nolan, M. J. "The Relationship Between Verbal and Nonverbal Communication." In G. J. Hanneman and W. J. McEwen (eds.), *Communication and Behavior*. Reading, Mass.: Addison-Wesley, 1975. Pp. 98–119.

Ruesch, J., and Kees, W. *Nonverbal Communication: Notes on the Visual Perception of Human Relations*. Berkeley and Los Angeles: University of California Press, 1956.

Sebeok, T.A., Hayes, A. S., and Bateson, M. C. (eds.). *Approaches to Semiotics*. The Hague: Mouton, 1964.

Spiegel, J. and Machotka, P. *Messages of the Body* (New York: Free Press, 1974).

Wertz, M. D. "Toward a Theory of Nonverbal Communication: A Critical Analysis of Albert Scheflen, Edward Hall, George Mahl and Paul Ekman." Unpublished Ph.D. dissertation, University of Michigan, 1972.

Wiener, M., Devoe, S., Rubinow, S., and Geller, J. "Nonverbal Behavior and Nonverbal Communication." *Pscyhological Review* 79 (1972): 185–214.

Bibliographies

Davis, M. *Understanding Body Movement: An Annotated Bibliography*. New York: Arno Press, 1972.

Harrison, R. P., Cohen, A. A., Crouch, W. W., Genova, B. K. L. and Steinberg, M. "The Nonverbal Communication Literature." *Journal of Communication* 22 (1972): 460–476.

Hore, T. and Paget, N. S. *Nonverbal Behavior: A Select Annotated Bibliography*. Victoria, Australia: Australian Council for Educational Research, 1975.

Key, M. R. *Nonverbal Communication: A Research Guide and Bibliography*. (Metuchen, N.J.: Scarecrow Press, 1977).

Key, M. R. *Paralanguage and Kinesics*. (Metuchen, N.J.: Scarecrow Press, 1977).

Stang, D. J. "Bibliography of Nonverbal Communication," *JSAS Catalog of Selected Documents in Psychology* 3 (1973): 8.

Textbooks

Argyle, M. *Bodily Communication* New York: International Universities Press, 1975.

Benson, T. W., and Frandsen, K. D. "An Orientation to Nonverbal Communication." In R. L. Applebaum and R. P. Hart (eds.), *Modcom: Modules in Speech Communication*. Chicago: SRA, 1976.

Bosmajian, H. (ed.). *The Rhetoric of Nonverbal Communication*. Glenview, Ill.: Scott-Foresman, 1971.

Nonverbal Communication: Basic Perspectives

Eisenberg, A. M. and Smith, R. R. *Nonverbal Communication* New York: Bobbs-Merrill, 1971.

Harrison, R. P. *Beyond Words*. Englewood Cliffs, N.J.: Prentice-Hall, 1974.

Leathers, D. G. *Nonverbal Communication Systems*. Boston: Allyn and Bacon, 1976.

McCardle, E. S. *Nonverbal Communication*. New York: Marcel Dekker, 1974.

Mehrabian, A. *Silent Messages*. Belmont, Calif.: Wadsworth, 1972.

Rosenfeld, L. B., and Civikly, J. M. *With Words Unspoken*. New York: Holt, Rinehart and Winston, 1976.

Weitz, S. (ed.). *Nonverbal Communication: Readings with Commentary*. New York: Oxford University Press, 1974.

Popularized Books for Mass Consumption

Davis, F. *Inside Intuition*. New York: McGraw-Hill, 1971.

Fast, J. *Body Language*. New York: M. Evans, 1970.

Nierenberg, G. I., and Calero, H. H. *How to Read a Person like a Book*. New York: Hawthorn, 1971.

Poiret, M. *Body Talk*. New York: Award Books, 1970.

Developmental Perspectives

Eibl-Eibesfeldt, I. *Ethology: The Biology of Behavior*. New York: Holt, Rinehart and Winston, 1970.

Hahn, M. E., and Simmel, E. C. (eds.). *Communicative Behavior and Evolution*. New York: Academic Press, 1976.

Hinde, R. A. (ed.). *Non-verbal Communication*. New York: Cambridge University Press, 1972.

The Environment

Drew, C. J. "Research on the Psychological-Behavioral Effects of the Physical Environment." *Review of Educational Research* 41 (1971): 447–463.

Mehrabian, A. *Public Places and Private Spaces*. New York: Basic Books, 1976.

Rohles, F. H. "Environmental Psychology: A Bucket of Worms." *Psychology Today* 1 (1967): 54–62.

Sommer, R. *Tight Spaces: Hard Architecture and How to Humanize It*. Englewood Cliffs, N.J.: Prentice-Hall, 1974.

Proxemics

Altman, I. *The Environment and Social Behavior*. Belmont, Calif.: Wadsworth, 1975.

Hall, E. T. *The Hidden Dimension*. Garden City, N.Y.: Doubleday, 1966.

Scheflen, A. E. *Human Territories: How We Behave in Space-Time*. Englewood

Cliffs, N.J.: Prentice-Hall, 1976.

Sommer, R. *Personal Space*. Englewood Cliffs, N.J.: Prentice-Hall, 1969.

Physical Appearance and Dress

Berscheid, E. and Walster, E. "Physical Attractiveness." In L. Berkowitz (ed.), *Advances in Experimental Social Psychology*, Vol. 7. New York: Academic Press, 1973.

Roach, M. E., and Eicher, J. B. (eds.). *Dress, Adornment and the Social Order*. New York: Wiley, 1965.

Ryan, M. S. *Clothing: A Study in Human Behavior*. New York: Holt, Rinehart and Winston, 1966.

Body Movements

Birdwhistell, R. L. *Kinesics and Context*. Philadelphia: University of Pennsylvania Press, 1970.

Efron, D. *Gesture, Race and Culture*. The Hague: Mouton, 1972.

Scheflen, A. E. *Body Language and Social Order*. Englewood Cliffs, N.J.: Prentice-Hall, 1972.

Spiegel, J., and Machotka, P. *Messages of the Body*. New York: The Free Press, 1974.

Touching Behavior

Frank, L. K. "Tactile Communication." *Genetic Psychology Monographs* 56 (1957): 123–155.

Montague, A. *Touching*. New York: Columbia University Press, 1971.

Facial Expressions

Ekman, P. (ed.). *Darwin and Facial Expression: A Century of Research in Review*. New York: Academic Press, 1973.

Ekman, P., and Friesen, W. V. *Unmasking the Face*. Englewood Cliffs, N.J.: Prentice-Hall, 1975.

Ekman, P., Friesen, W. V., and Ellsworth, P. *Emotion in the Human Face*. New York: Pergamon Press, 1972.

Eye Behavior

Argyle, M., and Cook, M. *Gaze and Mutual Gaze*. New York: Cambridge University Press, 1976.

Ellsworth, P. C., and Ludwig, L. M. "Visual Behavior in Social Interaction." *Journal of Communication* 22 (1972): 375–403.

Exline, R. V. "Visual Interaction: The Glances of Power and Preference." In J. K. Cole (ed.), *Nebraska Symposium on Motivation, 1971*. Lincoln: University of Nebraska Press, 1971. Pp. 163–206.

Nonverbal Communication: Developmental Perspectives

Vocal Behavior

Davitz, J. R. (ed.). *The Communication of Emotional Meaning*. New York: McGraw-Hill, 1964.

Kramer, E. "Judgment of Personal Characteristics and Emotions from Nonverbal Properties." *Psychological Bulletin* 60 (1963): 408–420.

Kramer, E. "Personality Stereotypes in Voice: A Reconsideration of the Data." *Journal of Social Psychology* 62 (1964): 247–251.

Mahl, G. F., and Schulze, G. "Psychological Research in the Extralinguistic Area." In T. Sebeok, A. S. Hayes, and M. C. Bateson (eds.), *Approaches to Semiotics*. The Hague: Mouton, 1964. Pp. 51–124.

Trager, G. L. "Paralanguage: A First Approximation." *Studies in Linguistics* 13 (1958): 1–12.

Observational Methodology

Reiss, A. J. "Systematic Observation of Natural Social Phenomena." In H. L. Costner (ed.), *Sociological Methodology*. San Francisco: Jossey-Bass, 1971.

Tagiuri, R. "Person Perception." In G. Lindzey and E. Aronson (eds.), *The Handbook of Social Psychology*, Vol. 3. Reading, Mass.: Addison-Wesley, 1969.

Weick, K. E. "Systematic Observational Methods." In G. Lindzey and E. Aronson (eds.), *The Handbook of Social Psychology*, Vol. 2 (second edition). Reading, Mass.: Addison-Wesley, 1968. Pp. 357–451.

Nonverbal Sending and Receiving Ability

Buck, R. "A Test of Nonverbal Receiving Ability: Preliminary Studies." *Human Communication Research* 2 (1976): 162–171.

Rosenthal, R., Archer, D., DiMatteo, M. R., Koivumaki, J., and Rogers, P. "Body Talk and Tone of Voice: The Language Without Words." *Psychology Today* 8 (1974): 64–68.

Snyder, M. "Self Monitoring of Expressive Behavior." *Journal of Personality and Social Psychology* 30 (1974): 526–537.

2 Nonverbal Communication: Developmental Perspectives

> There are no universal gestures. As far as we know, there is no single facial expression, stance or body position which conveys the same meaning in all societies.
> R. L. BIRDWHISTELL

> As we look back on a long phylogenetic history, which has determined our present day anatomical, physiological, and biochemical status, it would be simply astounding if it were found *not* to affect our behavior also.
> T. K. PITCAIRN and I. EIBL-EIBESFELDT

Children have been known to put parents "on the spot" momentarily and cause a fleeting frustration by innocently asking "Where did I come from?" When these same children reach adulthood, other questions of origin may be of interest—for example, "Am I doing this because of how I was raised or do all human beings do this?" The answers are often rapid, definite, and expressed with missionary zeal. On one side we hear scholars saying that behavior is innate, instinctive, inborn, or genetic; others argue that behavior is acquired, learned, culturally taught, imposed, imitated, or environmentally determined. It is the familiar nature/nurture dichotomy. The quotations above aptly illustrate these differing points of view. In the course of this chapter we will examine this issue concerning the origins of nonverbal behavior from two perspectives: phylogeny (the roots of nonverbal behavior in human evolutionary history) and ontogeny (the roots of nonverbal behavior in our current lifetime).

First, let's look at the dichotomy confronting us—innate vs. learned. As with most dichotomies, proponents of each side lose some of their capacity to explain things by supporting a polarized and inflexible position—trying to squeeze all observations into a single point of view. Instead of looking for a single origin, then, we might more productively look at the contribution of each side to the manifestation of any given behavior. No doubt much of our nonverbal behavior has *both* innate and learned (including imitation) aspects to it. Ekman and Friesen, whose work in this area we will detail later, outline three primary sources of our nonverbal behavior: (1) inherited neurological programs, (2) experiences common to all members of the species—for example, regardless of culture the hands will be used to place food in the mouth, and (3) experience which varies with culture, class, family, or individual.[1]

Biological and cultural forces overlap in many important ways. Some very common biological processes are later used to communicate—for example, breathing becomes a sigh of relief, grief, or boredom; a hiccough becomes an imitation of a drunk's behavior; audible blowing through one's nose may be interpreted as a snort of scorn; coughing becomes "ahem"; and so on. Later in this chapter we will discuss studies which suggest that some aspects of our facial expressions of emotion are inherited and are common to other members of the human species. This, however, does not mean that our cultural learning does not also play an important part in these expressions. The neurological program for any given facial expression can be altered or modified by learning display rules which are specific to our culture—for example, men shouldn't cry. Different stimuli may trigger a given facial expression—again depending on one's cultural training. A snake may evoke an expression of fear in one culture and bring out an expression of joy to those who see it as an important source of food. The society we grow up in is also largely responsible for the way we blend two or more emotional expressions—for example, showing some features of surprise and some features of anger at the same time. Lack's study of robins further illustrates this interrelationship between instinct and environment.[2] It seems that the European male robin will attack strange robins that enter his territory during the breeding season. Lack was able to demonstrate with stuffed models that the red breast alone will trigger this attack mechanism. The female robin who shared the nest, however, also had a red

[1]P. Ekman and W. V. Friesen, "The Repertoire of Nonverbal Behavior: Categories, Origins, Usage, and Coding," *Semiotica* 1 (1969): 49–98.

[2]D. Lack, "The Releaser Concept of Bird Behaviour," *Nature* 145 (1940): 107–108.

Nonverbal Communication: Developmental Perspectives

breast and was not attacked. Thus, this aggressive behavior which is believed to be innate is modified by certain conditions in the environment or the situation which calls forth the response. According to Thorpe, some birds instinctively sing a song common to their own species without ever having heard another bird sing the song.[3] These birds may, upon hearing the songs of their particular group, develop a variation on the melody which reflects a local dialect. And, even though a bird's song may not be learned, the bird may have to learn to whom the call should be addressed, under what circumstances it is to be used, and how to recognize signals from other birds. Much of the inherited components of human behavior can be similarly modified. It is like our human *predisposition for* or *capacity to learn* verbal language.[4] We are born with this capacity to learn language, but it will not be learned without cultural training. Children who have been isolated from human contact have not developed linguistic competence. There are probably some nonverbal signals which are primarily dependent on inherited neurological programs; there are others which probably depend primarily on environmental learning; and, of course, many behaviors are influenced by both. Furthermore, some behaviors which are primarily culturally taught at this time in human history may later be transmitted genetically if the behavior plays an important role in the continuance and survival of the species.

Finally, the answer to the nature/nurture issue concerning nonverbal behavior will vary with the behavior under consideration. We've already discussed the multiple origins of facial expressions of emotion. Adaptors may also have an inherited and learned derivation. You will recall that adaptors are habits associated with one's early coping with sensation, excretion, ingestion, grooming, and affect; early experiences in maintaining interpersonal relationships; and performing certain instrumental tasks. Illustrators and regulators, on the other hand, seem to be primarily learned by imitating others. Hence, we would expect to find variations in these behaviors across cultural, class, and ethnic lines. And, although there do seem to be some emblems which are found in several cultures, most seem to be very culture-specific—taught very much as verbal language is taught. Emblems which are observed in more than one culture may occasionally have similar meanings, but usually they have very different ones—for example, the circle made with the index finger and thumb which communicates "A-OK" to Americans may signify female genitalia to members of another culture.

So far we've focused entirely on nonverbal behavior. If we assume that our prehistoric ancestors were already communicating nonverbally while they

---

[3]W. H. Thorpe, "Vocal Communication in Birds" in R. Hinde (ed.), *Non-Verbal Communication* (Cambridge: Cambridge University Press, 1972).

[4]E. Lenneberg, *Biological Foundations of Language* (New York: Wiley, 1969).

Nonverbal Communication: Developmental Perspectives

were developing skills in verbal language, it is interesting to speculate on the role of nonverbal communication behavior in the development and origins of our verbal behavior.

The Development of Nonverbal Behavior in Human History: Phylogeny

Human beings, like other species, adapt to changing conditions around them. Some of these adaptations are important to our survival and are passed on from generation to generation. What are the nonverbal behaviors which have ancient roots in human history? On what basis do scientists conclude that a behavior or behavior pattern has an inherited component to it? Needless to say, it is not an easy task. Some of our current behavior displays are only fragments of larger patterns which are no longer enacted in their entirety; some behaviors which are now embedded in rituals have little to do with the original function of the behavior; and some behavior which seems to serve one function may be associated with something completely different—for example, grooming behavior may be the result of confusion or frustration in achieving a goal—rather than being enacted for some self-presentation, courtship, or cleanliness goals. Despite these and other difficulties inherent in any questions of phylogeny, researchers have made some important discoveries. Inferences about whether any given behavior has been inherited and is genetically transmitted to every member of the human species have been made primarily from three research strategies: (1) evidence from sensory deprivation—that is, noting the manifestation of a behavior in blind and/or deaf people who could not have learned it through visual or auditory channels; (2) evidence from nonhuman primates—that is, showing an evolutionary continuity of a behavior up to and including our closest relatives, nonhuman primates; and (3) evidence from multicultural studies—that is, observing the manifestation of similar behaviors used for similar purposes in other cultures around the world—literate and preliterate. Obviously, if we are able to compile evidence in all three categories our confidence in a phylogenetic dimension reaches the highest level of confidence. At present, few behaviors have been studied with such thoroughness; nor do we know much about how innate and learned factors combine and interact during infancy. Nevertheless, we can derive some important inferences from studies in each area.

Evidence from Sensory Deprivation.   Many have observed the early appearance of nonverbal behavior in children. Perhaps the behaviors are just learned quickly. In order to verify such a hypothesis, we need to examine children who, because of being blind and deaf at birth, could not learn such behaviors from visual or auditory cues. Eibl-Eibesfeldt began filming the behavior of several blind/deaf children in 1966.[5] His conclusions are similar to those of others who have systematically compared the behavior of blind/deaf children with sighted/hearing children. In short, the spontaneous expressions of sadness, crying, laughing, smiling, pouting, anger, surprise, and fear are not significantly different in blind/deaf children. Smiling and crying sequences filmed by Eibl-Eibesfeldt are shown in Figures 2.1, 2.2, and 2.3.

Some might argue that such expressions could be learned by touching or a slow reinforcement program. Eibl-Eibesfeldt points out, however, that even thalidomide babies who had no arms and children who could hardly be taught to raise a spoon to their mouth showed similar expressions.

In addition to facial expressions, these deaf/blind children sought contact with others by stretching out one or both hands, wanted to be embraced and

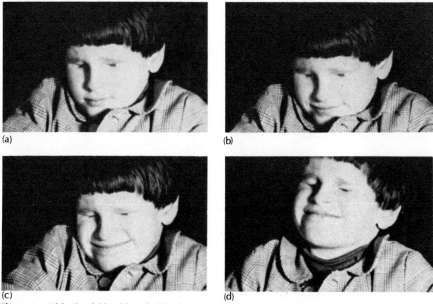

(a)

(b)

(c)

(d)

Figure 2.1 Eibl-Eibesfeldt's film of a blind/deaf smiling response. The head is liftd and tilted back as the intensity increases. From I. Eibl-Eibesfeldt, "The Expressive Behavior of the Deaf-and-Blind-Born," in M. von Cranach and I. Vine (eds.), *Social Communication and Movement* (New York: Academic Press, 1973).

[5]Cf. I. Eibl-Eibesfeldt, *Ethology: The Biology of Behavior*, 2 ed. (New York: Holt, Rinehart and Winston, 1975); I. Eibl-Eibesfeldt, "The Expressive Behaviour of the Deaf-and-Blind-Born," in M. von Cranach and I. Vine (eds.), *Social Communication and Movement* (New York: Academic Press, 1973); and T. K. Pitcairn and I. Eibl-Eibesfeldt, "Concerning the Evolution of Nonverbal Communication in Man," in M. E. Hahn and E. C. Simmel (eds.), *Communicative Behavior and Evolution* (New York: Academic Press, 1976).

Nonverbal Communication: Developmental Perspectives

48

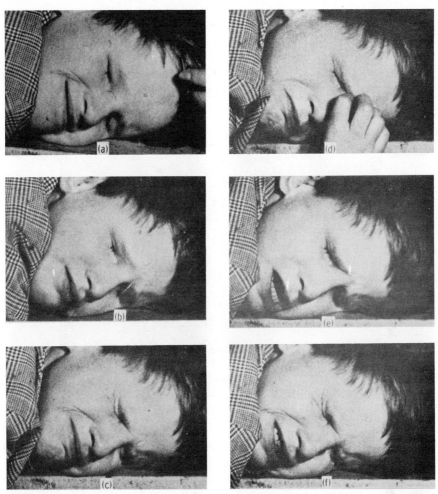

Figure 2.2 Blind/deaf crying response filmed by Eibl-Eibesfeldt. From T. K. Pitcarin and I. Eibl-Eibesfeldt, "Concerning the Evolution of Nonverbal Communication in Man," in M. E. Hahn and E. C. Simmel (eds.), *Communicative Behavior and Evolution* (New York: Academic Press, 1976).

caressed when distressed and, as the pictures in Figure 2.4 reveal, showed a remarkably familiar sequence of refusal gestures.

Eibl-Eibesfeldt also reports some interesting eye patterns of blind children. When he complimented a ten-year-old girl on her piano playing, she looked at him, coyly looked down and away and then looked at him again. A similar sequence was recorded for an eleven-year-old blind boy when asked about his girlfriend. This sequence of turning toward and away is also seen in sighted children under similar circumstances.

Naturally, blind/deaf children also show differences. The blind/deaf children do not show subtle gradations in expressions—for example, an expression may appear and suddenly disappear leaving the face blank. Some have noted

Nonverbal Communication: Developmental Perspectives

49

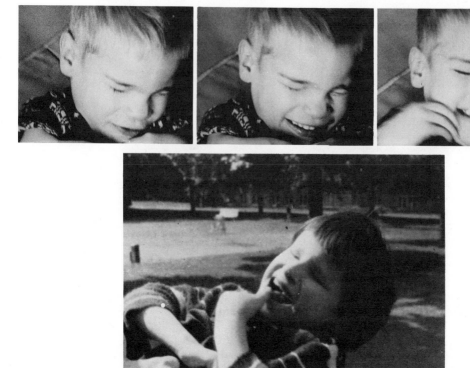

Figure 2.3 Laughing response of blind-deaf children filmed by Eibl-Eibesfeldt. From I. Eibl-Eibesfeldt, in M. von Cranach and I. Vine, 1973.

that the expressions are more restricted or restrained—for example, softer crying, and laughing which resembles a giggle. Blind/deaf children also show fewer facial expressions generally—with facial blends notably absent. Finally, when these blind/deaf children are asked to act out or mimic certain facial expressions they show less ability than sighted/hearing children.

After reviewing an extensive body of literature dealing with studies of normal, feral, isolated, institutionalized, and blind/deaf children, Charlesworth and Kreutzer conclude:

> . . . both the environment and innate factors have effects on expressive behavior. The environment may influence the time at which a behavior appears (many smiling individuals around a newborn may accelerate the appearance of the first social smile and may determine how often the behavior occurs once it first appears. The innate factors, on the other hand, seem to be mainly responsible for the morphological characteristics of expressive behaviors (and hence the fact that they occur at all as such) and for the connections such behaviors have to the emotional states associated with them.[6]

[6]W. R. Charlesworth and M. A. Kreutzer, "Facial Expressions of Infants and Children," in P. Ekman (ed.), *Darwin and Facial Expression: A Century of Research in Review* (New York: Academic Press, 1973), p. 160.

Nonverbal Communication: Developmental Perspectives

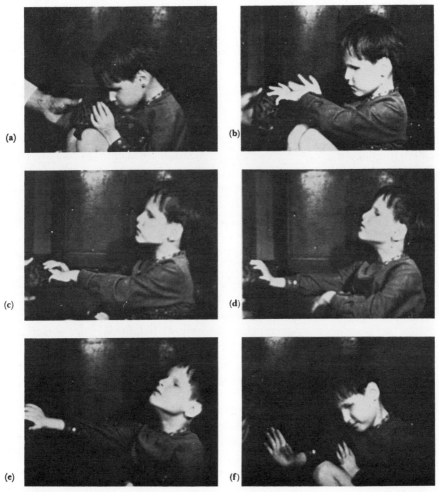

Figure 2.4 A blind/deaf child refusing an offer of a tortoise. The child sniffs at the object, pushes it back while simultaneously lifting her head in a movement of withdrawal. Finally she puts out her hand in a gesture of warding off. Filmed by Eibl-Eibesfeldt. From I. Eibl-Eibesfeldt, in M. von Cranach and I. Vine, 1973.

Evidence From Nonhuman Primates. Human beings are primates—but so are apes and monkeys. If we observe our nonhuman primate relatives manifesting behaviors similar to ours in similar situations, we have more confidence that such behavior has phylogenetic origins.

Before we begin emphasizing similarities, we should acknowledge some important differences in human and nonhuman primates. We humans make little use of changes in body color, but we do have an extensive repertoire of gestures which attend our verbal language. We also seem to have a greater

Nonverbal Communication: Developmental Perspectives

variety of facial blends. Our response repertoire is not nearly so limited to immediate and direct stimuli. And, although other animals are capable of complex acts, the level of complexity, control, and modification shown by the human animal may be hard to match—for example, smiling for purposes of ingratiation as well as to show pleasure.

Behavioral similarities are often linked to common biological and social problems which confront human and nonhuman primates—for example, mating, grooming, avoiding pain, expressing emotional states, rearing children, cooperating in groups, developing leadership hierarchies, defending, establishing contact, maintaining relationships, and so on. Figure 2.5 shows some of these similarities in grooming and bodily contact. There are many behaviors which might be explored for evolutionary roots.[7] We will focus on two: facial expressions and eye behavior during greetings.

Table 2.1 provides both written and visual descriptions of probable evolutionary paths for facial displays of anger in four living primates. It shows evolutionary dead ends for some expressions and a continuity for others. Chevalier-Skolnikoff has proposed similar phylogenetic chains for expressions of happiness (smiling and laughter) and sadness (with crying and without).[8] Although human beings have smaller and more discrete facial muscles, some of the similarities in facial displays to our primate relatives are striking. The activity which evokes the facial expression may also have similarities among the primates—for example, aggression, play, and the like. Like humans, nonhuman primates may accompany their emotional displays in the face with complementary cues in other body regions—for example, raised hair, muscle tenseness, and the like. And varying degrees of intensity (and blending) can be produced by nonhuman primates as well (see Figure 2.6). Like us, other primates can have the same facial display decoded in very different ways in different contexts—for example, a subordinate male monkey being chased by a dominant one can get the dominant one to leave by showing an expression of fear, but if the dominant male shows this fear expression while approaching a

[7]A most thorough description of chimpanzee behavior can be found in: J. A. R. A. M. van Hooff, "A Structural Analysis of the Social Behaviour of a Semi-Captive Group of Chimpanzees," in M. von Cranach and I. Vine (eds.), *Social Communication and Movement* (New York: Academic Press, 1973). For an extensive comparison of vocal cues, see W. H. Thorpe, "The Comparison of Vocal Communication in Animals and Man," in R. Hinde (ed.), *Non-verbal Communication* (Cambridge: Cambridge University Press, 1972).

A major literature review of communication in nonhuman primates can be found in S. A. Altmann, "Primates," in T. A. Sebeok (ed.), *Animal Communication* (Bloomington: Indiana University Press, 1968).

[8]S. Chevalier-Skolnikoff, "Facial Expression of Emotion in Nonhuman Primates," in P. Ekman (ed.), *Darwin and Facial Expression* (New York: Academic Press, 1973). Also see J. A. R. A. M. van Hooff, "A Comparative Approach to the Phylogeny of Laughter and Smiling," in R. Hinde (ed.), *Nonverbal Communication* (Cambridge: Cambridge University Press, 1972).

Nonverbal Communication: Developmental Perspectives

Figure 2.5 Upper left: Sonjo children clasping each other in fright. Middle left: Rhesus monkey mother with child. Upper right: An approximately four-year-old female with an older male chimpanzee. Middle right: A human couple. Lower left: Social grooming of vervet monkeys. Lower right: Social grooming among Bali women. All photographs except the two chimpanzees were taken by I. Eibl-Eibesfeldt. From I. Eibl-Eibesfeldt, *Ethology: The Biology of Behavior,* 2nd ed. (New York: Holt, Rinehart and Winston, 1975). Photograph of the chimpanzees by Baron Hugo van Lawick, © National Geographic Society. Originally published in Jane Goodall, *My Friends the Wild Chimpanzees,* National Geographic Society, p. 86.

Nonverbal Communication: Developmental Perspectives

Table 2.1   A Between-Species Analysis and Probable Evolutionary Paths for Facial Expressions of Anger

Lemurs	Macaques	Chimpanzees	Human Beings
	Confident Dominant ⟶ Threat; Anger Type I; "Stare" Eyes wide open; direct gaze, frequently with eye-to-eye contact. Brow often raised and lowered. Ears forward. Jaws closed; lips tightly closed. Confident Threat ⟶ Anger Type II; "Round-Mouthed Stare" Eyes wide open; direct gaze, frequently with eye-to-eye contact. Brow raised. Ears forward. Jaws open; lips contracted vertically and horizontally, covering the teeth and forming an "o" mouth opening. Often accompanied by a "roar."	Confident Dominant ⟶ Threat; Anger; Type I; "Glare" Direct gaze. Jaws closed; lips closed. Confident Dominant Threat; Anger; Type II; "Waa Bark" Direct gaze. Jaws half open; lips slightly extended and contracted, covering the teeth. Accompanied by a "bark."	Anger; Type I; "Angry Face" Direct gaze; frequently with eye-to-eye contact; no sclera (white part of eye) showing above and below iris (colored part of eye); upper lids appearing lowered; upper lids sometimes tense and squared; lower lids raised and tensed, often producing a squint. Brows lowered and pulled together. Jaws clenched; lips contracted vertically and tightly pressed together.

Confident Threat ⟶ Moderately Confident ⟶

Confident Threat
(anger)
Direct gaze. Jaws open; lips contracted, covering the teeth in some species. Invariably accompanied by a "bark" or "cough."

Moderately Confident Threat; Anger Type III; "Open-Mouthed Stare"
Eyes wide open; direct gaze, frequently with eye-to-eye contact. Brow raised and then lowered. Ears forward. Jaws slightly to moderately open; lips moderately contracted vertically, covering the upper teeth, but often not the lower teeth. Often accompanied by "hoarse roar."

Anger; Type II; "Angry Face"
Direct gaze; frequently with eye-to-eye contact; no sclera showing; upper lids appearing lowered; upper lids sometimes tense and squared; lower lids raised and tensed, often producing a squint. Brows lowered and pulled together. Jaws moderately open; lips moderately contracted vertically and horizontally, and extended, forming a rectangular opening with teeth showing.

Subordinate Threat ⟶ Subordinate Threat; ⟶ Subordinate Threat ⟶

Subordinate Threat
(fear-anger)
Alternation of jaws open and lips contracted, covering the teeth and lips retracted horizontally producing a "grin." Invariably accompanied by "shrieks."

Subordinate Threat;
Fear-Anger; "Bared-Teeth Stare"
Eyes wide open; alternation of direct gaze, often with eye-to-eye contact, and gaze avoidance. Brow lowered; forehead retracted. Ears back. Jaws and teeth repeatedly opened and closed; lips retracted vertically and horizontally, displaying the teeth. Often accompanied by "high-pitched scream."

Subordinate Threat
Fear-Anger; "Scream Calls"
Jaws half or wide open; lips retracted vertically and horizontally, displaying the teeth. Often accompanied by "screams."

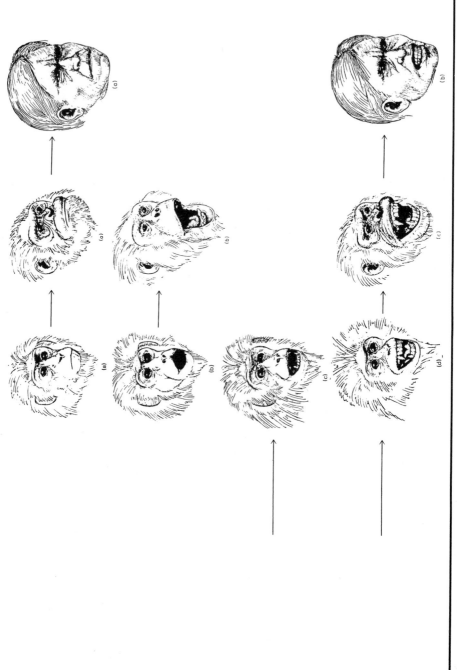

The information and drawings in Table 2.1 can be found in S. Chevalier-Skolnikoff, "Facial Expression of Emotion in Nonhuman Primates," in P. Ekman (ed.), *Darwin and Facial Expression* (New York: Academic Press, 1973). Drawn by Eric Stoelting.

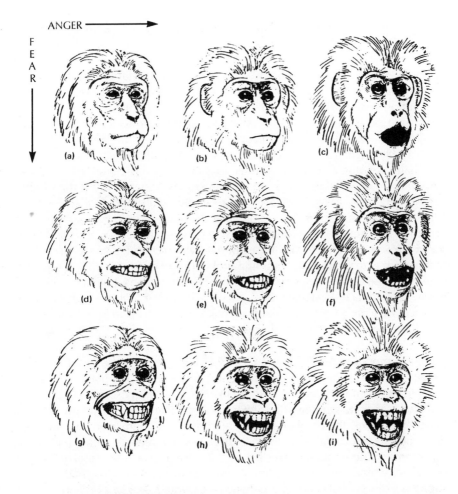

Figure 2.6 Facial expressions of *Macaca arctoides* according to intensity and emotion. (Note that on the anger axis [top row, left to right] as the monkey becomes increasingly angry, the stare intensifies, the ears are brought forward, the hair is raised over the head and neck, the lips are tightened and contracted, and the mouth is opened. On the fear axis [left column, top to bottom] as the animal's fear increases, the gaze is averted, the ears are drawn back against the head, where they do not show, and the lips are retracted horizontally and vertically, baring the teeth.) From Chevalier-Skolnikoff, op. cit., p. 27. Drawn by Eric Stoelting.

Reading left to right, and from top to bottom, the expressions are:
(a) Neutral face
(b) "Stare"; mild, confident threat.
(c) "Round-mouthed stare"; intense, confident threat.
(d) Slight "grimace"; slight fear.
(e) *No name*; a mild fear-anger blend.
(f) "Open-mouthed stare"; moderately confident, intense threat.
(g) Extreme "grimace"; extreme fear.
(h) Mild "bared-teeth stare"; extreme fear, blended with anger.
(i) "Bared-teeth stare"; intense fear-anger blend.

subordinate male, the subordinate may approach and embrace. Finally, we can note similarities in primate brains—that is, the parts of the brain which seem to mediate emotional responses in humans also seem to mediate facial expressions in nonhuman primates.

Many of our facial expressions have evolved from noncommunicative behaviors like attacking, moving toward or away from things, self-protective movements, and movements associated with respiration and vision. Chevalier-Skolnikoff argues, for instance, that "threat postures of most primates contain elements derived from attack (mouth open and ready for biting) and locomotion toward (body musculature tense and ready to advance), while the submissive postures contain elements derived from protective responses (retraction of lips and ears) and locomotion away from the sender." Thus, a behavior like flight from an enemy which was originally critical to survival may eventually become associated with feelings of fear and/or anger. It is possible, then, that an expression of fear and/or anger may appear even if the original behavior (fleeing) is unnecessary—for example, a monkey that feels fearful when approaching a female to copulate. The facial display has, over time, become associated with a particular feeling state and appears when that feeling state is aroused. It is likely that those animals who substituted facial expressions of threat for actual attack and fighting probably had a higher survival rate and, in turn, passed on this tendency to succeeding generations. In like manner, our heavy dependence on signals received visually (rather than through smell, for instance) may have been especially adaptive as our ancestors moved into open areas and increased in physical size.

We can also look at entire sequences of behavior which may have some genetic components and evolutionary origins. In greetings, for instance, many factors may affect the way they are handled—for example, place, time, relationship between the greeters, and the like. With so many sources of potential variation, then, it is noteworthy when we find seemingly invariant patterns. Pitcairn observed the eye behavior of adult humans, human infants and children, blind persons, and nonhuman primates in greeting rituals and found some remarkable similarities (see Figure 2.7).[9] Pitcairn believes this is a "stream of activity which, once started, must continue to the end" and that there is a strong possibility that there is a genetic or inherited program behind it.

Evidence from Multicultural Studies.   If we can observe human beings in different environments with different cultural guidelines encoding and/or decoding certain nonverbal behaviors in a similar manner, we develop

[9]T. K. Pitcairn and I. Eibl-Eibesfeldt, "Concerning the Evolution of Nonverbal Communication in Man," in M. E. Hahn and E. C. Simmel (eds.), *Communicative Behavior and Evolution* (New York: Academic Press, 1976).

Nonverbal Communication: Developmental Perspectives

increasing confidence that inherited components of the species may be responsible.

Because human beings around the world share certain biological and social functions, it should not be surprising to find areas of similarity. We've already mentioned the multicultural observations of emblems dealing with eating, sleeping, overeating, and pointing. Beier reports the decoding of vocal cues of emotion to have agreement across cultures[10]; Eibl-Eibesfeldt suggests we might find entire sequences of behavior to manifest cross-cultural similarities—for example, coyness, flirting, embarrassment, open-handed greetings, a lowered posture for communicating submission, and so on. On the other hand, the role of one's culture will surely contribute heavily to differences in nonverbal behavior because the circumstances which elicit the behavior will vary and the cultural norms and rules which govern the management of behavior will differ. Here we will detail two behaviors which seem to have widespread documentation in a variety of cultures—findings which urge us to look for the possibility of phylogenetic origins.

Eibl-Eibesfeldt has identified what he calls the "eyebrow-flash."[11] He has observed this rapid raising of the eyebrows (maintained for about one-sixth of a second before lowering) among Europeans, Balinese, Papuans, Samoans, South American Indians, Bushmen, and others (see Figure 2.8). Although it can often be seen in *friendly* greeting behavior, it has also been seen when people are giving approval or agreeing, seeking confirmation, flirting, thanking and when beginning and/or emphasizing a statement. The common denominator seems to be a yes to social contact—requesting or approving such contact. Smiles and nods sometimes accompany this gesture. The Japanese, however, are reported to suppress it as an indecent behavior. There are, however, other instances of eyebrow-raising which seem to indicate disapproval, indignation, or admonishment. These "no" eyebrow signals are often accompanied by a stare and/or head-lift with lowering of the eyelids—signaling a cutting off of contact. Since Eibl-Eibesfeldt observed eyebrow-lifting in some Old World monkeys, he began speculating on the possible evolutionary development. He reasoned that in both the "yes" and "no" displays a similar purpose was being served—that is, calling attention to someone or letting someone know (for sure) they were being looked at. When we display the expression of surprise, for instance, we raise our eyebrows and call attention to the object of our surprise. It may be a friendly surprise or an annoyed surprise. The entire evolutionary chain hypothesized by Eibl-Eibesfeldt is presented in Figure 2.9.

[10]E. G. Beier and Z. Zautra, "Identification of Vocal Communication of Emotions Across Cultures," ERIC 1972 Ed 056604.

[11]I. Eibl-Eibesfeldt, "Similarities and Differences Between Cultures in Expressive Movements," in R. Hinde (ed.), *Non-verbal Communication* (Cambridge: Cambridge University Press, 1972).

Nonverbal Communication: Developmental Perspectives

Figure 2.7 A Comparative Analysis of Gazing Patterns During Greeting Rituals (1 = Looking During Distant Salutation; 2 = Looking During Close Greeting; 3 = Looking as Interaction Begins; 4 = Looking Away; 5 = Looking As Interaction Continues.) (Filmed by T. K. Pitcairn)

Nonverbal Communication: Developmental Perspectives

a   b   c   d

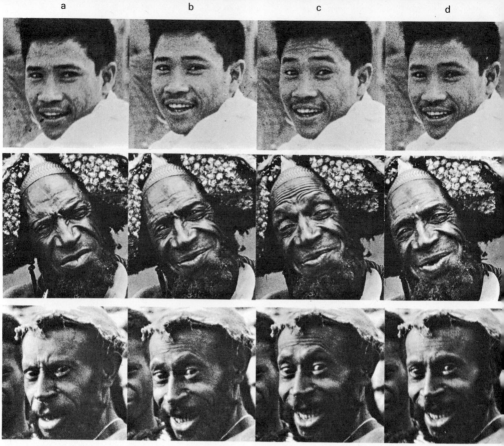

Figure 2.8 Eyebrow-flash during friendly greetings. Filmed by I. Eibl-Eibesfeldt. From I. Eibl-Eibesfeldt, *Ethology: The Biology of Behavior*, 2nd ed. (New York: Holt, Rinehart and Winston, 1975).

Perhaps the most conclusive evidence supporting the universality of facial expressions is found in the work of Ekman and his colleagues.[12] Photos of thirty faces expressing happiness, fear, surprise, sadness, anger and disgust/contempt were presented to subjects in five literate cultures. Faces were selected on the basis of meeting specific criteria for facial musculature associated with such expressions. As Table 2.2 shows, there was generally high agreement among the respondents regarding which faces fit which emotions. Ekman also asked his subjects to rate the intensity of each emotion and found no significant differences between the five cultures. Because these people were exposed to the mass media, one might argue that they may have learned to recognize unique aspects of faces in other cultures. However, in several studies with preliterate people (New Guinea) who did not have contact with the mass media and who had been almost completely isolated from contact with Western

[12]This research is summarized in P. Ekman, "Cross-Cultural Studies of Facial Expression," in P. Ekman (ed.), *Darwin and Facial Expression* (New York: Academic Press, 1973).

Nonverbal Communication: Developmental Perspectives

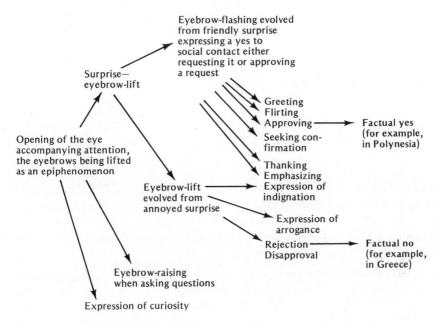

Figure 2.9 Eibl-Eibesfeldt's hypothesized evolution of eyebrow movements.

culture, Ekman found results comparable to those found in literate Eastern and Western cultures. In these studies, stories were told to the subjects who were then asked to select one of three facial photos which reflected the emotion of the story. Distinguishing fear from surprise was the most difficult discrimination to make. Perhaps, as Ekman says, fearful events in this culture are often surprising too. Interestingly, when Ekman obtained photos of expressions made by these New Guineans and asked Americans to judge them, the Americans accurately decoded all the expressions with high levels of accuracy—with the exception of fear, which was often judged as surprise and vice versa.

Finally, Ekman and his co-workers sought to answer the question of whether only *posed* expressions of emotion were universally understood and manifested. Thus, *spontaneous* facial expressions were obtained from Japanese and American subjects who watched a neutral and a stress-provoking film. The subjects showed similar facial configurations while they were alone watching the film, but during an interview with a member of their own culture the Japanese tended to mask their originally negative responses with polite smiling more than did the American subjects.

Although Ekman's program of research is perhaps the most complete, we

Nonverbal Communication: Developmental Perspectives

Table 2.2 Judgments of Emotion in Five Literate Cultures

	Japan	Brazil	Chile	Argentina	United States
Happiness	87%	97%	90%	94%	97%
Fear	71	77	78	68	88
Surprise	87	82	88	93	91
Anger	63	82	76	72	69
Disgust/Contempt	82	86	85	79	82
Sadness	74	82	90	85	73
Number of Subjects	29	40	119	168	99

find other studies of other cultures to support his findings. Thus, there does seem to be a universal association between particular facial muscular patterns and discrete emotions. It should be noted that this is only a specific element of universality and does not suggest that all aspects of facial affect displays are universal—as Ekman and Friesen testify:

> . . . we believe that, while the facial muscles which move when a particular affect is aroused are the same across cultures, the evoking stimuli, the linked effects, the display rules and the behavioral consequences all can vary enormously from one culture to another.[13]

Thus far we've explored three foci of research—none of which will *singly* offer "proof" of innate or inherited aspects for nonverbal behavior. When data is uncovered in each area, however, it provides us with the most conclusive evidence possible at this time. The primary facial expressions of emotion seem to meet this stringent test: They manifest themselves in children deprived of sight and hearing, in nonhuman primates, and in literate and preliterate cultures around the world. In view of such findings it would be hard to deny the existence of a genetic component passed along to members of the human species. Although the data supporting inherited aspects for other behaviors and behavior sequences we've reviewed is not currently as overwhelming, some strong indications have been noted. In keeping with the developmental perspective of this chapter, we now turn our attention to studies which have examined nonverbal behavior manifested during the early phases of the life-span.

[13]P. Ekman and W. V. Friesen, "The Repertoire of Nonverbal Behavior: Categories, Origins, Usage, and Coding," *Semiotica* 1 (1969): 49–98.

Nonverbal Communication: Developmental Perspectives

The Development of Nonverbal Behavior in Children: Ontogeny

The ontogenetic development of human speech has received considerably more attention than the development and origin of nonverbal behaviors. We do know that during the first few years of a child's life, an extensive repertoire of nonverbal signals is exhibited; we also know that shortly after birth the child is learning to interpret various nonverbal signals received from others. The following overview is in no way a comprehensive treatment of nonverbal behavior manifested by neonates, infants, children, and adolescents; instead we will attempt to highlight only *some* of the research and thinking in each of the areas treated later in this book.

Body Movements. Dittmann noticed that adults sometimes believe children are not listening to them—and badger them accordingly with questions like, "Did you hear me?" Dittmann reasoned that this common adult-child perception may be associated with what he calls "listener responses"—for example, head nods, some eyebrow raises, some types of smiles, "yeah," "I see," and so on.[14] His study of children in grades 1, 3, and 5 found these listener responses to be nearly absent except under "the strongest social pull" by the other interactant. Subsequent studies indicated the major deficiencies were in "m-hm" and head-nod responses. By eighth grade a dramatic increase in these listener responses is found. Now the early adolescent's peers are beginning to lengthen their response duration (providing more opportunity for such listener responses); the "response pull" from adult interactants is increasing; and there is a continuing movement away from a purely self-orientation and toward imagining instead, what others are going through.

Two research projects have focused on the use of emblems by children. Michael and Willis[15] asked children between the ages of four and seven to try to communicate the following messages without talking: "go away," "come here," "yes," "no," "be quiet," "how many," "how big," shape (for example, round, square), "I don't know," "good-bye," "hi," and "let me have your attention." They also tested the decoding ability of the children. In general, their results show that these children were better interpreters or decoders than encoders, that children with a year of school experience were better than preschool children, and that middle-class children showed a proficiency that

[14]A. T. Dittmann, "Development Factors in Conversational Behavior," *Journal of Communication* 22 (1972): 404–423.

[15]G. Michael and F. N. Willis, "The Development of Gestures as a Function of Social Class, Education and Sex," *Psychological Record* 18 (1968): 515–519; and G. Michael and F. M. Willis, "The Development of Gestures in Three Subcultural Groups," *Journal of Social Psychology* 79 (1969): 35–41.

lower-class children didn't. Kumin and Lazar presented a video tape of thirty emblems to two groups.[16] One group was aged 3 to 3½; the other group's ages ranged between 4 and 4½. In addition, observations of these same children were made in a nursery school free-play setting to see what emblems they actually used. Generally, the ability to decode emblems increases significantly from age 3–3½ to age 4–4½. Boys seemed to accurately interpret a greater number of emblems in the younger group, but girls scored better on the decoding task in the older group. Four-year-old children of both sexes accurately decoded the following emblems: "yes," "no," "come here," "quiet," "goodbye," "two," "I won't listen," blowing a kiss, "I'm going to sleep," "I won't do it." None of the four-year-olds were able to accurately decode "crazy." Three children in the 3–3½-year-old group could not decode a single emblem. Older children did not seem to encode or use more emblems than the younger age group, but girls at both age levels encoded more emblems in free play. The most frequently used emblems by both groups are listed in Table 2.3.

Table 2.3   Emblems Most Frequently Observed in Children's Free Play

	3–3½ year olds	4–4½ year olds
Both Girls And Boys	"I don't know."	"I don't know."
	"Yes."	—
	"No."	"No."
	"I'm tired."	—
	"Come here."	"Come here."
	"Stop."	—
	"Naughty."	—
	"Quiet."	"Quiet."
	"Out."	"Out."
	"Hello."	"Hello."
	—	"I won't listen."
	—	Blow kiss.
	—	"I won't do it."
Boys Primarily	Fist shaking.	Fist shaking.
Girls Primarily	"Go out."	—

[16]L. Kumin and M. Lazar, "Gestural Communication in Preschool Children," *Perceptual and Motor Skills* 38 (1974): 708–710.

Nonverbal Communication: Developmental Perspectives

66

Physical Appearance. At a very early age, children seem capable of making distinctions on the basis of physical appearance. Golomb found that most children at age two could not model a human figure out of clay, but by the end of the third year of life only a small percentage was unable to complete the task.[17] Before a child reaches age five, distinctions between skin color and incongruities in dress (for example, going barefoot in a wedding dress) are being made. Most of the research in this area has focused on general physical attractiveness and reactions to various body builds.

In Chapter 5 considerable evidence is cited to support the notion that people seem to agree generally on who is physically attractive and who isn't. When does this develop? According to Cavior and Lombardi, cultural guidelines for physical attractiveness are pretty well established by age six.[18] It is not surprising, then, to find peer popularity and physical attractiveness highly correlated in a number of elementary and secondary schools. Dion found that antisocial behavior (for example, throwing a brick through a window) was seen differently for attractive and unattractive children.[19] The transgression was seen as an enduring trait of the unattractive child, but only a temporary problem for the attractive one. The act was evaluated more negatively for the unattractive child, too. It does not surprise us, then, to find that juvenile delinquents were also rated as lower on attractiveness. The perceptions of attractiveness in a child's world are not limited to his or her peers. Teachers tend to see attractive children as more intelligent, more socially adept, higher in educational potential, and more positive in their attitudes toward school—even though the unattractive children used in the study had similar academic performance records.

Perceptions of body builds (endomorphs, ectomorphs, and mesoporphs) have also been studied developmentally. As early as kindergarten, children seem to prefer the more muscular mesomorph to either the thin or fat body

---

[17]C. Golomb, "Evolution of the Human Figure in a Three Dimensional Medium," *Developmental Psychology* 6 (1972): 385–391.

[18]N. Cavior and D. A. Lombardi, "Developmental Aspects of Judgments of Physical Attractiveness in Children," *Developmental Psychology* 8 (1973): 67–71; N. Cavior and P. R. Donecki, "Physical Attractiveness, Perceived Attitude Similarity and Academic Achievement As Contributors to Interpersonal Attraction Among Adolescents," *Developmental Psychology* 9 (1973): 44–54; K. K. Dion and E. Berschied, "Physical Attractiveness and Peer Perceptions Among Children," *Sociometry* 37 (1974): 1–12; K. K. Dion, "Young Children's Stereotypes of Facial Attractiveness," *Developmental Psychology* 9 (1973): 183–188; and J. F. Cross and J. Cross, "Age, Sex, Race and the Perception of Facial Beauty," *Developmental Psychology* 5 (1971): 433–439.

[19]K. Dion, "Physical Attractiveness and Evaluations of Children's Transgressions," *Journal of Personality and Social Psychology* 24 (1972): 207–213; and N. Cavior and L. R. Howard, "Facial Attractiveness and Juvenile Delinquency Among Black and White Offenders, *Journal of Abnormal Child Psychology* 1 (1973): 202–213.

Nonverbal Communication: Developmental Perspectives

types.[20] Youngsters seem to have a particular aversion to the fat physiques. Older children who select descriptive adjectives for these body types tend to see the mesomorph as "all things good," with ectomorphs and endomorphs attracting a host of unfavorable descriptors. In fact, ten- and eleven-year-olds seemed to consider body build as a more important characteristic in judging physical appearance than such things as deformities, disfigurements, and handicaps.[21] The psychological aversion to chubby figures results in children maintaining a greater physical distance from them.[22] In turn, we find that chubby children often tend to have a negative perception of their own bodies, which may later generalize to a negative self-image.[23]

Eye Behavior. An infant responds positively to its mother's eyes very early. Eye-to-eye contact between mother and child may even occur as early as the fourth week of life.[24] During the first two months, a smiling response can be elicited from the infant with a mask which portrays the eyes with two dots; the same response, however, will not occur with a real face which has the eyes covered.[25] It is not clear to what extent these eye patterns are innate, but it seems fair to conclude that the mutual gaze, the breaking of gaze, and facial responsiveness are crucial elements in establishing primitive bases for social relationships—even though the gaze duration may be fairly short. Pupil dilation has also been observed. At one month increased dilation occurs in response to faces; at four months the increased dilation is particularized to the mother's face.[26]

[20]R. M. Lerner and E. Gellert, "Body Build Identification, Preference and Aversion in Children," *Developmental Psychology* 1 (1969): 456–462; J. R. Staffieri, "Body Build and Behavioral Expectancies in Young Females," *Development Psychology* 6 (1972): 125–127; R. M. Lerner and S. J. Korn, "The Development of Body Build Stereotypes in Males," *Child Development* 43 (1972): 908–920; R. M. Lerner and C. Schroeder, "Physique Identification, Preference and Aversion in Kindergarten Children," *Developmental Psychology* 5 (1971): 538; and P. A. Johnson and J. R. Staffieri, "Stereotypic Affective Properties of Personal Names and Somatypes in Children," *Developmental Psychology* 5 (1971): 176.

[21]S. A. Richardson, N. Goodman, A. Hastorf, and S. Dornbusch, "Cultural Uniformities in Relation to Physical Disabilities," *American Sociological Review* 26 (1961): 241–247.

[22]R. M. Lerner, S. A. Karabenick, and M. Meisels, "Effect of Age and Sex on the Development of Personal Space Schemata Towards Body Build," *Journal of Genetic Psychology* 127 (1975): 91–101; and R. M. Lerner, J. Venning, and J. R. Knapp, "Age and Sex Effects on Personal Space Schemata Toward Body Build in Late Childhood," *Developmental Psychology* 11 (1975): 855–856.

[23]R. N. Walker, "Body Build and Behavior in Young Children," *Child Development* 34 (1963): 1–23.

[24]P. H. Wolff, "Observations on the Early Development of Smiling," in B. M. Foss (ed.), *Determinants of Infant Behaviour,* Vol. 2 (London: Methuen, 1963).

[25]R. A. Spitz and K. M. Wolf, "The Smiling Response: A Contribution to the Ontogenesis of Social Relationships," *Genetic Psychology Monographs* 34 (1946): 57–125.

[26]H. E. Fitzgerald, "Autonomic Pupillary Reflex Activity During Early Infancy and Its Relation to Social and Non-Social Stimuli," *Journal of Experimental Child Psychology* 6 (1968): 470–482.

Nonverbal Communication: Developmental Perspectives

Although a number of researchers have been interested in eye behavior during infancy, childhood gazing patterns have received very little attention. And, the two studies available seem to disagree on whether there is a gradually increasing or gradually decreasing trend in looking up to adolescence.[27] Data from both studies, however, does show that adolescence represents a nadir for eye gazing. Finally, Levine and Sutton-Smith suggest that we may find children less likely than adults to look at the beginnings and ends of their utterances.

Personal Space. From birth, the developing child is exposed to gradually increasing distances for various communication situations. The first few years provide a familiarity with what Hall calls "intimate" distance (see Chapter 4); then the child learns appropriate conversational distances for an increasing number of acquaintances obtained from family, neighborhood, and school; and by about age seven the child may have incorporated the concept of "public" distance into his or her behavioral repertoire. Several studies tend to support such a notion. For instance, when three-, five-, and seven-year-olds were asked to sit next to unknown peer working on a task, the three-year-olds sat significantly closer—sometimes touching the unknown peer.[28] Other studies using simulations, laboratory observations, and field observations tend to find younger children seeking less interaction distance.[29] Around the third grade, however, the gradually increasing interaction distance seems to stabilize—more closely reflecting adult norms. Like any generalization, the preceding developmental pattern will be modified by many factors. A child may learn patterns of conversational spacing in an ethnic environment and incorporate patterns of the larger culture at a later time.[30]

Sex of the child may also influence early interaction distancing. Sometimes the different experiences of males and females will manifest themselves in different spatial needs. Some observers, for instance, have suggested that the same stimuli may cause parents to put male infants on the floor or in a playpen, but hug or put the females in a nearby high chair. Boys, too, are frequently given toys which seem to encourage activities which demand more space—

---

[27]V. Ashear and J. R. Snortum, "Eye Contact in Children as a Function of Age, Sex, Social and Intellective Variables," *Developmental Psychology* 4 (1971): 479; and M. H. Levine and B. Sutton-Smith, "Effects of Age, Sex and Task on Visual Behavior During Dyadic Interaction," *Developmental Psychology* 9 (1973): 400–405.

[28]J. Lomranz, A. Shapira, N. Choresh, and Y. Gilat, "Children's Personal Space as a Function of Age and Sex," *Developmental Psychology* 11 (1975): 541–545.

[29]H. M. Bass and M. S. Weinstein, "Early Development of Interpersonal Distancing in Children," *Canadian Journal of Behavioural Science* 3 (1971): 368–376; J. C. Baxter, "Interpersonal Spacing in Natural Settings." *Sociometry* 33 (1970): 444–456; and C. J. Guardo and M. Meisels, "Factor Structure of Children's Personal Space Schemata," *Child Development* 42 (1971): 1307–1312.

[30]S. Jones and J. Aiello, "Proxemic Behavior of Black and White First-, Third-, and Fifth-Grade Children," *Journal of Personality and Social Psychology* 25 (1973) 21–27.

Nonverbal Communication: Developmental Perspectives

often away from the confines of the home itself—for example, footballs, cars, trains, and the like. Girls, on the other hand, may receive dolls, doll houses, and other domestic toys which require less space and encourage activity directed toward the home environment.[31] Observations of children at play tend to confirm the notion that many males learn the need for and use of greater territory at early ages. Boys spent more time outside, entered more areas than the girls, and maintained between 1.2 and 1.6 times the amount of space females did.[32]

Studies which have examined interaction distances with specific others during childhood offer few surprises. Greater distances seem to be maintained with teachers and unknown adults, endomorphs, unfriendly and/or threatening persons; closer distances are maintained with caretakers in unfamiliar environments. And, as social density increases, children tend to interact less and some will show increased aggressive tendencies.[33]

Vocalizations.   Newborns begin sound-making almost immediately. The infant's first cries are undifferentiated and reflexive. But soon the influence of the infant's environment is shown and cries begin to show differences related to the motivation for crying—for example, pain, anger, frustration, and the like. Other sounds, like laughter, cooing, and gurgling, are produced, but our focus will be on those sounds which are antecedent to and later attend spoken language—that is, pitch, pauses, loudness, and tempo.

At approximately three months of age, the child enters a stage called "babbling." Here the child is playfully experimenting with and exercising his or her sound-making equipment. Some sounds will be produced during this time which will not be reinforced by speakers of the child's native language and thus will receive minimal use later in life. Some feel that there is also an experimentation with intonation patterns at this stage—for example, expressing emotions, asking questions, and showing excitement through sounds alone. At the very least the child is imitating perceived differences in pitch levels. Lieberman recorded and analyzed samples of babbling for changes in pitch.[34] It was noted that infant pitch levels varied with the sex of the parent—lower for the father and higher for the mother. Further, pitch levels were lower when the

[31]H. L. Rheingold and K. V. Cook, "The Contents of Boys' and Girls' Rooms as an Index of Parents' Behavior," *Child Development* 46 (1975), 459–463.

[32]L. Harper and K. M. Sanders, "Preschool Children's Use of Space: Sex Differences in Outdoor Play," *Developmental Psychology* 11 (1975): 119.

[33]C. Hutt and M. J. Vaizey, "Differential Effects of Group Density on Social Behavior," *Nature* 209 (1967): 1371–1372; and C. Loo, "The Effects of Spatial Density on the Social Behavior of Children," *Journal of Applied Social Psychology* 4 (1972): 172–181.

[34]P. Lieberman, *Intonation, Perception, and Language* (Cambridge, Mass.: M.I.T. Press, 1966).

Nonverbal Communication: Developmental Perspectives

child was "conversing" (parent present) than when babbling alone. Others have observed that when adults are talking to children their pitch level will rise; even older children will sometimes raise their pitch when interacting with younger children. At roughly six months, the infant begins to imitate his or her own sounds—again for pleasure and practice. At approximately eight months, the child increases imitations of sounds made by others—and is rewarded accordingly. From this point on, the development of vocalizations necessary for human speech communication is a matter of practice and refinement.

Pitch goes through a number of changes from birth to puberty. A study of infants in their natural environments, using sophisticated recording equipment, found that during the first month pitch tended to decrease steadily.[35] During the second month pitch began to rise and kept rising until about four months. Generally, however, there is a gradual lowering of pitch which continues throughout childhood. At the onset of puberty, both male and female voices show a lowering of pitch—but the change for males is often dramatic.

Pausal patterns seem to be well established when the child enters school. A study which compared pausal patterns in the speech of children five to twelve years of age found no significant differences.[36] Tempo and loudness features of prosody also seem to be firmly established by the time children enter kindergarten.[37]

Thus far we've focused on the production of sounds. How do children decode or respond to vocal cues? Perhaps the first indication of responsiveness to adult voices is in the seemingly synchronized movements of babies as young as twelve hours old with rhythmic adult speech.[38] It is believed that by the age of three months, infants behave as if they knew they were the objects of the mothers' voices. And other work suggests that these first months are not too early for the infant to respond differently to friendly vs. hostile voices, inflected vs. noninflected voices, and baby-talk vs. normal talk.[39] Another study, using over two hundred children between five and twelve, examined the ability of these youngsters to accurately decode vocalized emotions. The speech content was controlled. As age increased, the ability to accurately decode vocal emotional expressions also increased. Sadness was most frequently identified correctly—followed by anger, happiness, and love. There was no marked pat-

[35]W. C. Sheppard and H. L. Lane, "Development of the Prosodic Features of Infant Vocalizing," *Journal of Speech and Hearing Research* 11 (1968): 94–108.

[36]H. Levin, I. Silverman, and B. Ford, "Hesitations in Children's Speech During Explanation and Description," *Journal of Verbal Learning and Verbal Behavior* 6 (1967): 560–564.

[37]B. Wood, *Children and Communication* (Englewood Cliffs, N.J.: Prentice-Hall, 1976). p. 224.

[38]W. S. Condon and L. W. Sander, "Synchrony Demonstrated Between Movements of the Neonate and Adult Speech," *Child Development* 45 (1974): 456–462.

[39]Lieberman, *Intonation, Perception, and Language.* Also see J. Kagan and M. Lewis, "Studies of Attention in the Human Infant," *Merrill-Palmer Quarterly* 4 (1965): 95–127.

Nonverbal Communication: Developmental Perspectives

tern of correct or incorrect responses by age level, suggesting about the same rate of development, in terms of understanding, for all the emotions studied.[40]

Facial Expressions. Exactly when the human infant begins to respond differentially to facial expressions in others is not well documented. At least two excellent reviews of this body of literature do exist.[41] Recognition studies with infants usually rely on mean attention time and eye movement photography to form the bases for inferences about reactions. Although the infant does fixate on a few facial features, it is not until sometime between two and five months that full facial scanning takes place. At about the middle of the infant's first year, it is making some discriminations of some aspects of facial expressions, and by the end of the first year facial expressions are probably recognized quite well—as long as they are pronounced and accompanied by the appropriate gestures and vocalizations. This generalization seems to be supported by a study of infants aged four, six, eight, and ten months.[42] The experimenter acted out angry, happy, sad, and "neutral" facial expressions—accompanied by the appropriate vocalizations. Videotapes were made of the infants' responses. At four months, reactions were indiscriminate; at six months (and beyond) infants seemed to discriminate between the expressions—sometimes mirroring the response given them. Gates conducted an early recognition study, and it is reported here because, although methodological problems did exist, the findings have not been seriously challenged.[43] It also suggests that recognition of various expressions of emotion will occur at different times with different expressions. Over four hundred children from age three to fourteen were shown adult photographs of emotional expressions. The youngest group could accurately identify only laughter. The majority were able to identify pain by the age of five or six, and anger at about age seven. Most could not identify fear until nine or ten, and identification of surprise came a year later. At age fourteen a majority could still not identify scorn.

Tentatively, we can also suggest some approximate times when children

[40]L. Dimitrovsky, "The Ability to Identify the Emotional Meaning of Vocal Expression at Successive Age Levels," in J. R. Davitz (ed.), *The Communication of Emotional Meaning* (New York: McGraw-Hill, 1964), pp. 69–86; and A. Fenster and A. M. Goldstein, "The Emotional World of Children 'Vis-A-Vis' the Emotional World of Adults: An Examination of Vocal Communication," *Journal of Communication* 21 (1971): 353–362.

[41]I. Vine, "The Role of Facial-Visual Signalling in Early Social Development," in M. Von Cranach and I. Vine (eds.), *Social Communication and Movement* (New York: Academic Press) 1973, pp. 195–298; and W. R. Charlesworth and M. A. Kreutzer, "Facial Expressions of Infants and Children," in P. Ekman (ed.), *Darwin and Facial Expression* (New York: Academic Press, 1973), pp. 91–168.

[42]Charlesworth and Kreutzer, "Facial Expressions of Infants and Children," p. 122.

[43]G. S. Gates, "An Experimental Study of the Growth of Social Perception," *Journal of Educational Psychology* 14 (1923) 449–461.

Nonverbal Communication: Developmental Perspectives

will *produce* facial expressions of emotion. Generally, children express their emotions with more body parts and in a less subtle fashion than adults. With increasing age we develop finer muscular control, our cognitive abilities become more complex, and we learn and respond to various social norms and pressures. As a result, we would expect to see a gradual increase in the ability to simulate facial expressions of emotion. Furthermore, the sudden shifts from one emotional display to another will likely decrease as age increases.

Smiling, as an early reflexive response, occurs early in life. The first social smile, however, probably occurs between the second and fourth month. Laughing seems to appear later than smiling. Persons familiar to the child may elicit laughing by tactile stimulation (tickling) sooner, but laughing without tactile stimulation does not seem to occur until the end of the first year. Sroufe and Waters, using about one hundred infants, had mothers employ numerous auditory, tactile, social, and visual stimuli to produce laughter in their children.[44] In children four months or younger, instances of laughter were not clear-cut, but unambiguous cases appeared after four months and were clearly apparent in most infants by eight months. It is hard to tell when affection responses first appear, but it seems reasonable to assume that before the age of three such responses will be directed primarily toward caretaking adults. During the third and fourth years we should see more peer-directed affection—frequently seen in role-played parental nurturing behavior with younger children. The child is now beginning experiences which may eventuate in the feeling that giving affection can be as satisfying as receiving it.

Expressions of anger seem to be well developed before six months of age, but increasing age seems to change the outward manifestations of this anger—for example, fewer explosive outbursts. As with affection, we would expect to see this anger directed primarily at parents first, with increasing anger displays directed toward peers as age increases. Environmental conditions will sometimes be very influential in the manifestations of this anger. In 69 percent of the angry outbursts that Ricketts observed in home settings, crying was involved; but crying was only a part of 39 percent of the anger responses at nursery school.[45]

Somewhere about the middle of the first year, expressions of fear seem to clearly manifest themselves, although some feel there may be two types of fear displays—one of which occurs very early. And, it is no surprise that expressions of fear seem to occur most often in response to large dogs, snakes, and dark rooms. Expressions of surprise are extremely difficult to locate on a devel-

[44]L. A. Sroufe and E. Waters, "The Ontogenesis of Smiling and Laughter," *Psychological Review* 83 (1976): 173–189.

[45]A. F. Ricketts, "A Study of the Behavior of Young Children in Anger," in L. Jack et al. (eds.), *University of Iowa Studies: Studies in Child Welfare* 9 (1934): 163–171.

Nonverbal Communication: Developmental Perspectives

opmental continuum. It is infrequently seen during the second half of the first year. One reason for this may be the nature of the infant's face. It is smooth with very light eyebrows, making observation difficult. Furthermore, a young child has not developed strong expectations which, when violated, produce a surprise reaction. The standard configuration of the face during surprise (mouth open, eyes opened wider, raised brows, momentary freezing) described by Darwin does not seem to occur much in elementary school children and may not change much from infancy through sixth grade.

Others have speculated on the occurrence of expressions of jealousy, sympathy, shyness, coyness, embarrassment, and shame, but credible data is yet to appear. Many of these reactions will appear after infancy because they require the performer to cognitively consider the behavior of others. Sympathy, for instance, requires you to sense distress in another; embarrassment occurs only when you care what others think of you—a condition which does not exist with infants.

If the preceding observations on the developmental nature of nonverbal behavior in children have seemed sketchy, they reflect the nature of the data available. Sometimes it is a matter of simply not having the necessary information. For instance, we need to develop criteria for the observation of children which are not entirely based on adult standards.[46] The coding of an expression of surprise in children may not involve all the elements necessary for noting adult surprise. In some cases, we try to generalize about the frequency of a particular behavior in children without any comparable norms for other stages in the life-span. It is difficult to say a child shows "little" or "a lot" of a particular behavior unless we have some referent for the frequency of that behavior at the same and other ages. Many researchers assume that once a behavior is observed, it continues to develop in the same manner until it reaches adult norms. Rarely is a nonlinear development hypothesized. The difficulty, of course, is that such an assumption inhibits the examination of a behavior after its earliest recorded moment—assuming that we "know" it exists. Sometimes nonverbal studies with children omit fundamental considerations such as social class, cultural background, level of cognitive development, language mastery, and personality characteristics of the children studied. Sometimes the stimuli used to evoke the behavior and the setting (school, home, and the like) are not reported. Some studies cannot be used because the age gradients are too gross—that is, lumping children age two to four in one category may obscure differences which occur by weeks and months rather than years. Currently there are many methods and many theoretical ap-

---

[46]There are attempts to develop such criteria. See N. G. Blurton Jones, "Criteria for Use in Describing Facial Expressions of Children," *Human Biology* 43 (1971): 365–413.

Nonverbal Communication: Developmental Perspectives

proaches to the study of the child's nonverbal behavior. While such diversity has its advantages, it does delay comparative analyses of the research and calls for tenuous conclusions.

Summary

The focus of this chapter has been on the origins and development of nonverbal behavior—development in the human species over geological time and development in the course of a single lifetime. With limited information available for other points in the life-span, our concern was mainly with the first part of the life-span.

We took the point of view that neither nature nor nurture is sufficient to explain the origin of many nonverbal behaviors. In many instances we inherit a neurological program that gives us the capacity to perform a particular act or sequence of acts; the fact that a particular behavior occurs at all may be genetically based. Our environment and cultural training, however, may be responsible for when the behavior appears, the frequency of its appearance, and the display rules which accompany it. We look at three sources of evidence for inborn behavior: (1) blind/deaf children, (2) nonhuman primates; and (3) multicultural studies. A number of behaviors and behavior sequences were examined, but facial expressions of emotion provided the consistent thread, deriving supporting data from all three categories.

Since the remainder of this book focuses on data which is heavily based on men and women between the ages of seventeen and twenty-five, this chapter presented some findings pertinent to infants and children. The development of touching behavior is treated fully in Chapter 7 and was not mentioned here. We did note some of the emblems used by children as young as 3½ and the fact that listener responses ("m-hm" and nodding) are infrequent in children until about the eighth grade. By the time children start at school they have established preferences for body builds (mesomorphs) and general attractiveness. Teachers also seem to respond to children on the basis of attractiveness. The eyes seem to be a part of the human face that infants observe very early, but we seem to know very little about the development of eye contact itself. The use of eye behavior to regulate the interaction flow seems infrequent in children. Most of the studies of personal space conducted thus far with children seem to confirm findings with adults. The stages of infant vocalizing, in preparation for using language are pretty well known. We know less about when children begin to recognize and respond to various vocal expressions. One intriguing line of research suggests that there is a synchrony between the parent's voice and the infant's movements as soon as twelve hours after birth.

Nonverbal Communication: Developmental Perspectives

Finally, we outlined some of the work on facial expressions, suggesting that a primitive type of discrimination begins at about six months but that recognition of an emotional expression in the face of another may be highly dependent on the emotion being portrayed (as well as other factors). After an attempt to collate the studies on which various facial expressions of emotion first appear, we concluded with an appraisal of this body of literature from the perspective of building a credible data bank.

SELECTED BIBLIOGRAPHY

Aiello, J., and Jones, S. "Field Study of the Proxemic Behavior of Young School Children in Three Subcultural Groups." *Journal of Personality and Social Psychology* 19 (1971): 351–356.

Als, H. "The Newborn Communicates," *Journal of Communication* 27 (1977): 66–73.

Altman, S. A. "Primates." In T. A. Sebeok (ed.), *Animal Communication*. Bloomington: Indiana University Press, 1968.

Ambrose, J. A. "The Development of the Smiling Response in Early Infancy." In B. M. Foss (ed.), *Determinants of Infant Behaviour*. London: Methuen, 1961, 179–196.

Andrew, R. J. "The Origin and Evolution of the Calls and Facial Expressions of the Primates." *Behaviour* 20 (1963): 1–109.

Ashear, V., and Snortum, J. R. "Eye Contact in Children as a Function of Age, Sex, Social and Intellective Variables." *Developmental Psychology* 4 (1971): 479.

Bass, H. M., and Weinstein, M. S. "Early Development of Interpersonal Distancing in Children." *Canadian Journal of Behavioural Science* 3 (1971): 368–376.

Baxter, J. C. "Interpersonal Spacing in Natural Settings." *Sociometry* 33 (1970): 444–456.

Blurton Jones, N. G. "Criteria for Use in Describing Facial Expressions of Children." *Human Biology* 43 (1971): 365–413.

Blurton Jones, N. G. (ed.) *Ethological Studies of Child Behavior* Cambridge: Cambridge University Press, 1972.

Blurton Jones, N. G. "Non-verbal Communication in Children." In R. Hinde (ed.) *Non-verbal Communication*. Cambridge: Cambridge University Press, 1972.

Brazelton, T. B., Kaslowski, B., and Main. M. "The Origins of Reciprocity: The Early Mother-Infant Interaction," in M. Lewis and L. A. Rosenblum (eds.), *The Effect of the Infant on its Caregiver*. New York: John Wiley and Sons, 1974, 49–76.

Bridges, K. "Emotional Development of Early Infancy." *Child Development* 3 (1932): 324–341.

Brooks, J., and Lewis, M., "Infants' Responses to Strangers: Midget, Adult and Child." *Child Development* 47 (1976): 323–332.

Buck, R. "Nonverbal Communication of Affect in Children." *Journal of Personality and Social Psychology* 31 (1975): 644–653.

Bugental, D. E., Kaswan, J. W., Love, L. R., and Fox, M. N. "Child Versus Adult Perception of Evaluative Messages in Verbal, Vocal, and Visual Channels." *Developmental Psychology* 2 (1970): 367–375.

Bugental, D., Love, L., and Gianetto, R. M. "Perfidious Feminine Faces." *Journal of Personality and Social Psychology* 17 (1971): 314–318.

Bullowa, M. "When Infant and Adult Communicate How Do they Synchronize Their Behavior?" In A. Kendon, R. M. Harris, and M. R. Key (eds.), *Organization of Behavior in Face-to-Face Interaction*. Chicago: Aldine, 1975.

Cairns, R. B. "The Ontogeny and Phylogeny of Social Interactions." In M. E. Hahn and E. C. Simmel (eds.), *Communicative Behavior and Evolution*. New York: Academic Press, 1976.

Capillari, M. J. L. "Gestures for Communication by Children Eighteen to Thirty-Six Months of Age." Unpublished Master's thesis, Purdue University, 1958.

Caron, A., Caron, R., Caldwell, R., and Weiss, S. "Infant Perception of the Structural Properties of the Face." *Developmental Psychology* 9 (1973): 385–399.

Carr, S. J., Dabbs, J., and Carr, T. S. "Mother-Infant Attachment: The Importance of the Mother's Visual Field." *Child Development* 46 (1975): 331–338.

Castell, R. "Effect of Familiar and Unfamiliar Environments on Proximity Behaviors of Young Children." *Journal of Experimental Psychology* 9 (1970): 342–347.

Cavior, N., and Donecki, P. R. "Physical Attractiveness, Perceived Attitude Similarity and Academic Achievement as Contributors to Interpersonal Attraction Among Adolescents." *Developmental Psychology* 9 (1973): 44–54.

Cavior, N., and Lombardi, D. A., "Developmental Aspects of Judgments of Physical Attractiveness in Children." *Developmental Psychology* 8 (1973): 67–71.

Charlesworth, W. R., and Kreutzer, M. A. "Facial Expressions of Infants and Children." In P. Ekman (ed.), *Darwin and Facial Expression*. New York: Academic Press, 1973.

Chevalier-Skolnikoff, S. "Facial Expression of Emotion in Nonhuman Primates." In P. Ekman (ed.), *Darwin and Facial Expression*. New York: Academic Press, 1973.

Condon, W. S., and Sanders, L. W. "Synchrony Demonstrated Between Movements of the Neonate and Adult Speech." *Child Development* 45 (1974): 456–462.

Cranach, M. Von, and Vine, I. (eds.). *Social Communication and Movement.* New York: Academic Press, 1973.

Darwin, C. R. "A Biographical Sketch of an Infant." *Mind* 2 (1877): 286–294.

Darwin, C. *The Expression of the Emotions in Man and Animals.* London: John Murray, 1872. Current edition: Chicago: University of Chicago Press, 1965.

DeLong, A. J. "Kinesic Signals at Utterance Boundaries in Preschool Children." *Semiotica* 11 (1974): 43–73.

Dimitrovsky, L. "The Ability to Identify the Emotional Meaning of Vocal Expression at Successive Age Levels." In J. R. Davitz (ed.), *The Communication of Emotional Meaning.* New York: McGraw-Hill, 1964. pp. 69–86.

Dion, K. K. "Physical Attractiveness and Evaluations of Children's Transgressions." *Journal of Personality and Social Psychology* 24 (1972): 207–213.

Dion, K. K. "Young Children's Stereotypes of Facial Attractiveness." *Developmental Psychology* 9 (1973): 183–188.

Dion, K. K., and Berschied, E. "Physical Attractiveness and Peer Perceptions Among Children." *Sociometry* 37 (1974): 1–12.

Dittmann, A. T. "Developmental Factors in Conversational Behavior." *Journal of Communication* 22 (1972): 404–423.

Eberts, E. H., and Lepper, M. R. "Individual Consistency in the Proxemic Behavior of Preschool Children." *Journal of Personality and Social Psychology* 32 (1975): 841–849.

Eibl-Eibesfeldt, I. *Ethology: The Biology of Behavior.* New York: Holt, Rinehart and Winston, 1970.

Eibl-Eibesfeldt, I. "Similarities and Differences Between Cultures in Expressive Movements." In R. Hinde (ed.), *Non-verbal Communications.* Cambridge: Cambridge University Press, 1972.

Eibl-Eibesfeldt, I. "The Expressive Behavior of the Deaf-and-Blind-Born." In M. von Cranach and I. Vine (eds.), *Social Communication and Movement.* New York: Academic Press, 1973.

Ekman, P. "Cross-Cultural Studies of Facial Expression." In P. Ekman (ed.), *Darwin and Facial Expression.* New York: Academic Press, 1973.

Ekman, P. (ed.). *Darwin and Facial Expression: A Century of Research in Review.* New York: Academic Press, 1973.

Ekman, P., and Friesen, W. V. "The Repertoire of Nonverbal Behavior: Categories, Origins, Usage, and Coding." *Semiotica* 1 (1969): 49–98.

Feinman, S., and Entwisle, D. R. "Children's Ability to Recognize Other Children's Faces." *Child Development* 47 (1976): 506–520.

Fenster, A., and Goldstein, A. M. "The Emotional World of Children 'Vis-À-Vis' the Emotional World of Adults: An Examination of Vocal Communication." *Journal of Communication* 21 (1971): 353–362.

Nonverbal Communication: Developmental Perspectives

Fitzgerald, H. E. "Autonomic Pupillary Reflex Activity During Early Infancy and Its Relation to Social and Non-social Stimuli." *Journal of Experimental Child Psychology* 6 (1968): 470–482.

Formby, D. "Maternal Recognition of Infant's Cry." *Developmental Medicine and Child Neurology* 9 (1967): 293–298.

Freedman, D. G. "Smiling in Blind Infants and the Issue of Innate Versus Acquired." *Journal of Child Psychology and Psychiatry* 5 (1964): 171–184.

Gates, G. S. "An Experimental Study of the Growth of Social Perception." *Journal of Educational Psychology* 14 (1923): 449–461.

Guardo, C. J. "Personal Space in Children." *Child Development* 40 (1969): 143–153.

Guardo, C. J., and Meisels, M. "Factor Structure of Children's Personal Space Schemata." *Child Development* 42 (1971): 1307–1312.

Hahn, M. E., and Simmel, E. C. (eds.). *Communicative Behavior and Evolution.* New York: Academic Press, 1976.

Harper, L., and Sanders, K. M. "Preschool Children's Use of Space: Sex Differences in Outdoor Play." *Developmental Psychology* 11 (1975): 119.

Hinde, R. A. *Biological Bases of Human Social Behavior.* New York: McGraw-Hill, 1974.

Hinde, R. (ed.). *Non-verbal Communication.* Cambridge: Cambridge University Press, 1972.

Hooff, J. A. R. A. M. Van. "A Comparative Approach to the Phylogeny of Laughter and Smiling." In R. Hinde (ed.), *Non-verbal Communication.* Cambridge: Cambridge University Press, 1972.

Hooff, J. A. R. A. M. Van. "A Structural Analysis of the Social Behavior of a Semi-captive Group of Chimpanzees." In M. von Cranach and I. Vine (eds.), *Social Communication and Movement.* New York: Academic Press, 1973.

Hutt, C., and Ounstead, C. "The Biological Significance of Gaze Aversion with Particular Reference to the Syndrome of Infantile Autism." *Behavioral Science* 11 (1966): 346–356.

Hutt, C., and Vaizey, M. J. "Differential Effects of Group Density on Social Behavior." *Nature* 209 (1967): 1371–1372.

Illingworth, R. "Crying in Infants and Children." *British Medical Journal* 75 (1955): 75–88.

Jones, S., and Aiello, J. "Proxemic Behavior of Black and White First-, Third-, and Fifth-Grade Children." *Journal of Personality and Social Psychology* 25 (1973): 21–27.

Kagan, J., and Lewis, M. "Studies of Attention in the Human Infant." *Merrill-Palmer Quarterly* 4 (1965): 95–127.

Kashinsky, M., and Wiener, M. "Tone in Communication and the Performance of Children from Two Socioeconomic Groups." *Child Development* 40 (1969): 1193–1202.

King, M. G. "Interpersonal Relations in Preschool Children and Average Approach Distance." *Journal of Genetic Psychology* 109 (1966): 109–116.

Kleck, R., Rishardson, S. A., Ronald L. "Physical Appearance Cues and Interpersonal Attraction in Children." *Child Development* 45 (1974): 305–310.

Kumin, L., and Lazar, M. "Gestural Communication in Preschool Children." *Perceptual and Motor Skills* 38 (1974): 708–710.

LaBarbara, J. D., Izard, C. E., Vietze, P., and Parisi, S. A. "Four and Six Month Infants' Visual Responses to Joy, Anger and Neutral Expressions." *Child Development* 47 (1976): 535–538.

Leach, E. "The Influence of Cultural Context on Non-verbal Communication in Man." In R. Hinde (ed.), *Non-verbal Communication*. Cambridge: Cambridge University Press, 1972.

Lenneberg, E. *Biological Foundations of Language*. New York: Wiley, 1969.

Lerner, R. M., and Gellert, E. "Body Build Identification, Preference and Aversion in Children." *Developmental Psychology* 1 (1969): 456–462.

Lerner, R. M., and Korn, S. J. "The Development of Body Build Stereotypes in Males." *Child Development* 43 (1972): 908–920.

Lerner, R. M., Karabenick, S. A., and Meisel, M. "Effect of Age and Sex on the Development of Personal Space Schemata Towards Body Build." *Journal of Genetic Psychology* 127 (1975): 91–101.

Levin, H., Silverman, I., and Ford, B. "Hesitations in Children's Speech During Explanation and Description." *Journal of Verbal Learning and Verbal Behavior* 6 (1967): 560–564.

Levine, M. H., and Sutton-Smith, B. "Effects of Age, Sex and Task on Visual Behavior During Dyadic Interaction." *Developmental Psychology* 9 (1973): 400–405.

Lieberman, P. *Intonation, Perception, and Language*. Cambridge, Mass.: M.I.T. Press, 1966.

Ling, D., and Ling, A. H. "Communication Development in the First Three Years of Life." *Journal of Speech and Hearing Research* 17 (1974): 146–159.

Lipsitt, L. P., Engen, T., and Kaye, H. "Developmental Changes in the Olfactory Threshold of the Neonate." *Child Development* 34 (1963): 371–376.

Lomranz, J., Shapira, A., Choresh, N., and Gilat, Y. "Children's Personal Space as a Function of Age and Sex." *Developmental Psychology* 11 (1975): 651–654.

Loo, C. "The Effects of Spatial Density on the Social Behavior of Children." *Journal of Applied Social Psychology* 4 (1972): 172–181.

Lord, C. "The Perception of Eye Contact in Children and Adults." *Child Development* 45 (1974): 1113–1117.

Maurer, D., and Salapatek, P. "Developmental Changes in the Scanning of Faces by Young Infants." *Child Development* 47 (1976): 523–527.

McGlone, R. "Vocal Pitch Characteristics of Children Aged One to Two Years." *Speech Monographs* 33 (1966): 178–181.

McGrew, P. "Social and Spacing Density Effects on Spacing Density in Preschool Children." *Journal of Child Psychology and Psychiatry* 11 (1970): 197–205.

McGrew, W. C. *An Ethological Study of Children's Behavior.* New York: Academic Press, 1972.

Mead, M. "Margaret Mead Calls 'Discipline-Centric' Approach to Research an 'Example of the Appalling State of the Human Sciences.' " *Journal of Communication* 25 (1975): 209–213.

Mehrabian, A. "Child Communication." In A. Mehrabian, *Nonverbal Communication.* Chicago: Aldine-Atherton, 1972. Pp. 159–177.

Meisels, M., and Guardo, C. J. "Development of Personal Space Schemata." *Child Development* 40 (1969): 1167–1178.

Michael, G., and Willis, F. M. "The Development of Gestures as a Function of Social Class, Education and Sex." *Psychological Record* 18 (1968): 515–519.

Michael, G., and Willis, F. M. "The Development of Gestures in Three Subcultural Groups." *Journal of Social Psychology* 79 (1969): 35–41.

Milmoe, S., Novey, M. S., Kagan, J., and Rosenthal, R. "The Mother's Voice: Postdictor of Aspects of Her Baby's Behavior." In S. Weitz (ed.), *Nonverbal Communication.* New York: Oxford University Press, 1974. Pp. 122–126.

Mollard, A. R., and Daniloff, R. G. "Glottal Cues for Parent Judgement of Emotional Aspects of Infant Vocalization." *Journal of Speech and Hearing Research* 16 (1973): 592–596.

Moss, H. A., and Robson, K. S. "Maternal Influences in Early Socio-visual Behavior." *Child Development* 39 (1968): 401–408.

Pedersen, D. "Developmental Trends in Personal Space." *Journal of Psychology* 83 (1973): 3–9.

Phillis, J. A. "Children's Judgements of Personality on the Basis of Voice Quality." *Developmental Psychology* 3 (1970): 411.

Pitcairn, T. K., and Eibl-Eibesfeldt, I. "Concerning the Evolution of Nonverbal Communication in Man." In M. E. Hahn and E. C. Simmell (eds.), *Communicative Behavior and Evolution.* New York: Academic Press, 1976.

Post, B., and Hetherington, E. M. "Sex Differences in the Use of Proximity and Eye Contact in Judgements of Affiliation in Preschool Children." *Developmental Psychology* 10 (1974): 881–889.

Rheingold, H. L., and Cook, K. V. "The Contents of Boys' and Girls' Rooms as an Index of Parents' Behavior." *Child Development* 46 (1975), 459–463.

Robson, K. S. "The Role of Eye-to-Eye Contact in Maternal-Infant Attachment." *Journal of Child Psychology and Psychiatry* 8 (1967): 13–25.

Rovee, C. V., Cohen, R. Y., and Shlapack, W. "Lifespan Stability in Olfactory

Sensitivity." *Developmental Psychology* 11 (1975): 311–318.

Schmidt, W., and Hore, T. "Some Nonverbal Aspects of Communication Between Mother and Child." *Child Development* 41 (1970): 889–896.

Self, P. A., Horowitz, F., and Paden. L. "Olfaction in Newborn Infants." *Developmental Psychology* 7 (1972): 349–363.

Sheppard, W. C., and Lane, H. L., "Development of the Prosodic Features of Infant Vocalizing." *Journal of Speech and Hearing Research* 11 (1968): 94–108.

Smith, W. J. "Displays and Messages in Intraspecific Communication." *Semiotica* 1 (1969): 357–369.

Spitz, R. A. *No and Yes: On the Genesis of Human Communication.* New York: International Universities Press, 1957.

Spitz, R., and Wolf, K. "The Smiling Response: A Contribution to the Ontogenesis of Social Relations." *Genetic Psychology Monographs* 34 (1946): 57–125.

Sroufe, L. A., and Waters, E. "The Ontogenesis of Smiling and Laughter." *Psychological Review* 83 (1976): 173–189.

Tautermannova, M. "Smiling in Infants." *Child Development* 44 (1973): 701–704.

Thorpe, W. H. "The Comparison of Vocal Communication in Animals and Man." In R. Hinde (ed.), *Non-verbal Communication.* Cambridge: Cambridge University Press, 1972.

Tinbergen, N. *The Study of Instinct.* London: Oxford University Press, 1951.

Tronick, E. D., Als, H. and Brazelton, T. B. "Mutuality in Mother-Infant Interaction." *Journal of Communication* 27 (1977): 74–79.

Turnure, C. "Responses to Voice of Mother and Stranger by Babies in the First Year." *Developmental Psychology* 4 (1971): 182–190.

Vine, I. "The Role of Facial-Visual Signalling in Early Social Development." In M. von Cranach and I. Vine (eds.), *Social Communication and Movement.* New York: Academic Press, 1973.

Walker, R. N. "Body Build and Behavior in Young Children." *Child Development* 34 (1963): 1–23.

Wasz-Hockert, O., Partanen, T., Vuorenkoski, V., Valanne, E., and Michelsson, K. "Effect of Training on Ability to Identify Preverbal Vocalization." *Developmental Medicine and Child Neurology* 6: (1964): 393–396.

Wolff, P. H. "Observations on the Early Development of Smiling." In B. M. Foss (ed.), *Determinants of Infant Behavior,* vol. 2. London, Methuen), 1963.

Wood, B. *Children and Communication.* Englewood Cliffs, N.J.: Prentice-Hall, 1976.

3 The Effects of the Environment on Human Communication

Every interior betrays the nonverbal skills of its inhabitants. The choice of materials, the distribution of space, the kind of objects that command attention or demand to be touched—as compared to those that intimidate or repel—have much to say about the preferred sensory modalities of their owners.

RUESCH and KEES

The ultimate influence on students of the student-teacher dialogue in America's classrooms is unknown. Few would disagree that this particular communication context is an extremely critical one for many students. What is the nature of the environment in which this important dialogue takes place? What difference does it make?

Most American classrooms are rectangular in shape with straight rows of chairs. They have wide windows which allow light to beam across the student's shoulder. This window placement determines the direction students will face and thus designates the "front" of the classroom. Most classroom seats are also permanently attached to the floor for ease of maintenance and tidiness. Most classrooms have some type of partition (usually a desk) which separates teacher from students. Most students and teachers can provide a long list of "problems" encountered in environments designed for learning. Such complaints center around poor lighting, acoustics, temperature which is too hot or too cold, outside construction noises, banging radiators, electrical outlets which do not work, seats which do not move, gloomy, dull, or distracting color schemes, unpleasant odors, and so on. Why do they complain? Because they recognize that such problems impede the purpose for gathering in these rectangular rooms—which is to increase one's knowledge through effective student-teacher communication. The whole question of the influence of the classroom environment on student and teacher behavior remains relatively unexplored. The following research by Sommer, however, provides us with some initial data on student participation in various classroom environments.[1]

Sommer selected six different kinds of classrooms for his study. He wanted to compare the amount of student participation in the different kinds of classrooms and to analyze the particular aspects of participatory behavior in each type. The types of classrooms included seminar rooms with movable chairs, usually arranged in the shape of a horseshoe; laboratories (complete with Bunsen burners, bottles, and gas valves), which represented an extreme in straight-row seating; one room which was windowless; and one in which had an entire wall of windows. Undergraduate students acted as observers to record participation by the students. A distaste for the laboratory rooms and the windowless room was demonstrated through several attempts by instructors and students to change rooms or hold classes outside. There were no differences between open and windowless rooms with respect to participation behavior. Comparisons between rooms showed that in seminar rooms fewer people participated, but for longer periods of time. In a related study, Sommer and his colleagues found that the average amount of participation did vary between large and small classes—2.5 minutes during one class period for the large lecture classes and 5.8 minutes for the classes of twenty and less.[2] Thus, the odds of a student participating in class discussion are greater for small classes—but not much. One important content-related aspect which Sommer hints at is a potentially significant difference in the *type* of participation. Student participation in the large classes seemed to be questions of clarification or requests for repeating an idea—a type of participation which differs radically from the intellectual give and take between two people seeking to understand, to refine, to see ramifications and related ideas, and so on.

When seminar rooms were analyzed separately, Sommer noted that most participation came from students seated directly opposite the instructor. Students generally avoided the two chairs on either side of the instructor—even when all other seats were filled. When a student did occupy the seat next to the

[1]R. Sommer, *Personal Space* (Englewood Cliffs, N.J.: Prentice-Hall, 1969), p. 110–119.

[2]R. Sommer, *Tight Spaces* (Englewood Cliffs, N.J.: Prentice-Hall, 1974). Another report of the variance of classroom participation with seating arrangements is found in R. Sommer, "Classroom Ecology," *Journal of Applied Behavioral Science* 3 (1967): 487–503.

The Effects of the Environment on Human Communication

instructor, he or she was generally silent throughout the entire period. In straight-row rooms, the following observations were made: (1) Students within eye contact range of the instructor participate more. (2) There is a tendency for more participation to occur in the center sections of each row and for participation to generally decrease from the front to the back. This tendency, however, is not evident when interested students sit in locations other than those which provide maximum visual contact with the instructor. (3) Participation decreases as class size increases.

A related research project offers additional support for Sommer's observations on participation in straight-row classrooms. Adams and Biddle noted a remarkably consistent pattern of interaction in Grades I, VI, and XI, which indicated most student participation comes from students sitting in the center of the room.[3] Sixty-three percent of the 1,176 behaviors observed came from students located in three positions, one behind the other, down the center of the room. Almost all pupil-initiated comments come from the shadowed area in Figure 3.1. In no instance did teachers select special students for placement in these locations. As the authors point out, "it is now possible to discriminate an area of the classroom that seems to be literally and figuratively the center of activity."

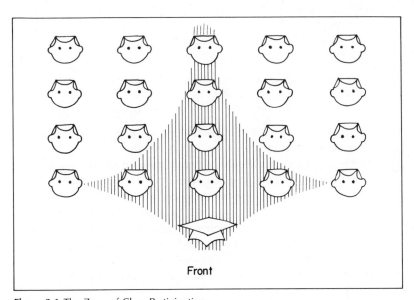

Figure 3.1 The Zone of Class Participation

[3]R. S. Adams and B. Biddle, *Realities of Teaching: Explorations With Video Tape* (New York: Holt, Rinehart and Winston, 1970).

The Effects of the Environment on Human Communication

Koneya felt that there were still some questions which Sommer and Adams and Biddle had not sufficiently explored.[4] First, do high participators choose certain seats or is there something about the dynamics of seat location which brings about high participation? After high and low participating students were identified, they were given the chance to choose a seat from a classroom diagram. High verbalizers did tend to select seats in the zone of participation more than low or moderate verbalizers. Secondly, Koneya wanted to put students who were previously identified as high, moderate, or low participators in different seats and observe their participation. Observations took place over seven class periods. Both the high and moderate participators talked more in the zone of participation than their counterparts in noncentral areas. Those who were low participators were consistently low—in or out of the central areas. From these studies we can conclude that classroom seating is not random, that certain types of people do gravitate to central and noncentral areas; and that the zone of participation, heavily influenced by teacher-student visibility, will promote participation for everyone except initially low participators. Even then, we might find increased participation at some point after the seventh class period with a teacher who rewards and supports participation. Why is participation important? It may assist in clarifying difficult ideas to be learned and it may link professor and student in a social bond which can create a better learning environment. And, to no student's surprise, "getting to know your instructor" may influence grades too.

Sommer concludes his observations on classroom behavior and environmental influences by saying:

> At the present time, teachers are hindered by their insensitivity to and fatalistic acceptance of the classroom environment. Teachers must be "turned on" to their environment lest their pupils develop this same sort of fatalism.[5]

The preceding discussion of the classroom was used as an illustrative example of a specific context in which the spatial relationships, the architecture, and the objects surrounding the participants influenced the amount and type of interaction which occurred. We will be examining other environmental factors which impinge on our human communication behavior, but we should remember that the environment is only one ingredient in structuring such behavior. If students, administrators, teachers, secretaries, and custodians want to run the university like a prison or a dehumanized bureaucracy, changes in the classroom structure may have very little overall impact.

Throughout this chapter we will be discussing a number of characteristics

---

[4]W. Koneya, "The Relationship Between Verbal Interaction and Seat Location of Members of Large Groups," Unpublished PhD dissertation, Denver University, 1973.
[5]Sommer, *Personal Space*, p. 119.

The Effects of the Environment on Human Communication

of environments, but let's initiate our exploration of environments by examining the way we perceive our surroundings.

Perceptions of Our Surroundings

The number of different places we communicate with others is limitless—buses, homes, apartments, public restaurants, offices, parks, hotels, sports arenas, factories, libraries, movie theaters, museums, and so on. Yet, despite this diversity, we probably evaluate these environments along similar dimensions. Once we have perceived our environment in a certain way, we may incorporate such perceptions in the development of the messages we send. And, once that message has been sent, the environmental perceptions of the other person have been altered. Thus, we are influenced by and influence our environments.

Mehrabian argues that we react emotionally to our surroundings.[6] And the nature of our emotional reactions can be accounted for in terms of how *arousing* the environment made us feel, how *pleasurable* we felt, and how *dominant* we are made to feel. Arousal refers to how active, stimulated, frenzied, or alert you are; pleasure refers to feelings of joy, satisfaction, or happiness; and dominance suggests that you feel in control, important—free to act in a variety of ways. Environments that are novel, surprising, crowded, and complex will probably produce feelings of higher arousal.

In another work, I proposed the following framework for classifying perceptions of interaction environments.[7] Although these perceptual bases are not intended to be completely relegated to emotional responses, it is not hard to see the overlap with Mehrabian's schema.

Perceptions of Formality.   One familiar dimension along which environments can be classified is a formal/informal continuum. Our reaction may be based on the objects present, the people present, the functions performed, or any number of other characteristics. Individual offices may be more formal than a lounge in the same building; a year-end banquet would seem to take on more formality than a "come as you are" party; an evening with one other couple in your home may be more informal than an evening with ten other couples; and so on. The greater the formality, the greater the chances that the communication behavior will be less relaxed and more superficial, hesitant, and stylized.

[6]A. Mehrabian, *Public Places and Private Spaces* (New York: Basic Books, 1976).
[7]M. Knapp, *Social Intercourse: From Greeting to Goodbye* (Boston: Allyn and Bacon, 1978).

Perceptions of Warmth.   Environments which make us feel psychologically warm encourage us to linger, to feel relaxed, and to feel comfortable. It may be some combination of the color of the drapes or walls, paneling, carpeting, texture of the furniture, softness of the chairs, soundproofing, and so on. Fast-food chains will try to retain some degree of warmth in their decor to remain inviting, but display enough coldness to encourage rapid turnover.

Perceptions of Privacy.   Enclosed environments usually suggest greater privacy, particularly if they will accommodate a few people. As long as the possibility of other people's entering and/or overhearing your conversation is small (even if you are outdoors), there is a greater feeling of privacy. Sometimes the objects in the setting will add to the perceptions of privacy—for example, toilet articles and other personal items. With greater privacy, we'll probably find close speaking distances and more personal messages, designed and adapted for the specific other person rather than "people in general."

Perceptions of Familiarity.   When we meet a new person, we are typically cautious, deliberate, and conventional in our responses. Ditto for unfamiliar environments. Unfamiliar environments are laden with ritual and norms which we do not yet know, so we are hesitant to move too quickly. We will probably go slowly until we can associate this unfamiliar environment with one we know. One interpretation for the rather stereotyped structures of quick-food stops is that they allow us (a mobile society) to readily find a familiar and predictable place which will guarantee minimum demands for active contact with strangers. In unfamiliar environments, the most likely topic of conversation will initially revolve around the environment itself—for example, "Have you ever been here before? What is it like? Who comes here? What's that for? Jeez, look at that!" and so on.

Perceptions of Constraint.   Part of our total reaction to an environment is based on our perception of whether (and how easily) we can leave it. Some students feel confined in their own homes during the Christmas break from school—but consider the differences between this constraint of two weeks with a permanent live-at-home arrangement. The intensity of these perceptions of constraint is closely related to the space available to us (and the privacy of this space) during the time we will be in the environment. Some environments seem to be only temporarily confining—for example, a long trip in an automobile; other environments seem more permanently confining—for example, prisons, spacecraft, nursing homes, and the like.

Perceptions of Distance.   Sometimes our responses within a given environment will be influenced by how close or far away we must conduct our

The Effects of the Environment on Human Communication

communication with another. This may reflect actual physical distance (an office on a different floor, a house in another part of the city), or it may reflect psychological distance (barriers clearly separating people who are fairly close physically). You may be seated close to someone and still not perceive it as a close environment—for example, interlocking chairs in an airport which are facing the same direction. When the setting forces us into close quarters with other people who are not well known (elevators, crowded buses), we will probably see efforts to increase distance psychologically to reflect a less intimate feeling—for example, less eye contact, body tenseness and immobility, cold silence, nervous laughter, jokes about the intimacy, and public conversation which is directed at all present.

The foregoing represent only some of the dimensions along which communication settings can be perceived. Generally, more intimate communication is associated with informal, unconstrained, private, familiar, close, and warm environments. In everyday situations, however, these dimensions combine in complex ways—for example, some formality with a lot of constraint and only a little bit of privacy. At present we don't know how these combinations affect the way we communicate. The mixture of intimate and nonintimate factors can be seen in an elevator if you perceive it as close, familiar, and temporarily confining, but also public, formal, and cold.

The remainder of this chapter will be devoted to the characteristics of environments—characteristics which go together to make up the perceptions we have just outlined. Each environment is made up of three major components: (1) the natural environment—geography, location, atmospheric conditions; (2) the presence or absence of other people; (3) architectural and design features, including movable objects.

The Natural Environment

For many years, behavioral scientists have hypothesized that those who choose to live in urban rather than rural areas will have fewer close personal relations. In the United States, however, there is less and less evidence to support this theory. Greater mobility and the influence of the mass media tend to offset the possibility that these differences exist. There is evidence to suggest, however, that the more physical mobility you have in a city, the less social intimacy you will have within your own neighborhood. If you are a resident new to the community, you will very likely associate with your neighbors more than do the old residents who know more people in other parts of town. And if the neighborhood is fairly homogeneous in terms of religious beliefs, social class, political attitudes, and the like, these relationships will tend to persist.

Some descriptive research, comparing characteristics of city and rural environments, reveals additional differences in city and country life—from which one may develop hypotheses concerning the effects of differing environments on the interaction patterns of the inhabitants. For instance: (1) there appears to be more political and religious tolerance in cities than in rural areas; (2) there appears to be less religious observance in cities than in rural areas; (3) there are more foreign immigrants in cities than in rural areas; (4) there is more change in cities, and more stability in the country; (5) there is a higher level of education in cities than in rural areas; (6) there are fewer married people in the cities than in rural areas; (7) there is a lower birth rate in cities than in rural areas; (8) there is more divorce in cities than in rural areas; (9) there is more suicide in cities than in rural areas. In slums or ghettos in urban areas, one often finds a social climate which encourages or fosters unconventional and deviant behavior—or at least tolerates it. Thus, slum areas show a high incidence of juvenile delinquency, prostitution, severe mental illness, alcoholism and drug addiction, physical and mental disability, and crimes of violence.

Some have even speculated on the effects of the moon and sunspots on human behavior. There is considerable skepticism of this work, partially because such forces seem too mystical to explain our behavior, and partially because the research studies of this type show that these things seem to vary together—but *not* that a particular moon position actually causes certain behaviors. While this line of inquiry may not be widely accepted, you may find some of the findings intriguing. A group of scientists and engineers who study the use of nuclear energy for the Atomic Energy Commission published a report entitled, "Intriguing Accident Patterns Plotted Against a Background of Natural Environment Features."[8] The report maintains that accident rates (and presumably other human behavior) are influenced by phases of the moon, solar cycles, and other natural phenomena. An examination of accident patterns for the past twenty years suggested that people's susceptibility to accidents was highest during the lunar phase similar to or 180 degrees away from the one in which they were born. Accidents also tended to peak in cycles of the new moon in apogee—the point at which the moon was farthest away from the earth. The sun's rotation also seems to alter the strength of the earth's magnetic field—alterations which seem to coincide with increases and decreases in accidents. These scientists conclude that these natural features of our environment, *in conjunction with other factors,* help to create misjudgments, pressures, and situations leading to accidents. Scientists who study wildlife have also found interesting covariations in an approximate ten-year lunar cycle and fluctuations in wildlife populations. It seems that population peaks and

[8]"Moonstruck Scientists," *Time* 48 (January 10, 1972).

The Effects of the Environment on Human Communication

declines coincide with the nodal cycle of the moon. This is true for populations which are widely separated from each other.

A former director of climatology with the U.S. Weather Bureau was elected the President of an organization called the American Institute of Medical Climatology.[9] This is a group of meteorologists, physicists, and physicians who exchange findings regarding the effects of temperature fluctuations and changes in humidity and barometric pressure on various illnesses such as heart attacks, asthma, arthritis, migraine headaches, intestinal disorders, hypertension, mental illness, and even the common cold.

We all know that we sometimes feel unusually depressed during dark, overcast days. Others have noted that the right combination of atmospheric pressure and high temperatures may lead to restlessness, irritability, temper tantrums, and even aggressive acts. The National Advisory Commission on Civil Disorders reported, in 1968, that the hot summer nights added to an already explosive situation which eventually resulted in widespread rioting in ghetto areas: "In most instances, the temperature during the day on which the violence erupted was quite high."[10] Griffitt varied heat and humidity under controlled laboratory conditions for students and confirmed a relationship to interpersonal responses. As temperature and humidity increased, evaluative responses for interpersonal attraction to another student decreased.[11] There may be more truth than fiction in the familiar explanation for a particularly unpleasant encounter. "Oh, he was just hot and irritable."

Obviously, the relationship between temperature and aggression is not a simple one. There are probably a number of things which interact with the temperature to increase the chances of one's aggression—for example, prior provocation, presence of aggressive models, perceived ability to leave the environment, and so on. Some laboratory studies by Baron and Bell provide some useful insights into this matter.[12] First, they had a confederate give some

[9]T. K. Irwin, "Weather and You: Your Illnesses, Your Moods in Rain or shine," *Family Weekly*, September 14, 1975, 4–6.

[10]"Report of the National Advisory Commission on Civil Disorders" (Washington: U.S. Government Printing Office, 1968), p. 71. Also see R. E. Goranson and D. King, "Rioting and Daily temperature: Analysis of the U.S. Riots in 1967," Unpublished manuscript, York University, Ontario, Canada, 1970.

[11]W. Griffitt, "Environmental Effects of Interpersonal Affective Behavior: Ambient Effective Temperature and Attraction," *Journal of Personality and Social Psychology* 15 (1970): 240–244. Also see W. Griffitt and R. Veitch, "Hot and Crowded: Influence of Population Density and Temperature on Interpersonal Affective Behavior," *Journal of Personality and Social Psychology* 17 (1971): 92–98.

[12]R. A. Baron and P. A. Bell, "Aggression and Heat: The Influence of Ambient Temperature, Negative Affect, and a Cooling Drink on Physical Aggression," *Journal of Personality and Social Psychology* 33 (1976): 245–255; Also see R. A. Baron and P. A. Bell, "Aggression and Heat: Mediating Effects of Prior Provocation and Exposure to An Aggressive Model," *Journal of Personality and Social Psychology* 31 (1975): 825–832.

The Effects of the Environment on Human Communication

male students a rather harsh, negative evaluation, while others got more positive feedback. Then, under the guise of another experiment, the men were given an opportunity to administer electric shocks to their partner—that is, the confederate who had evaluated them. Room temperatures were about 74 degrees Fahrenheit for some and about 94 degrees for others.

The results were just the opposite of what was expected. The higher temperatures facilitated aggressive acts (shocks) by those who were given the positive evaluations, while those receiving negative messages were more inhibited. The authors offer this explanation. The subjects who had been treated harshly were apparently so uncomfortable that escape from the environment or minimization of the discomfort was the primary goal—rather than aggression. They might have thought that if they gave strong electric shocks they would only prolong their already uncomfortable stay in this situation—delays caused either by protests from the person being shocked or censure by the experimenter. Furthermore, if they administered strong shocks they themselves might experience additional negative feelings, such as guilt, empathizing with signs of pain in the victim, and the like. So, if we are to hypothesize a relationship between high temperatures and aggression, we need to consider the amount of negative affect the person is experiencing from all sources.

In the early twentieth century, Huntington advanced a seemingly bizarre theory that for mental vigor, an average outdoor temperature of 50 to 60 degrees is better than one above 70 degrees.[13] More recently, scientists have suggested that: (1) monotonous weather is more apt to affect your spirits; (2) seasonally, you do your best mental work in late winter, early spring, and fall; (3) a prolonged blue sky reduces your productivity; and (4) the ideal temperature should average about 64 degrees Fahrenheit. McClelland, in his analysis of folk stories in primitive societies, found that achievement motivation was highest in areas where the mean annual temperature ranged between 40 and 60 degrees Fahrenheit.[14] He also concluded that temperature variation was important in determining achievement motivation with at least fifteen degrees daily or seasonal variation needed for high achievement motivation. Lee speculates that tropical climates produce mental and physical lethargy:

> Some loss of mental initiative is probably the most important single direct result of exposure to tropical environment. . . . Certainly, the usual pattern of life in tropical countries is more leisurely and less productive of material goods than that which is found in most temperate latitudes, and a case can be made for at least some influence of climate in this respect. Man in the temperate zones has built up his civilization around the important demands created by cold weather for securing food and shelter in advance. In so doing, he has developed a culture in which activity and making provisions for the future have high social values.

[13]E. Huntington, *Civilization and Climate* (New Haven: Yale University Press, 1915).
[14]D. McClelland, *The Achieving Society* (New York: Van Nostrand Reinhold, 1961).

The Effects of the Environment on Human Communication

In tropical populations, on the other hand, climate provides neither the social nor the psychological drive for activity and saving beyond the needs of the more or less immediate future. This difference in "spontaneous" activity marks one of the most important conflicts at the personal level between temperate and tropical modes of behavior.[15]

A final note—hardly worth reporting were it not for the fact that this author was born in July—some researchers have even argued that American babies born in the North, in the summer months, have slightly higher I.Q. scores in later life than those born at other times!

These reports on geography, climate, and celestial bodies provide us with little reliable and valid information. That our behavior is influenced by such factors seems a reasonable assumption, but the exact nature of this influence, the specific conditions under which this influence occurs, and the degree of the influence are still unknown.

Other People in the Environment

In the next chapter we will examine the reactions of people to environments which are overpopulated—that is, dense or crowded. For now, though, we just want to point out that other people can be perceived as part of the environment—and will have an effect on your behavior. These people may be perceived as "active" or "passive" participants, depending on the degree to which they are perceived as "involved" (speaking or listening) in your conversation. In many situations these people will be seen as "active," especially if they are able to overhear what you are saying. There are, however, situations when we grant another person or persons the dubious status of "nonperson"—and behave accordingly. This may occur in high-density situations, but it is also common with just one other person. Cab drivers, janitors, and children have been known to achieve nonperson status with some regularity. The presence of nonpersons, of course, allows the free uninhibited flow of interaction because as far as the active participants are concerned they are the only human interactants present. Parents will sometimes talk to others about very personal aspects of their child while the child is playing nearby. For the interactants, however, the child is perceived as "not here." Any relevant verbal or nonverbal responses on the part of the nonperson which are picked up by the interactants will immediately strip the person of the nonperson role.

[15]D. Lee, *Climate and Economic Development in the Tropics* (New York: Harper and Row, 1957), p. 100.

The Effects of the Environment on Human Communication

93

When others are perceived as an active ingredient in the environment, it may facilitate or inhibit certain kinds of communication. The chief difference in communication with active others is that messages must be adapted to multiple audiences rather than a single one. Even telephone conversations, where the third party can hear only one of the interactants, are altered to account for the uninvited listener. Sometimes the existence of these additional audiences presents such a strain or threat that one or both communicators leave the scene. On the other hand, the appearance of a third party provides an opportunity to ease out of a conversation with an undesirable other by "dumping" the focus of the interaction on this third party and making a polite exit.

The presence of others may increase our motivation to "look good" in what we say and do, which may be detrimental (distorting information) or may be beneficial. The benefits of looking good in the presence of others is exemplified in the form of constructive approaches to conflict. For instance, the presence of others may prohibit overt fighting from arising at all. But, of course, such benefits may be temporary in nature. The other people in the environment have insured a delay, which may act as a "cooling off" period or may further frustrate and aggravate the person who had to repress such feelings. If the people present are not highly interdependent on each other, the communication will probably be less personal, more conventional and stereotyped—a form of communication designed for broader, less specific audiences.

Architectural Design and Movable Objects

Hall has labeled the architecture and objects in our environment as either fixed-feature space or semi-fixed-feature space.[16] The term *fixed-feature* refers to space organized by unmoving boundaries (rooms of houses), while *semi-fixed-feature* refers to the arrangement of movable objects such as tables or chairs. Both of these aspects of our environments can have a profound impact on our communication behavior.

At one time in America's history, banks were deliberately designed to project an image of strength and security. The design frequently included large marble pillars, an abundance of metal bars and doors, uncovered floors, and barren walls. This style generally elicited a cold, impersonal reaction from visitors. Not too many years ago bankers perceived a need to change their environment—to present a friendly, warm, "homey" image of a place where people would enjoy sitting down and openly discussing their financial problems. The interiors of banks began to change. Carpeting was added; wood was

[16]E. T. Hall, *The Hidden Dimension* (Garden City, N.Y.: Doubleday, 1966).

The Effects of the Environment on Human Communication

used to replace metal; cushioned chairs were added; potted plants were used in some cases for additional "warmth," along with other, similar changes designed to create the same effect. This is but one example of a situation in which it was recognized that oftentimes the interior within which interaction occurs can significantly influence the nature of the interaction. Night club owners and restaurateurs are aware that dim lighting and sound-absorbing surfaces like carpets, drapes, and padded ceilings will provide greater intimacy and will cause patrons to linger longer than they would in an interior with high illumination and no soundproofing.

Sometimes we get very definite person-related messages from home environments. Our perception of the inhabitants of a home may be structured before we meet them—whether we think they decorated their house for themselves, for others, for conformity, for comfort, and so on. We may be influenced by the mood created by the wallpaper, by the symmetry and/or orderliness of objects displayed, by pictures on the walls, by the quality and apparent cost of the items placed around the house, and by many, many other things. Most of us have had the experience of being ushered into a living room which we perceive should be labeled an "unliving" room. We hesitate to sit down or touch anything because the room seems to say to us, "This room is for show purposes only; sit, walk, and touch carefully. It takes a lot of time and effort to keep this room neat, clean, and tidy; we don't want to clean it after you leave." The arrangement of other living rooms seems to say, "Sit down, make yourself comfortable, feel free to talk informally, and don't worry about spilling things." Interior decorators and product promotion experts often have experiential and intuitive judgments about the influence of certain colors, objects, shapes, arrangements, and the like, but there have been few attempts to empirically validate these feelings. Perhaps the best known empirical research into the influence of interior decoration on human responses were the studies of Maslow and Mintz.[17]

Maslow and Mintz selected three rooms for study: One was an "ugly" room (designed to give the impression of a janitor's storeroom in disheveled condition); one was a "beautiful" room (complete with carpeting, drapes, and the like), and one was an "average" room (a professor's office). Subjects were asked to rate a series of negative print photographs of faces. The experimenters tried to keep all factors, such as time of day, odor, noise, type of seating, and experimenter, constant from room to room so that any results could be attributed to the type of room. Results showed that subjects in the beautiful room tended to give significantly higher ratings to the faces than did participants in

[17]A. H. Maslow and N. L. Mintz, "Effects of Esthetic Surroundings: I. Initial Effects of Three Esthetic Conditions Upon Perceiving 'Energy' and 'Well-Being' in Faces," *Journal of Psychology* 41 (1956): 247–254. Also N. L. Mintz, "Effects of Esthetic Surroundings: II. Prolonged and Repeated Experience in a 'Beautiful' and 'Ugly' Room," *Journal of Psychology* 41 (1956): 459–466.

The Effects of the Environment on Human Communication

the ugly room. Experimenters and subjects alike engaged in various escape behaviors to avoid the ugly room. The ugly room was variously described as producing monotony, fatigue, headache, discontent, sleep, irritability, and hostility. The beautiful room, however, produced feelings of pleasure, comfort, enjoyment, importance, energy, and desire to continue the activity. In this instance, we have a well-controlled study which offers some evidence of the impact of visual-esthetic surroundings on the nature of human interaction. Similar studies have tested recall and problem solving in rooms similar to those used by Maslow and Mintz. In both cases, more effective performance is found in rooms which are well appointed or "beautiful."[18]

Color. Two newspaper accounts in 1972 indicated that prisons were being repainted in order to "cut down on prisoner mischief." The walls of the city jail in San Diego were reportedly painted pink, baby blue, and peach on the assumption that pastel colors would have a calming effect on the inmates. In Salem, Oregon, the cell bars of Oregon's Correctional Institution were done in soft green, blues, and buffs; some cell doors were painted bright yellow, orange, green, and blue. In addition, the superintendent of the institution said that the color schemes would be continually changed to keep it "an exciting place to work and live in." These are but two examples of organizations which have tried to use findings from environmental research, findings suggesting that colors, in conjunction with other factors, do influence moods and behavior.

A group of researchers in Munich, Germany, have been studying the impact of colors on mental growth and social relations since 1970.[19] Children who were tested in rooms they thought were beautiful scored about twelve points higher on an I.Q. test than those tested in rooms with ugly colors. Blue, yellow, yellow-green, and orange were considered beautiful; white, black, and brown were considered ugly. The beautifully colored rooms also seemed to stimulate alertness and creativity. And in the orange room, these psychologists found that positive social reactions (friendly words, smiles) increased 53 percent while negative reactions (irritability, hostility) decreased 12 percent.

Mehrabian says the *most pleasant* hues are, in order, blue, green, purple red, and yellow.[20] He goes on to suggest that the *most arousing* hues are red, followed by orange, yellow, violet, blue, and green. Although these proposals are not completely comparable with the following paper-and-pencil research on colors and mood tones, there are a number of similarities. Wexner

---

[18]H. Wong and W. Brown, "Effects of Surroundings upon Mental Work as Measured by Yerkes' Multiple Choice Method," *Journal of Comparative Psychology* 3 (1923): 319–331; and J. M. Bilodeau and H. Schlosberg, "Similarity in Stimulating Conditions as a Variable in Retroactive Inhibition," *Journal of Experimental Psychology* 41 (1959): 199–204.

[19]"Blue Is Beautiful," *Time*, September 17, 1973, p. 66.

[20]A. Mehrabian, *Public Places and Private Spaces* (New York: Basic Books, 1976).

The Effects of the Environment on Human Communication

presented eight colors and eleven mood-tones to ninety-four subjects. The results (see Table 3.1) show that for some mood-tones a single color is significantly related; for others there may be two or more colors.[21]

Table 3.1 Colors Associated with Moods

Mood tone	Color	Frequency of times chosen
Exciting-Stimulating	Red	61
Secure-Comfortable	Blue	41
Distressed-Disturbed-Upset	Orange	34
Tender-Soothing	Blue	41
Protective-Defending	Red	21
	Brown	17
	Blue	15
	Black	15
	Purple	14
Despondent-Dejected-Unhappy-Melancholy	Black	25
	Brown	25
Calm-Peaceful-Serene	Blue	38
	Green	31
Dignified-Stately	Purple	45
Cheerful-Jovial-Joyful	Yellow	40
Defiant-Contrary-Hostile	Red	23
	Orange	21
	Black	18
Powerful-Strong-Masterful	Black	48

A real problem in interpreting such research concerns whether people pick colors which are actually associated with particular moods or whether they are responding using learned verbal stereotypes. Another problem with some of the color preference research concerns the lack of association between color and objects. Pink may be your favorite color, but you may still dislike pink hair. Nevertheless, we cannot ignore the body of educational and design literature which suggests that carefully planned color schemes seem to have some influence on improving scholastic achievement. Obviously, we cannot make any final judgments about the impact of color on human interaction until behavioral studies link differently colored environments with different types of verbal behavior or communication patterns. In short, what configuration of circum-

[21]L. B. Wexner, "The Degree to Which Colors (Hues) Are Associated with Mood-Tones," *Journal of Applied Psychology* 38 (1954): 432–435. Also see D. C. Murray and H. L. Deabler, "Colors and Mood-Tones," *Journal of Applied Psychology* 41 (1957): 279–283.

The Effects of the Environment on Human Communication

stances is necessary for environmental color to affect human interaction to any appreciable degree?

Sound.   The types of sounds and their intensity also seem to affect interpersonal behavior. We may react very differently, however, to the drone of several people's voices, the overpowering sound of a nearby jackhammer, or the soothing or stimulating sounds of music. "Music," says Mehrabian, "can have a stronger and more immediate effect on arousal level and pleasure than, say, several cups of coffee."[22] That often unpleasant, arousing and powerful sound of the morning alarm clock may have a good deal to do with some people's irritability on rising. Generally, the more pleasant the music, the more likely we are to engage in "approaching" rather than "avoiding" behavior. The effect of slow, simple, soft and familiar music is to lower arousal levels while maintaining pleasure—eliciting an easygoing and satisfying feeling.

Glass and Singer conducted a series of studies on the impact of noise on performance.[23] People were asked to perform a variety of tasks, varying in complexity, while noises were manipulated by the experimenters. Noise levels were varied and some noise was predictable (followed a pattern) and some was unpredictable. Various noise sources were tested (for example, typewriters, machinery, people talking a foreign language, and so forth). Although noise alone did not seem to have a substantial effect on performance, deterioration was observed when noise interacted with other factors. For instance, performance decreased when the work load was high and the noise uncontrollable and unpredictable.

In some environments we want to change the sound to change behavior— for example, raising the volume of supermarket music to stimulate more purchases in a shorter time. In other instances, we may want to reduce unproductive noise through structural changes. In one mental institution, floor tiles were replaced with carpeting, which the authors feel made the patients less irritable, made the hospital seem warmer and more like a "home"—which, in turn, encouraged the patients to spend more time taking care of their environment.[24] Another study tested the effects of rooms of different sizes (150 cubic feet vs. 1600 cubic feet), different shapes (circular vs. rectangular), and different reverberation times (.8-1.0 seconds vs. .2-.3 seconds) upon a speaker's rate and intensity in reading aloud.[25] Generally, the data suggest that rate and intensity of reading were affected by the size of the room and the reverberation time—

[22]Mehrabian, *Public Places and Private Spaces*, p. 50.

[23]D. C. Glass and J. E. Singer, *Urban Stress* (New York: Academic Press, 1972).

[24]F. E. Cheek, R. Maxwell and R. Weisman, "Carpeting the Ward: An Exploratory Study in Environmental Psychiatry," *Mental Hygiene* 55 (1971): 109–118.

[25]J. W. Black, "The Effect of Room Characteristics upon Vocal Intensity and Rate," *Journal of the Acoustical Society of America* 22 (1950): 174–176.

The Effects of the Environment on Human Communication

but not by the shape. Rate seemed to be slower in the larger and less reverberant rooms; vocal intensity was greater in smaller and less reverberant rooms; and intensity consistently increased as the subject read through the twelve phrases provided in the less reverberant rooms.

Lighting. We know that lighting also helps to structure our perceptions of an environment and that these perceptions may very well influence the type of messages we send. If we enter a room which has dim lighting or candlelight, we may talk more softly and presume that more personal communication will take place. Bright lights, on the other hand, are more apt to be arousing— adding to initial discomfort in interacting with strangers—and indicative of less intimate interaction. Carr and Dabbs found that the combination of intimate questions and dim lighting with nonintimates caused a significant hesitancy in responding, a significant decrease in eye gaze, and a decrease in the average length of gaze.[26] All of these nonverbal behaviors appear to be efforts to create more psychological distance and decrease the perceived inappropriateness of the intimacy created by the lighting and the questions.

Several attempts have been made to test the effects of various types of colored lighting on human performance. Birren cites evidence suggesting that human reactions are 12 percent faster than average under red lighting conditions. Green lights, on the other hand, seem to generate reactions that are slower than normal.[27] Colored lighting also seems to influence judgments of time, length, and weight. Under red lighting, these judgments tend to be overestimated, while a green or blue light appears to generate underestimation.[28]

Movable Objects. If we know that the arrangement of certain objects in our environment can help structure the communication that takes place, it is not surprising that we often try to manipulate objects in order to bring about certain types of responses. Special, intimate evenings are often highlighted by candlelight, soft music, favorite drinks, fluffed pillows on the couch, and the absence of dirty dishes, trash, and other nonintimate materiel associated with daily living. Objects in our environment can also be arranged to reflect certain role relationships, to demarcate boundaries or to encourage greater affiliation. The interior of an executive suite may clearly indicate the perceived status of the inhabitant—for example, expensive wall paintings, large desk, plush sofa and chairs, drapes, and the like. Such an atmosphere may be very inappropriate for a personal counseling situation, but it may be rearranged to make it more conducive to such a purpose. And, of course, there are times when we

[26]S. J. Carr and J. M. Dabbs, "The Effects of Lighting, Distance and Intimacy of Topic on Verbal and Visual Behavior," *Sociometry* 37 (1974): 592–600.
[27]R. Birren, *Color Psychology and Color Therapy* (New York: University Books, 1965).
[28]K. Goldstein, "Some Experimental Observations Concerning the Influence of Color on the Function of the Organism," *Occupational Therapy and Rehabilitation* 21 (1942): 147–151.

The Effects of the Environment on Human Communication

are able to communicate well in seemingly "inappropriate" settings, as when lovers say good-bye in the relatively cold and public environs of an airport terminal.

Desks seem to be an important object in the analysis of interpersonal communication. An experiment conducted in a doctor's office suggests that the presence or absence of a desk may significantly alter the patient's "at ease" state.[29] With the desk separating doctor and patient, only 10 percent of the patients were perceived "at ease," whereas removal of the desk brought the figure of "at ease" patients up to 55 percent. Student-teacher relationships also seem to be affected by desk placement.[30] Faculty members were asked to sketch the furniture arrangement in their offices. These sketches were collected and analyzed with other information obtained from the professors and a school-wide teacher evaluation. Twenty-four out of thirty-three senior faculty members (full professors and associate professors) put their desks between themselves and their students, but only fourteen out of thirty junior faculty members (assistant professors and lecturers) did so. Furthermore, the "unbarricaded" professors were rated by students as more willing to "encourage the development of different viewpoints by students," as ready to give "individual attention to students who need it," and as less likely to show "undue favoritism." Even White House press briefings have apparently been affected by a barricade. During the Nixon administration, press briefings were formalized, and the press secretary stood behind a podium. Ron Nesson, President Ford's press secretary, felt this contributed to an unproductive "us and them" feeling, which prompted him to conduct briefings without the obstacle.

Less obvious barriers also exist. For instance, if you find a delicate *objet d'art* placed in front of some books in a bookcase you will likely feel hesitant about using the books. Keep in mind that desks and other "barriers" are not inherently good or bad. There will be some occasions when you want to keep a distant, formal relationship and the desk can help to create that feeling.

The arrangement of other items of furniture can facilitate or inhibit communication. The location of the television set in a room will very likely affect the placement of chairs, and, in turn, the pattern of conversations which occur in that room. Sommer and Ross found that some residents in a geriatric ward were "apathetic" and had few friends—in spite of a generally cheerful and bright environment. By rearranging the furniture to encourage interaction, they were able to double the frequency of resident conversations.[31] Even when you

[29]A. G. White, "The Patient Sits Down: A Clinical Note," *Psychosomatic Medicine* 15 (1953): 256–257.

[30]R. Zweigenhaft, "Personal Space in the Faculty Office: Desk Placement and the Student-Faculty Interaction," *Journal of Applied Psychology* 61 (1976): 529–532.

[31]R. Sommer and H. Ross, "Social Interaction in a Geriatric Ward," *International Journal of Social Psychiatry* 4 (1958): 128–133.

The Effects of the Environment on Human Communication

have tried to maximize the conversational possibilites, you may not get everyone to talk to everyone else. Consider the arrangement in Figure 3.2. We would predict exchanges marked by the arrows would be the most frequent, but the four people seated on the couch will probably talk to each other infrequently. The two groups of four on each end and the two people seated next to each other (F and G) are also likely to communicate infrequently. If the participants are periodically rearranged, the conversational groupings can be altered. Finally, notice that there are no other chairs in this arrangement, which poses the question of where one goes when "bored stiff" with his or her current conversational grouping.

In at least one case, a furniture designer has deliberately designed a chair to exert disagreeable pressure on a person's spine when occupied for more than a few minutes. The Larsen Chair was originally designed to keep patrons from becoming too comfortable and remaining in seats which could be occupied by other customers.[32] Hotel owners and airport designers apparently are already aware of the "too comfortable" phenomenon. Thus, seating arrangements are deliberately made uncomfortable for long seating and conversations so patrons will "move along" and perhaps drift into nearby shops where they can spend some of their money. Some environments seem to have an unwritten code which prohibits interaction. The lone men entering, sitting through, and leaving "girlie" movies without a word are a case in point.

Structure and Design.   We spend a lot of time in buildings. Most of us spend the day in a dwelling supposedly designed for the effective performance of our work; in the evening we enter another structure supposedly designed for the effective conduct of our personal and family life. The architecture can go a long way toward determining who shall meet whom, where, and perhaps for how long.

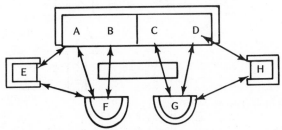

Figure 3.2 Conversation Flow and Furniture Arrangement (adapted from A. Mehrabian, *Public Places and Private Spaces*, New York: Basic Books, 1976, p. 92)

[32]Sommer, *Personal Space*, p. 121.

The Effects of the Environment on Human Communication

The life of domestic animals is, among other things, controlled through the erection of fences, flap doors, or the placement of food and water in particular locations. Although the control of human situations is implemented through verbal and nonverbal actions, manipulation of barriers, openings, and other physical arrangements is rather helpful. Meeting places can be appropriately rigged so as to regulate human traffic and, to a certain extent, the network of communication.[33]

American office buildings are often constructed from a standard plan—a plan which reflects a pyramidal organization—that is, a large number of people supervised by a few executives at the upper levels. And these executives generally have the most space, the most privacy, and the most desirable office locations, namely, on the highest floor of the structure. Achieving a height above the "masses" and acquiring a vast amount of space are only two indications of power which might be seen. Corner offices, large picture windows, and private elevators are also associated with status and power—and an office right next to an important executive may also hold a formidable power base. The offices of top-level executives are often hard to reach, the assumption being that the more you have to walk to get to the executive, the more powerful he or she seems. Figure 3.3 is a hypothetical, but not far-fetched, example of the long

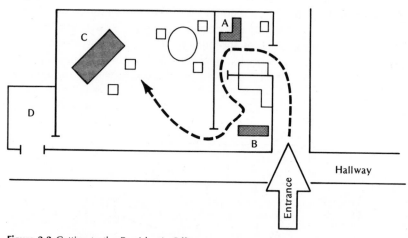

Figure 3.3 Getting to the President's Office
A = Receptionist   C = President
B = Private Secretary   D = Private Room With Rear Exit
              = Desks

[33]J. Ruesch and W. Kees, *Nonverbal Communication* (Berkeley and Los Angeles: University of California Press, 1956), p. 126.

The Effects of the Environment on Human Communication

and circuitous route to a president's office. In order to get to the office, the visitor must be screened by a receptionist and a private secretary and in either or both places may be asked to sit and wait. So, although the status and power of an executive may be related to his or her inaccessibility, secretaries and receptionists may value open views which allow them to act as a lookout and defender against unwanted intrusions on the executive. It is common for people on the lowest rungs of the organizational ladder to find themselves in a large open "pit." These "offices" (desks) have little or no privacy, and complaints are common. Although privacy is minimal, communication opportunities are plentiful.

Some dormitories are built from floor plans which resemble those in many office buildings and old hotels. Some have even speculated that these "corridor-type" dorms tend to encourage bureaucratic management approaches—approaches which seem to fit the orderly and uniform structure. Rigid rules are easier to enforce in structures with these designs, but interaction among the residents is discouraged. The sense of community and the resulting responsibility for one's living space is difficult to achieve. Lounges are sometimes intended to facilitate such interaction, but their usefulness has been questioned by architects and behavioral scientists. Lounges, like any other design feature, must be integrated into the entire architectural plan developed from an analysis of *human needs*—not inserted in places where they "fit nicely" or "look good" for parents and visitors.

If you look carefully, you can see any number of environmental structures which inhibit or prohibit communication. Fences separating yards create obvious barriers—even if they are only waist high; laundry rooms in apartment buildings and public housing which are located in dark, isolated places discourage use—particularly at night; homes with patios which are only accessible through a bedroom will probably discourage use; and so on.

Other environmental situations seem to facilitate interaction. Homes placed in the middle of a block seem to draw more interpersonal exchanges than those located in other positions on the block. Houses which have adjacent driveways seem to have a built in structure drawing the neighbors together and inviting communication. Cavan reports that the likelihood of interaction between strangers at a bar varies directly with the distance between them.[34] As a rule, a span of three bar stools is the maximum distance over which patrons will attempt to initiate an encounter. Two men conversing with an empty bar stool between them are likely to remain that way since they would be too close if they sat next to each other. However, if a man is talking to a woman and there is an empty stool between them, he will likely move onto it—to prevent someone else from coming between them. Most bars, however, are not designed for

[34]S. Cavan, *Liquor License* (Chicago: Aldine Publishing Co., 1966).

The Effects of the Environment on Human Communication

optimum interaction. Note that the three bar designs in Figure 3.4 provide very different opportunities for facing your interaction partner, for mutual eye gaze, and for getting physically close. Most bars are similar to type B—the type which seems to discourage interaction the most.

Some recent designs for housing elderly people have taken into consideration the need for social contact. These apartment dwellings have the doors of the apartments on a given floor open into a common entranceway. The probabilities for social exchange are then greatly increased over the situation in which apartment doors are staggered on either side of a long hallway so that no doorways face one another. If you desire a structure which encourages social interaction, you must have human paths crossing, but if you want them to interact, there must be something which will encourage them to linger for a time. Furthermore, the nature of the design may encourage or discourage certain types of communication—that is, the structure may determine how much interaction takes place and what the general content of that interaction will be. Drew reports an unpublished study of three different designs for nursing stations within a mental hospital.[35] In one, interaction had to take place by opening a door; in another interaction was conducted through a glass-enclosed counter; and in the third, interaction took place over an open counter. Although substantially more patients entered the nursing station with the door, interactions occurred less frequently than in the other two stations. An average of only one interaction per each fifteen-minute observation period occurred with the door; 5.3 interactions per period occurred in the glass-enclosed counter; and 8.7 occurred for the open counter. Although interaction was higher for the open counter, the author noted that there was a preponderance of social conversation here while the door design seemed to encourage more item requests and permission interactions. *In short, the more inaccessible setting decreased interaction frequency and increased task-oriented messages; the more accessible setting increased interaction frequency and increased the amount of "small talk."*

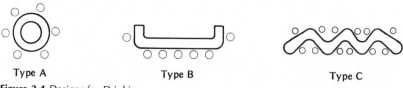

| Type A | Type B | Type C |

Figure 3.4 Designs for Drinking

[35]C. J. Drew, "Research on the Psychological-Behavioral Effects of the Physical Environment," *Review of Educational Research* 41 (1971): 447–465. The study cited was R. L. Proctor, "An Investigation of Mental Hospital Nursing Station Design on Aspects of Human Behavior," the Environmental Research Foundation, Topeka, Kansas, 1966 (mimeograph).

The Effects of the Environment on Human Communication

A more complete analysis of physical proximity and spatial distance will be made in Chapter 4, but it is clearly relevant to this chapter on the environment as well. As Stouffer puts it:

> Whether one is seeking to explain why persons go to a particular place to get jobs, why they go to trade at a particular store, why they go to a particular neighborhood to commit a crime, or why they marry the particular spouse they choose, the factor of spatial distance is of obvious significance.[36]

Several studies have confirmed Stouffer's remark. For instance, students tend to develop stronger friendships with students who share their classes, or their dormitory or apartment building, or who sit near them, than with others who are geographically distant. Workers tend to develop closer friendships with those who work close to them. Some research concludes that increased proximity of white persons and blacks will assist in reducing prejudice.[37] Several studies show an inverse relationship between the distance separating potential marriage partners and the number of marriages. For example, in New Haven in 1940, Kennedy reports 76 percent of the marriages were between persons living within twenty blocks of each other and 35 percent were between persons living within five blocks of each other.[38] Obviously, proximity allows us to obtain more information about the other person. The inescapable conclusion seems to be that as proximity increases, attraction is likely to increase. One might also posit that as attraction increases, proximity will tend to increase.

Perhaps the most famous study of proximity, friendship choice, and interpersonal contact was conducted by Festinger, Schachter, and Back in a housing development for married students.[39] Concern for what the authors called "functional distance" led to the uncovering of some data which clearly demonstrated that architects can have a tremendous influence on the social life of residents in these housing projects. Functional distance is determined by the number of contacts that position and design encourage—for example, which

[36]S. A. Stouffer, "Intervening Opportunities: A Theory Relating Mobility and Distance," *American Sociological Review* 5 (1940): 845–867.

[37]M. Deutsch and M. Collins, *Interracial Housing: A Psychological Evaluation of a Social Experiment* (Minneapolis: University of Minnesota Press, 1951). It is interesting that some attack social legislation designed to eliminate segregation because it does not change attitudes but only forces civil obedience. This study, and others, suggest there are times when bringing those of different races together in close proximity will indeed bring about corresponding positive attitude changes. Caution should be exercised in the generalization of such an idea, however. If the two groups are extremely polarized, proximity may only serve to magnify the hostilities.

[38]R. Kennedy, "Premarital Residential Propinquity," *American Journal of Sociology* 48 (1943): 580–584.

[39]L. Festinger, S. Schachter, and K. Back, *Social Pressures in Informal Groups: A Study of Human Factors in Housing* (New York: Harper and Row, 1950). For another interesting example of how architecture structures interaction, see R. R. Blake, C. C. Rhead, B. Wedge, and J. S. Mouton, "Housing Architecture and Social Interaction," *Sociometry* 19 (1956): 133–139.

The Effects of the Environment on Human Communication

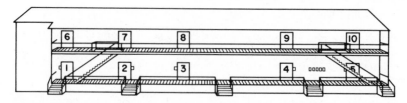

Figure 3.5

way apartments face, where exits and entranceways are located, location of stairways, mailboxes, and the like. Figure 3.5 shows the basic design of one type of building studied.

The researchers asked the residents of seventeen buildings (with the design of Figure 3.5) what people they saw most often socially and what friendship choices they made. Among the various findings from this study, the following are noteworthy: (1) There seemed to be a greater number of sociometric choices for those who were physically close to one another—on the same floor, in the same building, and so on. It was rare to find a friendship between people separated by more than four or five houses. (2) People living in apartments 1 and 5 gave and received from the upper floor residents more sociometric choices than the people living in any other apartment on the lower floor. (3) Apartments 1 and 6 exchanged more choices than apartments 2 and 7. Similarly, apartments 5 and 10 exchanged more choices than apartments 4 and 9. Although this represents the same physical distance, functional distance differed. (4) Apartment 7 chose 6 more than it chose 8; apartment 9 chose 10 more than it chose 8. This relationship did not hold true for corresponding first-floor apartments. (5) Because of the mailboxes, apartment 5 chose more upper-level friends—more of those choices being apartments 9 and 10. There are many ways of making friends, but functional distance seems to be highly influential—and functional distance is sometimes the result of architectural design.

Summary

The environment in which people communicate frequently contributes to the overall outcome of their encounters. We have seen that both the frequency and the content of our messages are influenced by various aspects of the setting in which we communicate. We have seen how the environment influences our behavior, but we also know that we can alter environments in order to elicit certain types of responses. Naturally, as our knowledge of environments increases, we may deliberately use them to help us obtain desired responses. In fact, this is the very point of a book by B. F. Skinner, perhaps the most renowned psychologist of this century.[40] Skinner believes we are a product of our environment and that if we want to change behavior we need only control the environment in which people interact.

Throughout this chapter we referred to a number of different types of environments—the classroom, dormitories, offices, prisons, homes, and bars. We suggested that there were several different ways of looking at environments. Mehrabian, following research in other domains of human perception, suggested that all environments could profitably be examined by looking at our emotional reactions to them. These emotions, or feelings, says Mehrabian, can be plotted on three dimensions—arousing/nonarousing; pleasant/unpleasant; and dominant/submissive. I suggested six perceptual bases for examining environments: formal/informal, warm/cold, private/public, familiar/unfamiliar, constraining/free, and distant/close.

Each environment seems to be composed of three major characteristics: (1) the natural environment, (2) the presence or absence of other people, and (3) architectural design and movable objects, including lighting, sound, color, and general visual-esthetic appeal. The quantity and quality of the research in each of these areas vary considerably, but it is clear that any analysis of human behavior must account for the influence of environmental features if it is to be a thorough analysis.

[40]B. F. Skinner, *Beyond Freedom and Dignity* (New York: Alfred A. Knopf, 1971).

SELECTED BIBLIOGRAPHY

Adams, R. S. "Location as a Feature of Instructional Interaction," *Merrill-Palmer Quarterly* 15 (1969): 309–321.

Allen, E. C., and Guilford, J. P. "Factors Determining the Affective Values of Color Combinations." *American Journal of Psychology* 48 (1936): 643–648.

Athanasion, R., and Uoshioka, G. A. "The Spatial Character of Friendship Formation." *Environment and Behavior* 5 (1973): 43–65.

Baird, D. A. "The Effects of Noise: A Summary of Experimental Literature." *Journal of the Acoustical Society of America* 1 (1930): 256–261.

Barker, R. *Ecological Psychology.* Palo Alto, Calif.: Stanford University Press, 1968.

Barker, R. G. "On the Nature of the Environment." *Journal of Social Issues* 19 (1963): 1–14.

Barker, R., and Wright, H. *Midwest and Its Children*. Lawrence, Kansas: University of Kansas Press, 1957.

Barnes, R. D. "Thermography of the Human Body," *Science* 140 (1963): 870–877.

Baron, R. A. "Aggression as a Function of Ambient Temperature and Prior Anger Arousal." *Journal of Personality and Social Psychology* 21 (1972): 183–189.

Baron, R. A., and Bell P. A. "Aggression and Heat: Mediating Effects of Prior Provocation and Exposure to an Aggressive Model." *Journal of Personality and Social Psychology* 31 (1975): 825–832.

Baron, R. A., and Bell, P. A. "Aggression and Heat: The Influence of Ambient Temperature, Negative Affect, and a Cooling Drink on Physical Aggression." *Journal of Personality and Social Psychology* 33 (1976): 245–255.

Baron, R. A., and Lawton, S. F. "Environmental Influences on Aggression: The Facilitation of Modeling Effects by High Ambient Temperatures." *Psychonomic Science* 26 (1972): 89–93.

Bechtel, R. B. "Human Movement and Architecture." *Trans-Action* 4 (1967): 53–56.

Bedford, T. "Researches on Thermal Comfort." *Ergonomics* 4 (1961): 289–310.

Bilodeau, J. M., and Schlosberg, H. "Similarity in Stimulating Conditions as a Variable in Retroactive Inhibition." *Journal of Experimental Psychology* 41 (1959): 199–204.

Birren, F. *Color Psychology and Color Therapy*. New York: McGraw-Hill, 1950.

Birren, F. *Light, Color and Environment*. New York: Van Nostrand Reinhold, 1969.

Black, J. W. "The Effect of Room Characteristics upon Vocal Intensity and Rate." *Journal of the Acoustical Society of America* 22 (1950): 174–176.

Blake, R. R., Rhead, C. C., Wedge, B. and Mouton, J. S. "Housing Architecture and Social Interaction." *Sociometry* 19 (1956): 133–139.

Breed, G., and Colaiuta, V. "Looking, Blinking, and Sitting: Nonverbal Dynamics in the Classroom." *Journal of Communication* 24 (1974): 75–81.

Byrne, D. "The Influence of Propinquity and Opportunities for Interaction on Classroom Relationships." *Human Relations* 14 (1961): 63–70.

Carr, S. J., and Dabbs, J. M. "The Effect of Lighting, Distance and Intimacy of Topic on Verbal and Visual Behavior." *Sociometry* 37 (1974): 592–600.

Cheek, F. E., Maxwell, R., and Weisman, R. "Carpeting the Ward: An Exploratory Study in Environmental Psychiatry." *Mental Hygiene* 55 (1971): 109–118.

Child, I. L. "Esthetics." In G. Lindsey and E. Aronson (eds.), *Handbook of Social Psychology*, Vol. 3. Reading, Mass.: Addison-Wesley, 1968. Pp. 853–916.

The Effects of the Environment on Human Communication

Deutsch, M., and Collins, M. *Interracial Housing: A Psychological Evaluation of a Social Experiment.* Minneapolis: University of Minnesota Press, 1951.

Drew, C. J. "Research on the Psychological-Behavioral Effects of the Physical Environment." *Review of Educational Research* 41 (1971): 447–463.

Ellis, D. S., and Brighouse, G. "Effects of Music on Respiration and Heart-Rate." *American Journal of Psychology* 65 (1952): 39–47.

Festinger, L. "Architecture and Group Membership." *Journal of Social Issues* 1 (1951): 152–163.

Festinger, L., Schachter, S., and Back, K. *Social Pressures in Informal Groups: A Study of Human Factors in Housing.* New York: Harper and Row, 1950.

Ford, C. S., Rothro, E. T., and Child, I. L. "Some Transcultural Comparisons of Esthetic Judgment." *Journal of Social Psychology* 68 (1966): 19–26.

Gans, H. J. "Planning and Social Life: Friendship and Neighbor Relations in Suburban Communities." *Journal of the American Institute of Planners* 27 (1961): 134–140.

Glass, D., and Singer, J. E. "Experimental Studies of Uncontrollable and Unpredictable Noise." *Representative Research in Social Psychology* 4 (1973): 165.

Goldstein, K. "Some Experimental Observations Concerning the Influence of Color on the Function of the Organism." *Occupational Therapy and Rehabilitation* 21 (1942): 147–151.

Goranson, R. E., and King, D. "Rioting and Daily Temperature: Analysis of the U.S. Riots in 1967." Unpublished manuscript, York University, Ontario, Canada, 1970.

Griffin, W. V., Mauritzen, J. H., and Kasmar, J. V. "The Psychological Aspects of the Architectural Environment: A Review." *American Journal of Psychiatry* 125 (1969): 1057–1062.

Griffitt, W. "Environmental Effects of Interpersonal Affective Behavior: Ambient Effective Temperature and Attraction." *Journal of Personality and Social Psychology* 15 (1970): 240–244.

Griffitt, W., and Veitch, R. "Hot and Crowded: Influence of Population Density and Temperature on Interpersonal Affective Behavior." *Journal of Personality and Social Psychology* 17 (1971): 92–98.

Guilford, J. P., and Smith, P. C. "A System of Color Preferences." *American Journal of Psychology* 72 (1959): 487–502.

Hall, E. T. *The Hidden Dimension.* Garden City, N.Y.: Doubleday, 1966.

Hazard, J. N. "Furniture Arrangement as a Symbol of Judicial Roles." *ETC* 19 (1962): 181–188.

Heilweil, M. (ed.). "Student Housing, Architecture, and Social Behavior." *Environment and Behavior* 5 (1973). Cf. entire issue.

Hutte, H. "Door-Knocks in Terms of Authority and Urgency." *European Journal of Social Psychology* 2 (1972): 98–99.

Isumi, K. "Psychological Phenomena and Building Design." *Building Research* 2 (1965): 9–11.

Jackson, P. W. *Life in Classrooms* New York: Holt, Rinehart and Winston, 1968.

Karmel, L. J. "Effects of Windowless Classroom Environment on High School Students." *Perceptual and Motor Skills* 20 (1965): 277–278.

Kasmar, J. V., Griffin, W. V., and Mauritzen, J. H. "The Effect of Environmental Surroundings on Outpatients' Mood and Perception of Psychiatrists." *Journal of Consulting and Clinical Psychology* 32 (1968): 223–226.

Katz, A. M., and Hill, R. "Residential Propinquity and Marital Selection: A Review of Theory, Method, and Fact." *Marriage and Family Living* 20 (1958): 327–335.

Kennedy, R. "Premarital Residential Propinquity." *American Journal of Sociology* 48 (1943): 580–584.

Koneya, M. "The Relationship Between Verbal Interaction and Seat Location of Members of Large Groups." Unpublished Ph.D. dissertation, Denver University, 1973.

Korda, M. "Office Power—You Are Where You Sit." *New York*, Jan. 13, 1975, 36–44.

Krieger, W. "The Effects of Visual Esthetics on Problem Solving and Mood." Unpublished Master's Thesis, Purdue University, 1972.

Lawton, M. P., and Cohen, J. "Environments and the Well-being of Elderly Inner-City Residents." *Environment and Behavior* 6 (1974): 194–211.

Lipman, A. "Building Design and Social Interaction." *The Architect's Journal* 147 (1968): 23–30.

Maslow, A. H., and Mintz, N. L. "Effects of Esthetic Surroundings: I. Initial Effects of Three Esthetic Conditions upon Perceiving 'Energy' and 'Well-being in Faces." *Journal of Psychology* 41 (1956): 247–254.

McClanahan, L. E., and Risly, T. R. "Design of Living Environments for Nursing Home Residents: Increasing Participation in Recreation Activities." *Journal of Applied Behavior Analysis* 8 (1975): 261–268.

McLuhan, M. "Inside on the Outside, or the Spaced-Out American." *Journal of Communication* 26 (1976): 46–53.

Mehrabian, A. *Public Places and Private Spaces* New York: Basic Books, 1976.

Mehrabian, A., and Diamond, S. G. "The Effects of Furniture Arrangement, Props, and Personality on Social Interaction." *Journal of Personality and Social Psychology* 20 (1971): 18–30.

Mehrabian, A., and Russell, J. A. "Environmental Effects on Affiliation Among Strangers." *Humanitas* 11 (1975): 219–230.

Mehrabian, A., and Russell, J. A. "The Basic Emotional Impact of Environments." *Perceptual and Motor Skills* 38 (1974): 283–301.

Merton, R. "The Social Psychology of Housing." In W. Dennis (ed.), *Current Trends in Social Psychology*. Pittsburgh: University of Pittsburgh Press, 1948.

Mintz, N. L. "Effects of Esthetic Surroundings: II. Prolonged and Repeated Experience in a 'Beautiful' and 'Ugly' Room." *Journal of Psychology* 41 (1956): 459–466.

Moos, R. H., Harris, R., and Schonborn, K. "Psychiatric Patients and Staff Reaction to Their Physical Environment." *Journal of Clinical Psychology* 25 (1969): 322–324.

Moriarty, B. M. "Socioeconomic Status and Residential Location Choice." *Environment and Behavior* 6 (1974): 448–469.

Murray, D. C. and Deabler, H. L. "Colors and Mood-Tones." *Journal of Applied Psychology* 41 (1957): 279–283.

Newman, O. *Defensible Space* New York: Macmillan, 1973.

Norman, R. D., and Scott, W. A. "Color and Affect: A Review and Semantic Evaluation." *Journal of General Psychology* 46 (1952): 185–223.

Odbert, H. S., Karwoski, T. F., and Eckerson, A. B. "Studies in Synesthetic Thinking: I. Musical and Verbal Associations of Color and Mood." *Journal of General Psychology* 26 (1942): 153–173.

Osmond, H. "Function as the Basis of Psychiatric Ward Design." *Mental Hospitals* 8 (1957): 23–29.

Pressey, J. L. "The Influence of Color on Mental and Motor Efficiency." *American Journal of Psychology* 32 (1921): 326–356.

Proshansky, H. M., Ittelson, W. H., and Rivlin, L. G. (eds.). *Environmental Psychology: Man and His Physical Setting*. New York: Holt, Rinehart and Winston, 1970.

Rice, A. H. "Color: What Research Knows About the Classroom." *Nation's Schools* 52 (1953): 1–8, 64.

Rieber, M. "The Effect of Music on the Activity Level of Children." *Psychonomic Science* 3 (1965): 325–326.

Roethlisberger, F. J., and Dickson, W. J. *Management and the Worker*. Cambridge, Mass.: Harvard University Press, 1939.

Rohles, F. H. "Environmental Psychology: A Bucket of Worms." *Psychology Today* 1 (1967): 54–62.

Rolfe, H. C. "Some Observable Differences in Space Use of Learning Situations in Large and Small Classrooms." Unpublished Ph.D. diss., University of California at Berkeley, 1961.

Ruesch, J., and Kees, W. *Nonverbal Communication*. Berkeley and Los Angeles: University of California Press, 1956.

Russell, J. A., and Mehrabian, A. "Environmental Variables in Consumer Research." *Journal of Consumer Research*, 3 (1976): 62–63.

Russell, J. A., and Mehrabian, A. "Some Behavioral Effects of the Physical Environment." In S. Wapner, S. Cohen, and B. Kaplan (eds.), *Experiencing the Environment. New York: Plenum, 1976.*

School Environments Research, College of Architecture and Design, University of Michigan, 1965.

Schwebel, A. I., and Cherlin, D. L. "Physical and Social Distancing in Teacher-Pupil Relationships." *Journal of Educational Psychology* 63 (1972): 543–550.

Smith, P. C., and Curnow, R. "'Arousal Hypothesis' and the Effects of Music on Purchasing Behavior," *Journal of Applied Psychology* 50 (1966): 255–256.

Smith, R. H., Downer, D. B., Lynch, M. T., and Winter, M. "Privacy and Interaction Within the Family as Related to Dwelling Space." *Journal of Marriage and the Family* 31 (1969): 559–566.

Solomon, P., Leiderman, P. H., Mendelson, J., and Wexler, D. "Sensory Deprivation: A Review." *American Journal of Psychiatry* 114 (1957): 357–363.

Sommer, R. "Classroom Ecology." *Journal of Applied Behavioral Science* 3 (1967): 489–503.

Sommer, R. *Design Awareness*. San Francisco: Rinehart Press, 1972.

Sommer, R. *Personal Space*. Englewood Cliffs, N.J.: Prentice Hall, 1969.

Sommer, R. *Tight Spaces: Hard Architecture and How to Humanize It*. Englewood Cliffs, N.J.: Prentice Hall, 1974.

Sommer, R., and Gilliland, G. W. "Design for Friendship." *Canadian Architect* 6 (1961): 59–61.

Sommer, R., and Ross, H. "Social Interaction on a Geriatric Ward." *International Journal of Social Psychiatry* 4 (1958): 128–133.

Staples, R., and Walton, W. E. "A Study of Pleasurable Experiences as a Factor in Color Preferences." *Journal of Genetic Psychology* 43 (1933): 217–223.

Stouffer, S. A. "Intervening Opportunities: A Theory Relating Mobility and Distance." *American Sociological Review* 5 (1940): 845–867.

Tars, S., and Appleby, L. "The Same Child in Home and Institution." *Environment and Behavior* 5 (1974): 3.

Wells, B. W. P. "The Psycho-Social Influence of Building Environment: Sociometric Findings in Large and Small Office Spaces." *Building Science* 1 (1965): 153–165.

Wexner, L. B. "The Degree to Which Colors (Hues) Are Associated with Mood-Tones." *Journal of Applied Psychology* 38 (1954): 432–435.

Wheeler, L. *Behavioral Research for Architectural Planning and Design*. Terre Haute, Indiana: Ewing Miller Associates, 1967.

White, A. G. "The Patient Sits Down: A Clinical Note." *Psychosomatic Medicine* 15 (1953): 256–257.

Whyte, W. *Street Corner Society*. Chicago: University of Chicago Press, 1943.

Whyte, W. *The Organization Man*. New York: Simon and Schuster, 1956.

Whyte, W. "The Social Structure of a Restaurant." *American Journal of Sociology* 54 (1949): 302–310.

Wilner, D., Walkley, R. P., and Cook, S. W. "Residential Proximity and Intergroup Relations in Public Housing Projects." *Journal of Social Issues* 8 (1952): 45–69.

Wong, H. and Brown, W. "Effects of Surroundings upon Mental Work as Measured by Yerkes' Multiple Choice Method." *Journal of Comparative Psychology* 3 (1923): 319–331.

Zweigenhaft, R. "Personal Space in the Faculty Office: Desk Placement and the Student-Faculty Interaction." *Journal of Applied Psychology* 61 (1976): 529–532.

4 The Effects of Personal Space and Territory on Human Communication

Spatial changes give a tone to a communication, accent it, and at times even override the spoken word.
E. T. HALL

"If you can read this, you're too close," announces a familiar automobile bumper sticker. This sign is an attempt to regulate the amount of space between vehicles for traffic safety. Signs reading, "Keep Out" and "Authorized Personnel Only" are also attempts to regulate the amount of space between human beings. We don't put up signs in daily conversation, but we use other signals to avoid uncomfortable crowding and other perceived invasions of our personal space. Our use of space (our own and others') can dramatically affect our ability to achieve certain desired communication goals—whether they involve romance, diplomacy, or aggression. A fundamental concept which interfaces with any discussion of human spatial behavior is the notion of territoriality. An understanding of this concept will provide a useful perspective for our later examination of conversational space.

The Concept of Territoriality

The term *territoriality* has been used for years in the study of animal and fowl behavior. Generally, it has come to mean behavior characterized by identification with an area in such a way as to indicate ownership and defense of this territory against those who may "invade" it. There are many different kinds of territorial behavior, and frequently these behaviors perform useful functions for a given species. For instance, territorial behaviors may help coordinate activities, regulate density, insure propagation of the species, provide places to hide, hold the group together, provide staging areas for courtship, for nesting, or for feeding.

Most behavioral scientists agree that territoriality exists in human behavior, too. It helps regulate social interaction, but it can also be the source of social conflict. Like animals, the more powerful, dominant humans seem to have control over more territory—as long as the group or societal structure is stable. Many would not support the position Ardrey put forth—based primarily on the study of animals and fowl—that territoriality is a genetically inherited trait somehow related to innate human aggressiveness.[1]

Some territorial behaviors around one's home are particularly strong—Dad's chair, or Mom's kitchen, or Billy's stereo, or Barbara's phone. Gamblers sometimes determine odds on sporting events based not on the skill of the players, but on where the game is being played. If it is being played on one of the teams' home territory—where players are familiar with exactly how many steps it takes to perform a particular action, or how solid the turf is in a particular area, or how high the mound is, or a multitude of other peculiar characteristics of the home territory—the odds favor the home team if all other factors are relatively equal.

Altman has identified three types of territories: primary, secondary, and public.[2] *Primary territories* are clearly the exclusive domain of the owner. They are central to the daily functioning of the owner, and they are carefully guarded against uninvited intruders. One's home or bedroom often qualifies as a primary territory. Goffman's description of possessional territories also seems to fit the requirements of primary territory.[3] Possessional territories include personal effects like jackets, purses, and even copresent dependents. In this same cate-

---

[1]R. Ardrey, *The Territorial Imperative* (New York: Atheneum, 1966). For a critique of Ardrey's position, see M. F. Ashley Montagu (ed.), *Man and Aggression* (New York: Oxford University Press, 1968). Also see P. H. Klopfer, "From Ardrey to Altruism: A Discourse on the Biological Basis of Human Behavior," *Behavioral Science* 13 (1968): 399–401.

[2]I. Altman, *The Environment and Social Behavior* (Belmont, Calif.: Wadsworth, 1975), pp. 111–120.

[3]E. Goffman, *Relations in Public* (New York: Basic Books, 1971), p. 38.

gory, Goffman discusses objects which can be temporarily claimed by people—for example, a magazine, a TV set, or eating utensils. These, however, seem to be more representative of what Altman calls "secondary territories." *Secondary territories* are not as central to the daily life of the owner, nor are they perceived as clearly exclusive to the owner. The neighborhood bar or the objects cited above are examples. We are apt to see more frequent conflicts develop over these territories because the public/private boundary is blurred—for example, "Let me watch my program on TV. You don't own it." *Public territories* are available to almost anyone for temporary ownership—for example, parks, beaches, streets, seats on public transportation, telephone booths, a place in line or an unobstructed line of vision to see a particular object of interest. The words *temporary occupancy* are important. Most of us would not consider it a territorial violation if a janitor entered our office to clean without our permission. It would be a different story if the janitor occupied the office all day or engaged in noncleaning activities, such as eating lunch.

While territorial behavior seems to be a standard part of our everyday contact with other people, it is also very much in evidence when social contact is denied. Altman and Haythorn analyzed the territorial behavior of socially isolated and nonisolated pairs.[4] For ten days, two individuals lived in a small room with no outside contact while a matched group received outside contacts. The men in the isolated groups showed a gradual increase in territorial behavior and a general pattern of social withdrawal. They desired more time alone. Their territorial behavior first evidenced itself with fixed objects (areas of the room) and personal objects (beds). Later the men began to lay claim to more mobile and less personal objects. Incompatibility of the two men living together with respect to characteristics such as dominance and affiliation resulted in high territoriality while incompatibility with respect to characteristics such as achievement and dogmatism did not have strong territorial outcomes.

Territoriality: Invasion and Defense

Instructions to police interrogators sometimes suggest sitting close to the suspect, not allowing a desk to intervene and provide any protection or comfort. This theory of interrogation assumes that invasion of the suspect's personal territory (with no chance for defense) will give the officer a psychological advantage. Interestingly, we noted in the last chapter that a desk or similar office barrier could inhibit "friendly" interaction and perceptions of "close-

[4]I. Altman and W. W. Haythorn, "The Ecology of Isolated Groups," *Behavioral Science* 12(1967): 169–182.

The Effects of Personal Space and Territory on Human Communication

116

ness." On a larger scale, we know that adolescent gangs, ethnic groups, and religious neighborhoods stake out territory in urban areas and defend it against intruders. Preserving national boundaries is often the underlying thread in international disputes. What happens when somebody invades "your" territory? For instance, how do you feel when the car behind you is tailgating? How do you feel when you have to stand in a crowded theater lobby or bus? How do you feel when somebody sits in "your" seat? What do you do? Some researchers have asked similar questions, and their answers will help us to understand further how we use the space around us.

Obviously, not all territorial encroachments are the same. Lyman and Scott[5] identify three types: (1) *Violation*. This involves the unwarranted use of another's territory. This may be done with the eyes (staring at someone trying to eat in a public restaurant); with the voice or other sounds (construction noise next to a classroom); or with the body (taking up two subway seats). (2) *Invasion*. Invasions have a more all-encompassing and permanent nature to them. Here there is an attempt to take over another's territory. This may be an armed invasion of another country, or it may be the act of a wife who has turned her husband's den into a sewing room. (3) *Contamination*. Sometimes we defile another's territory not by our presence but by what we leave behind. When we take temporary occupancy of a hotel room, for instance, we don't want to find the previous "owner's" toilet articles and soiled sheets. Similarly, we are frequently upset by dog feces in our yard or food particles on "our" silverware in restaurants.

Although it is clear that encroachments on your territory will sometimes produce defensive maneuvers, it is not always the case. The intensity of one's reaction to territorial encroachment will vary depending on a number of factors. Some of these include: (1) Who violated your territory? You may have very different reactions to friends as opposed to strangers; males as opposed to females; high-status individuals as opposed to low-status ones; objects as opposed to people; peers as opposed to the very old and very young. (2) Why did they violate your territory? If you feel that the violator "knew better" you might react more strongly than if you felt he or she "couldn't help it" or was "naive." (3) What type of territory was it? You may perceive a violation of your primary territory as far more serious than a violation of a public territory. (4) How was the violation accomplished? If your body is touched, you may be more aroused than if someone walked across your grass. (5) How long did the encroachment last? If the violation is perceived as temporary, reactions may be less severe. (6) Where did the violation occur? The population density and opportunities for negotiating new territorial boundaries will surely affect one's reaction. Later in

[5]S. M. Lyman and M. B. Scott, "Territoriality: A Neglected Sociological Dimension," *Social Problems* 15 (1967): 235–249.

The Effects of Personal Space and Territory on Human Communication

this chapter we will discuss high-density situations and the way people react. This section primarily addresses low-density situations. On a public beach, the territorial violations may not seem as important as those occurring in one's bathroom. On the beach there is more territory to negotiate, boundaries are easily redrawn, and it is considered public territory.

The two primary methods for territorial defense are prevention and reaction. Prevention is a means of staking out your territory so that others will recognize it as yours and go elsewhere. A person, by his or her mere presence in a place, can keep others from entering. If you stay in a place long enough or often enough, others think you "own" it—for example, a seat in a classroom. Sometimes you ask others to assist you in staking out and defending territory—for example, "Would you hold my seat while I go get some popcorn?" Neighbors' help will vary, of course, depending on how urgently you request their aid, how long you're gone, how important the territory appears, and so on. Objects are also used as territorial "markers"—to designate "your" spatial area.[6] In places which have relatively low density, markers like umbrellas, coats, notebooks, and the like, seem to be very effective. Sometimes these markers will reserve not only your seat in a public area, but an entire table! Markers which seem to be more personal will probably also be more effective in preventing violations. In public territories, it may be more effective to leave several markers since these areas are open to nearly everyone. Sometimes uniforms help identify the territory which can be legitimately used by a particular person. Often we construct fences and grow hedges to demarcate territory. And sometimes we stake out territory simply by the way we conduct our verbal interaction—for example, special jargon or dialects can warn others that a particular space is reserved for those who "know the language."

If the prevention of territorial violations does not work, how do people react? When people come close to us, we are physiologically aroused—heart rate and galvanic skin responses increase.[7] Patterson observed that arousal also varies with eye gaze and touch as well as distance.[8] Once aroused, we need to label our state as "positive" (liking, love, relief) or "negative" (dislike, embarrassment, stress, anxiety). If the aroused state is labeled as a positive one, Patterson predicts we will reciprocate the behavior; if it is labeled a negative one, we will take measures to compensate. So, if someone is aroused by

[6]F. D. Becker, "Study of Spatial Markers," *Journal of Personality and Social Psychology* 26 (1973): 439–445.

[7]G. McBride, M. G. King, and J. W. James, "Social Proximity Effects on Galvanic Skin Responses in Adult Humans," *Journal of Psychology* 61 (1965): 153–157; Also see S. J. Finando, "The Effects of Distance Norm Violation On Heart Rate and Length of Verbal Response," Unpublished PhD dissertation, Florida State University, 1973.

[8]M. L. Patterson, "An Arousal Model of Interpersonal Intimacy," *Psychological Review* 83 (1976): 235–245.

The Effect of Personal Space and Territory on Human Communication

another person's approach and identifies it as an undesirable state, we would predict behavior designed to restore the "proper" distance between the interactants—looking away, changing the topic to a less personal one, crossing one's arms to form a frontal barrier to the invasion, covering body parts, rubbing one's neck (which makes the elbow protrude sharply toward the invader), and so on.

Russo conducted a two-year study which consisted of invading the territory of female college students seated in a college library.[9] The study compared the responses of those invaded and a similar group which was not invaded. Several different invasion techniques were used—sitting next to subjects, across from them, and so on. The quickest departure or flight was triggered when the researcher sat next to a subject and moved her chair closer (approximately one foot). (Other researchers have suggested that males may feel more stress from frontal invasions while women react more unfavorably to adjacent invasions.) After about thirty minutes, about 70 percent of the people Russo approached at the one-foot distance moved. From this study, a whole vocabulary of defense was developed. For instance, there were defensive and offensive displays which included the use of position, posture, and gesture. Position refers to location in the room; a newcomer to the room will interpret the situation differently if you have selected a corner position rather than a position in the middle of the room. Posture refers to such things as whether a person has materials spread out "like he or she owned the place" or whether they are tightly organized. Gestures can be used to indicate receptivity or rejection of communication—for example, hostile glances, turning or leaning away, blocking with hands or arms, and so on. Finally, although under some circumstances verbal defense is less apt to occur, verbal defenses such as profanity (or generally obnoxious behavior) can be effectively used. Russo's work is summarized by Sommer:

> There were wide individual differences in the ways victims reacted—there is no single reaction to someone's sitting too close; there are defensive gestures, shifts in posture, and attempts to move away. If these fail or are ignored by the invader, or he shifts position too, the victim eventually takes to flight. . . . There was a dearth of direct verbal responses to the invasions. . . . Only one of the eighty students asked the invader to move over.[10]

Barash conducted a study similar to Russo's, but the library invaders' status was manipulated.[11] Students fled more quickly from the more formally dressed, "high status" invaders. And Knowles experimented with a type of invasion we

[9]R. Sommer, *Personal Space* (Englewood Cliffs, N.J.: Prentice-Hall, 1969), pp. 35, 46–48, 64.
[10]Ibid., 35–36.
[11]D. P. Barash, "Human Ethology: Personal Space Reiterated," *Environment and Behavior* 5 (1973): 67–73.

The Effect of Personal Space and Territory on Human Communication

are all familiar with—talking to somebody in a hallway while other people decide whether to walk through the conversants or around.[12] Only 25 percent of the people in this study walked through, but when the conversants were replaced by barrels, 75 percent of the passersby walked through. The fewest intrusions occurred with four-person groups (rather than a dyad) and "high status" conversants (older and more formally dressed). This study is reported to illustrate the fact that not only do we not want others to violate our territory, we generally do not like the role of invader either—as the mumbled apologies and bowed heads of some of Knowles' invaders testify.

Increasing the density of a species will also result in territorial violations. What happens when the population becomes so dense that one cannot exercise usual territorial behavior? The attention given to human overpopulation makes this a particularly important concern.

Density and Crowding

To begin, let us examine some interesting examples of animal behavior under conditions of high density or overpopulation. For years, scientists were intrigued by the large-scale suicides of lemmings, rabbits, and rats. Their interest was increased by the fact that at the time of the suicides, there seemed to be plenty of food, predators were not in evidence, and infection was not present. An ethnologist who had training in medical pathology hypothesized that such suicides were triggered by an endocrine reaction in the animals which resulted from stress built up during an increase of population.[13] This hypothesis was confirmed in a study of the deer population on James Island— an island one mile off the coast of Maryland in the Chesapeake Bay. Careful histological studies over a period of years showed that the deer on James Island died from overactive adrenal glands—resulting from stress. The adrenal glands play an important part in the regulation of growth, reproduction, and the level of the body's defenses. Thus, overpopulation caused death—not by starvation, infection, or aggression from others but by a physiological reaction to the stress created.

Calhoun's experiments go even further to suggest peculiar modes of behavior under conditions of overpopulation.[14] Calhoun noted that with plenty of

[12]E. S. Knowles, "Boundaries Around Group Interaction: The Effect of Group Size and Member Status on Boundary Permeability," *Journal of Personality and Social Psychology* 26 (1973): 327–332.

[13]J. J. Christian and D. E. Davis, "Social and Endocrine Factors Are Integrated in the Regulation of Mammalian Populations," *Science* 146 (1964): 1550–1560.

[14]J. B. Calhoun, "Population Density and Social Pathology." *Scientific American* 206 (1962): 139–148.

The Effect of Personal Space and Territory on Human Communication

food and no danger from predators, Norway rats in a quarter-acre outdoor pen stabilized their population at about 150. His observations, covering twenty-eight months, indicated that spatial relationships were extremely important. He then designed an experiment in which he could maintain a stressful situation through overpopulation while three generations of rats were reared. He labeled this experiment a "behavioral sink"—an area or receptacle where most of the rats exhibited gross distortions of behavior. Some of Calhoun's observations are worth noting: (1) Some rats withdrew from social and sexual intercourse completely; others began to mount anything in sight; courtship patterns were totally disrupted and females were frequently pursued by several males. (2) Nest building patterns—ordinarily neat—became sloppy or nonexistent. (3) Litters of young rats became mixed; newborn and young rats were stepped on or eaten by invading hyperactive males. (4) Unable to establish spatial territories, the dominant males would fight over positions near the eating bins; "classes" of rats shared territories and exhibited similar behaviors; the hyperactive males violated all territorial rights by running around in packs—disregarding any boundaries except those backed by force. (5) Pregnant rats frequently had miscarriages; disorders of the sex organs were numerous; only one-fourth of the 558 newborns in the sink survived to be weaned. (6) Aggressive behavior increased significantly.

Can we generalize from mice to men and women? Some early studies which found moderate correlations between various socially undesirable outcomes—such as crime, delinquency, and mental and physical disorders—and high population seemed to say yes. Others facetiously contend that the only generalization we can make from Calhoun's work is: "Don't crowd a rat!" On the basis of the research conducted thus far on human density and crowding, it is clear we don't have a simple "crowding is good or bad" answer.

One of the problems in interpreting this body of research concerns the many perspectives from which the subject has been studied. Density and crowding, for instance, are not the same. *Density refers to the number of people per unit of space; crowding is a feeling state* which may develop in high- or low-density situations. Your perception of being crowded may be influenced by (1) environmental factors—for example, available space, noise, or the availability of resources and your access to them; (2) personal factors, such as personality and behavioral styles or prior experiences in high-density situations; and (3) social factors—for example, frequency and duration of contact, the nature of the contact (cooperative vs. competitive), the people involved (friends vs. strangers), or the number of people involved (one, several, or an entire community). Definitions of density are also complex and varied. Correlational studies have used: number of people per city, per census tract, per dwelling unit, number of rooms per dwelling unit, number of buildings per neighborhood, and so on. Experimental studies sometimes put the same size group of people in different size rooms; others vary the number of people in the

The Effect of Personal Space and Territory on Human Communication

same room. Few studies have considered the rate at which high density evolves or whether participants feel they had any control over the development of a high-density situation. The point of this somewhat tedious list of contingencies is that people may react very differently under each of these conditions or combinations of conditions. Given these problems, what can we say about the effects of high density and human reactions to it?

The Effects of High Density. First, it should be clear that increased density does not automatically mean increased stress or antisocial behavior for human beings. Sometimes we even seek the pleasures of density. Football games and rock concerts are familiar examples. If we take responsibility for our presence in a highly populated situation and if we know the condition will terminate in a matter of hours, the chances of negative effects seem to be minimal. It is true that some studies have found results which might fit well into a "behavioral sink" theory—for example, aggression, stress, criminal activity, hostility toward others, and a deterioration of mental and physical health. However, in most every case we find other studies which do not find these effects. Usually, the difference lies in the fact that one of the variables we mentioned earlier was influential in reducing the undesirable effects. Rohe and Patterson, for instance, found that if you provided children with enough of the toys they wanted, increased density would not produce the withdrawal and aggression suggested by previous studies.[15] Some high density neighborhoods which are highly cohesive actually have a lower incidence of mental and physical health problems. Galle et al. looked at a number of density measures which had previously been associated with high criminal activity.[16] But unlike their predecessors, this research team tried to control for educational levels, ethnic background, occupational status, and the like. The person-per-room measure was the measure which provided the highest correlation between density and juvenile delinquency, higher death and fertility rates, and more public assistance. Yes, high density can produce a host of problems. But human beings do not stand passively by in situations which demand a long-term commitment to high density. Instead, we try various methods to cope with or offset potentially harmful effects. What are some of the methods of coping?

Coping with High Density. Milgram feels that city dwellers are exposed to an overload of information, people, things, problems, and the like.[17]

[15]W. Rohe and A. H. Patterson, "The Effects of Varied Levels of Resources and Density on Behavior in a Day Care Center," paper presented at Environmental Design and Research Association, Milwaukee, Wis., 1974. Cited in Altman, *The Environment and Social Behavior*, pp. 157, 165, and 182.

[16]O. R. Galle, W. R. Gove, and J. M. McPherson, "Population Density and Pathology: What Are the Relationships for Man?" *Science* 176 (1972): 23–30.

[17]S. Milgram, "The Experience of Living in Cities," *Science* 167 (1970): 1461–1468.

The Effects of Personal Space and Territory on Human Communication

As a result, these city dwellers engage in behavior designed to reduce this overload, which sometimes causes outsiders to see them as distant and emotionally detached from others. Some of these methods for coping in populated cities include: (1) spending less time with each input—for example, having shorter conversations with people; (2) disregarding low-priority inputs—for example, ignoring the drunk on the sidewalk or not talking to people you see on a commuter train every day; (3) shifting the responsibility for some transactions to others—for example, relieving bus drivers of the responsibility for making change; (4) blocking inputs—for example, using doormen to guard apartment buildings; and so on.

Western observers have been very interested in examining the life of the !Kung Bushmen in South-West Africa.[18] Here is a society which has one of the lowest population densities in the world (about one person per 10 square miles), but they deliberately build camps which create very close living conditions. The design of their huts produces a situation which approximates thirty people living in one room! There is close contact and extensive social interaction, but there seem to be no adverse effects. Several other facts may explain the coping methods of the !Kung. First, individuals or families are permitted to leave one camp and join another—typically fifteen or more miles away. This means that each person feels he or she can "escape" if the situation warrants it—and, perhaps more importantly, escape to a friendly place, a camp with the same life-style and values. A new environment can be found, but it is not staffed with inhospitable strangers. The fact that camps are widely separated may also be beneficial.

We now shift our attention from spatial relationships in overpopulated conditions to those involved in a two-person conversation.

Conversational Distance

You have probably had the experience (perhaps not conscious) of backing up or moving forward when speaking to another person. Sometimes this movement is caused by a need to find a comfortable conversational distance. In different situations, when discussing different topics, these "comfortable" distances vary. Is there any consistency to the distances chosen? Is there a specific distance most people select when talking to others?

Anthropologist Edward T. Hall's astute observations regarding human spatial behavior were published in a book called *The Silent Language*.[19] This book,

[18]P. Draper, "Crowding Among Hunter-Gatherers: The !Kung Bushmen," *Science* 182 (1973): 301–303.
[19](New York: Doubleday, 1959.)

The Effects of Personal Space and Territory on Human Communication

probably as much as any other single work, is responsible for a surge of scholarly interest in trying to answer the above and related questions. Hall identified several types of space, but our concern here is with what he called "informal" or "personal space." Informal space is carried with each individual and expands and contracts under varying circumstances—depending on the type of encounter, the relationship of the communicating persons, their personalities, and many other factors. Hall further classified informal space into four subcategories: intimate, casual-personal, social-consultative, and public. According to Hall, intimate distances range from actual physical contact to about eighteen inches; casual-personal extends from one and a half feet to four feet; social-consultative (for impersonal business) ranges from four to twelve feet; public distance covers the area from twelve feet to the limits of visibility or hearing. Hall is quick to note that these distances are based on his observations of a particular sample of adults from business and professional occupations, primarily middle class, and native to the northeastern U.S. and that generalization to various ethnic and racial groups in this country should be made with considerable caution.

Robert Sommer also sought answers to questions about comfortable conversational distance. He studied people who were brought into a room and told to discuss various "impersonal" topics.[20] The two sofas in this room were placed at various distances and subjects were observed to see whether they sat opposite or beside each other. It was hypothesized that when they began to sit side by side, it would mean the conversational distance was too far to sit opposite one another on the two couches. From one to three feet, the subjects sat on different couches facing one another. After three and a half feet, people sat side by side. If one measures "nose to nose," this would make the participants five and a half feet apart when they started to sit side by side. In a follow-up study, Sommer used chairs and, hence, was able to vary side-by-side distance as well as distance across. Here he found that people chose to sit across from one another until the across distance exceeded the side-by-side distance—then they sat side by side. How generalizable are these findings? A critical look at this study immediately leads us to question what other variables may affect the distance relationship. For instance, this study was conducted with people who knew each other slightly, who were discussing "impersonal" topics, and who were in a large lounge. How would other factors affect the distance relationship? Argyle and Dean have theorized that distance is based on the balance of approach and avoidance forces.[21] What are some of these forces? Burgoon and

[20]R. Sommer, "Leadership and Group Geography," *Sociometry* 24 (1961): 99–110. Also R. Sommer, "The Distance for Comfortable Conversation: A Further Study," *Sociometry* 25 (1962): 111–116.

[21]M. Argyle and J. Dean, "Eye Contact, Distance and Affiliation," *Sociometry* 28 (1965): 289–304.

The Effects of Personal Space and Territory on Human Communication

Jones say that the expected distance in a given conversation is a function of the social norms combined with idiosyncratic patterns of the interactants.[22] What are some of these norms and idiosyncratic patterns? What factors modify the distances we choose?

Answering these questions will be the focus of the remainder of this chapter. Again, however, we must sort through conflicting results due to variations in research methodology and conceptualization of personal space. Logically, we know that conversational distance is the product of both interactants' negotiations. But some research is based on the behavior of a single person; some research does not distinguish between actual physical distance and perceptions of distance; some research measures distance by floor tiles or space between chair legs and totally ignores the ability of the communicators to vary the distance by changes in topic, eye gaze, and body lean; and most research does not distinguish between initial distance and changes which take place over the course of a conversation. Since the methods of measuring personal space vary so much, we even have to be cautious about results which agree with other studies. Sometimes people fill out questionnaires about preferred distances; sometimes they are asked to approach nonhuman objects—for example, coat racks and life-size photographs; sometimes people are unknowingly approached at various distances by others; and sometimes they are asked to arrange miniature dolls, photographs, or silhouettes as if they were in various communication situations. With these factors in mind, the following sources of variation in conversational distance are presented.

1. Age and Sex. Willis studied standing speaking distance of 775 people in a variety of contexts and recorded speaking distance at the beginning of the interaction.[23] Among his conclusions were the following: (1) speakers stood closer to women than men, and (2) peers stood closer than did persons older than the listener. The first conclusion seems to be in line with other studies which suggest that mixed sex pairs interact at closer distances than all-female pairs—who choose closer distances than all-male pairs. Conversational space for males, then, may be greater than for females, but this will probably be highly variable as other factors in the situation are known. Age differences have not been carefully studied, but it seems reasonable to assume we would interact closer to people in our own general age range. The exceptions, of course, are the very old and very young who, for various reasons, often elicit interaction at closer quarters. Keep in mind that most of these generalizations about age and sex do not consider cultural or ethnic backgrounds.

[22]J. K. Burgoon and S. B. Jones, "Toward a Theory of Personal Space Expectations and Their Violations," *Human Communication Research* 2 (1976): 131–146.

[23]F. N. Willis, "Initial Speaking Distance as a Function of the Speaker's Relationship," *Psychonomic Science* 5 (1966): 221–222.

The Effects of Personal Space and Territory on Human Communication

2. Cultural and Ethnic Background. Volumes of folklore and isolated personal observations suggest that spatial relationships in other cultures with different needs and norms may produce very different distances for interacting. Watson and Graves found substantial and consistent differences between pairs of Arab students and pairs of American students in a conversational setting.[24] These differences included such things as: (1) Arabs confronted one another more directly; (2) Arabs moved closed together; (3) Arabs used more touch behavior; and (4) Arabs were apt to look each other squarely in the eye—an event which occurred less frequently with American student pairs. They also found a tendency toward subcultural homogeneity among Arabs from four different nations and among Americans from four regions of the country. These results are tempered by the statistical tests used to measure the differences and by the small number of pairs used—sixteen pairs of subjects for each culture. In a much more extensive treatment of cross-cultural proxemics, Watson reports numerous observations on individuals representing "contact" and "noncontact" cultures.[25] *Contact* refers to interactants who face one another more directly, interact closer to one another, touch one another more, look one another in the eye more, and speak in a louder voice. Contact groups in Watson's study were Arabs, Latin Americans, and Southern Europeans. Noncontact groups were Asians, Indians and Pakistanis, Northern Europeans, and Americans. Forston and Larson, however, found that Latin American students did not necessarily exhibit the traditional space differences of sitting closer than North Americans; in fact, their tendency was to sit further apart![26] Shuter's systematic field observations suggest that we are too imprecise when we talk about broad cultural groups.[27] He found, for instance, that there were significant differences within the so-called Latin American cultural group. Costa Ricans interacted more closely than did Panamanians or Colombians. Sommer found that when he asked students from five different countries to rank-order various seating arrangements according to degree of intimacy, there was agreement on the rank-order by all subjects.[28] Side by side seating was ranked most intimate, corner seating next, then face-to-face or opposite, followed by various distant arrangements.

The findings relevant to black Americans, white Americans, and Mexican

---

[24]O. M. Watson and T. D. Graves, "Quantitative Research in Proxemic Behavior," *American Anthropologist* 68 (1966): 971–985.

[25]O. M. Watson, *Proxemic Behavior: A Cross-Cultural Study* (The Hague: Mouton, 1970).

[26]R. F. Forston and C. U. Larson, "The Dynamics of Space: An Experimental Study in Proxemic Behavior Among Latin Americans and North Americans," *Journal of Communication* 18 (1968): 109–116.

[27]R. Shuter, "Proxemics and Tactility in Latin America," *Journal of Communication* 26 (1976): 46–52.

[28]Sommer, *Personal Space*, pp. 63–64.

The Effects of Personal Space and Territory on Human Communication

Americans are generally so haphazard that only a maze of contradictions remains. There is no consistent spatial pattern for comparing black interactants with white interactants, but a couple of studies show black-white pairs maintain greater distances than white-white or black-black dyads. A developmental study which examined black and white children in first, third, and fifth grade suggested that subcultural proxemic differences may exist when a child enters school, but by fifth grade these differences are minimized through maturation and acculturation.[29] Scherer feels that any differences between blacks, whites, and Mexican Americans is a socioeconomic difference and not a difference attributable to ethnic background.[30] This study found middle-class children maintained greater conversational distance than lower-class children, but there were no differences between middle-class blacks and whites nor lower-class blacks and whites. Finally, an intriguing aside offered by Connolly begs further research.[31] He said he observed black interactants moving around and altering the proxemic distances during the conversation more than white interactants. This observation may be of particular interest in light of Erickson's observation, reported next.

3. Topic of Subject Matter. Erickson wanted to find out if proxemic shifts (forward or backward) were associated with any other events in a conversation.[32] By coding co-occurring behavior, he determined that proxemic shifts may mark important segments of the encounter—for example, beginnings, endings, and topic changes.

Earlier we noted that Sommer, in his efforts to examine the limits of conversational distance, tried to use "impersonal" topics—topics which would not obviously influence the distances chosen. Leipold's work demonstrates how anticipated treatment of the same general topic can influence conversational distance.[33] Students entered a room and were given either stress ("Your grade is poor, and you have not done your best"), praise ("You are doing very well and Mr. Leipold wants to talk with you further"), or neutral ("Mr. Leipold is interested in your feelings about the introductory course") comments. Students in

[29]S. E. Jones and J. R. Aiello, "Proxemic Behavior of Black and White First, Third, and Fifth Grade Children," *Journal of Personality and Social Psychology* 25 (1973): 21–27.

[30]S. E. Scherer, "Proxemic Behavior of Primary School Children as a Function of Their Socioeconomic Class and Subculture," *Journal of Personality and Social Psychology* 29 (1974): 800–805.

[31]P. R. Connolly, "The Perception of Personal Space Among Black and White Americans," *Central States Speech Journal* 26 (1975): 21–28.

[32]F. Erickson, "One Function of Proxemic Shifts in Face-to-Face Interaction," in A. Kendon, R. M. Harris, and M. R. Keys (eds.), *Organization of Behavior in Face-to-Face Interactions* (Chicago: Aldine, 1975), pp. 175–187.

[33]W. E. Leipold, "Psychological Distance in a Dyadic Interview," Ph.D. diss., University of North Dakota, 1963.

the stress condition sat furthest from the experimenter and those given praise sat closest. Little asked subjects in several different countries to position dolls relative to one another for a variety of social situations and for pleasant, neutral, and unpleasant topics.[34] Pleasant topics clearly produced the closest placement of the figures, but neutral and unpleasant topic situations were not significantly different. Although we aren't able to obtain information about specific topics, it is worth noting that close distances may decrease the amount of talking—regardless of topic.[35]

4. Setting for the Interaction. Obviously the social setting makes a great deal of difference in how far we stand from others in conversation. A crowded cocktail party demands a different distance than a comfortable evening in the living room with your spouse. Lighting, temperature, noise, and available space will affect your interaction distance. Some authors have hypothesized that as room size increases, people tend to sit closer together. If you perceive the setting as a formal and/or unfamiliar one, we would predict greater distances from unknown others and closer distances to those you know. Little had people arrange actresses in certain settings to determine the interpersonal distances which were perceived as necessary in various situations.[36] Each student was a director and was to place the interactants in a street-corner setting, an office waiting room, the lobby of a public building, and a campus location. The maximum placement distance was in the office, while the closest placement was in the street scene.

5. Physical Characteristics. The size of your interaction partner (height and weight) may call for changes in interaction distance—to avoid overpowering or being overpowered or simply to achieve a better angle of gaze. A series of studies conducted by Kleck shows that persons interacting with stigmatized individuals (a left-leg amputation was simulated with a special wheel chair) choose greater initial speaking distances than with nonstigmatized, or "normal," persons, but that this distance decreases as the length of the interaction increases.[37] Perceived epileptics elicited similar reactions.

6. Attitudinal and Emotional Orientation. Kleck's work also included situations in which the subject was told the other person was "warm

[34]K. B. Little, "Cultural Variations in Social Schemata," *Journal of Personality and Social Psychology* 10 (1968): 1–7.

[35]R. Schulz and J. Barefoot, "Non-verbal Responses and Affiliative Conflict Theory," *British Journal of Social and Clinical Psychology* 13 (1974): 237–243.

[36]K. B. Little, "Personal Space," *Journal of Experimental Social Psychology* 1 (1965): 237–247.

[37]R. Kleck, "Physical Stigma and Task Oriented Interaction," *Human Relations* 22 (1969): 51–60.

and friendly" or "unfriendly." Not surprisingly, the subjects chose greater distances when interacting with a person perceived to be unfriendly. Similarly, when told to enter into conversation with another person and to behave in a friendly way, subjects chose closer distances than when told to "let him know you aren't friendly." This friendly-unfriendly relationship to distance even seems to manifest itself with preschool children.[38] The number of unfriendly acts was directly related to the distance maintained by the recipient of such acts during free-play situations. The distance could be reduced, however, by putting a prized toy near the aggressive child. In some instances our anger will cause us to withdraw from others, but if we seek retaliation, it may reduce distance.[39] Changes in our emotional state can sometimes make vast differences in how close or far away we want to be from others—for example, states of depression or fatigue vs. states of extreme excitement or joy.

An unpublished study mentioned by Patterson reveals we may make a whole host of interpersonal judgments about another person based on distance.[40] Subjects were told to interview others and secretly rate them on traits of friendliness, aggressiveness, dominance, extroversion, and intelligence. The interviewees were actually confederates who approached the interviewers at different distances and gave standard answers to the questions asked. The mean ratings for all the traits at four different distances were tabulated and revealed that the most distant position yielded significantly lower (less favorable) ratings. So, barring any contradictory information, closer people are often seen as warmer, liking one another more, and more empathic and understanding.

When we seek to win the approval of another person, there will also be a reduction in conversational distance as compared to instances when we are deliberately trying to avoid approval. Rosenfeld's female subjects seeking approval maintained a mean distance of fifty-seven inches; those trying to avoid approval averaged ninety-four inches. When the distance was held constant at five feet, approval seekers compensated by smiling more and engaging in gestural activity.[41] Mehrabian concluded his review of attitude-distance research by saying:

> . . . the findings from a large number of studies corroborate one another and indicate that communicator-addressee distance is correlated with the degree of negative attitude communicated to and inferred by the addressee. In addition,

[38]M. G. King, "Interpersonal Relations in Preschool Children and Average Approach Distance," *Journal of Genetic Psychology* 108 (1966): 109–116.

[39]M. Meisels and M. Dosey, "Personal Space, Anger Arousal, and Psychological Defense," *Journal of Personality* 39 (1971): 333–334.

[40]M. Patterson, "Spatial Factors in Social Interaction," *Human Relations* 21 (1968): 351–361.

[41]H. Rosenfeld, "Effect of Approval-Seeking Induction on Interpersonal Proximity." *Psychological Reports* 17 (1965): 120–122. Also: H. Rosenfeld, "Instrumental and Affiliative Functions of Facial and Gestural Expressions." *Journal of Personality and Social Psychology* 4 (1966): 65–72.

The Effects of Personal Space and Territory on Human Communication

studies carried out by sociologists and anthropologists indicate that distances which are too close, that is, inappropriate for a given interpersonal situation, can elicit negative attitudes when the communicator-addressee relationship is not an intimate one.[42]

7. Characteristics of the Interpersonal Relationship. Willis also found that strangers seemed to begin conversations further away than did acquaintances; women stood closer to close friends than did men, but further away from "just friends" (the author suggests this may be due to a more cautious approach used in making friends); and parents were found to be as distant as strangers![43] The range of distances measured in Willis' study was from 17.75 inches (close friends speaking to women) to 28 inches (Caucasian-black). Little, in a cross-cultural study, also found friends perceived as interacting closer together than acquaintances, and acquaintances closer than strangers.[44]

Also, in this culture status is associated with greater space or distance. Generally those with higher status have more and better space and greater freedom to move about. Theodore White, in *The Making of the President 1960,* tells of an instance in which John Kennedy's status was emphasized by the distance his fellow campaign workers maintained on a particular occasion— said to be about thirty feet. Hall recounts a problem of status and distance in the military.

> The Army, in its need to get technical about matters that are usually handled informally, made a mistake in the regulations on distance required for reporting to a superior officer. . . . Instructions for reporting to a superior officer were that the junior officer was to proceed up to a point three paces in front of the officer's desk, stop, salute, and state his name, his rank, and his business. . . . The normal speaking distance for business matters, where impersonality is involved at the beginning of the conversation, is five and a half to eight feet. The distance required by the Army regulations borders on the edge of what we would call "far." It evokes an automatic response to shout. This detracts from the respect which is supposed to be shown to the superior officer. There are, of course, many subjects which it is almost impossible to talk about at this distance. . . . [45]

Burns reports an experiment in which subjects consistently identified a man's status according to spatial relationships.[46] Short films depicted a man at a

[42]A. Mehrabian, "Significance of Posture and Position in the Communication of Attitude and Status Relationships," *Psychological Bulletin* 71 (1969): 363.

[43]Willis, "Initial Speaking Distance as a Function of the Speaker's Relationship."

[44]K. B. Little, "Cultural Variations in Social Schemata," *Journal of Personality and Social Psychology* 10 (1968): 5.

[45]Hall, *The Silent Language,* p. 163.

[46]T. Burns, "Nonverbal Communication," *Discovery* (Oct., 1964): 31–35.

The Effects of Personal Space and Territory on Human Communication

desk sorting through a card index. He stopped to answer the phone. Then the film switched to another man who stopped, knocked on the office door, entered, and approached the man seated at the desk. The second man pulled out some papers, and the two men discussed them. Two actors switched roles throughout the films. Audiences were asked to rate the relative status of the two men. The caller was consistently rated subordinate if he stopped just inside the door and conversed from that distance with the man at the desk. Time between the knock and the man at the desk rising was also related to status—the longer it took the man to respond to the knock, the higher his status was judged. Mehrabian cites two studies which suggest "that the distance between two communicators is positively correlated with their status discrepancy."[47]

8. Personality Characteristics.   Much has been written about the influence of introversion and extroversion on spatial relationships. It is difficult to draw any firm conclusions, however. Some find introverts tend to stand further away than extroverts—particularly in intimate situations. Some find that extroverts allow others to approach them more closely. Other find no differences in the distances which persons with these personality characteristics maintain when approaching others. Other studies suggest that anxiety-prone individuals will maintain greater distances, but closer distances are seen when people have a high self-concept, have high affiliative needs, are low on authoritarianism, and are "self-directed." People with various personality abnormalities can probably be counted on to show greater nonnormative spatial behavior—both too far away and too close.

In addition to studying human spatial behavior in overcrowded situations and in conversation, some researchers have examined such questions in the context of the small group—particularly with regard to seating patterns.

Seating Behavior and Spatial Arrangements in Small Groups

This body of work is known as small-group ecology. Results of these studies show that our seating behavior is not generally accidental or random. There are explanations for much of our seating behavior—whether we are fully conscious of them or not. The particular position we choose in relation to the other person or persons varies with the task at hand, the degree of relationship between the interactants, the personalities of the two parties, and the amount

[47]A. Mehrabian, "Significance of Posture and Position in the Communication of Attitude and Status Relationships," *Psychological Bulletin* 71 (1969): 363.

and kind of available space. Summaries of the findings about seating behavior and spatial positioning can be listed under the categories of leadership, dominance, task, sex and acquaintance, motivation, and introversion-extroversion.

1. Leadership. It seems to be a cultural norm that leaders are expected to be found at the head or end of the table. At a family gathering, we generally find the head of the household sitting at the head of the table.

Elected group leaders generally put themselves in the head positions at rectangular tables, and the other group members try to position themselves so they can see the leader. Strodtbeck and Hook set up some experimental jury deliberations which revealed that a man sitting at the head position was chosen significantly more often as the leader—particularly if he was perceived as a person from a high economic class.[48] If the choice was between two people at each end, the one perceived as of higher economic status was chosen. Howells and Becker add further support to the idea that one's position in a group is an important factor in leadership emergence.[49] They reasoned that spatial position determines the flow of communication which, in turn, determines leadership emergence. Five-person decision-making groups were examined. Three people sat on one side of a rectangular table and two sat on the other side. Since previous work suggested that communication usually flow across the table rather than around it, the researchers felt the side with two people would be able to influence the most people (or at least talk more) and therefore emerge more often as group leaders. This hypothesis was confirmed.

2. Dominance. The end positions also seem to carry with them a status or dominance factor. Russo found that people rating various seating arrangements on an "equality" dimension stated that if one person was at the head and one on the side, this was a more unequal situation in terms of status than if they were side by side or both on the ends.[50] In an analysis of talking frequency in small groups, Hare and Bales noted people in positions 1, 3, and 5 (at right) were frequent talkers.[51] Subsequent studies revealed that these people were

[48]F. Strodtbeck and L. Hook, "The Social Dimensions of a Twelve Man Jury Table," *Sociometry* 24 (1961): 297–415. Also see B. M. Bass and S. Klubeck, "Effects of Seating Arrangement on Leaderless Group Discussions," *Journal of Abnormal and Social Psychology* 47 (1952): 724–726.

[49]L. T. Howells and S. W. Becker, "Seating Arrangement and Leadership Emergence," *Journal of Abnormal and Social Psychology* 64 (1962): 148–150.

[50]N. Russo, "Connotation of Seating Arrangement," *Cornell Journal of Social Relations* 2 (1967): 37–44.

[51]A. Hare and R. Bales, "Seating Position and Small Group Interaction," *Sociometry* 26 (1963): 480–486.

The Effects of Personal Space and Territory on Human Communication

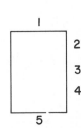

likely to be dominant personalities, while those who avoided the central or focal positions (by choosing seats 2 and 4) were more anxious and actually stated they wanted to stay out of the discussion. While further study is necessary, some preliminary work by students at the University of Wisconsin-Milwaukee suggests that deliberately placing nondominant persons in focal positions and dominant persons in nonfocal positions will not radically change the frequency of their communications. In groups composed only of nondominant individuals, the results may be much different. Positions 1, 3, and 5 were also considered to be positions of leadership, but leadership of a different type—depending on the position. The two end positions (1 and 5) attracted the task-oriented leader, while the middle position was determined to be for more of a socioemotional leader—one concerned about group relationships, getting everyone to participate, and so on. Lott and Sommer wanted to find out how others located themselves vis-à-vis higher- and lower-status people.[52] Generally, the results suggest that people (in this case, students) will sit further away from both higher-status (professor) and lower-status (flunking freshman) persons than from peers.

3. Task. Sommer's observations of seating behavior in student cafeterias and libraries led him to study how students would sit in different task situations.[53] The same study was conducted by Cook in the United Kingdom (U.K.) with Oxford University students and a sample of nonstudents—civil servants, schoolteachers, and secretaries.[54] In each case, persons were asked to imagine themselves sitting at a table with a friend of the same sex in each of the following four situations:

Conversation: Sitting and chatting for a few minutes before class. ("Before work" for nonstudents.)

Cooperation: Sitting and studying together for the same exam. ("Sitting doing a crossword or the like together" for nonstudents.)

Co-action: Sitting studying for different exams. ("Sitting at the same table reading" for nonstudents.)

Competition: Competing in order to see who will be the first to solve a series of puzzles.

Two types of tables were shown to each subject. One table was round and one was rectangular. Each had six chairs. The results of these two studies are presented in Table 4.1 for rectangular tables and Table 4.2 for circular tables.

[52]B. S. Lott and R. Sommer, "Seating Arrangements and Status," *Journal of Personality and Social Psychology* 7 (1967): 90–95.

[53]R. Sommer, "Further Studies of Small Group Ecology," *Sociometry* 28 (1965): 337–348.

[54]M. Cook, "Experiments on Orientation and Proxemics," *Human Relations* 23 (1970): 61–76.

The Effects of Personal Space and Territory on Human Communication

Table 4.1 Seating Preferences at Rectangular Tables

	×▢	▢ with × top and × bottom	×× ▢	×▢×	▢ ×	▢×
Conversation						
U.S. sample						
(151 responses)	42%	46%	11%	0%	1%	0%
U.K. (Univ.) sample						
(102 responses)	51	21	15	0	6	7
U.K. (nonuniv.) sample						
(42 responses)	42	42	9	2	5	0
Cooperation						
U.S. sample	19	25	51	0	5	0
U.K. (univ.) sample	11	11	23	20	22	13
U.K. (nonuniv.) sample	40	2	50	5	2	0
Co-action						
U.S. sample	3	3	7	13	43	33
U.K. (univ.) sample	9	8	10	31	28	14
U.K. (nonuniv.) sample	12	14	12	19	31	12
Competition						
U.S. sample	7	41	8	18	20	5
U.K. (univ.) sample	7	10	10	50	16	7
U.K. (nonuniv.) sample	4	13	3	53	20	7

    There are many similarities between the different groups in terms of order of preference, but there are also some differences worth noting. For instance, it is interesting that the nonuniversity sample differs less from the U.S. student sample than does the Oxford University group. Conversations before class (or work) primarily involved corner or "short" opposite seating at rectangular tables and side-by-side seating at round tables. Oxford students seemed to be more favorable toward distant seating for conversation than other groups, but the value of closeness and visibility for this task seems to prevail. Cooperation seems to elicit a preponderance of side-by-side choices from everyone except the Oxford group. The author suggests that since Oxford students are encouraged to do most of their work alone, they may not have realized the question meant cooperating with another person. Even more doubt is cast on the validity of the Oxford responses to this question since their responses to the co-action

The Effects of Personal Space and Territory on Human Communication

Table 4.2 Seating Preferences at Round Tables

	××◯	×◯	◯×
Conversation			
U.S. sample			
(116 responses)	63%	17%	20%
U.K. (univ.) sample			
(102 responses)	58	37	5
U.K. (nonuniv.) sample			
(42 responses)	58	27	15
Cooperation			
U.S. sample	83	7	10
U.K. (univ.) sample	25	31	44
U.K. (nonuniv.) sample	97	0	3
Co-action			
U.S. sample	13	36	51
U.K. (univ.) sample	16	34	50
U.K. (nonuniv.) sample	24	26	50
Competition			
U.S. sample	2	25	63
U.K. (univ.) sample	15	22	63
U.K. (nonuniv.) sample	9	21	70

question were similar. Co-action, studying for different exams or reading at the same table as another, necessitated plenty of room between the participants and the most distant seating positions were generally selected. The slightly different instructions for the nonuniversity sample may explain the greater variety of responses to the co-action question. Most persons wanted to compete in an opposite seating arrangement. However, the U.S. students wanted to establish a closer opposite relationship. Apparently this would afford them an opportunity not only to see how the other person is progressing, but would also allow them to use various gestures, body movements, and eye contact to "upset" their opponents. The more distant opposite position chosen by the United Kingdom samples would, on the other hand, prevent "spying."

In an attempt to replicate his work on seating arrangements and tasks with children, Sommer found that a widely used arrangement in adult groups, oppo-

The Effects of Personal Space and Territory on Human Communication

site seating, was infrequently used by children. The thirty-inch distance across the table was apparently a major factor. A related line of inquiry involved an attempt to determine the impact of discussion topics on seating arrangements. College women discussed topics ranging from very personal to very impersonal. The apparent lack of impact caused Sommer to conclude:

> It seems apparent that it is the nature of the relationship between the individuals rather than the topic itself that characterizes a discussion as personal or impersonal. Two lovers discussing the weather can have an intimate conversation, but a zoology professor discussing sex in a lecture hall containing 300 students would be having an impersonal session regardless of topic.[55]

4. Sex and Acquaintance. As the previous quote suggests, the nature of the relationship may make a difference in spatial orientation and, hence, in seating selection. Neither Sommer nor Cook found any differences between the sexes with respect to seat choices for different tasks; however, their studies were only concerned with the sex of the chooser. Perhaps cross-sex pairs choose differently. You may remember the previous studies were also concerned only with a "casual friend"; perhaps the degree of acquaintance will influence choices—for example, intimate friends may move closer. Such questions prompted Cook to conduct another questionnaire study and to obtain some actual observational data of persons interacting in a restaurant and several bars.[56] Subjects in the questionnaire study were asked to select seating arrangements when: (1) sitting with a casual friend of the same sex, (2) sitting with a casual friend of the opposite sex, and (3) sitting with a boyfriend or girlfriend. The results for the "public house" or bar are found in Table 4.3, and results for the restaurant are found in Table 4.4.

Table 4.3 Seating Preferences for a Bar or "Public House"

	×⃞× (corner)	⃞ (across)	×× ⃞ (side)	Other
Same-sex friend	70%	25%	45%	2%
Casual friend of opposite sex	63	37	29	7
Intimate friend	43	11	82	4

[55]Sommer, *Personal Space,* p. 65.
[56]Cook, "Experiments on Orientation and Proxemics."

The Effects of Personal Space and Territory on Human Communication

Table 4.4   Seating Preferences for a Restaurant

	x⌐x (corner)	x / x (opposite)	x x (side-by-side)	Other
Same-sex friend	30%	73%	34%	4%
Casual friend of opposite sex	43	64	28	4
Intimate friend	40	53	46	2

The predominant seating pattern, as stated by questionnaire respondents using a bar as a referent, was corner seating for same-sex friends and casual friends of the opposite sex. Intimate friends appear to desire side-by-side seating, however. In a restaurant, all variations of sex and acquaintance seem to select opposite seating—with more side-by-side seating occurring between intimate friends. There may be some very practical reasons for opposite seating in restaurants. For instance, others won't have to sit opposite you, which might create some uncomfortable situations with respect to eye contact and overheard conversation. In addition, you won't poke the other person with your elbow while eating. The actual observations of seating in a restaurant, presented in Table 4.5, seem to validate the questionnaire responses. Most people do select opposite seating in restaurants. However, the observations of people sitting in bars do not agree with the questionnaire study of seating preferences in bars (see Table 4.6). Although questionnaire preferences favored corner seating, actual observations show a marked preference for side-by-side seating. Cook suggests this may have been due to the fact that the bars were equipped with many seats located against the wall. Supposedly this allowed

Table 4.5   Observations of Seating Behavior in a Restaurant

	x / x (opposite)	x x (side-by-side)	x ⌐ x (corner)
Two males	6%	0%	0%
Two females	6	0	1
Male with female	36	7	1
Total	48	7	2

The Effects of Personal Space and Territory on Human Communication

Table 4.6 Observations of Seating Behavior in Three Bars

	×□ (×)	□ (× top, × bottom)	□ (×× top)
Bar A			
Two males	7%	8%	13%
Male with female	6	4	21
Total	13	12	34
Bar B			
Two males	1	0	9
Male with female	4	3	20
Total	5	3	29
Bar C			
Two males	0	11	7
Male with female	1	4	10
Total	1	15	17
Overall			
Two males	8	19	29
Male with female	11	11	51
Total	19	30	80

persons to sit side by side, not have their back to anyone, and have a good view of the other patrons. Thus, paper-and-pencil preferences were overruled by environmental factors. From this study we must conclude that sex and acquaintance with the other person do have an effect on one's actual and preferred seating positions. This is also consistent with a great deal of work which suggests we will try to reduce the distance between those we feel have attitudes similar to ours. And similarly, we seem more frequently to develop positive relationships with those whom we find in close proximity to us—at home or in a classroom.

5. Motivation. Earlier we mentioned the idea that one may regulate intimacy with another through either increasing eye contact or decreasing distance. Of course you may do both. What we did not know prior to another study by Cook was what conditions prompt the use of distance and what conditions prompt the use of eye contact.[57] Again respondents made seating selections based on different types (positive and negative) and different levels (high, medium, and low) of motivation. For example, high-positive motivation

[57]Cook, "Experiments on Orientation and Proxemics."

The Effects of Personal Space and Territory on Human Communication

was "sitting with your boy or girfriend" and low-negative motivation was "sitting with someone you do not like very much and do not wish to talk to." He found that as motivation increased, persons wanted to sit closer or to have more eye contact. When the motivation was affiliative the choice was to sit closer, and when the motivation was competitive, the choice was one which would allow more eye contact. It seems, then, that the choice of eye contact or proximity depends on the motives of the interacting pair. It is quite permissible to sit close to another when there is high affiliative motivation, but when there are high levels of nonaffiliative motivation, such proximity is not as permissible, so eye contact is used.

6. Introversion-Extroversion. We have already discussed the possible influence of introversion and extroversion on conversational distance. Cook found some relation between this personality variable and seating preference.[58] Extroverts chose to sit opposite (either across the table or down the length of it) and disregard positions which would put them at an angle. Many extroverts also chose positions which would put them in close physical proximity to the other person. Introverts generally chose positions which would keep them more at a distance, visually and physically.

The following example seems like a most appropriate way to conclude this chapter. It incorporates elements of territoriality and seating arrangements which are influenced by culture, attitudes, leadership perceptions, and the type of task undertaken. I am talking about the discussions of the size and shape of the negotiation table at the Paris peace talks in 1968. It took eight months to reach an agreement on the shape of the table! The diagrams in Figure 4.1 mark the chronology of the seating proposals.

"The United States (U.S.) and South Vietnam (S.V.) wanted a seating arrangement in which only two sides were identified. They did not want to recognize the National Liberation Front (NLF) as an equal party in the negotiations. North Vietnam (N.V.) and the NLF wanted equal status given to all parties, represented by a four-sided table. The final arrangement was such that both parties could claim "victory." The round table minus the dividing lines allowed North Vietnam and the NLF to claim all four delegations were equal. The existence of the two secretarial tables (interpreted as dividers), the lack of identifying symbols on the table, and an AA, BB speaking rotation permitted the United States and South Vietnam to claim victory for the two-sided approach. Considering the lives lost during the eight months needed to arrive at the seating arrangement, we must certainly conclude that proximity and territoriality are far from trivial concerns in some human encounters."[59]

[58]Ibid.
[59]J. C. McCroskey, C. E. Larson, and M. L. Knapp, *An Introduction to Interpersonal Communication* (Englewood Cliffs, N.J.: Prentice-Hall, 1971), p. 98.

The Effects of Personal Space and Territory on Human Communication

139

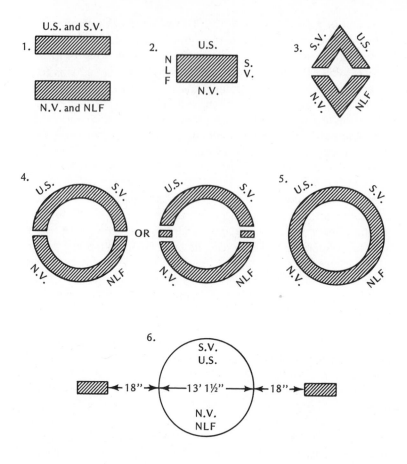

Figure 4.1 Proposals for a Table to Be Used at the Paris Peace Talks, 1968 (drawn from J. C. McCroskey, C. E. Larson, and M. L. Knapp, *An Introduction to Interpersonal Communication.* Englewood Cliffs, N.J.: Prentice-Hall, 1971, p. 98)

Summary

It is clear that our perceptions and use of space contribute extensively to various communication outcomes we seek. We know that some of our spatial behavior is related to a need to stake out and maintain territory. Our territorial behavior can be helpful in regulating social interaction and controlling density; it can also be the source of human conflict when territory is disputed or encroached upon. We identified three different types of territories (primary, secondary, and public) and several different levels at which territorial behavior exists (individual, group, community, nation). Although we often think people vigorously defend their territory, the type of defense is highly dependent on who the intruder is, why the intrusion is taking place, what type of territory is being encroached upon, what type of encroachment is used (violation, invasion, or contamination), how long the encroachment takes, and where it occurs. We often try to prevent people from moving into our territory by marking it as "ours." This can be done by our own physical presence or the presence of a friend who agrees to watch our territory. Territorial invasion can also be prevented by using various kinds of markers (fences, coats, and the like) or a special kind of language. When someone does invade another's territory, we sometimes find the "owner's" physiological arousal increased. In addition, various defensive maneuvers are seen—for example, flight, hostile looks, turning or leaning away, blocking advances with objects or hands and arms, or even verbal defenses. People don't like others to invade their territory, but we also find that they are often reluctant to invade the territory of others—often apologizing when it cannot be prevented.

We examined density and crowding from both animal and human perspectives. Animal studies found numerous undesirable effects from overpopulation. High-density human situations, however, are not always disruptive. Sometimes we want the company of many people. The best predictor of individually stressful and socially undesirable outcomes seems to be the number of people per room rather than other density measures. When we do feel the stress of a crowded situation, we will seek ways to cope with it—much like the !Kung or urban dwellers. We also distinguished between density (number of people per unit of space) and crowding (a feeling state brought on by the environment, personal factors, or social factors).

Our examination of spatial behavior in conversations revealed that there are many ways of conceptualizing and measuring this behavior. And, as a result, firm conclusions are difficult to make. We do know that each of us seeks a comfortable conversational distance—a distance which will vary depending on age, sex, cultural and ethnic background, setting, attitudes, emotions, topics, physical characteristics, personality, and our relationship with the other person.

Finally, we discussed seating arrangements in small groups. Distances and seats chosen do not seem to be accidental. Leaders and dominant personalities tend to choose specific seats, and seating will vary with the topic at hand, the nature of the relationship between the parties, and certain personality variables.

The Effects of Personal Space and Territory on Human Communication

141

SELECTED BIBLIOGRAPHY

Aiello, J. R., and Jones, S. E. "Field Study of the Proxemic Behavior of Young School Children in Three Subcultural Groups." *Journal of Personality and Social Psychology* 19 (1971): 351–356.

Albert, S., and Dabbs, J. M., Jr. "Physical Distance and Persuasion." *Journal of Personality and Social Psychology* 15 (1970): 265–270.

Allgeier, A. R., and Byrne, D. "Attraction Toward the Opposite Sex as a Determinant of Physical Proximity." *Journal of Social Psychology* 90 (1973): 213–219.

Altman, I. *The Environment and Social Behavior.* Belmont, Calif.: Wadsworth, 1975.

Altman, I., and Haythorn, W. W. "The Ecology of Isolated Groups." *Behavioral Science* 12 (1967): 169–182.

Ardrey, R. *The Territorial Imperative.* New York: Atheneum Press, 1966.

Argyle, M., and Dean, J. "Eye Contact, Distance and Affiliation." *Sociometry* 28 (1965): 289–304.

Bailey, K., Harnett, J., and Glover, H. "Modeling and Personal Space Behavior in Children." *Journal of Psychology* 85 (1973): 143–150.

Baird, J. E. "Some Nonverbal Elements of Leadership Emergence." *Southern Speech Communication Journal* 42 (1977): 352–361.

Barash, D. P. "Human Ethology: Personal Space Reiterated." *Environment and Behavior* 5 (1973): 67–73.

Barefoot, J. C., Hoople, H., and McClay, D. "Avoidance of an Act Which Would Violate Personal Space." *Psychonomic Science* 28 (1972): 205–206.

Bass, B. M. and Klubeck, S. "Effects of Seating Arrangements on Leaderless Group Discussions." *Journal of Abnormal and Social Psychology* 47 (1952): 724–727.

Bass, M. H. and Weinstein, M. S. "Early Development of Interpersonal Distance in Children." *Canadian Journal of Behavioral Science* 3 (1971): 368–376.

Baum, A., and Greenberg, C. I. "Waiting for a Crowd: The Behavioral and Perceptual Effects of Anticipated Crowding." *Journal of Personality and Social Psychology* 32 (1975): 671–679.

Baum, A., Riess, M., and O'Hara, J. "Architectural Variants of Reaction to Spatial Invasion." *Environment and Behavior* 6 (1974): 91–100.

Baxter, J. C. "Interpersonal Spacing in Natural Settings." *Sociometry* 33 (1970): 444–456.

Baxter, J. C. and Deanovitch, B. F. "Anxiety Effects of Inappropriate Crowding." *Journal of Consulting and Clinical Psychology* 35 (1970): 174–178.

Baxter, J. C., and Rozelle, R. M. "Nonverbal Expression as a Function of Crowding During a Simulated Police-Citizen Encounter." *Journal of Personality and Social Psychology* 32 (1975): 40–54.

Becker, F. D. "Study of Spatial Markers." *Journal of Personality and Social Psychology* 26 (1973): 439–445.

Becker, F. D., and Mayo, C. "Delineating Personal Distance and Territoriality." *Environment and Behavior* 3 (1971): 375–381.

Bickman, L., Teger, A., Gabriele, T., McLaughlin, C., Berger, M., and Sunaday, E. "Dormitory Density and Helping Behavior." *Environment and Behavior* 5 (1973): 465–490.

Boucher, M. "Effect of Seating Distance on Interpersonal Attraction in an Interview Situation." *Journal of Consulting Psychology* 38 (1972): 15–19.

Burgoon, J. K., and Jones, S. B. "Toward a Theory of Personal Space Expectations and Their Violations." *Human Communication Research* 2 (1976): 131–146.

Burns, T. "Nonverbal Communication." *Discovery*, October 1964, 31–35.

Byrne, D., and Buehler, J. A. "A Note on the Influence of Propinquity upon Acquaintanceships." *Journal of Abnormal and Social Psychology* 51 (1955): 147–148.

Calhoun, J. B. "Population Density and Social Pathology." *Scientific American* 206 (1962): 139–148.

Campbell, D. T., Kruskal, W. H., and Wallace, W. "Seating Aggregation as an Index of Attitude." *Sociometry* 29 (1966): 1–15.

Carey, G. W. "Density, Crowding, Stress and the Ghetto." *American Behavioral Scientist* 15 (1972): 495–508.

Carpenter, C. R. "Territoriality: A Review of Concepts and Problems." In A. Roe and G. G. Simpson (eds.), *Behavior and Evolution*. New Haven: Yale University Press, 1958. Pp. 224–250.

Castell, R. "Effect of Familiar and Unfamilar Environments on Proximity Behavior of Young Children." *Journal of Experimental Child Psychology* 9 (1970): 342–347.

Cheyne, J. A., and Efran, M. G. "The Effect of Spatial and Interpersonal Variables on the Invasion of Group Control Territories." *Sociometry* 35 (1972): 477–489.

Comer, R. J., and Piliavin, J. A. "The Effects of Physical Deviance upon Face-to-Face Interaction: The Other Side." *Journal of Personality and Social Psychology* 23 (1972): 33–39.

Connolly, P. R. "The Perception of Personal Space Among Black and White Americans." *Central States Speech Journal* 26 (1975): 21–28.

Cook, M. "Experiments on Orientation and Proxemics." *Human Relations* 23 (1970): 61–76.

Cummings, L. L., Huber, G. P., and Arendt, E. "Effects of Size and Spatial

The Effects of Personal Space and Territory on Human Communication

143

Arrangements on Group Decision Making." *Academy of Management Journal* 17 (1974): 460–475.

Daves, W. F., and Swaffer, P. W. "Effect of Room Size on Critical Interpersonal Distance." *Perceptual and Motor Skills* 33 (1971): 926.

Dawe, H. C. "The Influence of the Size of Kindergarten Groups upon Performance." *Child Development* 5 (1934): 295–303.

Day, A. T., and Day, L. H. "Cross-National Comparison of Population Density." *Science* 181 (1973): 1016–1023.

Dean, L. M., Willis, F. N., and Hewitt, J. "Initial Interaction Distance Among Individuals Equal and Unequal in Military Rank." *Journal of Personality and Social Psychology* 32: 294–299.

DeLong, A. J. "Dominance-Territorial Relations in a Small Group." *Environment and Behavior* 2 (1970): 190–191.

DeLong, A. J. "Territorial Stability and Hierarchial Formation." *Small Group Behavior* 4 (1973): 56–63.

Desor, J. A. "Toward a Psychological Theory of Crowding." *Journal of Personality and Social Psychology* 21 (1972): 79–83.

Dosey, M., and Meisels, M. "Personal Space and Self Protection." *Journal of Personality and Social Psychology* 11 (1969): 93–97.

Draper, P. "Crowding Among Hunter-Gatherers: The !Kung Bushmen," *Science* 182 (1973): 301–303.

Duke, M. P., and Nowicki, S. "A New Measure and Social Learning Model for Interpersonal Distance." *Journal of Experimental Research in Personality* 6 (1972): 1–16.

Edney, J. J. "Human Territoriality." *Psychological Bulletin* 31 (1974): 959–975.

Edney, J. J. "Place and Space: The Effects of Experience with a Physical Locale." *Journal of Experimental Social Psychology* 8 (1972): 124–135.

Edney, J. J. "Property, Possession and Permanence: A Field Study in Human Territoriality." *Journal of Applied Social Psychology* 3 (1972): 275–282.

Edney, J. J., and Jordan-Edney, N. L. "Territorial Spacing on a Beach." *Sociometry* 37 (1974): 92–103.

Edwards, D. J. A. "Approaching the Unfamiliar: A Study of Human Interaction Distances." *Journal of Behavioral Sciences* 1 (1972): 249–250.

Efran, M. G., and Cheyne, J. A. "Affective Concomitants of the Invasion of Shared Space: Behavioral, Physiological and Verbal Indicators." *Journal of Personality and Social Psychology* 29 (1974): 219–226.

Erickson, F. "One Function of Proxemic Shifts in Face-to-Face Interaction." In A. Kendon, R. M. Harris, and M. R. Key (eds.), *Organization of Behavior in Face-to-Face Interaction.* Chicago: Aldine, 1975.

Esser, A. H. (ed.). *Environment and Behavior: The Use of Space by Animals and Men.* New York: Plenum, 1971.

Evans, G. W., and Howard, R. B. "Personal Space." *Psychological Bulletin* 80 (1973): 334–344.

The Effects of Personal Space and Territory on Human Communication

Felipe, N. J., and Sommer, R. "Invasions of Personal Space." *Social Problems* 14 (1966): 206–214.

Fisher, J. D., and Byrne, D. "Too Close for Comfort: Sex Differences in Response to Invasions of Personal Space." *Journal of Personality and Social Psychology* 32 (1975): 15–21.

Forston, R. F., and Larson, C. U. "The Dynamics of Space: An Experimental Study in Proxemic Behavior Among Latin Americans and North Americans." *Journal of Communication* 18 (1968): 109–116.

Frankel, A. S., and Barrett, J. "Variations in Personal Space as a Function of Authoritarianism, Self-esteem and Racial Characteristics of a Stimulus Situation." *Journal of Consulting and Clinical Psychology* 37 (1971): 95–98.

Freedman, J. L. *Crowding and Behavior*. New York: Viking, 1975.

Freedman, J. L. "The Crowd: Maybe Not So Madding After All." *Psychology Today* 4 (1971): 58–61, 86.

Freedman, J. L., Klevansky, S., and Ehrlich, P. "The Effect of Crowding on Human Task Performance." *Journal of Applied Social Psychology* 1 (1971): 7–25.

Freedman, J. L., Levy, A. S., Buchanan, R. W., and Price, J. "Crowding and Human Aggressiveness." *Journal of Experimental Social Psychology* 8 (1972): 528–548.

Fried, M. L., and DeFrazio, V. "Territoriality and Boundary Conflicts in the Subway." *Psychiatry* 37 (1974): 47–58.

Fry, A. M., and Willis, F. N. "Invasion of Personal Space as a Function of the Age of the Invader." *Psychological Record* 2 (1971): 385–389.

Furbay, A. L. "The Influence of Scattered Seating vs. Compact Seating on Audience Responses." *Speech Monographs* 32 (1965): 144–148.

Galle, O. R., Gove, W. R., and McPherson, J. M. "Population Density and Pathology: What Are the Relationships for Man?" *Science* 176 (1972): 23–30.

Goffman, E. *Behavior in Public Places*. New York: Macmillan, 1963.

Goffman, E. *Relations in Public*. New York: Basic Books, 1971.

Goldberg, G. N., Kiesler, C. A., and Collins, B. E. "Visual Behavior and Face to Face Distance During Interaction." *Sociometry* 32 (1969): 43–53.

Gordon, T., and Ralph, D. C. "A Study of the Effect of Audience Proximity on Persuasion." *Speech Monographs* 26 (1959): 300–307.

Gottheil, E., Corey, J., and Parades, A. "Psychological and Physical Dimensions of Personal Space." *Journal of Psychology* 69 (1968): 7–9.

Guardo, C. J. "Personal Space in Children." *Child Development* 40 (1969): 145–151.

Guardo, C. J., and Meisels, M. "Child-Parent Spatial Patterns Under Praise and Reproof," *Developmental Psychology* 5 (1971): 365.

Guardo, C. J., and Meisels, M. "Factor Structure of Children's Personal Space Schemata." *Child Development* 42 (1971): 1307–1312.

The Effects of Personal Space and Territory on Human Communication

145

Haase, R. T. "The Relationship of Sex and Instructional Set to the Regulation of Interpersonal Interaction Distance in Counseling Analogue." *Journal of Counseling Psychology* 17 (1970): 223–236.

Haase, R. T., and DiMattia, D. J. "Proxemic Behavior: Counselor, Administrator and Client Preference for Seating Arrangement in Dyadic Interaction." *Journal of Counseling Psychology* 17 (1970): 319–325.

Hall, E. T. "A System for the Notation of Proxemic Behavior." *American Anthropologist* 65 (1963): 1003–1026.

Hall, E. T. *Handbook for Proxemic Research.* Washington, D.C.: Society for the Anthropology of Visual Communication, 1974.

Hall, E. T. "Proxemics." *Current Anthropology* 9 (1968): 83–108.

Hall, E. T. *The Hidden Dimension.* Garden City, N.Y.: Doubleday, 1966.

Hall, E. T. *The Silent Language.* Garden City, N.Y.: Doubleday, 1959.

Hansen, J. F. "Proxemics and the Interpretive Process in Human Communication." *Semiotica* 17 (1976): 165–179.

Hare, A., and Bales, R. "Seating Position and Small Group Interaction." *Sociometry* 26 (1963): 480–486.

Hartnett, J. J., Bailey, F., and Gibson, W. "Personal Space as Influenced by Sex and Type of Movement." *Journal of Psychology* 76 (1970): 139–144.

Hearn, G. "Leadership and the Spatial Factor in Small Groups." *Journal of Abnormal and Social Psychology* 104 (1957): 269–272.

Hediger, H. P. "The Evolution of Territorial Behavior." In S. L. Washburn (ed.), *Social Life of Early Man.* Chicago: Aldine Press, 1961. Pp. 34–57.

Heston, J. K. "Effects of Personal Space Invasion and Anomia on Anxiety, Nonperson Orientation and Source Credibility." *Central States Speech Journal* 25 (1974): 19–27.

Hildreth, A. M., Derogatis, L. R., and McCusker, K. "Body Buffer Zone and Violence: A Reassessment and Confirmation." *American Journal of Psychiatry* 127 (1971): 1641–1645.

Hollender, J. W., Duke, M. P., and Nowicki, S. "Interpersonal Distance: Sibling Structure and Parental Affection Antecedents." *Journal of Genetic Psychology* 123 (1973): 35–45.

Hoppe, R. A., Greene, M. S., and Kenney, J. W. "Territorial Markers: Additional Findings." *Journal of Social Psychology* 88 (1972): 305–306.

Horowitz, M. J. "Human Spatial Behavior." *American Journal of Psychotherapy* 19 (1965): 20–28.

Horowitz, M. J. "Spatial Behavior and Psychopathology." *The Journal of Nervous and Mental Disease* 146 (1968): 24–35.

Howells, L. T., and Becker, S. W. "Seating Arrangement and Leadership Emergence." *Journal of Abnormal and Social Psychology* 64 (1962): 148–150.

Hutt, C., and Vaizey, M. J. "Differential Effects of Group Density on Social Behavior." *Nature* 209 (1966): 1371–1372.

Jones, S. E. "A Comparative Proxemics Analysis of Dyadic Interaction in Selected Subcultures of New York City." *Journal of Social Psychology* 84 (1971): 35–44.

Jones, S. E., and Aiello, J. R. "Proxemic Behavior of Black and White First, Third, and Fifth Grade Children." *Journal of Personality and Social Psychology* 25 (1973): 21–27.

Jourard, S., and Friedman, R. "Experimenter-Subject 'Distance' and Self Disclosure." *Journal of Personality and Social Psychology* 15 (1970): 278–282.

Karabenick, S., and Meisels, M. "Effects of Performance Evaluation on Interpersonal Distance." *Journal of Personality* 40 (1972): 275–286.

Karlin, R. A., McFarland, D., Aiello, J. R., and Epstein, Y. M. "Normative Mediation of Reactions to Crowding." *Environmental Psychology and Nonverbal Behavior* 1 (1976): 30–40.

King, M. J. "Interpersonal Relations in Preschool Children and Average Approach Distance." *Journal of Genetic Psychology* 109 (1966): 109–116.

Kinzel, A. S. "Body Buffer Zone in Violent Prisoners." *American Journal of Psychiatry* 127 (1970): 59–64.

Kleck, R. "Interaction Distance and Non-verbal Agreeing Responses." *British Journal of Social and Clinical Psychology* 9 (1970): 180–182.

Kleck, R. "Physical Stigma and Nonverbal Cues Emitted in Face-to-Face Interaction." *Human Relations* 21 (1968): 19–28.

Kleck, R. "Physical Stigma and Task Oriented Interaction." *Human Relations* 22 (1969): 51–60.

Kleck, R., Buck, P. L., Goller, W. L., London, R. S., Pfeiffer, J. R., and Vukcevic, D. P. "The Effect of Stigmatizing Conditions on the Use of Personal Space." *Psychological Reports* 23 (1968): 111–118.

Klopfer, P. M. "From Ardrey to Altruism: A Discourse on the Biological Basis of Human Behavior." *Behavioral Science* 13 (1968): 399–401.

Klopfer, P. M. *Habitats and Territories: A Study of the Use of Space by Animals.* New York: Basic Books, 1969.

Knowles, E. S. "Boundaries Around Group Interaction: The Effect of Group Size and Member Status on Boundary Permeability." *Journal of Personality and Social Psychology* 26 (1973) 327–332.

Knowles, E. S. "Boundaries Around Social Space: Dyadic Responses to an Invader." *Environment and Behavior* 4 (1972): 437–447.

Korner, I. N., and Misra, R. K. "Perception of Human Relationship as a Function of Inter-individual Distance." *Journal of Psychological Researches* 11 (1967): 129–132.

Kutner, D. "Overcrowding: Human Responses to Density and Visual Exposure." *Human Relations* 26 (1973): 31–50.

Leibman, M. "The Effects of Sex and Race Norms on Personal Space." *Environment and Behavior* 2 (1970): 208–246.

Leipold, W. E. "Psychological Distance in a Dyadic Interview." Ph.D. diss., University of North Dakota, 1963.

Little, K. B. "Cultural Variations in Social Schemata." *Journal of Personality and Social Psychology* 10 (1968): 1–7.

Little, K. B. "Personal Space." *Journal of Experimental Social Psychology* 1 (1965): 237–247.

Little, K. B., Ulehla, F. J., and Henderson, C. "Value Congruence and Interaction Distance." *Journal of Social Psychology* 75 (1968): 249–253.

Loo, C. M. "The Effect of Spatial Density on the Social Behavior of Children." *Journal of Applied Social Psychology* 2 (1973): 372–381.

Lott, D. F., and Sommer, R. "Seating Arrangements and Status." *Journal of Personality and Social Psychology* 7 (1967): 90–94.

Lyman, S. M., and Scott, M. B. "Territoriality: A Neglected Sociological Dimension." *Social Problems* 15 (1967): 236–249.

Maisonneuve, J., Palmade, G., and Fourment, C. "Selective Choices and Propinquity." *Sociometry* 15 (1952): 135–140.

Mann, J. H. "The Effect of Interracial Contact on Sociometric Choices and Perceptions." *Journal of Social Psychology* 50 (1959): 143–152.

McBride, G., King, M. G., and James, J. W. "Social Proximity Effects on GSR in Adult Humans." *Journal of Psychology* 61 (1965): 153–157.

McDowell, K. V. "Violations of Personal Space." *Canadian Journal of Behavioral Science* 4 (1972): 210–217.

McGrew, P. L. "Social and Spatial Density Effects on Spacing Behavior in Preschool Children." *Journal of Child Psychology and Psychiatry* 11 (1970): 197–205.

Mehrabian, A. "Relationship of Attitude to Seated Posture, Orientation, and Distance." *Journal of Personality and Social Psychology* 10 (1968): 26–30.

Mehrabian, A. "Significance of Posture and Position in the Communication of Attitude and Status Relationships." *Psychological Bulletin* 71 (1969): 359–373.

Mehrabian, A., and Diamond, S. G. "Seating Arrangement and Conversation." *Sociometry* 34 (1971): 281–289.

Meisels, M., and Canter, F. M. "Personal Space and Personality Characteristics: A Non-confirmation." *Psychological Reports* 27 (1970): 287–290.

Meisels, M., and Dosey, M. "Personal Space, Anger Arousal, and Psychological Defense." *Journal of Personality* 39 (1971): 333–334.

Meisels, M., and Guardo, C. "Development of Personal Space Schemata." *Child Development* 40 (1969): 1167–1178.

Mitchell, R. "Some Social Implications of Higher Density Housing." *American Sociological Review* 36 (1971): 18–29.

Newman, O. *Defensible Space.* New York: Macmillan, 1972.

Norum, G. A. "Perceived Interpersonal Relationships and Spatial Arrangements." M.A. thesis, University of California, Davis, 1966.

The Effects of Personal Space and Territory on Human Communication

Pastalan, L., and Carson, D. H. (eds.). *Spatial Behavior of Older People.* Ann Arbor: University of Michigan/Wayne State University Press, 1970.

Patterson, M. "Spatial Factors in Social Interaction." *Human Relations* 21 (1968): 351–361.

Patterson, M. L. "Compensation and Nonverbal Immediacy Behaviors: A Review." *Sociometry* 36 (1973): 237–253.

Patterson, M. L., and Sechrest, L. B. "Interpersonal Distance and Impression Formation." *Journal of Personality* 38 (1970): 161–166.

Patterson, M. L., Mullens, S., and Romano, J. "Compensatory Reactions to Spatial Intrusion." *Sociometry* 34 (1971): 114–121.

Pedersen, D. M. "Developmental Trends in Personal Space." *Journal of Psychology* 83 (1973): 3–9.

Pedersen, D. M. "Relations Among Sensation Seeking and Simulated and Behavioral Personal Space." *Journal of Psychology* 83 (1973): 79–88.

Pedersen, D. M., and Shears, L. M. "A Review of Personal Space Research in the Framework of General System Theory." *Psychological Bulletin* 80 (1973): 367–388.

Porter, E., Argyle, M., and Salter, V. "What is Signalled by Proximity?" *Perceptual and Motor Skills* 30 (1970): 39–42.

Priest, R. F., and Sawyer, J. "Proximity and Peership: Bases of Balance in Interpersonal Attraction." *American Journal of Sociology* 72 (1967): 633–649.

Proshansky, H. M., Ittelson, W. H., and Rivlin, L. G. (eds.). *Environmental Psychology: Man and His Physical Setting.* New York: Holt, Rinehart and Winston, 1970.

Rawls, J. R., Trego, R. E., McGaffey, C. N., and Rawls, D. J. "Personal Space as a Predictor of Performance Under Close Working Conditions." *Journal of Social Psychology* 86 (1972): 261–267.

Rosegrant, T. J., and McCroskey, J. C. "The Effects of Race and Sex on Proxemic Behavior in an Interview Setting." *Southern Speech Journal* 40 (1975): 408–420.

Rosenfeld, H. "Effect of Approval-Seeking Induction on Interpersonal Proximity." *Psychological Reports* 17 (1965): 120–122.

Russo, N. "Connotation of Seating Arrangement." *Cornell Journal of Social Relations* 2 (1967): 37–44.

Scheflen, A. E. "Micro-territories in Human Interaction." In A. Kendon, R. M. Harris, and M. R. Key (eds.), *Organization of Behavior in Face-to-Face Interaction.* Chicago: Aldine, 1975.

Scheflen, A. E., and Ashcraft, N. *Human Territories: How We Behave in Space-Time.* Englewood Cliffs, N.J.: Prentice-Hall, 1976.

Scherer, S. E. "Proxemic Behavior of Primary School Children as a Function of Their Socioeconomic Class and Subculture." *Journal of Personality and Social Psychology* 29 (1974): 800–805.

The Effects of Personal Space and Territory on Human Communication

Schmitt, R. C. "Density, Health, and Social Disorganization." *American Institute of Planners Journal* 32 (1966): 38–40.

Schulz, R., and Barefoot, J. "Non-verbal Responses and Affiliative Conflict Theory." *British Journal of Social and Clinical Psychology* 13 (1974): 237–243.

Sherrod, D. R. "Crowding, Perceived Control, and Behavioral Aftereffects." *Journal of Applied Social Psychology* 4 (1974): 171–186.

Shuter, R. "Proxemics and Tactility in Latin America." *Journal of Communication* 26 (1976): 46–52.

Smith, G. H. "Personality Scores and Personal Distance Effect." *Journal of Social Psychology* 39 (1954): 57–62.

Smith, R. H., Downer, D. B., Lynch, M. T., and Winter, M. "Privacy and Interaction Within the Family as Related to Dwelling Space." *Journal of Marriage and the Family* 31 (1969): 559–566.

Sommer, R. "Further Studies of Small Group Ecology." *Sociometry* 28 (1965): 337–348.

Sommer, R. "Intimacy Ratings in Five Countries." *International Journal of Psychology* 3 (1968): 109–114.

Sommer, R. "Leadership and Group Geography." *Sociometry* 24 (1961): 99–110.

Sommer, R. *Personal Space,* Englewood Cliffs, N.J. Prentice-Hall, 1969.

Sommer, R. "Small Group Ecology." *Psychological Bulletin* 67 (1967): 145–152.

Sommer, R. "Studies in Personal Space." *Sociometry* 22 (1959): 247–260.

Sommer, R. "The Distance for Comfortable Conversation: A Further Study." *Sociometry* 25 (1962): 111–116.

Sommer, R., and Becker, F. D. "Territorial Defense and the Good Neighbor." *Journal of Personality and Social Psychology* 11 (1969): 85–92.

Sommer, R., and Ross, H. "Social Interaction on a Geriatrics Ward." *International Journal of Social Psychiatry* 4 (1958): 128–133.

Steinzor, B. "The Spatial Factor in Face to Face Discussion Groups." *Journal of Abnormal and Social Psychology* 45 (1950): 552–555.

Stokols, D. "On the Distinction Between Density and Crowding: Some Implications for Future Research," *Psychological Review* 79 (1972): 275–278.

Stokols, D., Rall, M., Pinner, B., and Schopler, J. "Physical, Social, and Personal Determinants of the Perception of Crowding." *Environment and Behavior* 5 (1973): 87–117.

Stratton, L. O., Tekippe, D. J., and Flick, G. L. "Personal Space and Self-Concept." *Sociometry* 36 (1973): 424–429.

Strodtbeck, F., and Hook, L. "The Social Dimensions of a Twelve Man Jury Table." *Sociometry* 24 (1961): 397–415.

Sundstrom, E. "An Experimental Study of Crowding: Effects of Room Size,

Intrusion, and Goal Blocking on Nonverbal Behavior, Self Disclosure, and Self-Reported Stress." *Journal of Personality and Social Psychology* 32 (1975): 645–654.

Thayer, S., and Alban, L. "A Field Experiment on the Effect of Political and Cultural Factors on the Use of Personal Space." *Journal of Social Psychology* 88 (1972): 267–272.

Tolor, A. "Popularity and Psychological Distance." *Personality* 1 (1971): 65–83.

Triandis, H. G., Davis, E., and Takezawa, Shin-Ichi. "Some Determinants of Social Distance Among American, German, and Japanese Students." *Journal of Personality and Social Psychology* 2 (1965): 540–551.

Vine, I. "Territoriality and the Spatial Regulation of Interaction." In A. Kendon, R. M. Harris, and M. R. Key (eds.), *Organization of Behavior in Face-to-Face Interaction.* Chicago: Aldine, 1975.

Ward, C. "Seating Arrangement and Leadership Emergence in Small Discussion Groups. *Journal of Social Psychology* 74 (1968): 83–90.

Watson, O. M. "Conflicts and Directions in Proxemic Research." *Journal of Communication* 22 (1972): 443–459.

Watson, O. M. *Proxemic Behavior: A Cross-Cultural Study.* The Hague: Mouton, 1970.

Watson, O. M. "Proxemics." In T. A. Sebeok (ed.), *Current Trends in Linguistics.* The Hague: Mouton Press, 1973.

Watson, O. M. "Symbolic and Expressive Uses of Space: An Introduction to Proxemic Behavior," Module No. 20. Reading, Mass.: Addison-Wesley, 1972.

Watson, O. M., and Graves, T. D. "Quantitative Research in Proxemic Behavior." *American Anthropologist* 68 (1966): 971–985.

Willerman, B., and Swanson, L. "An Ecological Determinant of Differential Amounts of Sociometric Choices Within College Sororities." *Sociometry* 15 (1952): 326–329.

Williams, J. L. "Personal Space and Its Relation to Extroversion-Introversion." *Canadian Journal of Behavioral Science* 3 (1971): 156–160.

Willis, F. N. "Initial Speaking Distance as a Function of the Speaker's Relationship." *Psychonomic Science* 5 (1966): 221–222.

Winnick, C., and Holt, H. "Seating Position as Nonverbal Communication in Group Analysis." *Psychiatry* 24 (1961): 171–182.

Winsborough, H. H. "The Social Consequences of High Population Density." *Law and Contemporary Problems* 30 (1965): 120–126.

Wolfgang, J., and Wolfgang, A. "Explanation of Attitudes via Physical Interpersonal Distance Toward the Obese, Drug Users, Homosexuals, Police and Other Marginal Figures." *Journal of Clinical Psychology* 27 (1971): 510–512.

The Effects of Personal Space and Territory on Human Communication

5 The Effects of Physical Appearance and Dress on Human Communication

> By a man's finger-nails, by his coat-sleeve, by his boots, by his trouser-knees, by the callosities of his forefinger and thumb, by his expression, by his shirt-cuffs—by each of these things a man's calling is plainly revealed. That all united should fail to enlighten the competent inquirer in any case is almost inconceivable.
>
> SHERLOCK HOLMES

Picture the following scene: Mr. and Mrs. American awake and prepare to start the day. Mrs. American takes off her nighttime bra and replaces it with a "slightly padded uplift" bra. After removing her chin strap, she further pulls herself together with her girdle. Then she begins to "put on her face." This involves an eyebrow pencil, mascara, lipstick, rouge, eye liner, and false eyelashes. Then she removes the hair under her arms and on her legs and places a hairpiece on her head. False fingernails, nail polish, and tinted contact lenses precede the deodorant, perfume, and endless decisions concerning clothes. Mr. American shaves the hair on his face, puts a toupee on his head, and carefully attaches his newly purchased sideburns. He removes his false teeth from a solution used to whiten them, gargles with a breath sweetener, selects his after-shave lotion, puts on his elevator shoes, and begins making his clothing decisions. This hypothetical example represents an extreme, but it is, nonetheless, true that people go to great lengths to make themselves attractive. Why? Does it make any difference to our interpersonal contacts?

The Associated Press reported two incidents in which a woman's appearance contributed heavily to the outcome of social contact. In 1971 a judge in Ragusa, Sicily, fined a Danish tourist for wearing hotpants; in 1972, the same judge fined a German woman $17 for crossing her legs in a way that bared one thigh while the woman was having coffee with friends at a sidewalk cafe. In 1975, Dr. Joan Lockard, professor of neurological surgery and psychology at the University of Washington, was reported to have conducted experiments which showed that a woman hitchhiker could double the number of rides she received by adding two inches of padding to her bust.

Some feel that antisocial behavior of convicts can be reduced by radical changes in appearance. It is reported, for instance, that a nineteen-year-old woman with a face "so deformed that little kids ran away crying" threw a brick through a bank window and waited for police to arrest her. "I was willing to die to get a better face," she said. The judge ordered extensive plastic surgery.[1] The same reasoning launched a massive plastic surgery program for reshaping noses, removing tattoos, tightening sagging skin, disguising ugly scars, reducing extensive ear protrusions, and removing other deformities of convicts at the Kentucky State Reformatory.[2] Authorities at this institution reasoned that every-day social ridicule and potential discrimination in hiring may lead to a feeling of rejection and frustration which can manifest itself in antisocial behavior. Similar programs by doctors at the University of Virginia and Johns Hopkins have not shown significant changes in postinstitutionalized behavior for convicts with changes in their appearance. Obviously appearance is only one factor which might contribute to antisocial behavior. For some, however, it may be the most important one.

Our Body: Its General Attractiveness

While it is not uncommon to hear people muse about how inner beauty is the only thing that really counts, research suggests that outer beauty, or physical attractiveness, plays an influential role in determining responses for a broad range of interpersonal encounters.

[1] "Deformed Brick-Thrower Eyes Future with New Face," *Lafayette Journal and Courier*, December 15, 1975, p. A-6.
[2] B. Watson, "Cons Get Cosmetic Surgery," *Lafayette Journal and Courier*, May 16, 1975, p. A-8.

The Effects of Physical Appearance and Dress on Human Communication

153

Consider, for instance, a fascinating study by Singer concerning the use of physical attractiveness by females as a manipulative device to obtain higher grades from college professors.[3] This phase of Singer's research occurred after he found no difference between the scores of males and females on a Machiavellian scale,[4] but could not identify the specific ways in which Machiavellian females expressed these attitudes behaviorally. He hypothesized that there were many sociocultural factors which militated against females using obviously devious, deceitful, or exploitative tactics; and that, therefore, they adopted a more socially acceptable method—capitalizing on their good looks! To test this, he first obtained 192 pictures of freshmen women and had the pictures rated by forty faculty members—with each picture being rated five times. When he compared these ratings with grade point averages and birth order, Singer found a positive relationship between being firstborn, attractive, and female, and grade point average. Naturally, he then asked, why was this true of firstborn women and not those born later? He reasoned that if firstborns engaged in more "exhibiting" behavior than their siblings, professors would be more likely to remember them and give them the benefit of the doubt on grades.

Observations of actual behavior and self-reports confirmed that firstborn women tend to sit in the front of the room, come up more frequently after class, and make more-frequent appointments to see instructors during office hours. Singer also sought to find out whether the higher grades given to attractive females were due to luck or whether there was manipulation by the women involved. Singer thought that if he could show that firstborns were more aware of, and socially concerned about, their looks, this finding would tend to support his attractiveness-manipulation interpretation. He therefore asked females to estimate ideal body measurements *and* their own measurements.[5] One group was told actual measurements would be taken after the paper and pencil estimates; another group was not told this would be done. Estimates were made of height, weight, bust, waist, and hips. Neck, ankle, and wrist size were added as control items. The results supported Singer's "manipulative intent" hypothesis because (1) firstborns had more accurate information about their body measurements, (2) they were more accurate in stating norms for the ideal female figure, and (3) they were more likely to distort their measurements in the direction of the ideal norms than were "later borns." Singer's conclusion is worth noting:

[3]J. E. Singer, "The Use of Manipulative Strategies: Machiavellianism and Attractiveness," *Sociometry* 27 (1964): 128–151.

[4]Machiavellianism is generally associated with the use of any means necessary, no matter how unscrupulous, to achieve a goal. It is frequently associated with cunning, duplicity, or bad faith.

[5]J. E. Singer and P. F. Lamb, "Social Concern, Body Size, and Birth Order," *Journal of Social Psychology* 68 (1966): 143–151.

The Effects of Physical Appearance and Dress on Human Communication

In some respects the results are not at all surprising. The suggestion that men live by their brains and women by their bodies was made as far back as Genesis. Although not astoundingly new, the implications are rather frightening. The documentation of the utility of manipulative skills was obtained from a population of freshmen in a university setting, with a criterion of academic success. The results imply that the poor college professor is a rather put-upon creature, hoodwinked by the male students (later born) and enticed by the female students (firstborn) as he goes about his academic and personal responsibilities. He is seemingly caught in a maelstrom of student intrigue and machination. The picture is bleak. In defense we can only offer the consolation that when 22 male members of the faculty at The Pennsylvania State University were administered the Machiavellian scale, their mean score was 10.44. When compared with the total sample values from the 994 subject study . . . the faculty appear significantly more manipulative than the students $(t = 2.43, p > 0.02)$. It is hoped that the academicians are fighting strategem with strategem.[6]

Other persuasive studies also show attractiveness to be important. Mills and Aronson found an attractive female could modify attitudes of male students more than an unattractive woman could.[7] Actually one woman was made up to look different under two conditions. In the unattractive condition she was rated repulsive by independent observers; she wore loose-fitting clothing, her hair was messy, makeup was conspicuously absent, a trace of a mustache was etched on her upper lip, and her complexion was oily and unwholesome looking. The experimenter suggested to a group of students that they would more quickly complete some measuring instruments if a volunteer would read the questions aloud and indicate what they meant. The "volunteer" was either the attractive or unattractive woman. While this study used a male audience, females are certainly not exempt from responding favorably to speaker attractiveness.[8] In Widgery's study, females attributed *higher* credibility ratings to attractive sources than males did. And Widgery and Webster offer some evidence that attractive persons, regardless of sex, will be rated high on the character dimension of credibility scales.[9] While more work needs to be done, attractiveness does seem to be an influential factor in perception of initial credibility—hence an influential factor in one's ultimate persuasiveness.

A number of studies which ask people to act as jurors in cases involving

[6]Ibid., p. 150.

[7]J. Mills and E. Aronson, "Opinion Change as a Function of the Communicator's Attractiveness and Desire to Influence," *Journal of Personality and Social Psychology* 1 (1965): 73–77.

[8]J. Horai, N. Naccari, and E. Faloultah, "The Effects of Expertise and Physical Attractiveness upon Opinion Agreement and Liking," *Sociometry* 37 (1974): 601–606. Also R. N. Widgery, "Sex of Receiver and Physical Attractiveness of Source as Determinants of Initial Credibility Perception," *Western Speech* 38 (1974): 13–17.

[9]R. N. Widgery and B. Webster, "The Effects of Physical Attractiveness upon Perceived Initial Credibility," *Michigan Speech Journal* 4 (1969): 9–15.

attractive and unattractive defendants show, as expected, that unattractive defendants are more likely to be judged guilty and more likely to receive longer sentences.[10] Obviously, a defendant's attractiveness is rarely assessed in isolation in the courtroom, and other factors will interact with attractiveness—for example, the extent to which the defendant expresses repentance, the degree of commitment jurors have toward impartiality, the extent to which jurors "discuss" the case, the perceived similarity of jurors and defendant, defendant verbalizations, and the nature of the crime being examined—that is, the extent to which attractiveness was a part of the crime, as in a swindle.

It is safe to say that the evidence from this culture overwhelmingly supports the notion that *initially* we respond much more favorably to those perceived as physically attractive than those seen as less attractive or ugly. Summarizing numerous studies in this area, it is not at all unusual to find physically attractive persons outstripping unattractive ones on a wide range of socially desirable evaluations, such as success, personality, popularity, sociability, sexuality, persuasiveness, and often happiness. Attractive women are more likely to be helped and less likely to be the objects of aggressive acts.[11] These judgments linked to a person's attractiveness begin early in life (preschool, kindergarten)—apparently reflecting similar attitudes and evaluations made by teachers and parents. Not only do teachers seem to interact less (and less positively) with the so-called unattractive elementary school child, but the child's peers also react unfavorably. We know there are many occasions in a child's life when adults ask, "Who dunnit?" It now seems that if there is an unattractive child available, the chances are stronger that he or she will be pointed out as the culprit.[12] As the unattractive child grows older, he or she probably won't be discriminated against as long as his or her task performance is impressive, but as soon as performance declines, the less attractive person will receive more sanctions than the attractive one.

[10]For summaries of this literature, see R. A. Kulka and J. B. Kessler, "Is Justice Really Blind?—The Influence of Litigant Physical Attractiveness on Juridical Judgment," *Journal of Applied Social Psychology* (in press). See also E. K. Solender and E. Solender, "Minimizing the Effect of the Unattractive Client on the Jury: A Study of the Interaction of Physical Appearance with Assertions and Self-Experience References," *Human Rights* 5 (1976): 201–214; and M. G. Efran, "The Effect of Physical Appearance on the Judgment of Guilt, Interpersonal Attraction and Severity of Recommended Punishment in a Simulated Jury Task," *Journal of Experimental Research in Personality* 8 (1974): 45–54.

[11]E. Berscheid and E. H. Walster, "Physical Attractiveness," in L. Berkowitz (ed.), *Advances in Experimental Social Psychology*, Vol. 7 (New York: Academic Press, 1974), 158–215.

[12]Articles which summarize some of these studies with children include R. Algozzine, "What Teachers Perceive—Children Receive?" *Communication Quarterly* 24 (1976): 41–47; E. Berscheid and E. Walster, "Beauty and the Best," *Psychology Today* 5 (1972): 42–46; G. Wilson and D. Nias, "Beauty Can't Be Beat," *Psychology Today* 10 (1976): 96–98, 103; and M. M. Clifford and E. Walster, "The Effect of Physical Attractiveness on Teacher Expectation," *Sociology of Education* 46 (1973): 248–258.

The Effects of Physical Appearance and Dress on Human Communication

Table 5.1 Attractiveness and the Ideal Man and Woman

	Male Respondents	Female Respondents
Ideal Man	26%	29%
Ideal Woman	47%	32%

Physical attractiveness also seems to be an extremely important factor in courtship and marriage decisions. Numerous studies provide testimony from unmarried men and women that physical attractiveness is a critical factor in mate selection. One early study asked students if they would marry a person who ranked low in such qualities as economic status, good looks, disposition, family religion, morals, health, education, intelligence, or age.[13] Men most frequently rejected women who were deficient in good looks, disposition, morals, and health. Women did not seem to worry as much about marrying a man who was deficient in good looks. Table 5.1, based on the responses of 28,000 readers of *Psychology Today*, shows a continued emphasis on female attractiveness—by both men and women. The percentages indicate the number of respondents who said attractiveness was "essential" or "very important" to the ideal.[14]

It was just such disproportionate concern for physical attractiveness which prompted Susan Sontag to argue against the social convention that aging enhances a man but progressively destroys a woman.[15] She points out that women are taught from childhood to care in a "pathologically exaggerated way" about their appearance. Men, she says, need only have a clean face, but a woman's face is a "canvas upon which she paints a revised, corrected portrait of herself." "Ruggedly attractive men" is a familiar concept, but is there a similar form of attractiveness for women who do not conform to the ideal? In many quarters *masculinity* means, among other things, not caring for one's looks; *femininity*, on the other hand, means caring a great deal. We've heard a lot about discrimination against women, but when men apply for jobs which have traditionally been held by women they often feel discriminated against. Could it be that a secretary, for instance, is perceived by the male employers as a

[13]R. E. Baber, *Marriage and Family* (New York: McGraw Hill, 1939).

[14]C. Tavris, "Men and Women Report Their Views on Masculinity," *Psychology Today* 10 (1977): 34–42, 82. Another study (of one thousand people at a "computer dance") also found women weighting physical attractiveness less than men. Cf. R. H. Coombs and W. F. Kenkel, "Sex Differences in Dating Aspirations and Satisfaction with Computer-Selected Partners," *Journal of Marriage and the Family* 28 (1966): 62–66.

[15]S. Sontag, "The Double Standard of Aging," *Saturday Review*, September 23, 1972, 29–38.

The Effects of Physical Appearance and Dress on Human Communication

"decoration" as well as a worker? A man may be able to type competently, but will male supervisors like to look at him all day?

On the other hand, gender seemed to make little difference in a study which asked persons to evaluate strangers of the same or opposite sex— strangers who had previously been rated as either physically attractive or unattractive.[16] Interpersonal attraction was greatest toward the physically attractive strangers—regardless of sex. In this phase of the study, subjects had no other information about the stranger; through subsequent study, the same researchers found that physical attractiveness was still an important determinant of attraction when subjects had additional information about the strangers—for example, information on several of the strangers' attitudes. These traits do not seem limited to the United States. A study conducted in India found that men wanted wives who were more physically beautiful than themselves, and women wanted husbands who were equal to them in physical beauty.[17]

In light of this general preference for a physically attractive partner, we might suspect actual dating patterns would reflect these preferences. Such a hypothesis would certainly be confirmed by a series of "computer dance" studies at the universities of Texas, Illinois, and Minnesota, where physical attractiveness superseded a host of other variables in determining liking for one's partner and desire to date in the future. Here's an example. Walster and her colleagues randomly paired 752 college students for a freshman dance.[18] A great deal of information was gathered from each student—including self-reports about popularity, religious preference, height, race, expectations for the date, self-esteem, high school academic percentile rank, scholastic aptitude score, and personality test scores. In addition, each student was rated by several judges for attractiveness. Physical attractiveness was by far the most important determinant of how much a date would be liked by his or her partner. It appears that physical attractiveness was just as important an asset for a man as for a woman, since it was a reliable predictor for both groups. Brislin and Lewis replicated this study with fifty-eight unacquainted men and women and again found a strong correlation (.89) between "desire to date again" and "physical attractiveness."[19] In addition, this study asked each person whether he or she would like to date anyone else at the dance. Of the thirteen other people named, all had previously, and independently, been rated very attractive.

[16]D. Byrne, O. London, and K. Reeves, "The Effects of Physical Attractiveness, Sex, and Attitude Similarity on Interpersonal Attraction," Journal of Personality 36 (1968): 259–272.

[17]B. N. Singh, "A Study of Certain Personal Qualities as Preferred by College Students in Their Marital Partners," Journal of Psychological Researches 8 (1964): 37–48.

[18]E. Walster, V. Aronson, D. Abrahams and L. Rohmann, "Importance of Physical Attractiveness in Dating Behavior," Journal of Personality and Social Psychology 4 (1966): 508–516.

[19]R. W. Brislin and S. A. Lewis, "Dating and Physical Attractiveness: Replication," Psychological Reports 22 (1968): 976.

The Effects of Physical Appearance and Dress on Human Communication

It seems that in many situations everyone prefers the most attractive date possible regardless of his or her own attractiveness and regardless of the possibility of being rejected by the most attractive date. There are obvious exceptions. Some gigolos argue that if they approach a woman somewhat less attractive—particularly in the company of some who are very attractive—their chances of succeeding are greatly increased. Some attractive persons have more dating opportunities than they desire; others, however, are almost untouched in the mainstream of dating behavior. Why? Walster and her colleagues proposed what they call the "matching hypothesis." Since this hypothesis was presented, other studies have confirmed its validity—including a study of middle-aged married couples. Essentially, the matching hypothesis argues that each person may be attracted to only the best-looking partners, but reality sets in when actual dates are made. You may face an unwanted rejection if you select only the best-looking person available, so the tendency is to select a person similar to yourself with respect to physical attractiveness. Hence, the procedure seems to be to try to maximize the attractiveness of your choice while simultaneously minimizing the possibilities of rejection. If you have high self-esteem, you might seek out highly attractive partners in spite of a considerable gap between your looks and theirs.[20] Self-esteem, in this case, will affect the perception of and possible reaction to rejection.

Sometimes we observe couples who seem to be "mismatched" with regard to their physical attractiveness. One study suggests that evaluations of males may change dramatically if they are viewed as "married" to someone very different in general physical attractiveness.[21] Unattractive men who were seen with attractive women were judged, among other things, as making more money, as being more successful in their occupation, and as being more intelligent than attractive men with attractive partners. Judges must have reasoned that for an unattractive man to marry an attractive woman, he must have to offset this imbalance by succeeding in other areas, such as making money. Handsome men don't seem to be able to significantly increase the ratings of unattractive women, however.

The whole question of "What is sex appeal?" seems relevant at this point.[22] The answer is far from clear-cut because so many aspects vary with the situation, the time (both time in a person's life and time in history), and the experiences and preferences of each individual. For instance, one may make different evaluations of another's sex appeal depending on whether the person is known

[20]E. Berscheid and E. H. Walster, *Interpersonal Attraction* (Reading, Mass.: Addison-Wesley, 1969), p. 113–114.

[21]D. Bar-Tal and L. Saxe, "Perceptions of Similarity and Dissimilarly Physically Attractive Couples and Individuals," *Journal of Personality and Social Psychology* 33 (1976): 772–781.

[22]B. I. Murstein, W. J. Gadpaile, and D. Byrne, "What Makes People Sexually Appealing?" *Sexual Behavior* 1 (1971): 75–77.

The Effects of Physical Appearance and Dress on Human Communication

or a stranger. A student attending a university, isolated from an urban environment, may consider another person particularly sexy—only to find his or her
judgment changed when returning to the city, where there is a greater variety to
choose from. Others may label sexy those with whom they feel they have some
chance of success in a sexual encounter. They may react to cues which suggest
readiness or openness. Still others may identify sex appeal with pleasant early
love experiences (with parents and relatives) and select people with the same
pleasantness, the same interests, or the same values. Possibly the most familiar
reaction to the question "What constitutes sex appeal?" involves judgments
about physical features—for example, "I'm a breast man," or "He's got a
rugged face," or "I'm a leg man," or "He looks like a stud." Frequently, these
responses to physical characteristics are defined by one's reference group or
the mass media (for example, movie idols)—and have relatively little to do with
sexual expertise. One effort to determine more precisely what women like in a
man's body surveyed seventy women from age eighteen to thirty. The favorite
male physique had a medium-wide trunk, a medium-thin lower trunk, and thin
legs. (V look). The most disliked physique had either a thin upper trunk or a
wide lower trunk (pear-shaped look). Women who saw themselves as traditionally feminine and conservative in their life-style favored "muscle men;"
more "liberated" women liked thinner, more linear bodies; big women went
for big men. The best clue to a woman's favorite male physique, however, was
the type of physique the man had who was "most important to them" at the
time of the survey.[23]

While some people would like to believe that "everything is beautiful in its
own way"—as a 1970 pop song put it—it should also be recognized that some
people are beautiful in much the same way to large segments of the population.
The stereotypes of American beauty promoted by Playboy and the Miss America Pageant, among numerous others, seem to be very influential in setting
cultural norms. Their recognition of this influence caused many women to
condemn Playboy's portrayal of ideal womanhood and prompted some black
leaders to organize a Miss Black America Pageant. It is not surprising to find
that in one case over four thousand judges, differing in age, sex, occupation,
and geographical location, exhibited high levels of agreement concerning pret-

[23]P. J. Lavrakas, "Female Preferences for Male Physiques," Journal of Research in Personality 9
(1975): 324–334. Although males tend to focus on female breasts, buttocks, and legs, specific
preferences do vary. See N. Wiggins and J. S. Wiggins, "A Typological Analysis of Male Preferences
for Female Body Types," Multivariate Behavioral Research 4 (1969): 89–102; and J. S. Wiggins, N.
Wiggins, and J. C. Conger, "Correlates of Heterosexual Somatic Preference," Journal of Personality
and Social Psychology 10 (1968): 82–90. Small buttocks seem to be preferred by females on both
males and females. Cf. S. B. Beck, C. I. Ward-Hull, and P. M. McLear, "Variables Related to
Women's Somatic Preferences of the Male and Female Body," Journal of Personality and Social
Psychology 34 (1976): 1200–1210.

The Effects of Physical Appearance and Dress on Human Communication

tiness in young women's faces.[24] Physical attractiveness seems to play an important role in persuading and/or manipulating others—whether in courtship, a classroom, or a public speaking situation. Certainly it is very influential on first impressions and expectations for an encounter.

It would not be fair to leave this section on attractiveness without at least noting that there are some important qualifications to the dictum that "what is beautiful is good." For instance, attractive people are *not consistently* rated more intelligent or more trustworthy. And unattractive couples have been judged by others to be more happily married than physically attractive couples. Handsome men do not seem to score any better on tests measuring happiness, self-esteem, and psychological well-being. Although attractive women seem to score slightly better on such measures than unattractive ones, this doesn't seem to be a lasting result. For example, middle-aged women who had been identified as attractive college students seemed to be less happy, less satisfied with their lives, and less well adjusted than their "plain" counterparts.[25]

Methodological issues may also provide comfort to those who perceive themselves as something short of attractive. Although it is not true of all studies of physical attractiveness, most use photographs which, prior to the study, are judged by a panel of "experts" to fall into the "beautiful" or "ugly" category. Hence, in most cases, we are not reporting results from live, moving, talking human beings in a particular environment and we are not generally dealing with subtle differences in physical attractiveness which lie between the extremes of beautiful and ugly. Furthermore, we must remember that one's appearance may be relative to the context in which it is judged—for example, you may perceive a popular singer on stage or on TV as "sexy," but the same person in your living room may seem much less glamorous. Some maintain that neither very attractive nor very unattractive women are the most likely to succeed in business in today's society—that is, extreme attractiveness may actually be a barrier to rapid and high-level achievement in this environment. And finally, we must remember that one's degree of attractiveness will, in most communication situations, interact with other factors which may offset or change perceptions of appearance—for example, the content of one's verbal messages.

Now that we've examined the global concept of attractiveness, we can ask: What *specific* aspects of another person's appearance do we respond to? Does it make any difference how we perceive our own body and appearance? The answers to these questions will be the focus for the remainder of this chapter.

[24]A. M. Iliffe, "A Study of Preferences in Feminine Beauty," *British Journal of Psychology* 51 (1960): 267–273.

[25]Cited as an unpublished manuscript by the authors and R. Campbell in E. Berscheid and E. H. Walster, "Physical Attractiveness," in L. Berkowitz (ed.), *Advances in Experimental Social Psychology*, Vol. 7 (New York: Academic Press, 1974), pp. 200–201.

The Effects of Physical Appearance and Dress on Human Communication

Our Body: Its Shape, Color, Smell, and Hair

Body Shape.   In order to add a personal dimension to some of the theory and research in this section, a short SELF-DESCRIPTION TEST is provided. By taking this test, you can gather some data on yourself which can be compared with that of others who have taken it.[26]

Instructions: Fill in each blank with a word from the suggested list following each statement. For any blank, three in each statement, you may select any word from the list of twelve immediately below. An exact word to fit you may not be in the list, but select the words that seem to fit *most closely* the way you are.

1. I feel most of the time _____, _____, and _____.

calm	relaxed	complacent
anxious	confident	reticent
cheerful	tense	energetic
contented	impetuous	self-conscious

2. When I study or work, I seem to be _____, _____, and _____.

efficient	sluggish	precise
enthusiastic	competitive	determined
reflective	leisurely	thoughtful
placid	meticulous	cooperative

3. Socially, I am _____, _____, and _____.

outgoing	considerate	argumentative
affable	awkward	shy
tolerant	affected	talkative
gentle-tempered	soft-tempered	hot-tempered

4. I am rather _____, _____, and _____.

active	forgiving	sympathetic
warm	courageous	serious
domineering	suspicious	soft-hearted
introspective	cool	enterprising

5. Other people consider me rather _____, _____, and _____.

generous	optimistic	sensitive
adventurous	affectionate	kind
withdrawn	reckless	cautious
dominant	detached	dependent

[26] J. B. Cortes and F. M. Gatti, "Physique and Self-Description of Temperament," *Journal of Consulting Psychology* 29 (1965): 434.

The Effects of Physical Appearance and Dress on Human Communication

6. Underline *one* word out of the three in each of the following lines which most closely describes the way you are:

(a) assertive, relaxed, tense
(b) hot-tempered, cool, warm
(c) withdrawn, sociable, active
(d) confident, tactful, kind
(e) dependent, dominant, detached
(f) enterprising, affable, anxious

This test has been given to numerous individuals participating in studies concerned with the relationship between certain personality and temperament characteristics and certain body types or builds. Generally, these studies are concerned with a person's physical similarity to three extreme varieties of human physique. These are shown in Figure 5.1.

Naturally, most of us do not fit these extremes exactly. So a system has been developed for specifying body type based on the assumption that we may have some features of all three types. Sheldon's work helps to explain this system.[27] A person's physical characteristics are rated on a scale from 1 to 7—7 representing the highest correspondence with one of the three extreme body types. An individual's "somatype" is represented by three numbers—the first referring to the degree of endomorphy, the second referring to the degree of mesomorphy and the third to the degree of ectomorphy. A grossly fat person would be 7/1/1; a broad shouldered, athletic person would be 1/7/1; and a very skinny person would be a 1/1/7. It is reported that Jackie Gleason is roughly 6/4/1, Muhammad Ali 2/7/1 and Abraham Lincoln 1/5/6. Scientific criticism of Sheldon's work has been plentiful. His work has, however, been the basis for many studies investigating the same general question—and in spite of critical errors in Sheldon's methodology, many of the later studies—using more precise measurements and research designs—have confirmed many of his early conclusions.

Now to the test you took earlier. Cortes and Gatti used this test to measure temperament. When they correlated the results with measures of physique, they found a very high correspondence. In other words, on the basis of this work we would expect to have a pretty good idea of your body build by the answers you gave on the SELF-DESCRIPTION TEST. To calculate your score on the test, simply add up the number of adjectives you chose from each of the endomorph, mesomorph, and ectomorph categories listed in Table 5.2.

If you chose six adjectives from the endomorph category, twelve from the mesomorph, and three from the ectomorph lists, your temperament score would be 6/12/3. If we assume a high correlation with body features we would assume you are primarily mesomorphic with a leaning toward endomorphism.

[27]W. H. Sheldon, *Atlas of Man: A Guide for Somatyping the Adult Male at All Ages* (New York: Harper and Row, 1954); W. H. Sheldon, *The Varieties of Human Physique* (New York: Harper and Row, 1940); W. H. Sheldon, *The Varieties of Temperament* (New York: Harper and Row, 1942).

The Effects of Physical Appearance and Dress on Human Communication

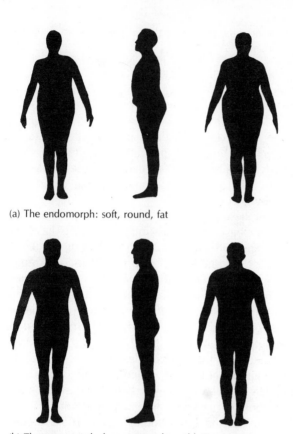

(a) The endomorph: soft, round, fat

(b) The mesomorph: bony, muscular, athletic

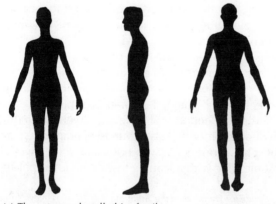

(c) The ectomorph: tall, thin, fragile

Figure 5.1

The Effects of Physical Appearance and Dress on Human Communication

164

Table 5.2

Endomorphic	Mesomorphic	Ectomorphic
dependent	dominant	detached
calm	cheerful	tense
relaxed	confident	anxious
complacent	energetic	reticent
contented	impetuous	self-conscious
sluggish	efficient	meticulous
placid	enthusiastic	reflective
leisurely	competitive	precise
cooperative	determined	thoughtful
affable	outgoing	considerate
tolerant	argumentative	shy
affected	talkative	awkward
warm	active	cool
forgiving	domineering	suspicious
sympathetic	courageous	introspective
soft-hearted	enterprising	serious
generous	adventurous	cautious
affectionate	reckless	tactful
kind	assertive	sensitive
sociable	optimistic	withdrawn
soft-tempered	hot-tempered	gentle-tempered

Your author is 5/11/5. This test and the body-personality research allow us to make some predictions based on probabilities, but, of course, in individual cases there may be exceptions. Nor can we assume from this work that the body causes temperament traits. The high correspondence between certain temperament traits and body builds may be due to life experiences, environmental factors, self-concept, and a host of other variables.

The obvious question at this point is, "What does all this have to do with human communication?" Simply this: If a case can be made that there are clearly defined and generally accepted physique-temperament stereotypes, we can reason that they will have a lot to do with the way you are perceived and responded to by others, and with the personality traits expected of you by others. Wells and Siegel uncovered some data supporting the existence of such stereotypes.[28] One hundred twenty adult subjects were shown silhouette draw-

[28]W. Wells and B. Siegel, "Stereotyped Somatypes" *Psychological Reports* 8 (1961): 77–78. Another study, using a written description of body extremes, asked personality questions about the written descriptions and found similar results. Cf. K. T. Strongman and C. J. Hart, "Stereotyped Reactions to Body Build," *Psychological Reports* 23 (1968): 1175–1178.

The Effects of Physical Appearance and Dress on Human Communication

ings of the endomorph, ectomorph, and mesomorph and asked to rate them on a set of twenty-four bipolar adjective scales such as lazy-energetic, fat-thin, intelligent-unintelligent, dependent–self-reliant; and so on. The investigators deliberately chose people who had not been to college—assuming these people would not be contaminated with information from previous studies which might structure their answers. Their results show that (1) the *endomorph* was rated fatter, older, shorter (silhouettes were the same height), more old-fashioned, less strong physically, less good-looking, more talkative, more warm-hearted and sympathetic, more good-natured and agreeable, more dependent on others, and more trusting of others; (2) the *mesomorph* was rated stronger, more masculine, better-looking, more adventurous, younger, taller, more mature in behavior, and more self-reliant; (3) the *ectomorph* was rated thinner, younger, more ambitious, taller, more suspicious of others, more tense and nervous, less masculine, more stubborn and inclined to be difficult, more pessimistic, and quieter. Several reports suggest that the relationship between body build and temperament also holds for young children.[29] For example, thin ectomorphic boys and girls were more anxious, more conscientious, and more meticulous than children with other body builds. The reactions to endomorphs, or obese individuals, are encountered frequently. They are discriminated against when seeking to obtain life insurance, adopt children, obtain jobs, and even in entrance to college.[30] One author suggests obesity is stamped with a stigma of moral turpitude.[31]

We have been trained for so long to believe that stereotypes are harmful distortions of the truth, we often fail to consider another equally plausible explanation—that a particular stereotype may be the result of a distillation of ages of social experience. In other words, a stereotype may be more accurate than we wish to admit—there may be some reason for the stereotype other than prejudicial whims. Clearly, the evidence shows we do associate certain personality and temperament traits with certain body builds. These expectations may or may not be accurate, but they do exist; they are a part of the psychological mortar in interpersonal communication. We must recognize these stereotypes as potential stimuli for communication responses, so we can deal with them more effectively.

Another dimension of body build which may influence interpersonal responses is height. In American society there seems to be a preference for the taller man; tall women, however, are often labeled "ungainly." Short

[29]R. N. Walker, "Body Build and Behavior in Young Children: II. Body Build and Parents' Ratings," *Child Development* 34 (1963): 1–23. See also R. W. Parnell, *Behavior and Physique: An Introduction to Practical and Applied Somatometry* (London: Edward Arnold, 1958).

[30]H. Channing and J. Mayer, "Obesity—Its Possible Effect on College Acceptance," *New England Journal of Medicine* 275 (1966): 1172–1174.

[31]W. J. Cahnman, "The Stigma of Obesity," *Sociological Quarterly* 9 (1968): 283–299.

The Effects of Physical Appearance and Dress on Human Communication

businesswomen, in fact, may have an advantage in not acquiring whatever "threatening" overtones may attend increased height. The ideal male lover is not *short*, dark, and handsome; male romantic leads are usually tall. The taller of the two national presidential candidates seems to have been a consistent winner since 1900—with five-foot-nine-inch Jimmy Carter a notable exception. Policemen and firemen are, in some areas, required to be at least five feet, eight inches tall. A survey at the University of Pittsburgh shows shorter men are shortchanged on job opportunities and salaries. Pittsburgh graduates six feet, two inches to six feet, four inches received average starting salaries 12.4 percent higher than those men under six feet. Further support for discrimination against the short man comes from a study of 140 corporate recruiters who were asked to make a choice between two men just by reading their applications for employment. The applications were exactly the same except that one listed a height of six feet, one inch and the other five feet, five inches. Only about 1 percent favored the short man. There are even cases on record where short men who did not measure up to the arbitrary height requirements set for policemen actually bludgeoned their heads in the hope that the swelling would make up the needed inches! Shorter children are encouraged to "drink your milk so you'll grow up and be healthy and strong"; attention is focused on shortness or tallness when children are asked to line up by height for various reasons in school. Tallness is often associated with power, but an interesting reversal occurs when the same behavior is labeled "competitive" in a taller man and a "Napoleonic complex" in a shorter one.

Does a tall person have a natural advantage in persuading people? Some preliminary evidence indicates he or she does not.[32] Photographs were taken of the same person (a male) from two different angles—one designed to make him look short; one to make him look tall. These pictures, plus a tape-recorded persuasive speech were the stimuli for various student groups. Attitude measures indicated there was no statistically significant difference between the "tall" and "short" speakers. It is more likely that tallness interacts with other factors such as general body size, girth, facial features, and numerous other variables. In Chapter 6, we discuss some of these other nonverbal dimensions of persuasiveness. In your own experience, you can probably recall some tall individuals who seemed almost frighteningly "overpowering," while others of the same height did not have this quality. Another investigator looked at height from the standpoint of the receiver—rather than the communicator or sender.[33] Will receivers perceive differences in height of people they think to be different in status? Again, only tentative conclusions can be drawn from some early

[32]E. E. Baker and W. C. Redding, "The Effects of Perceived Tallness in Persuasive Speaking: An Experiment," *Journal of Communication* 12 (1962): 51–53.

[33]P. R. Wilson, "Perceptual Distortion of Height as a Function of Ascribed Academic Status," *Journal of Social Psychology* 74 (1968): 97–102.

The Effects of Physical Appearance and Dress on Human Communication

work. A single individual was introduced to five similar groups of students. Each time he was introduced as a person with a different status—for example, student, lecturer, doctor, full professor. Students were then told they needed numerical data for their statistics lesson, so they were asked to estimate the height of the person just introduced. Results seem to suggest there is some perceptual distortion of height—the higher the ascribed status, the higher the judgments of height.

So far we have been discussing our perceptions of others. An equally important dimension of interpersonal communication is what we think of ourselves—our self-image. The self-image is the root system from which all of our overt communication behavior grows and blossoms. Our overt communication behavior is only an extension of the accumulated experiences which have gone into making up our understanding of self. In short, what you are, or think you are, organizes what you say and do. An important part of your self-image is body image—perhaps the first part formed in very young children. Jourard and Secord found males most satisfied with their bodies when they were somewhat larger than normal; females most satisfied when their bodies were smaller than normal—but when their busts were larger than average.[34] Sex researchers have frequently noted emotional problems in males resulting from perceived incongruence between their genital size and the supposed masculine ideal perpetuated by our literary and oral heritage. As we develop, we learn the cultural ideal of what the body should be like, and this results in varying degrees of satisfaction with the body—particularly during adolescence.[35]

Body Color.   In many respects, skin color has been the most potent body stimulus for determining interpersonal responses in this culture. There is no need to review the abuses heaped upon black persons in America on the basis of skin color alone. The words of a white man whose skin pigmentation was changed, and who experienced the dramatic and unforgettable life of a black man in America will be sufficient reminder:

> When all the talk, all the propaganda has been cut away, the criterion is nothing but the color of skin. My experience proved that. They judged me by no other quality. My skin was dark. That was sufficient reason for them to deny me those rights and freedoms without which life loses its significance and becomes a matter of little more than animal survival.

[34]S. M. Jourard and P. F. Secord, "Body Cathexis and Personality," *British Journal of Psychology* 46 (1955): 130–138.

[35]For an extensive treatment of body image research, see F. C. Shontz, *Perceptual and Cognitive Aspects of Body Experience* (New York: Academic Press, 1969):and W. Gorman, *Body Image and the Image of the Brain* (St. Louis: W. H. Green, 1969).

The Effects of Physical Appearance and Dress on Human Communication

I searched for some other answer and found none. I had spent a day without food and water and for no other reason than that my skin was black. I was sitting on a tub in the swamp for no other reason.[36]

In fact, such abuses frequently cause detrimental self-images for blacks—the effects of which only serve to confirm the self-fulfilling prophecy for the abusers. Brody reports tragic cases of young black boys who had great anxiety and guilt complexes stemming from a desire to be white.[37] He also reports deliberate, though unwitting indoctrination about color status by the mothers of these black children. The slogan "black is beautiful" and the Miss Black America Pageant are two of many attempts to cope with this identity problem. The whole concept of skin color has been further complicated by an attempt to label all Negroes *blacks*. Those who do not see themselves as "black" but some lighter shade, may have additional identity crises to face. While there is little doubt that blacks are at an immediate disadvantage in communicating with prejudiced persons, another interesting phenomenon has developed in recent years. There is almost a boomerang effect sometimes, with the black person still judged only by his or her skin color, but the judgment is indiscriminately positive instead of negative. Some explain this phenomenon as an over-reaction caused by widespread guilt feelings among whites. Most blacks would probably argue that this effect is not very widespread even today.

Numerous other judgments which we make about others are based heavily on body color. Expressions such as *red-necked* and *lily-white* are used to identify persons who are uncontrollably angry or who appear unusually white. A pale color may indicate a person is ill, and a healthy person is one whose skin is tanned. A rosy flush may indicate embarrassment.

Body Smell.   While it is obvious that vision and hearing are the most important sensors for social situations in Western societies, the sense of smell may also influence responses. The scientific study of the human olfactory system is in its infancy, but we know other animals obtain a great deal of information from their sense of smell—for example, the presence of an enemy, territorial markers, finding members of the same species or herd, sexual stimulation, and emotional states. Dogs are well known for their ability to sense fear, hate, or friendship in human beings and to track them with only the scent from clothing. The difficulty that dogs seem to have in distinguishing between the smells of identical twins prompted Davis to suggest that we each have an "olfactory signature."[38]

Generally, Americans do not rely on their sense of smell for interpersonal

[36]J. H. Griffin, *Black like Me* (Boston: Houghton Mifflin, 1960), p. 121–122.
[37]E. B. Brody, "Color and Identity Conflict in Young Boys," *Psychiatry* 26 (1963): 188–201.
[38]F. Davis, *Inside Intuition* (New York: McGraw Hill, 1971), p. 129.

The Effects of Physical Appearance and Dress on Human Communication

cues unless perspiration odor, breath, or some other smell is unusually strong. Some believe that this olfactory repression reflects an antisensual American bias. It is ironic that each year American men and women spend hundreds of thousands (if not millions) of dollars on deodorant sprays and soaps, mouthwashes, breath mints, perfumes, aftershave lotions, and other artificial scents. The so-called natural scent seems to have a low priority at this point in our cultural development, but we are not at all reluctant to buy a commercial product which will purportedly make us smell "*natural* and sexy." Meerloo's comments seem to strike a similar note:

> There is a good explanation for all my olfactory nostalgia. After all, smell is related to our first loving contacts in the world. The newborn infant lives first in a world of pure smells, although the world soon teaches him to forego his nostril pleasures. For him, mother is love at first smell. When he is older, he cannot sniff and smell keenly anymore because smelling has become taboo. Thanks to the enforced toilet taboos, our innate perception of smell degenerates into chemical irritation by soaps and antiseptics. While sexual odors are taboo, man borrows these odors from flowers and plants. The sexual organs of plant and animal—musk, civet, and the rose—bring him what he has suppressed in his own life. Nevertheless, something of the instinctual passion for smells remains in man. It cannot be totally suppressed by the most pristine sanitary habits or by chlorophyl-minded merchants. Modern culture has made people feel ashamed of body odor. Whole industries thrive on that artificially induced self-consciousness. They create diseases such as halitosis just to make people feel inferior. Many a girl has become neurotic because she has completely suppressed the role and delights of perspiration.[39]

Our reactions to odors may be consciously or unconsciously processed, but the message can be quite strong. For me there is a distinct smell associated with high schools and each time I enter one it triggers a chain of memories from my own history. Environmental odors are only one source. Human odors are primarily emitted through the sweat glands, but excrement, saliva, tears, and breath provide other sources. Another source of odor is the manipulation of flatulent air—generally adding a negative or insulting aura to an interpersonal encounter in this culture. In fact, anticipation of expelling flatus may lead to rapid termination of an interpersonal contact. Under certain conditions, however, emission of flatulent air may be used deliberately to draw attention to oneself.

Not all cultures are as reticent about odors in everyday human interaction, as Hall notes:

> Olfaction occupies a prominent place in the Arab life. Not only is it one of the distance-setting mechanisms, but it is a vital part of a complex system of behavior.

[39]J. A. M. Meerloo, *Unobtrusive Communication: Essays in Psycholinguistics* (Assen, Netherlands: Van Gorcum, 1964), pp. 168–169.

The Effects of Physical Appearance and Dress on Human Communication

170

Arabs consistently breathe on people when they talk. However, this habit is more than a matter of different manners. To the Arab good smells are pleasing and a way of being involved with each other. To smell one's friend is not only nice but desirable, for to deny him your breath is to act ashamed. Americans, on the other hand, trained as they are not to breathe in people's faces, automatically communicate shame in trying to be polite.[40]

Body Hair.   As previously mentioned, skin color has been an extremely influential cue in many human encounters in American society since its inception. During the late 1960s, body hair also took on major significance in structuring interpersonal responses. Males who allowed the hair on their head to grow over their ears and foreheads and sometimes to their shoulders found that they frequently attracted abuses similar to those leveled at black-skinned individuals. Cases of discrimination in housing, school attendance, jobs, and commercial establishments, to mention a few, were numerous. A professor who was concerned about the contribution of long hair to the generation gap took his own shorn locks and those of thirty other men, stuffed the hair in a pillow, and sent it to then Vice President Agnew. The professor said, "Stereotypes based on the way people look are so strongly ingrained that effective communication is impossible. Feelings about hair are as strong as on almost any subject." This observation would seem to be confirmed by the placement officer at Stanford University who stated that long-haired young men graduating from college in 1971 would likely find themselves lacking in job opportunities: "The length of a male's hair is directly proportionate to the job opportunities he can find. . . . In other words, the longer the hair, the fewer the jobs."[41] It is reported that Nader's Raiders must not have long hair because it may prohibit access to enterprises which are being investigated.

In late 1971 the U.S. Army dropped an advertising campaign using the slogan "We care more about how you think than how you cut your hair" apparently because too many servicemen believed it! The Army, the ad's original sponsor, later stated it does not condone long hair and that the youth featured in the ad campaign did not meet regulations set forth by the Army. Visitors to Taiwan in the early 1970s were greeted with cards saying, "Welcome to the Republic of China. No long hair or long beards, please." In fact, the mania against long hair may even be fatal: United Press International ran a story in April 1970 which reported a father had shot his son to death in a row over long hair and a "negative attitude toward society." The label *longhair* no longer refers exclusively to the revered and accomplished musicians and writers of the past; now it is also a label for young (and old) "undesirables."

[40]E. T. Hall, *The Hidden Dimension* (Garden City, N.Y.: Doubleday, 1966), pp. 159–160.
[41]Executive's Research Council, *Personnel Management Week*, January 25, 1971.

The Effects of Physical Appearance and Dress on Human Communication

The preceding accounts of the impact of one's hair refer to the period just preceding the publication of the first edition of this book. Since then, I've accumulated enough additional accounts to convince me that "the hair issue" has more than maintained the momentum it achieved in the late 1960s. The following paraphrased wire service accounts should amply illustrate the point.

PHILADELPHIA. (1971). Head coach of the Philadelphia Eagles Ed Khayat ordered his players to shave off their mustaches and trim their sideburns.

BEIRUT (1972). Palestinian guerrillas say long hair is "unmanly" and "It's very unrevolutionary and doesn't become people fighting for a cause."

WEST GERMANY (*Time* magazine, 1972). Fifteen months ago, Defense Minister Helmut Schmidt said members of the German Army could have beards and long hair as long as they were clean and well-groomed. The hoopla created by this order—including old soldiers who complained that long hair interfered with discipline and troop readiness—caused Schmidt to revise his order so that no soldier's hair falls below his collar.

BERLIN (1974). One officer (Lt. Carroll) and six enlisted men face courts-martial on charges of disobeying an order to trim their hair or beards. Regulations say mustaches must be neatly trimmed, beards are not allowed (although they were in the Navy), and hair on the head may not come over the ears or eyebrows or touch the collar except for closely cut hair at the back of the neck.

CONNECTICUT (1975). A woman was fired from her waitress job because she refused to shave her legs.

FRANKFURT (1975). The Army dropped charges against Lt. Carroll for violating haircut regulations because he agreed to leave the Army with an honorable discharge. Other servicemen, however, are serving terms in Army jails for such violations.

SCOTTSDALE, ARIZONA (1977). Chicago Cub outfielder, Jose Cardenal, said he was asked by General Manager Bob Kennedy to cut his hair. Cardenal pointed out that the length of his Afro haircut had been about the same for the last five years.

NEW JERSEY. The headmaster of Seton Hall Preparatory School (who sports a beard and mustache) said about 60 seniors will be suspended if they don't cut their hair to meet regulations on hair grooming. One student reported he was told by the headmaster, "I hold your diploma. Either you get a haircut or you don't get your diploma."

LINWOOD, KANSAS (1977). Eighth-grade cheerleader, Stacey Tinberg, was the recipient of an acid attack—apparently motivated by her Farrah Fawcett-Majors hair style. Nitric acid was thrown on her back and shoulders by another girl in an apparent attempt to damage Stacey's hair so it would have to be cut. Six girls, who had prior knowledge of the attack, seemed to confirm the belief that the hairdo was a primary cause of the attack.

A publication called *The Missionary*, sponsored by the Episcopal Diocese of Northern California, presented readers with this "sideburn chart." And last,

The Effects of Physical Appearance and Dress on Human Communication

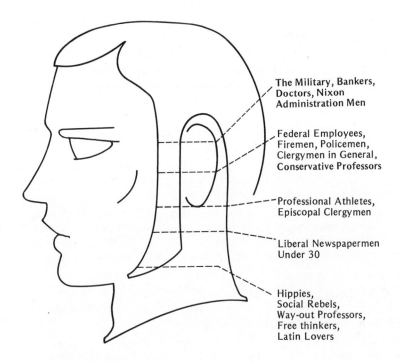

The Military, Bankers,
Doctors, Nixon
Administration Men

Federal Employees,
Firemen, Policemen,
Clergymen in General,
Conservative Professors

Professional Athletes,
Episcopal Clergymen

Liberal Newspapermen
Under 30

Hippies,
Social Rebels,
Way-out Professors,
Free thinkers,
Latin Lovers

but certainly not least, I offer the following item printed in the *Chicago Tribune*, May 22, 1973 (Section 3, p. 3). It is reprinted almost in its entirety because it seems to reflect so many of the stereotypes and biases regarding long hair which exist—but are rarely expressed:

AUSTIN, TEXAS, May 21 (UPI). Long hair on boys and men is the sign of a sissy and should be banned from American athletic fields, according to the lead article in the May issue of the Texas High School Coaches Association's magazine.

Tony Simpson, head football coach at Northshore Junior High School in the Houston suburb of Galena Park, said God made man to dominate woman and, therefore, meant for man to wear short hair.

"It's time that American coaches stopped allowing themselves to be personally represented by male athletic teams and individuals that look like females," Simpson said in his article in "Texas Coach."

"Only in the animal world is the male designed to be the most attractive or the prettiest—for example, the male lion has the mane, the male peacock has the feathers," Simpson said. "This is normal in the animal world only.

"However, a male with long hair is cute, he is pretty and he is sweet," said Simpson, who wears his blond hair cropped short. "If the coaches of America would grow

The Effects of Physical Appearance and Dress on Human Communication

long hair like their athletes, we might be able to scare the Russian and Chinese Communists to death with our lack of masculinity.

"It should be pointed out here that the only reason males are free to look like females and their coaches are free to permit this is because we had real men that were not cute, not sweet and not pretty, with courage and sense enough to kill our enemies on battlefields all over the globe," Simpson said.

The article came within weeks of the Texas High School Coaches Association's decision to ban long hair on athletes in its annual high school football and basketball all-star games.

Two Houston athletes, including the most sought-after prep basketball player in Texas—Eddie Owens of Houston Wheatley—said they would boycott the games before they would trim back their sideburns and long afros.

"If common sense dictates that long hair on a man is a disgrace, let's stop compromising our common sense by allowing it," Simpson told his fellow coaches in the article. "A good hair code will get the abnormals out of athletics before they become coaches and bring their 'losers' standards into the coaching profession."

Simpson said keeping his hair short is a sign of male discipline. . . . He said a woman who wants a man with long hair is not "a real woman in her soul."

"But the American male youth—and many not so young—wear their hair long simply because they know the female will like it."

Equally undesirable reactions would probably result if people went to the other extreme by shaving all the hair off their heads—as an antihair group called the Skinheads actually did. In 1974 an organization called Bald-Headed Men of America was formed to "cultivate a sense of pride and eliminate the vanity associated with the loss of one's hair." The motivation for negative responses to these extreme hair styles by some members of our culture is an interesting question, but not our major concern here. The fact that body hair, in and of itself, elicits feelings either of appreciation or repugnance is the important point. Other body hair also seems to be important in judgments of attractiveness—illustrated by the comment, "I like him, but he's so hairy." For years, Playboy magazine, a primary reference work for many men on the nude female figure, neatly "brushed out," or did not display pubic hair on its models. Even magazines depicting human figures in nudist colonies were so well known for such alterations of pubic hair that many of them now advertise their magazines as "unretouched." It is reported that the Chacobo Indians of the Amazon rain forest carefully trim and groom their head hair, but feel that other body hair is not attractive, and they methodically eliminate eyebrows by completely plucking them. The lack of eyebrows on the Mona Lisa is some evidence that it may at one time have been desirable to pluck them for beauty's sake.

Finally, the beard. Freedman's work, though far from a conclusive treatise, offers some interesting hypotheses.[42] In 1969 he asked a group of undergraduate students how they felt about beardedness. None of the men wore a beard. The majority of both men and women used adjectives of youthfulness to describe unbearded men. Of the men, 22 percent described the personalities of bearded men as independent, and 20 percent described them as extroverted. Women were envisioning an idealized husband, says Freedman, when they described bearded men as masculine, sophisticated, and mature—which accounted for 55 percent of the adjectives they used. Further interviews with women suggested a beard heightens sexual magnetism—it makes a man seem more masculine to a woman, and she feels more feminine toward him. Freedman goes on to say that people will stand closer to beardless men while bearded men report they are less tense with unbearded male strangers than with other bearded men. In another study, photos were taken of eight men fully bearded, only with a goatee, only with a mustache, and clean-shaven.[43] These photos were shown to 128 students who judged the men at various stages in the process. The more hair the man had, the more he was judged to be masculine, mature, good-looking, self-confident, dominant, courageous, liberal, nonconformist, and industrious. Whether these findings extend beyond the campus environment is still open to question.

Obviously, there are many other body-related cues we have not covered, such as freckles, moles, acne, and so-called beauty marks, all of which may be very important in a given situation. The numerous individuals who have had "nose jobs" must have felt a great communicative potential for the nose. However, our responses to body shape, color, smell, and hair seem to be the major factors involved, aside from dress and other artifacts, such as cosmetics, eyeglasses, jewelry, and the like.

Our Body: Clothes and Other Artifacts

Examine the clothing types shown in Figure 5.2 (see page 177). What are your first impressions?

On the list below you will find twenty characteristics which may be associated with one or more of these clothing types. Check the spaces which you think apply to specific clothing types and compare your impressions with those of your friends, family, or associates.

[42]D. G. Freedman, "The Survival Value of the Beard," *Psychology Today* 3 (1969): 36–39.
[43]R. Pellegrini, "The Virtue of Hairiness," *Psychology Today* 6 (1973): 14.

Males				Females				
1	2	3	4	1	2	3	4	
——	——	——	——	——	——	——	——	1. Has smoked marijuana.
——	——	——	——	——	——	——	——	2. Has "hippie" friends.
——	——	——	——	——	——	——	——	3. Is a fraternity or sorority member.
——	——	——	——	——	——	——	——	4. Is a Democrat.
——	——	——	——	——	——	——	——	5. Is involved in athletics.
——	——	——	——	——	——	——	——	6. Is married.
——	——	——	——	——	——	——	——	7. Is generous.
——	——	——	——	——	——	——	——	8. Drives a sports car.
——	——	——	——	——	——	——	——	9. Is a Republican.
——	——	——	——	——	——	——	——	10. Is vocationally oriented.
——	——	——	——	——	——	——	——	11. Is active politically.
——	——	——	——	——	——	——	——	12. Is dependable.
——	——	——	——	——	——	——	——	13. Was against the war in Vietnam.
——	——	——	——	——	——	——	——	14. Lives with parents.
——	——	——	——	——	——	——	——	15. Has long hair.
——	——	——	——	——	——	——	——	16. Has many friends.
——	——	——	——	——	——	——	——	17. Is intelligent.
——	——	——	——	——	——	——	——	18. Is religious.
——	——	——	——	——	——	——	——	19. Is open-minded.
——	——	——	——	——	——	——	——	20. Is older.

Did you find any similarities in your responses and those of your peers? Were there any major differences between your responses and the responses of people with distinctly different backgrounds? Later in this chapter we will focus on what particular impressions are communicated by clothes, but first we need to answer an even more basic question, "Do clothes communicate?" Anecdotal evidence is plentiful. For instance, a newspaper article based on a story from the Associated Press not too long ago reported that the Lutheran Church felt the attire worn by clergymen in the pulpit was responsible for some churchgoers' switching denominations. There are numerous tailors, manufacturers, and sellers of clothes who claim to be "wardrobe engineers"—engineering your outward appearance in order to increase your sales, assert your authority, or win more cases in court. In the early 1970s the Associated Press reported that an eighth-grade girl in Clifton, Arizona was sent home from her graduation ceremony because she didn't have on the right style of dress. After admitting the girl's dress met the "pastel" requirement, the head of the local school board said, however, that the dress had flowers on it and "we couldn't have everybody different. She was defying authority."

You may have had the experience in a restaurant of responding only to the uniform of the waiter or waitress and later, when you were ready to leave, not

The Effects of Physical Appearance and Dress on Human Communication

Males

Females

Figure 5.2

knowing who waited on your table. It is reasonable to assume that, in most instances, our perception of others is influenced partly by clothes and partly by other factors. In order to determine whether our judgments of others are ever made on the basis of clothes alone, it is necessary to measure the effects of changing the type of clothing while keeping everything else the same. Experiments by Hoult were designed on this basis.[44] First, forty-six students rated thirteen male students of similar background on such things as "best-looking," "most likely to succeed," "most intelligent," "most like to date or double date

[44]R. Hoult, "Experimental Measurement of Clothing as a Factor in Some Social Ratings of Selected American Men," *American Sociological Review* 19 (1954): 324–328.

The Effects of Physical Appearance and Dress on Human Communication

with," "best personality," and "most like to have as class president." The four men with the highest ratings were told to "dress down," while the four with the lowest ratings were told to "dress up." Others were told to dress the same. Two weeks later, when ratings were again obtained. Hoult found no evidence that the clothes had been influential in changing the ratings—even though independent ratings of the clothes showed they did, indeed, indicate "dressing up" or "dressing down" from the previous outfits. A high correlation between the social closeness of the raters and models and the social ratings prompted Hoult to conduct another study using models who were complete strangers to the raters. In this study, he used photos of male strangers who were rated by 254 students from two colleges. Having obtained independent ratings of clothes and the models' heads, Hoult was able to place high-ranked outfits on models with low-ranked heads. Lower-ranked clothing was placed on models with higher-ranked heads. He found that higher-ranked clothing was associated with an increase in rank, while lower-ranked clothing was associated with loss of rank. Clothing, then, did seem to be a significant factor affecting the judgments students made about these strangers.

While Hoult's work is helpful in demonstrating the communicative value of clothes, an equally important conclusion can be derived from the failure of his first experiment. This first experiment demonstrates one of the conditions under which clothing may not be a highly influential factor in interpersonal perception of others—when the observer is well acquainted with the person being observed. Changes in the clothing of a family member or close friend may indicate a temporary change of mood, but it is likely that we will not perceive any basic changes in values, attitudes, or personality traits unless the clothing change becomes permanent for that individual. In addition to social closeness to the person being observed, there are other factors which may modify responses to clothes, such as the psychological-social orientation and background of the observer and the particular task or situation within which the observation is made. We should also remember that any given item of clothing can convey several different meanings. For instance, a tie a person selects to wear may reflect "sophistication" or "high status," but the way the tie is worn—that is, tightly knotted, loosened, thrown over one's shoulder, and so on—may provide additional information about the wearer and evoke different reactions.

To understand the relationship between clothes and communication, we should be familiar with the various functions clothes may fulfill: decoration, protection (both physical and psychological), sexual attraction, self-assertion, self-denial, concealment, group identification, and display of status or role.[45]

[45]One author sees the differences in consumption of clothes by black and white men as reflecting a need by blacks to compensate for inferior social position and as an anthropometric disguise rather than simply the result of economic differences. Cf. J. Schwartz, "Men's Clothing and the Negro," *Phylon* 24 (1963): 224–231.

The Effects of Physical Appearance and Dress on Human Communication

178

Since there are some widely accepted cultural rules for combining certain colors and styles of dress, clothes may also function to inform the observer of one's knowledge of such rules. With such a variety of functions, it is interesting to ponder the effects a trend toward unisexism in dress would have. Perhaps the type of incident in which one customer in a store mistakenly asks another customer (dressed in coat and tie) for assistance would occur more frequently. Obviously some clothing may serve more than one function—a woman's bra is, in one sense, used for concealment but in another sense it may also fulfill the sexual attraction function. An interesting study by Lefkowitz, Blake, and Mouton shows not only how clothes fulfill a particular function, but how they affect the behavior of others.[46] They found pedestrians will violate the instructions given by a traffic signal light more often when another person violates it ahead of them. More important, there were significantly more violations when the original violator was dressed to represent a high-status person. Additional studies of this type find that a variety of requests (making change, accepting leaflets, giving detailed street directions, returning a dime left in a phone booth, and so on) are more easily granted if one is dressed to fit the situation or is dressed in what would be considered higher-status clothing. Bickman, for example, had four men stop 153 adults on the streets of Brooklyn and make various requests.[47] The men's clothing varied and included civilian (sports jacket and tie), milkman (uniform, white pants, milk bottles), and guard (uniform, badge, insignia, no gun). The men asked pedestrians either to pick up a bag, to put a dime in a parking meter for someone else, or to stand on the opposite side of a bus stop sign. In each case, the guard uniform received greater compliance. In fact, 83 percent of those who were asked to put a dime in the parking meter obeyed even after the person in the guard uniform had left the scene. Lawyers have long known that their client's manner of dress may have an impact on the judgments made by the judge and/or jury. Some defendants have even been encouraged to put on a simulated wedding ring to offset any prejudice against single persons. This brings us to the question of what specific things are communicated by clothes.

To make a list of the things invariably communicated by clothes would be impossible; such a list would vary with the demands of each particular situation and would also change with time. If the fashion industry could devise such a list, it would need to spend far less on advertising designed to persuade women that a particular cosmetic or dress actually does communicate "beauty." Some of the potential personal attributes which may be communicated by dress include: sex, age, nationality, relation to opposite sex (a func-

[46]M. Lefkowitz, R. Blake, and J. Mouton, "Status Factors in Pedestrian Violation of Traffic Signals," *Journal of Abnormal and Social Psychology* 51 (1955): 704–706.

[47]L. Bickman, "The Social Power of a Uniform," *Journal of Applied Social Psychology* 4 (1974): 47–61. Also, see L. Bickman, "Social Roles and Uniforms: Clothes Make the Person," *Psychology Today* 7 (1974): 48–51.

The Effects of Physical Appearance and Dress on Human Communication

tion, sometimes, of matched sweaters), socioeconomic status, identification with a specific group, occupational or official status, mood, personality, attitudes, interests, and values. Clothes also set our expectations for the behavior of the wearer—especially if it is a uniform of some type. Obviously, the accuracy of such judgments varies considerably—the more concrete items such as age, sex, nationality, and socioeconomic status being signaled with greater accuracy than more abstract qualities like attitudes, values, and personality. Personality judgments are probably dependent on the traits being judged. Observers may depend more on clothes for judging such things as efficiency or aggressiveness and more on facial characteristics for friendliness or shyness. For some personality judgments, clothes probably play a minimal role. Another factor which influences the accuracy of such judgments is the similarity of the observer to the person being observed with respect to the traits being rated. If you belong to the same group or have characteristics similar to those of the person being observed, your accuracy in judging those characteristics may increase. One research project found considerable agreement in judgments on such abstract characteristics as political and social liberalism/conservatism as represented by clothing behavior.[48] The fact that these judgments were made on a college campus may have contributed to the accuracy. Interviews were conducted with 410 students using photos of color drawings of various clothing types, ranging from conventional to unconventional (cf. Figure 5.2). Subjects were asked to judge their own appearance and provide information on stereotypes they felt were associated with dress. Associated consistently with less conventional dress were such items as: "against the war in Vietnam," "pro-Negro," "label self a radical," "used marijuana," "used LSD," and "active in left-wing politics." Associated with conventional dress were such things as "vocational orientation," and "oriented toward the traditional fun and football college culture." Interest in joining the Peace Corps was associated with the two middle clothing styles—not extremely conventional or extremely "earthy." There was little association between dress and judgments on whether the person might have an interest in academic work or in artistic or literary culture, or whether he or she might tutor deprived children. Kelley concludes his analysis this way:

> Dress may be considered as a form of non-verbal communication: in a university community it gives a rough indication of political and social ideology. The communication is reasonably accurate largely because the wearer chooses, perhaps inadvertently, a dress style that indicates his position. Inaccuracy in communication

[48]J. Kelley, "Dress as Non-verbal Communication," paper presented to the Annual Conference of the American Association for Public Opinion Research, May 1969. Also see J. Kelley and S. A. Star, "Dress and Ideology: The Nonverbal Communication of Political Attitudes," paper presented to the Annual Meeting of the American Sociological Association, August 1971.

The Effects of Physical Appearance and Dress on Human Communication

arises for several reasons: dress symbolism is not sufficiently elaborated to express atypical combinations of political and social attitudes; information on the meaning of dress styles is acquired by informal processes subject to appreciable inaccuracy; finally, there is sometimes pressure on individuals not to wear the styles appropriate to their beliefs. By making political position more visible, dress somewhat facilitates the formation of politically homogeneous friendship circles and so sharpens political cleavages.

We have talked previously about the effect of one's self-image on his or her communication behavior. Extending this same idea, we should consider the possible effects of clothes on the wearer. Some authors feel clothes help satisfy a personal image of one's ideal self. Gibbins, in his work with fifteen- and sixteen-year-old girls, for instance, found a definite relationship between dresses which were liked and ratings of ideal self. Clothing was a means of communicating messages about the wearer, and liking for a particular outfit was "related to the extent to which this message is similar to the subject's ideal self image.[49] In another fascinating discovery, we see a potential link between clothing and self-concept. High school boys who had much higher "achievement scores" but who wore clothing deemed "unacceptable" by their peers were found to have lower grade point averages than those who wore "acceptable" clothing. This latter group also found themselves in less conflict and in more school activities. Clothes, then, may encourage or discourage certain patterns of communication. A new outfit may promote feelings of gaiety and happiness; you may feel less efficient in shoes which hurt you; self-consciousness may result from wearing an "inappropriate" outfit—a common feeling for adolescents trying to understand their own self-image. Some graduate teaching assistants wear suits and ties to class to distinguish themselves as teachers because frequently they are almost peers of their students. In addition to distinguishing them as the teacher, some report such attire also gives them added confidence or assurance in dealing with their students.

Hypothesizing that one's self-image is expressed in one's selection of clothing fabrics, Compton compared color and design preferences of 145 freshmen women, with other measures of their physical and personality characteristics.[50] None of the physical characteristics such as eye color, hair color, and weight/stature were related to any of the color and design preferences. However, three personality measures were strongly associated with selection of a small (less bold) design size. These factors included: interest in clothing merchandising, femininity, and a personality measure indicating a woman

[49]K. Gibbins, "Communication Aspects of Women's Clothes and Their Relation to Fashionability," *British Journal of Social and Clinical Psychology* 8 (1969): 301–312.

[50]N. Compton, "Personal Attributes of Color and Design Preferences in Clothing Fabrics," *Journal of Psychology* 54 (1962): 191–195.

The Effects of Physical Appearance and Dress on Human Communication

presents herself as natural, unaffected, and modest. Women high in sociability (outgoing) consistently chose deep shades and saturated colors rather than tints, which were chosen by quiet, submissive, and passive women. Admittedly, Compton's study only provides a very rough, exploratory attempt to investigate this question. There is much to do.

Closely related to Compton's work is that of Aiken.[51] Aiken wanted to determine whether the selection of certain types of clothing was related to certain personality traits. His clothing opinionnaire tested five factors on a female population: (1) *Interest in dress*. Personality traits related to this factor included: "conventional," "conscientious," "compliant before authority," "stereotyped in thinking," "persistent," "suspicious," "insecure," and "tense"—that is, uncomplicated and socially conscientious, with indications of adjustment problems. Two student term papers at the University of Wisconsin-Milwaukee found sorority women scored highest in this category. The following factors are listed in the rank order obtained from these sorority women. (2) *Economy in dress*. Personality measures related to this factor included: "responsible," "conscientious," "alert," "efficient," "precise," "intelligent," and "controlled." Another student paper using Aiken's opinionnaire found that marital status and increasing age contributed heavily to economy orientation. (3) *Decoration in dress*. Personality measures related to this factor included: "conscientious," "conventional," "stereotyped," "nonintellectual," "sympathetic," "sociable," and "submissive"—that is, uncomplicated and socially conscientious. (4) *Conformity in dress*. Personality variables associated with this factor included a large number of conformity variables: "restraint," "socially conscientious," "moral," "sociable," "traditional," "submissive," "emphasis on economic, social and religious values," and "minimized aesthetic values." (5) *Comfort in dress*. Personality measures related to this factor included "self-controlled," "socially cooperative," "sociable," "thorough," and "deferent to authority"—that is, controlled extrovert.

An extensive follow-up study of Aiken's work was conducted by Rosenfeld and Plax.[52] This study obtained responses from both males and females on a questionnaire about clothing attitudes. A massive battery of personality tests were also given to this group of 371 men and women. The results of these personality tests were then matched with the scores on four dimensions of the clothing questionnaire. These results are listed as follows according to the males and females who scored high or low on each dimension.

[51]L. Aiken, "Relationships of Dress to Selected Measures of Personality in Undergraduate Women," *Journal of Social Psychology* 59 (1963): 119–128.
[52]L. B. Rosenfeld and T. G. Plax, "Clothing as Communication." *Journal of Communication* 27 (1977): 24–31.

The Effects of Physical Appearance and Dress on Human Communication

1. *Clothing Consciousness* ("The people I know always notice what I wear.")

   High Males were: deliberate; guarded; deferential to authority, custom and tradition. They did not value beauty, form, and unity very highly and they believed people were easily manipulated.

   High Females were: inhibited; anxious; compliant before authority; kind; sympathetic; loyal to friends.

   Low Males were: aggressive; independent; and did not believe people could be easily manipulated.

   Low Females were: forceful, independent; dominant; clear thinking; and had low motivation for heterosexual relationships or for manipulating others.

2. *Exhibitionism* ("I approve of skimpy bathing suits and wouldn't mind wearing one myself.")

   High Males were: aggressive; confident; outgoing; unsympathetic; unaffectionate; moody; impulsive; and had a low self-concept regarding their familial interactions.

   High Females were: radical; detached from interpersonal relationships; and had a high opinion of their own self-worth and moral-ethical beliefs.

   Low Males were: guarded about self-revelations. They had a low self-concept regarding their familial interactions and they believed people were easily manipulable.

   Low Females were: timid; sincere; accepting of others; patient; and had a low motivation for heterosexual relationships. They also had feelings of inferiority.

3. *Practicality* ("When buying clothes, I am more interested in practicality than beauty.")

   High Males were: inhibited; cautious; rebellious; dissatisfied; and had a low motivation to make friends, sustain relationships, or gain recognition of authorities.

   High Females were: clever; enthusiastic; confident; outgoing; and guarded about personal self-revelations. They had feelings of superiority, but did not wish to lead.

   Low Males were: success oriented; mature; forceful; serious; analytical; and tried to predict responses of others in various situations.

   Low Females were: self-centered; independent; detached.

4. *Designer* ("I should love to be a clothes designer.")

   High Males were: cooperative; sympathetic; warm; helpful; impulsive; irritable; demanding; and conforming. They worried about their behavior and sought encouragement from others.

The Effects of Physical Appearance and Dress on Human Communication

High Females were: irrational; uncritical; stereotyped in thinking; quick; expressive; ebullient.

Low Males were: adventurous; egotistic; dissatisfied; and anxious. They had feelings of superiority and were not highly motivated to form friendships.

Low Females were: efficient; clear thinking; resourceful; persistent; and easily disorganized under pressure. They believed that people were easily manipulated and they were pessimistic about their occupational future.

Reed used a somewhat different methodology in another attempt to delineate broad fashion categories and the attitudinal and personality characteristics which seem to typify these categories.[53] Over two-hundred women responded to a questionnaire which first asked questions about what a person should wear to various places such as concerts, beer parties and so on. The second part of the questionnaire tapped background, attitudes and personality features. Reed's respondents fell into the following four categories:

1. *High Fashion* (Establishment; latest styles)
   These women, among other things, were the most interested in fashion and spent the most on clothing. They had the lowest grade point average and were the least likely to disagree with their parents on social issues. They were the most likely to attach importance to religious activities and the least likely to advocate a "new left" philosophy. They were most often enrolled in programs related to the humanities.
2. *Low Fashion* (Casual)
   These women, among other things, perceived themselves as wanting to be most attractive. In most other areas this group tended to be moderate.
3. *Non-Fashion* (Simple lines; not faddish; Wear clothes that are several years old and somewhat out of style)
   These women, among other things, were from the lowest socioeconomic background but had the highest grade point averages. They were the most dogmatic, the most politically conservative and scored the highest on Machiavellian tactics. They tended to be older than persons in the other three groups and they used drugs less than any of the other groups.
4. *Counter-Fashion* (Opposite of establishment dress; emphasis on comfort, not on neatness)

[53]J. A. P. Reed, "Clothing: A Symbolic Indicator of the Self." Unpublished Ph.D. dissertation, Purdue University, 1973.

The Effects of Physical Appearance and Dress on Human Communication

These women, among other things, were the youngest and the least interested in fashion, athletic competition, or religion. They were the least dogmatic, but the most likely to disagree with their parents on social issues. They were the most likely to advocate a "new left" philosophy and were the most likely to use drugs. They perceived themselves as being individualistic, conscientious, tender, apprehensive, and liberal. They also perceived themselves as being less status conscious, less formal, and less sophisticated than did people from other groups.

Each person adorns him- or herself with a number of other objects and cosmetics, such as badges, tatoos, masks, earrings, other jewelry, and the like. We have termed these *artifacts*. Any discussion of clothing must take these artifacts into consideration because they are also potential communicative stimuli. A ring worn on a particular finger, a fraternity or sorority pin worn in a particular configuration, and a man's ring worn around the neck of a woman all signify a close relationship with a member of the opposite sex. There is a dearth of research on such artifacts. Thornton found people who wore eyeglasses were rated higher in intelligence and industriousness by college students in 1944.[54] Argyle and McHenry, twenty-seven years later, found the same effect for brief exposure (fifteen seconds), but intelligence ratings showed a decrease after about five minutes.[55] McKeachie had female interviewees rated by male interviewers after a ten-minute interview.[56] Females behaved similarly but varied with respect to whether they wore lipstick or not. With lipstick, they were rated more frivolous than serious, more placid than worrying, less talkative, more conscientious than not conscientious, and less interested in the opposite sex. Although studies like these make efforts to keep everything constant except the eyeglasses or lipstick or whatever, generalizations are limited to the shade of lipstick, the type of eyeglasses, and many other factors. Cosmetics and other artifacts interact with other clothing, facial, verbal, and body features;[57] but under some yet unspecified conditions, they may be the primary source of information communicated about a particular person.

[54]G. Thornton, "The Effect of Wearing Glasses upon Judgments of Personality Traits of Persons Seen Briefly," *Journal of Applied Psychology* 28 (1944): 203–207.

[55]M. Argyle and R. McHenry, "Do Spectacles Really Affect Judgments of Intelligence?" *British Journal of Social and Clinical Psychology* 10 (1971): 27–29.

[56]W. McKeachie, "Lipstick as a Determiner of First Impressions of Personality: An Experiment for the General Psychology Course," *Journal of Social Psychology* 36 (1952): 241–244.

[57]Cf. P. N. Hamid, "Some Effects of Dress Cues on Observational Accuracy, a Perceptual Estimate, and Impression Formation," *Journal of Social Psychology* 86 (1972): 279–289. This study attempts to show interactions between makeup, glasses, and the sex of the observer.

The Effects of Physical Appearance and Dress on Human Communication

Summary

The exact role of appearance and dress in the total system of non-verbal communication is still unknown. We do know, however, that appearance and dress are part of the total nonverbal stimuli which influence interpersonal responses—and under some conditions they are the primary determiners of such responses. Physical attractiveness may be influential in determining whether you are sought out, it may have a bearing on whether you are able to persuade or manipulate others, it is often an important factor in the selection of dates and marriage partners, it may determine whether a defendant is deemed guilty or innocent, it may even have an effect on whether the prisoner is able to decrease the antisocial behavior responsible for his or her imprisonment, it may be a major factor contributing to how others judge your personality, your sexuality, your popularity, your success, and often your happiness. Fortunately for some and unfortunately for others, such judgments begin early in life. Not all children are "beautiful." There are indications that teachers not only make attractiveness judgments about young children, but treat the unattractive ones with fewer and less-positive communications. A sizable proportion of the American public still thinks of the ideal man or woman in terms of physical attractiveness.

In spite of the overwhelming evidence that physical attractiveness is a highly desirable quality in interpersonal situations, there are other factors to consider which temper these general findings. For instance, all positive findings for attractiveness are based on probabilities—not certainty. Some unattractive persons will not be evaluated unfavorably. Why? There are many reasons—for example, the persons they are seen with, the environment in which they are judged, other communicative behavior they engage in and/or the time of life at which they are evaluated. In addition, many of the attractiveness studies have used photographs rather than live, interacting human beings.

In addition to the importance of general physical attractiveness in influencing the responses of others, we have some information on stereotyped responses to specific features—for example, general body build, skin color, odor, hair, and clothes. These specific features may have a profound influence on your self-image and hence, on your patterns of communication with others. Future work in this area will have to approach such basic questions as: Under what conditions do physical appearance and dress make a critical difference in the total communication event? What is the relative impact of physical appearance and dress when combined with other verbal and nonverbal cues? Are there any specific features of physical appearance which consistently act as primary sources of information for the perceiver? If not, which features act as primary sources of informaton under certain circumstances? Is there any valid-

The Effects of Physical Appearance and Dress on Human Communication

ity to the various stereotypes associated with physical appearance and dress? What effect does your self-image with respect to your own appearance and dress have on your interpersonal communication behavior?

SELECTED BIBLIOGRAPHY

Aiken, L., "Relationship of Dress to Selected Measures of Personality in Undergraduate Women." *Journal of Social Psychology* 59 (1963): 119–128.

Argyle, M., and McHenry, R. "Do Spectacles Really Affect Judgments of Intelligence?" *British Journal of Social and Clinical Psychology* 10 (1971): 27–29.

Aronson, E., and Golden, B. W. "The Effect of Relevant and Irrelevant Aspects of Communicator Credibility on Opinion Change." *Journal of Personality* 30 (1962): 135–146.

Baker, E. E., and Redding, W. C. "The Effects of Perceived Tallness in Persuasive Speaking: An Experiment." *Journal of Communication* 12 (1962): 51–53.

Barker, R. "The Social Interrelatedness of Strangers and Acquaintances." *Sociometry* 5 (1942): 1969–1979.

Bar-Tal, D., and Saxe, L. "Perceptions of Similarly and Dissimilarly Attractive Couples and Individuals." *Journal of Personality and Social Psychology* 33 (1976): 772–781.

Beck, S. B., Ward-Hull, C. I., and McLear, P. M. "Variables Related to Women's Somatic Preferences of the Male and Female Body." *Journal of Personality and Social Psychology* 34 (1976): 1200–1210.

Bedichek, R. *The Sense of Smell*. Garden City, N.Y.: Doubleday, 1960.

Berscheid, E., and Walster, E. "Beauty and the Best." *Psychology Today* 5 (1972): 42–46.

Berscheid, E., and Walster, E. H. *Interpersonal Attraction*. Reading, Mass.: Addison-Wesley, 1969.

Berscheid, E., and Walster, E. H. "Physical Attractiveness." In L. Berkowitz (ed.), *Advances in Experimental Social Psychology*, Vol. 7. New York: Academic Press, 1974. Pp. 158–215.

Berscheid, E., Dion, K., Walster, E., and Walster, G. W. "Physical Attractiveness and Dating Choice: Tests of the Matching Hypothesis." *Journal of Experimental Social Psychology* 7 (1971): 173–189.

Bickman, L. "The Effects of Social Status on the Honesty of Others." *Journal of Social Psychology* 85 (1971): 87–92.

Bickman, L. "Social Roles and Uniforms: Clothes Make the Person." *Psychology Today* 7 (1974): 48–51.

Bickman, L. "The Social Power of a Uniform." *Journal of Applied Social Psychology* 4 (1974): 47–61.

Brislin, R. W., and Lewis, S. A. "Dating and Physical Attractiveness: Replication." *Psychological Reports* 22 (1968): 976.

Brody, E. B. "Color and Identity Conflict in Young Boys." *Psychiatry* 26 (1963): 188–201.

Bush, G., and London, P. "On the Disappearance of Knickers: Hypotheses for the Functional Analysis of Clothing." *Journal of Social Psychology* 51 (1960): 359–366.

Byrne, D., Ervin, C. R., and Lamberth, J. "Contiguity Between the Experimental Study of Attraction and Real-Life Computer Dating." *Journal of Personality and Social Psychology* 16 (1970): 157–165.

Byrne, D., London, O., and Reeves, K. "The Effects of Physical Attractiveness, Sex, and Attitude Similarity on Interpersonal Attraction." *Journal of Personality* 36 (1968): 259–272.

Cahnman, W. J. "The Stigma of Obesity." *Sociological Quarterly* 9 (1968): 283–299.

Cavior, N., and Dokecki, P. R. "Physical Attractiveness, Perceived Attitude Similarity and Academic Achievement as Contributors to Interpersonal Attractiveness." *Developmental Psychology* 9 (1972): 44–54.

Cavior, N., and Lombardi, D. H. "Developmental Aspects of Judgment of Physical Attractiveness in Children." *Developmental Psychology* 8 (1973): 67–71.

Charkin, A., et al. "The Effects of Appearance in Compliance." *Journal of Social Psychology* 92 (1974): 199–200.

Clifford, M. M., and Walster, E. "The Effect of Physical Attractiveness on Teacher Expectation." *Sociology of Education* 46 (1973): 248–258.

Comfort, A. "Likelihood of Human Pheromones." *Nature* 230 (1971): 432–433.

Compton, N. "Personal Attributes of Color and Design Preferences in Clothing Fabrics." *Journal of Psychology* 54 (1962): 191–195.

Coombs, R. H., and Kenkel, W. F. "Sex Differences in Dating Aspirations and Satisfaction with Computer-Selected Partners." *Journal of Marriage and the Family* 28 (1966): 62–66.

Corson, R. *Fashions in Hair: The First Five Thousand Years*. New York: Hastings House, 1965.

Cortes, J. B., and Gatti, F. M. "Physique and Motivation." *Journal of Consulting Psychology* 30 (1966): 408–414.

Cortes, J. B., and Gatti, F. M. "Physique and Propensity." *Psychology Today* 4 (1970): 42.

Cortes, J. B., and Gatti, F. M. "Physique and Self-Description of Temperament." *Journal of Consulting Psychology* 29 (1965): 432–439.

Curran, J. P. "Correlates of Physical Attractiveness and Interpersonal Attraction in the Dating Situation." *Social Behavior and Personality* 1 (1973): 153–157.

Curran, J. P., and Lippold, S. "The Effects of Physical Attraction and Attitude Similarity on Dating Dyads." *Journal of Personality* 43 (1975): 528–539.

Dabbs, J. M., and Stokes, N. A. "Beauty Is Power: The Use of Space on the Sidewalk." *Sociometry* 38 (1975): 551–557.

Dannenmaier, W., and Thumin, F. "Authority Status as a Factor in Perceptual Distortion of Size." *Journal of Social Psychology* 63 (1964): 361–365.

Darden, E. "Masculinity-Femininity Body Rankings by Males and Females." *Journal of Psychology* 80 (1972): 205–212.

Darley, J. M., and Cooper, J. "The 'Clean Gene' Phenomenon: The Effect of Students' Appearance on Political Campaigning." *Journal of Applied Social Psychology* 2 (1972): 24–33.

Dibiase, W. J., and Hjelle, L. A. "Body-Image Stereotype and Body-Type Preferences Among Male College Students." *Perceptual and Motor Skills* 27 (1968): 1143–1146.

Dion, K. K. "Physical Attractiveness and Evaluation of Children's Transgressions." *Journal of Personality and Social Psychology* 24 (1972): 207–213.

Dion, K. K. "Young Children's Stereotyping of Facial Attractiveness." *Developmental Psychology* 9 (1973): 183–188.

Dion, K., and Berscheid, E. "Physical Attractiveness and Peer Perception Among Children." *Sociometry* 37 (1972): 1–12.

Dion, K., Berscheid, E., and Walster, E. "What Is Beautiful Is Good." *Journal of Personality and Social Psychology* 24 (1972): 285–290.

Douty, H. I. "Influence of Clothing on Perception of Persons." *Journal of Home Economics* 55 (1963): 197–202.

Efran, M. G. "The Effect of Physical Appearance on the Judgment of Guilt, Interpersonal Attraction and Severity of Recommended Punishment in a Simulated Jury Task." *Journal of Experimental Research in Personality* 8 (1974): 45–54.

Fisher, S. "Sex Differences in Body Perception." *Psychological Monographs* 78 (1964): No. 14 (Whole No. 591).

Flugel, J. *The Psychology of Clothes*. London: Hogarth Press, 1930.

Freedman, D. G. "The Survival Value of the Beard." *Psychology Today* 3 (1969): 36–39.

Friend, R. M., and Vinson, M. "Leaning Over Backwards: Jurors' Responses to Defendants' Attractiveness." *Journal of Communication* 24 (1974): 124–129.

Gibbins, K. "Communication Aspects of Women's Clothes and Their Relation to Fashionability." *British Journal of Social and Clinical Psychology* 8 (1969): 301–312.

Giles, H., and Chavasse, W. "Communication Length as a Function of Dress Style and Social Status." *Perceptual and Motor Skills* 40 (1975): 961–962.

The Effects of Physical Appearance and Dress on Human Communication

Goffman, E. *The Presentation of Self in Everyday Life,* Garden City, N.Y.: Doubleday, 1959.

Goldberg, P. A., Gottesdiener, N., and Abramson, P. R. "Another Put-down of Women?: Perceived Attractiveness as a Function of Support for the Feminist Movement." *Journal of Personality and Social Psychology* 32 (1975): 113–115.

Gorman, W. *Flavor, Taste and the Psychology of Smell.* Springfield, Ill.: Charles C Thomas, 1964.

Gottesfeld, M. "Body and Self-Cathexis of Super-obese Patients." *Journal of Psychonomic Research* 6 (1962): 177–183.

Green, W. P., and Giles, H. "Reactions to a Stranger as a Function of Dress Style: The Tie." *Perceptual and Motor Skills* 37 (1973): 676.

Gross, L. H. "Short, Dark and Almost Handsome." *Ms.,* June 1975, 33–34, 37–38.

Gurel, L., Wilbur, J. C., and Gurel, L. "Personality Correlates of Adolescent Clothing Styles." *Journal of Home Economics* 60 (1972): 42–47.

Hallpike, C. R. "Social Hair." *Man* 4 (1969): 256–264.

Hamid, P. "Some Effects of Dress Cues on Observational Accuracy, A Perceptual Estimate, and Impression Formation." *Journal of Social Psychology* 86 (1972): 279–289.

Hamid, P. N. "Styles of Dress as a Perceptual Cue in Impression Formation." *Perceptual and Motor Skills* 26 (1968): 904–906.

Hamilton, J., and Warden, J. "Student's Role in a High School Community and His Clothing Behavior." *Journal of Home Economics* 58 (1966): 789–791.

Harris, M. B., and Baudin, H. "The Language of Altruism: The Effects of Language, Dress, and Ethnic Group." *Journal of Social Psychology* 91 (1973): 37–41.

Harrison, A. "Exposure and Popularity." *Journal of Personality* 37 (1969): 359–377.

Hartmann, G. W. "Clothing: Personal Problem and Social Issue." *Journal of Home Economics* 41 (1949): 295–298.

Hendricks, S. H., Kelley, E. A., and Eicher, J. B. "Senior Girls' Appearance and Social Acceptance." *Journal of Home Economics* 60 (1968): 167–172.

Horai, J., Naccari, N., and Faloultah, E. "The Effects of Expertise and Physical Attractiveness upon Opinion Agreement and Liking." *Sociometry* 37 (1974): 601–606.

Hoult, R. "Experimental Measurement of Clothing as a Factor in Some Social Ratings of Selected American Men." *American Sociological Review* 19 (1954): 324–328.

Hunt, R. G., and Feldman, M. J. "Body Image and Ratings of Adjustment on Human Figure Drawings." *Journal of Clinical Psychology* 16 (1960): 35–38.

Hurlock, E. B. "Motivation in Fashion." *Archives of Psychology* 3 (1929).

Iliffe, A. H. "A Study of Preferences in Feminine Beauty." *British Journal of Psychology* 51 (1960): 267–273.

Jacobson, S. K., and Berger, C. R. "Communication and Justice: Defendant Attributes and Their Effects on the Severity of His Sentence." *Speech Monographs* 41 (1974): 282–286.

Jourard, S. M., and Secord, P. F. "Body-Cathexis and Personality." *British Journal of Psychology* 46 (1955): 130–138.

Jourard, S. M., and Secord, P. F. "Body-Cathexis and the Ideal Female Figure." *Journal of Abnormal and Social Psychology* 50 (1955): 243–246.

Kelley, J. "Dress as Non-verbal Communication." Paper presented to the Annual Conference of the American Association for Public Opinion Research, May 1969.

Kenny, C., and Fletcher, D. "Effects of Beardedness on Person Perception." *Perceptual and Motor Skills* 37 (1973): 413–414.

Keunaleguen, A. "Selected Perceptual and Personality Variables Related to Orientation to Clothing." *Perceptual and Motor Skills* 36 (1973): 843–848.

Kiesler, S. B., and Baral, R. L. "The Search for a Romantic Partner: The Effects of Self-Esteem and Physical Attractiveness on Romantic Behavior." In K. J. Gergen and D. Marlowe (eds.), *Personality and Social Behavior.* Reading, Mass.: Addison-Wesley, 1970. Pp. 155–165.

Kitson, H. D. "Height and Weight as Factors in Salesmanship." *Journal of Personnel Research* 1 (1922).

Kleck, R. E., Richardson, S. A., and Ronald, L. "Physical Appearance Cues and Interpersonal Attraction in Children." *Child Development* 45 (1974): 305–310.

Kleck, R., and Rubinstein, C. "Physical Attractiveness, Perceived Attitude Similarity and Interpersonal Attraction in an Opposite Sex Encounter." *Journal of Personality and Social Psychology* 31 (1975): 107–114.

Krebs, D., and Adinolfi, A. A. "Physical Attractiveness, Social Relations and Personality Style." *Journal of Personality and Social Psychology* 31 (1975): 245–253.

Kretschmer, E. *Physique and Character.* New York: Harcourt Brace Jovanovich, 1925.

Lambert, S. "Reactions to a Stranger as a Function of Style of Dress." *Perceptual and Motor Skills* 35 (1972): 711–712.

Landy, D., and Sigall, H. "Beauty Is Talent: Task Evaluation as a Function of the Performer's Physical Attractiveness." *Journal of Personality and Social Psychology* 29 (1974): 299–304.

Lavrakas, P. J. "Female Preferences for Male Physiques." *Journal of Research in Personality* 9 (1975): 324–334.

Lefkowitz, M., Blake, R., and Mouton, J. "Status Factors in Pedestrian Violation of Traffic Signals." *Journal of Abnormal and Social Psychology* 51 (1955): 704–706.

Lerner, R. M. "Some Female Stereotypes of Male Body Build–Behavior Relations." *Perceptual and Motor Skills* 28 (1969): 363–366.

Lerner, R. M., Karalnick, S. A., and Stuart, J. L. "Relations Among Physical Attractiveness, Body Attitudes, and Self Concept in Male and Female College Students." *Journal of Psychology* 85 (1973): 119–129.

Martin, J. G. "Racial Ethnocentrism and Judgment of Beauty." *Journal of Social Psychology* 63 (1964): 59–63.

McKeachie, W. "Lipstick as a Determiner of First Impressions of Personality: An Experiment for the General Psychology Course." *Journal of Social Psychology* 36 (1952): 241–244.

Mills, J., and Aronson, E. "Opinion Change as a Function of the Communicator's Attractiveness and Desire to Influence." *Journal of Personality and Social Psychology* 1 (1965): 73–77.

Moss, M. K., Miller, R., and Page, R. A. "The Effects of Racial Context on the Perception of Physical Attractiveness." *Sociometry* 38 (1975): 525–535.

Murstein, B. I. "Physical Attractiveness and Marital Choice." *Journal of Personality and Social Psychology* 23 (1972): 8–12.

Murstein, B. I., and Christy, P. "Physical Attractiveness and Marriage Adjustment in Middle-Aged Couples." *Journal of Personality and Social Psychology* 34 (1976): 537–542.

Murstein, B. I., Gadpaille, W. J., and Byrne, D. "What Makes People Sexually Appealing?" *Sexual Behavior* 1 (1971): 75–77.

Nemmeth, C., and Hyland, R. "A Simulated Jury Study: Characteristics of the Defendant and the Jurors." *Journal of Social Psychology* 90 (1973): 223–229.

Parnell, R. W. *Behavior and Physique: An Introduction to Practical and Applied Somatometry.* London: Edward Arnold, 1958.

Patterson, D. G., and Ludgate, K. E. "Blond and Brunette Traits." *Journal of Personnel Research* 1 (1922).

Perutz, K. *Beyond the Looking Glass: Life in the Beauty Culture.* London: Hodder and Stroughton, 1970.

Popplestone, J. A. "A Syllabus of the Exoskeletal Defenses." *Psychological Record* 13 (1963): 15–25.

Ray, W. S. "Judgments of Intelligence Based on Brief Observation of Physiognomy." *Psychological Reports* 13 (1958): 478.

Raymond, B., and Unger, R. "The Apparel Oft Proclaims the Man." *Journal of Social Psychology* 87 (1972): 75–82.

Reed, J. A. P. "Clothing: A Symbolic Indicator of the Self." Unpublished Ph.D. dissertation, Purdue University, 1973.

Roach, M. E., and Eicher, J. B. (eds.). *Dress, Adornment, and the Social Order*. New York: Wiley, 1965.

Robinson, D. E. "Style Changes: Cyclical, Inexorable, and Forseeable." *Harvard Business Review* 53 (1975): 121–131.

Rosencranz, M. L., "Clothing Symbolism." *Journal of Home Economics* 54 (1962): 18–22.

Rosenfeld, L. B. and Plax, T. G. "Clothing as Communication." *Journal of Communication* 27 (1977): 24–31.

Rosenthal, T. L., and White, G. M. "On the Importance of Hair in Student's Clinical Inferences." *Journal of Clinical Psychology* 28 (1972): 43–47.

Rudofsky, B. *The Unfashionable Human Body*. Garden City, N.Y.: Doubleday, 1971.

Rump, E. E., and Delin, P. S. "Differential Accuracy in the Status-Height Phenomenon and an Experimenter Effect." *Journal of Personality and Social Psychology* 28 (1973): 343–347.

Ryan, M. S. *Clothing: A Study in Human Behavior*. New York: Holt, Rinehart and Winston, 1966.

Salzman, L. "Psychodynamics of Seduction." *Sexual Behavior* 1 (1971): 57–62.

Schiavo, R. S., Sherlock, B., and Wicklund, G. "Effect of Attire on Obtaining Directions." *Psychological Reports* 34 (1974): 245–246.

Schwartz, J. "Men's Clothing and the Negro." *Phylon* 24 (1963): 224–231.

Secord, P. F., and Jourard, S. M. "The Appraisal of Body-Cathexis: Body-Cathexis and the Self." *Journal of Consulting Psychology* 17 (1953): 343–347.

Sheldon, W. H. *Atlas of Man: A Guide for Somatyping the Adult Male at All Ages*. New York: Harper and Row, 1954.

Sheldon, W. H. *The Varieties of Human Physique*. New York: Harper and Row, 1940.

Sheldon, W. H. *The Varieties of Temperament*. New York: Harper and Row, 1942.

Sigall, H., and Landy, D. "Radiating Beauty: Effects of Having a Physically Attractive Partner on Person Perception." *Journal of Personality and Social Psychology* 26 (1973): 218–223.

Sigall, H., and Ostrove, N. "Beautiful but Dangerous: Effects of Offender Attractiveness and Nature of the Crime on Juridic Judgment." *Journal of Personality and Social Psychology* 31 (1975): 410–414.

Silverman, I. "Physical Attractiveness and Courtship." *Sexual Behavior* 1 (1971): 22–25.

Singer, J. E. "The Use of Manipulative Strategies: Machiavellianism and Attractiveness." *Sociometry* 27 (1964): 128–151.

Singer, J. E., and Lamb, P. F. "Social Concern, Body Size, and Birth Order." *Journal of Social Psychology* 68 (1966): 143–151.

Singh, B. N. "A Study of Certain Personal Qualities as Preferred by College Students in Their Marital Partners." *Journal of Psychological Researches* 8 (1964): 37–48.

Smith, K., and Sines, J. O. "Demonstration of a Peculiar Odor in the Sweat of Schizophrenic Patients." *Archives of General Psychiatry* 2 (1960): 184–188.

Solender, E. "Attractiveness, Deception and Adjudication: Implications for Jury Decision-Making." Unpublished M.A. Thesis, Purdue University, 1975.

Solender, E. K., and Solender, E. "Minimizing the Effect of the Unattractive Client on the Jury: A Study of the Interaction of Physical Appearance with Assertions and Self-Experience References." *Human Rights* 5 (1976): 201–214.

Stephan, C. "Sex Prejudice in Jury Simulation." *Journal of Psychology* 88 (1974): 305–312.

Stewart, R. A., Tutton, S. J., and Steel, R. E. "Stereotyping and Personality: Sex Differences in Perception of Female Physiques." *Perceptual and Motor Skills* 36 (1973): 811–814.

Stroebe, W., et al. "Effects of Physical Attractiveness, Attitude Similarity and Sex on Various Aspects of Interpersonal Attraction." *Journal of Personality and Social Psychology* 18 (1971): 79–91.

Strongman, K. T. and Hart, C. J. "Stereotyped Reactions to Body Build." *Psychological Reports* 23 (1968): 1175–1178.

Suedfeld, P., Bochner, S., and Matas, C. "Petitioner's Attire and Petition Signing by Peace Demonstrators: A Field Experiment." *Journal of Applied Social Psychology* 1 (1971): 278–283.

Sugerman, A. A., and Haronian, F. "Body Type and Sophistication of Body Concept." *Journal of Personality* 32 (1964): 380–394.

Sybers, R., Roach, M. E. "Clothing and Human Behavior." *Journal of Home Economics* 54 (1962): 184–187.

Szzett, R., and Lefinski, W. "Group Discussion and the Influence of Defendant Characteristics in a Simulated Jury Setting." *Journal of Social Psychology* 93 (1974): 271–279.

Taylor, L. C. and Compton, N. H. "Personality Correlates of Dress Conformity." *Journal of Home Economics* 60 (1968): 653–656.

Thornton, G. "The Effect of Wearing Glasses upon Judgments of Personality Traits of Persons Seen Briefly." *Journal of Applied Psychology* 28 (1944): 203–207.

Unger, R., and Raymond, B. "External Criteria as Predictors of Values: The Importance of Race and Attire." *Journal of Social Psychology* 93 (1974): 295–296.

The Effects of Physical Appearance and Dress on Human Communication

Walker, R. N. "Body Build and Behavior in Young Children: II. Body Build and Parents' Ratings." *Child Development* 34 (1963): 1–23.

Walster, E., Aronson, V., Abrahams, D., and Rohmann, L. "Importance of Physical Attractiveness in Dating Behavior." *Journal of Personality and Social Psychology* 4 (1966): 508–516.

Warr, P. B., and Knapper, C. *The Perception of People and Events*. New York: Wiley, 1968.

Wells, W., and Siegel, B. "Stereotyped Somatypes." *Psychological Reports* 8 (1961): 77–78.

Widgery, R. N. "Sex of Receiver and Physical Attractiveness of Source as Determinants of Initial Credibility Perception." *Western Speech* 38 (1974): 13–17.

Widgery, R. N., and Webster, B. "The Effects of Physical Attractiveness upon Perceived Initial Credibility." *Michigan Speech Journal* 4 (1969): 9–15.

Wiener, H. "External Chemical Messengers: I. Emission and Reception in Man." *New York State Journal of Medicine* 66 (1966): 3153.

Wiggins, J. S., Wiggins, N., and Conger, J. C. "Correlates of Heterosexual Somatic Preference." *Journal of Personality and Social Psychology* 10 (1968): 82–90.

Wiggins, N., and Wiggins, J. S. "A Topological Analysis of Male Preferences for Female Body Types." *Multivariate Behavioral Research* 4 (1969): 89–102.

Wilson, G., and Nias, D. "Beauty Can't Be Beat." *Psychology Today* 10 (1976): 96–98, 103.

Wilson, P. R. "Perceptual Distortion of Height as a Function of Ascribed Academic Status." *Journal of Social Psychology* 74 (1968): 97–102.

6 The Effects of Physical Behavior on Human Communication

We respond to gestures with an extreme alertness and, one might almost say, in accordance with an elaborate and secret code that is written nowhere, known by none, and understood by all.
E. SAPIR

If someone asked you, "What does the word *model* mean?" you might very well reply that its meaning depends on the context in which it is used and the characteristics of the person interpreting its meaning. We have all heard the familiar admonition: "Meanings are in people, not in words." If someone asked you how to make the sound *l* you could legitimately reply that it would depend on the phonemic context. The *l* in *lit* is made differently from the *l* in *law*. Suppose someone asked you what a clenched fist, or a wink, means? We should apply the same reasoning to nonverbal body movements that we use with verbal behavior. Most body movements do not have precise social meanings. To say that a woman's crossed legs indicate she is sexually closing out those around her is just as dangerous as the assumption that the word *model* always means a small-scale replica of a larger project. Common meanings of words, as found in a variety of contexts, are studied, and individual differences are compared to these common usage patterns. Similarly, movements can be studied within a range of contexts to determine their usual meaning. The importance of considering the specific context and individuals involved in the study of body movements is clear, but not all the empirical research has operated on this assumption. In the interests of experimental control, some studies eliminate context and personality completely.

Before we look at these studies (both contextual and non-contextual)— before we ask what information, attitudes, and feelings are communicated through body movements, and how, we need some understanding of the component parts of the system we are observing. Some communication experts argue we can better understand verbal communication behavior if we begin by analyzing the verbal building blocks of spoken language. Ray Birdwhistell, whose life work has been describing the structural units of movement, would probably support a similar priority in studying nonverbal behavior.[1] To understand these descriptive units is to understand the basic building blocks of human body language. Some readers may find the following section somewhat more difficult than the work reported in other chapters, because it deals with seemingly minute and technical matters rather than broad behavioral manifestations. It is, however, an important ingredient of any treatment of nonverbal behavior because (1) it outlines the basic assumptions of the original work which tried to break the nonverbal code, and (2) it was, for many years, the most noteworthy theoretical construct available to researchers in this area.

The Linguistic-Kinesic Analogy

The description of behavioral units of body movement has largely been conducted in analogical terms—using verbal analogies to examine nonverbal behavior. The analogy is particularly useful in clarifying some of the very elementary units, and in reminding us of the interlocking nature of verbal and nonverbal systems. The difficulty with this analogy is most apparent when we attempt to identify nonverbal movement comparable to such things as grammar and syntax. The identification of these complex movement patterns—which may be similar to sentences, paragraphs, and their relation to one another—is the last and most difficult area to analyze, and, at present, information is not available on which we can base explicit analogical descriptions. Preliminary investigations do, however, suggest that there are at least some body movements which parallel a linguistic system built on formal rules of language.

What are some of the specific characteristics of the linguistic-kinesic analogy? Birdwhistell began his systematic empirical study of body motion in the early 1950s to determine the role of such movement in multichannel com-

[1]R. Birdwhistell, *Kinesics and Context* (Philadelphia: University of Pennsylvania Press, 1970).

The Effects of Physical Behavior on Human Communication

munication. He called this area *kinesics*. The analog of kinesics is *linguistics*. Just as there are subdivisions of linguistic study (descriptive and historical), there are also subdivisions of kinesic study (microkinesics, prekinesics, and social kinesics). While there is no kinesic analog to *historical linguistics*, such work will be plausible in future kinesic study—using the vast number of reels of films and video tapes currently capturing human body motions in a variety of contexts and in a variety of cultures. Microkinesics and prekinesics seem to parallel descriptive linguistics. Prekinesics deals with the physiological study of the limits of movement and the physiological determinants of movement; microkinesics deals with the derivation of units of movement. Social kinesics concerns the study of units and patterns of movement in context in order to determine their function in communication. Birdwhistell acknowledges that most of his work has been focused on middle-class Americans, and that specific findings will vary when analyzed in other cultures and subcultures. Like spoken language, body movements have dialects and regionalisms. Further, it is said we use only a small number of the total sounds and motions available to us. Our reading vocabulary is larger than our speaking vocabulary. Similarly, our awareness of visible movement and gestures is greater than our actual use of various movement patterns. Broadly, then, these represent some of the parallelisms or analogs between linguistic and kinesic systems:

The voice has intonations, qualifiers (intensity, pitch, height, and the like), qualities (tempo, resonance, pitch range, vocal lip control, and the like), which are designated *paralinguistic* phenomena. There are also parakinesic phenomena. These are motion qualifiers which serve to modify small stretches of kinesic behavior or activity modifiers which describe an entire body in motion. Illustrative parakinesic phenomena include (1) the degree of muscular tension involved in forming a movement pattern (intensity), (2) the length of time involved in a movement (duration), and (3) the extent of the movement (range).

Another parallel of linguistic to kinesic behavior concerns the smallest units of analysis. In vocal behavior, these are termed *allophones;* in kinesic behavior they are termed *allokines*. Allokines are the smallest structural building blocks of body language. To understand this concept, let us first examine the characteristics of allophones. Take, for instance, the *t* sound in the word *team*. Physically, there are many ways of making this sound—all slightly different from one another. Some speech scientists believe we never make exactly the same sound twice. Hence, all the minute variations which may exist in producing a specific sound (for example, the *t* in *team*) are allophones. Like the allophone, an allokine is the smallest and simplest unit of movement which can be discriminated as different from another movement. These are such minor differences that we rarely pay any attention to the possibility that they exist, because this

The Effects of Physical Behavior on Human Communication

198

does not have any bearing on how well we understand one another when communicating. Physiologists estimate the facial musculature is capable of producing some twenty thousand different facial expressions.

Rather than treat each individual allophone or allokine as a distinct and separate unit for analyzing linguistic or kinesic behavior, we must use a larger category which encompasses several allophones or allokines which are similar in nature. Otherwise, we might have an infinite number of categories for analyzing spoken and body language. These larger groups are called *phones* and *kines*. A phone, for example, is really a category of sounds which includes all the allophonic variations of a given sound—for example, the t sound in *team* is the phone which includes all the slight variations in making that sound; the t sound in *butter* is another phone and it includes all the slight variations in making *that* sound.

The t sounds in *team* and *butter* are two ways of forming the t sound. They are phones of the phoneme [t]. All the phones (with allophonic variations) go together to make up a *phoneme*. The relationships between allophones, phones, and phonemes are illustrated in Figure 6.1.

The two t phones can be used interchangeably within words without a change in meaning. Meaning is the feature that sounds of a phoneme have in common. For instance, there may be many ways to say the e sound in the word *pen*. When one stretches the acceptable sound range so the word is heard and interpreted as *pan* or *pin*, one moves into another phonemic unit. A *kineme* is similar to a phoneme because it consists of a group of movements which are not identical, but which may be used interchangeably without affecting social meaning. Birdwhistell once reported the observations of five nurses who picked out twenty-three different positions of the eyelids—or twenty-three kines. These same observers, however, agreed that only about four positions had differential meaning. While the human eye could note numerous distinct positions, only four made any major change in communicational meaning— the other positions were kines for the four kinemes.

Birdwhistell hypothesized that general American movement consists of ap-

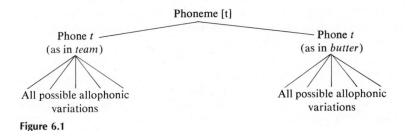

Figure 6.1

proximately fifty to sixty kinemes. About thirty-three of these have been isolated in the face and head area.

3 head nod kinemes (single nod, double nod, triple nod)
2 kinemes of lateral head sweeps (single sweep, double sweep)
1 kineme of head cock
1 kineme of head tilt
3 junctural or connective kinemes which use the entire head (1 of head raise and hold; 1 of head lower and hold; and 1 of head position hold)
4 kinemes of brow behavior (lifted brow, knit brow, lowered brow, and single brow movement)
4 kinemes of lid closure (over-open, slit, closed, squeezed)
4 kinemes of the nose (wrinkled nose, compressed nostrils, bilateral nostril flare, unilateral nostril flare)
7 kinemes (tentative) around the mouth (compressed lips, protruded lips, retracted lips, apically withdrawn lips, snarl, lax open mouth, and mouth over-open)
1 kineme of anterior chin thrust
1 kineme of puffed cheeks
1 kineme of sucked cheeks
1 kineme of lateral chin thrust

Phonemes rarely occur in isolation; the same is true of kinemes. A wink or gesture generally occurs as a part of a multimovement complex. Sequences of phonemes constitute words, and the minimum sequence of phonemes with communicational meaning is called a *morpheme*. The word *house* is monomorphemic while the word *unchildlike* is multimorphemic. As we noted earlier, it is believed that kinemes also combine to form *kinemorphemes;* the exact nature of these kinemorphemes is still under study. Several gestures performed in sequence may be put together in the form of a sentence or even a paragraph. A person makes a complex statement about his hostilities, Birdwhistell says, when he clenches his fist, scratches himself and rubs under his nose with his finger, because each of these gestures indicates a different aspect of his hostility. Birdwhistell notes some of these more complicated relationships when he says:

> These kinemes combine to form *kinemorphs,* which are further analyzable into *kinemorphemic classes* which behave like linguistic morphemes. These, analyzed, abstracted and combined in the full body behavioral stream, prove to form *complex kinemorphs* which may be analogically related to words. Finally, these are combined by syntactic arrangements, still only partially understood, into extended

The Effects of Physical Behavior on Human Communication

linked behavioral organizations, the *complex kinemorphic constructions,* which have many of the properties of the spoken syntactic sentence.[2]

Not everyone agrees with Birdwhistell that kinesics forms a communication system which is the same as spoken language. Dittmann presents a rather convincing argument that there are at least *some* very fundamental differences between the two systems.[3] He selects two criteria which linguists identify as necessary for classifying a communication system as a language: (1) that its smallest units be discrete and go together to form some sort of "alphabet," and (2) that there be rules to govern the organization of these small units into larger ones.

He then analyzed two gesture languages: American Sign Language (ASL) and Indian Sign Language (ISL). In both, but particularly in ASL, Dittmann finds that ideas are "boiled down, organized and presented in ways that both the signer and viewer have come to a tacit agreement about, so that when a string of signs comes along the two people can both know what the original idea was." His analysis of the research conducted on body movement forces him to conclude that very few of these movements meet the criteria for a body language similar to spoken language or even ASL. Most of our movements, Dittmann argues, serve more as cues from which we make inferences—rather than a formalized language code. Most movements seem to derive their organization from speech rhythm and the state of the person. And extended discourse in our everyday body movements which might parallel spoken language or ASL does not seem to occur. Dittmann concludes that there are many types of information in body movements:

1. There are some body movements which are discrete information sources. These behaviors form a category of movement and have meanings which are agreed upon by members of the language community. These behaviors would, indeed, be similar to what Birdwhistell calls "kinemes." Emblems are probably the best example of such behaviors, but Dittmann also suggests the possible inclusion of eye gaze, smiles, kinesic markers, head nods and shakes, arms akimbo, and open/closed positions of the arms and legs.

2. There are some body movements which may be discrete as performed, but which cannot be described as movement categories—and therefore are not similar to kinemes. He includes posture shifts and gesticulations which accompany speech as examples.

[2]R. Birdwhistell, "Communication Without Words," in P. Alexandre (ed.), *L'Aventure Humaine* (Paris: Société d'Etudes Litteraires et Artistiques, 1965), pp. 36–43.

[3]A. T. Dittmann, "Review of *Kinesics in Context,*" *Psychiatry* 34 (August 1971): 334–342. Also see A. T. Dittmann, "The Role of Body Movement in Communication," in A. W. Siegman and S. Feldstein (eds.), *Nonverbal Behavior and Communication* (Potomac, Md.: Lawrence Erlbaum Associates, 1977).

The Effects of Physical Behavior on Human Communication

3. There are other body movements which researchers appear to have measured in discrete categories, but which behaviorally seem to be continuous. Dittmann says these are "possibly discrete and categorical." Behavioral examples include all variations of posture and position such as forward and backward lean; distance between persons; and body orientation.

4. There are other movements of the body which are clearly continuous information sources. Adaptors such as rubbing your hands together are the clearest example. Other nondiscrete behavior may be the swinging of your foot while your legs are crossed or the tapping of your fingers or feet. Summarizing his analyses, Dittmann says:

> ... there is no evidence that movements are assembled into groupings based upon any set of rules internal to the movements themselves. There is evidence that there are groupings of movements, but the boundaries of these groups are determined by unit formation in the speech which is going on at the same time.
> ... the basic hypothesis of kinesics as a communication system with the same structure as spoken language is not a viable one.[4]

This book is not meant to explore in detail all the possible similarities and dissimilarities of the linguistic-kinesic analogy. Instead, this brief overview should serve as an introduction to one framework within which we can view the structural units of body language.

Now, let us turn our attention to the work of other researchers who have analyzed specific information, attitudes, and feelings communicated through body movements—generally using methods other than Birdwhistell's linguistic schema. First, we will return to the category system formulated by Ekman and Friesen and discussed in Chapter 1—that is, emblems, illustrators, regulators, and adaptors. Our discussion here will assume an understanding of the category descriptions found in Chapter 1. Facial expressions were also a part of this taxonomy, but this behavior is fully discussed in Chapter 8.

Emblems

Emblems are those nonverbal acts which have a specific verbal translation which is known by most members of a communicating group. Until now, few researchers have systematically investigated emblems. In Chapter 2 we reported a study of emblem usage by children.[5] Efron recorded a glossary of emblems for immigrant Italians and Jews in 1941.[6] Saitz and Cervenka have

[4]Dittmann, "Review of *Kinesics in Context.*"

[5]L. Kumin and M. Lazar, "Gestural Communication in Preschool Children," *Perceptual and Motor Skills* 38 (1974): 708–710.

[6]D. Efron, *Gesture and Environment* (New York: King's Crown Press, 1941).

also developed a list of American and Colombian emblems.[7] Some of the similarities between emblem usage in these two different cultures were reported to be the head nod for agreement, shaking one's fist for anger, clapping for approval, raising one's hand for attention, yawning for boredom, waving a hand during leave-taking, rubbing hands to indicate coldness, and the "thumbs down" gesture for disapproval.

Johnson, Ekman, and Friesen have initiated a systematic study of American emblems.[8] The authors do not claim to have identified a complete list of American emblems, but it is the most comprehensive effort available at the time of this writing. Respondents were asked to produce emblems which were associated with a list of verbal statements and phrases. To qualify as a "verified" emblem, at least 70 percent of the encoders had to perform the action in a similar way. The emblems which were similarly encoded (plus some added by the authors) were then presented to a group of decoders who were asked to identify the meaning of the gesture and the extent to which it reflected natural usage in everyday situations. Gestures used primarily for games like charades were generally not considered "natural." Criteria for the status of a "verified" American emblem required at least 70 percent of the decoders to match the encoder's meaning and judge it to be used naturally in everyday communication situations. The list of verified emblems from this study are presented in Table 6.1.

Illustrators and Other Body Movements Linked With Human Speech

Illustrators are those nonverbal acts which are intimately linked to spoken discourse. A few studies focusing specifically on illustrators were reviewed in Chapter 1. Our major concern in this chapter will be with a number of attempts to carefully scrutinize the patterns of movement co-occurring with various patterns of speech—that is, speech–body movement synchrony. Generally, this research has not separated gestures intentionally used to illustrate verbal behavior from other body movements. The findings, however, have obvious implications for studying illustrators and other movement categories. This research amply illustrates that movements are not produced randomly during the stream of speech; speech behavior and movement behavior are inextricably linked—part and parcel of the same system.

[7]R. Saitz and E. Cervenka, *Colombian and North American Gestures* (the Hague: Mouton Press, 1973).

[8]H. G. Johnson, P. Ekman, and W. V. Friesen, "Communicative Body Movements: American Emblems," *Semiotica* 15 (1975): 335–353.

The Effects of Physical Behavior on Human Communication

Table 6.1 Verified American Emblems (From H. G. Johnson, P. Ekman, and W. V. Friesen, "Communicative Body Movements: American Emblems," *Semiotica* 15 (1975): 335–353.)

Message Type	Encoded Message Meaning	Decoded Message Meaning	% Decoded Correctly	% Considered Natural Usage
Interpersonal Directions (Commands)	Sit down beside me	Sit down beside me	100	100
	Be silent, hush	Be silent, hush	100	100
	Come here	Come here	100	100
	I can't hear you	I can't hear you	100	100
	Wait—hold it	Wait—hold it	100	100
	I warn you	I warn you	100	94
	Get lost	*Get lost or get out or go away	100	93
	Be calm	Be calm	100	93
	Follow me	*Follow me or this way	100	88
	‡Time to go	*Time to go or what time is it	100	87
	Stop	*Stop or halt	100	81
	Go the other way	*Go the other way or no, not that way	96	96
	§I want to smoke and got a cigarette?	*I want to smoke or got a cigarette?	96	74
	Look!	*Look or I see something or look over there	91	100
	Go away	Go away or rejection or get out of here	91	96
	Take it away	*Take it away or go away or get out of here	90	87
	Go this way	*Go this way or over	89	86

	§Hurry and quickly	*Quickly or hurry or come here quickly	85	100
	‡What time is it?	*What time is it? or time to go	77	100
	Stay here	*Stay here or down here	77	100
Own Physical State	§I'm hot and it's hot	*I'm hot or hard work or a close shave	100	88
	§Hard work	*Hard work or I'm hot or a close shave	81	100
	§A close shave	*A close shave or I'm hot or hard work	81	100
	§It's cold and I'm cold	*It's cold or I'm cold	100	70
	I'm full of food	I'm full of food	93	93
	I've got a headache	I've got a headache	93	93
	I've got a toothache	I've got a toothache	87	87
	I've got an earache	I've got an earache	70	81
	Tastes good	Tastes good	93	70
	I am smart	I am smart	93	73
	How could I be so dumb?	How could I be so dumb?	100	95
Insults	†Fuck you (finger)	*Screw you or up yours or fuck you	100	100
	†Fuck you (arm)	*Fuck you or up yours or screw you	100	81

Table 6.1 Verified American Emblems (Continued)

Message Type	Encoded Message Meaning	Decoded Message Meaning	% Decoded Correctly	% Considered Natural Usage
	§The hell with you and rejection	*The hell with you or rejection	100	94
	§He's crazy and he's stupid	*He's crazy or he's stupid	100	75
	Shame on you	Shame on you	100	70
Replies	OK (fingers)	OK	100	100
	§No (head) and I disagree	*No or I disagree	100	100
	I don't know	I don't know	100	100
	§Yes and I agree and I like it	*Yes or I agree or I like it	100	100
	Absolutely no	*Absolutely no or no way	100	95
	I dislike it	*I dislike it or no way	100	93
	I promise	*I promise or cross my heart	100	74
	Absolutely yes	Absolutely yes	93	81
	§Hard to think about this and thinking	*Hard to think about this or puzzlement or thinking	89	100
	I doubt it	I doubt it	70	81
Own Affect	I'm angry	I'm angry	100	94
	§I'm disgusted and something stinks	*Something stinks	100	81

	I'm surprised	I'm surprised	95	88
	Whoopee!	*Whoopee! or hooray!	88	74
Greetings and Departures	Good-bye	Good-bye	94	100
	Hello	Hello	80	100
Physical Appearance of Person	§Woman and nice figure	*Woman or nice figure	100	100
Unclassified	You (finger point)	You	100	100
	Me (own chest)	Me	100	100
	Hitchhiking	Hitchhiking	100	94
	Counting	Counting	100	70
	Gossip	*Gossip or talk-talk-talk	96	91
	Fighting	Fighting	96	73
	§Peace and victory	*Peace or victory	94	87
	Good luck	Good luck	92	100
	Money	Money	92	79
	It's far away	*It's far away or over there	87	96
	Suicide (gun)	*Suicide or shoot myself	83	73
	Finished	*It's finished or that's enough	78	83

*Either decoded message was accepted, although the first message was given more often than the second.
§The same action was performed for each encoded message.
†Two different actions were performed as alternatives for the same message.
‡Two subtly different actions were performed for two subtly different messages.

207

Condon's analysis of interaction films shown in slow motion is one cornerstone of this body of information.[9] Condon and others believe normal human beings manifest a pattern of synchronous speech–body acts. This means that a change in one behavior (a body part, for instance) will coincide or be coordinated with the onset or change in another behavior (phonological segment or some other body part). Our head and eyes often mark spoken "sentences," a shift in posture may forecast a new topic or change in viewpoint, speaker gazes may coincide with grammatical pauses. Condon argues that a similar synchrony exists between two interactants. In some cases, this interactional synchrony may be imitative or a mirror image of the other's behavior. This is probably most evident at the beginning and end of utterances. Other researchers have shown how we tend to match the other person's utterance duration, loudness, precision of articulation, conversational latency, silence duration, and speech rate.[10] Sometimes our feedback in the form of facial expressions or head movements will also appear at specific junctures in the speech of the other person. Flora Davis described her reaction to one of Condon's films in this way:

> The third film clip Condon showed me was an example of heightened synchrony. A man and a woman—employer and job applicant—sat facing each other in a sequence that at normal speed seemed merely to involve rather a lot of shifting around, as the man first uncrossed and then recrossed his legs and the woman stirred in her chair. But when the film was run through a few frames at a time, their synchrony became clear. In the same frame, the two began to lean toward each other. They stopped at the same split second, both raised their heads, and then they swept backwards together into their chairs, stopping in the same frame. It was very like the elaborate courtship dances of some birds, or—in Condon's favorite analogy—they were like puppets moved by the same set of strings. Condon told me that this kind of heightened synchrony happens often between male and female. During courtship, it's one of the ways in which vast statements can be made between a man and a woman without a word being said.[11]

The implications of this research on speech–body movement synchrony may be far-reaching. Condon suggests that people suffering from various pathologies will manifest "out of sync" behavior; synchrony may assist in the identification of the quality of an ongoing relationship—for example, determining listening behavior, rapport, or the degree of intimate interpersonal knowl-

[9]W. S. Condon and W. D. Ogston, "Soundfilm Analysis of Normal and Pathological Behavior Patterns," *Journal of Nervous and Mental Disease* 143 (1966): 338-347. Also W. S. Condon and W. D. Ogston, "A Segmentation of Behavior," *Journal of Psychiatric Research* 5 (1967): 221-235.

[10]Some specific references to this work can be found in Chapter 10. Also see J. T. Webb, "Interview Synchrony: An Investigation of Two Speech Rate Measures," in A. W. Siegman and B. Pope (eds.) *Studies in Dyadic Communication* (Elmsford, N.Y.: Pergamon Press, 1972).

[11]F. Davis, *Inside Intuition* (New York: McGraw-Hill, 1971), p. 103.

The Effects of Physical Behavior on Human Communication

edge of the other person. It may even be a precursor of language learning. Condon and Sander found babies twelve-hours old whose head, hands, elbows, hips, and leg movements tended to correspond to the rhythms of human speech.[12] When the babies were exposed to disconnected speech or to plain tapping sounds, however, the rhythmic pattern was not observed. If this finding is validated by other researchers it may mean that an infant has participated in and laid the groundwork for various linguistic forms and structures long before formal language learning begins.

Kendon's detailed analysis of a single speaker confirmed the notion of self-synchrony and reveals some additional aspects of the relationship between speech and body movement.[13]We know, for instance, that there are different-size speech units which include small, frequently used syllables and larger, less frequent verbal "paragraphs." Kendon argues that there is also a hierarchy of body movements which act in conjunction with our speech behavior. He found that the wrist and fingers tended to change positions most often, followed by the forearm, then the upper arm; elements of the face generally changed more often than the head; trunk and lower limb movements were rare. The larger units of body movement were related to the larger units of speech; the smaller body units were related to the smaller verbal units.

Kendon also made some important observations on when movements occur in relation to the speech stream. There are some movements which accompany speech, but there are also many which precede speech units. The time between the speech preparatory body movement and the onset of speech is apparently related to the size of the impending speech unit—with earlier and more extensive behavior (more body parts involved) for larger speech units. A change in body posture, for instance, may precede a long utterance and be held for the duration of the utterance, but various arm movements are made during subparts of the long utterance. Like other researchers in this area, Kendon believes that the hierarchically structured body movements probably convey information about verbal structure and communicative involvement, that the positions of the head, limb, and body will sometimes forecast information to a listener, such as length of utterance, change in argument strategy or viewpoint and the like.

The work of Dittmann and his co-workers represents yet another approach to understanding the interrelationships between speech and body move-

[12]W. S. Condon and L. W. Sander, "Neonate Movement Is Synchronized with Adult Speech: Interactional Participation and Language Acquisition," *Science*, January 11, 1974, 99–101.

[13]A. Kendon, "Some Relationships Between Body Motion and Speech: An Analysis of an Example," in A. W. Siegman and B. Pope (eds.) *Studies in Dyadic Communication* (Elmsford, N.Y.: Pergamon Press, 1972). Also see A. Scheflen, *Communicational Structure: Analysis of a Psychotherapy Transaction* (Bloomington, Ind.: Indiana University Press, 1973).

The Effects of Physical Behavior on Human Communication

ments.[14] This research is based on the idea that some movements are so closely tied to the speech encoding process that they are virtually motor manifestations of that process. You can probably recall instances when you were trying to communicate an exciting idea, an idea which was difficult to conceptualize, or an idea that you felt was very important. In such cases you can get a "general feel" for the connections between the flow of your thoughts and the flow of your body movements. Dittmann's work provides us with some specific data regarding timing and location of body movements in the speech stream. He finds that movements tend to occur early in an encoding unit or following pauses in speech. He also provides further evidence of interactional synchrony. Listener responses in the form of vocalizations ("mm-hmm," "I see," and other comments), head nods, and movements of hands and feet tend to occur at the ends of rhythmical units of the talker's speech—that is, at pauses within phonemic clauses, but mainly at junctures between these clauses. There also seems to be a tendency for vocally stressed words to be accompanied by movements.

Birdwhistell's analysis of nonverbal activity which accompanies verbal behavior led him to postulate what he calls *kinesic markers*.[15] These nonverbal markers seemed to generally mark a specific oral language behavior. Markers seem to operate at several different levels. For instance, we might see an eyeblink at the beginning and end of some words; a microlateral head sweep may be seen during the expression of a compound word which we would originally hyphenate in the written form. Figure 6.2 shows head, hand, and eyelid markers occurring at the end of statements and questions. Similarly, after making a point the head may turn to one side, or tilt, or one may flex or extend his or her neck, signaling the transition to another point. Another level of markers is characterized by gross shifts in postural behavior—involving half the body—indicating or marking a sequence of points or point of view expressed by the speaker. One marker on this level is simply the shift from leaning back when listening to leaning forward when talking. Markers on the next level are frequently complete changes in location, following the presentation of one's total position during an interaction.

[14] A. T. Dittmann and L. G. Llewellyn, "The Phonemic Clause as a Unit of Speech Decoding," *Journal of Personality and Social Psychology* 6 (1967): 341-349; A. T. Dittmann and L. G. Llewellyn, "Relationship Between Vocalization and Head Nods as Listener Responses," *Journal of Personality and Social Psychology* 9 (1968): 79-84; A. T. Dittmann and L. G. Llewellyn, "Body Movement and Speech Rhythm in Social Conversation," *Journal of Personality and Social Psychology* 11 (1969): 98-106; and A. T. Dittmann, "The Body Movement—Speech Rhythm Relationship as a Cue to Speech Encoding," in A. W. Siegman and B. Pope (eds.), *Studies in Dyadic Communication* (Elmsford, N.Y.: Pergamon Press, 1972).

[15] R. L. Birdwhistell, "Some Relations Between American Kinesics and Spoken American English," in A. G. Smith (ed.), *Communication and Culture* (New York: Holt, Rinehart and Winston, 1966).

The Effects of Physical Behavior on Human Communication

Regulators

Regulators are nonverbal acts which maintain and regulate the back and forth nature of speaking and listening between two or more interactants. Regulators also play a prominent role in initiating and terminating conversations.

Greetings and Goodbyes. Greetings perform a regulatory function by signaling the beginning of interaction. Greetings also convey information about the relationship between the two communicators which helps structure the ensuing dialogue. Verbal and nonverbal behavior during greetings may signal status differences (subordinate/supervisor) and the degree of intimacy (acquaintance/lover). An emotionally charged greeting may reflect one's desired involvement with the other person or it may reflect a long absence of contact. Goffman proposed an "attenuation rule" which states that the expansiveness of a greeting with a particular person will gradually subside as you are continually brought into contact with that person, for example, a co-worker at an office.[16] Kendon and Ferber found the following six stages characterized greetings which were initiated from a distance:[17]

1. *Sighting, Orientation and Initiation of the Approach.*
2. *The Distant Salutation.* This is the "official ratification" that a greeting sequence has been initiated and who the participants are. A wave, smile, or call may be used for recognition. Two types of head movements were noted at this point. One, the head toss, is a fairly rapid back and forward tilting motion. Some people tended to lower their head, hold it for a while, then slowly raise it.
3. *The Head Dip.* This movement has been noted by researchers in other contexts as a marker for transitions between activities or shifts in psychological orientation. Interestingly, this movement was not observed by Kendon and Ferber if the greeter did not continue to approach his or her partner.
4. *Approach.* As the greeting parties continued to move toward each other, several behaviors were observed. Gazing behavior probably helped signal that the participants were cleared for talking. An aversion of this gaze was seen just prior to the close salutation stage, however. Grooming behavior and one or both arms moved in front of the body were also observed at this point.
5. *Final Approach.* Now the participants are less than ten feet from each

[16]E. Goffman, *Relations in Public* (New York: Basic Books, 1971) pp. 84-85.

[17]A. Kendon and A. Ferber, "A Description of Some Human Greetings," in R. P. Michael and J. H. Crook (eds.), *Comparative Ecology and Behaviour of Primates* (London: Academic Press, 1973).

other. Mutual gazing, smiling, and a positioning of the head not seen in the sequence thus far can be seen. The palms of the hands may also be turned toward the other person.

6. *Close Salutation*. As the participants negotiate a standing position, we will hear the more stereotyped, ritualistic verbalizations so characteristic of the greeting ceremony, for example, "Hi, Steve! How ya doin'?? and so on. If the situation calls for body contact (handshakes, embraces, and the like), it will occur at this time.

Our study of greeting behavior confirmed some of the observations of Kendon and Ferber.[18] The specific nature of greetings will vary according to the relationship between the communicators, the setting, and the attendant verbal behavior. Our major concern here is with the nonverbal behavior. The greetings we observed were frequently initiated by a vertical or sideways motion of the head accompanied by eye gaze. Smiles, regardless of the degree of acquaintanceship, were also common. Perhaps the smile serves the function of setting a positive, friendly initial mood. The eye gaze signals that the communication channels are open and an obligation to communicate exists. Other eye-related greeting behaviors included winks and the eyebrow flash (discussed in Chapter 2). The hands are often active in the greeting process with salutes, waves, handshakes,[19] handslaps, and various emblematic gestures such as the peace sign, the raised fist, or the "thumbs up" gesture. Hands may also be engaged in grooming—that is, running fingers through your hair. Touching may take the form of embraces, kisses, or hitting on the hands or arm. The mouth may smile or assume an oval shape, suggesting a possible readiness for talk.

Our analysis of everyday leave-taking situations prompted us to conclude that the rhetoric of good-bye serves three functions.[20] The primary regulatory function is signaling the end of the interaction—that is, immediate physical and/or vocal contact will soon be terminated. Again, specific nonverbal manifestations of these functions will vary with the relationship between the communicators, the preceding dialogue, body position (standing/sitting), the anticipated time of separation, and other factors. Decreasing eye gaze and positioning one's body toward the nearest exit were the two most frequent nonverbal behaviors observed in our study and seem to adequately signal impending absence. Leave-taking rituals also serve to summarize the substance of the

[18]P. D. Krivonos and M. L. Knapp, "Initiating Communication: What Do You Say When You Say Hello?" *Central States Speech Journal* 26 (1975): 115-125.

[19] For an interesting discussion of the handshake, see D. Schiffrin, "Handwork as Ceremony: The Case of the Handshake." *Semiotica* 12 (1974): 189-202.

[20] M. L. Knapp, R. P. Hart, G. W. Friedrich, and G. M. Shulman, "The Rhetoric of Goodbye: Verbal and Nonverbal Correlates of Human Leave-Taking," *Speech Monographs* 40 (1973): 182-198.

The Effects of Physical Behavior on Human Communication

discourse sometimes. This is usually done verbally, but a good-night kiss may sufficiently capture the evening's pleasantries to qualify as a summarizer. Finally, departures tend to signal supportiveness. Supportiveness tends to offset any negativity which might arise from encounter termination signals while simultaneously setting a positive mood for the next encounter—that is, our conversation has terminated but our relationship hasn't. Nonverbal supportiveness may be found in a smile, a handshake, a touch, head-nodding and forward body lean. Since signaling supportiveness seems so important we often use the more direct verbal signals—for example, "Thanks for your time. I'm glad we got a chance to talk."

Head-nodding and forward lean, of course, serve several functions at the same time. Rapid head-nodding toward the end of a conversation serves to reinforce the speaker for what he or she is saying, but it is a rather empty reinforcement since it also signals a desire to terminate the conversation. After all, if there is no apparent disagreement or lack of understanding, the speaker will feel no need to expand on his or her remarks. And, although it is true that people accompany their feelings of liking by sometimes leaning toward another person, it is also necessary to lean forward in order to stand up prior to exiting. So, like words, movements have multiple meanings and serve several functions.

Other nonverbal leave-taking included looking at one's watch; placing hands on thighs for leverage in getting up—which also signals the other person that the catapult is imminent; gathering one's possessions together in an orderly fashion; and accenting the departure ritual by nonvocal sounds, such as slapping your thighs as you rise, stomping the floor with your feet as you rise, or tapping a desk or wall with your knuckles or palm. Finally, we noticed that nearly all the nonverbal variables we studied tended to increase in frequency during the last minute of interaction—with a peak during the fifteen seconds just prior to standing. This increasing activity in at least ten body areas just prior to termination may suggest why we are so frustrated when our partings "fail"—that is, when our partner calls us back with "Oh, just one more thing. . . ." It means we have to go through the entire process of leave-taking again!

Turn-Taking in Conversations   Conversations begin and they are eventually terminated. Between these two points, however, it is necessary to exchange speaking and listening roles—that is, to take turns. Without much awareness for what we are doing, we use body movements, vocalizations, and some verbal behavior which often seems to accomplish this turn-taking with surprising efficiency. The act of smoothly exchanging speaking and listening turns is an extension of our discussion of interaction synchrony. And, since a number of the turn-taking cues are visual, it is understandable that we might

The Effects of Physical Behavior on Human Communication

have a harder time synchronizing our exchanges during telephone and intercom conversations.

Turn-taking behavior is not just an interesting curiosity of human behavior. We seem to make important judgments about others on the basis of how the turns are allocated and how smoothly exchanges are accomplished. Effective turn-taking may elicit the perception that you and your partner "really hit it off well" or that your partner is a very competent communicator; ineffective turn-taking may prompt evaluations of "rude" (too many interruptions) or "dominating" (not enough turn-yielding) or "frustrating" (unable to make an important point).

The turn-taking behaviors we are about to outline have generally been derived from analyses of adult white, middle and upper socioeconomic class interactants. Some of these behaviors and behavior sequences may not apply to other groups. LaFrance and Mayo, for instance, found black interactants gazed more while speaking while Caucasians gazed more while listening.[21] Other groups may develop speaking patterns with more unfilled pauses which may communicate turn-yielding to those unfamiliar with the group norm. Children who are learning turn-taking rules engage in behaviors we rarely see in adults, such as tugging at their parent's clothing and hand-raising to request a speaking turn.

Speakers engage in two turn-taking behaviors: (1) turn-yielding and (2) turn-maintaining; listeners also initiate two types of turn-taking behaviors: (1) turn-requesting and (2) turn-denying. The behaviors associated with these acts are derived from careful analyses of both audio and visual elements enacted at junctures where interactants exchange or maintain the speaking turn.[22] It should be noted, however, that a familiarity with the rules of interaction is also an important part of effective turn-taking—for example, before any specific turn-taking behaviors are observed, most people enter conversations with the knowledge that speaking roles will generally alternate in an *ababab* sequence and that when one person "finishes" an utterance, the other person is generally obligated to "take the conversational ball."

1. *Turn-Yielding.* To "yield" literally means that you are giving up your

[21]M. LaFrance and C. Mayo, "Racial Differences in Gaze Behavior During Conversations: Two Systematic Observational Studies," *Journal of Personality and Social Psychology* 33 (1976): 547–552.

[2]The turn-taking behaviors listed here were derived from many sources. For an examination of the foremost researcher in this area, see S. Duncan, Jr. "Interaction Units During Speaking Turns in Dyadic, Fact-to-Face Conversations," in A. Kendon, R. M. Harris, and M. R. Key (eds.), *Organization of Behavior in Face-to-Face Interaction* (Chicago: Aldine, 1975). Also See S. Duncan, Jr. and D. W. Fiske, *Face-to-Face Interaction: Research, Methods, and Theory* (Hillsdale, N.J.: Lawrence Erlbaum Associates, 1977). For a summary of a number of studies, see J. M. Wiemann and M. L. Knapp, "Turn-Taking in Conversations," *Journal of Communication* 25 (1975): 75–92. The vocal elements of turn-taking are treated more extensively in Chapter 10.

The Effects of Physical Behavior on Human Communication

turn and you expect the other person to start talking. Figure 6.2 shows how the termination of one's utterance can be communicated with kinesic markers which rise or fall with the speaker's pitch level. Questions are clearly an indication that a speaker yields his or her turn and expects the partner to respond. If it is a rhetorical question which the speaker plans to answer, we will probably see some turn-maintaining cues, but if the listener is eager to get into the conversation, he or she may attempt to answer even the rhetorical question. Vocally we can also indicate the end of our utterance by a decreased loudness, a slowed tempo, a drawl on the last syllable, or an utterance "trailer" such as "you know," "or something," or "but, uh." Naturally an extended unfilled pause is also used to signal turn-yielding. More often than not, however, the silence becomes awkward, and the speaker adds a trailer onto the utterance. Body movements which have been accompanying the speech may also be terminated—for example, illustrative gestures come to rest, body tenseness

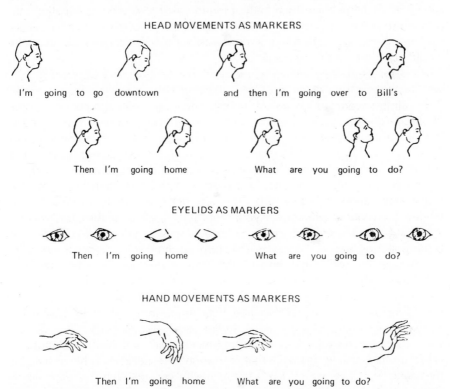

Figure 6.2 Some postural-kinesic markers of American syntactic sentences. [From A. E. Scheflen, "The Significance of Posture in Communication Systems," *Psychiatry* 27 (1964): 321. Used by permission of the author and publisher.]

The Effects of Physical Behavior on Human Communication

215

becomes relaxed. Gazing at the other person will also help to signal the end of your utterance. If the listener does not perceive these yielding cues (and gives no turn-denying cues), the speaker may try to convey more explicit cues, such as touching the other, raising and holding the eyebrows in expectation, or saying something like "Well?"

2. *Turn-Maintaining.* If, for some reason, you do not want to yield a speaking turn, several behaviors are likely to be seen. The voice loudness will probably increase as turn-requesting signals are perceived in the listener. Gestures will probably not come to rest at the end of verbal utterances, creating a gestural equivalent to the filled pause. Filled pauses will probably be increased while the frequency and duration of silent pauses will be decreased. This minimizes the opportunities for the other person to start speaking without interrupting or speaking simultaneously. Sometimes we see a light touching of the other person by the speaker which seems to say, "Hold on a little bit longer. I want to make a few more points and then you can talk." This touching is sometimes accompanied by a patting motion as if to sooth the impatient auditor. In some respects, this act of touching has the effect of the speaker putting his hand over the mouth of the auditor—an act which interpersonal etiquette would not allow in this society.

3. *Turn-Requesting.* When we do not have the floor and we want to talk, we may exhibit one or more of the following behaviors. An upraised index finger almost seems to symbolize an instrument for creating a conversational "hole" in the speaker's stream of words, but it also approximates a familiar formal turn-requesting signal learned in school—a raised hand. Sometimes this upraised index finger is accompanied by an audible inspiration of breath and a straightening and tightening of posture, signaling the imminence of talk. In some cases, certain self-adaptors classified as "preening" behavior may also signal preparation for a new role. The very act of simultaneous talking (extended interruption) will convey your request for a speaking turn, but to make sure that request is granted, you may have to speak louder than your partner, begin gesturing, and look away as if the turn was now yours. When the speaker and listener are well synchronized, the listener will anticipate the speaker's juncture for yielding and will prepare accordingly—getting the rhythm before the other person has stopped talking, much like a musician tapping a foot preceding his or her solo performance. If the requestor's rhythm does not fit the speakers, we might observe some stutter starts—for example, "I . . . I . . . I wa . . ." Sometimes the turn-requesting mechanism will consist of efforts to speed up the speaker, realizing that the sooner the speaker has his or her say, the sooner you'll get yours. This same behavior was noted in our leave-taking study when people were anxious to terminate the conversation. The most common method for encouraging the other person to finish quickly is the use of rapid head nods, often accompanied by verbalizations of pseudoagreement,

such as "yeah," "mm-hmm," and the like. The requestor hopes the speaker will perceive that these comments are given much too often and do not logically follow ideas expressed to be genuine signs of reinforcement.

4. *Turn-Denying.* There are instances when we receive turn-yielding cues from the speaker, but we do not want to talk. At such times we will probably maintain a relaxed listening pose, maintain silence or gaze intently at something in the surrounding environment. More often, we exhibit behavior which shows our continuing involvement in the content of the speaker's words, but denies that we are seeking a turn. This might take the form of smiling, nodding or shaking the head; completing a sentence started by the speaker; briefly restating what the speaker just said; briefly requesting clarification of the speaker's remarks; or showing approval by appropriately placed "mm-hmms," "Yeahs," or other noises such as the "clicking" sound which suggests, "You shouldn't have said that."

Nonverbal Audience Feedback. Another group of investigators have examined positive and negative nonverbal listener responses in the context of audience feedback to a speaker and its impact on the speaker's behavior. Although this ongoing audience feedback is primarily nonverbal, it is usually more subtle than most researchers have conceptualized it for experiments. When I sent students into the field to observe audience reactions, they were generally unable to find the extreme cases of continual head-nodding and shaking, smiling, eye gaze, frowning, note-taking, audible verbalizations of "good" or "no," and the like, which are so characteristic of the laboratory feedback studies.

There is evidence, however, that speakers can accurately perceive audience feedback and that it does affect their behavior. Certain individual predispositions, such as a high need for approval, however, may severely affect the accuracy of perceived feedback and/or the amount of behavioral change adopted as a result. Speaker fluency, utterance rate, length of speaking, voice loudness, heart rate, stage fright, eye gaze, and movement may all be affected by perceived positive or negative nonverbal audience feedback.[23] One study suggested that the sex of the person observing the feedback is not as crucial in accurately perceiving this feedback as the sex of the audience members.[24] Female audience members' attitudes were more accurately judged than males; highly ego-involved persons were also judged more accurately. Further evidence of sex differences was uncovered by Hackney.[25] His subjects produced

[23]J. C. Gardiner, "A Synthesis of Experimental Studies of Speech Communication Feedback," *Journal of Communication* 21 (1971): 17–35.

[24]J. Ayres, "Observers' Judgments of Audience Members' Attitudes," *Western Speech* 39 (1975): 40–50.

[25]H. Hackney, "Facial Gestures and Subject Expression of Feelings," *Journal of Counseling Psychology* 21 (1974): 173–178.

significantly more "feeling" responses and self-reference feeling responses when supportive feedback (head nods and smiles) was given by females to females. Similar feedback given by males to females did not increase the frequency of expressions of feeling.

Adaptors

Adaptors, as the term implies, are behavioral adaptations we make in response to certain learning situations—for example, to perform some bodily or instrumental action, learning to manage our emotions, learning to satisfy our needs, or learning to get along with other people. These behaviors (or some residue of them) seem to appear, then, in situations which the person feels approximate the conditions of the early learning experiences. Generally we are not aware of performing these behaviors, but frequent feedback may heighten our sensitivity—for example, "Stop picking your nose!" Although the research on adaptors is not extensive, there seems to be some consensus that adaptors are generally associated with negative feelings—for oneself or another person. There are also some useful classifications of different types of adaptors. These classifications include both the probable referent for the behavior (self, other, object) and the type of behavior (scratch, rub). Some attempts are now being made to link various adaptors to specific emotional or mood states. Most of the research has focused on self-adaptors.

Ekman and Friesen's examination of psychiatric patients and normal individuals finds that self-adaptors increase as a person's psychological discomfort and anxiety increase.[26] If, however, the anxiety level is too high, a person may "freeze" and engage in little movement at all. The finding that self-adaptors were also associated with guilt feelings in the patients studied illuminates one aspect of the deception research reviewed later in this chapter. Specifically, Ekman and Friesen discovered picking and scratching self-adaptors to be related to a person's hostility and suspiciousness. Theoretically, this picking and scratching is a manifestation of aggression against oneself or aggression felt for another person which is projected upon oneself. Other speculations and hypotheses about self-adaptors include the possibility that rubbing may be designed to give self-assurance, that covering one's eyes is associated with shame, and that self-grooming may show a concern for one's self-presentation.

Freedman and his colleagues have combined self and object adaptors into

[26]P. Ekman and W. V. Friesen, "Hand Movements," Journal of Communication 22 (1972): 353-374.

The Effects of Physical Behavior on Human Communication

218

one category called "body focused movements."[27] They do distinguish, however, between continuous hand-to-hand movements, continuous body-touching, and discrete body-touching. Discrete body-touching generally lasts less than three seconds and has a definite termination point, as in pulling down one's skirt. This research finds that covert hostility is associated with hand-to-hand movements—apparently acting as a substitute for what is not said. Further, Freedman says there may be a close link between body-touching and preoccupation with oneself, reduction of communicative intent, withdrawal from interaction, and a possible impoverishment of symbolic activity. Body-focused activity also seems to be manifested differently for people diagnosed as paranoid or depressed. In a ten-minute segment of an interview, depressed patients had a mean duration of continuous body-focused activity of 150.6 seconds, while paranoids showed only 41.2. Paranoids, however, had a mean of 154.4 seconds of hand-to-hand activity, while the depressed patients showed only 16.2 in this category.

In spite of some methodological problems associated with the work of Krout, it is significant that he identified over five thousand distinct hand gestures.[28] He asked his subjects personal questions designed to arouse different emotional and motivational states. Subjects were asked to delay their verbal response until Krout signaled them—the signal being given when a hand gesture appeared. He did not specifically label any of his hand movements as adaptors, but some of his hypotheses about certain regularities found in his study seem to have relevance—for example, fear being represented by hand-to-nose gestures; aggression being represented by fist gestures; shame represented by fingers at the lips; frustration represented by an open hand dangling between one's legs.

Sainesbury[29] and Dittmann[30] were not concerned with adaptors per se, but their work did show that high degrees of emotional arousal are associated with a lot of bodily movement. This movement may vary with the particular mood.

[27]N. Freedman, T. Blass, A. Rifkin, and F. Quitkin, "Body Movements and the Verbal Encoding of Aggressive Affect," *Journal of Personality and Social Psychology* 26 (1973): 72–85; N. Freedman, "The Analysis of Movement Behavior During the Clinical Interview," in A. W. Siegman and B. Pope, *Studies in Dyadic Communication* (Elmsford, N.Y.: Pergamon Press, 1972); N. Freedman and S. P. Hoffman, "Kinetic Behavior in Altered Clinical States: Approach to Objective Analysis of Motor Behavior During Clinical Interviews," *Perceptual and Motor Skills* 24 (1967); 527–539.

[28]M. Krout, "An Experimental Attempt to Determine the Significance of Unconscious Manual Symbolic Movements," *Journal of General Psychology* 51 (1954); 296–308. Also M. Krout, "An Experimental Attempt to Produce Unconscious Manual Symbolic Movements," *Journal of General Psychology* 51 (1954): 121–152.

[29]P. Sainesbury, "Gestural Movement During Psychiatric Interviews," *Psychosomatic Medicine* 17 (1955): 458–469.

[30]A. T. Dittmann, "The Relationship Between Body Movements and Moods in Interviews," *Journal of Consulting Psychology* 26 (1962): 480.

The Effects of Physical Behavior on Human Communication

For instance, Dittmann found the depressed mood indicated by fewer movements of the head and hands, but many leg movements.

Since our discussion of adaptors has proposed a number of relationships between various body movements and affective or mood states, we will conclude this section with Ekman's ideas regarding the type of emotional information carried by different body parts.[31] On the basis of his research, Ekman suggests that the head-face area carries information about the affect being experienced (anger, joy, and the like), while the body cues communicate primarily information about the intensity of the affective experience. Although some affect information may be communicated though bodily cues, it is probably infrequent and difficult for observers to perceive. More specifically, Ekman says facial expressions and body acts (movements of some duration) communicate specific emotional states, while body positions (nonmoving positions of some duration) and head orientations (tilts, leaning) may communicate gross affective states, but not specific emotions—usually. Body acts are capable of showing moderate to high intensity in the emotion while body positions portray a full range of intensity cues.

Communicating Attitudes, Status, and Deception Through Gestures, Postures, and Other Body Movements

Some of the investigations of body movements and posture have examined various communication outcomes rather than specific types of nonverbal behavior. Several specific types of behavior combine with each other to communicate a particular impression. We will be concerned with the following outcomes or communicative goals: (1) attitudes of liking/disliking; (2) status and power; and (3) deception.

We must remember that most of the body movements we are discussing are learned and vary from culture to culture. Efron, for instance, found that the sharp contrasts in gestural styles of Eastern European Jews and Southern Italians gradually disappeared and were assimilated into American gestural norms when these people emigrated to the U.S.[32] Hewes further emphasizes this point when he concludes that while over one thousand different steady postures are available to human beings (see Figure 6.3), the postural choices we make are

---

[31]P. Ekman, "Differential Communication of Affect by Head and Body Cues," *Journal of Personality and Social Psychology* 2 (1965): 726-735. Also P. Ekman, "Head and Body Cues in the Judgment of Emotion: A Reformulation," *Perceptual and Motor Skills* 24 (1967): 711-724.

[32]D. Efron, *Gesture and Environment* (New York: Kings's Crown Press, 1941).

The Effects of Physical Behavior on Human Communication

largely determined by cultural influences—for example, being punished for "poor" posture; nutrition; cold or wet ground which inhibits sitting; clothing; terrain; or house construction.[33] Thus, unless otherwise specified, our discussion of body movements should be considered culture specific—that is, primarily derived from and generalizable to adult, white middle and upper socioeconomic class people in the United States.

Attitudes. Body movements and attitudes have been studied in the context of liking or disliking toward another person. Mehrabian's work is one baseline from which to draw generalizations in this area.[34] First, he was interested in the degree of liking for the other person as related to general body orientation. Body orientation is the degree to which a communicator's shoulders and legs are turned in the direction of, rather than away from, the addressee. In measuring seated male communicators, he found no major difference except when they were interacting with a person they liked very much—revealing a less direct body orientation. Seated female communicators used very indirect body orientation with intensely disliked addressees, most direct with neutral addressees, and relatively direct with liked addressees. The slight decrease in directness of orientation of males and females toward intensely liked addressees may be explained by their tendency to assume a side-by-side position or very close proximity to one another. For standing communicators, body orientation did not seem to change significantly when people interacted with others who were extremely liked or extremely disliked. Another variable studied by Mehrabian concerned what he called the "accessibility of the body" or the openness of the arms and legs. He found no significant differences in the openness of arms and legs of communicators addressing persons they liked or disliked. However, when he posed models in varying degrees of openness (open, normal, closed) and asked subjects to infer the attitude of the model he found the following: (1) Male models displaying open postures were not perceived as communicating a more positive attitude by either males or females, while (2) females displaying openness of arms and legs, who were either younger or older than the subject (but not the same age) were perceived as communicating a more positive attitude. These findings on body accessibility do not show consistent correlates with attitude or degree of liking and were explained by Mehrabian in terms of relaxation.

> . . . an open arm position of seated communicators may more appropriately be considered an index of relaxation, with relatively more open positions indicating greater relaxation. In contrast, for standing communicators, a folded arm position

[33]G. W. Hewes, "The Anthropology of Posture," *Scientific American* 196 (1957): 123–132.
[34]For a summary of this work through 1972, see A. Mehrabian, *Nonverbal Communication* (Chicago: Aldine, 1972).

The Effects of Physical Behavior on Human Communication

POSTURE TYPES are shown in this sampling from the classification scheme of Hewes. The figures numbered 301 through 306 (*top row on this page*) are common resting positions; by contrast, the arm-on-shoulder postures of the next four figures are found mainly among western American Indians. In the next row are variations of the one-legged Nilotic stance, found in the Sudan, Venezuela and elsewhere. Chair-sitting (*third row*) spread from the ancient Near East, but the Arabs there have replaced it with floor-sitting

Figure 6.3

The Effects of Physical Behavior on Human Communication

postures (*fourth and fifth rows*). Sitting cross-legged (*top row on this page*) predominates south and east of Near Eastern influence. Sedentary kneeling postures (102 *to* 104) are typically Japanese; sitting with the legs folded to one side (106 *through* 108) is a femi-nine trait, a rare exception being the male Mohave Indians. The deep squat (*fourth row on this page*) is uncomfortable for adult Europeans but replaces the sitting posture for at least a fourth of mankind. The last two rows show various asymmetrical postures.

Figure 6.3 (Continued)

The Effects of Physical Behavior on Human Communication

may be more relaxed than one with the arms hanging. Given these considerations, then, the experimental data need to be reexamined in terms of degree of relaxation which can be inferred from arm or leg arrangement, rather than the accessibility they provide the body. Thus, for instance, although the folded arm position of seated females may be a more "proper" and tense position, that same closed arm position while standing may be considered a more relaxed position and may thus occur more with lower status addressees.[35]

The use of an arms-akimbo position by a standing communicator was also indicative of communicator attitude according to Mehrabian. The arms-akimbo position was used with greater frequency while interacting with disliked persons than with liked.

Two indices of relaxation (reclining and sideways-leaning angles) have also shown significant relations to attitude in Mehrabian's work. Seated male and female communicators both perceived a person leaning backward and away from them as having a more negative attitude than one who was leaning forward. When communicating with others, subjects did not demonstrate significantly different reclining angles for neutral or disliked addressees, but the angles decreased as their attitudes toward the addressee became more positive. Sideways-lean elicited different results from males and females. Males exhibited less sideways-lean and generally less body relaxation with intensely disliked males (not with females), whereas females exhibited most sideways-lean with intensely disliked male or female addressees. Thus, degree of relaxation is either very high or very low for a disliked addressee and moderate for a liked addressee. These sex differences suggest preferred modes of expressing dislike through variations in relaxation. Possibly males see a potential physical threat from disliked males and therefore assume a greater degree of body tension and vigilance.

Mehrabian and Williams found general support for their hypotheses that the degree of liking communicated nonverbally to an addressee is a direct correlate of the intended persuasiveness of a communicator and the perceived persuasiveness of his communication.[36]

In an attempt to broadly summarize Mehrabian's research, we would say that liking is distinguished from disliking by more forward lean, a closer proximity, more eye gaze, more openness of arms and body, more direct body orientation, more touching, postural relaxation, and more positive facial and vocal expressions.

Other investigators have explored similar liking/disliking behaviors under the labels of warm/cold. Reece and Whitman identified the body language

[35]A. Mehrabian, "Significance of Posture and Position in the Communication of Attitude and Status Relationships," Psychological Bulletin 71 (1969): 368.

[36]A. Mehrabian and M. Williams, "Nonverbal Concomitants of Perceived and Intended Persuasiveness." Journal of Personality and Social Psychology 13 (1969): 37–58.

The Effects of Physical Behavior on Human Communication

components which lead to being perceived as a "warm" person.[37] Warmth indicators included a shift of posture toward the other person, a smile, direct eye contact, and hands remaining still. A "cold" person looked around the room, slumped, drummed fingers, and did not smile. The warmth cues, coupled with the verbal reinforcer "mm-hmm," was effective for increasing verbal output (a particular kind of output) from the other person. The verbal reinforcer alone was not sufficient.

Clore and his colleagues collected a large number of verbal statements which described nonverbal liking and disliking.[38] These behaviors were limited to a female's actions toward a male. The large number of behavioral descriptions were narrowed down by asking people to rate the extent to which the behavior accurately conveyed liking or disliking. Table 6.2 lists (in order) the behaviors which were rated highest and lowest. An actress then portrayed these behaviors in an interaction with a male, and the interaction was video-taped. To no one's surprise, viewers of the tape felt the warm behaviors would elicit greater liking from the male addressee. The interesting aspect of these studies is what happened when viewers were exposed to a combined tape in which the actress' behavior was initially warm, then turned cold; or when her behavior was initially cold, then turned warm. The reactions to these video-tapes were compared with responses to video-tapes which showed totally warm or totally cold portrayals by the actress. People judged that the man on the video-tape would be more attracted to the woman who was cold at first and warm later than he would to the woman who was warm for the entire interaction. Further, people felt that the woman whose behavior turned from warm to cold was less attractive to the man than the woman who was cold during the entire interaction.

One contribution by Scheflen to the literature on interpersonal attitudes of liking and disliking is related to his observations related to American courtship patterns.[39] He made sound films of numerous therapeutic encounters, business meetings, and conferences. His content analysis of these films led him to conclude that there were consistent and patterned quasi-courtship behaviors exhibited in these settings. He then developed a set of classifications for such behaviors. *Courtship readiness* defines a category of behaviors characterized by constant manifestations of high muscle tone, reduced eye bagginess and

[37]M. Reece and R. Whitman, "Expressive Movements, Warmth, and Verbal Reinforcement," *Journal of Abnormal and Social Psychology* 64 (1962): 234–236.

[38]G. L. Clore, N. H. Wiggins, and S. Itkin, "Judging Attraction from Nonverbal Behavior: The Gain Phenomenon," *Journal of Consulting and Clinical Psychology* 43 (1975): 491–497; and G. L. Clore, N. H. Wiggins, and S. Itkin, "Gain and Loss in Attraction: Attributions from Nonverbal Behavior," *Journal of Personality and Social Psychology* 31 (1975): 706–712.

[39]A. E. Scheflen, "Quasi-Courtship Behavior in Psychotherapy," *Psychiatry* 28 (1965): 245–257.

The Effects of Physical Behavior on Human Communication

Table 6.2 Behaviors Rated as Warm and Cold (adapted from Clore, Wiggins, and Itkin, *Journal of Consulting and Clinical Psychology,* 1975)

Warm Behaviors	Cold Behaviors
Looks into his eyes	Gives a cold stare
Touches his hand	Sneers
Moves toward him	Gives a fake yawn
Smiles frequently	Frowns
Works her eyes from his head to his toes	Moves away from him
Has a happy face	Looks at the ceiling
Smiles with mouth open	Picks her teeth
Grins	Shakes her head negatively
Sits directly facing him	Cleans her fingernails
Nods head affirmatively	Looks away
Puckers her lips	Pouts
Licks her lips	Chain smokes
Raises her eyebrows	Cracks her fingers
Has eyes wide open	Looks around the room
Uses expressive hand gestures while speaking	Picks her hands
Gives fast glances	Plays with her hair's split ends
Stretches	Smells her hair

jowl sag, lessening of slouch and shoulder hunching, and decreasing belly sag. *Preening behavior* is exemplified by such things as stroking of the hair, rearrangement of makeup, glancing in the mirror, rearranging clothes in a sketchy fashion, leaving buttons open, adjusting suit coats, tugging at socks, and readjusting tie knots. *Positional cues* were reflected in seating arrangements which suggested, "We're not open to interaction with anyone else." Arms, legs, and torsos were arranged so as to inhibit others from entering the conversation. *Actions of appeal or invitation* included flirtatious glances, gaze-holding, rolling of the pelvis, crossing legs to expose a thigh, exhibiting wrist or palm, protruding the breasts, and others.

Others have discussed Scheflen's *positional cues* in terms of who is excluded and who is included. The positioning of the torsos and legs in Figure 6.4 clearly suggests, "We're not open to others" in (a) and "I'm with you—not him," (b).

Open and closed body positions may also help or hinder your ability to change another person's attitude.[40] Female communicators in open and closed

[40]H. McGinley, R. LeFevre, and P. McGinley, "The Influence of a Communicator's Body Position on Opinion Change in Others," *Journal of Personality and Social Psychology* 31 (1974): 686–690.

The Effects of Physical Behavior on Human Communication

Figure 6.4

body positions were viewed by other women whose attitudes were tested before and after exposure to the communicator. Open positions showed the communicator in various combinations of the following: leaning backward, legs stretched out, knees apart, one ankle crossed over the other knee, elbows away from her body, hands held outward, and arms held outward from her body—either directly at her side or elevated. Closed positions showed the communicator in some sort of combination of the following: elbows next to her body, arms crossed, hands folded in her lap, knees pressed together, feet together, and legs crossed at either knees or ankles. Women who saw the open persuader showed significantly more change toward the speaker's position and evaluated her more positively than did the women who viewed the closed speaker.

Rosenfeld designed an experiment in which female undergraduate students were trying either to win or avoid approval from other female students.[41] Smiles, head-nodding, and a generally higher level of gestural activity characterized the approval seekers. Rosenfeld, like Ekman, felt the larger amount of gestural activity gave information about the intensity of the affective state—approval seeking inducing more intense emotion. Although smiles and head nods have other meanings in other contexts, they seem to be nonverbal concomitants of approval seeking behavior.

Some believe people who have very similar attitudes will share a common interaction posture, while noncongruent postures may reflect attitudinal or relationship distance. There may, of course, be a number of other reasons for congruent or noncongruent postures—for example, relaxation postures. Therapists have reported the use of posture-matching to promote greater client-therapist rapport, and one study of counselor behavior did find that empathic responses were communicated primarily by nonverbal behaviors.[42]

[41]H. Rosenfeld, "Instrumental Affiliative Functions of Facial and Gestural Expressions," *Journal of Personality and Social Psychology* 4 (1966): 65–72.

[42]R. F. Haase and D. T. Tepper, "Nonverbal Components of Empathic Communication," *Journal of Counseling Psychology* 19 (1972): 417–424.

The Effects of Physical Behavior on Human Communication

Nonverbal signals used in this study included forward lean, direct body orientation, eye gaze, and a distance of seventy-two inches.

It should be clear by now that we do communicate interpersonal attitudes of liking and disliking through our body movements. Davis reports that in the trial of the Chicago Seven, defense attorney William Kunstler objected that Judge Julius Hoffman effectively communicated his attitude for all to see—leaning forward in an attentive position during the prosecutor's summation and leaning so far back that he almost seemed to be asleep during the concluding arguments of the defense.[43]

Status. Mehrabian's work also provides us with some information concerning the role of status in kinesic communication. For instance, in standing positions, shoulder orientation was found to be more direct with a high-status addressee than with a low-status addressee, regardless of attitude toward the addressee. The arms-akimbo position is more likely when you are talking to a person you see as having a lower status than your own. Mehrabian also found that his subjects would raise their heads more when speaking to a high-status person—especially male subjects speaking to high-status males. Observational evidence seems to confirm that those assuming inferior roles more often lower their heads, while those assuming superior roles more frequently keep their heads raised. Leg and hand relaxation was found to be greater for standing communicators communicating with lower-status addressees. Also, sideways-lean was greater when communicating with lower-status persons than with high-status persons. Goffman's observations of staff meetings in a psychiatric hospital confirm this finding.[44] Goffman noted that high-status individuals (psychiatrists) sat in relaxed postures, putting their feet on the table and lying slumped in their seats. Lower-status people more often sat formally, straight in their chairs.

To summarize Mehrabian's research on nonverbal indicators of status/power, we would say that high-status persons are associated with less eye gaze; postural relaxation; greater voice loudness; more frequent use of arms akimbo; dress ornamentation with power symbols; greater territorial access; more expansive movements and postures; greater height; and more distance. All of these characteristics are in the context of comparisons to lower-status behavior. It should be noted that the higher-status person will sometimes exhibit constant eye gaze (for example, to intimidate). Similarly, a lower-status person is often seen as "keeping distance" between him or herself and the higher status person, but this may be partly a result of the need for the higher-status person to maintain a large territory or to emphasize his or her prominence.

[43]Davis, *Inside Intuition*, p. 93.
[44]E. Goffman, *Encounters* (Indianapolis: Bobbs-Merrill) 1961.

The Effects of Physical Behavior on Human Communication

Henley reviewed literature pertaining to the verbal and nonverbal behavior of men and women and compared it to behavioral indicators of status and power.[45] The comparisons of the nonverbal behaviors are summarized in Table 6.3.

Deception and Leakage.　Freud once said, "He that has eyes to see and ears to hear may convince himself that no mortal can keep a secret. If his lips are silent, he chatters with his fingertips; betrayal oozes out of him at every pore."[46] An increasing number of researchers are exploring the specific nature of Freud's hypothesis—asking what particular nonverbal cues give a person away when he or she is trying to deceive someone. Unsystematic observations like the liar's "shifty eyes" are plentiful. The famous trial lawyer Louis Nizer suggests that jurors may associate deception with witnesses who (1) scissor their legs when asked certain questions, (2) look at the ceiling (as if for help), (3) pass their hands over their mouths before answering questions in a certain area—as if to say, "I wish I didn't have to say what I am about to say."[47]

Scholarly investigations have found a variety of nonverbal behaviors associated with liars rather than truthful communicators. According to these studies, liars will have a higher pitch;[48] less gaze duration and longer adaptor duration;[49] fewer illustrators (less enthusiastic), more hand-shrug emblems (uncertainty), more adaptors—particularly face play adaptors;[50] and less nodding, more speech errors, slower speaking rate and less-immediate positions relative to their partners.[51] Findings have not always been consistent, and researchers have used many methods of creating a deception situation to study. Furthermore, we don't know which, if any, of the cues just listed are used by observers when attempting to detect deception. We do know, however, that most studies show that untrained human observers can detect deceptive communications by strangers at about chance level—about 50 percent of the time.

Ekman and Friesen developed a theoretical framework regarding the manifestation of nonverbal signals relating to deception.[52] Attention was given

---

[45]N. M. Henley, *Body Politics: Power, Sex, and Nonverbal Communication* (Englewood Cliffs, N.J.: Prentice-Hall, 1977).

[46]S. Freud, "Fragment of an Analysis of a Case of Hysteria (1905)" *Collected Papers* Vol. 3 (New York: Basic Books, 1959).

[47]L. Nizer, *The Implosion Conspiracy* (Greenwich, Conn.: Fawcett, 1973), p. 16.

[48]P. Ekman, W. V. Friesen, and K. R. Scherer, "Body Movement and Voice Pitch in Deceptive Interaction," *Semiotica* 16 (1976): 23–27.

[49]M. L. Knapp, R. P. Hart, and H. S. Dennis, "An Exploration of Deception as a Communication Construct," *Human Communication Research* 1 (1974): 15–29.

[50]P. Ekman and W. V. Friesen, "Hand Movements," *Journal of Communication* 22 (1972): 353–374.

[51]A. Mehrabian, *Nonverbal Communication* (Chicago: Aldine Atherton, 1972).

[52]P. Ekman and W. V. Friesen, "Nonverbal Leakage and Clues to Deception," *Psychiatry* 32 (1969): 88–106.

The Effects of Physical Behavior on Human Communication

Table 6.3   Henley's Summary of Status and Power Gestures

Behavior	Between Status Equals		Between Status Nonequals		Between Men And Women	
	Intimate	Nonintimate	Used by Superior	Used by Subordinate	Used by Men	Used by Women
Posture	Relaxed	Tense (less relaxed)	Relaxed	Tense	Relaxed	Tense
Personal space	Closeness	Distance	Closeness (optional)	Distance	Closeness	Distance
Touching	Touch	Don't touch	Touch (optional)	Don't touch	Touch	Don't touch
Eye gaze	Establish	Avoid	Stare, ignore	Avert eyes, watch	Stare, ignore	Avert eyes, watch
Demeanor	Informal	Circumspect	Informal	Circumspect	Informal	Circumspect
Emotional expression	Show	Hide	Hide	Show	Hide	Show
Facial Expression	Smile*	Don't smile*	Don't smile	Smile	Don't smile	Smile

*Behavior not known.

particularly to the face, hands, and feet/legs since Ekman and Friesen felt posture was so easy to simulate it would not be a major source of leakage (revealing specific hidden information) or deception clues (revealing that a deception is taking place, without indicating specific information). Considering sending capacity, internal feedback, and external feedback, the face ranks highest on all three dimensions; hands next; and feet/legs last. The availability of leakage and deception clues reverses this pattern—the feet/legs being a good source of leakage and deception clues; hands next; and face last. It is reasoned that you will not expend much effort inhibiting or dissimulating with areas of the body largely ignored by others. Equally important, you cannot inhibit or dissimulate actions in areas of the body about which you have learned to disregard internal feedback, or about which you receive little external feedback.

Leakage and deception clues in the face generally come from microfacial movements (rarely observed in everyday conversation) and imperfectly performed simulations—the smile drawn out too long, the frown that is too severe.[53] Hands are easier to inhibit than the face because you can hide them from view without the hiding itself becoming a deception clue. Hands, however, may be digging into your cheek, tearing at your fingernails or protectively holding your knees while your face is smiling and pleasant. Leakage cues in the legs or feet might include aggressive footkicks, flirtatious leg displays, autoerotic or soothing leg squeezing, or abortive, restless flight movements. Deception clues might be tense leg positions, frequent shifts of leg posture, or restless or repetitive leg and foot acts. Obviously, failure to perform nonverbal acts which ordinarily accompany verbal acts is a sign something is wrong.

Ekman and Friesen, were not testing specific nonverbal behaviors in the preceding hypotheses, but they did obtain some interesting data on information communicated by different parts of one's body during deception. Observers watched films of patients who had previously been identified as engaging in deception. Some watched only the head and face; some only from the neck down; and some the entire body. The most dramatic results came from a patient who was withholding information about confusion, anxiety, and delusions—simulating well-being and health. Observers of only the head perceived the patient as cooperative, friendly, cheerful, sensitive, affectionate, appreciative, pleasant, warm, kind, talkative, considerate, good-natured, and honest. Those who saw only the body cues perceived the patient as tense, nervous, defensive, confused, cautious, and worrying. Those who saw the entire body saw the person as active, changeable, and alert.

[53]Ekman and Friesen elaborate on how people try to lie with their face and some sources of leakage which will help observers, such as, facial morphology, timing and location of the expression, and micromomentary expressions. Cf. Chapter 11, "Facial Deceit," in P. Ekman and W. V. Friesen, *Unmasking the Face* (Englewood Cliffs, N.J.: Prentice-Hall, 1975).

The Effects of Physical Behavior on Human Communication

Subsequent experimentation confirmed the idea that most people pay attention to their facial behavior when attempting to deceive another, but observers who were unfamiliar with the communicators could not isolate deceivers by examining body cues only—unless they were also exposed to the person's behavior under honest message-sending conditions.[54]

If you fail at deception because of nonverbal leakage or deception clues, it may be because of a conscious wish to be caught, secondary guilt, or shame or anxiety about engaging in deception or possibly about being discovered; or because you simply cannot monitor and disguise forms of behavior you do not have any feedback about and that you have learned most people will not attend to—forgetting that the slightest hint of deception will cause intense monitoring of these traditionally neglected areas.

At this point, let us reiterate an important point. The nonverbal behaviors associated with the areas surveyed in this chapter must be kept in a contextual perspective—that is, while a given configuration of nonverbal cues seems to convey the feeling of interpersonal warmth, the same configuration may take on a completely different meaning in a context in which the warmth behaviors are neutralized, added to, or canceled out by other factors.

Summary

This chapter dealt with the heart of human nonverbal study—the human body and the movement it makes during interpersonal contacts. Dozens of studies have been reviewed, summarized, and categorized. Any time we subdivide and categorize a complex set of behaviors, we should remember that behaviors are not, in actuality, seen alone—they work together and form clusters of cues. We should also remember that the meaning of these behaviors will ultimately be found in a specific context by the specific people in that context. This is not to say that a particular behavior may not be weighted more heavily than another in any given situation; it is simply a reminder to avoid oversimplification in analyzing nonverbal behavior.

What does the information in this chapter teach us? We know that in looking at body language, we are looking at a system which has some parallels to spoken language. Some of the elementary or basic "building blocks" of spoken language have parallels in body language. Whether the linguistic-

[54]P. Ekman and W. V. Friesen, "Detecting deception from the Body or Face," *Journal of Personality and Social Psychology* 29 (1974): 288–298.

The Effects of Physical Behavior on Human Communication

kinesic analogy can be carried through more complex dimensions such as grammar, paragraphs, and syntax, or whether we will need separate classifications for kinesic language, remains to be seen. Current evidence suggests kinesics is not a communication system with exactly the same structure as spoken language. Larger and smaller body movements do, however, seem to have a distinct relationship to correspondingly large and small speech units. Movements do not seem to be produced randomly—they are inextricably linked to human speech. From birth there seems to be an effort to synchronize speech and body movements, and adults have manifested both self-synchrony and interactional synchrony. People whose body movements and speech are out of sync may have some pathology; two people who are out of sync may not know each other well, or there may be an absence of listening behavior. Some of these body movements which accompany speech are made prior to the speech unit, some during, and some after. Dittmann's work showed that vocalizations, head nods and movements of the hands and feet of listeners tended to occur at the end of rhythmical units of the talker's speech—that is, at pauses within phonemic clauses, but mainly at the junctures between these clauses.

We also presented sixty-seven American emblems which have been verified. Regulators were discussed in the contexts of greetings and good-byes, conversational turn-taking, and nonverbal audience feedback. We found that head movements and eye behavior were central in initiating and terminating dialogue. Some of the body behaviors we examined seemed to serve several functions and carry the potential for several different meanings—within the greeting and departure rituals. The methods which we use to exchange speaking turns were analyzed as an extension of the concept of interactional synchrony. We noted how the speaker can yield or maintain his or her speaking turn through nonverbal behavior and how the listener can nonverbally request or deny a speaking turn. The research on adaptors generally suggested they were linked to negative feelings, anxiety, discomfort, covert hostility, preoccupation with self, and low involvement in the communicative event.

The last part of the chapter attempted to show how clusters of nonverbal behavior can help communicate several common and important ideas. Attitudes of liking and disliking were examined under several related labels: interpersonal warmth or coldness; approval seeking; quasi-courtship behavior; and open and closed positioning. We outlined a number of nonverbal behaviors which seem to be related to perceptions of status and power. Interestingly, Henley's analysis revealed that many of the behaviors associated with status and power were not used by or encouraged in women, but they were in men. We concluded the chapter with several nonverbal behaviors linked to deceivers and Ekman and Friesen's theoretical framework for studying deception.

The Effects of Physical Behavior on Human Communication

SELECTED BIBLIOGRAPHY

Allport, G. W., and Vernon, P. E. *Studies in Expressive Movement.* (Boston: Houghton Mifflin, 1933.

Argyle, M., Salter, V., Nicholson, H., Williams, M., and Burgess, P. "The Communication of Inferior and Superior Attitudes by Verbal and Non-verbal Signals." *British Journal of Social and Clinical Psychology* 9 (1970): 221–231.

Ayres, J. "Observers' Judgments of Audience Members' Attitudes." *Western Speech* 39 (1975): 40–50.

Baxter, J. C., Winters, E. P., and Hammer, R. E. "Gestural Behavior During a Brief Interview as a Function of Cognitive Variables." *Journal of Personality and Social Psychology* 8 (1968): 303–307.

Benthall, J., and Polhemus, T. *The Body as a Medium of Expression.* New York: E. P. Dutton, 1975.

Birdwhistell, R. L. "Background to Kinesics." *ETC* 13 (1955): 10–18.

Birdwhistell, R. L. *Introduction to Kinesics.* Louisville: University of Louisville Press, 1952. (Now available on microfilm only. Ann Arbor, Michigan: University Microfilms.)

Birdwhistell, R. L. "Kinesic Analysis in the Investigation of Emotions." In *Expression of the Emotions in Man.* P. Knapp (ed.), New York: International Universities Press, 1963. Pp. 123–139.

Birdwhistell, R. L. "Kinesics and Communication." In E. Carpenter and M. McLuhan (eds.), *Explorations in Communication.* New York: Beacon, 1960.

Birdwhistell, R. L. *Kinesics and Context.* Philadelphia: University of Pennsylvania Press, 1970.

Birdwhistell, R. L. "Some Body Motion Elements Accompanying Spoken American English." In L. Thayer (ed.) *Communication: Concepts and Perspectives.* Washington, D.C.: Spartan Books, 1967. Pp. 53–76.

Blass, T., Freedman, N. and Steingart, I. "Body Movement and Verbal Encoding in the Cogenitally Blind." *Perceptual and Motor Skills* 39 (1974): 279–293.

Blubaugh, J. A. "Effects of Positive and Negative Audience Feedback on Selected Variables of Speech Behavior." *Speech Monographs* 36 (1969): 131–137.

Brewer, W. D. "Patterns of Gesture Among the Levantine Arabs." *American Anthropologist* 53 (1951): 232–237.

Carmichael, L., Roberts, S., and Wessell, N. "A Study of the Judgment of Manual Expression as Presented in Still and Motion Pictures." *Journal of Social Psychology* 8 (1937): 115–142.

Charney, E. J. "Postural Configurations in Psychotherapy." *Psychosomatic Medicine* 28 (1966): 305–315.

Clore, G. L., Wiggins, N. H., and Itkin, S. "Gain and Loss in Attraction:

The Effects of Physical Behavior on Human Communication

234

Attributions from Nonverbal Behavior." *Journal of Personality and Social Psychology* 31 (1975): 706–712.

Clore, G. L. Wiggins, N. H., and Itkin, S. "Judging Attraction from Nonverbal Behavior: The Gain Phenomenon." *Journal of Consulting and Clinical Psychology* 43 (1975): 491–497.

Cohen, A. A. "The Communication Functions of Hand Illustrators." *Journal of Communication* (in press).

Cohen, A. A., and Harrison, R. P. "Intentionality in the Use of Hand Illustrators in Face-to-Face Communication Situations." *Journal of Personality and Social Psychology* 28 (1973): 276–279.

Condon, W. S., and Ogston, W. D. "A Segmentation of Behavior." *Journal of Psychiatric Research* 5 (1967): 221–235.

Condon, W. S., and Ogston, W. D. "Soundfilm Analysis of Normal and Pathological Behavior Patterns." *Journal of Nervous and Mental Disease* 143 (1966): 338–347.

Condon, W. S., and Ogston, W. D. "Speech and Body Motion Synchrony of the Speaker-Hearer." In D. L. Horton and J. J. Jenkins (eds.), *Perception of Language.* Columbus, O.: Merrill, 1971.

Condon, W. S., and Sander, L. W. "Neonate Movement is Synchronized with Adult Speech: Interactional Participation in Language Acquisition." *Science,* January 11, 1974, 99–101.

Corbin, E. "Muscle Action as Nonverbal and Preverbal Communication." *Psychoanalytic Quarterly* 31 (1962): 351–363.

Critchley, M. *The Language of Gesture.* London: Arnold, 1939.

Davis, F. *Inside Intuition.* New York: McGraw-Hill, 1971.

Deutsch, F. "Analysis of Postural Behavior." *Psychoanalytic Quarterly* 16 (1947): 195–213.

Dibner, A. "Cue-Counting: A Measure of Anxiety in Interviews." *Journal of Consulting Psychology* 20 (1956): 475–478.

Dickens, M., and Krueger, D. H. "Speakers' Accuracy in Identifying Immediate Audience Response During a Speech." *Speech Teacher* 18 (1969): 303–307.

Dittmann, A. T. "Review of *Kinesics in Context." Psychiatry* 34 (August, 1971): 334–342.

Dittmann, A. T. "The Body Movement-Speech Rhythm Relationship as a Cue to Speech Encoding." In A. W. Siegman and B. Pope (eds.) *Studies in Dyadic Communication.* New York: Pergamon Press, 1971.

Dittmann, A. T. "The Relationship Between Body Movements and Moods in Interviews." *Journal of Consulting Psychology* 26 (1962): 480.

Dittmann, A. T. "The Role of Body Movement in Communication. " In A. W. Siegman and S. Feldstein (eds.), *Nonverbal Behavior and Communication.* Potomac, Md.: Lawrence Erlbaum Associates, 1977.

The Effects of Physical Behavior on Human Communication

Dittmann, A. T., and Llewellyn, L. G. "Body Movement and Speech Rhythm in Social Conversation." *Journal of Personality and Social Psychology* 11 (1969): 98–106.

Dittmann, A. T., and Llewellyn, L. G. "Relationships Between Vocalizations and Head Nods as Listener Responses." *Journal of Personality and Social Psychology* 9 (1968): 79–84.

Dittmann, A. T., and Llewellyn, L. G. "The Phonemic Clause as a Unit of Speech Decoding." *Journal of Personality and Social Psychology* 6 (1967): 341–349.

Dittmann, A. T., Parloff, M. B., and Boomer, D. S. "Facial and Bodily Expression: A Study of Receptivity of Emotional Cues." *Psychiatry* 28 (1965): 239–244.

Duncan, S. "Interaction Units During Speaking Turns in Dyadic, Face-to-Face Conversations." In A. Kendon, R. M. Harris, and M. R. Key (eds.), *Organization of Behavior in Face-to-Face Interaction*. Chicago: Aldine, 1975.

Duncan, S. "Some Signals and Rules for Taking Speaking Turns in Conversations." *Journal of Personality and Social Psychology* 23 (1972): 283–292.

Duncan, S. "Toward a Grammar for Dyadic Conversation." *Semiotica* 9 (1973): 29–46.

Duncan, S. and Fiske, D. W. *Face-To-Face Interaction: Research, Methods, and Theory*. Hillsdale, N.J.: Lawrence Erlbaum Associates, 1977.

Duncan, S., and Niedereche, G. "On Signaling That It's your Turn to Speak." *Journal of Experimental Social Psychology* 10 (1974): 234–254.

Duvall, E. N. *Kinesiology: the Anatomy of Motion*. Englewood Cliffs, N.J.: Prentice-Hall, 1959.

Efron, D. *Gesture and Environment*. New York: King's Crown Press, 1941.

Ekman, P. "Body Position, Facial Expression, and Verbal Behavior During Interviews." *Journal of Abnormal and Social Psychology* 48 (1964): 295–301.

Ekman, P. "Communication Through Nonverbal Behavior: A Source of Information About an Interpersonal Relationship." In S. S. Tomkins and C. E. Izard (eds.), *Affect, Cognition and Personality*. New York: Springer 1965. Pp. 390–442.

Ekman, P. "Differential Communication of Affect by Head and Body Cues." *Journal of Personality and Social Psychology* 2 (1965): 726–735.

Ekman, P., and Friesen, W. V. "Detecting Deception from the Body or Face." *Journal of Personality and Social Psychology* 29 (1974): 288–298.

Ekman, P., and Friesen, W. V. "Hand Movements." *Journal of Communication* 22 (1972): 353–374.

Ekman, P., and Friesen, W. V. "Head and Body Cues in the Judgment of Emotion: A Reformulation." *Perceptual and Motor Skills* 24 (1967): 711–724.

Ekman, P., and Friesen, W. V. "Nonverbal Behavior and Psychopathology." In R. J. Friedman and M. M. Katz (eds.), *The Psychology of Depression: Contemporary Theory and Research.* Washington: Winston & Sons, 1974.

Ekman, P., and Friesen, W. V. "Nonverbal Leakage and Clues to Deception." *Psychiatry* 32 (1969): 88–106.

Ekman, P., and Friesen, W. V. "The Repertoire of Nonverbal Behavior: Categories, Origins, Usage, and Coding," *Semiotica* 1 (1969): 49–98.

Ekman, P., Friesen, W. V., and Scherer, K. R. "Body Movement and Voice Pitch in Deceptive Interaction." *Semiotica* 16 (1976): 23–27.

Freedman, N. "The Analysis of Movement Behavior During the Clinical Interview." In A. W. Siegman and B. Pope (eds.), *Studies in Dyadic Communication.* Elmsford, N.Y.: Pergamon Press, 1972.

Freedman, N., and Hoffman, S. "Kinetic Behavior in Altered Clinical States: Approach to Objective Analysis of Motor Behavior During Clinical Interviews." *Perceptual and Motor Skills* 24 (1967): 527–539.

Freedman, N., Blass, T., Rifkin, A., and Quitkin, F. "Body Movements and the Verbal Encoding of Aggressive Affect." *Journal of Personality and Social Psychology* 26 (1973): 72–85.

Fretz, B. R., "Postural Movements in a Counseling Dyad." *Journal of Counseling Psychology* 13 (1966): 335–343.

Frey, S. "Tonic Aspects of Behavior in Interaction." In A. Kendon, R. M. Harris, and M. R. Key (eds.), *Organization of Behavior in Face-to-Face Interaction.* Chicago: Aldine, 1975.

Gardiner, J. C. "A Synthesis of Experimental Studies of Speech Communication Feedback." *Journal of Communication* 21 (1971): 17–35.

Goffman, E. *Relations in Public.* New York: Basic Books, 1971.

Goldstein, I. B. "The Role of Muscle Tension in Personality Theory." *Psychological Bulletin* 61 (1964): 413–425.

Haase, R. F., and Tepper, D. T. "Nonverbal Components of Empathic Communication." *Journal of Counseling Psychology* 19 (1972): 417–424.

Hackney, H. "Facial Gestures and Subject Expression of Feelings." *Journal of Counseling Psychology* 21 (1974): 173–178.

Hamalian, L. "Communication by Gesture in the Middle East." *ETC* 22 (1965): 43–49.

Hayes, F. "Gestures: A Working Bibliography." *Southern Folklore Quarterly* 21 (1957): 218–317.

Henley, N. *Body Politics: Power, Sex, and Nonverbal Communication.* Englewood Cliffs, N.J.: Prentice-Hall, 1977.

Hewes, G. "Primate Communication and the Gestural Origin of Language." *Current Anthropology* 14 (1973): 1-2, 5-12.

Hewes, G. W. "The Anthropology of Posture." *Scientific American* 196 (1957): 123–132.

The Effects of Physical Behavior on Human Communication

237

Hoffman, S. P. "An Empirical Study of Representational Hand Movements." Unpublished Ph.D. dissertation, New York University, 1968.

Jacobson, R. "Motor Signs for 'Yes' and 'No.' " *Language in Society* 1 (1972): 91–96.

Jaffe, J., and Feldstein, S. *Rhythms of Dialogue.* New York: Academic Press, 1970.

James, W. "A Study of the Expression of Bodily Posture." *Journal of General Psychology* 7 (1932): 405–436.

Johnson, H. G., Ekman, P., and Friesen, W. V. "Communicative Body Movements: American Emblems." *Semiotica* 15 (1975): 335–353.

Jurich, A. P., and Jurich, J. A. "Correlations Among Nonverbal Expressions of Anxiety." *Psychological Reports* 24 (1974): 199–204.

Karns, C. F. "Speaker Behavior to Nonverbal Aversive Stimuli from the Audience." *Speech Monographs* 36 (1969): 26–30.

Kendon, A. "Gesticulation, Speech and the Gesture Theory of Language Origins," *Sign Language Studies* 9 (1975), 349–373.

Kendon, A. "Movement Coordination in Social Interaction: Some Examples Described." *Acta Psychologica* 32 (1970): 101–125.

Kendon, A. "Review of Birdwhistell: *Kinesics and Context.*" *American Journal of Psychology* 85 (1972): 441–456.

Kendon, A. "Some Relationships Between Body Motion and Speech." In A. W. Siegman and B. Pope (eds.), *Studies in Dyadic Communication.* New York: Pergamon Press, 1971.

Kendon, A., and Ferber, A. "A Description of Some Human Greetings." In R. P. Michael and J. H. Crook (eds.), *Comparative Ecology and Behaviour of Primates.* (London: Academic Press, 1973.

Kendon, A., Harris, R. M., and Key, M. R. (eds.). *Organization of Behavior in Face-to-Face Interaction.* Chicago: Aldine, 1975.

Kimura, D. "Manual Activity During Speaking: 1. Right-Handers." *Neuropsychologia* 11 (1973): 45–50. Also see pp. 51-55 of the same issue for an analysis of left-handers.

Knapp, M. L., Hart, R. P., and Dennis, H. S. "An Exploration of Deception as a Communication Construct." *Human Communication Research* 1 (1974) 15–29.

Knapp, M. L., Hart, R. P., Friedrich, G. W., and Shulman, G. M. "The Rhetoric of Goodbye: Verbal and Nonverbal Correlates of Human Leave-Taking." *Speech Monographs* 40 (1973): 182–198.

Knapp, R. H. "The Language of Postural Interpretation." *Journal of Social Psychology* 67 (1965): 371–377.

Krivonos, P. D., and Knapp, M. L. "Initiating Communication: What Do You Say When You Say Hello?" *Central States Speech Journal* 26 (1975): 115–125.

Krout, M. "An Experimental Attempt to Determine the Significance of Unconscious Manual Symbolic Movements." *Journal of General Psychology* 51 (1954): 121–152.

Krout, M. "An Experimental Attempt to Produce Unconscious Manual Symbolic Movements." *Journal of General Psychology* 51 (1954): 93–120.

LaBarre, W. "Paralinguistics, Kinesics, and Cultural Anthropology." In T. A. Sebeok, A. S. Hayes, and M. C. Bateson (eds.), The Hague: Mouton, 1964. Pp. 191–220.

LaBarre, W. "The Cultural Basis of Emotions and Gestures." *Journal of Personality* 16 (1947): 49–68.

LaFrance, M., and Mayo, C. "Racial Differences in Gaze Behavior During Conversations: Two Systematic Observational Studies." *Journal of Personality and Social Psychology* 33 (1976): 547–552.

Lamb, W. *Posture and Gesture.* London: Gerard Duckworth and Co., 1965.

Laver, J. "Communicative Functions of Phatic Communion." In A. Kendon, R. M. Harris, and M. R. Key (eds.), *Organization of Behavior in Face-to-Face Interaction.* Chicago: Aldine, 1975.

Loeb, F. F., Jr. "The Fist: The Microscopic Film Analysis of the Function of a Recurrent Behavioral Pattern in a Psychotherapeutic Session." *Journal of Nervous and Mental Disease* 147 (1968): 605–618.

Mahl, G. F. "Gestures and Body Movements in Interviews." In J. Shlien (ed.), *Research in Psychotherapy*, Vol. 3. Washington: American Psychological Association, 1968.

Mahl, G., Danet, B., and Norton, N. "Reflection of Major Personality Characteristics in Gestures and Body Movements." *American Psychologist* 7 (1959): 357.

Mallery, G. "Sign Language Among North American Indians." *First Annual Report of the Bureau of American Ethnology.* Washington: U.S. Government Printing Office, 1881. Pp. 263–552. Republished by Mouton Press, The Hague, 1972.

Markel, N. N. "Coverbal Behavior Associated with Conversation Turns." In A. Kendon, R. M. Harris, and M. R. Key (eds.), *Organization of Behavior in Face-to-Face Interaction.* Chicago: Aldine, 1975.

McGinley, H., LeFevre, R., and McGinley, P. "The Influence of a Communicator's Body Position on Opinion Change in Others." *Journal of Personality and Social Psychology* 31 (1974): 686–690.

Mehrabian, A. "Inference of Attitude from the Posture, Orientation and Distance of a Communicator." *Journal of Consulting and Clinical Psychology* 32 (1968): 296–308.

Mehrabian, A. *Nonverbal Communication.* Chicago: Aldine, 1972.

Mehrabian, A. "Orientation Behaviors and Nonverbal Attitude Communication." *Journal of Comunication* 17 (1967): 324–332.

The Effects of Physical Behavior on Human Communication

239

Mehrabian, A. "Relationship of Attitude to Seated Posture, Orientation, and Distance." *Journal of Personality and Social Psychology* 10 (1968): 26–30.

Mehrabian, A. "Significance of Posture and Position in the Communication of Attitude and Status Relationships." *Psychological Bulletin* 71 (1969): 359–372.

Mehrabian, A., and Williams, M. "Nonverbal Concomitants of Perceived and Intended Persuasiveness." *Journal of Personality and Social Psychology* 13 (1969): 37–58.

Pike, K. "On Kinesic Triadic Relations in Turn-Taking." *Semiotica* 13 (1975): 389–394.

Raskin, A. "Observable Signs of Anxiety or Distress During Psychotherapy." *Journal of Consulting Psychology* 26 (1962): 389.

Reece, M., and Whitman, R. "Expressive Movements, Warmth, and Verbal Reinforcement." *Journal of Abnormal and Social Psychology* 64 (1962): 234–236.

Rosenberg, B. G., and Langer, J. "A Study of Postural–Gestural Communication." *Journal of Personality and Social Psychology* 2 (1965): 593–597.

Rosenfeld, H. M. "Approval-Seeking and Approval-Inducing Functions of Verbal and Nonverbal Repsonses in the Dyad." *Journal of Personality and Social Psychology* 4 (1966): 597–605.

Rosenfeld, H. "Instrumental Affiliative Functions of Facial and Gestural Expressions." *Journal of Personality and Social Psychology* 4 (1966): 65–72.

Rosenfeld, H. M. "Nonverbal Reciprocation of Approval: An Experimental Analysis." *Journal of Experimental Social Psychology* 3 (1967): 102–111.

Sainesbury, P. "Gestural Movement During Psychiatric Interviews." *Psychosomatic Medicine* 17 (1955): 458–469.

Saitz, R. L., and Cervenka, E. J. *Columbian and North American Gestures.* The Hague: Mouton Press, 1973.

Scheflen, A. E. "Communication and Regulation in Psychotherapy." *Psychiatry* 27 (1964): 126–136.

Scheflen, A. *Communicational Structure: Analysis of a Psychotherapy Transaction.* Bloomington, Ind.: University of Indiana Press, 1973.

Scheflen, A. E. "Quasi-Courtship Behavior in Psychotherapy." *Psychiatry* 28 (1965): 245–257.

Scheflen, A. E. "The Significance of Posture in Communicative Systems." *Psychiatry* 27 (1964): 316–331.

Scheflen, A. E., and Scheflen, A. *Body Language and the Social Order.* Englewood Cliffs, N.J.: Prentice-Hall, 1972.

Schiffrin, D. "Handwork as Ceremony: The Case of the Handshake." *Semiotica* 12 (1974): 189–202.

Siegman, A. W., and Pope, B. (eds.). *Studies in Dyadic Communication.* Elmsford, N.Y.: Pergamon Press, 1972.

Spiegel, P., and Machotka, P. *Messages of the Body*. New York: Free Press, 1974.

Stokoe, W. C. "Face-to-Face Interaction: Signs to Language." In A. Kendon, R. M. Harris, and M. R. Key (eds.), *Organization of Behavior in Face-to-Face Interaction*. Chicago: Aldine, 1975.

Stokoe, W. "Motor Signs as the First Form of Language." *Semiotica* 10 (1974): 117–130.

Stokoe, W. C. *Semiotics and Human Sign Languages*. The Hague: Mouton, 1972.

Trevoort, B. "Could There Be a Human Sign Language." *Semiotica* 9 (1974): 347–382.

Wachtel, P. L. "An Approach to the Study of Body Language in Psychotherapy," *Psychotherapy: Theory, Research & Practice* 4 (1967): 97–100.

Wallach, M. A., and Gahm, R. C. "Personality Functions of Graphic Constriction and Expansiveness." *Journal of Personality* 28 (1960): 73–88.

Webb, J. T. "Interview Synchrony: An Investigation of Two Speech Rate Measures." In A. W. Siegman and B. Pope (eds.), *Studies in Diadic Communication*. Elmsford, N.Y.: Pergamon Press, 1972.

Wiemann, J. M., and Knapp, M. L. "Turn-Taking in Conversations." *Journal of Communication* 25 (1975): 75–92.

Wolff, C. *A Psychology of Gesture*. London: Methuen, 1945.

Wolff, P., and Gustein, J. "Effects of Induced Motor Gestures on Vocal Output." *Journal of Communication* 22 (1972): 277–288.

Wundt, W. *The Language of Gestures*. The Hague: Mouton, 1973.

Yngve, V. H. "On Getting a Word in Edgewise." In M. A. Campbell et al. (eds.), *Papers from the Sixth Regional Meeting, Chicago Linguistics Society*. Chicago: Department of Linguistics, University of Chicago, 1970.

7 The Effects of Touching Behavior on Human Communication

We often talk about the way we talk, and we frequently try to see the way we see, but for some reason we have rarely touched on the way we touch.

D. MORRIS

The scene is a university library. It could just as easily be the local supermarket, bank, or restaurant. What happens takes about half a second, and it is not noticed by the recipients. Remarkably, however, this act apparently affects their evaluation of their experience in the library. Let's begin at the beginning. Researchers at Purdue University wanted to systematically investigate the effects of a brief, "accidental" touch in a nonintimate context.[1] They had male and female clerks return library cards to some students by placing their hand directly over the other's palm, making physical contact; other students were not touched. Outside the library students were given instruments to measure their feelings toward the library clerk and the library in general. Students who were touched—especially the females—evaluated the clerk and the library significantly more favorably than those who weren't touched. This was

[1] J. D. Fisher, M. Rytting, and R. Heslin, "Hands Touching Hands: Affective and Evaluative Effects of an Interpersonal Touch," *Sociometry* 39 (1976): 416–421.

true for both students who were aware of being touched and those who weren't. Obviously, the clerks may have been doing other things when they touched (for example, smiling), even though they were trained to maintain consistent behaviors for all students. So we know touch was influential, but it may have worked in conjunction with other aspects of the setting, the relationship to the other, experiences with touch, other behaviors, and so on.

Another study suggests some people may prefer touch over verbal and visual communication.[2] Subjects interacted with what they thought were three different people under three different conditions. Actually, they were interacting with the same person each time. The three situations included touch only (no talking, blindfolded); visual only (no talking, not blindfolded, no touching); and verbal only (no touching, blindfolded). After the interaction was finished, subjects picked adjectives which they felt were most descriptive of their encounters under each condition. The touch-only encounter was described as "trustful, sensitive, natural, mature, serious, and warm." The verbal encounter was described as "distant, noncommunicative, artificial, insensitive, and formal." The visual condition was labeled "artificial, childish, arrogant, comic, and cold." Each subject was then asked which of the three persons with whom they had communicated they would select as a partner for future interactions. The person encountered by touch only was chosen by 47 percent of the subjects. Although there are some major shortcomings in this study, it is reported here because it is one of the few attempts to empirically test the effects of tactile communication in a social situation. Most data on the effects of touch behavior consist of testimonials from participants in various personal-growth workshops and encounter groups. While such information provides a useful foundation, it severely limits any generalizations we can make for larger segments of the population.

Touch is a crucial aspect of most human relationships. It plays a part in giving encouragement, expressing tenderness, showing emotional support, and many other things. The growth of body-awareness and personal-growth workshops testifies that many Americans feel a need to rediscover communication through touch. These workshops encourage physical contact as a way of breaking through some psychological barriers. People try to become more aware of themselves, other people, and the world around them through physical experiences rather than through words or sight. It is, as some say, a widespread movement reflecting a yearning for human contact. It may also be a movement to restore some unfilled tactile needs. As Montagu says:

> When affection and involvement are conveyed through touch, it is those meanings as well as the security-giving satisfactions, with which touch will become

[2]J. P. Bardeen, "Interpersonal Perception Through the Tactile, Verbal, and Visual Modes," paper presented at the convention of the International Communication Association, Phoenix, 1971.

The Effects of Touching Behavior on Human Communication

associated. Inadequate tactile experience will result in a lack of such associations and a consequent inability to relate to others in many fundamental human ways.[3]

Perhaps the most dramatic testimony to the communicative potential of touch comes from the blind. Helen Keller's diary tells of an incident when she was touching her dog: "He was rolling on the grass . . . his fat body revolved, stiffened and solidified into an upright position, and his tongue gave my hand a lick. . . . If he could speak, I believe he would say with me that paradise is attained by touch."

Obviously, the act of touching is like any other message we communicate—it may elicit negative reactions as well as positive ones depending on the configuration of people and circumstances. We would, then, be very careful about the extent to which we generalize the findings from the two studies discussed above. We know that sometimes people get "uptight," anxious, and/or uncomfortable when touched; we know that touching which is perceived as inappropriate for the relationship can be met with aggressive reactions—that is, "touching" back, in the form of slapping or hitting. Everyday observation would lead us to assume that there are some people who evaluate almost all touching negatively. In some cases this dislike for touching may be related to early experiences with touch. What do we know about touching as it occurs throughout the life-span?

Touching and Human Development

Tactile communication is probably the most basic or primitive form of communication. In fact, tactual sensitivity may be the first sensory process to become functional. In fetal life, the child begins to respond to vibrations of the mother's pulsating heartbeat which impinge on the child's entire body and are magnified by the amniotic fluid. In one sense, our first input about what "life" is going to be like comes from the sense of touch. Newborn children continue to gain knowledge of themselves and the world around them through tactile explorations. Some of the common touch experiences include the touch of the obstetrician's hands, the hands that change their diapers, feed them, bathe them, rock them, and comfort them. During early childhood, words accompany touch until the child associates the two; then words replace touch entirely. For example, a mother may gently stroke or pat an infant to console him or her. As the child grows older, she strokes and pats while murmuring encouraging words. Eventually, the mother may call from another room, "It's all

---

[3]M. F. A. Montagu, *Touching: The Human Significance of the Skin* (New York: Columbia University Press, 1971), p. 292.

right dear—mummy's here." As words replace touching, an intimate closeness is replaced by distance. Frank has hypothesized an important relationship from this sequence.[4] He says that symbols without primary tactile validation in childhood may be less clearly and less effectively established as basic codes of communication later in life.

There have been several efforts to examine parental touching of infants and children. It would seem reasonable to assume that the neonate and infant receive more tactile stimulation than children aged fourteen months to two years. In view of infant needs, this would seem both needed and predictable. However, Clay's results indicate children begin to receive more touching between fourteen months and two years of age than as infants. This study also indicates that girl babies tend to receive more of these physical acts of affection than boy babies.[5] Lewis, however, summarizing several research projects, reports that for the first six months of life, boys receive more physical contact than girls. After six months of age, the girls are not only allowed, but encouraged, to spend more time touching and staying near their parents than boys.[6]

Willis and his colleagues observed children in elementary school and junior high school.[7] From kindergarten through sixth grade the amount of touching steadily declines but still surpasses most reports of adult touching. This same trend occurs in junior high—showing about half as much touching as in the primary grades. Some other interesting findings emerged from these studies. The most touching occurred between same-sexed dyads. Black children—especially black females—tended to exhibit more touching behavior. Although the touching in the primary grades is more often initiated with the hands, the junior high students showed much more shoulder to shoulder and elbow to elbow touching. Junior high females began to show more aggressive touching and junior high boys were touched in more places—primarily because of the play fighting so common at that age.

Following childhood, the American child goes through a "latency" period in which tactile communication plays only a small role. Then, during adolescence, tactile experiences with members of the same, and then opposite, sex become increasingly important. The use of touch to communicate emotional and relational messages to the elderly may be crucial—particularly as the reliance on verbal/cognitive messages wanes. Although we seem to give the

[4]L. K. Frank, "Tactile Communication." *Genetic Psychology Monographs* 56 (1957): 209–255.

[5]V. S. Clay, "The Effect of Culture on Mother-Child Tactile Communication," Ph.D. dissertation, Columbia University, 1966.

[6]M. Lewis, "Culture and Gender Rules: There is No Unisex in the Nursery." *Psychology Today* 5 (1972): 54–57.

[7]F. N. Willis and G. E. Hoffman, "Development of Tactile Patterns in Relation to Age, Sex, and Race," *Developmental Psychology* 11 (1975): 866. See also F. N. Willis and D. L. Reeves, "Touch Interactions in Junior High Students in Relation to Sex and Race," *Developmental Psychology* 12 (1976): 91–92.

The Effects of Touching Behavior on Human Communication

aged in this country a greater "license" to touch others, it is not clear how much others touch them. No doubt the infirmities of age will require more touching, but it may make a big difference whether this increased touching is just "functional/professional" or expresses affectionate feelings.

Early tactile experiences seem crucial to later mental and emotional adjustment. Youngsters who have little physical contact during infancy may walk and talk later; many schizophrenic children are reported to have been deprived of handling and mothering as infants; some instances of difficulties and retardation in reading and speech are also associated with early deprivation of, and confusion in, tactile communication. Ashley Montagu cites vast numbers of animal and human studies to support the theory that tactile satisfaction during infancy and childhood is of fundamental importance to subsequent healthy behavioral development of the person. He maintains that we cannot handle a child too much since "there is every reason to believe that, just as the salamander's brain and nervous system develops more fully in response to peripheral stimulation, so does the brain and nervous system of the human being."[8] Harlow's famous "surrogate mother" experiments offer some supporting evidence from the animal world for the importance of touch to infants. Harlow constructed a monkey mother-figure out of wire which could provide milk and protection; then he constructed another one out of sponge rubber and terry cloth which did not provide milk. Since infant monekys consistently chose the terry cloth mother, Harlow concluded "contact comfort" was a more important part of the mother-child relationship for monkeys, and that nursing was less important as a food source and more a source of reassuring touch.

Who Touches Whom, Where, and How Much?

The amount and kind of contact in adulthood vary considerably with the age, sex, situation, and relationship of the parties involved. There are reports of some married couples who either have so little to say to each other or who find it so difficult to establish closeness through verbal contact, that physical contact during sexual encounters becomes a primary mode of communication for establishing "closeness." In fact, Masters and Johnson, the famous sex researchers, claim they are trying to help people achieve more effective communication: "We believe that effective sexual intercourse is the ultimate in communication." Many factors in the development of American society have led to a common expectation that touching will only be conducted in extremely personal and intimate relationships, which makes most touching sensual in nature. For some individuals, the contact involved in a crowded com-

[8]Montagu, *Touching,* p. 188.

The Effects of Touching Behavior on Human Communication

muter train or theater lobby is very discomforting—particularly if these contacts are with a member of the same sex. Explanations for such feelings are numerous. Some children grow up learning "not to touch" a multitude of animate and inanimate objects; they are told not to touch their own body and later not to touch the body of their dating partner; care is taken so children do not see their parents "touch" one another intimately; some parents demonstrate a noncontact norm through the use of twin beds; touching is associated with admonitions of "not nice" or "bad" and is punished accordingly—and frequent touching between father and son is thought to be something less than masculine.

Certain *situations* will have a facilitating or inhibiting effect on touching behavior too. Henley's research suggests that people may be more likely to touch when:[9] (1) giving information or advice rather than asking for it; (2) giving an order rather than responding to it; (3) asking a favor rather than agreeing to do one; (4) trying to persuade rather than being persuaded; (5) the conversation is "deep rather than casual; (6) at a party rather than at work; (7) communicating excitement rather than receiving it from another; and (8) receiving messages of worry from another rather than sending such messages. Heslin and Boss found that 60 percent of the people they observed greeting or saying good-bye to someone at an airport were touching.[10] Extended embraces and greater intimacy of touch was observed more frequently in departures or good-byes than in greetings. The greater the emotional feeling (as reflected in facial expressions) and the closer the perceived relationship, the greater the chances of increased touching. This study also reconfirmed another important finding, namely, that touching behavior is often initiated by men.

Henley has explored this recurrent finding that men seem to be the touchers and women the touchees in the context of status relationships.[11] Henley asks us to consider whom we would expect to initiate touching behavior in dyads like the following: teacher-student; police-accused; doctor-patient; master-slave; foreman-worker; advisor-advisee; and so on. Most people tend to see the person of higher status initiating the touch. For a "subordinate" to initiate (or even reciprocate, sometimes) touching is often perceived as out of line, presumptuous, or an affront. Thus, Henley argues that the predominantly male-initiated touch is just as likely (if not more so) to be an indication of power as a reflection of affection. When women initiate touch with men it is fre-

[9]N. M. Henley, *Body Politics: Power, Sex and Nonverbal Communication* (Englewood Cliffs, N.J.) 1977, p. 105.
[10]R. Heslin and D. Boss, "Nonverbal Intimacy in Arrival and Departure at an Airport," Unpublished manuscript, Purdue University, 1976.
[11]N. Henley, "The Politics of Touch," in P. Brown (ed.), *Radical Psychology* (New York: Harper & Row, 1973), pp. 421–433. Also see Henley's chapter "Tactual Politics" in her book *Body Politics* (Englewood Cliffs, N.J.: Prentice-Hall) 1977.

The Effects of Touching Behavior on Human Communication

quently associated with sexual intent—since, as Henley concludes, "the implication of power is unacceptable."

Jourard counted the frequency of contact between couples in cafés in various cities and reports the following contacts per hour: San Juan, Puerto Rico, 180; Paris, 110; Gainesville, Florida, 2; London, 0.[12] In addition, Jourard wanted to know what parts of the body are touched most often. He administered a questionnaire to students who indicated which of twenty-four body parts they had seen or touched on, or had had seen or touched by, four other persons: mother, father, same-sex friend, and opposite-sex friend, within the past twelve months. Among other findings, Jourard's study found females considerably more accessible to touch by all persons than males. Opposite-sex friends and mothers did the most touching, while many fathers touched not much more than the hands of the subjects.

Jourard's data for Figure 7.1 was gathered in 1963–1964. A replication of this study over a decade later revealed about the same results—with one exception.[13] It seems that both males and females are even more accessible to opposite-sex friends than they were a decade ago, with increased touching reported for body parts normally considered more intimate, such as chest, stomach, hips, thigh. In the early 1970s, Barnlund conducted a comparative study of Japanese and American touching patterns.[14] Figure 7.2 indicates that in almost every category, the amount of physical contact reported by Americans is twice that reported by Japanese. In general, then, Americans seem to be both more accessible to and more physically expressive toward others in the area of touch. This data was obtained from 120 college students in each culture—60 female and 60 male.

Although our primary interest is in everyday social communication, the study of touch also has important implications for institutionalized persons. Watson found that there was more touching of residents in a home for the elderly if the following conditions were present: (1) the area of touch was far from the genital region, (2) staff and resident were of the same sex, (3) the touch initiator was perceived to have high status, and (4) the resident was relatively free of stigmatizing physical impairments.[15] Watson goes on to point out that severely impaired residents and males (because the staff is largely female) will probably receive relatively little touching.

[12]S. M. Jourard, "An Exploratory Study of Body-Accessibility," *British Journal of Social and Clinical Psychology* 5 (1966): 221–231.

[13]L. B. Rosenfeld, S. Kartus, and C. Ray, "Body Accessibility Revisited," *Journal of Communication* 26 (1976): 27–30.

[14]D. C. Barnlund, "Communicative Styles in Two Cultures: Japan and the United States," in A. Kendon, R. M. Harris, and M. R. Key (eds.), *Organization of Behavior in Face-to-Face Interaction* (The Hague: Mouton, 1975).

[15]W. H. Watson, "The Meanings of Touch: Geriatric Nursing," *Journal of Communication* 25 (1975): 104–112.

The Effects of Touching Behavior on Human Communication

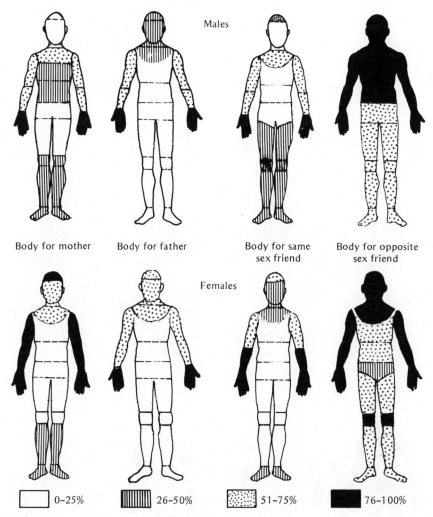

Males

Body for mother   Body for father   Body for same   Body for opposite
                                      sex friend   sex friend

Females

| | 0–25% | | 26–50% | | 51–75% | | 76–100% |

Figure 7.1 Areas of the body involved in bodily contact.

Different Types of Touching Behavior

Argyle says that the following kinds of bodily contact are most common in Western culture:[16]

[16]M. Argyle, *Bodily Communication* (New York: International Universities Press, 1975), p. 287. I made the following alterations in the original list: (1) changed *bottom* to *buttocks*, (2) added *genitals* to four categories, and (3) added *shoulders* to the "shaking" category.

The Effects of Touching Behavior on Human Communication

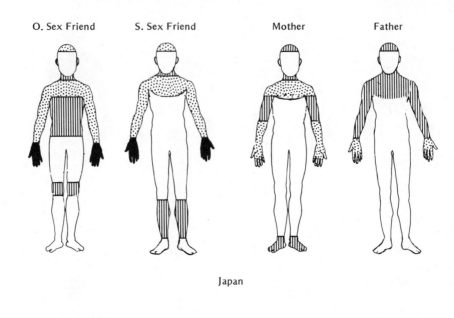

Japan

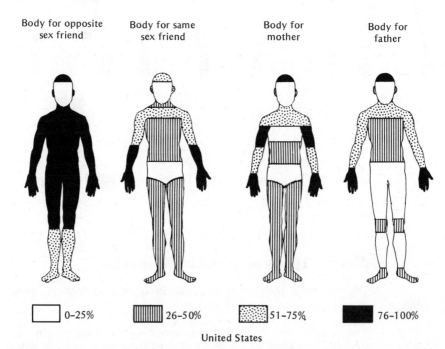

Figure 7.2 Physical contact patterns in Japan (above) and the United States (below).

The Effects of Touching Behavior on Human Communication

Type of Touch	Body Areas Typically Involved
Patting	Head, back
Slapping	Face, hand, buttocks
Punching	Face, chest
Pinching	Cheek
Stroking	Hair, face, upper body, knee, genitals
Shaking	Hands, shoulders
Kissing	Mouth, cheek, breasts, hand, foot, genitals
Licking	Face, genitals
Holding	Hand, arm, knee, genitals
Guiding	Hand, arm
Embracing	Shoulder, body
Linking	Arms
Laying-on	Hands
Kicking	Legs, buttocks
Grooming	Hair, face
Tickling	Almost anywhere

Heslin categorized the various types of touching according to the messages communicated.[17] His taxonomy reflects a continuum, from very impersonal touching to very personal touching.

1. Functional-Professional. The communicative intent of this impersonal, often "cold" and businesslike touching is to accomplish some task—to perform some service. The other person is considered as an object or nonperson in order to keep any intimate or sexual messages from interfering with the task at hand. Examples of such situations may include a golf pro with his or her student, a tailor with a customer, or a physician with his or her patient.

Like other forms of nonverbal behavior, touching may support or contradict information communicated by other systems. A doctor may explain that you need not worry about your pending operation, and his or her touch may add confirmation; but it may contradict the verbalization if the doctor is nervous, still, and abrupt. Agulera reports an instance in which touch behavior by nurses increased verbal output of the patients and improved patient attitudes toward nurses.[18] The phrase *verbal output* does not necessarily mean a deeper level of self-disclosure; it may just mean more small talk. In fact, a positive relationship

---

[17]R. Heslin, "Steps Toward a Taxonomy of Touching," paper presented to the Midwestern Psychological Association, Chicago, May 1974.

[18]D. C. Agulera, "Relationships Between Physical Contact and Verbal Interaction Between Nurses and Patients," *Journal of Psychiatric Nursing* 5 (1967): 5–21.

The Effects of Touching Behavior on Human Communication

between the amount of tactile contact and self-disclosure has not been established.[19]

2. Social-Polite.   The purpose of this type of touching is to affirm the other person's identity as a member of the same species, operating by essentially the same rules of conduct. Although the other is treated as a "person," there is still very little perceived involvement between the interactants. The handshake is the best example of this type of touching. Although the handshake is only about 150 years old, it was preceded by a hand-clasp, which goes back at least as far as ancient Rome.

3. Friendship-Warmth.   This kind of touching behavior begins to recognize more of the other person's uniqueness and expresses a liking for that person. In short, this type of touching is oriented toward the other person as a friend.

4. Love-Intimacy.   When you lay your hand on the cheek of a person of the opposite sex or when you fully embrace another person, you are probably expressing an emotional attachment or attraction through touch. The other person is the object of one's feelings of intimacy or love. The various kinds of touching at this point will probably be the least stereotyped and the most adapted to the specific other person.

5. Sexual Arousal.   Although sexual arousal is sometimes an integral part of love and intimacy, it may also have characteristics distinct from that category. Here we are primarily looking at touch as an expression of physical attraction only. The other person is, in common parlance, a sex object.

Morris believes that heterosexual couples in Western culture normally go through a sequence of steps—like courtship patterns in other animal species—on the road to sexual intimacy.[20] Notice that each step, aside from the first three, involves some kind of touching: (1) eye to body, (2) eye to eye, (3) voice to voice, (4) hand to hand, (5) arm to shoulder, (6) arm to waist, (7) mouth to mouth, (8) hand to head, (9) hand to body, (10) mouth to breast, (11) hand to genitals, (12) genitals to genitals and/or mouth to genitals. Morris feels that these steps generally follow the same order, although he admits there are variations. One form of skipping steps or moving to a level of intimacy beyond what would be expected is found in socially formalized types of bodily

[19]S. M. Jourard and J. E. Rubin, "Self-Disclosure and Touching: A Study of Two Modes of Interpersonal Encounter and Their Inter-Relation," *Journal of Humanistic Psychology* 8 (1968): 39–48.

[20]D. Morris, *Intimate Behaviour* (New York: Random House, 1971), pp. 71–101.

The Effects of Touching Behavior on Human Communication

252

contact—for example, a good-night kiss or a hand-to-hand introduction. It should be pointed out here that although mouth-to-mouth touching in heterosexual pairs may frequently reflect an advancing stage of intimacy, it may also occur in the most nonintimate settings with the most nonintimate meaning attached to it—as, for example, when a host of a TV quiz show dutifully "pecks" the female contestants as they are greeted or as they depart.

Morris also provides a fascinating discussion of the full embrace and its various permutations in modern society's touching behavior. He says we find the full embrace occurring in amorous contact between lovers; between friends and relatives at greetings, departures, and reunions; and between same-sex individuals following a triumph at a sporting event—for example, scoring a goal or touchdown.

In the full embrace the two parties are pressed close together frontally with the sides of their heads in contact and their arms wrapped around one another's bodies. There are, however, other forms of touching which contain only fragments of these behaviors, evolving from various social and cultural constraints—for example, side-to-side contact, one arm wrapped around the other person and keeping heads apart. Morris says his observations would predict that these partial embraces are six times as likely to occur as full embraces with adults in public places. The most common partial embrace, a predominantly masculine act, seems to be the shoulder embrace. The hand-on-shoulder and the arm-link follow in frequency. Holding hands is a still more distant cousin of the full embrace—again, primarily a heterosexual act. However, males may be seen holding hands during a community sing or a curtain call for a play or when politicians signal a joint victory. Head contacts (touching another's head with your hand or putting two heads together) and the kiss are the remaining permutations of the original full embrace, according to Morris.[21]

We also engage in self-touching. This, again from the observations of Desmond Morris, may include: (1) shielding actions to reduce input or output—for example, putting your hand over your mouth or over your ears; (2) cleaning actions—bringing the hand up to the head to scratch, rub, pick, wipe, and the like; (3) specialized signals to communicate specific messages—for example, holding a hand under your chin to signal "I'm fed up to here" or thumbing your nose at someone; and (4) self-intimacies—holding your own hands, hugging your legs, masturbating, and so on.[22] Freedman has studied the self-touching of psychiatric patients. He was concerned only with these "body-focused" touches during the patient's speech—and under conditions

[21]Ibid., pp. 117–134.
[22]Ibid., pp. 213–227.

The Effects of Touching Behavior on Human Communication

where the subject was expected to speak rather than listen.[23] Some of his preliminary studies show that acutely depressed patients may show a preponderance of these body-focused hand movements. He further suggests that there may be a close linkage between body touching and preoccupation with self. He summarizes his observations by saying:

> . . . body-focused activity implies a reduction in communicative intent, a withdrawal from the interchange and the possible impoverishment of symbolic activity. Yet this reduction varies with the different categories of body-focused movement, each representing different constellations of conflict between what is and is not verbalized. The formal organization of the movement categories may have a bearing on the ability to verbalize experiences associated with these movements.[24]

Morris sums up the various kinds of intimate touching which form the substance of his book through this example:

> (1) When we are feeling nervous or depressed, a loved one may attempt to reassure us by giving us a comforting hug or a squeeze of the hand. (2) In the absence of a loved one, it may have to be one of the specialist touchers, such as a doctor, who pats our arm and tells us not to worry. (3) If our only company is our pet dog or cat, we may take it in our arms and press our cheek to its furry body to feel the comfort of its warm touch. (4) If we are completely alone and some sinister noise startles us in the night, we may hug the bed-clothes tightly around us to feel secure in their soft embrace. (5) If all else fails, we still have our own bodies, and we can hug, embrace, clasp and touch ourselves in a great variety of ways to help soothe away our fears.[25]

The Meanings of Touching Behavior

The meaning of any message will vary according to a multitude of factors—for example, cultural and environmental context, the relationship between the communicators, the intensity and duration of the message, whether it was perceived as intentional or unintentional, and so on. For instance, you could plot the following touch behavior along an intimacy continuum: touch and release (least intimate), touch and hold; touch and stroke. The available data on the meaning of touch is scarce, and the following efforts represent early ground-breaking efforts.

Argyle feels that touch can be decoded as communicating various interper-

---

[23]N. Freedman, "The Analysis of Movement Behavior During the Clinical Interview," in A. W. Siegman and B. Pope (eds.), *Studies in Dyadic Communication* (New York: Pergamon, 1972), pp. 153–175.

[24]Ibid., p. 173.

[25]Morris, *Intimate Behaviour*, p. 214.

The Effects of Touching Behavior on Human Communication

sonal attitudes—for example, it may mean sexual interest, nurturance-dependence (cradling or caressing an infant), affiliation (establishing friendly relations), and aggression (establishing unfriendly relations). Other touching signals may simply be interpreted as managing the interaction itself. These management touches may guide someone without interrupting verbal conversation, may get somebody's attention by tugging at that person's arm or tapping him or her on the shoulder, may indicate or mark the beginning (greeting) or end (good-bye) of a conversation, or may fulfill some ritualistic function, such as congratulating a person at graduation or touching a baby's head at a baptism. We can also interpret touching as "accidental" or "meaningless" when in overcrowded situations or when a passerby brushes against you. Like any other message, the two communicators may not have a similar meaning for the touch—or one person may deliberately try to mislead another. A not unfamiliar example of the latter deception is when one person touches another in a joking context but intends the touch to be a step toward intimacy.

The meanings of touch behavior will also vary somewhat with the parts of the body used to touch. In one study, there seemed to be five meanings commonly attributed to various manipulations of the hands.[26] Hand-to-hand messages included the following: (1) detached (indifferent, unfeeling), (2) "mothering" (tender, caring, comforting), (3) fearful (insecure, afraid), (4) playful (carefree, fun), and (5) angry (irritated).

Nguyen, Heslin, and Nguyen conducted two studies on the meaning of touch.[27] First, they presented unmarried people with the body parts diagramed in Figure 7.3. Each person was asked to indicate what it meant to them to be touched in each of the eleven areas—that is, patted, squeezed, stroked, or brushed. To focus reactions, subjects were asked to respond only in the context of touching by an opposite-sex friend (and not parents, siblings, or relatives). The method of responding was limited to scales representing various degrees of playfulness, warmth/love, friendship/fellowship, pleasantness, and sexual desire.

Generally, married persons tended to react more positively toward touch and tended to associate it with sex more often than did unmarried respondents. Unless the touch was in the genital region, sexual desire was not a common response for the unmarrieds.

The type of touch seemed to be closely linked to one's judgments of playfulness and warmth/love—for example, patting is associated with play, but

[26]A. I. Smith, "'Non-verbal Communication Through Touch," Unpublished PhD dissertation, Georgia State University, 1970.

[27]T. Nguyen, R. Heslin, and M. L. Nguyen, "The Meanings of Touch: Sex Differences," *Journal of Communication* 25 (1975): 92–103; and M. L. Nguyen, R. Heslin, and T. Nguyen, "The Meaning of Touch: Sex and Marital Status Differences," *Representative Research in Social Psychology* 7 (1976): 13–18.

The Effects of Touching Behavior on Human Communication

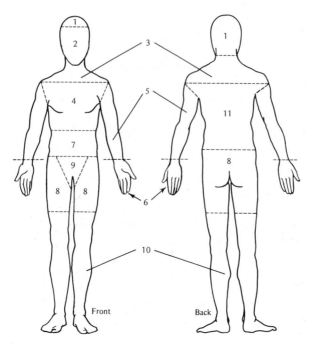

Figure 7.3 The human body diagrammed into eleven areas.

stroking is associated with warmth/love and sexual desire. On the other hand (no pun intended), friendliness and sexuality seem most closely linked to the location of the touch—for example, hands, no matter how they were touched, were seen as pleasant, warm, and friendly; the genital area was not seen as very "playful"—regardless of what kind of touching was being evaluated.

Although unmarried women did not perceive sexual touching to be as pleasant and as warm as unmarried men, married women did. Married men attributed less warmth/love and pleasantness to sexual touching than either single men or married women.

In view of what seems to be a widespread sensitivity to sexual touching, one would think that those body parts are strongly represented in the cerebral cortex. To the contrary, Nguyen, Heslin, and Nguyen found an inverse correlation between ratings of sexual desire for various body parts and the amount of sensory cortex representing that part. If we drew a body as it is represented in our brain, it would look like Figure 7.4.

The Effects of Touching Behavior on Human Communication

256

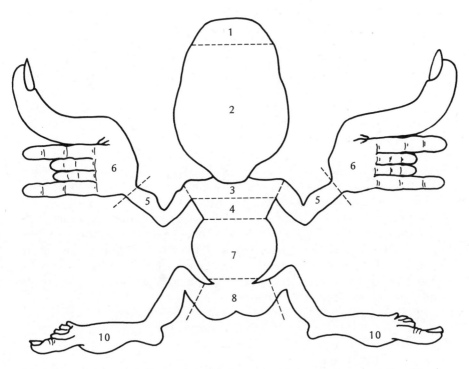

Figure 7.4 Relative size of body parts based on the extent of their cortical representation. (Numbers on the diagram refer to corresponding areas in Figure 7.3).

Cultural Differences in Touching Behavior

To anyone who travels, it seems like there are vast differences in the amount of touching behavior in some countries when compared with our own. This idea has received a lot of anecdotal support, and there is probably considerable accuracy in the concept of "contact" vs. "noncontact cultures"—that is, some cultures encourage more touching of various kinds than others. The United States has traditionally been labeled a noncontact culture, but we are probably touching more now that at any time in our history. In some ethnic pockets people probably touch a great deal, and Davis has quoted Erving Goffman as saying that we *do* live in a contact culture, but that "we read it out"—that is, our expectations either don't facilitate our observation of it or we do observe it but treat it as atypical.[28]

Just as there are differences within this so-called noncontact culture based on one's ancestry, social status, and living conditions, Shuter's observations led him to conclude that there may be significant differences in what we have traditionally called "contact cultures" as well.[29] Shuter systematically observed people interacting in natural settings in Costa Rica, Panama, and Colombia. His data seems to show that as one moves southward from Central America, the amount of touching and holding decreases.

Aside from a rich store of anecdotal material, we don't know much about the specifics of cultural differences in touching. We do know that there seem to be enormous differences—for example, two males interacting in some countries may hold hands or intertwine their legs.

The human skin has hundreds of thousands of tactile receptors—submicroscopic nerve endings—specialized to detect pressure, temperature, texture, pain, stroking, tickling, and the like. Skin tissue, similar to that of the eardrum, is also sensitive to vibration. Several experimenters have been trying to teach people to receive and respond to language transmitted through the skin by vibrations—and other means.[30]

Summary

Our first information about ourselves, others, and the environment in which we live probably comes from touching. The act of touching or being touched by another can have a powerful impact on our response to a situation—even if that touch was unintentional or accidental. In some cases, touching is the most effective method for communicating; in others, it can elicit negative or hostile reactions. The meanings we attach to touching behavior vary according to what body part is touched, how long the touch lasts, the strength of the touch, the method of the touch (for example, open or closed fist!) and the frequency of the touch. Touch also means different things in different environments (institutions, airports, and so on) and with communicators varying in age, sex, and stage of relationship.

Touching behavior can be used to communicate interpersonal attitudes (such as dominance, affection, and the like). Henley believes that the prepon-

[28]F. Davis, Inside Intuition (New York: McGraw-Hill, 1971), p. 137.

[29]R. Shuter, "Proxemics and Tactility in Latin America," Journal of Communication 26 (1976): 46–52.

[30]For a comprehensive review of this literature, see: J. W. Kirman, "Tactile Communication of Speech: A Review and an Analysis," Psychological Bulletin 80 (1973): 54–74.

derance of male-initiated touch to females represents a consistent reinforcement of perceived status differences. We also use touch to help us manage the interaction—guiding another person, touching to get attention, accenting some verbal or facial message—perhaps by squeezing or embracing the other person, and so on. Heslin classified the various types of touching behavior as: (1) functional/professional, (2) social/polite, (3) friendship/warmth, (4) love/ intimacy, and (5) sexual arousal.

Although anecdotal reports and a few isolated studies would suggest that America represents a noncontact culture, there appear to be several indications that this may be changing. At the least, it seems clear that there are sizable variations in the amount of contact within this culture, regardless of what we choose to label the entire culture. There are some indications that children in this culture touch more than adults, but there seems to be a decreasing amount of touch from kindergarten through junior high. Some research reports that boys and girls get differential early experiences with touch from parents, but most agree that early experiences with touch are crucial for later adjustment.

SELECTED BIBLIOGRAPHY

Agulera, D. C. "Relationships Between Physical Contact and Verbal Interaction Between Nurses and Patients." *Journal of Psychiatric Nursing* 5 (1967): 5–21.

Bardeen, J. P. "Interpersonal Perception Through the Tactile, Verbal, and Visual Modes." Paper presented at the convention of the International Communication Association. Phoenix, 1971.

Barnett, K. E. "The Development of a Theoretical Construct of the Concepts of Touch as They Relate to Nursing." Ph.D. dissertation. North Texas State University-Denton, 1970.

Bodermann, A., Freed, D. W., and Kinnucan, M. T. " 'Touch Me, Like Me': Testing an Encounter Group Assumption." *Journal of Applied Behavioral Science* 8 (1972): 527–533.

Bosanquet, C. "Getting in Touch." *Journal of Analytical Psychology* 15 (1970): 42–58.

Burton, A., and Heller, L. G. "The Touching of the Body." *Psychoanalytic Review* 51 (1964): 122–134.

Casher, L., and Dixson, B. K. "The Therapeutic Use of Touch," *Journal of Psychiatric Nursing and Mental Health Service* 5 (1967): 442–451.

Casler, L. "The Effects of Extra Tactile Stimulation on a Group of Institutionalized Infants." *Genetic Psychology Monographs* 71 (1965): 137–175.

The Effects of Touching Behavior on Human Communication

Clay, V. S. "The Effect of Culture on Mother-Child Tactile Communication." Ph.D. dissertation. Columbia University, 1966.

Cooper, C. L., and Bowles, D. "Physical Encounter and Self-Disclosure." *Psychological Reports* 33 (1973): 451–454.

Dresslar, F. B. "Studies in the Psychology of Touch." *American Journal of Psychology* 6 (1894): 313–368.

Fisher, J. D., Rytting, M., and Heslin, R. "Hands Touching Hands: Affective and Evaluative Effects of an Interpersonal Touch." *Sociometry* 39 (1976): 416–421.

Frank, L. K. "Tactile Communication." *Genetic Psychology Monographs* 56 (1957): 209–255.

Freedman, N. "The Analysis of Movement Behavior During the Clinical Interview." In A. W. Siegman and B. Pope (eds.), *Studies in Dyadic Communication*. New York, Pergamon, 1972.

Geis, F., and Viksne, V. "Touching: Physical Contact and Level of Arousal." *Proceedings of the Annual Convention of the APA* 7 (1972): 179–180.

Geldhard, F. A. "Body English." *Psychology Today* 2 (1968): 42–47.

Gibson, J. J. "Observations on Active Touch." *Psychological Review* 69 (1962): 477–491.

Gunther, B. *Sense Relaxation: Below Your Mind.* New York: Collier Books, 1968.

Harlow, H. F. "The Nature of Love." *American Psychologist* 13 (1958): 678–685.

Henley, N. *Body Politics: Power, Sex and Nonverbal Communication* (Englewood Cliffs, N.J.: Prentice-Hall) 1977.

Henley, N. "Power, Sex and Non-verbal Communication." *Berkeley Journal of Sociology* 18 (1973–1974): 1–26.

Henley, N. "Status and Sex: Some Touching Observations." *Bulletin of the Psychonomic Society* 2 (1973): 91–93.

Henley, N. "The Politics of Touch." In Brown, P. (ed.), *Radical Psychology.* New York: Harper & Row, 1973. Pp. 421–433.

Heslin, R. "Steps Toward a Taxonomy of Touching." Paper presented to the Midwestern Psychological Association, Chicago, May 1974.

Hibbard, J. A. "Attitudes Toward Sexual and Non-sexual Touch in Dating Couples as A Function of Level of Romantic Love." Unpublished Master's thesis, Purdue University, 1974.

Hollender, M. H. "The Need or Wish to be Held." *Archives of General Psychiatry* 22 (1970): 445–453.

Howard, J. *Please Touch: A Guided Tour of the Human Potential Movement.* New York: McGraw-Hill, 1970.

Hunton, V. D., and Summer, F. C. "The Affective Tone of Tactual Impressions." *Journal of Psychology* 26 (1948): 235–242.

The Effects of Touching Behavior on Human Communication

260

Jourard, S. M. "An Exploratory Study of Body-Accessibility." *British Journal of Social and Clinical Psychology* 5 (1966): 221–231.

Jourard, S. M. *Disclosing Man to Himself.* New York: Van Nostrand Reinhold, 1968.

Jourard, S. M., and Rubin, J. E. "Self-Disclosure and Touching: A Study of Two Modes of Interpersonal Encounter and Their Inter-relation." *Journal of Humanistic Psychology* 8 (1968): 39–48.

Julesz, B. "Texture and Visual Perception." *Scientific American* 212 (1965): 38–48.

Kaufman, L. E. "Tacesics, the Study of Touch: A Model for Proxemic Analysis." *Semiotica* 14 (1971): 149–161.

Kirman, J. H. "Tactile Communication of Speech: A Review and an Analysis." *Psychological Bulletin* 80 (1973): 54–74.

Korner, A., and Thoman, M. "The Relative Efficacy of Contact and Vestibular-Proprioceptive Stimulation in Soothing Neonates." *Child Development* 43 (1972): 443–453.

Levine, S. "Stimulation in Infancy." *Scientific American* 202 (1960): 80–86.

Lewis, M. "Culture and Gender: There Is No Unisex in the Nursery." *Psychology Today* 5 (1972): 54–57.

Lobsenz, N. M. "The Loving Message in Touch." *Woman's Day* 31 (February 1970): 94–96.

McCorkle, R. "Effects of Touch on Seriously Ill Patients." *Nursing Research* 23 (1974): 125–132.

Montagu, M. F. A. *Touching: The Human Significance of the Skin.* New York: Columbia University Press, 1971.

Morris, D. *Intimate Behaviour.* New York: Random House, 1971.

Murphy, A. J. "Effect of Body Contact on Performance of a Simple Cognitive Task." *British Journal of Social and Clinical Psychology* 11 (1972): 402–408.

Nguyen, M. L., Heslin, R., and Nguyen, T. "The Meaning of Touch: Sex and Marital Status Differences." *Representative Research in Social Psychology* 7 (1976): 13–18.

Nguyen, T., Heslin, R., and Nguyen, M. L. "The Meanings of Touch: Sex Differences." *Journal of Communication* 25 (1975): 92–103.

Pattison, J. E. "Effects of Touch on Self-Exploration and the Therapeutic Relationship." *Journal of Consulting and Clinical Psychology* 40 (1973): 170–175.

Rosenfeld, L. B., Kartus, S., and Ray, C. "Body Accessibility Revisited." *Journal of Communication* 26 (1976): 27–30.

Schaffer, H., and Emerson, E. "Patterns of Response to Physical Contact in Early Human Development." *Journal of Child Psychology and Psychiatry* 5 (1964): 1–13.

The Effects of Touching Behavior on Human Communication

Schindler-Rainman, E. "The Importance of Non-verbal Communication in Laboratory Training." *Adult Leadership* 16 (1968): 383.

Schutz, W. *Joy.* New York: Grove Press, 1967.

Shevrin, H., and Toussieng, P. W. "Vicissitudes of the Need for Tactile Stimulation in Instinctual Development." *The Psychoanalytic Study of the Child* 20 (1965): 310–339.

Shuter, R. "Proxemics and Tactility in Latin America." *Journal of Communication* 26 (1976): 46–52.

Silverman, A. F., Pressman, M. E., and Bartel, H. W. "Self-Esteem and Tactile Communication." *Journal of Humanistic Psychology* 13 (1973): 73–77.

Silverthorne, N., and Hunt, R. "The Effects of Tactile Stimulation on Visual Experience." *Journal of Social Psychology* 88 (1972): 153–154.

Smith, A. I. "Non-verbal Communication Through Touch." Unpublished Ph.D. dissertation, Georgia State University, 1970.

Sokoloff, N., Yaffe, S., Weintraub, D., and Blase, B. "Effects of Handling on the Subsequent Development of Premature Infants." *Developmental Psychology* 1 (1969): 765–768.

Spitz, R. "Hospitalism: Genesis of Psychiatric Conditions in Early Childhood." *Psychoanalytic Study of the Child* 1 (1945): 53–74.

Spotnitz, H. "Touch Countertransference in Group Psychotherapy." *International Journal of Group Psychotherapy* 22 (1972): 455–463.

Walker, D. N. "Openness to Touching: A Study of Strangers in Nonverbal Interaction." Unpublished Ph.D. dissertation, University of Connecticut, 1971.

Watson, W. H. "The Meanings of Touch: Geriatric Nursing." *Journal of Communication* 25 (1975): 104–112.

Weinstein, S. "Intensive and Extensive Aspects of Tactile Sensitivity as a Function of Body Part, Sex, and Laterality." In D. R. Kenshalo (ed.), *The Skin Senses.* Springfield, Ill.: Charles C. Thomas, 1968.

Williams, T. "Cultural Structuring of Tactile Experience in a Borneo Society." *The American Anthropologist* 68 (1966): 27–39.

Willis, F. N., and Hoffman, G. E. "Development of Tactile Patterns in Relation to Age, Sex, and Race." *Developmental Psychology* 11 (1975): 866.

Willis, F. N., and Reeves, D. L. "Touch Interactions in Junior High Students in Relation to Sex and Race." *Developmental Psychology* 12 (1976): 91–92.

8 The Effects of the Face on Human Communication

Your face, my thane, is as a book where men
May read strange matters
SHAKESPEARE, MacBeth, *Act 1*

The face is rich in communicative potential. It is the primary site for communication of emotional states, it reflects interpersonal attitudes, it provides nonverbal feedback on the comments of others, and some say it is the primary source of information next to human speech. For these reasons, and because of its visibility, we pay a great deal of attention to the messages we receive from the faces of others. Frequently we place considerable reliance on facial cues when making important interpersonal judgments. This begins when, as infants, we take special interest in the huge face peering over our crib and tending to our needs. Most of the research on facial expressions (and various component parts of the face) has focused on the display and interpretation of emotional states. While this will be the major focus of this chapter, we should at least mention the fact that the face may also be the basis for judging another person's personality and that it can (and does) provide information other than one's emotional state.

The Face and Personality Judgments

The human face comes in many sizes and shapes. There are triangular, square, and round faces; foreheads may be high and wide, high and narrow, low and wide, low and narrow, protruding or sunken; the complexion of a face may be light, dark, coarse, smooth, wrinkled, or blemished; eyes may be balanced, close, far apart, recessed or bulging; noses can be short, long, flat, crooked, "humpbacked," a "bag," or a "ski slope"; mouths are large and small with thin and thick lips; ears, too, may be large or small, short or long; and cheeks can bulge or appear sunken. In addition to the fact that there are many features in the face which we can respond to, we know that we pay a lot of attention to the face. We look to the face as a primary source of information about other people. Do we judge another's personality by facial characteristics? It seems reasonable to assume that such judgments are made, but at the present time there is almost no reliable, scientific data which provides us with a full understanding of this process.[1]

Secord and his colleagues made an early exploratory investigation into the relationship of facial features and personality judgments and found some consistent associations—for example, high foreheads and intelligence, thin lips and conscientiousness, thick lips on females and "sexiness," and so on.[2] Undesirable persons were portrayed by Secord's subjects as having more extreme features—that is, features which extended beyond the perceived normative boundaries. This included such things as eyes which were too close or too far apart, a nose which was very narrow or very bulbous, and the like. While such studies provide a beginning, we need information on a broad range of facial features from a variety of people, we need information from faces which are not "posed," and we need to discover the role of personality judgments in combination with the context, verbal information, and other facial features—all aspects of daily social situations.

In spite of the fact that the research doesn't provide us with much help, we can speculate on how perceptions of others are generalized from facial characteristics. For instance, you may see someone with a face similar to someone you know and, without further information, infer similar personality characteristics. You may make an initial judgment of age, sex, or race from facial information and then infer associated characteristics from these perceptions—for example, this person is young so he or she is probably also carefree, energetic, and impatient. And sometimes a particular feature has been stereotypically associated with a particular group of people—for example, a "Jewish" nose.

---

[1]Other publications, however, do not hesitate to make grandiose (and unsubstantiated) claims: "The face reveals facts not only about a person's mood, but also about his character, health, personality, sex life, popularity, ability to make money, social status and life expectancy." Cf. B. DeMente, *Face Reading for Fun and Profit* (West Nyack, N.Y.: Parker Publishing, 1968).

[2]P. F. Secord, W. F. Dukes, and W. Bevan, "Personalities in Faces, I: An Experiment in Social Perceiving," *Genetic Psychology Monographs* 49 (1959): 231–279.

The Effects of the Face on Human Communication

264

The Face and Interaction Management

Our faces are also used to facilitate and inhibit responses in daily interaction. Component parts of the face are used to (1) open and close channels of communication, (2) complement or qualify verbal and/or nonverbal responses, and (3) replace speech. Behaviors can, of course, serve several functions simultaneously—for example, a yawn may replace the spoken message "I'm bored" and serve to shut down the channels of communication at the same time.

Channel Control. When we are desirous of a speaking turn, we sometimes open our mouth in readiness to talk—often accompanied by an inspiration of breath. As we noted in Chapter 2, the eyebrow flash (frequently accompanied by a smile) is found in greeting rituals and signals a desire to interact. Interestingly, smiles are also found in situations where there is a desire to close the channels of communication—for example, a smile of appeasement as you back away from a person threatening you with physical harm. Smiling and winking are also used to flirt with others—an invitation which not only opens the channels of communication, but suggests the type of communication desired!

Complementing or Qualifying Other Behavior. In the normal conversational give and take, there are instances when we wish to "underline," magnify, minimize, or support messages. These signals may be given by the speaker or listener. A sad verbal message may acquire added emphasis with the eyebrows, which normally accompany the emotional expression of sadness. A smile may temper a message you feel may otherwise be interpreted as extremely negative. Or you may accompany the hand emblem for "A-OK" with a wink—which tends to leave little doubt you are communicating approval.

Replacing Spoken Messages. Ekman and Friesen have identified what they call facial emblems.[3] Like hand emblems, these displays have a fairly consistent verbal translation. The facial emblems identified thus far are different from the actual emotional expressions in that the sender is trying to talk about an emotion while indicating he or she is not actually feeling it. These facial emblems will usually occur in contexts which would likely not trigger the actual emotion, they are usually held for a longer or shorter time than the actual expression, and they are usually performed by using only a part of the face. When you drop your jaw and hold your mouth open without displaying other features of the surprise expression, you may be saying that the other person's

[3]P. Ekman and W. V. Friesen, *Unmasking the Face* (Englewood Cliffs, N.J.: Prentice-Hall, 1975).

The Effects of the Face on Human Communication

comment is surprising or that you were dumbfounded by what was said. Widened eyes (without other features of the surprise and fear expressions) may serve the same purpose as a verbal "Wow!" If you want to nonverbally comment on your disgust for a situation, a nose wrinkle or raising your upper lip or raising one side of your upper lip should get your message across. Sometimes the eyebrows will communicate "I'm puzzled" or "I doubt that." There are other facial messages which have common verbal translations but are not associated with expressions of emotion—for example, the "You know what I mean" wink; the insult or disapproval associated with sticking your tongue out;[4] or the excessive blinking and lip biting which does not require the verbal statement "I'm anxious (nervous)."

Although the preceding discussion does provide an overview of how the face is used in managing the interaction, it does not sufficiently reflect the complexity a thorough analysis would require. For instance, we did not deal with concomitant gaze behavior and other subtle movements like head tilts. We talked about smiles as if a smile comes in only one variety. Brannigan and Humphries have identified nine smiles—representing various types and degrees of intensity—many of which seem to occur in distinctly separate situations.[5]

The Face and Expressions of Emotion

Because of its importance in displaying our emotional states, researchers have frequently subjected the face to empirical study. The central questions of this research have been "What emotions does the face portray?" and "How accurately can we judge facial expressions of emotion?" Recently there has been some interest in the effects of facial displays of emotion on others and on the sender's subsequent behavior. We will examine each of these questions, but first we need to look more closely at the nature of the face itself.

The Face—A Complex Stimulus. Consider the following situations:

1. A student feels sure he is doing "C" work and is told by his instructor he is doing "A" work. His immediate reaction is total surprise (probably followed by glee), but how does he react? His face shows mild surprise

[4]W. J. Smith, J. Chase, and A. K. Lieblich, "Tongue Showing: A Facial Display of Humans and Other Primate Species," *Semiotica* 11 (1974): 201–246.

[5]C. R. Brannigan and D. A. Humphries, "Human Non-verbal Behaviour, A Means of Communication," in N. Blurton Jones (ed.), *Ethological Studies of Child Behaviour* (New York: Cambridge University Press, 1972).

and he makes some comment to the effect that he thought he was doing pretty good work in the course.
2. A poker player draws his fourth ace in a game with no wild cards. His face would lead the other players to believe he was unmoved.
3. A woman receives a Christmas present which she is pleasantly surprised about and happy to receive, but it is nothing spectacular. Her facial expression and comments, however, lead the giver (who is present) to believe it was the only thing she ever wanted in her entire life.
4. The wife of a fledgling executive is forced to attend the boss's party and told explicitly her behavior will have a profound impact on the promotion of her fledgling executive husband. She is nervous and upset. According to those who describe the party later, however, Mrs. Fledgling was the life of the party—happy and gay, carefree and content.

These four examples illustrate certain display rules we tend to follow. Example I illustrated a de-intensified affect—strong surprise was made to look like mild surprise; in example 2, the poker player was trying to neutralize an affect—make it appear there was no affect at all; the person reacting to the Christmas present tried to make mild surprise appear to be strong surprise—an overintensification of the affect; Mrs. Fledgling was trying to mask an affect of tenseness or despondency with happiness, coolness, and confidence. These display rules are learned, but they are not always at a conscious level of awareness when we use them. We learn that there are culturally prescribed display rules—for example, not laughing at funerals; we also develop personal display rules based on our needs or perhaps the demands of our occupation—for example, politicians or salespersons. We learn that some affect displays are appropriate in some places and not others, for some status and role positions and not others, for one sex and not another; we may use different expressions responding to the same event at a different time and with different people.

Ekman and Friesen have developed a classification system for various styles of facial expression.[6] These are heavily based on personal display rules and represent extremes. A style may be displayed in a less extreme fashion only in some situations or at a certain time in your life—but some people tend to manifest a given style with consistency. These styles include the following: (1) The Withholders. The face inhibits expressions of actual feeling states. There is little facial movement. (2) The Revealers. This is just the opposite of the Withholder. The face leaves little doubt how the person feels—continually. (3) The Unwitting Expressors. This pattern usually pertains to a limited number of expressions which a person may feel have been masked—that is, "How did you know I was angry?" (4) The Blanked Expressors. In this style, the person is

[6]*Unmasking the Face* (Englewood Cliffs, N.J.: Prentice-Hall, 1975).

The Effects of the Face on Human Communication

convinced an emotion is being portrayed, but others see only a blank face! (5) The Substitute Expressors. Here the facial expression shows an emotion other than the one the person thinks is being displayed. (6) The Frozen-Affect Expressors. This style manifests at least a part of an emotional display at all times. Some people are born with a facial configuration which, in a supposedly relaxed, neutral state, shows the downturned mouth of sadness; others habitually experience an emotion (like sadness) enough so traces of the emotional display are permanently etched into the face. (7) The Ever-Ready Expressors. This style refers to a tendency to display a given emotion, as an initial response, to almost any stimulus. Even though you expected to be reprimanded by your boss, you might initially respond with surprise—followed, perhaps, by anger. (8) The Flooded-Affect Expressors. This is a style Ekman and Friesen have observed primarily with disturbed individuals and people experiencing intense life crises. If a person is flooded with fear, for instance, he or she may not only maintain some of these features constantly, but when another emotion is provoked it will likely be colored or eradicated by the fearful state. As a final note on styles of expression, it has been noted by Seaford that there may even be "facial dialects." He found, for instance, that people in some Southern states seemed to show certain facial configurations that were not common to other regions of the United States.[7]

The preceding discussion of display rules and styles of emotional facial expression demonstrates that we have considerable control over our facial expressions—and this control is manifested in a variety of ways. Yes, we can present facial messages which we don't feel, but sometimes we lie imperfectly—enacting an expression at the wrong time; enacting an expression too often or for too long a time, as when we insincerely display a smile too long; or enacting expressions with an inappropriate use of various facial muscles. Any or all of these factors may help us separate genuine from pseudoexpressions of emotion on the face. We can't deny, however, that we are aware of the communicative potential of our face and we tend to monitor it carefully—inhibiting when desired and exhibiting when desired. With the constant feedback we receive about our facial expressions, we become rather proficient at controlling them. As Ekman and Friesen put it:

> Although we usually are aware of our facial affect displays, they may occur with or without a deliberate intention to communicate. Similarly, inhibition of facial display, control of facial display, or dissimulation of an affect (looking cool even when tense), may or may not be intentional. Because we have such good feedback about our facial behavior, we usually are aware of what happens the moment we change facial movements.[8]

[7]H. W. Seaford, "Facial Expression Dialect: An Example," in A. Kendon, R. M. Harris, and M. R. Key (eds.), *Organization of Behavior in Face-to-Face Interaction* (Chicago: Aldine, 1975).
[8]P. Ekman and W. V. Friesen, "The Repertoire of Nonverbal Behavior: Categories, Origins, Usage, and Coding," *Semiotica* 1 (1969): 76.

The Effects of the Face on Human Communication

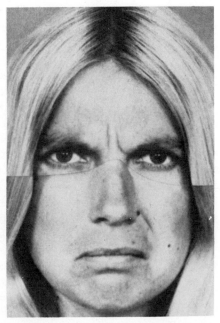

Figure 8.1 Facial Blends [Figures 8.1 and 8.3–8.8 are from: P. Ekman and W. V. Friesen, *Unmasking the Face: A Guide to Recognizing Emotions from Facial Clues,* 1975. Reprinted by permission of Prentice-Hall, Inc., Englewood Cliffs, New Jersey.]

Another important aspect of our facial expressions is that we don't always portray "pure" or single emotional states in which, for example, all the parts of our face show anger. Instead, the face conveys multiple emotions. These are called *affect blends.* These facial blends of several emotions may appear on the face in a number of different ways: (1) One emotion is shown in one facial area and another is shown in another area—for example, brows are raised as in surprise, and lips are pressed as in anger. (2) Two different emotions are shown in one part of the face—for example, one brow is raised as in surprise and the other lowered as in anger. (3) A facial display is produced by muscle action associated with two emotions, but containing specific elements of neither.[9] In Figure 8.1 you will see two examples of facial blends. The brows/forehead area and the eyes/lids area show anger while the mouth shows sadness. This might occur, for example, if your instructor told you that your grade on an exam you considered unfair was an "F." You feel sad about the low grade and angry at

[9]P. Ekman, W. V. Friesen, and S. S. Tomkins, "Facial Affect Scoring Technique: A First Validity Study," *Semiotica* 3 (1971): 53.

The Effects of the Face on Human Communication

the instructor. The other photograph shows a blend of happiness (mouth area) and surprise (eyebrows/forehead, eyes/lids, and a slight dropping of the jaw). Such an expression could occur if you thought you were going to get an "F" on an exam but you received an "A."'

A final note about the complexity of our face concerns what Haggard and Issacs have called "micromomentary facial expressions."[10] While searching for indications of nonverbal communication between therapist and patient, they ran some film at slow motion and noticed that the expression of the patient's face would sometimes change dramatically—from a smile to a grimace to a smile for example—within a few frames of the film. Further analysis revealed that when they ran their films at four frames per second instead of the normal twenty-four frames, there were 2½ times as many changes of expression. At normal speed, expressions which came and went in about one-fifth second escaped notice; expressions which took about two-fifths second were seen as changes, but the kind of change could not be identified; expressions lasting longer than two-fifths second were usually identified, but not always the same way. It is thought these micromomentary expressions reveal actual emotional states but are condensed in time because of repressive processes. They are often incompatible with both the apparent expression and the patient's words. One patient, saying nice things about a friend, had a seemingly pleasant facial expression; slow motion films revealed a wave of anger cross her face. We are now ready to return to one of our original questions: "What emotions does the face portray?"

Primary Affect Displays.   Although the face is capable of making hundreds of distinct movements and communicating many emotional states, those which have been uncovered by virtually every researcher since 1940 are surprise, fear, anger, disgust, happiness, and sadness. Others such as interest and shame are also frequently discussed, but the exact facial muscle movements associated with these states are not well known at this time. In addition to information about specific emotions, people also seem to judge facial expressions primarily along the following dimensions: pleasant/unpleasant; active/passive; and intense/controlled. Comparatively few researchers have actually measured changes in facial musculature and matched these with various emotional states. This is why the work of Paul Ekman and his colleagues represents a major advance in the study of facial expressions of emotion. Ekman has developed a coding system for the six emotions which seem to be at the foundation of most expressions—namely, surprise, fear, anger, disgust, happiness, and sadness. From these expressions, we can derive many emotions

[10]E. A. Haggard and F. S. Issacs, "Micromomentary Facial Expressions as Indicators of Ego Mechanisms in Psychotherapy," in L. A. Gottschalk and A. H. Auerback (eds.), *Methods of Research in Psychotherapy*, (New York: Appleton-Century-Crofts, 1966).

The Effects of the Face on Human Communication

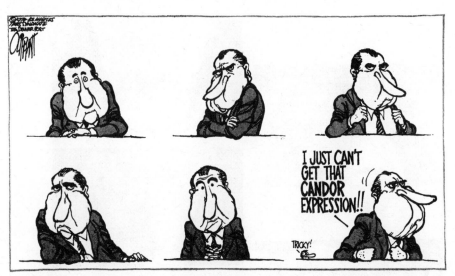

Pat Oliphant, Copyright © 1974, The Denver Post. Reprinted with permission, Los Angeles Times Syndicate.

which differ only in intensity or which are simply blends of these primary emotions. Ekman calls his system the Facial Affect Scoring Technique (FAST).[11] Coding is broken down into three areas of the face: the brows/forehead area; the eyes/lids/bridge of the nose area; and the lower face—including the cheek-nose-mouth-chin-jaw. This system recognizes that for each component part of the face, there is an acceptable range of movement or positions which can be enacted and will still communicate the intended emotion. Figure 8.2 shows the FAST items for surprise. Coders are trained to recognize the various components of each emotion from photographic examples and verbal descriptions. After about six hours of training, coders were able to identify emotional expressions with high levels of accuracy. Since twenty-eight different people were used for the stimulus expressions, it is felt that the FAST technique overcomes many of the differences in facial expressions associated with age, sex, physiognomy, and lighting. From this research, we can learn some very specific details about facial movement for different emotional expressions.

For instance, there does not seem to be any one area of the face which best

[11]P. Ekman, W. V. Friesen, and S. S. Tomkins, "Facial Affect Scoring Technique: A First Validity Study," *Semiotica* 3 (1971): 37–58. An important extension of this work is the development of Facial Action Code which measures visibly different movements of the face according to their anatomical bases. See: P. Ekman and W. V. Friesen, "Measuring Facial Movement." *Environmental Psychology and Nonverbal Behavior* 1 (1976): 56–75.

The Effects of the Face on Human Communication

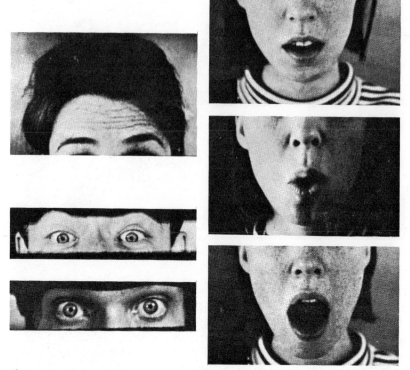

Figure 8.2 FAST items for surprise. [From P. Ekman, W. V. Friesen, and S. S. Tomkins, "Facial Affect Scoring Technique: A First Validity Study," *Semiotica* 3 (1971): 41.]

Figure 8.3 Surprise (facing page top)
—The brows are raised, so that they are curved and high.
—The skin below the brow is stretched.
—Horizontal wrinkles go across the forehead.
—The eyelids are opened; the upper lid is raised and the lower lid drawn down; the white of the eye—the sclera—shows above the iris, and often below as well.
—The jaw drops open so that the lips and teeth are parted, but there is no tension or stretching of the mouth.

Figure 8.4 Fear (facing page bottom)
—The brows are raised and drawn together.
—The wrinkles in the forehead are in the center, not across the entire forehead.
—The upper eyelid is raised, exposing sclera, and the lower eyelid is tensed and drawn up.
—The mouth is open and the lips are either tensed slightly and drawn back or stretched and drawn back.

The Effects of the Face on Human Communication

272

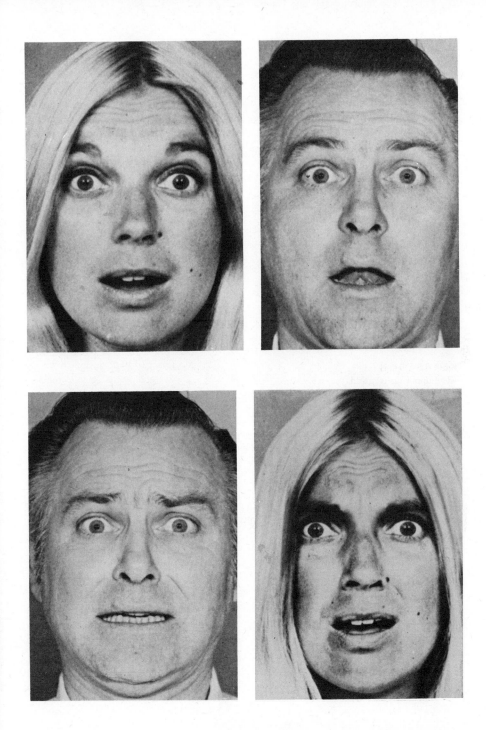

The Effects of the Face on Human Communication

273

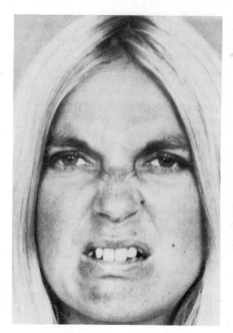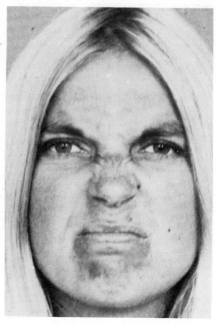

Figure 8.5 Disgust

—The upper lip is raised.

—The lower lip is also raised and pushed up to the upper lip, or is lowered and slightly protruding.

—The nose is wrinkled.

—The cheeks are raised.

—Lines show below the lower lid, and the lid is pushed up but not tense.

—The brow is lowered, lowering the upper lid.

The Effects of the Face on Human Communication

 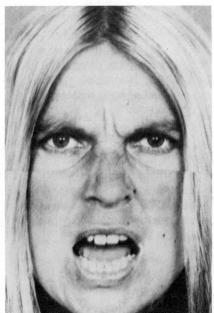

Figure 8.6 Anger
—The brows are lowered and drawn together.
—Vertical lines appear between the brows.
—The lower lid is tensed and may or may not be raised.
—The upper lid is tense and may or may not be lowered by the action of the brow.
—The eyes have a hard stare and may have a bulging appearance.
—The lips are in either of two basic positions: pressed firmly together, with the corners straight or down; or open, tensed in a squarish shape as if shouting.
—The nostrils may be dilated, but this is not essential to the anger facial expression and may also occur in sadness.
—There is ambiguity unless anger is registered in all three facial areas.

The Effects of the Face on Human Communication

Figure 8.7 Happiness
—Corners of lips are drawn back and up.
—The mouth may or may not be parted, with teeth exposed or not.
—A wrinkle (the naso-labial fold) runs down from the nose to the outer edge beyond the lip corners.
—The cheeks are raised.
—The lower eyelid shows wrinkles below it, and may be raised but not tense.
—Crow's-feet wrinkles go outward from the outer corners of the eyes (covered by hair in these photographs).

reveals emotions, but for any given emotion, a particular area of the face may carry the most important information for identification. For disgust the nose/cheeks/mouth area is crucial; for fear it is the eyes/eyelids; for sadness we would do well to examine the brows/forehead and eyes/eyelids; the important areas for happiness seem to be the cheeks/mouth and eyes/eyelids; anger relies heavily on the cheeks/mouth and brows/forehead areas; and surprise can be seen in any of the three areas of the face.

The Effects of the Face on Human Communication

276

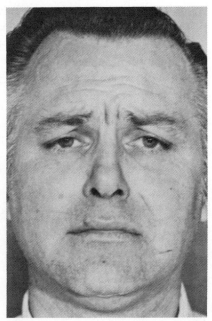

Figure 8.8 Sadness
—The inner corners of the eyebrows are drawn up.
—The skin below the eyebrow is triangulated, with the inner corner up.
—The upper eyelid inner corner is raised.
—The corners of the lips are down or the lip is trembling.

Now that we have examined the face itself and explored the characteristics of some basic emotional expressions, we shall return to our question of whether facial expressions of emotion can be accurately judged.

Judging Facial Expressions of Emotion. An in-depth analysis of all the important studies of facial expression prompted Ekman, Friesen, and Ellsworth to draw the following conclusion: "Contrary to the impression conveyed by previous reviews of the literature that the evidence in the field is contradictory and confusing, our reanalysis showed consistent evidence of accurate judgment of emotion from facial behavior."[12] Ekman and his col-

[12]P. Ekman, W. V. Friesen, and P. Ellsworth, *Emotion in the Human Face: Guidelines for Research and an Integration of Findings* (Elmsford, N.Y.: Pergamon, 1972), p. 107.

The Effects of the Face on Human Communication

leagues rightly acknowledge that this conclusion pertains primarily to posed expressions, but an increasing number of studies of spontaneous expressions also show accurate perceptions. Because of the difficulty involved in measuring responses to facial expressions, and because so much of the literature concerns itself with these measurement problems, we will discuss measurement more than we have in previous chapters. The whole question of how we measure responses to facial expressions is central to any statement about how accurate we are in judging these expressions.

Examine the three faces shown in Figure 8.9. Then consider the following methods of responding. Would your responses differ depending on the method used? Is one method easier or harder than another? Is one likely to elicit greater accuracy?

1. In the space below, write in the emotion being expressed in each of the faces you observed.
   A.＿＿＿＿   B.＿＿＿＿   C.＿＿＿＿
2. From the choices below, select the one emotion which best describes Face A; Face B; and Face C.
   A. Rage＿＿   B. Happiness＿＿   C. Sadness＿＿
      Anger＿＿   Joy＿＿   Despair＿＿
      Wrath＿＿   Delight＿＿   Solemnity＿＿
      Indignation＿＿   Amusement＿＿   Despondency＿＿
      Resentment＿＿   Pleasure＿＿   Melancholy＿＿
3. From this list of emotions, select the one which best describes Face A, Face B, and Face C: Happiness, Sadness, Surprise, Fear, Anger.

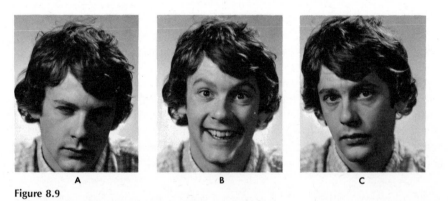

A   B   C

Figure 8.9

The Effects of the Face on Human Communication

This example illustrates one of the many problems involved in testing the accuracy of judgments about facial expressions—the type of response required from the judge. In this case, judging accuracy would depend a great deal on which set of instructions the judge got. In the first testing condition, we have a totally open or free response from the judge. This will provide a wide range of responses, and the researcher will be faced with the problem of deciding whether the judge's label corresponds with his or her label for the emotion. Sometimes the researcher elicits a label which, under other testing conditions, may be perceived as a blend—for example, smugness may contain facial features found in both happiness and anger expressions. The labels used by the experimenter and the responder may be different, but both of them may respond the same way to the actual emotion in real life. This also raises the problem of the gap between perceiving and naming emotional responses so that others understand. In the second testing condition, the discriminatory task is too difficult—the emotions listed in each category are too much alike. We can predict low accuracy for judges given these instructions. In some cases, the labels may all focus on variants of the same emotion and the perceiver sees something completely different—but is prohibited from adding new categories. For example, photograph "C" seems to be perceived by the researcher as a form of sadness, but a judge might see it as neutral. The last set of instructions is just the opposite of the second set—the discriminatory task is very easy. Since the emotion categories are discrete, we can predict high accuracy for the third condition.

Accuracy is also likely to vary based on whether the emotion presented to the judge is "real" rather than simulated or acted. Obviously, acted emotions are based on perceptions of real ones, but they are frequently exaggerated, based on stereotypes, and, hence, easier to identify. We are also concerned here with the fact that in "real" situations, a person may or may not be trying to communicate a particular state to others, while an actor is, by the nature of the experiment, trying his best to communicate the emotion he is instructed to portray.

Studies have varied with respect to how these emotions are elicited. Some simply describe a situation and tell the actor to react as if he or she were in that situation, others give a list of emotions and tell the actor to portray the emotion, and some use candid photos of people in real situations. One laboratory study reached an almost comic extreme.[13] A camera was set up in a laboratory—ready to catch the subject's expressions at the proper moment. To elicit an expression of pain, the experimenter would bend the subject's finger backward

[13]K. Dunlap, "The Role of Eye-Muscles and Mouth-Muscles in the Expression of the Emotions." *Genetic Psychology Monographs* 2 (1927): 199–233.

The Effects of the Face on Human Communication

forcibly; to produce a startled look, the experimenter fired a pistol behind the subject at an unexpected moment; apprehension was elicited by telling the subject the pistol would be fired again close to his ear on the count of three; at the count of two the photo was taken; amusement was captured when the experimenter told the subject some jokes; disgust resulted from the subject's smelling the odor from the test tube which contained tissues of a dead rat, reposed, and corked for several months; and finally—an unbelievable manipulation in the name of science—to elicit an expression of grief, a subject was hypnotized and told several members of his family had been killed in a wreck! "Unfortunately," the camera could not catch intense grief because the subject bowed his head and cried—so the experimenter said he had to settle for an expression of mild grief to be used in the study! Another interesting point from this particular study brings us back to our discussion of facial control and display rules. Dunlap found all of his women subjects made facial expressions which approached amusement under what were supposed to be pain conditions. This was not true for the men, nor did it match the women's verbal description of how they felt. It did hurt! This material on how emotions were elicited is reported simply to demonstrate that this factor can make a difference in judging accuracy.

Some studies have even found that positive or pleasant expressions are perceived more accurately than unpleasant ones. This finding is sometimes the result of using stimulus faces which do not adequately portray the emotion in each facial area. Accurate identifications of anger, for instance, need to show the appropriate facial components in all three areas of the face outlined previously.

Sometimes even the smallest changes in faces can make a considerable difference in what we observe. Stritch and Secord found that very slight changes in faces can make critical differences in personality and physiognomic judgments of faces.[14] They had an artist retouch photos so as to systematically change such things as grooming of the hair, mouth curvature, eye wrinkles, heaviness of eyebrows, and brightness of eyes. In some cases, such minute changes caused significantly different evaluations by the judges with respect to dimensions of personality and physiognomic features. For instance, when mouth curvature was changed to appear "straight" (rather than up and down), judges perceived changes in the lips (thicker) and complexion (lighter) although these features had not been changed.

Another variable which confounds interpretation of facial research is the variety of methods by which the facial stimuli have been presented to judges. Are they "live" faces, still photographs, drawings, sketches, video tapes or

[14]T. Stritch and P. Secord, "Interaction Effects in the Perception of Faces," *Journal of Personality* 24 (1956): 272–284.

The Effects of the Face on Human Communication

films? Some research suggests greater accuracy is achieved when filmed expressions are used. Frequently, the length of observation differs from study to study, and there is always the question of advantages and disadvantages in seeing faces which are larger (on movie screen) or smaller (small photos) than those seen in everyday interaction situations. Earlier, in Chapter 2, we mentioned research by Ekman which found high levels of agreement on posed facial expressions across a variety of literate and preliterate cultures. This led Ekman and his colleagues to propose that posed expressions differ little from spontaneous expressions in *form*. However, there are differences in such things as duration of the expression, the absence of control or manipulation of the expression in posed examples, and the higher frequency of single emotion faces (rather than blends) in posed expressions. One obvious advantage in using filmed expressions is that the judge can easily tell whether a particular feature is part of the person's permanent facial configuration or whether it is only a part of a given emotional expression.

Prior exposure to a face will make a difference in emotional judgment accuracy. If you are familiar with the face and have seen it express other emotions, you are more likely to correctly identify another emotion you have not seen before. If you are familiar with the person, you again have a better reference point for making judgments. For instance, a person who is frequently smiling and who you see not smiling may seem very sad. With another person, absence of a smile may simply be part of a normal, neutral expression. Laughery et al. found that the longer one was exposed to an expression of emotion on a face and the earlier this face appeared in a test series, the greater were the chances of accurate recognition.[15]

Several studies make it clear that additional knowledge concerning the context in which a particular facial expression occurs will affect accuracy in judging the emotion expressed. We can accurately identify facial expressions of emotion without any knowledge of the context in which it occurs, but co-occurring perceptions of the social context, the environment, and other people will surely affect our judgments. Although a number of investigators have pursued the question of whether context or expression dominates perceptions, the issue is far from resolved. Perhaps the most often cited study regarding the influence of context in face judging is one by Munn.[16] Facial expressions taken from *Life* and *Look* magazines were shown with and without background context. The background information was very helpful in the identification of these facial expressions. Verbal cues describing the situation also seem

[15]K. R. Laughery, J. F. Alexander, and A. B. Lane, "Recognition of Human Faces: Effects of Target Exposure Time, Target Position, Pose Position, and Type of Photograph," *Journal of Applied Psychology* 55 (1971): 477–483.

[16]N. L. Munn, "The Effect of Knowledge of the Situation upon Judgment of Emotion from Facial Expression," *Journal of Abnormal and Social Psychology* 35 (1940): 324–338.

The Effects of the Face on Human Communication

to increase accuracy. Munn's study sampled a limited number of faces, emotions, and contexts, but it does bring to our attention another important dimension to consider in studying facial expressions. One of my students, as part of a term project assignment, showed two faces to groups of judges with only the background color varied. The facial expressions were previously identified as "neutral." This student found in her limited study that even changing the background color can change interpretation of the facial expression. Warm, bright colors resulted in more positive or "happy" responses; dark or dull tones produced more negative or "not particularly happy" responses. Cline used line drawings to test the effect of having another face as part of the total context.[17] He found that the expression on one face influenced interpretation of the other face and vice versa. As an example, when the smiling face in Figure 8.10 was paired with a glum face. it was seen as the dominant face, that of a vicious, gloating, taunting bully. When seen with the frowning face, the smiling face seemed peaceful, friendly, and happy. Cline probably summed up many of the studies of context and facial expression when he made the following observations about his own study: "Certain psychological properties of the drawings appear to inhere in the faces independently of their perceived social matrix, while others are clearly a function of the nature of interaction."[18]

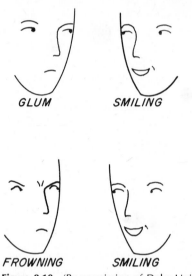

GLUM   SMILING

FROWNING   SMILING

Figure 8.10 (By permission of Duke University Press)

Finally, we must be concerned about the characteristics of the people photographed and the people doing the judging. Although this seems to be an extremely important variable in testing accuracy, consistent and reliable findings are not always available. Some preliminary work by Ekman's research team, which required individuals to imitate certain expressions, uncovered reliable individual differences in ability to make certain facial movements. The proficiency of the expression "portrayer" may make a vast difference in how accurately others perceive his or her expressions. It is clear that you, as a judge, will probably be influenced by the type and structure of the face you see.

[17]M. Cline, "The Influence of Social Context on the Perception of Faces," *Journal of Personality* 25 (1956): 142–158.
[18]Ibid., p. 157.

The Effects of the Face on Human Communication

Eiland and Richardson, for instance, report significantly different interpretations of faces differing in age, sex, and race.[19] Several studies by Buck and others suggest females are better senders (portrayers), as well as receivers or decoders.[20] Others, however, find the sex of the person presenting the emotion has little influence on observer interpretations.[21] At present, all of these conclusions must remain tentative; differences in the facial properties of emotion portrayers (and the resulting effect) is just beginning to be understood.

We also suspect that some people are able to judge emotions from faces with greater accuracy than others—but again, we have only hints at what those characteristics might be. Obviously, the observer's own emotional state and degree of attentiveness are important. In everyday interaction, some expressions may be enacted so quickly we may miss them during a normal period of gaze aversion. Individuals who monitor their own behavior closely may be better judges of expressions in others; people who are very facially expressive may perceive more than those who exert a lot of self-control on their expressiveness. Some feel intelligence accounts for a small portion of one's sensitivity to facial cues; some feel age is a factor, with youthful judges having insufficient experience and older judges possibly having difficulty picking up visual cues in the facial area; some feel women have perceptual superiority in this area; some feel that individual differences are related to perceiving particular emotions and not all emotions; but some feel there are those who have a "general ability" for judging emotional meaning in a wide variety of situations—vocal, musical, facial, and the like. Shapiro's work shows that some people do have a predilection for observing facial cues while others consistently choose to respond to linguistic cues. If this is true, perhaps those who choose facial cues have been reinforced for their previous accuracy.

If we are seeking the ideal conditions under which a person could be most accurate in judging facial expressions of emotion—and we based our conditions on the research to date—we might suggest something like this: (1) Give the judges some prior experience in judging emotion in faces; train them. (2) Give the judges some exposure to the face they will be judging prior to the experiment, showing it in emotional states other than the one to be judged. (3) Use good actors to portray the emotions and ask them to exaggerate. (4) Use films. (5) Make the judge's discriminatory task easy, use terminology which is

[19] R. Eiland and D. Richardson, "The Influence of Race, Sex and Age on Judgments of Emotion Portrayed in Photographs," *Communication Monographs* 43 (1976) 167–175.

[20] R. Buck, R. E. Miller, and W. F. Caul, "Sex, Personality, and Physiological Variables in the Communication of Affect via Facial Expression," *Journal of Personality and Social Psychology* 30 (1974): 587–596; M. Zuckerman, J. A. Hall, R. S. DeFrank, and R. Rosenthal, "Encoding and Decoding of Spontaneous and Posed Facial Expressions," *Journal of Personality and Social Psychology* 34 (1977): 966–977.

[21] R. Dunhame and J. Herman, "Development of a Female Faces Scale for Measuring Job Satisfaction," *Journal of Applied Psychology* 60 (1975): 629–631.

The Effects of the Face on Human Communication

familiar, and make the emotions form discrete categories. (6) Make sure the judges can see the entire face; the more of the person they can see, the better. (7) Make sure the judges are not of subnormal intelligence and do not represent extremes in age. (8) Allow the judges to be aware of the context of the expression and what evoked it. (9) Allow the judges plenty of time to observe. (10) Make sure they can see the face clearly—preferably on a large screen.

Thus far we have been examining the sending and receiving of messages relevant to one's emotional state. A few researchers have asked questions which go beyond the momentary expression of emotion—that is, does the facial expression of emotion tell us anything about how others will react or what behavior the sender is likely to engage in following a given expression?

Facial Expressions and Subsequent Reactions. Ekman and his colleagues were interested in whether facial expressions displayed while watching televised violence would be related to subsequent aggressiveness.[22] They predicted that facial expressions of emotion showing happiness, pleasantness, and interest would predict more subsequent aggressive behavior than unpleasant, sad, painful, and disinterested expressions. Some five- and six-year-old children watched a sports program, while others saw a scene from "The Untouchables" which included a killing, a chase, the shooting and death of one villain, and an extended fist fight involving a second villain. The segment was only 3½ minutes long. Then the children were put into a situation where they could help or hurt another child who was supposedly working in the next room. Hurting behavior (making another's task more difficult) was deemed to be a manifestation of aggressiveness. The boys who displayed the pleasant expressions did engage in more aggressive behavior; the girls did not. It remains to be seen whether the portrayal of violence using female role models would evoke similar behavior.

Savitsky et al. were interested in whether facial expressions of emotion on the part of a "victim" would have any effect on the aggressor's behavior.[23] When individuals thought they were controlling the amount of electric shock that another person (victim) would get, they gave more shocks to victims who responded with expressions of happiness and smiles and fewer to victims who displayed expressions of anger. Expressions of fear and neutrality did not differ from each other nor did they affect shock behavior.

[22]P. Ekman, R. M. Liebert, W. V. Friesen, R. Harrison, C. Zlatchin, E. J. Malstrom, and R. A. Baron, "Facial Expressions of Emotion While Watching Televised Violence as Predictors of Subsequent Aggression," in *Television and Social Behavior,* Vol. 5: *Television's Effects: Further Explorations,* report to the Surgeon General's Scientific Advisory Committee on Television and Social Behavior (Washington: U.S. Government Printing Office, 1972).

[23]J. C. Savitsky, C. E. Izard, W. E. Kotsch, and L. Christy, "Aggressor's Response to the Victim's Facial Expression of Emotion," *Journal of Research on Personality* 7 (1974): 346–357.

The Effects of the Face on Human Communication

In another study, Savitsky and Sim tried to find out what effect facial expressions had on evaluations of a defendant's account of his crime.[24] Defendants told the story of their crime (petty thefts and vandalism) and varied their emotional expressions. Anger, happiness, sadness, and neutral expressions were used. Sad/distressed and neutral defendants were apparently seen most favorably—that is, their crimes were rated as less severe, they were perceived as less likely to commit another crime, and they were given the least amount of punishment. Angry (and to a lesser degree, happy) defendants were evaluated the most harshly.

Summary

This discussion of the face and its role in human communication should leave you with several impressions.

First, the face is a multimessage system. It can communicate information regarding your personality, your interest and responsiveness during interaction, and your emotional states. Although there is little doubt that people do associate certain personality characteristics with certain faces and facial features, the research to date does not tell us much. We know the face is used as a conversational regulator—opening and closing communication channels, complementing and qualifying other behaviors, and replacing spoken messages.

We learned that facial expressions are very complex entities to deal with. Of all the areas of the body, the face seems to elicit the best external and internal feedback, which makes it easy for us to follow a variety of facial display rules. Not all facial displays represent single emotions; some are "blends" of several emotions. Sometimes we will show some aspects of an emotional display when we aren't actually feeling it, as with facial "emblems" which represent commentary on emotions. When we subject the face to microscopic analysis (using slow-motion film), we uncover rapidly changing facial expressions which reflect repressed affective states. These are called micromomentary facial expressions. They are so fleeting that they are rarely noticed in everyday conversation. We also listed a number of common expressive styles and suggested there may even be regional dialects in facial expressions.

We noted some of the measurement problems involved in the study of facial expressions: the complexity of the decisions observers are asked to make, simulated as opposed to "real" expressions, the skill of the "portrayer," the method of presenting the face to the observer (films, photos, and the like), prior exposure to the face, knowledge of the context, and characteristics of the target face and the perceiver. Naturally, all these factors may impinge on one's accu-

---

[24]J. C. Savitsky and M. E. Sim, "Trading Emotions: Equity Theory of Reward and Punishment," *Journal of Communication* 24 (1974): 140–146.

The Effects of the Face on Human Communication

racy in identifying facial expressions of emotion, but Ekman's research suggests we can be accurate in our assessments of emotion from the face if we are given proper training. His Facial Affect Scoring Technique (FAST) seems to provide us with a useful device for providing that training. Ekman and his colleagues, after studying many people and many emotions in a variety of contexts, have developed what amounts to a facial dictionary for at least six primary facial affects and thirty-three blends. We outlined the components of the six emotions which seem to be uncovered in almost every study of facial expressions to date: anger, sadness, fear, surprise, happiness, and disgust/contempt.

We concluded this chapter with reports from a few studies which suggest that the identification of facial expressions of emotion may help us predict subsequent behaviors—of the person showing the affect and of people responding to it. Generally, we would predict more immediate aggressiveness from male children who view violent TV programs with pleasant affect, we would expect more aggressive reactions from people who see pleasant reactions on the faces of their victims, and we would predict that neutral or sad/distressed looks will be most favorably responded to as judge and jury scrutinize the defendant's expressions.

SELECTED BIBLIOGRAPHY

Abelson, R. P., and Sermat, V. "Multidimensional Scaling of Facial Expressions." *Journal of Experimental Psychology* 63 (1962): 546–551.

Andrew, R. J. "Evolution of Facial Expression." *Science* 142 (1963): 1034–1041.

Andrew, R. J. "The Origins of Facial Expression." *Scientific American* 213 (1965): 88–94.

Bokander, I. "Precognitive Perception of Facial Photographs." *Scandinavian Journal of Psychology* 6 (1965): 103–108.

Bokander, I., and Radeborg, K. "The Solution of Perceptual Conflict Between Stereoscopically Presented Facial Photographs." *Scandinavian Journal of Psychology* 8 (1967): 187–192.

Boucher, J. D. "Facial Displays of Fear, Sadness, and Pain." *Perceptual and Motor Skills* 28 (1969): 239–242.

Boucher, J. D., and Ekman, P. "Facial Areas of Emotional Information." *Journal of Communication* 25 (1975): 21–29.

Brannigan, C. R., and Humphries, D. A. "Human Non-verbal Behaviour, A Means of Communication." In N. Blurton Jones (Ed.), *Ethological Studies of Child Behaviour.* New York: Cambridge University Press, 1972.

Buck, R. "Nonverbal Communication of Affect in Children." *Journal of Personality and Social Psychology* 31 (1975): 644–653.

Buck, R., Miller, R. E., and Caul, W. F. "Sex, Personality, and Physiological Variables in the Communication of Affect via Facial Expression." *Journal of Personality and Social Psychology* 30 (1974): 587–596.

Buck, R. W., Savin, V. J., Miller, R. E., and Caul, W. F. "Communication of Affect Through Facial Expressions in Humans." *Journal of Personality and Social Psychology* 23 (1972): 362–371.

Bugental, D. E., Love, L. R., and Gianetto, R. M. "Perfidious Feminine Faces." *Journal of Personality and Social Psychology* 17 (1971): 314–318.

Buzby, D. E. "The Interpretation of Facial Expression." *American Journal of Psychology* 35 (1924): 604.

Chance, J., Goldstein, A. G., and Schicht, W. "Effects of Acquaintance and Friendship on Children's Recognition of Classmates' Faces." *Psychonomic Science* 7 (1967): 223–224.

Cline, M. "The Influence of Social Context on the Perception of Faces." *Journal of Personality* 25 (1956): 142–158.

Coleman, J. D. "Facial Expressions of Emotions." *Psychological Monographs* 63, No. 1, whole No. 296 (1949).

Cuceloglu, D. M. "Facial Code in Affective Communication." *Comparative Group Studies* 3 (1972): 395–408.

Cuceloglu, D. M. "Perception of Facial Expressions in Three Different Cultures." *Ergonomics* 13 (1970): 93–100.

Darwin, C. *The Expression of Emotions in Man and Animals*. London: John Murray, 1872. Reprint, Chicago: University of Chicago Press, 1965.

Davitz, J. R. "A Review of Research Concerned with Facial and Vocal Expressions of Emotion." In J. R. Davitz (ed.), *The Communication of Emotional Meaning*. New York: McGraw-Hill, 1964. Pp. 13–23.

Dickey, E. C., and Knower, F. H. "A Note on Some Ethnological Differences in Recognition of Simulated Expressions of the Emotions." *American Journal of Sociology* 47 (1941): 190–193.

Drag, R. M., and Shaw, M. E. "Factors Influencing the Communication of Emotional Intent by Facial Expression." *Psychonomic Science* 8 (1967): 137–138.

Dunhame, R., and Herman, J. "Development of a Female Faces Scale for Measuring Job Satisfaction." *Journal of Applied Psychology* 60 (1975): 629–631.

Dunlap, K. "The Role of Eye-Muscles and Mouth Muscles in the Expression of the Emotions." *Genetic Psychology Monographs* 2 (1927): 199–233.

Dusenberry, D., and Knower, F. H. "Experimental Studies of the Symbolism of Action and Voice. I. A Study of the Specificity of Meaning in Facial Expression." *Quarterly Journal of Speech* 24 (1938): 424–435.

Eiland, R., and Richardson, D. "The Influence of Race, Sex and Age on Judgments of Emotion Portrayed in Photographs." *Communication Monographs* 43 (1976): 167–175.

The Effects of the Face on Human Communication

Ekman, P. "Constants Across Cultures in the Face and Emotion." *Journal of Personality and Social Psychology* 17 (1971): 124–129.

Ekman, P. (ed.), *Darwin and Facial Expression*. New York: Academic Press, 1973.

Ekman, P. "Universals and Cultural Differences in Facial Expressions of Emotion." In J. Cole (ed.), *Nebraska Symposium on Motivation, 1971*. Lincoln: University of Nebraska Press, 1972.

Ekman, P. "VID-R and SCAN: 'Tools and Methods in the Analyses of Facial Expression and Body Movement.' " In G. Gerbner, O. Holsti, K. Krippendorff, W. Paisley, and P. Stone (eds.), *Content Analysis*. New York: Wiley, 1969.

Ekman, P., and Friesen, W. V. "Head and Body Cues in the Judgment of Emotion: A Reformulation." *Perceptual and Motor Skills* 24 (1967): 711–724.

Ekman, P., and Friesen, W. V. "Measuring Facial Movement." *Environmental Psychology and Nonverbal Behavior* 1 (1976): 56–75.

Ekman, P., and Friesen, W. V. *The Facial Atlas* (in preparation).

Ekman, P., Friesen, W. V., and Ellsworth, P. *Emotion in the Human Face*. Elmsford, N.Y.: Pergamon Press, 1972.

Ekman, P., Friesen, W. V., and Tomkins, S. S. "Facial Affect Scoring Technique: A First Validity Study." *Semiotica* 3 (1971): 37–58.

Ekman, P., Sorenson, E. R., and Friesen, W. V. "Pan-cultural Elements in Facial Displays of Emotion." *Science* 164 (1969): 86–88.

Ekman, P., Liebert, R. M., Friesen, W. V., Harrison, R., Zlatchin, C., Malmstrom, E. J., and Baron, R. A. "Facial Expressions of Emotion While Watching Televised Violence as Predictors of Subsequent Aggression. In *Television and Social Behavior*, Vol. 5: *Television's Effects: Further Explorations*. Report to the Surgeon General's Scientific Advisory Committee on Television and Social Behavior. Washington: U.S. Government Printing Office, 1972.

Engen, T., and Levy, N. "Constant-Sum Judgments of Facial Expressions." *Journal of Experimental Psychology* 51 (1956): 396–398.

Engen, T., Levy, N., and Schlosberg, H. "The Dimensional Analysis of a New Series of Facial Expressions." *Journal of Experimental Psychology* 55 (1958): 454–458.

Feleky, A. M. "The Expression of the Emotions." *Psychological Review* 21 (1914): 33–41.

Fields, S. J. "Discrimination of Facial Expression and Its Relation to Personal Adjustment." *American Psychologist* 5 (1950): 309.

Frijda, N. "Facial Expression and Situational Cues." *Journal of Abnormal and Social Psychology* 57 (1958): 149–154.

Frijda, N. H. "Recognition of Emotion." In L. Berkowitz (ed.), *Advances in*

Experimental Social Psychology, Vol. 4. New York: Academic Press, 1969.

Frijda, N. H. "The Relation Between Emotion and Expression." In M. von Cranach and I. Vine (eds.), *Social Communication and Movement*. New York: Academic Press, 1973.

Frijda, N. H. "The Understanding of Facial Expression of Emotion." *Acta Psychologica* 9 (1953): 294–362.

Frijda, N. H., and Philipszoon, E. "Dimensions of Recognition of Emotion." *Journal of Abnormal Social Psychology* 66 (1963): 45–51.

Frois-Wittman, J. "The Judgment of Facial Expression." *Journal of Experimental Psychology* 13 (1930): 113–151.

Fulcher, J. S. " 'Voluntary' Facial Expression in Blind and Seeing Children." *Archives of Psychology* 38 (1942): 272.

Gates, G. S. "A Test for Ability to Interpret Facial Expressions." *Psychological Bulletin* 22 (1925): 120.

Gladstones, W. H. "A Multidimensional Study of Facial Expression of Emotion." *Australian Journal of Psychology* 14 (1962): 95–100.

Goodenough, F. L., and Tinker, M. A. "The Relative Potency of Facial Expression and Verbal Description of Stimulus in the Judgment of Emotion." *Journal of Comparative Psychology* 12 (1931): 365–370.

Grant, E. C. "Human Facial Expression." *Man* 4 (1969): 525–536.

Gubar, G. "Recognition of Human Facial Expressions Judged Live in a Laboratory Setting." *Journal of Personality and Social Psychology* 4 (1966): 108–111.

Haggard, E. A., and Isaacs, F. S. "Micromomentary Facial Expressions as Indicators of Ego Mechanisms in Psychotherapy." In L. A. Gottschalk and A. H. Auerback (eds.), *Methods of Research in Psychotherapy*. New York: Appleton-Century-Crofts, 1966.

Hamilton, M. L. "Imitation of Facial Expression of Emotion." *Journal of Psychology* 80 (1972): 345–350.

Hamilton, M. L. "Imitative Behavior and Expressive Ability in Facial Expressions of Emotions." *Developmental Psychology* 8 (1973): 138.

Hanawalt, N. G. "The Role of the Upper and the Lower Parts of the Face as a Basis for Judging Facial Expressions—II. In Posed Expression and 'Candid Camera' Pictures." *Journal of General Psychology* 31 (1944): 23–36.

Harrison, R. "Pictic Analysis: Toward a Vocabulary and Syntax for the Pictorial Code, with Research on Facial Communication." Ph.D. dissertation, Michigan State University, 1964.

Hastorf, A. H., Osgood, C. E., and Ono, H. "The Semantics of Facial Expressions and the Prediction of the Meanings of Stereoscopically Fused Facial Expressions." *Scandinavian Journal of Psychology* 7 (1966): 179–188.

Haviland, J. M. "Sex-Related Pragmatics in Infants' Nonverbal Communication." *Journal of Communication* 27 (1977): 80–84.

The Effects of the Face on Human Communication

Howell, R. J., and Jorgenson, E. C. "Accuracy of Judging Emotional Behavior in a Natural Setting—A Replication." *Journal of Social Psychology* 81 (1970): 269–270.

Huber, E. *Evolution of Facial Musculature and Facial Expression*. Baltimore: Johns Hopkins Press, 1931.

Hulin, W. S., and Katz, D. "The Frois-Wittmann Pictures of Facial Expressions." *Journal of Experimental Psychology* 18 (1935): 482–498.

Izard, C. E. *The Face of Emotion*. New York: Appleton-Century-Crofts, 1971.

Kanner, L. "Judging Emotions from Facial Expressions." *Psychological Monographs* 41 (1931): 45.

Kauranne, U. "Qualitative Factors in Facial Expression." *Scandinavian Journal of Psychology* 7 (1964): 1–30.

Kier, R. J., and Harter, S. "Children's Ability to Order Facial and Non Facial Continua as a Function of MA, CA, and I.Q." *Journal of Genetic Psychology* 120 (1972): 241–251.

Knapp, P. (ed.). *Expression of the Emotions in Man*. New York: International Universities Press, 1963.

Laird, J. D. "Self-Attribution of Emotion: The Effects of Expressive Behavior on the Quality of Emotional Experience." *Journal of Personality and Social Psychology* 29 (1974): 475–486.

Langfeld, H. S. "The Judgment of Emotions from Facial Expressions." *Journal of Abnormal Psychology* 13 (1918): 172–184.

Lanzetta, J. T., Cartwright-Smith, J., and Kleck, R. E. "Effects of Nonverbal Dissimulation on Emotional Experience and Autonomic Arousal." *Journal of Personality and Social Psychology* 33 (1976): 354–370.

Laughery, K. R., Alexander, J. F., and Lane, A. B. "Recognition of Human Faces: Effects of Target Exposure Time, Target Position, Pose Position, and Type of Photograph." *Journal of Applied Psychology* 55 (1971): 477–483.

Leventhal, H., and Sharp, E. "Facial Expressions as Indicators of Distress." In S. S. Tomkins and C. E. Izard (eds.), *Affect, Cognition and Personality: Empirical Studies*. New York: Springer, 1965. Pp. 296–318.

Levitt, E. A. "The Relationship Between Abilities to Express Emotional Meanings Vocally and Facially." In J. R. Davitz (ed.), *The Communication of Emotional Meaning*. New York: McGraw-Hill, 1964. Pp. 87–100.

Levy, L. H., Orr, T. B., and Rosenzweig, S. "Judgments of Emotion from Facial Expression by College Students, Mental Retardates, and Mental Hospital Patients." *Journal of Personality* 28 (1960): 342–349.

Levy, N., and Schlosberg, H. "Woodworth Scale Values of the Lightfoot Pictures of Facial Expression." *Journal of Experimental Psychology* 60 (1960): 125.

Manis, M. "Context Effects in Communication." *Journal of Personality and Social Psychology* 5 (1967): 326–334.

Mead, M. "Margaret Mead Calls 'Discipline-Centric' Approach to Research an 'Example of the Appalling State of the Human Sciences.' " *Journal of Communication* 25 (1975): 209–213.

Munn, N. L. "The Effect of Knowledge of the Situation upon Judgment of Emotion from Facial Expression." *Journal of Abnormal and Social Psychology* 35 (1940): 324–338.

Odom, R. D., and Lemond, C. M. "Developmental Differences in the Perception and Production of Facial Expressions." *Child Development* 43 (1972): 359–370.

Osgood, C. E. "Dimensionality of the Semantic Space for Communication via Facial Expressions." *Scandinavian Journal of Psychology* 7 (1966): 1–30.

Osgood, C. E., and Heyer, A. W. "Objective Studies in Meaning. II. The Validity of Posed Facial Expressions as Gestural Signs in Interpersonal Communication." *American Psychologist* 5 (1950): 298.

Plutchik, R. *The Emotions: Facts, Theories, and a New Model.* New York: Random House, 1962.

Rubenstein, L. "Facial Expressions: An Objective Method in the Quantitative Evaluation of Emotional Change." *Behavior Research Methods and Instrumentation* 1 (1969): 305–306.

Ruckmick, C. A. "A Preliminary Study of Emotions." *Psychological Monographs* 30 (1921): 30–35.

Rump, E. E. "Facial Expression and Situational Cues: Demonstration of a Logical Error in Frijda's Report." *Acta Psychologica* 17 (1960): 31–38.

Saral, T. B. "Cross-Cultural Generality of Communication via Facial Expressions." *Comparative Group Studies* 3 (1972): 473–486.

Savitsky, J. C., and Sim, M. E. "Trading Emotions: Equity Theory of Reward and Punishment." *Journal of Communication* 24 (1974): 140–146.

Savitsky, J. C., Izard, C. E., Kotsch, W. E., and Christy, L. "Aggressor's Response to the Victim's Facial Expression of Emotion." *Journal of Research on Personality* 7 (1974): 346–357.

Schiffenbauer, A. "Effects of Observer's Emotional State on Judgments of the Emotional State of Others." *Journal of Personality and Social Psychology* 30 (1974): 31–35.

Schlosberg, H. A. "A Scale for the Judgment of Facial Expressions." *Journal of Experimental Psychology* 29 (1941): 497–510.

Schlosberg, H. "The Description of Facial Expressions in Terms of Two Dimensions." *Journal of Experimental Psychology* 44 (1952): 229–237.

Schlosberg, H. "Three Dimensions of Emotion." *Psychological Review* 61 (1954): 81–88.

Seaford, H. W. "Facial Expression Dialect: An Example." In A. Kendon, R. M. Harris, and M. R. Key (eds.), *Organization of Behavior in Face-to-Face Interaction.* Chicago: Aldine, 1975.

Secord, P. "Facial Features and Influence Processes in Interpersonal Perception." In R. Tagiuri and L. Petrullo (eds.), *Person Perception and Interpersonal Behavior*. Palo Alto, Calif.: Stanford University Press, 1958.

Secord, P. F., and Muthard, J. E. "Personalities in Faces—IV: A Descriptive Analysis of the Perception of Women's Faces and the Identification of Some Physiognomic Determinants." *Journal of Psychology* 39 (1955): 269–278.

Secord, P., Bevan, W., and Katz, B. "The Negro Stereotype and Perceptual Accentuation." *Journal of Abnormal and Social Psychology* 53 (1956): 78–83.

Secord, P., Dukes, W., and Bevan, W. "Personalities in Faces: I. An Experiment in Social Perceiving." *Genetic Psychology Monographs* 49 (1954): 231–279.

Shannon, A. "Facial Expression of Emotion: Recognition Patterns in Schizophrenics and Depressives." *Proceedings: 1971 ANA Research Conference*. New York: American Nurses' Association, 1971.

Shapiro, J. G. "Responsivity to Facial and Linguistic Cues." *Journal of Communication* 18 (1968): 11–17.

Shapiro, J. G., Foster, C. P., and Powell, T. "Facial and Bodily Cues of Genuineness, Empathy, and Warmth." *Journal of Clinical Psychology* 24 (1968): 233–236.

Smith, W. J., Chase, J., and Lieblich, A. K. "Tongue Showing: A Facial Display of Humans and Other Primate Species." *Semiotica* 11 (1974): 201–246.

Snyder, M. "Self-Monitoring of Expressive Behavior." *Journal of Personality and Social Psychology* 30 (1974): 526–537.

Sorce, J. F., and Campos, J. J. "The Role of Expression in the Recognition of a Face." *American Journal of Psychology* 87 (1974): 71–82.

Spitz, R. A., and Wolf, K. M. "The Smiling Response: A Contribution to the Ontogenesis of Social Relations." *Genetic Psychology Monographs* 34 (1946): 57–125.

Stevenson, M. A., and Ferguson, L. W. "The Effects on Personality-Impression Formation of the Cold-Warm Dimension, The Grown-Smile Dimension, and the Negro-White Dimension." *Psychological Record* 18 (1968): 215–224.

Stringer, P. "Cluster Analysis of Non-verbal Judgments of Facial Expressions." *British Journal of Mathematical and Statistical Psychology* 20 (1967): 71–79.

Stringer, P. H. "Do Dimensions Have Face Validity?" In M. von Cranach and I. Vine, (eds.), *Social Communication and Movement*. New York: Academic Press, 1973.

Stritch, T., and Secord, P. "Interaction Effects in the Perception of Faces." *Journal of Personality* 24 (1956): 272–284.

Thayer, S., and Schiff, W. "Eye-Contact, Facial Expression and the Experience of Time." *Journal of Social Psychology* 95 (1975): 117–124.

Thompson, D. F., and Meltzer, L. "Communication of Emotional Intent by Facial Expression." *Journal of Abnormal and Social Psychology* 68 (1964): 129–135.

Tolch, C. J. "The Problem of Language and Accuracy in Identification of Facial Expression." *Central States Speech Journal* 14 (1963): 12–16.

Tomkins, S. S. *Affect, Imagery, Consciousness*, Vols. I and II. New York: Springer, 1962, 1963.

Tomkins, S. S., and McCarter, R. "What and Where are the Primary Affects? Some Evidence for a Theory." *Perceptual and Motor Skills* 18 (1964): 119–158.

Triandis, H. G., and Lambert, W. W. "A Restatement and Test of Schlosberg's Theory of Emotions, with Two Kinds of Subjects in Greece." *Journal of Abnormal and Social Psychology* 56 (1958): 321–328.

Van Rooijen, L. "Talking About the Bright Side . . . Pleasantness of the Referent as a Determinant of Communication Accuracy." *European Journal of Social Psychology* 3 (1973): 473–478.

Vinacke, W. E. "The Judgment of Facial Expressions by Three National-Racial Groups in Hawaii—I: Caucasian Faces." *Journal of Personality* 17 (1949): 407–429.

Vinacke, W. E., and Fong, R. W. "The Judgment of Facial Expressions by Three National-Racial Groups in Hawaii: II. Oriental Faces." *Journal of Social Psychology* 41 (1955): 184–195.

Vine, I. "Communication by Facial-Visual Signals." In J. H. Cook (ed.), *Social Behavior in Animals and Men*. New York: Academic Press, 1969.

Watson, S. G. "Judgments of Emotion from Facial and Contextual Cue Combinations." *Journal of Personality and Social Psychology* 24 (1972): 334–342.

Westbrook, M. "Sex Differences in the Perception of Emotion." *Australian Journal of Psychology* 26 (1974): 139–146.

Williams, F., and Tolch, J. "Communication by Facial Expression." *Journal of Communication* 15 (1965): 17–27.

Young, P. T. *Emotion in Man and Animal*. Huntington, N.Y.: R. E. Krieger, 1973. First published in 1943.

Zuckerman, M., Hall, J. A., DeFrank, R. S., and Rosenthal, R. "Encoding and Decoding of Spontaneous and Posed Facial Expressions." *Journal of Personality and Social Psychology* 34 (1977): 966–977.

9 The Effects of Eye Behavior on Human Communication

He speaketh not; and yet there lies
A conversation in his eyes.
HENRY WADSWORTH LONGFELLOW

Throughout history we have been preoccupied with the eye and its effects on human behavior. Do you recall the last time you used one of these phrases: "She could look right through you"; "It was an icy stare"; "He's got shifty eyes"; "She's all eyes'"; "Did you see the gleam in his eye?"; "We're seeing eye to eye now"; "He looked like the original Evil Eye"; "His eyes shot daggers across the room"; "She could kill with a glance"?

Greenacre reported that some Bushmen in South Africa believe the glance of a menstruating girl's eye can fix a man in whatever position he is in and change him into a tree![1] Psychiatric literature reveals numerous cases in which the eye is used as a symbol for either male or female sex organs.

We associate various eye movements with a wide range of human expressions: Downward glances are associated with modesty; wide eyes may be associated with frankness, wonder, naiveté, or terror; raised upper eyelids along with contraction of the orbicularis may mean displeasure; generally

[1]P. Greenacre, "The Eye Motif in Delusion and Fantasy." *American Journal of Psychiatry* 5 (1926): 553.

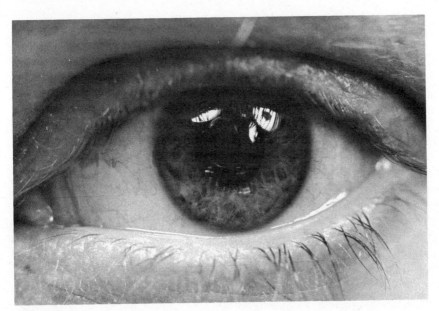

Figure 9.1

immobile facial muscles with a rather constant stare are frequently associated with coldness; eyes rolled upward may be associated with fatigue or a suggestion that another's behavior is a bit weird.

Our society has established a number of eye-related norms—for example, we don't look too long at strangers in public places, we aren't supposed to look at various body parts except under certain conditions, and so on.

Our fascination with eyes has led to the exploration of almost every conceivable feature of the eyes (size, color, position) and surrounding parts (eyebrows, rings, wrinkles). Some feel that excessive blinking may be associated with various states of anxiety—as if attempting to cut off reality. Psychiatrists report some patients who blink up to one hundred times per minute; normal blinking, needed to lubricate and protect the eyeball, occurs about six to ten times per minute in adults. There is some evidence that when a person is attentive to objects in the environment or during concentrated thought, blinking rate will decrease. Eye-rings are mainly found in other animals, but some speculate that our eyebrows are residual rings—raised during surprise and fear and lowered for focus during threat and anger. Eye patches are the colored eyelids sometimes seen in nonhuman primates. These patches are not a part of the natural human communicative repertoire, although women often use eyeliner and eyeshadow to achieve a similar effect. Another nonhuman feature

The Effects of Eye Behavior on Human Communication

which has received scholarly attention is eyespots—eye-shaped images located on other body parts. These can be seen in peacock feathers, butterflies and fish.

Some people have examined the degree to which eyes open as a reflection of various emotional states. There is also a condition known as *sanpaku* where the whites of your eyes show below the pupils when you look straight ahead. This condition is supposed to be associated with individuals who have an emotional imbalance or, more mystically, are "out of tune with the elements." One nonscientific publication reported on a psychologist who, through measurements of eye color, pupil dilation, and focus change, claimed 100 percent accuracy in reading unspoken responses to questions![2] Changes in eye color were purportedly detected as the experimenter projected a light source (retinoscope) into the subject's pupil while asking questions. Another approach to the study of eye color attempted to find correlates of eye color and motor performance.[3] Worthy's main thesis is that dark-eyed animals, human and nonhuman, specialize in behaviors that require sensitivity, speed, and reactive responses; light-eyed animals specialize in behaviors that require hesitation, inhibition, and self-paced responses. His analyses of various sports show dark-eyed persons are more likely to be running backs in football and effective hitters in baseball; light-eyed persons are more likely to be quarterbacks or offensive linemen in football, effective free throwers in basketball, and proficient pitchers in baseball!

Now that we've outlined the variety of eye-related concerns, it is time to focus on the two main subjects of this chapter. One of these is known by such terms as *eye contact, mutual glances, visual interaction, gazing,* or *line of regard;* the other area concerns pupil dilation and constriction under various social conditions.

Gaze and Mutual Gaze

Let's begin by looking at the terminology we have chosen—*gaze* and *mutual gaze.*[4] *Gaze* refers to an individual's looking behavior, which may or may not be at the other person; *mutual gaze* refers to a situation where the two interactants are looking at each other—usually in the region of the face. Eye contact (looking specifically in each other's eyes) does not seem to be reliably distinguished by receivers or observers from gazing at the area surrounding the eyes.[5] Gazing and mutual gazing, however, can be reliably as-

[2]W. Lazarus, "The Eyes Have It," *New Times,* June 14, 1974, 37–39.

[3]M. Worthy, *Eye Color, Sex and Race* (Anderson, S.C.: Droke House/Hallux, 1974).

[4]Two excellent summaries of the research in this area include M. Argyle and M. Cook, *Gaze and Mutual Gaze* (Cambridge: Cambridge University Press, 1976), and P. C. Ellsworth and L. M. Ludwig, "Visual Behavior in Social Interaction," *Journal of Communication* 22 (1972) 375–403.

sessed. At a distance of three meters, face-directed gazing can be distinguished; shifting the direction of one's gaze by one centimeter can reliably be detected from a distance of one meter.

We know we don't look at another person during the entire time we're talking to him or her—nor do we avert our gaze 100 percent of the time. So, what would be considered "normal" gazing patterns? Obviously, the answer will vary according to the background and personalities of the participants, the topic, the other person's gazing patterns, objects of mutual interest in the environment, and so on. Keeping such qualifications in mind, we can get a general idea of normal gazing patterns from two studies of focused interaction between two people.[6] See Table 9.1.

Table 9.1 Amount of Gazing in Two-Person Conversations

	Average	Range	Talking	Listening	Mutual Gaze	Average Length of Gaze	Average Length of Mutual Gaze
Nielsen	50%*	8-73%	38%	62%	—	—	—
Argyle & Ingham	61%	—	41%	75%	31%	2.95 sec.	1.18 sec.

*Percentages reflect the amount of time gazing relative to the total interaction time.

Kendon has identified four functions of gazing: (1) cognitive—subjects tend to look away when having difficulty encoding; (2) monitoring—subjects may look at their interactant to indicate the conclusions of thought units and to check their interactant's attentiveness and reactions; (3) regulatory—responses may be demanded or suppressed by looking; and (4) expressive—the degree of involvement or arousal may be signaled through looking.[7] Our discussion will follow a similar pattern: (1) regulating the flow of communication, (2) monitoring feedback, (3) expressing emotions, and (4) communicating the nature of the interpersonal relationship. These functions do not take place independently— that is, visual behavior not only sends information, but is one of the primary methods for collecting it; looking at the other person as you finish an utterance may not only tell the other it is his or her turn to speak, but is an occasion to monitor feedback regarding the utterance.

[5]M. von Cranach and J. H. Ellgring, "Problems in the Recognition of Gaze Direction," in M. von Cranach and I. Vine (eds.), Social Communication and Movement (New York: Academic Press, 1973).

[6]G. Nielson, Studies in Self Confrontation (Copenhagen: Monksgaard, 1962); M. Argyle and R. Ingham, "Gaze, Mutual Gaze and Proximity," Semiotica 6 (1972): 32–49.

[7]A. Kendon, "Some Functions of Gaze-Direction in Social Interaction," Acta Psychologica 26 (1967): 22–63. Also see M. Argyle, R. Ingham, F. Alkema, and M. McCallin, "The Different Functions of Gaze," Semiotica 7 (1973): 19–32.

The Effects of Eye Behavior on Human Communication

Regulating the Flow of Communication. Visual contact occurs when we want to signal that the communication channel is open. In some instances, eye gaze can almost establish an obligation to interact. When you seek visual contact with your waiter in a restaurant, you are essentially indicating the communication channel is open, and you want to say something to him. You may recall instances when your classroom instructor asked a question of the class, and you were sure you did not know the answer. Establishing eye contact with the instructor was the last thing you wanted to do. You did not wish to signal the channel was open. We behave the same way when we see someone coming toward us, and we do not wish to talk to the person. As long as we can avoid eye gaze (in a seemingly natural way), it is a lot easier to avoid having to interact. When you want to disavow social contact, your eye gaze will likely diminish. Thus, we see mutual gazing in greeting sequences and greatly diminished gazing when one wishes to bring an encounter to a halt.

In addition to opening and closing the channel of communication, eye behavior also regulates the flow of communication by providing turn-taking signals. We've already noted that white, adult speakers generally look less often than listeners.[8] But speakers do seem to glance at grammatical breaks, at the end of a thought unit or idea and at the end of the utterance. Although glances at these junctures can signal that the other person can assume the speaking role, we also use these glances to obtain feedback, to see how we're being received, and to see if the other will let us continue. This feedback function will be addressed in the next section. The speaker-listener pattern seems to be choreographed as follows: As the speaker comes to the end of an utterance or thought unit, gazing at the listener will continue as the listener assumes the speaking role; the listener will maintain gaze until the speaking role is assumed when he or she will look away. When the speaker does not yield a speaking turn by glancing at the other, the listener will probably delay a response or fail to respond. Further, when a speaker begins an anticipated lengthy response, less gazing is apt to occur—often accompanied by an initially lengthy pause too. This pattern of adult gazing and looking away during speech seems to have its roots in early childhood development. Observations of the gazing patterns of three-to-four-month-old infants and their parents revealed gross temporal similarities in the looking at and looking away sequence with the vocalizing and pausing sequences in adult conversations.[9]

---

[8]One study, however, suggests that this pattern may be limited to Caucasians. In this study, whites gazed more while listening and blacks more while speaking. See M. LaFrance and C. Mayo, "Racial Differences in Gaze Behavior During Conversations: Two Systematic Observational Studies," *Journal of Personality and Social Psychology* 33 (1976): 547–552.

[9]J. Jaffe, D. N. Stern, and C. Peery, " 'Conversational' Coupling of Gaze Behavior in Prelinguistic Human Development," *Journal of Pyscholinguistic Research* 2 (1973): 321–329.

The Effects of Eye Behavior on Human Communication

When two people are jointly watching a third object or person we can again see how this may be the basis for initiating or sustaining an interaction. This process does, however, require monitoring the other person's gaze.

Monitoring Feedback. When people seek feedback concerning the reactions of others, they gaze at the other person. If you find that the other person is looking at you, this is usually interpreted as a sign that the other is attentive to what you are saying. In fact, such a notion seems so firmly held that when people were *told* that their partner looked at them less than normal—regardless of their actual gaze—the partner was rated as "less attentive."[10] Listener facial expressions and gazing suggests not only attention, but whether the listener is interested in what you're saying (for example, "Good. Continue.").

Both listeners and speakers seem to have a tendency to look away when they are trying to process difficult or complex ideas. This may reflect a shift in attention from external to internal matters. Interestingly, Day found that when we look away during difficult encoding situations it is not a random pattern.[11] We seem to look away more on reflective questions than factual ones. Bakan reports studies in which subjects were asked "thought provoking" questions and eye movement was measured.[12] It was found that people tend to make about 75 percent of these movements in the same direction. Typical questions used were: "How many letters are there in the word *Washington?*" "Multiply twelve by thirteen," and "What is meant by the proverb 'It is better to have a bad peace than a good war?' " Then, after classifying "right movers" and "left movers," other data was collected to further characterize the two groups. Left movers seem more susceptible to hypnosis, have more alpha brain waves, score higher on "verbal" parts of the Scholastic Aptitude Test, show greater fluency in writing, have more-vivid imagery, are more likely to major in classical/humanistic areas, are more sociable, more likely to be alcoholic if a male, and report themselves as more musical and more religious. Right movers appear more likely to show tension in large postural muscles, tend to have higher "quantitative" scores on the Scholastic Aptitude Test, are more likely to

[10]C. L. Kleinke, A. A. Bustos, F. B. Meeker, and R. A. Staneski, "Effects of Self-Attributed and Other-Attributed Gaze in Interpersonal Evaluations Between Males and Females," *Journal of Experimental Social Psychology* 9 (1973): 154–163.

[11]M. E. Day, "Eye Movement Phenomenon Relating to Attention, Thought, and Anxiety," *Perceptual and Motor Skills* 19 (1964): 443–446.

[12]P. Bakan, "The Eyes Have It," *Psychology Today* 4 (1971): 64–67; and P. Bakan and F. F. Strayer, "On Reliability of Conjugate Lateral Eye Movements," *Perceptual and Motor Skills* 36 (1973): 429–430.

The Effects of Eye Behavior on Human Communication

major in science/quantitative areas, have more tics and twitches, spend less time asleep if male, pay more attention to the right side of the body if male, prefer cool colors, and make career choices earlier. Bakan cautions against too much generalization from these findings due to the integrative nature of the brain. In fact, women were found not to be as frequent left or right movers—they were more likely than men to move their eyes in both directions.

Expressing Emotions.   Rarely is the eye area tested separately from the entire face in judging emotions. Sometimes, however, a glance at the eye area may provide us with a good deal of information about the emotion being expressed. In one study of this type, fifty-one faces were used as stimuli for judges.[13] The eyes were better than the brows-forehead or lower face for the accurate perception of fear, but less accurate for anger and disgust.

The extensive studies of Paul Ekman and his colleagues have given us valuable insights into facial configurations for six common emotions. The following descriptions pertain to the brow and eye area.[14]

Surprise. Brows are raised so they are curved and high. Skin below the brow is stretched. Eyelids are opened; the upper lid is raised, and the lower lid drawn down; the white of eye shows above the iris and often below as well.

Fear. Brows are raised and drawn together. The upper eyelid is raised, exposing the white of the eye, and the lower eyelid is tensed and drawn up.

Disgust. Disgust is shown primarily in the lower face and in the lower eyelids. Lines show below the lower lid, and the lid is pushed up but not tense. The brow is lowered, lowering the upper lid.

[13]P. Ekman, W. V. Friesen, and S. S. Tomkins, "Facial Affect Scoring Technique: A First Validity Study," *Semiotica* 3 (1971): 37–58.

[14]P. Ekman and W. V. Friesen, *Unmasking the Face* (Englewood Cliffs, N.J.: Prentice-Hall, 1975).

The Effects of Eye Behavior on Human Communication

Anger. The brows are lowered and drawn together. Vertical lines appear between the brows. The lower lid is tensed and may or may not be raised. The upper lid is tense and may or may not be lowered by the action of the brow. The eyes have a hard stare and may have a bulging appearance.

Happiness. Happiness is shown primarily in the lower face and lower eyelids. The lower eyelid shows wrinkles below it, and may be raised but is not tense. Crow's feet wrinkles go outward from the outer corners of the eyes.

Sadness. The inner corners of the eyebrows are drawn up. The skin below the eyebrow is triangulated, with the inner corner up. The upper eyelid inner corner is raised.

We should also recognize that some expressions of emotion show a lot of changes in the eye area (surprise, fear) and others do not (happiness, disgust). Furthermore, an expression of anger can be ambiguous unless the entire face manifests anger signals. Similarly, in everyday interaction we are likely to see facial blends where the eyes may tell one story and other parts of the face another. And, of course, some clues to expressions of emotion can be derived from gazing patterns—for example, sadness may be accompanied by increased looking downward and generally reducing the amount of gaze.

Communicating the Nature of the Interpersonal Relationship. Gazing and mutual gazing is often indicative of the nature of the relationship between two interactants. Relationships characterized by different status levels may be reflected in the eye patterns. With all other variables held relatively constant, Hearn found gazing and mutual gazing is moderate with a very high status addressee, maximized with a moderately high status addressee

The Effects of Eye Behavior on Human Communication

301

and minimal with a very low status addressee.[15] Another experiment, with a freshman addressing a senior-freshman pair, adds some support to Hearn's work, since the senior consistently received more eye glances.[16] Mehrabian's work shows less visual contact on the part of both males and females (sitting and standing) with low status addressees.[17] It may be that if you perceive a low amount of gazing from a higher status person it is related to interpersonal needs. The higher status person may not feel the need to monitor your behavior as closely as you monitor his or hers. There will, however, be predictable differences based on how much a person likes another and how many rewards are derived.

Obviously, we make more eye contact when we look at something rewarding to us. Efran and Broughton, using male subjects and experimenters, found that their subjects engaged in more visual interaction with the person they had had a friendly conversation with just prior to the experiment and who nodded and smiled during the subject's presentation.[18] Exline and Winters report that subjects avoided the eyes of an interviewer and disliked him after he had commented unfavorably on their performance.[19] Using the same verbal communication, Exline and Eldridge found that it was decoded by a subject as being more favorable when associated with more eye contact than when it was presented with less eye contact.[20]

Closely related to looking at persons and objects which are rewarding is the factor of positive or negative attitude toward the other person. Generally, we seem to gaze more at people we like, but, as we'll see later, we sometimes look long and hard at people we don't like too. It makes sense to predict that we will look more at those who like us—if for no other reason than to observe signs of approval and friendliness. Mehrabian asked a group of people to imagine they liked another and to engage this person in conversation. Even in this role-playing situation, increased gazing was associated with increased liking.[21] Wiemann confronted subjects with a simulated employment interview in which the interviewer's gaze was varied across four conditions—100 percent,

[15]G. Hearn, "Leadership and the Spatial Factor in Small Groups," *Journal of Abnormal and Social Psychology* 54 (1957): 269–272.

[16]J. S. Efran, "Looking for Approval: Effect on Visual Behavior of Approbation from Persons Differing in Importance," *Journal of Personality and Social Psychology* 10 (1968): 21–25.

[17]A. Mehrabian, *Nonverbal Communication* (Chicago: Aldine/Atherton, 1972).

[18]J. Efran and A. Broughton, "Effect of Expectancies for Social Approval on Visual Behavior," *Journal of Personality and Social Psychology* 4 (1966): 103–107.

[19]R. Exline and L. Winters, "Affective Relations and Mutual Glances in Dyads," in S. Tomkins and C. Izard (eds.), *Affect, Cognition and Personality* (New York: Springer, 1965).

[20]R. Exline and C. Eldridge, "Effects of Two Patterns of a Speaker's Visual Behavior upon the Perception of the Authenticity of His Verbal Message," paper presented to the Eastern Psychological Association, Boston, 1967.

[21]Mehrabian, *Nonverbal Communication*.

The Effects of Eye Behavior on Human Communication

75 percent, 25 percent, and 0 percent. When subjects were asked to evaluate the interviewers, the level of "friendliness" decreased as the amount of gaze decreased. Interestingly, however, "applicants" did not seem to evaluate the interviewer's dominance, potency, or confidence as lower with decreasing gaze.[22]

The term *making eyes* is frequently used in the context of a courtship relationship. Indeed, several sources confirm an increase in eye behavior between two people who are seeking to develop a more intimate relationship. Rubin's analysis of engaged couples indicated more mutual gaze;[23] Kleinke et al. found that longer glances or reciprocated glances were perceived as an indicator of a longer relationship;[24] Kleck and Rubinstein varied the physical attractiveness of female confederates by altering makeup and hair styling and found that male subjects looked more at the attractive confederates.[25] It may be that the amount of gazing increases as relationships become more intimate, but it may also be true that after maintaining an intimate relationship for years, gazing may return to levels below those used during more intense stages of development. Argyle and Dean have proposed an intimacy equilibrium model.[26] This model suggests that intimacy is a function of the amount of eye gazing, physical proximity, intimacy of topic, and amount of smiling. Argyle believes it is most appropriate to established relationships. Clearly, there are other variables which might be inserted into the equation—for example, body orientation, the form of address used, tone of voice, facial expression, forward lean, and the like. The central idea behind this proposal is that as one component of the model is changed, one or more of the other components will also change—in the opposite direction—for example, if one person looks too much, the other may look less, move further away, smile less, talk less about intimate matters, and so on. Although this notion has received some support, there are occasions when, rather than complement the other's behavior, we seem to imitate it—that is, gazing will elicit gazing.

When the relationship between the two communicators is characterized by negative attitudes, we might see a decrease in gazing and mutual gazing. But,

[22]J. M. Wiemann, "An Experimental Study of Visual Attention in Dyads: The Effects of Four Gaze Conditions on Evaluations by Applicants in Employment Interviews," paper presented to the Speech Communication Association, Chicago, 1974.

[23]Z. Rubin, "The Measurement of Romantic Love," *Journal of Personality and Social Psychology* 16 (1970): 265–273.

[24]C. L. Kleinke, A. A. Bustos, F. B. Meeker, and R. A. Staneski, "Effects of Self-Attributed and Other Attributed Gaze in Interpersonal Evaluations Between Males and Females."

[25]R. E. Kleck and S. Rubinstein, "Physical Attractiveness, Perceived Attitude Similarity, and Interpersonal Attraction in an Opposite-Sex Encounter," *Journal of Personality and Social Psychology* 31 (1975): 107–114.

[26]M. Argyle and J. Dean, "Eye-Contact, Distance and Affiliation," *Sociometry* 28 (1965): 289–304.

as we previously suggested, a hostile or aggressive orientation may trigger the use of staring to produce anxiety in others. A gaze of longer than ten seconds is likely to induce irritation—if not outright discomfort—in many situations. We can express our hostility toward another by visually and verbally ignoring him or her—especially when the other person knows we are deliberately doing so. But we can insult another person by looking at that person too much—that is, by not according him or her the public anonymity that each of us requires at times. There are times when you can elicit aggressive behavior from others just because you happen to look too long at a stranger's behavior. Sometimes threats and aggressive motions can be elicited by human beings who stare too long at monkeys in a zoo! Desmond Morris, in his popular book *The Naked Ape*, hypothesized that this tendency to produce anxiety in others through staring is due to our biological antecedents as a species—for example, the aggressiveness and hostility signified by the ape's stare.

Thus, if we are looking for a unifying thread to link gazing patterns motivated by positive and negative feelings toward the other, it would seem to be this: *People tend to look at those with whom they are interpersonally involved.* Gazing motivated by hostility or affection, then, both suggest an interest and involvement in the interpersonal relationship.

Now that we've outlined several major functions of eye behavior, we can look at a number of conditions which seem to influence the amount of gazing: (1) distance, (2) physical characteristics, (3) personal and personality characteristics, (4) topics and tasks, and (5) cultural background.

Distance. Gazing and mutual gazing seem to increase as the communicating pair increases the distance between them. In this case, gazing psychologically reduces the distance between the communicators. There may be less visual contact when the two parties are too close together—especially if they are not well acquainted. Reducing one's gaze in this situation, then, psychologically increases the physical distance.

Physical Characteristics. One would think that when interacting with a person who was perceived as disabled or stigmatized in some way (identified as an epileptic or made to look like an amputee) that eye gaze would be less frequent. However, Kleck found the amount of gazing between normal and disabled interactants did not differ significantly from normal-normal interactions.[27] One possible explanation is that in such situations, the normal person is desperately seeking information which might suggest the proper mode of behavior. This counteracts any tendency to avoid eye gaze.

[27] R. Kleck, "Physical Stigma and Nonverbal Cues Emitted in Face-to-Face Interaction," *Human Relations* 21 (1968) 19-28.

The Effects of Eye Behavior on Human Communication

Personal and Personality Characteristics. Generally, the relationships between gazing patterns and personality traits are weak. In most cases, however, the meanings attributed to various gaze patterns seem to reflect the message sender's mood, intent, or disposition. Kleck and Nuessle's study reflects a number of personality characteristics commonly associated with gaze and averted gaze.[28] A film of people looking either 15 or 80 percent of the time was shown to observers who were asked to select characteristics which typified the interactants. The 15 percent lookers were labeled as cold, pessimistic, cautious, defensive, immature, evasive, submissive, indifferent, and sensitive; the 80 percent lookers were seen as friendly, self-confident, natural, mature, and sincere. The two traits which seem to show the least correspondence between encoding and decoding are judgments of anxiety and dominance. Observers seem to associate anxiety with too little gazing and dominance with too much gazing. From what we know at this time, such associations are less frequently true than we think. Gazing may more appropriately be associated with efforts to *establish* dominance or to maintain it when someone seems to challenge one's authority. Further, it does seem that dominant persons are more apt to control the other person's gazing patterns in reprimand situations—for example, "You look straight ahead while I'm talking to you, soldier!" or "Look at me when I talk to you (chew you out)!" Dependent individuals, on the other hand, seem to use eye behavior not only to communicate more positive attitudes, but also to elicit such attitudes when they are not forthcoming.[29] Dependent males made more eye gaze with a listener who provided them with few, as compared to many, social reinforcers—whereas dominant males decreased their eye gaze with less reinforcing listeners.

Extroverts seem to gaze more frequently than introverts and for longer periods of time.[30] This seems to be true especially while talking.

In an early study of aggression, Moore and Gilliland found eye behavior to be a good predictor of aggressiveness:

> Thus the simple behavioristic fact of the ability to look another person in the eye seems to have such a high significance regarding the presence or absence of aggressiveness as to warrant giving it an extremely prominent place in any scoring method devised as a measure of this trait aggressiveness.[31]

[28] R. E. Kleck and W. Nuessle, "Congruence Between the Indicative and Communicative Functions of Eye-Contact in Interpersonal Relations," *British Journal of Social and Clinical Psychology* 7 (1968): 241-246.

[29] R. Exline and D. Messick, "The Effects of Dependency and Social Reinforcement upon Visual Behavior During an Interview," *British Journal of Social and Clinical Psychology* 6 (1967): 256-266.

[30] N. Mobbs, "Eye Contact in Relation to Social Introversion/Extroversion," *British Journal of Social and Clinical Psychology* 7 (1968): 305-306.

[31] R. T. Moore and A. R. Gilliland, "The Measurement of Aggressiveness," *Journal of Applied Psychology* 5 (1921): 97-118.

The Effects of Eye Behavior on Human Communication

These authors also report that an unaggressive person is three times more likely than an aggressive person to be deterred to a considerable degree when stared at.

There have been a number of research studies which suggest special gazing patterns (usually less gaze) for autistic, schizophrenic, depressed, and neurotic persons.

Finally, it seems that males and females can be expected to differ in the amount of gaze shown. Females seem to look more than males on almost all measures of gaze frequency, duration, and reciprocity—and such differences have been observed in early elementary school. Henley has observed that while women tend to look at others more, they also tend to avert their eyes more than men.[32] One of her students observed another pattern of eye behavior which seems to be enacted primarily by females. This pattern involves a repeated sequence of glancing and glancing away in response to being stared at by a man. Only one male from the thirty observed performed this behavior while it was seen in twelve of the thirty females.

Most of the results of these efforts to link gazing patterns to personality and/or personal characteristics may be accounted for by the following: (1) The existing need for affiliation, involvement, or inclusion: Those with high affiliative needs will tend to glance and return glances more often. (2) Other looking motivations: Persons who are highly manipulative and/or need a lot of information in order to control their environment (high Machiavellian types) will predictably look more. (3) The need to avoid unduly high levels of arousal caused by gazing (mutual gazing especially): Autistic children, for instance, are thought to have a high level of arousal and will avoid gaze in order to keep arousal down. (4) A feeling of shame or low self-esteem: The lower level of gaze sometimes seen in adolescents may reflect the well-known uncertainties about ourselves which most of us have experienced during this period.

Topics and Tasks.   Common sense would suggest that the topic being discussed and/or the task at hand will affect the amount of gazing. People who have not developed an intimate relationship can be expected to gaze less when discussing intimate topics—providing other factors like the need for affiliation or inclusion are controlled. We would expect competitive situations and cooperative situations to elicit different patterns of gaze.

Discussions on topics which cause embarrassment, humility, shame, guilt, or sorrow might be expected to engender gazing less at the other person. Looking away during such situations may be an effort to insulate oneself against threats, arguments, information, or even affection from the other party. Have you noticed how *some* men look away rather quickly after having made visual

[32] N. M. Henley, *Body Politics: Power, Sex, and Nonverbal Communication* (Englewood Cliffs, N.J.: Prentice-Hall) 1977.

The Effects of Eye Behavior on Human Communication

contact with a braless woman? When subjects were caused to fail at an anagram task and publicly criticized for their work, they not only reported feeling embarrassed but the amount of gaze slipped from 30 percent to 18 percent.[33] When people want to hide some aspect of their inner feelings, they may try to avoid visual contact—for example, in situations where you are trying to deceive your partner. Exline and his colleagues designed a fascinating, if not ethically suspect, experiment.[34] A paid confederate induced subjects to cheat on an experimental task. Later the experimenter interviewed the subjects with the supposed purpose of understanding and evaluating their problem-solving methods. For some subjects the experimenter grew increasingly suspicious during the interview and finally accused the student subject of cheating and demanded an explanation. Subjects included those who scored high on tests of Machiavellianism and those who scored low. Machiavellianism is often associated with those who use cunning and shrewdness to achieve a goal—without much regard for how unscrupulous the means might be. Figure 9.2 shows that the high Machs seem to use gazing to present the appearance of innocence after being accused of cheating; low Machs, on the other hand, continued to look away. Some people will tend to look away from others just to avoid seeing signs of rejection or threat. And mutual gaze during deception could be a source of dissonance since, as we said before, this signals a free flow of communication and mutual openness.

Another communicative task we all undertake is that of persuasion. We know that gazing can add emphasis to a particular point, but Mehrabian and Williams report that a person trying to be more persuasive will tend to look more generally.[35] We don't know what the relationship between actual attitude change in a listener and speaker gazing is. But listeners do seem to judge speakers with more gaze as more persuasive, truthful, sincere and credible. Beebe manipulated the amount of gaze in an informative speech of about seven minutes.[36] Gaze seemed to primarily affect audience ratings on the following characteristics: skilled, informed, experienced and honest, friendly and kind. Similarly, Wills found that speakers rated as sincere had an average of 63.4 percent eye gaze while those rated insincere had an average of 20.8 percent.[37]

[33] A. Modigliani, "Embarrassment, Facework and Eye-Contact: Testing a Theory of Embarrassment," *Journal of Personality and Social Psychology* 17 (1971): 15–24.

[34] R. V. Exline, J. Thibaut, C. B. Hickey, and P. Gumpert, "Visual Interaction in Relation to Machiavellianism and an Unethical Act," in R. Christie and F. L. Geis (eds.), *Studies in Machiavellianism* (New York: Academic Press, 1970).

[35] A. Mehrabian and M. Williams, "Nonverbal Concomitants of Perceived and Intended Persuasiveness," *Journal of Personality and Social Psychology* 13 (1969): 37–58.

[36] S. A. Beebe, "Eye-Contact: A Nonverbal Determinant of Speaker Credibility," *Speech Teacher* 23 (1974): 21-25.

[37] J. Wills, "An Empirical Study of the Behavioral Characteristics of Sincere and Insincere Speakers," Unpublished Ph.D. dissertation, University of Southern California, Los Angeles, 1961.

The Effects of Eye Behavior on Human Communication

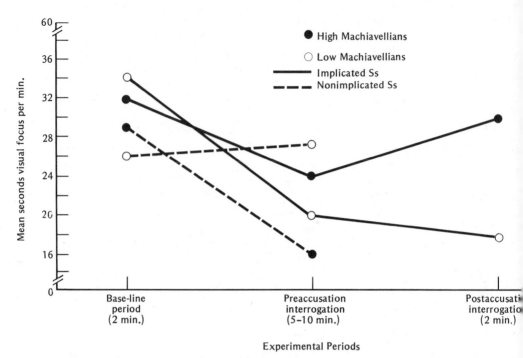

Figure 9.2 Gazing, Machiavellianism, and Deception

Cultural Background. Eye behavior will also vary according to the environment in which one learns social norms. Sometimes gazing patterns show differences between "contact" (Arabs) and "noncontact" (Northern Europeans) cultures; sometimes the differences may be in duration of gaze rather than frequency—for example, it has been said that Swedes look less frequently, but for longer periods, than the English; sometimes it is a question of "where" we analyze gaze that differences between cultures are revealed—for example, looking more in public places; sometime there are rules regarding "whom" you should or shouldn't look at—for example, a person of high status. One report suggests that a conversation between some men in Kenya and their mothers-in-law is conducted by each turning their back to the other. As we suggested earlier, we may find different patterns within our own culture—for example, the possible black-white differences in gazing during speaking and listening. Although patterns differ, we may find that perceived extremes in gaze elicit similar meanings in different cultures. For instance, too much gazing may signal anger, threat, or disrespect; too little may signal dishonesty, inattention,

The Effects of Eye Behavior on Human Communication

or shyness. These studies of multicultural perceptions of meaning in gaze patterns remain to be done.

Pupil Dilation and Constriction

Most of us are aware that the pupils of the eyes constrict in the presence of bright light and dilate in the absence of light. In the early 1960s, however, Eckhard Hess and his colleagues at the University of Chicago renewed the interest of the scientific community in pupil dilation and constriction as a possible indicator of mental and emotional states. At one point dozens of universities were conducting pupil dilation research and advertising agencies were testing magazine ads, package designs, television pilot films, and television commercials using the results of Hess' pupil dilation measures.

In an early experiment, Hess and Polt presented five pictures to male and female subjects.[38] Male pupils dilated more than female pupils to pictures of female nudes; females' pupils dilated more than males' to pictures of a partially clothed "muscle man," a woman with a baby, and a baby alone. Thus it seemed pupil dilation and interest value of the stimulus were related. Hess, Seltzer, and Schlien found the pupils of male homosexuals dilating more when viewing pictures of males than did the pupils of heterosexual males—who dilated to female pictures.[39] Studies since then have had similar results. For instance, Barlow preselected subjects with particular political preferences—subjects who actively supported either liberal or conservative candidates.[40] He photographed the pupil of the right eye while they watched slides of political figures. There seemed to be a perfect correlation between pupillary response and verbal response. White conservatives dilated to slides of George Wallace and constricted to Lyndon B. Johnson and Martin Luther King. Black liberals reacted in an exact opposite manner.

Several of Hess' studies suggested pupil response might be an index of attitudes—that is, that pupils will dilate for positive attitudes and constrict for negative ones. His oft-cited study supporting this theory was the eventual constriction of subjects' pupils who viewed pictures of concentration camp victims, dead soldiers, and a murdered gangster. In Hess' words: "The changes in

---

[38] E. H. Hess and J. M. Polt, "Pupil Size as Related to Interest Value of Visual Stimuli," *Science* 132 (1960): 349-350.

[39] E. H. Hess, A. L. Seltzer, and J. M. Shlien. "Pupil Response of Hetero- and Homosexual Males to Pictures of Men and Women: A Pilot Study." *Journal of Abnormal Psychology* 70 (1965): 165-168.

[40] J. D. Barlow. "Pupillary Size as an Index of Preference in Political Candidates." *Perceptual and Motor Skills* 28 (1969): 587-590.

emotions and mental activity revealed by changes in pupil size are clearly associated with changes in attitude."[41] His most recent work continues to maintain this position.[42] He cites a study which showed photographs like those in Figure 9.3, where the woman's pupils were retouched so she had large pupils in one photo and smaller ones in the other. Although male subjects did not tend to pick either picture as consistently more friendly or attractive, there was a tendency to associate positive attributes with the woman who had larger pupils and negative attributes to the one with smaller pupils. Woodmansee set out to test Hess' theory. While Woodmansee tried to improve on Hess' methodology and measuring instruments, he could find no support for pupil dilation and constriction as an index of attitudes toward blacks.[43] Hays and Plax found their subject's pupils dilated when they received supportive statements ("I am very much interested in your speech.") but constriction did not follow from nonsupportive statements ("I disagree completely with the development of your speech.")[44] One study found dilation from positive *and* negative feedback.[45] Other research has found the reflex dilation reaction of the pupil to be associated with arousal, attentiveness, interest, and perceptual orientation— but it does not seem to be an attitudinal index. Tightening muscles anywhere on the body, anticipation of a loud noise, drugs, lid closure, and mental effort will all alter pupil size. Even the advertising agencies seem to have lost interest in pupils as an involutionary measure of viewer attitudes.

Some of the potential problems facing ad testing include: (1) The viewer's pupil response may be affected by light and dark colors on the ad itself. (2) It is difficult to know what the viewer is focusing on. In one ad for french fries, viewers' pupils dilated, but subsequent analysis suggested the dilation may have been due to a steak which was also contained in the ad! (3) One advertising executive, commenting on the viability of a theory of attitudes and pupil dilation for his products, asked: "How excited can a person get about a laundry detergent?" (4) In some experiments it was noted that the pupils did not immediately return to their predilated state after seeing an arousing piture. Hence, the following stimuli were viewed with eyes which were still partially dilated.

[41]E. H. Hess, "The Role of Pupil Size in Communication," *Scientific American*, 233 November, 1975, 110–112, 116-119.

[42]E. H. Hess. *The Tell-Tale Eye* (New York: Van Nostrand Reinhold, 1975). Another historical-critical account of the development of Hess' work can be found in B. Rice, "Rattlesnakes, French Fries and Pupillometric Oversell," *Psychology Today* 7 (1974): 55-59.

[43]J. J. Woodmansee, "The Pupil Response as a Measure of Social Attitudes," in G. F. Summers (ed.), *Attitude Measurement* (Chicago: Rand McNally. 1970). pp. 514–533.

[44]E. R. Hays and T. G. Plax, "Pupillary Response to Supportive and Aversive Verbal Messages," *Speech Monographs* 38 (1971): 316–320.

[45]M. P. Janisse and W. S. Peavler, "Pupillary Research Today: Emotion in the Eye," *Psychology Today* 7 (1974): 60–63.

The Effects of Eye Behavior on Human Communication

310

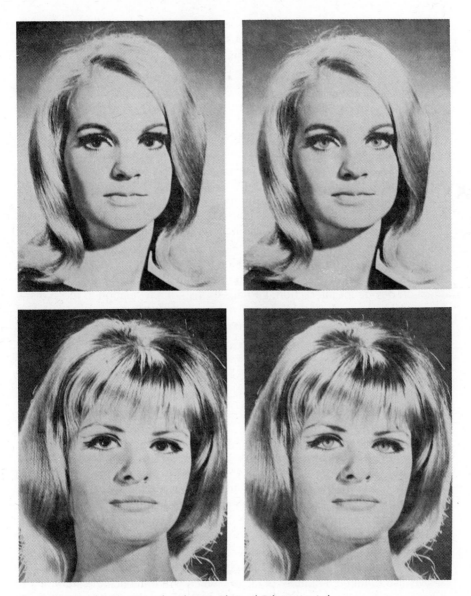

Figure 9.3 Some of Hess' Stimulus Photos with Pupil Dilation Varied

The Effects of Eye Behavior on Human Communication

(5) Since dilation occurs in response to so many different stimuli, it is difficult to state positively that the dilation is exclusively due to an attitudinal orientation.

While pupil dilation reveals emotional arousal, it is still not clear how much people notice it, or how close they have to be to see it. However, at least one study suggests pupil dilation may be influential in selecting interaction partners—or even dates. Stass and Willis dealt with live subjects rather than pictures.[46] Subjects were told they would be in an experiment and they had to choose a partner—one they could trust and one who was pleasant and easy to talk to on an intimate basis. They were taken to a room where two other persons waited. These two persons had previously been independently rated as about the same in general attractiveness. Eye gazing and pupil dilation (through use of a drug) were varied. Once the naive subject left the waiting room, the experimenter asked him or her to choose one of the persons and give reasons for the choice. Results show eye gazing is an overwhelming factor in choice making, but pupil dilation is also a factor. A few people mentioned visual contact as a reason for their choice, but none mentioned pupil dilation. Thus, for both women and men, pupil dilation seems to play an influential role as an attraction device for interaction. Perhaps this is not a revelation to those many women who, since the Middle Ages, have put belladona in their eyes to increase attractiveness; or to those expert romancers who suggest a dimly lighted place to meet.

Summary

Although researchers have examined the size, color, and position of the eyes, eye-rings, eyebrows, and eyespots, our major concern was with gaze and mutual gaze. The term eye *contact* was not used because it did not seem to accurately represent the phenomena studied or perceived by the interactants. We said that gazing served many interpersonal functions: (1) regulating the flow of communication—opening the channels of communication and assisting in the turn-taking process; (2) monitoring feedback; (3) expressing emotions; and (4) communicating the nature of the interpersonal relationship—for example, variations due to status, liking, and disliking.

We also outlined a number of factors which will influence the amount and duration of gaze in human relationships—for example, distance, physical characteristics, personal and personality characteristics, topics and tasks, and cultural background. From this review, we would predict *more* gazing when:

[46]J. W. Stass and F. N. Willis, Jr. "Eye Contact. Pupil Dilation, and Personal Preference," *Psychonomic Science* 7 (1967): 375–376.

The Effects of Eye Behavior on Human Communication

you are physically distant from your partner.

you are discussing easy, impersonal topics.

there is nothing else to look at.

you are interested in your partner's reactions—interpersonally involved.

you are interested in your partner—that is, like or love the partner.

you are of a lower status than your partner.

you are trying to dominate or influence your partner.

you are from a culture which emphasizes visual contact in interaction.

you are an extrovert.

you have high affiliative or inclusion needs.

you are dependent on your partner (and the partner has been unresponsive).

you are listening rather than talking.

you are female.

We would predict *less* gazing when:

you are physically close.

you are discussing difficult, intimate topics.

you have other relevant objects, people, or backgrounds to look at.

you are not interested in your partner's reactions.

you are talking rather than listening.

you are not interested in your partner—that is, dislike the partner.

you perceive yourself as a higher-status person than your partner.

you are from a culture which imposes sanctions on visual contact during interaction.

you are an introvert.

you are low on affiliative or inclusion needs.

you have a mental disorder like autism, schizophrenia, and the like.

you are embarrassed, ashamed, sorrowful, sad, submissive, or trying to hide something.

Obviously, the preceding lists are not exhaustive. Indeed, some of them are dependent on certain important qualifications—for example, you may have less gaze and mutual gaze when you are physically close—*unless* you happen to love your partner and want to get as close, physically and psychologically, as you can! The lists are not intended to replace the qualified principles as they appear in the chapter.

The last part of this chapter dealt with pupil dilation and constriction. We reviewed the major writer in this area, Eckhard Hess, and others who have pursued his ideas. At this time, pupil dilation has been associated with arousal, attentiveness mental effort, interest, and perceptual orientation. Aside from

The Effects of Eye Behavior on Human Communication

313

Hess' own work, however, no support has been found for the idea that pupils reflect attitudinal states. Dilation has been found to occur under conditons which seem to represent positive attitudes, but there is little or no support for the belief that constriction of pupils is associated with negative attitudes toward objects and people. Finally, we examined one study which intimates that pupil dilation may be a factor in our desire to interact with another person.

SELECTED BIBLIOGRAPHY

Aiello, J. "A Test of Equilibrium Theory: Visual Interaction in Relation to Orientation, Distance and Sex of Interactants." *Psychonomic Science* 27 (1972): 335–336.

Argyle, M. "Eye Contact and Distance: A Reply to Stephenson and Rutter." *British Journal of Psychology* 61 (1970): 395-396.

Argyle, M., and Cook, M. *Gaze and Mutual Gaze.* Cambridge: Cambridge University Press, 1976.

Argyle, M., and Dean J. "Eye Contact, Distance and Affiliation." *Sociometry* 28 (1965): 289–304.

Argyle, M., and Ingham, R. "Gaze, Mutual Gaze and Proximity." *Semiotica* 6 (1972): 32–49.

Argyle, M., Ingham, R., Alkema, F., and McCallin, M. "The Different Functions of Gaze." *Semiotica* 7 (1973): 19–32.

Argyle, M., Lalljee, M., and Cook, M. "The Effects of Visibility on Interaction in a Dyad." *Human Relations* 21 (1968): 3–17.

Argyle, M., Lefebvre, L., and Cook, M. "The Meaning of Five Patterns of Gaze." *European Journal of Social Psychology* 4 (1974): 125–136.

Ashear, V., and Snortum, J. R. "Eye Contact in Children as a Function of Age, Sex, Social and Intellective Variables." *Developmental Psychology* 4 (1971): 479.

Bakan, P. "The Eyes Have It." *Psychology Today* 4 (1971): 64–67, 96.

Bakan, P., and Strayer, F. F. "On Reliability of Conjugate Lateral Eye Movements." *Perceptual and Motor Skills* 36 (1973): 429–430.

Barlow, J. D. "Pupillary Size as an Index of Preference in Political Candidates." *Perceptual and Motor Skills* 28 (1969): 587–590.

Beebe, S. A. "Eye Contact: A Nonverbal Determinant of Speaker Credibility." *Speech Teacher* 23 (1974): 21–25.

Bernick, N., and Oberlander, N. "Effect of Verbalization and Two Different Modes of Experiencing on Pupil Size." *Perception and Psychophysics* 3 (1968): 327–330.

Birren, J. E., Casperson, R. C., and Botwinick, J. "Age Changes and Pupil Size." *Journal of Gerontology* 5 (1950): 216–221.

The Effects of Eye Behavior on Human Communication

314

Bond, M. H., and Komai, H. "Targets of Gazing and Eye Contact During Interviews: Effects on Japanese Nonverbal Behavior," *Journal of Personality and Social Psychology* 34 (1976): 1276–1284.

Bradshaw, J. L. "Pupil Size and Problem Solving." *Quarterly Journal of Experimental Psychology* 20 (1968): 116–122.

Breed, G., and Colaiuta, V. "Looking, Blinking and Sitting: Nonverbal Dynamics in the Classroom." *Journal of Communication* 24 (1974): 75–81.

Chapman, L. J., Chapman, J. P., and Brelje, T. "Influence of the Experimenter on Pupillary Dilation to Sexually Provocative Pictures." *Journal of Abnormal Psychology* 74 (1969): 396–400.

Cline, M. G. "The Perception of Where a Person Is Looking." *American Journal of Psychology* 80 (1967): 41–50.

Collins, B. E., Ellsworth, P. C., and Helmreich, R. L. "Correlations Between Pupil Size and the Semantic Differential: An Experimental Paradigm and Pilot Study." *Psychonomic Science* 9 (1967): 627-628.

Cook, M., and Lalljee, M. G. "Verbal Substitutes for Visual Signals in Interaction." *Semiotica* 6 (1973): 212–221.

Cook, M., and Smith, J. M. C. "The Role of Gaze in Impression Formation." *British Journal of Social and Clinical Psychology* 14 (1975): 19–25.

Coss, R. G. "Reflections on the Evil Eye." *Human Behavior*, 3 October, 1974, 16–22.

Cranach, M. von, and Ellgring, J. H. "Problems in the Recognition of Gaze Direction." In M. von Cranach and I. Vine (eds.), *Social Communication and Movement*. (New York: Academic Press, 1973.

Day, M. E. "Eye Movement Phenomenon Relating to Attention, Thought, and Anxiety." *Perceptual and Motor Skills* 19 (1964): 443–446.

Efran, J. S. "Looking for Approval: Effects on Visual Behavior of Approbation from Persons Differing in Importance." *Journal of Personality and Social Psychology* 10 (1968): 21–25.

Efran, J., and Broughton, A. "Effect of Expectancies for Social Approval on Visual Behavior." *Journal of Personality and Social Psychology* 4 (1966): 103–7.

Ellsworth, P. C., and Carlsmith, J. M. "Effects of Eye Contact and Verbal Content on Affective Response to a Dyadic Interaction." *Journal of Personality and Social Psychology* 10 (1968): 15–20.

Ellsworth, P. C., and Carlsmith, J. M. "Eye Contact and Gaze Aversion in an Aggressive Encounter." *Journal of Personality and Social Psychology* 28 (1973): 280–292.

Ellsworth, P. C., Carlsmith, J. M., and Henson, A. "The Stare as a Stimulus to Flight in Human Subjects: A Series of Field Experiments." *Journal of Personality and Social Psychology* 21 (1972): 302–311.

Ellsworth, P. C., and Langer, E. J. "Staring and Approach: An Interpretation of the Stare as a Nonspecific Activator." *Journal of Personality and Social Psychology* 33 (1976): 117–122.

Ellsworth, P. C., and Ludwig, L. M. "Visual Behavior in Social Interaction." *Journal of Communication* 22 (1972): 375–403.

Exline, R. "Explorations in the Process of Person Perception: Visual Interaction in Relation to Competition, Sex and Need for Affiliation." *Journal of Personality* 31 (1963): 1–20.

Exline, R. V., and Eldridge, C. "Effects of Two Patterns of a Speaker's Visual Behavior upon the Perception of the Authenticity of his Verbal Message." Paper presented to the Eastern Psychological Association, Boston, 1967.

Exline, R. V., and Messick, D. "The Effects of Dependency and Social Reinforcement upon Visual Behavior During an Interview." *British Journal of Social and Clinical Psychology* 6 (1967): 256–266.

Exline, R., and Winters, L. "Affective Relations and Mutual Glances in Dyads." In S. Tomkins and C. Izard (eds.), *Affect, Cognition and Personality*. New York: Springer, 1965.

Exline, R., Gray, D., and Schuette, D. "Visual Behavior in a Dyad as Affected by Interview Content and Sex of Respondent." *Journal of Personality and Social Psychology* 1 (1965): 201–209.

Exline, R., Thibaut, J., Hickey, C. B., and Gumpert, P. "Visual Interaction in Relation to Machiavellianism and an Unethical Act." In P. Christie and F. Geis (eds.), *Studies in Machiavellianism*. New York: Academic Press, 1970. pp. 53–75.

Fitzgerald, H. E. "Autonomic Pupillary Reflex Activity During Early Infancy and Its Relation to Social and Nonsocial Visual Stimuli." *Journal of Experimental Child Psychology* 6 (1968): 470–482.

Fromme, D. K., and Beam, D. C. "Dominance and Sex Differences in Nonverbal Responses to Differential Eye Contact." *Journal of Research in Personality* 8 (1974): 76–87.

Fugita, S. S. "Effects of Anxiety and Approval on Visual Interaction." *Journal of Personality and Social Psychology* 29 (1974): 586–592.

Galin, D., and Ornstein, R. "Individual Differences in Cognitive Style—I. Reflective Eye Movements." *Neuropsychologia* 12 (1974): 367–376.

Gardner, W. H. "The Study of the Pupillary Reflex of Special Reference to Stuttering." *Psychology Monographs* 49 (1945): 1–31.

Gibson, J. J., and Pick, A. D. "Perception of Another Person's Looking Behavior." *American Journal of Psychology* 76 (1963): 386–394.

Giesen, M. "Eye Contact, Video Context and Impressions of a Persuasive Speaker." Unpublished Ph.D. dissertation, Kent State University, 1973.

Goldberg, G. N., and Mettee, D. R. "Liking and Perceived Communication Potential as Determinants of Looking at Another." *Psychonomic Science* 16 (1969): 277–278.

Goldberg, G. N., Kiesler, C. A., and Collins, B. E. "Visual Behavior and Face-to-Face Distance During Interaction." *Sociometry* 32 (1969): 43–53.

Gough, D. "The Visual Behaviour of Infants in the First Few Weeks of Life." *Proceedings of the Royal Society of Medicine* 55 (1962): 308–310.

Harris, C. S., Thackray, R. I., and Schoenberger, R. W. "Blink Rate as a Function of Induced Muscular Tension and Manifest Anxiety." *Perceptual and Motor Skills* 22 (1966): 155–160.

Hart, H. H. "The Eye in Symbol and Symptom." *Psychoanalytic Review* 36 (1949): 1–21.

Hays, E. R., and Plax, T. G. "Pupillary Response to Supportive and Aversive Verbal Messages." *Speech Monographs* 38 (1971): 316–320.

Hess, E. H. "Attitudes and Pupil Size." *Scientific American* 212 (1965): 46–54.

Hess, E. H. "Pupillometric Assessment." In J. M. Shlien (ed.), *Research in Psychotherapy*. Pp. 573–583. Washington: American Psychological Assn., 1968.

Hess, E. H. "The Role of Pupil Size in Communication." *Scientific American*, 233 November 1975, 110–112; 116–119.

Hess, E. H. *The Tell-Tale Eye*. New York: Van Nostrand Reinhold, 1975.

Hess, E. H., and Polt, J. M. "Changes in Pupil Size as a Measure of Taste Difference." *Perceptual and Motor Skills* 23 (1966): 451–455.

Hess, E. H., and Polt, J. M. "Pupil Size as Related to Interest Value of Visual Stimuli." *Science* 132 (1960): 349–350.

Hess, E. H., and Polt, J. M. "Pupil Size in Relation to Mental Activity During Simple Problem Solving." *Science* 143 (1964): 1190–1192.

Hess, E. H., Seltzer, A. L., and Shlien, J. M. "Pupil Response of Hetero- and Homosexual Males to Pictures of Men and Women: A Pilot Study." *Journal of Abnormal Psychology* 70 (1965): 165–168.

Hindmarch, I. "Eye-Spots and Pupil Dilation in Non-verbal Communication." In M. von Cranach and I. Vine (eds.), *Social Communication and Movement*. New York: Academic Press, 1973.

Hobson, G. N., Strongman, K. T., Bull, D., and Craig, G. "Anxiety and Gaze Aversion in Dyadic Encounters." *British Journal of Social and Clinical Psychology* 12 (1973): 122–129.

Hutt, C., and Ounsted, C. "The Biological Significance of Gaze Aversion with Particular Reference to the Syndrome of Infantile Autism." *Behavioral Science* 11 (1966): 346–356.

Jaffe, J., Stern, D. N., and Peery, C. "'Conversational' Coupling of Gaze Behavior in Prelinguistic Human Development." *Journal of Psycholinguistic Research* 2 (1973): 321–329.

Janisse, M. P. "Pupil Size and Affect: A Critical Review of the Literature Since 1960." *Canadian Psychologist* 14 (1973): 311–329.

Janisse, M. P., and Peavler, W. S. "Pupillary Research Today: Emotion in the Eye." *Psychology Today* 7 (1974): 60–63.

Jellison, J. M. and Ickes, W. J. "The Power of the Glance: Desire to See and Be Seen in Cooperative and Competitive Situations." *Journal of Experimental Social Psychology* 10 (1974): 444–450.

Kahneman, D., and Beatty, J. "Pupil Diameter and Load on Memory." *Science* 54 (1966): 1583–1585.

Kahneman, D., and Peavler, W. S. "Incentive Effects and Pupillary Changes in Association with Learning." *Journal of Experimental Psychology* 79 (1969): 312–318.

Kahneman, D., Peavler, W. S., and Onuska, L. "Effects of Verbalization and Incentive on the Pupil Response to Mental Activity." *Canadian Journal of Psychology* 22 (1968): 186–196.

Kanfer, F. H. "Verbal Rate, Eyeblink, and Content in Structured Psychiatric Interviews." *Journal of Abnormal and Social Psychology* 61 (1960): 341–347.

Kendon, A. "Some Functions of Gaze-Direction in Social Interaction." *Acta Psychologica* 26 (1967): 22–63.

Kendon, A., and Cook, M. "The Consistency of Gaze Patterns in Social Interaction." *British Journal of Psychology* 60 (1969): 481–494.

Kleck, R. E., and Nuessle, W. "Congruence Between the Indicative and Communicative Functions of Eye-Contact in Interpersonal Relations." *British Journal of Social and Clinical Psychology* 7 (1968): 241—246.

Kleinke, C. L., and Pohlen, P. D. "Affective and Emotional Responses as a Function of Other Person's Gaze and Cooperativeness in a Two-Person Game." *Journal of Personality and Social Psychology* 17 (1971): 308–313.

Kleinke, C. L., Meeker, F. B., and La Fong, C. "Effects of Gaze, Touch and Use of Name on Evaluation of 'Engaged' Couples." *Journal of Research in Personality* 7 (1974): 368–373.

Kleinke, C. L., Bustos, A. A., Meeker, F. B., and Staneski, R. A. "Effects of Self-Attributed and Other-Attributed Gaze in Interpersonal Evaluations Between Males and Females." *Journal of Experimental Social Psychology* 9 (1973): 154–163.

Krugman, H. E. "Some Applications of Pupil Measurement." *Journal of Marketing Research* 1 (1964): 15–18.

LaFrance, M., and Mayo, C. "Racial Differences in Gaze Behavior During Conversations: Two Systematic Observational Studies." *Journal of Personality and Social Psychology* 33 (1976): 547–552.

LeCompte, W. F., and Rosenfeld, H. M. "Effects of Minimal Eye Contact in the Instruction Period on Impressions of the Experimenter." *Journal of Experimental Social Psychology* 7 (1971): 211–220.

Lefebvre, L. "Encoding and Decoding of Ingratiation in Modes of Smiling and Gaze." *British Journal of Social and Clinical Psychology* 14 (1975): 33–42.

Levine, M. H., and Sutton-Smith, B. "Effects of Age, Sex, and Task on Visual Behavior During Dyadic Interaction." *Developmental Psychology* 9 (1973): 400–405.

Libby, W. L. "Eye Contact and Direction of Looking as Stable Individual Differences." *Journal of Experimental Research in Personality* 4 (1970): 303–312.

Libby, W. L., and Yaklevich, D. "Personality Determinants of Eye Contact and Direction of Gaze Aversion." *Journal of Personality and Social Psychology* 27 (1973): 197–206.

Libby, W. L., Lacey, B. C., and Lacey, J. I. "Pupillary and Cardiac Activity During Visual Attention." *Psychophysiology* 10 (1973): 270–294.

Llewellyn, T. E. "Movements of the Eye." *Scientific American* 219 (1968): 88–95.

Loewenfeld, I. E. "Mechanisms of Reflex Dilation of the Pupil. Historical Review and Experimental Analysis." *Documents Ophthalmologia* 12 (1958): 185–448.

Lord, C., and Haith, M. M. "The Perception of Eye Contact." *Perception and Psychophysics* 16 (1974): 413–416.

Lowenstein, O., and Loewenfeld, I. E. "Electronic Pupillograph." *AMA Archives of Ophthalmology* 59 (1958): 352–363.

Mehrabian, A. *Nonverbal Communication*. Chicago: Aldine-Atherton, 1972.

Mobbs, N. "Eye Contact in Relation to Social Introversion/Extroversion." *British Journal of Social and Clinical Psychology* 7 (1968): 305–306.

Modigliani, A. "Embarrassment, Facework and Eye-Contact: Testing a Theory of Embarrassment." *Journal of Personality and Social Psychology* 17 (1971): 15–24.

Moore, H. T., and Gilliland, A. R. "The Measure of Aggressiveness." *Journal of Applied Psychology* 5 (1921): 97–118.

Nachson, I., and Wapner, S. "Effect of Eye Contact and Physiognomy on Perceived Location of Other Person." *Journal of Personality and Social Psychology* 7 (1967): 82–89.

Nevill, D. "Experimental Manipulation of Dependency Motivation and Its Effects on Eye Contact and Measures of Field Dependency." *Journal of Personality and Social Psychology* 29 (1974): 72–79.

Nichols, K. A., and Champness, B. G. "Eye Gaze and the GSR." *Journal of Experimental Social Psychology* 60 (1969): 481–494.

Nunnally, J. C., Knott, P. D., Duchnowski, A., and Parker, R. "Pupillary Responses as a General Measure of Activation." *Perception and Psychophysics* 2 (1967): 149–155.

Paivio, A., and Simpson, H. M. "The Effect of Word Abstractness and Pleasantness on Pupil Size During an Imagery Task." *Psychonomic Science* 5 (1966): 55–56.

Peavler, W. S., and McLaughlin, J. P. "The Question of Stimulus Content and Pupil Size." *Psychonomic Science* 8 (1967): 505–506.

Pellegrini, R. J., Hicks, R. A., and Gordon, L. "The Effects of an Approval-Seeking Induction on Eye-Contact in Dyads." *British Journal of Social and Clinical Psychology* 9 (1970): 373–374.

Polt, J. M., and Hess, E. H. "Changes in Pupil Size to Visually Presented Words." *Psychonomic Science* 12 (1968): 389–390.

Poock, G. K. "Information Processing vs. Pupil Diameter." *Perceptual and Motor Skills* 37 (1973): 1000–1002.

Rice, B. "Rattlesnakes, French Fries and Pupillometric Oversell." *Psychology Today* 7 (1974): 55–59.

Riemer, M. D. "Abnormalities of the Gaze—A Classification." *Psychiatric Quarterly* 29 (1955): 659–672.

Robson, K. S. "The Role of Eye-to-Eye Contact in Maternal-Infant Attachment." *Journal of Child Psychology and Psychiatry* 8 (1967): 13–25.

Rutter, D. R. "Visual Interaction in Psychiatric Patients: A Review." *British Journal of Psychiatry* 123 (1973): 193–202.

Rutter, D. R., and Stephenson, G. M. "Visual Interaction in a Group of Schizophrenic and Depressive Patients," *British Journal of Social and Clinical Psychology* 11 (1972): 57–65.

Rutter, D. R., Morley, I. E., and Graham, J. C. "Visual Interaction in a Group of Introverts and Extroverts." *European Journal of Social Psychology* 2 (1972): 371–384.

Schaefer, T., Ferguson, J. B., Klein, J. A., and Rawson, E. B. "Pupillary Responses During Mental Activities." *Psychonomic Science* 12 (1968): 137–138.

Scherwitz, L., and Helmreich, R. "Interactive Effects of Eye Contact and Verbal Content on Interpersonal Attraction in Dyads." *Journal of Personality and Social Psychology* 25 (1973): 6–14.

Schnelle, J. F., Kennedy, M., Rutledge, A. W., and Golden, S. B. "Pupillary Response as an Indication of Sexual Preference in a Juvenile Correctional Institution." *Journal of Clinical Psychology* 30 (1974): 146–150.

Simmel, G. "Sociology of the Senses: Visual Interaction." In R. E. Park and E. W. Burgess (eds.) *Introduction to the Science of Sociology*. Chicago: University of Chicago Press, 1921.

Simms, T. M. "Pupillary Response of Male and Female Subjects to Pupillary Difference in Male and Female Picture Stimuli." *Perception and Psychophysics* 2 (1967): 553–555.

Simpson, H. M., and Paivio. A. "Effects on Pupil Size of Manual and Verbal

Indicators of Cognitive Task Fulfillment." *Perception and Psychophysics* 3 (1968): 185–190.

Smythe, M. J. "Eye Contact as a Function of Affiliation, Distance, Sex and Topic of Conversation." Unpublished Ph.D. dissertation, Florida State University, 1973.

Snyder, M., Grether, J., and Keller, C. "Staring and Compliance: A Field Experiment on Hitchhiking." *Journal of Applied Social Psychology* 4 (1974): 165–170.

Spence, D. P., and Feinberg, C. "Forms of Defensive Looking: A Naturalistic Experiment." *Journal of Nervous and Mental Disorders* 145 (1967): 261–271.

Stass, J. W., and Willis, F. N., Jr. "Eye Contact, Pupil Dilation, and Personal Preference." *Psychonomic Science* 7 (1967): 375–376.

Stephenson, G. M., and Rutter, D. R. "Eye Contact, Distance and Affiliation: A Re-evaluation." *British Journal of Psychology* 61 (1970): 385–393. Also note the reply by M. Argyle on p. 395–396 of the same journal.

Stephenson, G. M., Rutter, D. R., and Dore, S. R. "Visual Interaction and Distance." *British Journal of Psychology* 64 (1973): 251–257.

Strongman, K. T., and Champness, B. G. "Dominance Hierarchies and Conflict in Eye Contact." *Acta Psychologica* 28 (1968): 376–386.

Tankard, J. W. "Effects of Eye Position on Person Perception." *Perceptual and Motor Skills* 31 (1970): 883–893.

Thayer, S. "The Effect of Interpersonal Looking Duration on Dominance Judgments." *Journal of Social Psychology* 79 (1969): 285–286.

Thayer, S., and Schiff, W. "Eye-Contact, Facial Expression, and the Experience of Time." *Journal of Social Psychology* 95 (1975): 117–124.

Thayer, S., and Schiff, W. "Observer Judgment of Social Interaction: Eye Contact and Relationship Inferences." *Journal of Personality and Social Psychology* 30 (1974): 110–114.

Thomas, E. L. "Movements of the Eye." *Scientific American* 219 (1968) 88–95.

Vacchiano, R. B., Strauss, P. S., Ryan, S., and Hochman, L. "Pupillary Response to Value-Linked Words." *Perceptual and Motor Skills* 27 (1968): 207–210.

Vine, I. "Judgment of Direction of Gaze: An Interpretation of Discrepant Results." *British Journal of Social and Clinical Psychology* 10 (1971): 320–331.

Wardwell, E. "Children's Reactions to Being Watched During Success and Failure." Ph.D. dissertation. Cornell University, 1960.

Woodmansee, J. J. "The Pupil Response as a Measure of Social Attitudes." In G. F. Summers (ed.), *Attitude Measurement.* Chicago: Rand McNally, 1970. pp. 514–533.

Worthy, M. *Eye Color, Sex and Race.* Anderson, S. C.: Droke House/Hallux, 1974.

10 The Effects of Vocal Cues Which Accompany Spoken Words

I understand a fury in your words
But not the words
SHAKESPEARE, Othello, Act IV

Ideally, this chapter should not be read; it should not have been written! Instead, this chapter should be a recording you can listen to. A recording would give you a greater appreciation for the vocal nuances which are the subject of this chapter—or, as the cliché goes, "*how* something is said rather than *what* is said." As we will find out shortly, the dichotomy set up by this cliché is misleading, because *how* something is said is frequently *what* is said.

Some responses to vocal cues are elicited because we deliberately try to manipulate our voice in order to communicate various meanings. Robert J. McCloskey, a major spokesman for the State Department during the Nixon Administration, reportedly exemplified such behavior:

> McCloskey has three distinct ways of saying, "I would not speculate": spoken without accent, it means the department doesn't know for sure; emphasis on the "I" means "I wouldn't, but you may—and with some assurance"; accent on "speculate" indicates that the questioner's premise is probably wrong.[1]

[1]*Newsweek*, October 5, 1970, p. 106.

Most of us do the same kind of thing when we emphasize a particular word in a message. Notice how different vocal emphases influence the interpretation of the following message:

1. *He's* giving this money to Herbie.
   1a. HE is the one giving the money; nobody else.
2. He's *giving* this money to Herbie.
   2a. He is GIVING, not lending, the money.
3. He's giving *this* money to Herbie.
   3a. The money being exchanged is not from another fund or source; it is THIS money.
4. He's giving this *money* to Herbie.
   4a. MONEY is the unit of exchange, not a check or wampum.
5. He's giving this money to *Herbie*.
   5a. The recipient is HERBIE, not Eric or Bill or Rod.

We manipulate our voice to indicate the end of a declarative sentence (by lowering it) or a question (by raising it). Sometimes we consciously manipulate our voice, so the vocal message contradicts the verbal one. In certain situations, this may be perceived as sarcasm. For instance, you can say the words, "I'm having a wonderful time" so they mean "I'm having a terrible time." You may say "I'd much rather hear Gordon Lightfoot than Willie Nelson," and your voice says, "I can't think of anything worse than listening to Gordon Lightfoot." If you are perceived as being sarcastic, the vocal cues you have given have probably superseded the verbal cues.

It was just such an assumption (the predominance of vocal cues in forming attitudes based on contradictory vocal and verbal content) that initiated some work of Mehrabian and his colleagues. In one study he used single words, previously rated as positive, neutral, or negative and presented them to listeners in positive or negative vocal tones. From this experiment, it was concluded:

> The variability of inferences about communicator attitude on the basis of information available in content and tone combined is mainly contributed by variations in tone alone. For example, when the attitude communicated in content contradicted the attitude communicated by negative tone, the total message was judged as communicating negative attitude.[2]

A study conducted in a similar fashion, pitting the vocal cues against facial and verbal cues, found the facial more influential. From these studies, Mehrabian

[2]A. Mehrabian and M. Wiener, "Decoding of Inconsistent Communication." *Journal of Personality and Social Psychology* 6 (1967): 109. Also see A. Mehrabian and S. R. Ferris, "Inference of Attitudes from Nonverbal Communication in Two Channels," *Journal of Consulting Psychology* 31 (1967): 248–252.

The Effects of Vocal Cues Which Accompany Spoken Words

devised a formula which illustrates the differential impact of verbal, vocal, and facial cues.

Perceived attitude = .07 (verbal) + .38 (vocal) + .55 (facial)

Obviously the formula is limited by the design of Mehrabian's experiments. For instance, we don't know how the formula might change if some of the variables were manipulated more vigorously, we don't know whether the formula would apply to verbal materials longer than one word, we don't know whether these respondents were reacting to the inconsistency itself as a source of attitudinal information—and just the fact that subjects resolved their inconsistency by relying on the vocal cues does not mean that evaluative information is conveyed by vocal cues alone.

Questions such as these prompted the work of Hart and Brown.[3] They reasoned, like Markel before them, that the vocal channel probably carries a greater percentage of some classes of information and a lesser percentage of others. Markel's work has suggested support for the idea that evaluative information (like-dislike; good-bad) is most often based on listener perceptions of content, while potency judgments (strong-weak; superior-subordinate) are based primarily on information derived from vocal cues.[4] Hart and Brown tried to use stimuli which more closely approximated natural speech—that is, speech samples representing thought units rather than single words, and natural verbal/vocal interplay rather than exclusively inconsistent patterns. Unfortunately, the scales used for responding to these stimuli did not reflect those commonly used in studies measuring evaluative, potency, and activity dimensions. Thus, we cannot match these results with Markel's. However, the results do show a complex response pattern with several evaluative-type reactions related to verbal content and information on "social attractiveness" apparently conveyed by vocal characteristics. The potency-type information was communicated by both vocal and verbal cues for males, but primarily through vocal cues for females.

In spite of the little research conducted thus far and the problems associated with these studies, it is significant that vocal cues (manipulated or not) seem to exert a great deal of influence on listener perceptions—particularly with certain classes of information or for certain kinds of responses. Generally, these responses are based on stereotypes associated with various vocal qualities, intonations, characteristics, and the like. Some research even suggests we have

[3]R. J. Hart and B. L. Brown, "Interpersonal Information Conveyed by the Content and Vocal Aspects of Speech," *Speech Monographs* 41 (1974): 371–380.

[4]N. N. Markel and G. L. Robin, "The Effect of Content and Sex-of-Judge on Judgments of Personality from Voice," *International Journal of Social Psychiatry* 11 (1965): 295–300. Also see N. N. Markel, M. Meisels, and J. E. Houck, "Judging Personality from Voice Quality," *Journal of Abnormal and Social Psychology* 69 (1964): 458–463.

The Effects of Vocal Cues Which Accompany Spoken Words

sound preferences as we have visual, tactile, and olfactory preferences. Psychiatrists tell us of critical insights into patient problems derived from vocal cues; researchers find vocal cues during the explanation of experimental instructions can drastically effect the results of an experiment; psychologists report a relationship between vocal cues and ability to identify certain personal characteristics—including some personality characteristics; students of speech communication find important relationships between vocal cues and the effects of various messages on retention and attitude change; the identification of various emotional states from vocal cues has been studied extensively; some have even suggested an important communicative role for nonlanguage vocalizations such as coughs, sneezes, belches, and the like. Glossolalia, or "speaking in tongues," is a vocal and linguistic phenomenon associated with certain religious experiences. Although the sounds are not similar to any known language, listeners often claim to "understand" the message—deriving their interpretation of the message from contextual and vocal cues.[5] Whistle speech, where fluted notes represent the prosodic features of spoken words and sentences, is an example of vocal cues substituting for, rather than accompanying, verbal content.[6]

Aside from this whistle speech which assumes more formalized linguistic features, our responses to vocal cues are often based on stereotypes. Obviously we may question whether such stereotyped responses to vocal cues are accurate. Indeed, the research suggests that there are a great many vocal stereotypes which have no basis in fact. However, since we are concerned with the complexities of the process of interpersonal communication, we need to be as much concerned with inaccurate stereotypes as with accurate ones. Inaccurate stereotypes do exist and are operating in our communicative behavior; we must recognize them before we can then begin to deal with them.

It is clear we are talking about a phenomenon which is extremely influential in many interpersonal judgments. In some situations, we intentionally use our voice in a particular way; in other situations people respond to vocal cues we are largely unaware of—making inferences about our personality, emotional state, attitudes, and the like. As we mentioned in the first chapter of this book, the vocal cues accompanying our spoken language have often been termed "paralanguage." Let us briefly review the ingredients of paralanguage before we examine the research on responses to paralanguage.

[5]J. Laffal, J. Monahan, and P. Richman, "Communication of Meaning in Glossolalia," *Journal of Social Psychology* 92 (1974): 277–291.

[6]A. R. Tayloe, "Nonverbal Communication Systems in Native North America," *Semiotica* 13 (1975): 329–374. Also see T. Stern, "Drum and Whistle Languages: An Analysis of Speech Surrogates," *American Anthropologist* 59 (1957): 487–506.

The Effects of Vocal Cues Which Accompany Spoken Words

The Ingredients of Paralanguage

You may be tempted to regard the next few paragraphs as unduly technical, dry, or even dull. Hang on. This section is not designed to give you the tools to observe and record paralanguage scientifically. The rather technical categories are outlined to give you a detailed account of the specific acoustic phenomena signified by the fairly abstract phrase *vocal cues*. These categories of acoustic phenomena are outlined here so you can see what specific cues others may be responding to when they make judgments of emotion, personality, attitude, and the like. Unfortunately, many researchers have obtained judgments based on vocal cues without further specifying the specific vocal characteristics responsible for the judgments made. We should, at least, be aware of the range of vocal cues which may be influential in such judgments.

Trager identifies the following components in his "first approximation" of paralanguage: (1) *Voice qualities*—pitch range (spread, narrowed); vocal lip control (sharp transition, smooth transition); articulation control (forceful, relaxed); rhythm control (smooth, jerky); resonance (resonant, thin); tempo (increased, decreased). (2) *Vocal characterizers*—laughing, crying, whispering, snoring, yelling, moaning, groaning, yawning, whining, stretching, sucking, spitting, sneezing, coughing, clearing of the throat, sniffing, sighing, swallowing, heavily marked inhaling or exhaling, belches, and hiccups. (3) *Vocal qualifiers*—intensity (overloud, oversoft); pitch height (overhigh, overlow); extent (drawl, clipping). (4) *Vocal segregates*—"uh," "um," "uh-huh," and variants, silent pauses (beyond junctures), and intruding sounds.[7] Vocal segregates seem to be identical with actual linguistic sounds in the language but do not appear in the kinds of sequences that can be called words.

Some related phenomena, which Mahl and Schulze place under the broad heading of *extralinguistic* phenomena, are also relevant for any discussion of communication and vocal behavior.[8] This would include reactions to such things as dialect or accent, nonfluencies, speech rate, latency of response, duration of utterance and interaction rates. Obviously, there is some overlap here and some paralinguists include these additional aspects within the classification *paralanguage*.

How reliably can trained judges use such a paralinguistic taxonomy to identify these behaviors in actual interaction? In other words, if we observed

---

[7]G. L. Trager, "Paralanguage: A First Approximation," *Studies in Linguistics* 13 (1958): 1–12.

[8]G. F. Mahl and G. Schulze, "Psychological Research in the Extralinguistic Area," in T. Sebeok, A. S. Hayes, and M. C. Bateson (eds.) *Approaches to Semiotics* (The Hague: Mouton, 1964). For an extensive discussion of vocal alternants (Trager's vocal segregates), see F. Poyatos, "Cross-Cultural Study of Paralinguistic 'Alternants' in Face-to-Face Interaction," in A. Kendon, R. M. Harris and M. R. Key (eds.) *Organization of Behavior in Face-to-Face Interaction* (Chicago: Aldine, 1975).

The Effects of Vocal Cues Which Accompany Spoken Words

and recorded the paralinguistic behaviors of two speakers today, would we make the same observations three months from now? While there is still further work to be done, we have some evidence that certain paralanguage dimensions are scored more reliably than others—that is, high reliability is typically reported for the various hesitation phenomena, three independent studies found high reliability in scoring for loudness and pitch, two studies found high reliabilty in measuring tempo, one study obtained high reliability in measuring voice openness, and one obtained reliable measures of extent.

Now that we have a basic referent for the ingredients of paralanguage, we can ask the next logical question: What reactions do vocal cues elicit and how are they important in communicating?

Vocal Cues and Speaker Recognition

You may have had this experience: A person calls you on the telephone and, apparently assuming you will recognize his or her voice, does not provide any verbal content which would help you identify that person—for example, you pick up the phone and say: "Hello." The voice on the other end says: "Hi, how ya doin'?" At this point you realize two things: (1) The greeting suggests an informality found among people who are supposed to know each other, and (2) you don't know who it is! So you try to extend the conversation without admitting your ignorance, hoping some verbal clue will be given or that you'll eventually recognize the caller's voice. As a result, you say something like, "Fine. What have you been up to?"

Each time we speak we produce a complex acoustic signal. It's not exactly the same each time we speak (even if it's the same word); nor is the acoustic signal you produce exactly the same as the one produced by other speakers. The knowledge that there are greater differences between the voices of two different speakers than the voice of a single speaker at two different times has led to considerable interest in the process of identifying speakers by their voices alone.

There are three primary methods for identifying speakers: (1) listening, (2) visual comparison of spectrograms (voiceprints), and (3) recognition through machine analysis of the speech signals.

After reviewing an extensive body of literature in this area, Hecker argues that the recognition accuracy for listening compares very favorably with the other two techniques.[9] There are, however, many variables which will affect

[9]M. H. L. Hecker, "Speaker Recognition: An Interpretive Survey of the Liturature," *ASHA Monographs*, Number 16 (Washington: American Speech and Hearing Association, 1971).

The Effects of Vocal Cues Which Accompany Spoken Words

Figure 10.1 Sound Waves Being Translated into Pictures on Spectograph (Albert Fenn, *Life Magazine*, © Time, Inc.)

accuracy, such as familiarity with the speaker, the judge's desire to accurately identify the speaker, the type of spectrogram used, the amount of training the judges obtain, the amount of noise or masking accompanying or distorting the signal, the method of identification and discrimination used by the judge, the duration of the speech sample, the number of phonemes represented in the sample, the psychological state or bias of the hearer or reader, and so on.

Even when listeners accurately pinpoint a speaker's voice, they aren't able to explain the perceptual bases for their decision—that is, we don't know what features of the voice listeners are reacting to. From the many characteristics of the voice, listeners probably utilize very few in speaker recognition attempts.

Law enforcement and judicial agencies have had a special concern for being able to identify speakers objectively from their vocal characteristics. At the famous trial of Bruno Hauptman, the accused kidnapper of the Lindbergh baby, Lindbergh claimed he recognized Hauptman's voice as the voice of the kidnapper, even though it had been about three years since he had heard it. While it is not beyond the realm of possibility that such an identification could have been accurate, McGehee found that accuracy tends to drop off sharply after three weeks and after five months it dips to about 13 percent.[10] Uncertain-

[10]F. McGehee, "The Reliability of the Identification of the Human Voice," *Journal of General Psychology* 17 (1937): 249–271.

The Effects of Vocal Cues Which Accompany Spoken Words

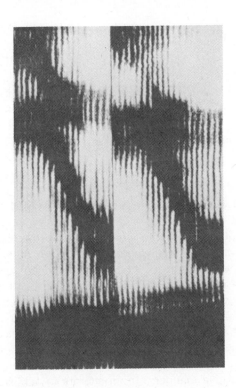

Figure 10.2 Similar Spectrograms of the Word *You* Uttered by Two Arbitrarily Selected Speakers

ties of this nature have encouraged a search for more objective methods. One of these attempts to gather more objective data on voice recognition is to get a visual picture of a person's speech—a spectrogram (see Figure 10.1).

Some people have made strong claims for the accuracy and reliability of spectrographic analysis, but the experimental data only reminds us that we still face human error in the interpretation of the visual data. The interpreter's skill becomes particularly relevant when one looks at Figure 10.2[11] Here are two similar spectrograms—admittedly featuring only one word—but sufficient to point out that our reliance on spectrograms as evidence at trials must be weighed very carefully. Spectrograms are not entirely like fingerprints. It is true that no two voices are exactly alike, but depending on the voice sample obtained and the equipment used, two different voices may appear very similar. On the other hand, fingerprints, unlike voices, will show little variability from one time to the next—unless, of course, smudges or smears have occurred. One study which asked speakers to produce the same sentence using their

[11]P. Ladefoged and R. Vanderslice, "The Voiceprint Mystique," *Working Papers in Phonetics*, 7, November 1967, University of California, Los Angeles.

The Effects of Vocal Cues Which Accompany Spoken Words

normal voice and a number of "disguises"—speaking like an old person, using a hypernasal voice, a hoarse voice, a slow rate of speech, and a disguise of one's own choosing.[12] These voice samples were then submitted to spectrographic analysis by experts who were paid fifty dollars if they achieved the highest accuracy of identification. Normal voices were matched with about 57 percent accuracy, but all the disguises significantly interfered with identification—with the least accuracy being achieved when speakers chose their own type of disguise.

Vocal Cues and Personality Judgments

One cultural syndrome which aptly illustrates our association of vocal cues with certain personality characteristics concerns what some speech scientists call our "vocal neurosis" about the low, deep voice. We find salesmen, radio and TV announcers, receptionists, lawyers, and many others trying to emulate the low vocal tones, which they perceive somehow as being more sophisticated, appealing, sexy, or masculine than higher-pitched voices. In many respects we have been trained to such stereotypes—noting vocal characteristics of such movie stars as Marlene Dietrich, Lauren Bacall, Charles Boyer, Humphrey Bogart, and others. Some people equate the low-pitched voice with security and a "positive manner." In an attempt to achieve this vocal ideal, however, it is also quite possible that we may develop nodes, polyps, and ulcers of the larynx—in short, we may be committing vocal suicide in an effort to achieve vocal desirability!

There have been numerous research efforts aimed at determining whether certain personality traits are expressed in one's voice and whether others are sensitive to these cues. The results of these studies have been mixed. It is common to find: (1) a great amount of agreement among judges of the voices regarding the presence of certain personality characteristics; (2) little agreement between the judges' personality perceptions and the speaker's actual score on personality tests; (3) for some voices and some personality traits, a very high correspondence between the judges' perceptions and actual criterion measures. Kramer, in his interpretation of this data, makes several worthwhile observations:[13] First, the criterion measures (personality tests) are also frequently imperfect measures—that is, a judge may rate a voice as representative

---

[12]A. R. Reich, K. L. Moll, and J. F. Curtis, "Effects of Selected Vocal Disguises upon Spectrographic Speaker Identification," *Journal of the Acoustical Society of America* 60 (1976): 919–925.

[13]E. Kramer, "Personality Stereotypes in Voice: A Reconsideration of the Data," *Journal of Social Psychology* 62 (1964): 247–251.

of a particular personality trait and, when matched with a score on a personality test taken by that speaker, the two measures only correlate as much as would be predicted by chance. However, since the personality test is not a totally accurate measure, it is possible there might be a higher correspondence than this data seems to indicate. Second, Kramer points out that almost all these studies have used a speaker giving a monologue—to which the judges respond. Perhaps some personality characteristics associated with vocal cues only "come out" in dialogue form—a possibility which has not been adequately tested. Finally, Kramer points out that the research has generally ignored differences among listeners with respect to such things as personality, culture, and developmental and psychophysical traits—which may have a profound impact on the listener's accuracy in perceiving personality traits based on vocal cues. It would also seem highly desirable to obtain acoustical records on spectrograms to find out how acoustically similar voices are perceived.

Thus, we find there are a series of studies which have had little success in relating judgments of vocal cues and personality test scores on extroversion, introversion, sociability, intelligence, and leadership. On the other hand, we find studies which relate breathiness to low dominance, while high introversion scores on the Bernreuter Personality Inventory appear negatively related to loudness, low pitch, and resonance; there seems to be a slight positive correlation between dominance and low pitch, loudness, and resonance; some preliminary work suggests that "dominant" vocal characteristics seem to be closely associated with "dominant" personality scores on the Minnesota Multiphasic Personality Inventory.[14] Some researchers have had success in matching summary personality sketches with voices. Such is the nature of the phrase *mixed results*.

Perhaps one of the most complete studies in this area was conducted by Addington.[15] He recognized that stereotyped judgments of vocal cues regularly occur and decided to explore the specific nature of these stereotypes. Male and female speakers simulated nine vocal characteristics, and judges responded to the voices by rating them on forty personality characteristics. Judges were most reliable in ratings of masculine-feminine, young-old, enthusiastic-apathetic, energetic-lazy, good-looking–ugly. The least reliable ratings occurred on the following personality dimensions: extroverted-introverted, honest-dishonest, law abiding-criminal, and healthy-sickly. Addington factor-analyzed his personality data and concluded that the male personality was generally perceived in terms of physical and emotional power, while the female personality was apparently perceived in terms of social faculties. Table 10.1 summarizes his

[14]J. C. Weaver and R. J. Anderson, "Voice and Personality Interrelationships," *Southern Speech Communication Journal* 38 (1973): 262–278.

[15]D. W. Addington, "The Relationship of Selected Vocal Characteristics to Personality Perception," *Speech Monographs* 35 (1968): 492–503.

The Effects of Vocal Cues Which Accompany Spoken Words

Table 10.1 Simulated Vocal Cues and Personality Stereotypes

Simulated vocal cues*	Speakers	Stereotyped perceptions
Breathiness	Males	Younger, more artistic
	Females	More feminine, prettier, more petite, more effervescent, more high-strung, and shallower
Thinness	Males	Did not alter listener's image of the speaker; no significant correlations
	Females	Increased social, physical, emotional, and mental immaturity; increased sense of humor and sensitivity
Flatness	Males	More masculine, more sluggish, colder, more withdrawn
	Females	More masculine, more sluggish, colder, more withdrawn
Nasality	Males	A wide array of socially undesirable characteristics
	Females	A wide array of socially undesirable characteristics
Tenseness	Males	Older, more unyielding, cantankerous
	Females	Younger; more emotional, feminine, high-strung; less intelligent
Throatiness	Males	Older; more realistic, mature; sophisticated; well adjusted
	Females	Less intelligent; more masculine; lazier; more boorish, unemotional, ugly, sickly, careless, inartistic, naive, humble, neurotic, quiet, uninteresting, apathetic. In short, "Cloddish or oafish" (Addington)
Orotundity	Males	More energetic, healthy, artistic, sophisticated, proud, interesting, enthusiastic. In short, "hardy and aesthetically inclined." (Addington)
	Females	Increased liveliness, gregariousness, esthetic sensitivity, and "increasingly proud and humorless" (Addington)
Increased Rate	Males	More animated and extroverted
	Females	More animated and extroverted
Increased Pitch Variety	Males	More dynamic, feminine, esthetically inclined
	Females	More dynamic and extroverted

*For descriptions of these cues, see P. Heinberg, *Voice Training for Speaking and Reading Aloud* (New York: Ronald Press, 1964). Pp. 152–181.

results. Addington concludes his study by posing some interesting questions for researchers studying vocal cues and personality. For instance, to what extent are these stereotyped impressions of personality maintained in the face of conflicting personality information? Another question concerns the nature of the relationship between a given personality impression and vocal cue. For example, Addington's research indicated increased pitch variety led to more positive personality impressions, but is it not possible that at some point, increasing pitch variety could become so exaggerated as to evoke negative perceptions? These questions await further study.

A related line of study involves the association of various personality characteristics with voices representative of large groups of people. These studies deal with judgments of group personality rather than individual personality. For instance, Anisfeld, Bogo, and Lambert asked Jewish and Gentile students to evaluate voices—some speaking standard English; some speaking English with a Jewish accent.[16] The same speakers did both voice samples. Both Gentiles and Jews rated the accented voices low in height, good looks, and leadership. Gentiles did not rate the accented voices higher on any trait, while Jews rated accented voices higher on humor, entertainingness, and kindness. Jews saw many more nonaccented voices as being Jewish than did the Gentiles. There seemed to be no relationship between a measure of attitudes toward Jews and the personality traits chosen. Another fascinating group to group study centered on the long-standing tension between French- and English-speaking Canadians.[17] An initial study, using bilingual speakers, presented judges with the same messages in English-Canadian and French-Canadian. The English-Canadian message was rated significantly better than the French-Canadian message. In fact, the French-Canadian judges rated the English-Canadian speaker higher on such traits as intelligence, likability, dependability, and character. Thus, certain subgroups of college age French-Canadians seemed to have a bias against their own linguistic group. A follow-up study tried to determine at what age this bias is present. With girls the bias appears about age twelve, but the ultimate fate of this attitude depends to a great extent on social class background. Girls who came from upper-middle-class French-Canadian homes, and especially those who had become bilingual, were particularly likely to maintain this view—at least into their young adult years. Obviously, one possible factor here is the upper-middle-class desire to associate with those who have power and prestige. Perhaps among certain middle-class American blacks, the same phenomenon has occurred.

[16]M. Anisfeld, N. Bogo, and W. Lambert, "Evaluation Reactions to Accented English Speech," *Journal of Abnormal and Social Psychology* 65 (1962): 223–231.

[17]W. E. Lambert, H. Frankel, and G. R. Tucker, "Judging Personality Through Speech: A French-Canadian Example," *Journal of Communication* 16 (1966): 305–321.

The Effects of Vocal Cues Which Accompany Spoken Words

Closely related to these studies of group personalities and voices are the many efforts to show how people evaluate various dialects and accents. You may recall that Liza Doolittle in Shaw's *Pygmalion* spent considerable time and effort trying to correct her dialect so she could rise in social standing. (Professor Higgins: "Look at her—a pris'ner of the gutters; Condemned by ev'ry syllable she utters." Act 1, Scene 1, *My Fair Lady*). Liza's training, according to one study, was most appropriate—suggesting that if we expect a speaker to reflect a nonstandard and/or "lower class" dialect and the speaker actually presents him/or herself in accord with standard or "upper class" models, the evaluation will be very positive; the reverse was also true—speakers expected to speak "up" who spoke "down" were evaluated negatively.[18] Obviously, there is a fine line between "adapting to your audience" and severely violating expectations of your own background.

Although some of the studies which form the foundation for the following conclusions seemed to use stimuli representing something more than just vocal cues, they still represent a significant corpus of material relevant to our understanding of vocal cues. While there are some exceptions, ordinarily we find dialects other than the one spoken by the listener/evaluators receive less favorable evaluations than those considered "standard." Generally, these negative responses occur because the listener associates the speaker's dialect with an ethnic or regional stereotype and then evaluates the voice in accord with the stereotype. Typical of this type of response are studies which found the following; (1) Chicano English speakers were rated lower on success, ability, and social awareness; (2) native-born Americans rated Europeans (speaking English) less positively than other native-born speakers; (3) teachers will tend to label a child as "culturally disadvantaged" especially if the speech exhibits perceived irregularities in grammar, silent pausing, and pronunciation; and (4) "standard" dialects were preferred and judged more competent than "nonstandard"—regardless who spoke—except standard dialects were more often associated with white speakers than black.[19]

Do regional varieties of speech in the United States differ in prestige value?

---

[18]F. E. Aboud, R. Clement, and D. M. Taylor "Evaluational Reactions to Discrepancies Between Social Class and Language," *Sociometry* 37 (1974): 239–150.

[19]A. Bradford, D. Ferror, and G. Bradford, "Evaluation Reactions of College Students to Dialect Differences in the English of Mexican-Americans," *Language and Speech* 17 (1974): 255–270. A. Mulac, T. D. Hanley, and D. Y. Prigge, "Effects of Phonological Speech Foreignness upon Three Dimensions of Attitude of Selected American Listeners," *Quarterly Journal of Speech* 60 (1974): 411–420; F. Williams and G. W. Shamo, "Regional Variations in Teacher Attitudes Toward Children's Language," *Central States Speech Journal* 23 (1972): 73–77; F. Williams. "The Psychological Correlates of Speech Characteristics: On Sounding 'Disadvantaged,' " *Journal of Speech and Hearing Research* 13 (1970): 472–488, J. Buck, "The Effects of Negro and White Dialectical Variations upon Attitudes of College Students," *Speech Monographs* 35 (1968): 181–186.

The Effects of Vocal Cues Which Accompany Spoken Words

Some people in Maine, Lousiana, New York City, Arkansas, and Michigan rated twelve voice samples of American dialects and one foreign accent.[20] The most unfavorably regarded were the foreign accent and the example of "New Yorkese." Although this study is about thirty years old, you may be able to think of some current dialect or accent stereotypes which may influence your own judgments of a speaker's status today. Certainly a lot of people had a chance to test their Southern stereotypes as they evaluated the speech of President Carter. Miller's work appears to be the only current effort to go beyond the theory that dialects evoke stereotypes of groups which influence the judgment of that dialect. In this study we find some support for the notion that there may be aspects of certain dialects which are evaluated independently of the stereotype—that is, some listeners may respond negatively to a French Canadian speaker because of a negative stereotype *and/or* because of some dislike for the dialect itself.[21]

Several investigators have pursued the question of how we tend to judge the speech and dialects of others. Lambert's work shows accents rated along the dimensions of competence, integrity, and attractiveness.[22] Williams found teachers evaluating children's speech along two dimensions, which he labeled "confidence-eagerness" and "ethnicity-nonstandardness."[23] By far the most extensive work in this direction is that of Mulac.[24] Mulac's experiments have used regional and foreign dialects, broadcasters, various speech pathologies, prose and spontaneous speech, and different modes of presentation, such as written, audio tape, video tape, sound film, and the like. This work shows we tend to look at samples of speech along three primary dimensions: (1) socio-intellectual status—for example, high or low social status, blue or white collar, rich or poor, and literate or illiterate; (2) esthetic quality—pleasing or displeasing, nice or awful, sweet or sour, beautiful or ugly; and (3) dynamism—aggressive or unaggressive, active or passive, strong or weak, loud or soft. These results are but another confirmation of studies in many other areas of perception which show we tend to see our world and the things in it according to evaluative, power, and activity dimensions.

As we have mentioned several times in this book, our main concern is not

[20]W. Wilke and J. Snyder, "Attitudes Toward American Dialects," *Journal of Social Psychology* 14 (1941): 349–362.

[21]D. T. Miller, "The Effect of Dialect and Ethnicity on Communicator Effectiveness," *Speech Monographs* 42 (1975): 69–74.

[22]W. E. Lambert, R. C. Hodgson, R. C. Gardner, and S. Fillenbaum, "Evaluational Reactions to Spoken Languages," *Journal of Abnormal and Social Psychology* 60 (1960): 44–51.

[23]F. Williams, "The Psychological Correlates of Speech Characteristics: On Sounding 'Disadvantaged,'" *Journal of Speech and Hearing Research* 13 (1970): 472–488.

[24]A. Mulac, "Assessment and Application of the Revised Speech Dialect Attitudinal Scale," *Communication Monographs* 43 (1976): 238–245.

The Effects of Vocal Cues Which Accompany Spoken Words

with pathological behavior. It should be noted, however, that there is a significant body of literature concerning various vocal cues and their relationship to personality adjustment or psychopathology. Schizophrenia in particular has been studied for special vocal cues associated with it.

Vocal Cues and Judgments of Personal Characteristics

Over forty years ago Pear was doing pioneering work on vocal cues and judgments of personal characteristics.[25] Using nine speakers and over four thousand radio listeners, he found a speaker's age could be estimated fairly accurately, the speaker's sex with remarkable accuracy, birthplace with little accuracy, and occasionally vocation with surprising accuracy. The actor and clergyman were consistently identified from among the nine professions represented. Since that time, others have been interested in judgments of such characteristics as body type, height, weight, age, occupation, status or social class, race, sex, education, and dialect region.

Nerbonne found listeners able to differentiate accurately between male and female, Negro and Caucasian, big and small speakers; among twenty-to-thirty-year-old, forty-to-sixty-year-old, and sixty-to-seventy-year-old speakers (age differentiation being easiest from spontaneous cues); among speakers with less than a high school education, high school graduates, and college graduates; and among speakers from Eastern, Southern, and General American dialect regions.[26] For some reason, age and dialect were more accurately judged in Nerbonne's study when aural cues were provided by telephone speech rather than under conditons simulating face-to-face conversation. An undergraduate student at the University of Wisconsin–Milwaukee doubted the validity of distinctions between Negroes and Caucasians on the basis of voice alone—particularly if the characteristics of the social community in which the speakers were born and raised were kept constant. She conducted an informal telephone survey using Negroes and Caucasians—all of whom were raised from childhood in the same neighborhood in Milwaukee. Her results show no more than chance accuracy in making such distinctions. Thus, although black and white speakers can sometimes be distinguished by their vocal cues at high levels of accuracy, there will be other times when such identifications will be very difficult. For instance, West Indian blacks in a British community were

[25]T. H. Pear. Voice and Personality (London: Chapman and Hall, 1931).
[26]G. P. Nerbonne, "The Identification of Speaker Characteristics on the Basis of Aural Cues," Ph.D. dissertation. Michigan State University, 1967.

The Effects of Vocal Cues Which Accompany Spoken Words

misattributed as whites 8 percent of the time when voice samples were judged.[27]

Weitz, in a slightly different approach, looked at interracial interaction and voice tone.[28] She found that voice tone seemed to be a better predictor of "friendliness" for whites interacting with blacks than overtly expressed verbal attitudes. Weitz has also speculated that in crossed sex interactions, vocal tones may also help identify underlying attitudes, such as patronizing, friendly, or hostile.

Listeners who heard six recorded vowels of twenty speakers were able to identify the sex of the speaker 96 percent of the time when the tape was not altered in any way. Accuracy decreased to 91 percent for a filtered tape and to 75 percent for a whispered voice sample.[29] These authors argue that the laryngeal fundamental frequency is a more important acoustic cue in speaker sex identification tasks than the resonance characteristics of the voices. Sometimes women and men may be identified on the basis of their intonation patterns. Some believe, for instance, that women might end a sentence on a higher pitch, relative to where they started the sentence, than men. Pitch may be another basis for discrimination. Again, the nature of the vocal stimuli will be most influential in determining exactly how well we can discriminate male from female voices. For instance, males and females *interacting* may manifest different vocal cues than when they present monologues or interact with a member of the same sex;[30] the topic of discussion may affect voice production and perceptions; and if, as we noted earlier with the black speakers, there is a gradual narrowing of differences as adaptations to the social community are made, we might speculate that the vocal tones of working women in predominately male organizations may be harder to distinguish—particularly if the sample is taken in the work milieu. Instead of children shaping their voices to sound like the adult version of their sex,[31] this may be an instance of adults acquiring some vocal characteristics of the opposite sex. It may also be, of

[27]H. Giles and R. Y. Bourhis, "Voice and Racial Categorization in Britian," *Communication Monographs* 43 (1976): 108–114. Some of the vocal features which judges may respond to or look for in making such identifications can be found in F. S. Dubner, "Nonverbal Aspects of Black English," *Southern Speech Communication Journal* 37 (1972): 361–374.

[28]S. Weitz, "Attitude, Voice, and Behavior: A Repressed Affect Model of Interracial Interaction." *Journal of Personality and Social Psychology* 24 (1972): 14–21.

[29]N. J. Lass, K. R. Hughes, M. D. Bowyer, L. T. Waters, and V. T. Broune, "Speaker Sex Identification from Voiced, Whispered and Filtered Isolated Vowels," *Journal of the Acoustical Society of America* 59 (1976): 675–678.

[30]N. N. Markel, L. D. Prebor, and J. F. Brandt, "Biosocial Factors in Dyadic Communication: Sex and Speaking Intensity," *Journal of Personality and Social Psychology* 23 (1972): 11–13.

[31]J. Sachs, P. Lieberman, and D. Erickson, "Anatomical and Cultural Determinants of Male and Female Speech," in R. W. Shuy and R. W. Fasold (eds.) *Language Attitudes: Current Trends and Prospects* (Washington: Georgetown University Press, 1973), pp. 74–84.

The Effects of Vocal Cues Which Accompany Spoken Words

course, that females whose voices are at some variance with a traditional female-stereotyped voice are selectively hired by male employers for traditionally male-held jobs.

The literature on height and weight judgments is mixed—some studies report accuracy and others do not. One source of variance might be the range allowed for an accurate answer—for example, we would predict greater accuracy if we had to guess a person's height within five inches than within two. As long as the response category is not too discriminating, height and weight can probably be judged with greater than chance accuracy from vocal cues.[32] When Lass and his colleagues asked people to estimate exact height and weight, however, the *average* difference between actual height (for all speakers—male and female) and estimated height (for all speakers) was only .80 inches. The weight discrepancy was only 3.48 pounds. And height and weight of the speakers was not limited to a narrow range. As judges we might attach various heights and weights to certain vocal characteristics. Test your own stereotypes and compare them with your friends. Would you associate an extremely low-pitched voice with a heavier person? Does loudness suggest a weight category for you? Think of people you know who are very tall, very short, very light, and very heavy. Would your reaction to an unknown voice be influenced by your experiences with and memory of these other people? There are many characteristics which influence our judgments. These have only been a few. Others include breathiness, rate, intonation, and resonance.

When listeners are asked to match voice samples with photographs, we again find the task performed with better than chance accuracy—but again, the accuracy level will depend heavily on the preciseness of the judgment to be made.[33] Fay and Middleton studied body type as one variable which might be associated with vocal cues.[34] Unfortunately, they did not verify the actual body types of the speakers by precise measurements (only observed guesstimates), so it is advisable to weigh their findings with caution. Listeners were asked to write in the body type they thought fit the voice they heard. Listeners heard nine different speakers and were asked to determine whether they were:

Pyknic— round, thickset body; a soft, well-proportioned face; short legs, thick neck, and a relatively large barrel-shaped trunk; short stocky person; fat or stout.

[32]N. J. Lass and M. Davis, "An Investigation of Speaker Height and Weight Identification," *Journal of the Acoustical Society of America* 60 (1976): 700–707.

[33]N. J. Lass and L. A. Harvey, "An Investigation of Speaker Photograph Identification," *Journal of the Acoustical Society of America* 59 (1976):1232–1236.

[34]P. Fay and W. Middleton, "Judgments of Kretschmerian Body Types from the Voice as Transmitted Over a Public Address System," *Journal of Social Psychology* 12 (1940): 151–162.

The Effects of Vocal Cues Which Accompany Spoken Words

Leptosomatic— long extremities and small trunk; underdeveloped; small proportions and sharp lean features; may be quite childlike physically; lean, slender, skinny.

Athletic— bony; muscular body of an athlete; symmetrical development of limbs; rather long extremities and relatively small trunk; approaches ideal type of masculine development.

Fay and Middleton report the pyknic and leptosomatic types were judged with far more than chance accuracy while the athletic type was at about chance. It seems that for extreme body types, there may be vocal stereotypes which have some validity.

Judgments of occupation from vocal cues also seems to vary from study to study. Generally the judges agree with one another, but their judgments do not always match the actual occupations. Some early studies reported a fairly consistent identification of occupation from voices, but Fay and Middleton only found the voice of a preacher identified at a rate better than chance—and it was frequently mistaken for the voice of a lawyer![35]

Several studies show age to be fairly accurately assessed from vocal cues. Davis concluded her research by saying: "the results of this study seem to indicate clearly that voice alone can suggest age to the listener."[36] Why is this? Several studies have investigated pitch of males during infancy, childhood, adolescence, early adulthood, and middle and advanced age. There seems to be a general lowering of pitch level from infancy through middle age. Then a reversal occurs, and pitch level rises slightly with advancing age. Mysak, for instance, found that males in his 80–92year-old study group were characterized by higher measures of average fundamental pitch levels than males aged 65–79.[37] He says age 80 is a very sensitive dividing line in terms of pitch change. Pitch changes were explained by physical changes and increasing tension. A similar, but less complete, series of studies have been completed on the developing female voice. McClone and Hollien, using research methods similar to Mysak's, found no significant difference in the mean pitch level of two groups (aged 65–79 and 80–94).[38] The data on pitch from the 65–79 group was compared with data gathered by another investigator on some young adult women. Since again there were no differences, McGlone and Hollien conclude

[35]P. Fay and W. Middleton, "Judgment of Occupation from the Voice as Transmitted over a Public Address System." *Sociometry* 3 (1940): 186–191.

[36]P. B. Davis. "An Investigation of the Suggestion of Age Through Voice in Interpretative Reading," M.A. thesis, University of Denver, 1949, p. 69.

[37]E. D. Mysak. "Pitch and Duration Characteristics of Older Males," *Journal of Speech and Hearing Research* 2 (1959): 46–54.

[38]R. E. McClone and H. Hollien. "Vocal Pitch Characteristics of Aged Women." *Journal of Speech and Hearing Research* 6 (1963): 164–170.

The Effects of Vocal Cues Which Accompany Spoken Words

that speaking pitch level of women probably varies little throughout adult life, even though data for middle-aged women was not compared. If, as some gerontological studies suggest, our voices change in pitch flexibility, rate, loudness, vocal quality, articulatory control and the like, this may give clues to age that we are largely unaware of. It is also quite possible we are responding to other vocal characteristics that have not been reported in these developmental studies—they only give us possible clues.

Finally, we find several studies which show listeners amazingly accurate in judging social class or status on the basis of voice alone. Harms obtained independent scores from nine speakers on the Hollingshead Two Factor Index of Status Position.[39] The speakers were then categorized as either high, middle, or low status. Each speaker recorded a forty-to-sixty-second conversation in which he responded to questions and statements like "How are you?" "Ask for the time," and so on. Adult listeners rated the speakers according to status and credibility. Results show that these listeners were not only able to identify the speakers' status, but many of them said they made their decision after only ten to fifteen seconds of listening to the recording. Responses also showed those perceived as high in status were also perceived as most credible. This finding is consistent with other studies of status and vocal cues. Ellis even conducted a study in which he told speakers to try to fake status and imitate upper class.[40] Listener judgments still correlated .65 with independent measures of status for these speakers. As we've intimated so many times, it appears we learn to talk like those around us—those in our neighborhoods, those in our vocational environment, and those in our educational environments.

If voice and status are so intimately related, the following dialogue from *The Selling of the President 1968* takes on a definite note of realism: "The announcer who was to do the opening called to ask if his tone was too shrill. 'Yeah, we don't want it like a quiz show,' Roger Ailes said. 'He's going to be presidential tonight so announce presidentially.' "[41]

Vocal Cues and Judgments of Emotion

Would you know if someone were happy? sad? afraid? "Of course I would," you say. What if we removed this person from your sight? "Sure," you say. "The kinds of things the person says will tell me whether he or she is

[39]L. S. Harms, "Listener Judgments of Status Cues in Speech," *Quarterly Journal of Speech* 47 (1961): 164–168. This study was replicated with similar results in J. D. Moe, "Listener Judgments of Status Cues in Speech: A Replication and Extension," *Speech Monographs* 39 (1972): 144–147.

[40]D. S. Ellis, "Speech and Social Status in America," *Social Forces* 45 (1967): 431–451.

[41]J. McGinniss, *The Selling of the President 1968* (New York: Trident 1969): p. 155.

The Effects of Vocal Cues Which Accompany Spoken Words

happy, sad, angry, or afraid." What if we eliminate any words you might respond to—the voice is the only stimulus for judging emotional expressions. "Maybe" you say. Some researchers might be more optimistic, but *maybe* may, indeed, be the best answer as we will show later.

Starkweather, in 1961, summarized a series of studies which attempted to specify the relationship between the voice and judgments of emotion. His conclusion reiterates the frequent finding in studies of personality judgments from vocal cues—consistent agreement between the judges.

> Studies of content free speech indicate that the voice alone can carry information about the speaker. Judges agree substantially, both when asked to identify the emotion being expressed and when given the task of estimating the strength of the feeling. Judgments appear to depend on significant changes in pitch, rate, volume and other physical characteristics of the voice, but untrained judges cannot describe these qualities accurately.[42]

Three years later, Davitz seemed to suggest that such judgments are not only reliable, but also valid: "Regardless of the technique used, all studies of adults thus far reported in the literature agree that emotional meanings can be communicated accurately by vocal expression."[43]

Beier and Zautra even feel there may be some sort of universality of meaning for emotions expressed vocally.[44] They obtained responses to vocal expressions of the following moods: angry, sad, happy, flirtatious, fearful, and indifferent. Each mood was portrayed by Americans and interpreted by American, Polish, and Japanese subjects. Accuracy was high, but increased as the duration of the stimulus increased.

In order to understand these conclusions fully, it is necessary to elaborate on the factors which may cause differences in judging emotions accurately from vocal cues. Certainly the authors of the aforementioned conclusions do not intend to imply invariable consistency in judging emotions accurately.

There have been several *methods* used to eliminate or control the verbal information usually accompanying vocal cues. Accuracy may vary depending on the method used. Some studies attempt to use what is assumed to be "meaningless content." This usually takes the form of having the speaker say numbers or letters while trying to convey various emotional states. Davitz and Davitz conducted a typical study of this type.[45] Speakers were instructed to

---

[42]J. A. Starkweather. "Vocal Communication of Personality and Human Feelings," *Journal of Communication* 11 (1961): 69.

[43]J. R. Davitz. *The Communication of Emotional Meaning* (New York: McGraw-Hill, 1964), p. 23.

[44]E. G. Beier and A. Zautra, "Identification of Vocal Communication of Emotions Across Culture," *ERIC* (1972) Ed 056504.

[45]J. R. Davitz and L. Davitz. "The Communication of Feelings by Content-Free Speech," *Journal of Communication* 9 (1959): 6–13.

The Effects of Vocal Cues Which Accompany Spoken Words

express ten different feelings by reciting parts of the alphabet. These expressions were recorded and played before judges who were asked to identify the emotion being expressed by choosing from a list of ten emotions. Generally, emotions or feelings were communicated far beyond chance expectation. It is difficult to tell, in this type of study, whether the communicators were using the same tonal or vocal cues which would be used in "real life" emotional reactions.

Other studies have attempted to control the verbal cues by using "constant content." In other words, a speaker reads a standard passage while attempting to simulate different emotional states. The assumption underlying this technique is that the passage selected is neutral in emotional tone. An independent study of the passage used in one early study which used this method found the so-called "neutral" passage most frequently associated with "anger"![46]

Another approach is to simply try to ignore content and focus attention on the pauses, breathing rate, and other characteristics which may give clues to the person's emotional state. This method is frequently used in psychotherapy to identify signs of anxiety.

Finally, some of the more recent studies have used electronic filtering to eliminate verbal content. A low pass filter will hold back the higher frequencies of speech upon which word recognition depends. The finished product sounds much like a mumble you might hear through a wall. Although this type of speech sample is commonly referred to as "content-free," this is, in many respects, a misnomer. Since such voice samples are not literally content-free, some prefer to use terms like *word-free voice* or *vocalic communication*. Certainly a recording which communicates emotional content is not content-free—particularly since for some messages, emotion is the major or most critical content. An example of the electronically filtered technique is the work of Starkweather, who used the actual spoken transcriptions from the Army-McCarthy hearings of 1954.[47] His results suggest a tendency for judges to be able to discriminate "pleasantness" and "emotion being expressed" in these word-free samples. Another study by Starkweather found judges discriminating between aggressive and submissive speakers. One common problem with the electronically filtered technique is that some of the nonverbal vocal cues may be eliminated in the filtering process, creating an artificial stimulus. Starkweather admits some aspects of vocal quality may be lost in the filtering process, but a listener can still adequately perceive pitch, rate, and loudness in order to make judgments of emotional content.

[46]E. Kramer, "Judgment of Personal Characteristics and Emotions from Non-verbal Properties," *Psychological Bulletin* 60 (1963): 408–420.

[47]J. A. Starkweather, "The Communication Value of Content-Free Speech," *American Journal of Psychology* 69 (1956): 121–123. Another method for filtering the content of natural speech is described in P. L. Rogers, K. R. Scherer, and R. Rosenthal, "Content Filtering Human Speech: A Simple Electronic System," *Behavior Research Methods and Instrumentation* 3 (1971): 16–18.

The Effects of Vocal Cues Which Accompany Spoken Words

Another method which eliminates the continuity and rhythm of the speaking voice, but which still maintains the affective tone and emotional information is randomized splicing.[48] With this method, the voice is recorded on tape, cut into short segments, and pasted back together in random order to mask the speech content.

Earlier we spoke of the merit of the answer "maybe" to a question concerning our ability to judge emotional expression from vocal cues. One reason for such a qualified answer involves the differing methods by which such observations may be made. Other reasons for equivocation include:

(1) Speakers vary in their ability to produce expressed emotion. Several studies show distinct differences in perceived accuracy between speakers as a result. In the Davitz and Davitz study one speaker's expressions were correctly identified only 23 percent of the time while another speaker communicated accurately well over 50 percent of the time.[49] Some researchers who have studied speakers from vastly different socioeconomic levels suggest there are differences in the "affective tone" of these speakers. It is clear there are distinct differences in encoding behavior for emotional expressions, but we know very little about this phenomenon from empirical studies conducted so far.

(2) We also know that listeners vary in their ability to perceive emotional expressions. In the Davitz and Davitz study, listeners ranged from 20 percent correct to over 50 percent correct. Again we have limited information on the correlates of listener sensitivity to vocal cues. The best available information suggests the following: (a) Listeners sensitive to emotions expressed vocally by others are also likely to be able to express emotions accurately to others and to identify their own vocal expressions of feelings accurately; (b) listeners able to accurately express emotions vocally are likely to be able to accurately express emotions facially as well; (c) sensitive listeners must be able to make auditory discriminations; (d) sensitive listeners must have some abstract symbolic ability; (e) listeners sensitive to feelings expressed vocally must have a knowledge of vocal characteristics of emotional expressions; (f) sensitive listeners should score well on tests of verbal intelligence; (g) general intellectual ability is a valuable asset for listeners sensitive to vocal cues, but a high I.Q. is no guarantee of emotional sensitivity; (h) sensitive listeners must have had exposure to a wide range of emotional expressions carried by the voice.[50] Some researchers talk about a "general factor" of sensitivity which influences a wide range of behaviors involved in nonverbal emotional communication, but most

[48]K. R. Scherer, "Randomized Splicing: A Note on A Simple Technique for Masking Speech Content," *Journal of Experimental Research in Personality* 5 (1971): 155–159. Also see K. R. Scherer, J. Koivumaki, and R. Rosenthal, "Minimal Cues in the Vocal Communication of Affect: Judging Emotions from Content-Masked Speech," *Journal of Psycholinguistic Research* 1 (1972): 269–285.

[49]Davitz and Davitz, "The Communication of Feelings by Content-Free Speech," 6–13.

[50]Davitz, *The Communication of Emotional Meaning.*

The Effects of Vocal Cues Which Accompany Spoken Words

agree it only accounts for a small part of the total sensitivity to any one feature—like the voice. Snyder finds that some people are more conscious of and have more control over their expressive behavior. He calls this process "self-monitoring." Extensive testing brought him to the conclusion that people who are high in self-monitoring behavior are better able to intentionally express emotions in both vocal and facial channels. There also seems to be a tendency for high self-monitors to be better judges of expressed emotions of others.[51]

(3) Several studies show vast differences in the accuracy of judging emotional vocal expressions—depending on the emotions being tested. One study found anger identified 63 percent of the time while pride was only identified correctly 20 percent of the time. Another study found that joy and hate were easily recognized, but shame and love were the most difficult to recognize. The similarity of some feelings may account for some of the difference. For instance, certain errors are consistent in some studies—for example, fear is mistaken for nervousness, love is mistaken for sadness, pride is mistaken for satisfaction. Some have suggested that when two subjectively similar feelings are sought to be communicated, the "stronger" of the two is perceived more accurately, more often. Another possible explanation is that we have not been socially trained to deal with the finer discriminations involved in two "similar" emotions. General semanticians frequently remind us of our tendency to communicate in polar extremes like black-white, hot-cold, good-bad, and the like. Perhaps such verbal behavior has influenced the way we perceive nonverbal emotional expression. It is also possible that as we develop, we rely on context to discriminate emotions with similar characteristics. Thus, when confronted with such cues and no context, we find discriminations difficult.

(4) Finally, we must consider that the context of everyday communication will not duplicate the often well-controlled environment in the laboratory. Your ability to identify a given emotion expressed vocally will be influenced by the context (conversational and/or environmental), how well you know the other person, supplementary cues given through other channels (visual), and so on.

If one of the necessary requirements for developing sensitivity to emotional vocal expressions is knowledge of the vocal characteristics of emotional expression, it would seem worthwhile to outline these characteristics at this point. Unfortunately, the development of such a dictionary of emotions—defined by nonverbal vocal characteristics—is extremely difficult. The same emotion may be expressed differently by different people at different times. Several isolated studies do provide some information on the vocal characteristics associated with various vocalized emotional states, but few generalizations can be made

[51]M. Snyder, "Self-Monitoring of Expressive Behavior," *Journal of Personality and Social Psychology* 30 (1974): 526–537.

The Effects of Vocal Cues Which Accompany Spoken Words

from them. Rather than report these isolated findings, we have reproduced the scoring table (Table 10.2) developed by Davitz which represents, as well as anything, a composite statement of vocal cues associated with various emotional expressions.[52] The table was developed to test subjects on their knowledge of vocal characteristics.

Again, this table should not be interpreted as a summary of research or as "fact." It simply represents one way of devising the Emotion-Vocal Cue Dictionary. Any shortcomings you find in Table10.2—any exceptions you find—only serve to demonstrate the difficulty in developing such a compendium.

Even when we take a broad concept like "anxiety" and try to list the vocal characteristics associated with it, we face the relativity problem again. There are wide individual differences in vocal expression by anxious people. Some say normally anxious people talk slower under experimentally induced anxiety: those not normally anxious speak faster under such conditions. There is some indication that under stress, dialects become stronger. Silent pause frequency and duration, raised pitch level, nonfluencies, and other factors tend to be associated with anxiety in some studies, and not in others. Cook feels certain speech disturbances are associated with anxiety.[53] Table 10-3 presents the categories of speech disturbance investigated by Cook. "Non-Ah" speech errors (categories 2 through 8) seem to increase with induced anxiety or discomfort while "Ah" errors (category 1) do not. Some feel that "Ah" errors increase as the difficulty of the speaking task increases—to allow for "thinking time." Other researchers studying speech errors believe some of these "Non-Ah" speech errors correlate with anxiety as a personality trait. The major assumption behind a much-talked-about lie detector system today is that people who lie are under stress and this stress or anxiety will reflect itself in a measure of vocalizations. It is called the P.S.E. (Psychological Stress Evaluator). It takes an ordinary tape recording of a voice and feeds it into a machine which measures muscular microtremors—faint quivers that come from the muscles in the larynx and cause slight changes in pitch during unstressed speech. These changes are generally not detectable by the unaided ear. Theoretically, the throat muscles of a person under stress are so tense they produce hardly any microtremors. The inventors claim to have monitored the TV program "To Tell the Truth" with 94.7 percent accuracy in identifying the truth-tellers. Despite the fact that the reliability of the machine has not been satisfactorily proved, it has been used in several court cases. Dependence on one nonverbal cue to detect liars seems indeed risky. Further, even if the machine identifies a person under stress, the assumption of lying does not necessarily follow. In fact, for some of

[52]Davitz, *The Communication of Emotional Meaning,* p. 63

[53]M. Cook, "Anxiety, Speech Disturbances, and Speech Rate," *British Journal of Social and Clinical Psychology* 4 (1965): 1–7.

The Effects of Vocal Cues Which Accompany Spoken Words

Table 10.2 Characteristics of Vocal Expressions Contained in the Test of Emotional Sensitivity

Feeling	Loudness	Pitch	Timbre	Rate	Inflection	Rhythm	Enunciation
Affection	Soft	Low	Resonant	Slow	Steady and slight upward	Regular	Slurred
Anger	Loud	High	Blaring	Fast	Irregular up and down	Irregular	Clipped
Boredom	Moderate to low	Moderate to low	Moderately resonant	Moderately slow	Monotone or gradually falling	—	Somewhat slurred
Cheerfulness	Moderately high	Moderately high	Moderately blaring	Moderately fast	Up and down; overall upward	Regular	
Impatience	Normal	Normal to moderately high	Moderately blaring	Moderately fast	Slight upward	—	Somewhat clipped
Joy	Loud	High	Moderately blaring	Fast	Upward	Regular	
Sadness	Soft	Low	Resonant	Slow	Downward	Irregular pauses	Slurred
Satisfaction	Normal	Normal	Somewhat resonant	Normal	Slight upward	Regular	Somewhat slurred

Table 10.3 Speech Disturbance Categories, Frequency of Occurrence, and Examples

Category	% of total	Example
1. 'Er.' 'Ah.' or 'Um'	40.5	Well . . . er . . . when I go home
2. Sentence change	25.3	I have a book which . . . the book I need for finals.
3. Repetition	19.2	I often . . . often work at night.
4. Stutter	7.8	It sort of I . . . I . . . leaves me.
5. Omission (that is, leaving out a word or leaving it unfinished)	4.5	I went to the lib . . . the Bod.
6. Sentence incompletion	1.2	He said the reason was . . . anyway I couldn't go.
7. Tongue slip	0.7	I haven't much term (that is, time) these days.
8. Intruding incoherent sound	1.2	I don't really know why . . . dh . . . I went.

the lies we tell, stress is not much of an issue. Motley's spectrographic analysis of one-word, nonsalient lies revealed that the only characteristic which discriminated true from false responses was duration.[54] The lie responses were invariably the shortest in duration. After this brief detour into the specific vocal features of anxiety or stress, let's return to the broader question of vocal characteristics associated with a wide range of emotions.

Scherer approached the problem of which vocal features are associated with which emotions using artificial sounds rather than spontaneous speech.[55] Using a Moog synthesizer he had subjects rate each acoustic stimulus on a ten-point scale of pleasantness, potency, activity, and evaluation. He also asked the respondents if they felt the stimuli could or could not be an expression of interest, sadness, fear, happiness, disgust, anger, surprise, elation, or boredom. Generally speaking, tempo and pitch variation seem to be very influential factors for a wide range of judgments about emotional expressions. Although Table 10.4 represents the results of a follow-up study, it closely resembles the results of several of Scherer's studies. The nature of Table 10.4

[54]M. T. Motley, "Acoustic Correlates of Lies," *Western Speech* 38 (1974): 81–87.
[55]K. R. Scherer, "Acoustic Concomitants of Emotional Dimensions: Judging Affect from Synthesized Tone Sequences," in S. Weitz (ed.), *Nonverbal Communication: Readings with Commentary* (New York: Oxford University Press, 1974), pp. 105–111.

The Effects of Vocal Cues Which Accompany Spoken Words

Table 10.4 Acoustic Concomitants of Emotional Dimensions

Amplitude Variation	Moderate	Pleasantness, Activity, Happiness
	Extreme	Fear
Pitch Variation	Moderate	Anger Boredom, Disgust, Fear
	Extreme	Pleasantness Activity, Happiness, Surprise
Pitch Contour	Down	Pleasantness, Boredom, Sadness
	Up	Potency, Anger,Fear, Surprise
Pitch Level	Low	Pleasantness, Boredom, Sadness
	High	Activity, Potency, Anger Fear, Surprise
Tempo	Slow	Boredom, Disgust, Sadness
	Fast	Pleasantness, Activity, Potency, Anger, Fear, Happiness, Surprise
Duration Shape	Round	Potency, Boredom, Disgust, Fear, Sadness
	Sharp	Pleasantness, Activity, Happiness, Surprise
Filtration (Lack of Overtones)	Low	Sadness
		Pleasantness, Boredom, Happiness
	Moderate	
		Potency, Activity
	Extreme	Anger, Disgust, Fear, Surprise
	Atonal	
		Disgust
Tonality	Tonal-	
	Minor	Anger
	Tonal-	
	Major	Pleasantness, Happiness
Rhythm	Not rhythmic	Boredom
	Rhythmic	Activity, Fear, Surprise

The Effects of Vocal Cues Which Accompany Spoken Words

may seem unduly technical for some readers, but it is an important effort in showing how we attribute meaning from auditory stimuli based on characteristic patterns of acoustic cues.

The researchers who are now plotting vocal characteristics on spectrograms will certainly provide more precision for our dictionary, but they are faced with the problem of generalizing to the communication situation—they must ask what is perceived and responded to rather than what is produced.

In addition to its role in personality and emotional judgments, the voice also seems to play a part in retention and attitude change—primarily studied in the public speaking situation.

Vocal Cues, Comprehension, and Persuasion

For many years introductory public speaking textbooks have stressed the importance of the ancient canon of delivery to the rhetorical situation. Delivery of the speech (rather than the message or "content") was perhaps the first area of rhetoric to receive quantitative examination by speech researchers. In almost every study which isolated delivery as a variable for study, it was shown that delivery did matter—it had positive effects on the amount of information remembered, the amount of attitude change elicited from the audience, and the amount of credibility audience members attributed to the speaker. Some authors maintain that poor delivery decreases one's chances for accomplishing intended goals, but that good delivery does not, in and of itself, produce desirable changes—it only allows such effects to take place.

Our purpose, however, is not to argue the merits of good delivery. We are only concerned with one aspect of this larger concept. We want to know if we examine only vocal cues (and exclude gestures, facial expressions, movements, and other elements of delivery), whether we will still be able to significantly affect comprehension, attitude change, and speaker credibility.

Typical prescriptions for use of the voice in delivering a public speech include: (1) Use variety in volume, rate, pitch, and articulation. The probabilities of desirable outcomes are less when one uses a constant rate, volume, pitch, and articulation. Being consistently overprecise may be as ineffective as being overly sloppy in your articulation. Although it has not been formally studied, it is quite possible that when vocal variety is perceived as rhythmic or patterned, it is no longer variety and this decreases the probabilities of desirable outcomes. (2) Decisions concerning loud-soft, fast-slow, precise-sloppy, or high-low should be based on what is appropriate for a given audience in a given situation. (3) Excessive nonfluencies are to be avoided. How are these prescriptions reflected in the research on vocal cues?

The Effects of Vocal Cues Which Accompany Spoken Words

349

Vocal Cues, Comprehension, and Retention. Several studies tend to support the prescriptions for vocal variety in increasing audience comprehension or retention. Woolbert, in perhaps the earliest study of this type found large variations of rate, force, pitch, and quality produced high audience retention when compared with a no-variation condition.[56] Glasgow, using prose and poetry, established two conditions for study: "good intonation" and "mono-pitch."[57] Multiple-choice tests, following exposure to these differing vocal samples, showed mono-pitch decreased comprehension by more than 10 percent for both prose and poetry. Diehl, White, and Satz, using similar methods, however, found several ways of varying pitch did not significantly affect comprehension scores.[58] Other research data suggests that moderately poor vocal quality, pitch patterns, nonfluencies,[59] mispronunciation,[60] and even stuttering[61] do not interfere significantly with comprehension—although listeners generally find these conditions unpleasant. Diehl and McDonald found that simulated breathy and nasal voice qualities significantly interfered with comprehension, but simulated harsh and hoarse voice qualities did not appear to have a very negative effect.[62] All of these studies indicate that listeners are rather adaptable; it probably takes constant and extreme vocal unpleasantries to affect comprehension—and even then, the listener may adapt to the extent that he or she retains important information being communicated. Probably poor vocal qualities contribute more to a listener's perception of the speaker's personality or mood than to a decrease in comprehension.

The study of speaking rate only yields additional evidence of listener flexibility and lack of impact on comprehension of seemingly "poor" voice related phenomena. The normal speaking rate is between 125 and 190 words per minute. Some feel comprehension begins to decrease once the rate exceeds 200 words per minute, but experts in speeded speech place the level of significant decline in comprehension at between 275 and 300 words per.minute. Obviously, there are wide differences in individual ability to process informa-

---

[56]C. Woolbert, "The Effects of Various Modes of Public Reading." *Journal of Applied Psychology* 4 (1920): 162–185.

[57]G. M. Glasgow. "A Semantic Index of Vocal Pitch." *Speech Monographs* 19 (1952): 64–68.

[58]C. F. Diehl, R. C. White, and P. H. Satz, "Pitch Change and Comprehension." *Speech Monographs*, 28 (1961): 65–68.

[59] V. A. Utzinger, "An Experimental Study of the Effects of Verbal Fluency upon the Listener," Ph.D. dissertation, University of Southern California, 1952. Utzinger found varying degrees of fluency ranging from four to sixty-four breaks in two minutes did not affect recall.

[60] R. J. Kibler and L. L. Barker, "Effects of Selected Levels of Misspelling and Mispronunciation on Comprehension and Retention," *Southern Speech Communication Journal* 37 (1972): 361–374.

[61] H. N. Klinger, "The Effects of Stuttering on Audience Listening Comprehension," Ph.D. dissertation, New York University, 1959.

[62] C. F. Diehl and E. T. McDonald, "Effect of Voice Quality on Communication." *Journal of Speech and Hearing Disorders* 21 (1956): 233–237.

The Effects of Vocal Cues Which Accompany Spoken Words

tion at rapid rates. The inescapable conclusion from studies of speech rate, however, is that we can comprehend information at much more rapid rates than we ordinarily have to cope with. In an experiment in which individual listeners were allowed to vary the rates of presentation at will, the average choice was 1½ times normal speed.[63]

Vocal Cues and Persuasion.　What is the role of the voice in persuasive situations? It is clear we can communicate various attitudes with our voice alone—for example, friendliness, hostility, superiority, and submissiveness. What contribution, if any, then do vocal cues make toward changing people's attitudes? We know that we can sometimes be persuaded by ordinarily positive words spoken in negative tones—for example, disliking someone who calls you "honey" in a nasty voice.

Mehrabian and Williams conducted a series of studies on the non-verbal correlates of intended and perceived persuasiveness.[64] Extracting only findings on vocal cues, the following seem to be associated with both "increasing intent to persuade and decoded as enhancing the persuasiveness of a communication": more intonation, more speech volume, higher speech rate, and less halting speech. One might think frequent nonfluencies would work against attitude change, but this does not seem to be the case. In a speech characterized by 0, 50, 75, 100, and 125 nonfluencies of five types ("ah," sentence change, repetition, tongue slip, and stutter) Sereno and Hawkins found no significant differences in audience attitude change after exposure to the various versions of the speech.[65]

Considerable evidence from the persuasion literature suggests a speaker's perceived credibility may profoundly affect his or her persuasive impact. We also find some studies which show communicators with "good delivery" are consistently observed to have higher credibility at the end of the speech than those with poor delivery. Therefore, it is not surprising to find Pearce asking whether vocal cues alone affect judgments of credibility—and hence, potential for achieving audience attitude change.[66] Pearce developed a speech arguing that marijuana is pleasant, useful, and not harmful and had it recorded by a professionally experienced actor using two different styles of delivery. One

[63] D. B. Orr, "Time Compressed Speech—A Perspective," *Journal of Communication* 18 (1968): 288–292.

[64] A. Mehrabian and M. Williams, "Nonverbal Concomitants of Perceived and Intended Persuasiveness," *Journal of Personality and Social Psychology* 13 (1969): 37–58.

[65] K. K. Sereno and G. J. Hawkins, "The Effect of Variations in Speakers' Nonfluency upon Audience Ratings of Attitude Toward the Speech Topic and Speakers' Credibility," *Speech Monographs* 34 (1967): 58–64.

[66] W. B. Pearce and F. Conklin, "Nonverbal Vocalic Communication and Perceptions of a Speaker," *Speech Monographs* 38 (1971): 235–241. Also see W. B. Pearce, "The Effect of Vocal Cues on Credibility and Attitude Change," *Western Speech* 35 (1971): 176–184.

The Effects of Vocal Cues Which Accompany Spoken Words

type of delivery epitomized a "scholarly, dispassionate, yet very involved person, serious about his subject." This version had a smaller range of inflections, greater consistency of rate and pitch, less volume, and generally lower pitch than the second version. The second type of delivery epitomized a "person who was passionately involved in his subject, unalterably committed to his position, and highly emotional." This version had more pauses, used primarily the upper portion of the speaker's pitch range, and had more variations in volume that the first type. Pearce says neither type was what he would call extreme. Each represented good, but different delivery techniques used by spokesmen in society. The tapes were electronically filtered to eliminate the influence of the speaker's words and used as vocal stimuli for three studies. The results of these studies show vocal cues affected judgments about trustworthiness, dynamism, and likableness, but not competence. Furthermore, the conversational style elicited higher ratings on several socioeconomic characteristics and honesty, and was perceived as more person-oriented than the dynamic-vocalic delivery style. Although there was no evidence from this study to suggest that style of delivery had a direct effect on the effectiveness of the message in changing audience attitudes toward the topic, later study did show that initial credibility (induced through an introduction) and vocal cues did affect the message's persuasive impact.[67] Although many studies do show dramatic effects of speaker credibility in creating attitude change, it is not always a foregone conclusion that high credibility will insure a corresponding attitude change.

You will recall earlier we mentioned the Sereno and Hawkins study in which they found large numbers of nonfluencies did not seem to affect audience attitude change. The same study seems to show, however, that increasing numbers of nonfluencies do have an impact on ratings of speaker credibility. As nonfluencies increase, ratings for a speaker's competence and dynamism decrease, but not ratings on trustworthiness. This finding was confirmed by Miller and Hewgill.[68] Another study found that speech rate seemed to function as a general cue that augmented credibility ratings, and that rapid speech was more likely to enhance persuasion or attitude change than slower speech.[69]

At this point you may legitimately ask, "So what?" What if we know the voice's potential for eliciting various responses related to comprehension, attitude change, and speaker credibility? Obviously in real-life situations, there will be visual cues, prior publicity and experiences with the speaker, verbal

[67] W. B. Pearce and B. J. Brommel, "Vocalic Communication in Persuasion," *Quarterly Journal of Speech* 58 (1972): 298–306.

[68] G. R. Miller and M. A. Hewgill, "The Effect of Variations in Nonfluency on Audience Ratings of Source Credibility," *Quarterly Journal of Speech* 50 (1964): 36–44.

[69] N. Miller, G. Maruyama, R. J. Beaber, and K. Valone, "Speed of Speech and Persuasion," *Journal of Personality and Social Psychology* 34 (1976): 615–624.

The Effects of Vocal Cues Which Accompany Spoken Words

cues, and a multitude of other interacting factors which will greatly reduce the importance of vocal cues. In short, vocal cues do not operate in an isolated fashion in human interaction as they do in the experiments reported in this section. True. Vocal cues do not operate alone, but we do not know what their role is in context—they may even be more influential. Earlier we pointed out that a book which focuses only on nonverbal communication distorts reality by not integrating the role of verbal and nonverbal cues. The study of vocal cues also distorts reality. However, in this case, it is necessary to divide the process and study the component parts to understand them better—so that when we develop methods for studying more complex phenomena, we will know a little more about the nature of the parts we are putting together.

Vocal Cues and Turn-Taking in Conversations

Thus far we've talked about the role of vocal cues in communicating interpersonal attitudes, emotions, and information about oneself. Vocal cues also play an important role in *managing* the interaction. Vocal cues are part of a system of cues which help us structure our interactions—that is, who speaks, when, to whom, and for how long. Turn-taking, or "floor apportionment," rules may have as much to do with how a conversation "comes off" or is perceived as the actual verbal content of the interaction.[70] Most of us can recall instances where turn-taking rules played a significant role in our responses—for example, when a long-winded speaker wouldn't let you get a word in edgewise, when a passive respondent refused to "take the conversational ball" that you offered, when you were confronted with an "interrupter," or those awkward moments when two people were talking simultaneously. Obviously vocal cues compose only some of the signals we use to manage our turn-taking; these can be found in previous chapters. We do know that only rarely do we explicitly verbalize this information—for example, "OK, Lillian, I'm finished talking. Now it's your turn to talk." Vocal signals may be a part of the following management behaviors:

Turn Yielding.   To "yield" a turn means to signal you are finished and the other person can start talking. Sometimes we do this by asking a question—causing the pitch to rise at the end of our comment. Another unwritten rule most of us operate by is that questions require (or demand) answers.

---

[70] J. M. Wiemann and M. L. Knapp, "Turn-Taking in Conversations," *Journal of Communication* 25 (1975): 75–92. Also see S. Duncan, Jr., "Toward a Grammar for Dyadic Conversation," *Semiotica* 9 (1973): 24–46.

We can also drop our pitch (sometimes with a drawl on the last syllable) as we do when finishing a declarative statement which concludes our monologue. If the cues are not sufficient for the other person to start talking, we may have to add a "trailer" on the end. The "trailer" may be just silence or it may take the form of a filled pause—for example, "ya know," "so, ah," or "or something" to reiterate the fact that you are yielding, and to fill a silence which might otherwise indicate the other's insensitivity to your signals (or your own inability to make them clear!).

Turn-Requesting. We can also show others that we want to say something through the use of some vocal cues. Although an audible inspiration of breath may not be a sufficient cue by itself, it does help to signal turn-requesting. The mere act of interrupting or simultaneous talking (without a knowledge of the verbal content) may signal an impatience to get the speaking turn. Sometimes you can inject vocalizations during normal pausing of the other speaker. These "stutter starts" may be the beginning of a sentence ("I. . . I. . . I. . . ") or they may just be vocal buffers ("Ah. . . Er. . . Ah. . . "). Another method used to request a turn is to assist the other person in finishing quickly. This can be done by increasing the rapidity of one's responses—much like the increased rapidity of the head nods when people are anxious to leave a situation where the other person has the floor. These "back-channel" cues are vocalizations like "Uh-huh," "Yeah," and "Mm-hmm." But the message from the rapid use of these cues is "Get finished so I can talk."

Turn-Maintaining. Sometimes we want to keep the floor. It may be to show our status or to avoid unpleasant feedback or perhaps some exaggerated sense of importance attached to our own words and ideas. Common vocal cues in these instances may include: (1) increasing volume and rate when turn-requesting cues are sensed, (2) increasing the frequency of filled pauses, and (3) decreasing the frequency and duration of silent pauses[71] Although Lalljee and Cook's research does not support the use of pauses for control,[72] Rochester cites several studies which give support to the following: (1) More filled pauses and fewer silent pauses are found more often in dialogue than monologue, (2) more filled pauses and fewer silent pauses are *not* found when people want to break off speaking, and (3) more filled pauses and fewer silent pauses are more likely when the speaker lacks visual means of controlling the conversation.[73]

[71]Probably the first hypothesis of this behavior can be found in H. Maclay and C. E. Osgood, "Hesitation Phenomena in Spontaneous English Speech," *Word* 15 (1959): 19–44.

[72]M. G. Lalljee and M. Cook, "An Experimental Investigation of the Function of Filled Pauses in Speech," *Language and Speech* 12 (1969): 24–28.

[73]S. R. Rochester, "The Significance of Pauses in Spontaneous Speech," *Journal of Psycholinguistic Research* 2 (1973): 51–81.

The Effects of Vocal Cues Which Accompany Spoken Words

Turn-Denying. There may also be instances where we want the other person to keep talking—to deny the turn when offered. The back-channel cues noted earlier may serve to keep the other person talking by giving reinforcement for what is being said. The rate with which these are delivered, however, is probably slower than when we are requesting a turn. And, of course, just remaining silent may dramatically communicate a turn denial. Silence and pauses are the subjects of our next section.

Hesitations, Pauses, Silence, and Speech

It is quite possible that hesitations or pauses in speech have received more research than any other paralinguistic phenomenon. You will soon see why. This research offers us some potentially valuable insights into human communication behavior. Spontaneous speech is actually highly fragmented and discontinuous. Goldman-Eisler says that even when speech is at its most fluent, two-thirds of spoken language comes in chunks of less than six words—strongly suggesting that the concept of fluency in spontaneous speech is an illusion.[74] Pauses range in length from milliseconds to minutes. Pauses seem to be subject to considerable variation based on individual differences, the kind of verbal task, the amount of spontaneity, and the pressures of the particular social situation.

Location or Placement of Pauses. Pauses are not evenly distributed throughout the speech stream. Goldman-Eisler outlines places where pauses do occur—at grammatical junctures and at nongrammatical junctures.

Grammatical

1. "Natural" punctuation points, e.g., the end of a sentence.
2. Immediately preceding a conjunction whether (i) co-ordinating, such as and, but, neither, therefore, or (ii) subordinating, such as if, when, while, as, because.
3. Before relative and interrogative pronouns, e.g., who, which, what, why, whose.
4. When a question is direct or implied, e.g., "I don't know whether I will."
5. Before all adverbial clauses of time (when), manner (how) and place (where).
6. When complete parenthetical references are made, e.g., "You can tell that the words—this is the phonetician speaking—the words are not sincere."

Nongrammatical

1. Where a gap occurs in the middle or at the end of a phrase, e.g., "In each of//the cells of the body// . . ."

[74]F. Goldman-Eisler, *Psycholinguistics: Experiments in Spontaneous Speech* (London and New York: Academic Press, 1968).

The Effects of Vocal Cues Which Accompany Spoken Words

2. Where a gap occurs between words and phrases repeated, e.g., (i) "The question of the//of the economy." (ii) "This attitude is narrower than that//that of many South Africans."
3. Where a gap occurs in the middle of a verbal compound, e.g., "We have//taken issue with them and they are//resolved to oppose us."
4. Where the structure of a sentence is disrupted by a reconsideration or a false start, e.g., "I think the problem of de Gaulle is the//what we have to remember about France is . . ."[75]

Analysis of spontaneous speech shows that only 55 percent of the pauses fall into the grammatical category, whereas oral readers of prepared texts are extremely consistent in pausing at clause and sentence junctures.

Types of Pauses.   The two major types of pauses are the unfilled pause (silent) and the filled pause. A filled pause is simply filled with some type of phonation such as "um," "uh," stutters, false starts, repetitions, and slips of the tongue. A variety of sources associate filled pauses with a range of generally undesirable characteristics. Some people associate filled pauses and repetitions with emotional arousal; some feel filled pauses may reduce anxiety, but jam cognitive processes. Goldman-Eisler found, in four studies, that unfilled pausing time was associated with "superior (more concise) stylistic and less probable linguistic formulations" while higher rates of filled pauses were linked to "inferior stylistic achievement (long winded statement) of greater predictability."[76] Livant found the time required to solve addition problems was significantly greater when the subject filled his pauses than when he was silent.[77] Several experimenters reached similar conclusions—that when speakers fill pauses they also impair their performance. Thus, in a heated discussion you may maintain control of the conversation by filling the pauses, but you may also decrease the quality of your contribution. Too many filled or too many unfilled pauses may receive negative evaluations from listeners. Lalljee found too many unfilled pauses by the speaker caused listeners to perceive the speaker as anxious, angry, or contemptuous; too many filled pauses evoked perceptions of the speaker as anxious or bored.[78] Specialized receivers (like counselors) may have different reactions. For example, variations in filled and unfilled pauses did not affect counselors' perceptions of a patient's genuineness or anxiety, but unfilled (3–7 seconds) pauses seemed to make the counselor

[75]Goldman-Eisler, *Psycholinguistics*, p. 13.

[76] F. Goldman-Eisler, "A Comparative Study of Two Hesitation Phenomena," *Language and Speech* 4 (1961): 18–26.

[77] W. P. Livant, "Antagonistic Functions of Verbal Pauses: Filled and Unfilled Pauses in the Solution of Additions," *Language and Speech* 6 (1963): 1–4.

[78] M. C. Lalljee, "Disfluencies in Normal English Speech," unpublished Ph.D. dissertation, Oxford University, 1971.

The Effects of Vocal Cues Which Accompany Spoken Words

think the ensuing message was revealing more about the person.[79] Some feel that there is an interrelationship between filled and unfilled pauses. It goes something like this: When you increase the frequency and duration of unfilled pauses it won't affect the occurrence of filled pauses, but when you decrease the frequency and duration of unfilled pauses, it will increase the rate of filled pauses.

Reasons Why Pauses Occur. During the course of spontaneous speech, we are confronted with situations which require decisions as to what to say and what lexical or structural form to put it in. One school of thought relates hesitancy in speech to the uncertainty of predicting the cognitive and lexical activity while speaking. The speaker may be reflecting on decisions about the immediate message or may even be projecting into the past or future—that is, "I don't think she understood what I said earlier" or "If she says no, what do I say then?" Working on the assumption that these hesitation pauses were actually delays due to processes taking place in the brain whenever speech ceased to be the automatic vocalization of learned sequences, Goldman-Eisler conducted an experiment designed to "make thought construction an indispensible and controlled part of the speaking process." Subjects were presented with cartoons and given tasks of describing and interpreting. Pause time while "interpreting" was twice as long as while "describing." It was also observed that with each succeeding trial (a reduction in spontaneity), there was a decline in pausing. Another possible explanation for some pausing behavior involves what is described as *disruption behavior*. Instead of representing time for planning, the pause may indicate a disruption due to an emotional state which may have developed from negative feedback or time pressures. These disruptions may take many forms; fears about the subject matter under discussion, desire to impress the listener with verbal and/or intellectual skills, pressure to perform other tasks simultaneously, pressure to produce verbal output immediately and so on.

Further study of pauses and breathing suggests that the cognitive and lexical decision processes are also regulators of the incidence of breathing during speech. While reading passages of prose aloud, speakers took breaths exclusively at the gaps occasioned by grammatical junctures. During spontaneous speech, approximately one-third of the breaths were taken at gaps which were in the nongrammatical category. The frequency and length of pauses may also be due to certain predispositions to certain listeners, adaptations to certain audience situations, the number of potential speakers, and one's desire to speak.

[79] M. J. Fisher and R. A. Apostal, "Selected Vocal Cues and Counselors' Perceptions of Genuineness, Self-Disclosure, and Anxiety," *Journal of Counseling Psychology* 22 (1975): 92–96.

The Effects of Vocal Cues Which Accompany Spoken Words

Response Latency and Talking Time. Thus far we've considered hesitations and pauses primarily from the standpoint of the speaker. Now we will consider the interaction process and the effect of one person's interpersonal timing on another. Since the 1930s Chapple has been exploring the rhythms of dialogue—that is, the degree of synchrony found in the give and take of conversations.[80] Ordinarily this involves noting who talks, when, and for how long. He has developed a standardized interview in which the interviewer alternates "normal" attentive responding with silences and later, interruptions. As you might suspect, there are many reactions. Some people respond to a nonresponse, or silence, by speeding up, others match the nonresponse, most try some combination of the two. Chapple feels we can learn a great deal from these behaviors—for example, manifested dominance, reactions to another's dominance and stress, and other behavioral proclivities. He backs up his work with data which indicates success in employee selection. Whether talk time and latency of response are indeed manifestations of a person's personality is largely irrelevant in everyday social interaction if people believe they are. For instance, speech errors and length of talk time were found to play a part in self-fulfilling prophecies in interracial interviews.[81]

Matarazzo's studies of interviewing behavior found most latencies of response were between 1 and 2 seconds with the mean about 1.7 seconds.[82] The interviewer, however, can have considerable influence on the length of pauses. For example, when the interviewer did not respond to a statement by the interviewee, almost 65 percent of the interviewees began to talk again, but the pause was now closer to 4.5 seconds. In the same manner, Matarazzo demonstrated the impact of *response matching*—showing how the interviewer can also control the length of utterance by increasing the length of his own utterances. Figures 10.3 and 10.4 show the results of several experiments involving three 15-minute segments of a 45-minute interview with the interviewer varying his responses during different periods. As the interviewer extended the length of his responses, there was a corresponding increase in the length of responses from the interviewee. In the same manner, there must be times when pauses beget pauses.

[80]E. D. Chapple, "The Interaction Chronograph: Its Evolution and Present Application," *Personnel* 25 (1949): 295–307; E. D. Chapple, "The Standard Experimental (Stress) Interview as Used in Interaction Chronograph Investigations," *Human Organizations* 12 (1953): 23–32; and E. D. Chapple and L. R. Sayles, *The Measure of Management* (New York: Macmillan, 1961).

[81] C. C. Word, M. P. Zanna, and J. Cooper, "The Nonverbal Mediation of Self-Fulfilling Prophecies in Interracial Interaction," *Journal of Experimental Social Psychology* 10 (1974): 109–120.

[82]J. D. Matarazzo, A. N. Wiens, and G. Saslow, "Studies in Interviewer Speech Behavior," in L. Krasner and U. P. Ullman (eds.), *Research in Behavior Modification*, (New York: Holt, Rinehart and Winston, 1965).

The Effects of Vocal Cues Which Accompany Spoken Words

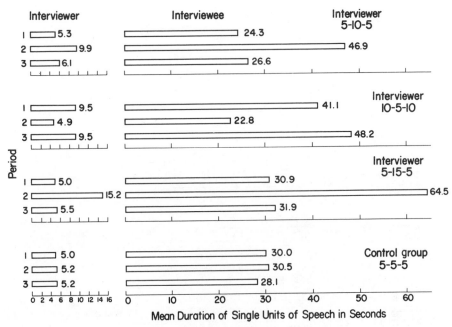

Figure 10.3 Interviewer influence on duration of interviewee speech

The interviewer can also control response duration by head-nodding or saying "Mm-hmm" during the interviewee's response as shown in Figure 10.4. Some have even suggessted that increased talking speed is not an increased rate of articulation, but a decrease in the length of pauses.

Obviously one's latency of response will be influenced by many factors. We've focused primarily on the behavior of the other person, but a sudden topic shift, a changing interpersonal distance, an intimate setting with an intimate, and many other factors may affect this behavior. Similarly it would be dangerous to conclude that on the basis of length of response exhibited in one interaction that a person was exhibiting dominance. The person may, on closer examination, have talked longer, but fewer times—or the person may have been responding to other needs than dominance. Latency of response and talk time can be valuable data in assessing features of an interaction, but like other features they comprise only a part of the whole.

Silence. Most of the hesitations and pauses we've discussed are of relatively short duration. Sometimes silences may be extended. They may be imposed by the nature of the environment—for example, in churches, libraries,

The Effects of Vocal Cues Which Accompany Spoken Words

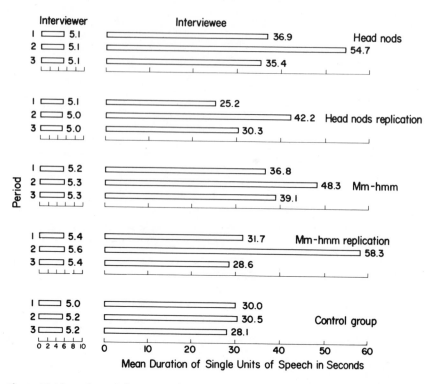

Figure 10.4 Interviewer influence on duration of interviewee speech

courtrooms, or hospitals; they may be imposed for the duration of a given event—for example at a funeral, during the playing of taps, when praying, or when singing the national anthem; or they may be self-imposed—remaining quiet in the woods to hear other sounds or enjoying with a lover the mutual closeness that silence may bring. Silence can mean virtually anything— anything that can be said verbally at least. Silence is charged with those words which have just been exchanged; words which have been exchanged in the past; words which haven't or will not be said, but which are fantasized; and words which may actually be said in the future. For this reason it would be absurd to provide a list of meanings for silence. The meaning of silence, like the meaning of words, can only be deduced after careful analysis of the communicators, subject matter, time, place, culture, and the like.

Some of the many interpersonal functions served by silence[83] include: (1)

[83]J. V. Jensen, "Communicative Functions of Silence," *ETC* 30 (1973): 249–257. Also see T. J. Bruneau, "Communicative Silences: Forms and Functions," *Journal of Communication* 23 (1973): 17–46.

The Effects of Vocal Cues Which Accompany Spoken Words

punctuation or accenting—drawing attention to certain words or ideas; (2) evaluating—providing judgments of another's behavior, showing favor or disfavor, agreement or disagreement, attacking (for example, not responding to a comment, greeting, or letter); (3) revelation—making something known or hiding something by being silent; (4) expression of emotions—the silence of disgust, sadness, fear, anger, or love; (5) mental activity—showing thoughtfulness and reflection or ignorance through silence.

Summary

In the course of reading this chapter, you have been exposed to a considerable number of research studies and a considerable amount of descriptive material. What do they mean for you as a communicator and as an observer of nonverbal behavior in human interaction?

Generally, this chapter should have left you with the overall impression that vocal cues frequently play a major role in determining responses in human communication situations. You should be quick to challenge the cliché that vocal cues only concern *how* something is said—frequently they are *what* is said. *What* is said might be an attitude ("I like you" or "I'm superior to you"), it might be an emotion, it might be the coordination and management of the conversation, or it might be the presentation of some aspect of your personality, background, or physical features. Vocal cues will, depending on the situation and the communicators, carry a great deal of information in some classes and perhaps little in others.

As a communicator and observer of the human species, you should also recognize the important role vocal stereotypes play in determining responses. Whether judges are trying to estimate your occupation, sociability, race, degree of introversion, body type, or any of various other qualities about you, they will be very apt to respond to well-learned stereotypes. These stereotypes may not accurately describe you, but they will be influential in the interaction which takes place between you and the judge. Almost all the research reviewed in this chapter demonstrated considerable interjudge agreement. So far it is difficult to identify any personality trait which seems to be judged with consistent accuracy. This is partly due, of course, to the imperfect nature of the personality measures. Moreover, a particular person, judging a particular voice, may be very accurate in judging the personality behind that voice. Our judgments of large groups of people are also influential in our judgments of a single person's vocal personality. Although it is not uncommon for a person speaking a dialect other than your own to be perceived negatively, speakers who try to correct for speech differences and severely violate expectations for their speech may also be perceived negatively. There is considerable support for the idea that a voice

The Effects of Vocal Cues Which Accompany Spoken Words

may evoke an ethnic stereotype which will then overlay one's perceptions of an individual's voice; however, one study suggests that we may also react to vocal aspects of the dialect itself which we either like or dislike.

Accurate judgments (beyond chance) of age, sex, and status from vocal cues alone tend to be fairly consistently reported in the literature. Furthermore, we seem to be able to identify specific speakers from their voice alone, but recently greater attention has been given to spectrographic and electronic means of speaker identification.

Although studies of judgments of emotions from vocal cues have used different methods, different emotions, listeners with differing sensitivity, and speakers with differing abilities for portraying the emotions, the results have been amazingly consistent. We can make pretty accurate judgments of emotions and feelings from wordless vocal messages. Obviously, we should consistently remind ourselves that any given individual may vocally express the same emotion differently on different days, in different situations, and with different provoking stimuli.

There is some indication that moderately poor vocal behaviors do not interfere with a listener's comprehension of a message, and that if we use variety in our volume, pitch, and rate we may increase our chances of achieving audience comprehension in making public speeches. Unchanging, constant vocal behavior (particularly at the extremes) may be less advantageous in achieving audience comprehension.

Preliminary findings suggest the voice may also be important in some aspects of persuasion. Nonfluencies do not seem to affect attitude change, but more intonation, higher rate, more volume, and less halting speech seem related to intent to persuade and perceived persuasiveness. We know that the credibility of the speaker plays an important role in persuasion in some situations. We now know that some decisions concerning credibility (trustworthiness, dynamism, likableness, competency) are made from word-free samples of the voice alone. Increasing nonfluencies also tend to impair credibility.

Vocal cues also help us manage the give and take of speaking turns. In turn-yielding, turn-requesting, turn-maintaining, and turn-denying we can use vocal cues to make our intentions clear.

You should also be more conscious now of the important role of hesitations or pauses in spontaneous speech. Such pauses, ordinarily between one and two seconds long, may be greatly influenced by the other interactant, the topic being discussed, and the nature of the social situation. Several reports suggest "impaired performance" in a number of areas may result from excessive use of filled pauses. Pauses may be the overt manifestation of time used to make decisions about what to say and how to say it, or they may represent disruptions in the speech process.

Taken together, these findings show that vocal cues alone can give much

The Effects of Vocal Cues Which Accompany Spoken Words

information about a speaker—and that our total reaction to another individual is at least somewhat colored by our reactions to these vocal cues. Our *perceptions* of vocal cues combine with other verbal and nonverbal stimuli to mold *conceptions* used as a basis for communicating. Perhaps future study will provide some information on how our responses to our own voices affect self-images and hence, our communication behavior. First, however, we need to have more attention given to voices manifested in naturalistic *interaction*—particularly with partners other than strangers. Some of the preceding results may need modification as we look at spontaneous speech at different stages in relationships.

SELECTED BIBLIOGRAPHY

Aboud, F. E., Clement, R., and Taylor, D. M. "Evaluational Reactions to Discrepancies Between Social Class and Language." *Sociometry* 37 (1974): 239–250.

Addington, D. W. "The Effect of Vocal Variations on Ratings of Souce Credibility." *Speech Monographs* 38 (1971): 242–247.

Addington, D. W. "The Relationship of Selected Vocal Characteristics to Personality Perception." *Speech Monographs* 35 (1968): 492–503.

Albas, D. C., McCluskey, K. W., and Albas, C. A. "Perception of the Emotional Content of Speech: A Comparison of Two Canadian Groups." *Journal of Cross Cultural Psychology* 7 (1976): 481–490.

Allport, G., and Cantril, H. "Judging Personality from Voice." Journal of Social Psychology 5 (1934): 37–54.

Anderson, B. "The Emergence of Conversational Behavior." *Journal of Communication* 27 (1977): 85–91.

Anisfeld, M., Bogo, N., and Lambert, W. "Evaluation Reactions to Accented English Speech." *Journal of Abnormal and Social Psychology* 65 (1962): 223–231.

Beier, E. G., and Zautra, A. "Identification of Vocal Communication of Emotions Across Cultures." *ERIC* (1972), Ed 056504.

Black, J. W. "A Study of Voice Merit." *Quarterly Journal of Speech* 28 (1942): 67–74.

Bochner, B., and Bochner, A. "The Effects of Social Status and Social Dialect on Listener Responses." *Central States Speech Journal* 24 (1973): 75–82.

Boomer, D. S. "Hesitation and Grammatical Encoding." *Language and Speech* 8 (1965): 148–158.

Boomer, D. S., and Dittmann, A. T. "Hesitation Pauses and Juncture Pauses in Speech," *Language and Speech* 5 (1962): 215–220.

Boomer, D. S., and Dittmann, A. T. "Speech Rate, Filled Pause, and Body

Movements in Interviews." *Journal of Nervous and Mental Disease* 139 (1964): 324–327.

Bradford, A., Ferror, D., and Bradford, G. "Evaluation Reactions of College Students to Dialect Differences in the English of Mexican-Americans." *Language and Speech* 17 (1974): 255–270.

Bruneau, T. J. "Communicative Silences: Forms and Functions." *Journal of Communication* 23 (1973): 17–46.

Bryden, J. D. "An Acoustic and Social Dialect Analysis of Perceptual Variables in Listener Identification and Rating of Negro Speakers." Unpublished Ph.D. dissertation, University of Virginia, 1968.

Buck, J. "The Effects of Negro and White Dialectical Variations upon Attitudes of College Students." *Speech Monographs* 35 (1968): 181–186.

Burns, K. L., and Beier, E. G. "Significance of Vocal and Visual Channels in the Decoding of Emotional Meaning." *Journal of Communication* 23 (1973): 118–130.

Chapple, E. D. "The Standard Experimental (Stress) Interview as Used in Interaction Chronograph Investigations." *Human Organizations* 12 (1953): 23–32.

Charlip, W. S. "The Aging Female Voice: Selected Fundamental Frequency Characteristics and Listener Judgments." Ph.D. dissertation. Purdue University, 1967.

Cook, M. "Anxiety. Speech Disturbances, and Speech Rate." *British Journal of Social and Clinical Psychology* 8 (1969): 13–21.

Cook, M., Smith, J., and Lalljee, M. G. "Filled Pauses and Syntactic Complexity." *Language and Speech* 13 (1974): 11–16.

Crawford, C. C., and Michael W. "An Experiment in Judging Intelligence by the Voice.," *Journal of Educational Psychology* 18 (1927): 107–114.

Crider, C. C. "Regional Variations in the Estimation of Social Class from Auditory Stimuli." Ph.D. dissertation, University of Southern California, 1962.

Crystal, D., and Quirk, R. *Systems of Prosodic and Paralinguistic Features in English*. The Hague: Mouton. 1964.

Davis, P. B. "An Investigation of the Suggestion of Age Through Voice in Interpretative Reading." M.A. thesis. University of Denver, 1949.

Davitz, J. R. *The Communication of Emotional Meaning*. New York: McGraw-Hill, 1964.

Davitz, J. R., and Davitz, L. "Correlates of Accuracy in the Communication of Feelings." *Journal of Communication* 9 (1959): 110–117.

Davitz, J. R., and Davitz, L. "Nonverbal Vocal Communication of Feeling." *Journal of Communication* 11 (1961): 81–86.

Davitz, J. R., and Davitz, L. "The Communication of Feelings by Content-Free Speech." *Journal of Communication* 9 (1959): 6–13.

De La, N., Flores, Z., and Hopper, R. "Mexican-Americans' Evaluations of Spoken Spanish and English." *Speech Monographs* 42 (1975): 91–98.

The Effects of Vocal Cues Which Accompany Spoken Words

Dickens, M., and Sawyer, G. M. "An Experimental Comparison of Vocal Quality Among Mixed Groups of Whites and Negroes." *Southern Speech Journal* 18 (1962): 178–185.

Diehl, C. F., and McDonald, E. R. "Effect of Voice Quality on Communication." *Journal of Speech and Hearing Disorders* 21 (1956): 233–237.

Diehl, C., White, R., and Satz, P. "Pitch Change and Comprehension." *Speech Monographs* 28 (1961): 65–68.

Dittmann, A. T. "The Body Movement–Speech Rhythm Relationship as a Cue to Speech Encoding." In A. W. Siegman and B. Pope (eds.), *Studies in Dyadic Communication.* New York: Pergamon Press, 1971.

Dittmann, A. T., and Llewellyn, L. G. "Body Movement and Speech Rhythm in Social Conversation." *Journal of Personality and Social Psychology* 11 (1969): 98–106.

Dittmann, A. T., and Llewellyn, L. G. "The Phonemic Clause as a Unit of Speech Decoding." *Journal of Personality and Social Psychology* 6 (1967): 341–349.

Dubner, F. S. "Nonverbal Aspects of Black English." *Southern Speech Communication Journal* 37 (1972): 361–374.

Duncan, S. "Some Signals and Rules for Taking Speaking Turns in Conversations." *Journal of Personality and Social Psychology* 23 (1972): 283–292.

Duncan, S. "Toward a Grammar for Dyadic Conversation." *Semiotica* 9 (1973): 24–46.

Duncan, S., and Niederehe, G. "On Signalling That It's Your Turn to Speak." *Journal of Experimental Social Psychology* 10 (1974): 234–247.

Duncan, S. D., Jr., and Rosenthal, R. "Vocal Emphasis in Experimenters' Introduction Reading as Unintended Determinant of Subjects' Responses." *Language and Speech* 11 (1968): 20–26.

Duncan, S. D., Jr., Rice, L. N., and Butler, J. M. "Therapists' Paralanguage in Peak and Poor Psychotherapy Hours." *Journal of Abnormal Psychology* 73 (1968): 566–570.

Duncan, S. D., Jr., Rosenberg, M. J., and Finkelstein, J. "The Paralanguage of Experimenter Bias." *Sociometry* 32 (1969): 207–219.

Dusenbury, D., and Knower, F. "Experimental Studies of the Symbolism of Action and Voice—II: A Study of the Specificity of Meaning in Abstract Tonal Symbols." *Quarterly Journal of Speech* 25 (1939): 67–75.

Eisenberg, P., and Zalowitz, E. "Judging Expressive Movement, III. Judgments of Dominance Feeling from Phonograph Records of the Voice." *Journal of Applied Psychology* 22 (1939): 620–631.

Eisenson, J. "Affective Behavior (Emotion) and Speech." In J. Eisenson, J. J. Auer, and J. V. Irwin (eds.), *The Psychology of Communication.* New York: Appleton-Century-Crofts, 1963. pp 68–83.

Ellis, D. S. "Speech and Social Status in America." *Social Forces* 45 (1967): 431–437.

Fairbanks, G., and Pronovost, W. "An Experimental Study of the Pitch Characteristics of the Voice During the Expression of Emotion." *Speech Monographs* 6 (1939): 87–104.

Fay, P., and Middleton, W. "Judgment of Introversion from the Voice as Transmitted over a Public Address System." *Quarterly Journal of Speech* 28 (1942): 226–228.

Fay, P., and Middleton, W. "Judgment of Kretschmerian Body Types from the Voice as Transmitted over a Public Address System." *Journal of Social Psychology* 12 (1940): 151–162.

Fay, P., and Middleton, W. "Judgment of Leadership from Transmitted Voice." *Journal of Social Psychology* 17 (1943): 99–102.

Fay, P., and Middleton, W. "Judgment of Occupation from the Voice as Transmitted over a Public Address System." *Sociometry* 3 (1940): 186–191.

Fay, P., and Middleton, W. "Judgment of Spranger Personality Types from the Voice as Transmitted over a Public Address System." *Character and Personality* 8 (1939): 144–155.

Fay, P., and Middleton. W. "Rating a Speaker's Natural Voice When Heard over a Public Address System." *Quarterly Journal of Speech* 27 (1941): 120–124.

Fay, P., and Middleton, W. "The Ability to Judge Sociability from the Voice as Transmitted over a Public Address System." *Journal of Social Psychology* 13 (1941): 303–309.

Fay, P., and Middleton, W. "The Ability to Judge the Rested or Tired Condition of a Speaker from his Voice as Transmitted over a Public Address System." *Journal of Applied Psychology* 24 (1940): 645–650.

Fay, P., and Middleton, W. "The Ability to Judge Truth Telling or Lying from the Voice as Transmitted over a Public Address System." *Journal of General Psychology* 24 (1941): 211–215.

Fisher, M. J., and Apostal, R. A. "Selected Vocal Cues and Counselors' Perceptions of Genuineness, Self-Disclosure and Anxiety." *Journal of Counseling Psychology* 22 (1975): 92–96.

Gallois, C., and Markel, N. M. "Turn Taking: Social Personality and Conversational Style." *Journal of Personality and Social Psychology* 31 (1975): 134–140.

Gates, G. S. "The Role of the Auditory Element in the Interpretation of Emotions." *Psychological Bulletin* 24 (1927): 175.

Giles, H. "Ethnocentrism and the Evaluation of Accented Speech." *British Journal of Social and Clinical Psychology* 10 (1971): 187–188.

Giles, H., and Bourhis, R. Y. "Voice and Racial Categorization in Britain." *Communication Monographs* 43 (1976): 108–114.

Giles, H., and Powesland, P. F. *Speech Style and Social Evaluation* New York: Academic Press, 1975.

Glasgow, G. "A Semantic Index of Vocal Pitch." *Speech Monographs* 19 (1952): 64–68.

Goldhaber, G. M. "PAUSAL: A Computer Program to Identify and Measure Pauses." *Western Speech* 37 (1973): 23–26.

Goldman-Eisler, F. "A Comparative Study of Two Hesitation Phenomena." *Language and Speech* 4 (1961): 18–26.

Goldman-Eisler, F. "Continuity of Speech Utterance, Its Determinants and Its Significance." *Language and Speech* 4 (1961): 220–231.

Goldman-Eisler F. "On the Variability of the Speed of Talking and on Its Relation to the Length of Utterances in Conversations." *British Journal of Psychology* 45 (1954): 94–107.

Goldman-Eisler, F. *Psycholinguistics: Experiments in Spontaneous Speech.* New York: Academic Press, 1968.

Goldman-Eisler, F. "Sequential Temporal Patterns and Cognitive Processes in Speech." *Language and Speech* 10 (1967): 122–132.

Goldman-Eisler, F. "The Distribution of Pause Durations in Speech." *Language and Speech* 4 (1961): 232–237.

Goldman-Eisler, F. "The Predictability of Words in Context and the Length of Pauses in Speech." *Journal of Communication* 11 (1961): 95–99.

Goldman-Eisler, F. "The Significance of Changes in the Rate of Articulation." *Language and Speech* 4 (1961): 171–174.

Gottschalk, L. A., and Frank, E. C. "Estimating the Magnitude of Anxiety from Speech," *Behavioral Science* 12 (1967): 289–295.

Gunderson, D. F. and Hopper, R. "Relationships Between Speech Delivery and Speech Effectiveness." *Communication Monographs* 43 (1976): 158–165.

Harms, L. S. "Listener Judgments of Status Cues in Speech." *Quarterly Journal of Speech* 47 (1961): 164–168.

Harris, R. M. and Rubinstein, D. "Paralanguage, Communication and Cognition," in A. Kendon, R. M. Harris and M. R. Key (eds.) *Organization of Behavior in Face-to-Face Interaction* (Chicago: Aldine) 1975.

Hart, R. J., and Brown, B. L. "Interpersonal Information Conveyed by the Content and Vocal Aspects of Speech." *Speech Monographs* 41 (1974): 371–380.

Hayes, D. P., and Bouma, G. P. "Patterns of Vocalization and Impression Formation." *Semiotica* 13 (1975): 113–128.

Hecker, M. H. L. "Speaker Recognition: An Interpretive Survey of the Literature." *ASHA Monographs*, Number 16. Washington: American Speech and Hearing Association, 1971.

Hunt, R. G., and Lin, T. K. "Accuracy of Judgments of Personal Attributes from Speech." *Journal of Personality and Social Psychology* 6 (1967): 450–453.

Hurt, H. T., and Weaver, C. H. "Negro Dialect, Ethnocentrism and the Distortion of Information in the Communication Process." *Central States Speech Journal* 23 (1972): 118–125.

Jensen, J. V. "Communicative Functions of Silence." *ETC* 30 (1973): 249–257.

Johannesen, R. L. "The Functions of Silence: A Plea for Communication Research." *Western Speech* 38 (1974): 25-35.

Jones, P. A. "Elaborated Speech and Hesitation Phenomena." *Language and Speech* 17 (1974): 199–203.

Kasl, S. V., and Mahl, G. F. "The Relationship of Disturbances and Hesitations in Spotaneous Speech to Anxiety." *Journal of Personality and Social Psychology* 1 (1965): 425–433.

Key, M. R. *Paralanguage and Kinesics.* Metuchen, N. J.: Scarecrow Press, 1975.

Kibler, R. J., and Barker, L. L. "Effects of Selected Levels of Misspelling and Mispronunciation on Comprehension and Retention." *Southern Speech Communication Journal* 37 (1972): 361–374.

Knower, F. H. "Analysis of Some Experimental Variations of Simulated Vocal Expressions of the Emotions." Journal of Social Psychology 14 (1941): 369–372.

Kramer, E. "Judgment of Personal Characteristics and Emotions from Non-verbal Properties." *Psychological Bulletin* 60 (1963): 408–420.

Kramer, E. "Personality Stereotypes in Voice: A Reconsideration of the Data." *Journal of Social Psychology* 62 (1964): 247–251.

Ladefoged, P., and Vanderslice, R. "The Voiceprint Mystique." Working papers in Phonetics, 7. University of California, Los Angeles, November, 1967.

Laffal, J., Monahan, J., and Richman, P. "Communication of Meaning in Glossolalia." *Journal of Social Psychology* 92 (1974): 277–291.

Lalljee, M. G. "Disfluencies in Normal English Speech." Unpublished Ph.D. dissertation, Oxford University, 1971.

Lalljee, M. G., and Cook, M. "An Experimental Investigation of the Function of Filled Pauses in Speech." *Language and Speech* 12 (1969): 24–28.

Lambert, W. E., Frankel H., and Tucker, G. R. "Judging Personality Through Speech: A French-Canadian Example." *Journal of Communication* 16 (1966): 305–321.

Lambert, W., Hodgson, R., Gardner, R, and Fillenbaum, S. "Evaluational Reactions to Spoken Languages." *Journal of Abnormal and Social Psychology* 60 (1960): 44–51.

Lass, N. J., and Davis, M. "An Investigation of Speaker Height and Weight Identification." *Journal of the Acoustical Society of America* 60 (1976): 700–703.

Lass, N. J., and Harvey, L. A. "An Investigation of Speaker Photograph Identification." *Journal of the Acoustical Society of America* 59 (1976): 1232–1236.

The Effects of Vocal Cues Which Accompany Spoken Words

Lass, N. J., Hughes, K. R., Bowyer, M. D., Waters, L. T., and Broune, V. T. "Speaker Sex Identification from Voiced, Whispered and Filtered Isolated Vowels." *Journal of the Acoustical Society of America* 59 (1976): 675–678.

Leginski, W., and Izzett, R. R. "Linguistic Styles as Indices for Interpersonal Distance." *Journal of Social Psychology* 91 (1973): 291–304.

Leonard, L. B. "The Role of Intonation in the Recall of Various Linguistic Stimuli." *Language and Speech* 16 (1975): 327–336.

Levin, H., and Silverman. I. "Hesitation Phenomena in Children's Speech." *Language and Speech* 8 (1965): 67–85.

Licklider, J. C. R., and Miller, G. A. "The Perception of Speech." In S. S. Stevens (ed.), *Handbook of Experimental Psychology*. New York: Wiley, 1951.

Lindenfeld, J. "Verbal and Non-verbal Elements in Discourse." *Semiotica* 3 (1971): 223–233.

Linke, C. E. "A Study of Pitch Characteristics of Female Voices and Their Relationship to Vocal Effectiveness." *Folia Phoniatrica.* 25 (1973): 173–186.

Livant, W. P. "Antagonistic Functions of Verbal Pauses: Filled and Unfilled Pauses in the Solution of Additions." *Language and Speech* 6 (1963): 1–4.

Lounsbury, F. G. "Pausal, Juncture, and Hesitation Phenomena." In C. E. Osgood and T. A. Sebeok (eds.), *Psycholinguistics: A Survey of Theory and Research Problems*. Bloomington: Indiana University Press, 1954.

Luft, J. "Differences in Prediction Based on Hearing Versus Reading Verbatim Clinical Interviews." *Journal of Consulting Psychology* 15 (1951): 115–119.

Maclay, H., and Osgood, C. E. "Hesitation Phenomena in Spontaneous English Speech." *Word* 15 (1959): 19–44.

Mahl, G. F. "Disturbances and Silences in the Patient's Speech in Psychotherapy." *Journal of Abnormal and Social Psychology* 53 (1956): 1–15.

Mahl, G. F., and Schulze, G. "Psychological Research in the Extralinguistic Area." In T. Sebeok, A. S. Hayes, and M. C. Bateson (eds.), *Approaches to Semiotics*. The Hague: Mouton, 1964.

Mallory, E., and Miller, V. "A Possible Basis for the Association of Voice Characteristics and Personality Traits." *Speech Monographs* 25 (1958): 255–260.

Markel, N. N. "The Reliability of Coding Paralanguage: Pitch, Loudness, and Tempo." *Journal of Verbal Learning and Verbal Behavior* 4 (1965): 306–308.

Markel, N., and Roblin, G. "The Effect of Content and Sex of Judge in Judgments of Personality from Voice." *International Journal of Social Psychiatry* 11 (1965): 295–300.

Markel, N. N., Bein, M. F., and Phillis, J. "The Relationship Between Words and Tone-of-Voice." *Language and Speech* 16 (1973): 15–21.

Markel, N., Eisler, R. M., and Reese, H. W. "Judging Personality from Dialect." *Journal of Verbal Learning and Verbal Behavior* 6 (1967): 33–35.

Markel, N. N., Meisels, M., and Houck, J. E. "Judging Personality from Voice Quality." *Journal of Abnormal and Social Psychology* 69 (1964): 458–463.

Markel, N. N., Prebor, L. D., and Brandt, J. F. "Biosocial Factors in Dyadic Communication: Sex and Speaking Intensity." *Journal of Personality and Social Psychology* 23 (1972): 11–13.

Matarazzo, J. D., Wiens, A. N., and Saslow, G. "Studies in Interviewer Speech Behavior." In L. Krasner and U. P. Ullman (eds.), *Research in Behavior Modification*. New York: Holt, Rinehart and Winston, 1965.

McDavid, R. I. "Dialect Differences and Intergroup Tensions." *Studies in Linguistics* 9 (1951): 27–33.

McGehee, F. "The Reliability of the Identification of the Human Voice." *Journal of General Psychology* 17 (1937): 249–271.

McGlone, R. E., and Hollien, H. "Vocal Pitch Characteristics of Aged Women." *Journal of Speech and Hearing Research* 6 (1963): 164–170.

McKelvy, D. P. "Voice and Personality." *Western Speech* 17 (1953): 91–94.

Mehrabian, A. "Nonverbal Communication." In J. Cole (ed.), *Nebraska Symposium on Motivation 1971*. Lincoln: University of Nebraska Press, 1972.

Mehrabian, A. *Silent Messages*. Belmont, California: Wadsworth, 1972.

Mehrabian, A., and Ferris, S. R. "Inference of Attitudes from Nonverbal Communication in Two Channels." *Journal of Consulting Psychology* 31 (1967): 248–252.

Mehrabian, A., and Wiener, M. "Decoding of Inconsistent Communication." *Journal of Personality and Social Psychology* 6 (1967): 109–114.

Mehrabian, A., and Williams, M. "Nonverbal Concomitants of Perceived and Intended Persuasiveness." *Journal of Personality and Social Psychology* 13 (1969): 37–58.

Miller, D. T. "The Effect of Dialect and Ethnicity on Communicator Effectiveness." *Speech Monographs* 42 (1975): 69–74.

Miller, G. R., and Hewgill, M. A. "The Effect of Variations in Nonfluency on Audience Ratings of Source Credibility." *Quarterly Journal of Speech* 50 (1964): 36–44.

Miller, N., Maruyama, G., Beaber, R. J., and Valore, K. "Speed of Speech and Persuasion." *Journal of Personality and Social Psychology* 34 (1976): 615–624.

Milmoe, S., Novey, M. S., Kagan, J., and Rosenthal, R. "The Mother's Voice: Postdictor of Aspects of Her Baby's Behavior." In S. Weitz (ed.), *Nonverbal Communication: Readings with Commentary*. New York: Oxford University Press, 1974. pp. 122–126.

Milmoe, S., Rosenthal, R., Blane, H. T., Chafetz, M. E., and Wolf, I. "The Doctor's Voice: Postdictor of Successful Referral of Alcoholic Patients." *Journal of Abnormal Psychology* 72 (1967): 78–84.

The Effects of Vocal Cues Which Accompany Spoken Words

Moe, J. D. "Listener Judgments of Status Cues in Speech: A Replication and Extension." *Speech Monographs* 39 (1972): 144–147.

Moses, P. "The Study of Personality from Records of the Voice." *Journal of Consulting Psychology* 6 (1942): 257–261.

Moses, P. *The Voice of Neurosis*. New York: Grune and Stratton, 1954.

Motley, M. T. "Acoustic Correlates of Lies." *Western Speech* 38 (1974): 81–87.

Motley, M. T. "An Analysis of Spoonerisms as Psycholinguistic Phenomena." *Speech Monographs* 40 (1973): 66–71.

Mulac, A. "Assessment and Application of the Revised Speech Dialect Attitudinal Scale." *Communication Monographs* 43 (1976): 238–245.

Mulac, A. "Evaluation of Speech Dialect Attitudinal Scale." *Speech Monographs* 42 (1975): 184–189.

Mulac, A., Hanley, T. D., and Prigge, D. Y. "Effects of Phonological Speech Foreignness upon Three Dimensions of Attitude of Selected American Listeners." *Quarterly Journal of Speech* 60 (1974): 411–420.

Murray, D. C. "Talk, Silence and Anxiety." *Psychological Bulletin* 75 (1971): 244–260.

Mysak, E. D. "Pitch and Duration Characteristics of Older Males." *Journal of Speech and Hearing Research* 2 (1959): 46–54.

Nerbonne, G. P. "The Identification of Speaker Characteristics on the Basis of Aural Cues." Ph.D. dissertation, Michigan State University, 1967.

Orr, D. B. "Time Compressed Speech—A Perspective." *Journal of Communication* 18 (1968): 288–292.

Ostwald, P. F. "A Method for the Objective Denotation of Sound of the Human Voice." *Journal of Psychosomatic Research* 4 (1960): 301–305.

Ostwald, P. F. *Soundmaking*. Springfield, Ill.: Chas. C. Thomas, 1963.

Packwood, W. T. "Loudness as a Variable in Persuasion." *Journal of Counseling Psychology* 21 (1974): 1–2.

Paivio, A. "Audience Influence, Social Isolation and Speech." *Journal of Abnormal and Social Psychology* 67 (1963): 247–253.

Panek, D. M., and Martin, B. "The Relationship Between GSR and Speech Disturbance in Psychotherapy." *Journal of Abnormal and Social Psychology* 58 (1959): 402–405.

Paul, J. E. "An Investigation of Parent-Child Relationships in Speech: Intensity and Duration." Ph.D. dissertation, Purdue University, 1951.

Paves, L. A. "A Study to Determine Relationships Between Voice Qualities and Attributed Traits of Personality." Ph.D. dissertation, New York University, 1965.

Pear, T. H. *Voice and Personality*. London: Chapman & Hold, 1931.

Pearce, W. B. "The Effect of Vocal Cues on Credibility and Attitude Change." *Western Speech* 35 (1971): 176–184.

Pearce, W. B., and Brommel, B. J. "Vocalic Communication in Persuasion." *Quarterly Journal of Speech* 58 (1972): 298–306.

The Effects of Vocal Cues Which Accompany Spoken Words

Pearce, W. B., and Conklin, F. "Nonverbal Vocalic Communication and Perceptions of a Speaker." *Speech Monographs* 38 (1971): 235–241.

Pettas, M. "An Exploratory Study of Oral Communication Characteristics in a Population of Aged Women." Ph.D. dissertation, University of Florida, 1963.

Pfaff, P. L. "An Experimental Study of Communication of Feeling Without Contextual Material." *Speech Monographs* 21 (1954): 155–156.

Pittenger, R. E., and Smith, H. L., Jr. "A Basis for Some Contributions of Linguistics to Psychiatry." *Psychiatry* 20 (1957): 61–78.

Pittenger, R. E., Hockett, C. F., and Danehy, J. J. *The First Five Minutes: A Sample of Microscopic Interview Analysis*. Ithaca, N.Y.: Martineau, 1960.

Poyatos, F. "Cross-Cultural Study of Paralinguistic 'Alternants' in Face-to-Face Interaction." In A. Kendon, R. M. Harris, and M. R. Key (eds.), *Organization of Behavior in Face-to-Face Interaction*. Chicago: Aldine, 1975.

Ptacek, P. H., and Sander, E. K. "Age Recognition from Voice." *Journal of Speech and Hearing Research* 9 (1966): 273–277.

Putnam, G. N., and O'Hearn, E. M. "The Status Significance of an Isolated Urban Dialect." *Language* 31 (1955): 1–32.

Reardon, R. C. "Individual Differences and the Meanings of Vocal Emotional Expressions." *Journal of Communication* 21 (1971): 72–82.

Reardon, R., and Amatea, E. "The Meaning of Vocal Emotional Expressions: Sex Differences for Listeners and Speakers." *International Journal of Social Psychiatry* 18 (1972): 214–219.

Reich, A. R., Moll, K. L., and Curtis, J. F. "Effects of Selected Vocal Disguises upon Spectrographic Speaker Identification." *Journal of the Acoustical Society of America* 60 (1976): 919–925.

Reid, D. W., and Ware, E. E. "A Factorial Study of Judgments of Vocally Expressed Emotion and Meaning." *Journal of Social Psychology* 84 (1971): 161–162.

Renneker, R. "Microscopic Analysis of Sound Tape." *Psychiatry* 23 (1960): 347–355.

Ringel, R. L., and Kluppel, D. D. "Neonatal Crying: A Normative Study." *Folia Phoniatrica* 16 (1964): 1–9.

Rochester, S. R. "The Significance of Pauses in Spontaneous Speech." *Journal of Psycholinguistic Research* 2 (1973): 51–81.

Rogers, P. L., Scherer, K. R., and Rosenthal, R. "Content Filtering Human Speech: A Simple Electronic System." *Behavior Research Methods and Instrumentation* 3 (1971): 16–18.

Sachs, J., Lieberman, P., and Erickson, D. "Anatomical and Cultural Determinants of Male and Female Speech." In R. W. Shuy and R. W. Fasold (eds.), *Language Attitudes: Current Trends and Prospects*. Washington: Georgetown University Press, 1973.

Sanford, F. H. "Speech and Personality." *Psychological Bulletin* 39 (1942): 811–845.

Scherer, K. R. "Acoustic Concomitants of Emotional Dimensions: Judging Affect from Synthesized Tone Sequences." In S. Weitz, (ed.), *Nonverbal Communication: Readings with Commentary*. New York: Oxford University Press, 1974. Pp. 105–111.

Scherer, K. R. "Judging Personality from Voice: A Cross Cultural Approach to An Old Issue in Interpersonal Perception." *Journal of Personality* 40 (1972): 191–210.

Scherer, K. R. "Randomized Splicing: A Note on a Simple Technique for Masking Speech Content." *Journal of Experimental Research in Personality* 5 (1971): 155–159.

Scherer, K. R., Koivumaki, J., and Rosenthal, R. "Minimal Cues in the Vocal Communication of Affect: Judging Emotions from Content-Masked Speech." *Journal of Psycholinguistic Research* 1 (1972): 269–285.

Schweitzer, D. A. "The Effect of Presentation on Source Evaluation." *Quarterly Journal of Speech* 56 (1970): 33–39.

Scott, R. L. "Rhetoric and Silence." *Western Speech* 36 (1972): 146–158.

Sereno, K. K., and Hawkins, G. J. "The Effects of Variations in Speakers' Nonfluency upon Audience Ratings of Attitudes Toward the Speech Topic and Speakers' Credibility." *Speech Monographs* 34 (1967): 58–64.

Sewell, E. H. "Speech, Silence and Authenticity." *Southern Speech Communication Journal* 40 (1975): 169–179.

Shipp, F. T., and Hollien, H. "Perception of the Aging Male Voice." *Journal of Speech and Hearing Research* 12 (1969): 703–710.

Snyder, M. "Self-Monitoring of Expressive Behavior." *Journal of Personality and Social Psychology* 30 (1974): 526–537.

Soskin, W. F., and Kauffman, P. E. "Judgment of Emotions in Word-Free Voice Samples." *Journal of Communication* 11 (1961): 73–81.

Stagner, R. "Judgments of Voice and Personality." *Journal of Educational Psychology* 27 (1936): 276–277.

Starkweather, J. "Content-Free Speech as a Source of Information About the Speaker." *Journal of Abnormal and Social Psychology* 52 (1956): 394–402.

Starkweather, J. "The Communication Value of Content-Free Speech." *American Journal of Psychology* 69 (1956): 121–123.

Starkweather, J. A. "Vocal Communication of Personality and Human Feelings." *Journal of Communication* 11 (1961): 63–72.

Steer, A. B. "Sex Differences, Extroversion and Neuroticism in Relation to Speech Rate During the Expression of Emotion." *Language and Speech* 17 (1974): 80–86.

Summerfield, A. B. "Errors in Decoding Tone of Voice During Dyadic Interaction." *British Journal of Social and Clinical Psychology* 14 (1975): 11–17.

Tayloe, A. R. "Nonverbal Communication Systems in Native North America." *Semiotica* 13 (1975): 329–374.

Taylor, H. "Social Agreement on Personality Traits as Judged from Speech." *Journal of Social Psychology* 5 (1934): 224–248.

Thompson, C., and Bradway, K. "The Teaching of Psychotherapy Through Content-Free Interviews." *Journal of Consulting Psychology* 14 (1950): 321–323.

Thorndike, E. L. "Euphony and Cacophony of English Words and Sounds." *Quarterly Journal of Speech* 30 (1944): 201–207.

Trager, G. L. "Paralanguage: A First Approximation." *Studies in Linguistics* 13 (1958): 1–12.

Trager, G. L. "The Typology of Paralanguage." *Anthropological Linguistics* 3 (1961): 17–21.

Truby, H. M., Bosma, J. F., and Lind, J. *Newborn Infant Cry*. Uppsala, Sweden: Almqvist & Wiksells, 1965.

Voiers, W. D. "Perceptual Bases of Speaker Identity." *Journal of the Acoustical Society of America* 36 (1964): 1065–1073.

Weaver, A. T. "Experimental Studies in Vocal Expression." *Quarterly Journal of Speech Education* 10 (1924): 199–204.

Weaver, J. C., and Anderson, R. J. "Voice and Personality Interrelationships." *Southern Speech Communication Journal* 38 (1973): 262–278.

Weitz, S. "Attitude, Voice, and Behavior: A Repressed Affect Model of Interracial Interaction." *Journal of Personality and Social Psychology* 24 (1972): 14–21.

Whitehead, J. L., and Miller, L. "Correspondence Between Evaluations of Children's Speech and Speech Anticipated upon the Basis of Stereotype." *Southern Speech Communication Journal* 37 (1972): 375–386.

Whitehead, J. L., Williams, F., Civikly, J. M., and Albino, J. W. "Latitude of Attitude in Ratings of Dialect Variations." *Speech Monographs* 41 (1974): 397–408.

Wiemann, J. M., and Knapp, M. L. "Turn-Taking in Conversations." *Journal of Communication* 25 (1975): 75–92.

Wiener, M. and Mehrabian, A. *Language Within Language: Immediacy, A Channel in Verbal Communication*. New York: Appleton-Century-Crofts, 1968.

Wiggins, S. L., McCranie, M. L., and Bailey, P. "Assessment of Voice Stress in Children." *Journal of Nervous and Mental Disease* 160 (1975): 402–408.

Wilke, W., and Snyder, J. "Attitudes Toward American Dialects." *Journal of Social Psychology* 14 (1941): 349–362.

Williams, F. "The Psychological Correlates of Speech Characteristics: On Sounding 'Disadvantaged.' " *Journal of Speech and Hearing Research* 13 (1970): 472–488.

Williams, F., and Naremore, R. C. "Language Attitudes: An Analysis of Teacher Differences." *Speech Monographs* 41 (1974): 391–396.

Williams, F., and Shamo, G. W. "Regional Variations in Teacher Attitudes Toward Children's Language." *Central States Speech Journal* 23 (1972): 73–77.

Williams. F., and Sundene, B. "Dimensions of Recognition: Visual vs. Vocal Expression of Emotion." *Audio-Visual Communication Review* 13 (1965): 44–51.

Williams, F., Hopper, R., and Natalicio, D. S. *The Sounds of Children*. Englewood Cliffs, N.J.: Prentice-Hall, 1976.

Williams, F., Whitehead, J. L., and Traupmann, J. "Teachers' Evaluations of Children's Speech." *Speech Teacher* 20 (1971): 247–254.

Wolf, G., Gorski, R., and Peters, S. "Acquaintance and Accuracy of Vocal Communication of Emotions." *Journal of Communication* 22 (1972): 300–305.

Wolff, P., and Gutstein, J. "Effects of Induced Motor Gestures on Vocal Output." *Journal of Communication* 22 (1972): 277–288.

Woolbert, C. "The Effects of Various Modes of Public Reading." *Journal of Applied Psychology* 4 (1920): 162–185.

Word, C. O., Zanna, M. P., and Cooper, J. "The Nonverbal Mediation of Self-Fulfilling Properties in Interracial Interaction." *Journal of Experimental Social Psychology* 10 (1974): 109–120.

Zahn, G. L. "Cognitive Integration of Verbal and Vocal Information in Spoken Sentences." *Journal of Experimental Social Psychology* 9 (1973): 320–334.

11 Observing and Recording Nonverbal Behavior

**Why do you still keep looking
at me that way, Daddy?**
HILARY KNAPP, age 11½

Examine Figure 11.1. What do you see? Write down your observations.

Given such an open-ended or unstructured task, it is likely that you, as an observer, will report such findings as a brick structure, abstract modern art, a line drawing, a group of squares, rectangles, and other odd shapes, nothing, a bunch of lines, a maze, and so forth. If, however, you were instructed to be particularly observant of letters of the alphabet, it is highly probable that you (the observer) would see the capital letter *E* when confronting this stimulus. In Figure 11.1 the vertical and horizontal lines acted as visual interference or "noise" and kept the *E* well concealed. Interference in human observational situations can be a hundredfold more distracting if we attempt to examine it without any sense of perspective—or system for oberving. We need to kow what to look for and how to record it if we want to look at it later. One could certainly argue that rigid adherence to a particular observational schema will eventually bias what we see—making us unable to notice behaviors not on our list. While this can happen and we should be careful to avoid it, we need to start somewhere; we need to give some order to a very complex set of events.

Obviously, observing and recording nonverbal behavior is of great concern to the scientist conducting research, but it can also be of great value to anyone interested in improving his or her own communication skills. It seems reason-

Observing and Recording Nonverbal Behavior

376

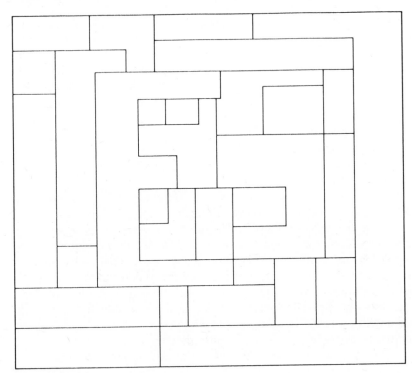

Figure 11.1

able that if we are told what to look for and how to rapidly record it, each successive observational experience will increase our sensitivity to these cues. In a broad sense we are trying to synthesize the previous chapters into a formal system which can be used in observing nonverbal behavior. You may wish to use the elaborate systems developed by scholars in specialized areas in order to conduct controlled research studies. References to these systems are available following this chapter. You may simply wish to read this chapter in order to increase your observational sensitivity to nonverbal behavior in the classroom, at cocktail parties, at work, and so forth. This chapter is also intended to meet such needs.

The Process of Systematic Observation

The study of nonverbal behavior, like the study of human behavior in general, can be profitably examined in a number of different ways. Some seek published material in the library, some make observations in controlled laboratory settings, and some observe people as they go about their everyday

Observing and Recording Nonverbal Behavior

activities. Commonly, investigators set up a role-played or simulated "real-life" situation in the laboratory and ask the participants or other observers for their reactions. Self-reports and rating scales are common instruments in quantifying the meaning of nonverbal behavior. Some observers of nonverbal behavior do not even ask what a particular gesture or movement means to another person. They are concerned only with how a gesture or movement fits into the total system of observed behaviors. They are concerned with describing the structure of our nonverbal behavior—the "building blocks." Given the total range of behaviors which might be performed, the structural analyst asks, Which ones actually occur in a given communication, in a given situation, in a given culture? And do these behaviors occur in characteristic sequences or clusters with other behaviors? The slight rising of the head at the end of questions and slight lowering at the end of declarative sentences (head "markers") are the sort of behaviors observed by structuralists. In short, these researchers are seeking communication rules concerning types and contexts of communication behavior. They are less concerned with the meaning attached to a particular behavior by a judge or group of judges. Scheflen, one of the main proponents of structural research in nonverbal communication, says he is trying to find out how "the pieces are organized into standard units . . . recognizable at a glance and recordable with a stroke."[1]

Needless to say, each approach has its strengths and weaknesses and to derive useful conclusions means obtaining the best information from each approach. Since the process of observation is crucial to all approaches it will be our focus.

Occasions for Observation.   There are times when the process of observation seems especially critical and should be given high priority. For instance, if you were planning a study of leave-taking behavior and you didn't know what cues might be important, you'd observe people saying good-bye in different situations until you felt you knew the general parameters within which you'd be working. Observational methods are also well suited for situations where you suspect people cannot or will not give you accurate information about themselves. For instance, you may not want to rely solely on a child's response to an introspective question like, "How do you react when your father tells you you've been bad?" Similarly, there are times when we all have a hard time remembering exactly how and why we reacted the way we did. We may not even know the answer to a question about common self-adaptors we perform. Or, if we can remember a sequence of behavior, we may not be able to communicate it adequately—using abstract terms with ambiguous referents.

[1]A. E. Scheflen, "Natural History Method in Psychotherapy: Communicational Research," in *Methods of Research in Psychotherapy*, edited by L. A. Gottschalk and A. H. Auerbach (New York: Appleton-Century-Crofts, 1966), p. 277.

Observing and Recording Nonverbal Behavior

There are other times when the person may get defensive and be unwilling to provide certain types of information. Sometimes the nature of the act to be studied will suggest observational methods. It may be a behavior that occurs so quickly a person may not notice it, such as micromomentary facial expressions. Mutual gaze is also a fleeting phenomenon, but people may feel it occurs more than it actually does. As an observer, you may also be interested in observing something which neither interactant could individually provide because the phenomenon is the product of both interactants. And finally, you may decide to use observational methods with people going about their daily activities when you cannot adequately construct a realistic situation in the laboratory.

Ethical Considerations. In any observational situation, you will have to consider matters of potential harm or injury to the participants—the observed. To what extent, for instance, will your presence harm or alter courses of action for the persons observed? To what extent are you violating the personal rights and privacy of the persons under scrutiny? How important is the acquisition of your information relative to the problems created for those observed? To what extent should you reveal the purposes of your observational role? These and other questions must be addressed, but we may not all answer them in the same way. One person may feel no ethical constraints in attending a cocktail party, acting like a participant, observing behaviors, and occasionally retiring to the bathroom to record such observations. Another person may feel obligated to tell the host and/or participants more details, making it clear that he or she is performing a role which goes beyond that expected at a cocktail party.

Participant and Nonparticipant Roles. There are two common approaches which observers use. They vary in the degree to which the observer is a part of the situation being observed. In one cae, the observer attempts to stay out of the action being examined. This has been dubbed the "potted palm" approach by some. It has the potential advantage of reducing the observer's influence on what he or she is observing. Sometimes, however, the very act of being a nonparticipant in a social setting can make one look very conspicuous. And, in spite of strong efforts to observe communicators without participating, sometimes the communicators will notice you and drag you into the action. This, of course, assumes you are not sufficiently concealed. It is possible for people to lose their conscious awareness of you over a period of time—even if you are clearly visible and they know you set out to observe them. We don't know, however, the extent to which they behave differently because of your presence. As a result, some advocate gathering observations in unobtrusive ways.[2] You might, for instance, determine which toilet received the most use by

---

[2] E. J. Webb, D. T. Campbell, R. D. Schwartz, and L. Sechrest, *Unobtrusive Measures* (Chicago: Rand McNally, 1966).

Observing and Recording Nonverbal Behavior

379

examining the amount of paper used, you might infer radio listening habits by looking at the frequency to which radios are tuned, you might examine public records to increase your knowledge of certain participants, or you might ask people to recall what they observed others doing in a given situation. In each case, the observer does not have to worry about any influence his or her presence may have on the behavior of those observed. The limitations of this approach are obvious, but it is a method of obtaining data which should not be overlooked.

Many sociologists and anthropologists opt for the participant-observer role. Here we see a deliberate attempt to *decrease* the social distance between the observed and the observer. Sometimes this involvement means a commitment of weeks, months, or years in which you share the hopes, frustrations, and problems of the observed.

> It . . . is my belief that any group of persons—prisoners, primitives, pilots, or patients—develop a life of their own that becomes meaningful, reasonable, and normal once you get close to it, and that a good way to learn about any of these worlds is to submit oneself in the company of the members to the daily round of petty contingencies to which they are subject.[3]

Again, over time the participant observers may blend into the activities of the observed, but they must be extremely cautious of generalizations about behavior which they helped mold.

The Observer

Aristotle and Darwin. When we look back at especially good observers of human behavior these two names inevitably come up. It is not wholly clear why some people seem to make more insightful observations than others, but we can offer a few ideas based on our own experience. The effective observer should be able to maintain a delicate balance between assuming the knowledgeable role as an expert in his or her field and the ignorance and wide-eyed naiveté of a child or alien from Mars. When you are feeling very confident about your understanding of what is taking place around you, it is time to shift the emphasis to that of the child; when you feel a great deal of chaos and disorder in your observation field, it is time to shift to that of the expert. Just as effective speakers are highly motivated to have their audience understand their ideas, an effective observer probably has a strong interest and drive to understand the behavior of the observed. This does not mean, however, that the observer can't achieve a sense of detachment from those being observed when necessary.

[3] E. Goffman, *Asylums* (New York: Anchor Books, 1961).

Observing and Recording Nonverbal Behavior

Effective observers probably have had a variety of educational and personal experiences. This experiential base assists the observer in processing complex and fleeting ongoing stimuli and in putting isolated observations in their proper perspective later. Put another way, the observer should have skills necessary for slow, careful, detailed work *and* the skills necessary to see unifying threads and broad concepts which tie the many isolated observations together. This, then, also suggests a need for patience and perseverance. And, finally, if people are going to be effective observers of others, it seems reasonable that they will also show some skill at self-insight—seeing and accepting both positive and negative qualities in themselves. Not everyone will agree with this last point. And, it is true that we don't know if those who are best at understanding themselves are also the best at understanding others, or whether those who are skilled at observing and interpreting the behavior of friends are equally proficient at similar processes with strangers.

Another approach to the characteristics of successful observers is to look at the information they seek and obtain. The following list can be useful to observers of any human transaction. Obviously, there will be times when some of the following information will contribute to observer bias, but the information may be necessary at some point to fully interpret the observations: (1) Find out about the *participants*—age, sex, position, or status, relationship to each other, previous history, and the like. (2) Find out about the *setting* of the interaction—kind of environment, relationship of the participants to the environment, expected behavior in that environment, and so on. (3) Find out about the *purposes* of the interaction—hidden goals, compatibility of goals, and so on. (4) Find out about the *social behavior*—who does what to or with whom, form of the behavior, its intensity, toward whom it is directed, what initiates it, apparent objective of the behavior, effect on the other interactants, and so forth. (5) Find out about the *frequency* and *duration* of such behavior—when it occurs, how long it lasts, whether it recurs, frequency of recurrence, how typical such behavior is in this situation, and so on.

The Fallibility of Human Perception.   It is not unusual for several observers of the same event to see very different things; nor is it unusual for one observer to see very different things in the same event at two different times. Sometimes an observer will perceive a sequence of action as one perceptual unit; another observer may see the same sequence as several units—or only part of a unit. The following are but some of the factors which may contribute to differences in perception—factors which successful observers must be aware of and take into account.

First, we must recognize that our perceptions are structured by our own cultural conditioning, education, and personal experiences. Adults teach children what they think are critical dimensions of others by what they choose to talk about and make note of. Thus, we form associations which inevitably enter

Observing and Recording Nonverbal Behavior

into our observations. For instance, we may be unable to see what we consider to be contradictory traits or behaviors in others—that is, can you conceive of a person who is both quiet and active? wealthy and accessible? short and romantic? Another aspect of this internally consistent world view which may affect our observations concerns preconceived notions about what we will see—for example, "My observations will take place in a nursing home. Therefore, the people I will observe will be old, noncommunicative, sick, inactive, and so on." Admittedly, such expectations and stereotypes can sometimes be helpful; sometimes they prevent accurate observations. In the United States, we are taught to rely primarily on visual and auditory systems for reliable information, missing, at times, useful data derived from other senses like touch and smell.

We should also be aware that we will sometimes project our own qualities onto the object of our attention—after all, if it is worth being a part of us, it must be true of others! We do reverse the process sometimes when we want to see ourselves as unique—for example, "I am a rational person, but most people aren't." This interaction between our own needs, desires, or even temporary emotional states and what we see in others sometimes causes us to see only what we want to see or to miss what may be obvious to others. This is the process known as selective perception. To show the mental gyrations which we can perform in the pursuit of selective perception, let's assume we have observed a mother slapping her child—a mother who was previously perceived to be incapable of such an act. We can ignore the stimulus—for example, "She's a wonderful mother, so she couldn't have been slapping her child"; we can reduce the importance of the contradictory information—for example, "Kids can be exasperating sometimes, and it's understandable that parents have to 'get tough' sometimes—besides it wasn't a hard slap"; we can change the meaning of the inconsistency—"It couldn't have been slapping because the child would have recoiled more and cried harder —it must have been a 'love tap' "; we can reinterpret previously observed traits to fit the contradictory information—"I always felt that her 'wonderful mother' image was just a front and this slapping incident only confirms it"; or we can infer new traits in the person—"I think she is an energetic, committed, and generous person, but she may be quick-tempered and overly punitive." Thus, it is not uncommon that observations which contradict what we believe to be true will often be twisted into a shape so they "make sense" to us. When adults observe animals or infants, it is difficult to resist analyses which are deeply rooted in adult human activity. Because we have these perceptual biases, it is important that observers check their observations against the independent reports of others—or check the consistency of their own observations at several different points over an extended period of time.

We must also recognize that our perceptions will be influenced by what we choose to observe. We probably don't use the same criteria for observing our friends, our parents, and strangers. To see our own children or our spouse as

Observing and Recording Nonverbal Behavior

382

others do is about as difficult as hearing a tape recording of ourselves as others do. We may attribute more positively perceived behaviors to our friend's personality and negatively perceived behaviors to situational constraints. Familiarity can assist observation or it can create observational "noise"—but it does affect our perceptions. Furthermore, some phenomena will cause us to zero in on one particular kind of behavior, observing it very closely but missing simultaneous behaviors occurring elsewhere. It may be that the behavior receiving the scrutiny is bigger or more active or just more interesting. It might be that we monitor deviant behavior more closely than normative or expected behavior. When observing a conversation, we can't possibly attend to everything as it happens. Sometimes we'll look for, see, respond to, and interpret a particular set of cues and at other times the same cues will go unnoticed or disregarded. Sometimes observers will fall prey to the natural tendency to follow the conversational speaking turns, viewing the speaker and missing other nonverbal events associated with the nonspeaker. And, of course, some phenomena are so complex, so minute, or so frequent that observer fatigue becomes a major concern.

Even if two people observe the same event and attach similar meanings to it, they may choose to express their observations differently. Others may suspect, then, that the two observers saw two different things. It's the difference between describing a facial expression as happiness, joy, delight, pleasure, or amusement. Or it might be the difference between saying, "She struck him" vs. "She pushed him." Hence, the language we use to express our perceptions can be an important variable in judging the accuracy of those perceptions.

Observers must also be sensitive to the possible influence of order effects. Sometimes we will observe some feature of another's behavior which will influence the perceptions of what follows. And sometimes it is a person's last act which causes us to reanalyze and reinterpret all the behavior preceding it.

Finally, we must be concerned about factual, nonevaluative descriptions of behavior and the interpretations we give to these descriptions. At the most basic level, we can say that a successful observer is careful not to confuse pure description with the inferences or interpretations about the behavior. Failure at the "inference stage" is aptly illustrated by the familiar story of the scientist who told his frog to jump and, after a few minutes, the frog jumped. The scientist recorded this behavior and amputated one of the frog's hind legs. Again he told the frog to jump. He repeated his instruction "Jump!" several times and, in time, the frog made a feeble attempt to jump with one hind leg. Then the scientist cut off the other hind leg, repeatedly ordered the frog to jump, and when no jumping behavior occurred, the scientist recorded in his log: "Upon amputation of one of the frog's hind legs, it begins to lose it's hearing; upon severing both hind legs, the frog becomes totally deaf." Another valuable lesson to be drawn from this story concerns the problem of simple explanations for complex behavioral acts. It is very tempting to note when

Observing and Recording Nonverbal Behavior

someone seems to avoid eye contact with you that this suggests he or she is hiding something from you. We should constantly be on guard against such simple cause-effect explanations of observed behavior. Only after considering the total context of the event can we even begin to make inferences about why such behavior occurred—even then, we only speak with varying degrees of probability—never with complete certainty.

When observers do wish to make interpretations of observed behaviors, considerable caution must be exercised. For instance, let's suppose you observed me from a distance and you saw me using what you thought was an inordinate number of illustrators. Whether this was just my usual communicative "style" or whether it was the result of the situation (for example, talking to a person who didn't speak my language very well) would not be clear until you obtained further information. Sometimes we are faced with the question of whether a behavior is attributable to a person's personality or to something in the immediate situation. We might look for a situational cause for some "undesirable" behavior, but if we don't find a plausible explanation, we may attribute it to the person's personality with even more confidence. We should, however, recognize that we could have missed the situational cause, being unable to view the situation as the participant does. If we err in any direction, I suppose we are more apt to attribute actions to enduring dispositions of others and minimize situational demands. Obviously, if a behavior is a part of a person's personality and is carried from place to place, our predictions about this person are made considerably easier.

The preceding perceptual tendencies are only some of the matters that a successful observer must be aware of, adapt to, and account for.

The Observational Record

What should we observe? What categories of behavior should be coded? We know that in addition to a lengthy list of nonverbal behaviors per se there may be a number of other factors which will ultimately determine the meaning of any given behavior. Ekman and Friesen list five: (1) other simultaneous body behavior—for example, smiling while moving toward someone may mean recognition or pleasure, but a similar smile performed while moving away may serve to hide fear; (2) any concomitant verbal behavior—for example, a smile may be perceived much differently if you hear the other person say, "Smile when you say that!"; (3) the setting in which the behavior occurs—smiling at a cocktail party and a funeral will surely be interpreted differently; (4) physical characteristics of the interactants—when a small, frail person challenges a huge muscle-bound person to a fight, the act takes on a different meaning than when the two interactants have similar physiques; and (5) verbal and nonverbal behavior of the other person—you may smile on two different occasions, but one is in response to friendly behavior and the other is in response to hostile behavior.[4] Thus, while we will concentrate our discussion on specific nonverbal behaviors of a single individual, it should be clear that a full understanding will require the notation of many other aspects of the situation.

The question of which behaviors you choose to study will vary with the object of your concern—for example, deception, turn-taking, leave-taking, and so on. Initial categories will probably be developed by the observer's own informal observation; examining previous studies, audiovisual records, and anecdotal reports; asking others for reports of informal observations in a wide variety of settings; and pretesting a category system in a limited number of naturalistic and laboratory settings prior to conducting the actual observational task. Final category refinements or additions can be made after you have tested the system on a situation similar to the one you ultimately want to observe. If you are breaking new ground, you may not want to enter the situation with any preconceived categories. For whatever behaviors are being coded, the category system should be inclusive enough so that every observable (or potentially influential) behavior is classifiable. Sometimes you will want to adapt your categories for co-occurrence coding. In other words, two or more verbal categories can be coded as co-occurring, verbal and nonverbal categories can be coded as co-occurring, and/or two or more nonverbal categories may co-occur. While the complexity of the coding does increase, it is sometimes necessary to increase the precision of the observations—and hence, our understanding of what actually occurred.

The precision of these category descriptions is another difficult, but important task. For instance, touching may be a behavior one wishes to code. Yet, there may be vast differences in the touch of an open palm lightly placed on the shoulder of the other interactant and the hard touch of a closed fist on the other's jaw! Hence, one not only has to be aware of possible differences in strength of touch, but place of touch, kind of touch (open or closed fist), duration of touch, and frequency of touch. The amount of category specificity is largely dependent on your purposes and hypotheses, but nonverbal observers should at least be aware of differences that may make a difference before they start coding. As we've seen, such information may have a profound impact on interpreting the data and inferences made from it. For instance, one may code the frequency of verbal reinforcers such as "Yeah," "Right," or "Uh-huh," and conclude that one party was giving a lot of support to the other. However, we know the same words can be said in a sarcastic fashion (with the addition of certain vocal cues), which changes the interpretation completely;

[4]P. Ekman and W. V. Friesen, "Nonverbal Behavior in Psychotherapy Research," in J. Schlien (ed.), *Research in Psychotherapy*, Vol. 3 (American Psychological Association, 1968).

Observing and Recording Nonverbal Behavior

we also know that such verbal devices are also used to "get the floor" when conversational openings are otherwise absent.

In the development of your categories for observation it may be tempting to assume common referents for "common" behaviors. I recall one study we conducted in which we were going to code smiling behavior. It seemed like there was little need to describe exactly what we meant by a *smile*. After all, everyone knew what a smile was, didn't they? Apparently not. Out of twelve behaviors coded for that study, the lowest agreement among the observers was on the frequency of smiling. We spent less time specifying (visually and verbally) what constituted a smile, and the reliability obtained from our observers was understandably low. The more intangible or abstract the behavior to be coded, the more your reliability among observers is likely to suffer. In any case, observers and coders should be given a thorough training program prior to performing their tasks. They should be given a thorough description of the behavior to be coded and enough time to practice on events which closely approximate their eventual task.

Closely intertwined with the development of categories is the method of recording the behaviors. Efficiency is always an important criterion in recording procedures, but equally important is the criterion of accuracy. For instance, it would be efficient to simply record whether a given behavior occurred or didn't occur; however, the subtleties of some nonverbal behaviors demand scales of various lengths to record the degree to which a given behavior was performed. One must determine, for instance, whether it is important to record that a "forward lean" occurred (yes/no) or what degree of forward lean occurred (ten degree, thirty degree, forty-five degree, and so on) or how long a forward lean occurred (1–5 seconds, 6–10 seconds, 11–15 seconds and so on) or at what point in the interaction the forward lean occurred (first 10 seconds of the interaction, last 10 seconds, etc.) or all four. Such judgments can only be made in the context of a specific study, but it is very tempting to select a bipolar scale when a five- or seven-point scale would provide more accurate data. Furthermore, the intensity and significance of an event may be lost if all the behaviors in your category system are given the same weight. The importance of fine discriminations in recording behavior in relation to the eventual interpretation of that behavior can be seen in an examination of nodding behavior. There are many different types of nodding—fast or slow, short or long vertical sweep, clustered or evenly paced, and so on. Hence, if you only recorded frequency of nods, you might not be able to separate nods of agreement or support from nods used to regulate the interaction—that is, for turn-taking or leave-taking.

Some of the observational systems currently being used will illustrate the variety of approaches to categorizing and recording nonverbal behavior. Some of these category systems report intercoder reliability and some don't. Some deal with a specific part of the body and some are concerned with clusters of

Observing and Recording Nonverbal Behavior

cues found throughout the body. Scales of various lengths are used by some, while others use pictographic or photographic notations. Some deal with only one communicator, while others gather data on both interactants. Some are concerned exclusively with nonverbal dimensions, while others attempt to integrate verbal and nonverbal behavior. All have been used with some success to quantify portions of human interaction, but it is clear that there is no one category system for nonverbal observations which currently enjoys the same widespread acceptance and use achieved by Bales[5] for observing and recording primarily verbal behavior. Nonverbal observational systems are in an early developmental stage, and most researchers develop their own category systems specific to their own research goals. Hopefully, in the long run, this approach will filter out useful categories and methods which, in turn, will lead to greater standardization of methods and greater integration of research findings.

This chapter will not discuss all the extant (or even all the well-known) observational systems pertinent to nonverbal behavior. For instance, those who wish to study vocal cues or paralanguage are indebted to Trager, who provided the pioneering work on the development of an observational category system for paralanguage.[6] A rather extensive and complex notation system has been developed for stylized movements in dance and may be applied to the observation and recording of human movement in other settings.[7] And several nonverbal category systems have been used for observing teacher nonverbal behavior in classroom settings.[8]

Proxemic Analysis. Anthropologist Edward T. Hall was a pioneer in the study of human spatial behavior. He was also the first to develop a proxemic notation system, which he has now extensively revised.[9] Originally, Hall believed there were eight factors which regulated and structured the distance between people during interaction. In the revised system, nineteen factors are recorded. In addition, the revised system also provides for finer discriminations by extending the length of the scales used.

1. Posture. On a 0 to 9 point scale, the interactants' posture is recorded—for example, 2 is standing; 3 is leaning; 4 is sitting; 5 is squatting; 6 is prone; and so on.

[5]R. Bales, *Interaction Process Analysis* (Reading, Mass.: Addison Wesley, 1950).

[6]G. L. Trager, "Paralanguage: A First Approximation," *Studies in Linguistics* 13 (1958): 1–12. For a detailed application of this system, see R. E. Pittenger, C. F. Hockett, and J. J. Danehy, *The First Five Minutes* (Ithaca, NY: Martineau, 1960).

[7]A. Hutchinson, *Labanotation: The System of Analyzing and Record Movement* (New York: Theater Arts Books, 1970).

[8]B. M. Grant and D. G. Hennings, *The Teacher Moves: An Analysis of Non-verbal Activity* (New York: Columbia Teachers College Press, 1971). Also P. Amidon, *Nonverbal Interaction Analysis* (Minneapolis: P. S. Amidon and Associates, 1971).

[9]See E. T. Hall, "A System for the Notation of Proxemic Behavior," *American Anthropologist* 65 (1963): 1003–1026; and E. T. Hall, *Handbook for Proxemic Research* (Washington: Society for the Anthropology of Visual Communication, 1974).

2. Body Orientation. The observer records the various positions (again 0-9) of the interactants' bodies in relation to each other. The scale begins with 0 or the two persons standing back to back ⊲⊳ . If the two people are standing in line, ⊳⊳ , a 4 would be noted. A face-to-face orientation would be a 9 on the scale and would be characterized as ⊳⊲ .

3. Lateral Displacement of Bodies, Displacement simply refers to the fact that even if two people are face to face, they may not be standing directly in front of one another. A 7 on this scale represents the lining up of the interactants' shoulders—for example, ⌒ ⌄ . A 4 shows two elbows extended—for example, ⌒⌒ ⌄⌄ .

‾4. Change of Orientation. If the participants, during the interaction, begin to "close" or "open" their body orientation toward each other, the observer can record it. A 5 would mean "no change" in orientation.

5. Change of Distance. Like the preceding category, this one allows the observer to record distance changes. A slight movement away from the other person would be recorded as a 4 and a slight movement toward the other person would be noted as a 6.

6. Body Distance. This measure relies on distances which are a function of the potential for touching with one's limbs or body—for example, two persons who are barely able to touch each other by leaning ⌒ would receive a 1. Other distances are measured by whether participants could touch with elbows or forearms or with body and head.

7. Gestures (Degree of Movement). This is a nine-point scale which records the degree of animation people use during interaction. A 1 indicates no detectable movement while an 8 indicates virtually all body parts in active movement.

8. Kinesic Isomorphism. This scale attempts to record the degree to which the two participants are mirroring each other's actions or body positions. No mirroring would be 0, while maximum mirroring would be 9.

9. Affect: Kind. This is a measure of the emotional tone of the interaction. Negative affect or hostilities would be coded with numbers from 0 to 3: positive expressions of emotion would be coded from 6 to 9.

10. Affect: Intensity. In order to determine the intensity with which emotions are displayed, we have a scale which records intensity from 0 (low) to 9 (extremely intense).

11. Eye Behavior. Complete avoidance of visual contact would be recorded as a 0, looking at some part of the other's body or looking away but still

Observing and Recording Nonverbal Behavior

retaining peripheral vision would be coded a 5, looking in the general facial area would be an 8, and mutual gaze or direct eye contact would be a 9.

12. Auditory Code: Number Talking. If both interactants are silent, a 0 is noted; one person talking is represented by a 4; and a 9 is given if both people are talking.

13. Auditory Code: Linguistic Style. This category considers the type of communication event—that is, a lecture given in a public setting at a public distance would be coded a 1, a monologue with a small audience in a personal or social setting would be a 2, a conversation would be a 5, and a tirade would be an 8.

14. Auditory Code: Voice Loudness. This scale, as the category title suggests, moves through silence, whispering, soft voices, normal voices, loud voices, shouting and screaming—again on a nine-point scale.

15. Auditory Code: Listening Behavior. Here the observer tries to assess the degree to which the person is paying attention or listening to the other.

16. Olfaction Code. While it may be very difficult for observers to identify, the goal is to assess the role of olfaction in the interaction. Are there odors which will help regulate or structure the distances between the interactants? Certain perfumes are advertised as promoting closer contact; certain body odors, smelly feet, and flatus frequently tend to extend distances between communicating partners. Are these breath and body odors detectable?

17. Thermal Code. Hall admits we know very little about thermal zones and heat gain or loss in structuring distance relationships. Some of Hall's subjects did, however, report sensing heat from another body and a resultant movement either toward or away from the source. Obviously, an observer in such a situation has to rely heavily on reports from the persons he is observing, which certainly suggests limitations. One of Hall's subjects, a rather voluptuous young female, noted that when she danced with certain young males she could detect a rise in temperature in the abdominal region, which foreshadowed genital tumescence and which could be differentiated from a temperature rise due to exertion. Further, this rise in temperature could be detected several inches from the dance partner! Heat is recorded on a continuum from 0 (no heat) to 9 (bodily contact heat).

18. Bodily Involvement. This scale attempts to measure the amount of physical contact between the communicators. We begin with 0 (no touching) and move up through brushing, spot touching, holding hands or extremities, caressing and embracing, and extensive body involvement.

19. Seeking or Avoiding Touching. This scale is based on the belief that persons will either seek contact, avoid it, or remain neutral. For instance, one person may reach to shake another's hand and would be coded as an 8—seeking contact. If, however, the other person makes no move to take the offered hand, this person is recorded as a 2—passive avoidance of contact.

Observing and Recording Nonverbal Behavior

389

Kinesic Analysis. David Efron's seminal work *Gesture and Environment* was first published in 1941 and was republished in 1972.[10] Efron's study focused on the observation, recording, and analysis of hand and head movements—with some attention given to space and posture. Conceptually and methodologically, this treatise represents the intellectual springboard for some of the later observational systems of Birdwhistell, Hall, Ekman, and others. Efron applied his observational methods to hundreds of different interactive settings, environments, and types of people; he accumulated over two thousand sketches by an artist of communicators in natural settings; and he analyzed more than five thousand feet of film from these same subjects. While the details of this system will not be presented in full, we can outline the general categories:[11]

1. Spatio-Temporal Measures—gestures considered simply as movement, independent from their interactive or referential aspects.
    A. Radius of the gesture: size of the radius of movement and axis of the movement, whether elbow, wrist, and so forth.
    B. Form: Sinuous, elliptical, angular, or straight.
    C. Plane: sideways—transversal; toward auditor—frontal; up-down—vertical; away from speaker and auditor—lateral centrifugality; or away from speaker toward auditor—dorsoventral centrifugality.
    D. Bodily Parts: involved in gesticulation and ways in which they are employed.
        (1) Head gestures: area of movement, rate and frequency, and whether used as a substitute for hands.
        (2) Digital gestures: variety of positions and shapes of hands.
        (3) Unilaterality versus bilaterality in hand movement.
        (4) Ambulatory gestures: sequential transfer of motion from one arm to the other.
    E. Tempo: abrupt, dischronic versus flowing transitions from one movement to another.
2. Interlocutional Aspects—communicational or interactive elements of gestures without regard for referential aspects.
    A. Familiarity with the other person by touch: to interrupt or capture attention; also compared with contacting own body.
    B. Simultaneous gesturing of all interactants.
    C. Gesturing with objects: using an inaminate object as an arm extension.
    D. Conversational grouping: use of space and distance between speakers and auditors.

[10]D. Efron, *Gesture and Environment* (New York: Kings Crowns Press, 1941); and D. Efron, *Gesture, Race and Culture* (the Hague: Mouton, 1972).
[11]This outline is taken from the preface to the 1972 ed. of Efron's *Gesture, Race and Culture* compiled by P. Ekman, pp. 9–11.

Observing and Recording Nonverbal Behavior

3. Linguistic Aspects—a consideration of the referential meaning of a gesture (or gestures)—including a distinction between gestures which have
meaning independent of and in conjunction with speech.
   A. Logical-discursive: gestures which do not refer to an object or
   thought but to the course of the ideational process. They lend emphasis to the content of the verbal-vocal behavior. They are related
   more to the *how* than to the *what* of the idea they enact. They are
   bodily re-enactments of the ideational process, of the logical pauses,
   intensities, inflections, and the like.
      (1) Batons: gestures which time out with the hands the successive
      stages of referential activity. They beat the tempo of mental
      locomotion.
      (2) Ideographic: gestures which trace or sketch out in the air the
      path and direction of thought.
   B. Objective: gestures which have meaning independent of speech to
   which they may or may not be an adjunct.
      (1) Deictic: gestures which indicate a visually present object, usu-
      ally by pointing.
      (2) Physiographic: gestures which visually show what they mean.
         (a) Iconographic: gestures which depict the form of a visual
         object.
         (b) Kinetographic: gestures which depict a bodily action.
      (3) Emblematic or symbolic: gestures which represent either a
      visual or a logical object by means of pictorial or nonpictorial
      form which has no morphological relationship to the thing rep-
      resented. These have standardized meaning within a culture and
      are culture specific. If the emblem is morphologically similar to
      that which it represents, it is considered a hybrid emblem.

For over twenty-five years, Ray Birdwhistell has been trying to refine and
further specify the various human movements which have meaning. This system is so comprehensive it cannot be presented in much detail, but interested
readers are referred to the latest report of his notation system.[12] We will simply
review the eight broad categories which compose Birdwhistell's notation system. Within each category, Birdwhistell has attempted to classify every movement and posture which may evoke "meaning" in interpersonal transactions.
Pictorial notation devices (pictographs) are used to record not only movement
and positions, but other "modifiers" such as stress, junctures, action modifiers,
tension, relaxation, and so on. Hundreds of notations are possible for filmed
interaction sequences no longer than a few minutes. The difficulty in learning

[12]R. L. Birdwhistell, *Kinesics and Context* (Philadelphia: University of Pennsylvania Press, 1970).

Observing and Recording Nonverbal Behavior

the coding system is probably one reason the system has not been widely applied. It is primarily used by those researchers who wish to describe the structure of the nonverbal system—in a manner similar to structural linguistics. Communicologists and social psychologists who are more concerned with the relationship of a particular nonverbal behavior (or cluster of behaviors) to other external variables such as status, acquaintance, personality, and the like, generally avoid the Birdwhistell system and opt for the development of their own systems adapted to their particular research project. It should be noted, however, that the structural approach does provide useful information on the range of influential cues and the possible interrelationship between spoken words and kinesic behavior.

1. Total Head. Under this heading, observations are made of head nods (which way and how much), head sweeps, whether the head is cocked, and so on.

2. Face. In this category are recorded such things as blank face, brow movements, wide eyes, winks, squints, closed eyes, sideways looks, staring, rolled eyes, nostril flare and pinch, wrinkled nose, sneers, droopy mouth, pouting mouth, toothy smile, slow licking of the lips, lip biting, pursed lips, tightened temples, ear wiggle, and total scalp movement—among others.

3. Trunk and Shoulders. Here various graphic symbols represent such things as spinal positions (upright "stiff," anterior slump, leaning back, curvature beginning at buttocks, and the like); and shoulder positions (hunched, shrugging, one shoulder raised or drooped, one shoulder back, and the like). Also in this category are pectoral muscle tension, chest tension or relaxation, and stomach muscle tension and relaxation.

4. Shoulder, Arm, and Wrist. This category involves a rather complex method for recording activity or movements in the shoulder, arm, and wrist area.

5. Hand and Finger Activity. After labeling various sections of the hand and fingers, it is possible to make notations of their positions and activity. For instance, a single finger may be extended lax, extended tense, hooked, curled, closed, touching an object, grasping an object, caressing, drumming, and so on. Then add observations of the whole hand and palm and the activity of the other hand, palm, and fingers (nail picking, clapping, cupping, and the like) and you begin to understand the detailed level upon which Birdwhistell is working.

6. Hip, Upper Leg, Lower Leg, Ankle. This is a system similar to the shoulder, arm, and wrist method—including notations for various positions of the legs while seated: furled umbrella, leg wind, balls of feet touching with legs semiextended, leg dangling, swinging, stuttering, and the like.

7. Foot Behavior. While standing, we make numerous identifiable foot movements: the toe teeter (standing, rising on toes and dropping back on heel and toe), the full teeter (standing, rocking back and forth from toe to heel to

toe), the toe dig (toes of one foot scratch surface of support while other supports weight), knee teeter (knees bend while weight rests on toes), and several others. Birdwhistell also notes several categories of walking behavior in this section: the bent-knee walk, the straight-knee walk, the bounce, the glide, the high step, the foot drag, the shuffle, the duck walk, and the Indian walk. He also mentions the fact that Arabs describe a woman who walks gracefully as "walking like a chicken," while the Indian describes a graceful woman as "walking like an elephant." This, he says, should make an observer cautious about making value judgments of something like a duck walk for instance.

8. Neck. This category records such behaviors as the Adam's-apple jump, neck twists, neck projections, swallowing, and neck tensing or sagging.

Since Birdwhistell's system is so detailed and extensive, it would not be practical to illustrate his notational markings here. However, Kendon developed a kinesic notation system from which we will extract and illustrate markings for five possible configurations of the brow and forehead area, sixteen possible configurations of the mouth, and five notations for direction of gaze.[13] The full notation system also includes: seven possible configurations of the eyes; seven positions of the head and two of the neck; three positions of the arms and hands; and nine positions of the shoulders and trunk.

A. *Brows (including forehead)*

1. G Normal, or baseline position.

2. $\cap\cap$ Raised brows.

3. $/\setminus$ Sloping brows. The brows are drawn upward and together.

4. W Knitted brows. The brows are drawn together over the nose as in a frown.

5. $\sum$ The brows are drawn downward over the nose, with transverse wrinkling above nose bridge.

B. *Mouth*

1. ——   Normal or inexpressive mouth.

2. —⊖—   Normal or inexpressive mouth, open.

3. $\smile\smile$ Mouth with slight smile at corners.

4. $\smile$ Smiling mouth.

5. $\mathsf{\smile}$ Smiling mouth, open.

[13]A. Kendon and J. Ex, "Progress Report of an Investigation into Aspects of the Structure and Function of the Social Performance in Two-Person Encounters," cited in M. Argyle, *Social Interaction* (New York: Atherton, 1969), pp. 123–126.

Observing and Recording Nonverbal Behavior

6.   \w/   Smiling mouth, lips parted to expose teeth.

7.   \w/   Smiling mouth, open, lips drawn back to expose teeth.

8. t_____t Mouth with corners slightly tightened.

9.   =   Lips drawn tightly together.

10.   =>   Lips rolled inward into the mouth.

11.   ◎   Lips pushed outward, closed. "Pouting."

12.   ◉   Lips pushed outward, open.

13.   ⊗   Lips pushed outward, pressed together. "Pursed."

14.   ⌒   Corners of the mouth drawn downward.

15.   ≡   Lips together, tongue protruding.

16.   —∪—   Lower lips protruding. "Half-pout."

C. *Direction of gaze*

1.   O   P looking at q, that is, looking at his eyes, or looking at the point where he would meet q's eyes if q looked up at him.

2.   ♀   P looking down.

3.   ─O   P looking to left.

4.   O─   P looking right.

5.   ⚲   P looking upward.

For the downward and upward positions, numerical subscripts may be used to indicate the degree to which p is looking in one or another of these directions.

Mehrabian has used a variety of categories and recording techniques to identify behaviors associated with his tripartite concept of nonverbal semantic space—immediacy (liking/disliking), power (status), and responsiveness.[14] In this system, several different methods are used for observing and recording variables in five categories: (1) distance, (2) relaxation, (3) movements, (4) facial expressions, and (5) verbalizations. For instance, the reclining angles of the communicators are estimates by coders to the nearest ten-degree angle; for voice intonation, coders may make judgments on a five-point scale or more precise measures may be made by spectrographic analysis; isolated movements may be recorded by frequency, but continuous movements are coded by occurrence every five seconds; distance measures may be estimated by coders

[14]A. Mehrabian, "Methods and Designs: Some Referents and Measures on Nonverbal Behavior," *Behavior Research Methods and Instrumentation* 1 (1969): 203–207.

Observing and Recording Nonverbal Behavior

or measured precisely by floor tiles (some proxemic researchers have devised formulas for estimating actual distance by stop-action measurements of distance on video tapes); some variables are coded as either occurring or not occurring, while others are scored on the basis of the degree to which the act was performed; and communication length is measured by a simple summation of total words emitted.

Verbal-Nonverbal Interaction Analysis. As we have often mentioned in this book, the verbal and nonverbal systems are so interwoven that it is conceptually inadequate to concern ourselves with only one system at a time. A system based on simultaneous observation of spoken and unspoken behaviors would be most desirable. Unfortunately, few efforts have been made to develop such a system. Some even argue that, on everything but a very general level, it is impossible. From a strictly perceptual point of view, it may be impossible to make the many observations required for a sophisticated verbal-nonverbal system. Nevertheless, it is important enough for us to consider the possibilities.

A very general (nonspecific) verbal-nonverbal interaction analysis system was presented by Harrison.[15] His system only records whether verbal or nonverbal communication is being used, when, and for how long. In this context, nonverbal communication obviously does not include vocal tones. The term covers only overt, observable movements. Since this system is not designed for analysis of content, it can be used across a variety of interaction events for comparisons or summary analyses. Table 11.1 shows the thirteen categories in Harrison's system of analysis.

Although no message "content" in the usual sense is analyzed, one may make some inferences about the relative intensity of the situation, who was in control, who was involved or uninvolved, who spoke and who was silent and for how long, at what point in the interaction shifts in verbal and nonverbal behavior took place, and so on. By obtaining other measures, such as relative status of the two parties, judged "satisfaction" with the interaction, effectiveness as an interviewer, and the like, we can then compare these measures against the record of gross verbal and nonverbal behavior to note differences, if any.

Harrison also suggests the use of video tape to increase the reliability of the observations—viewing the verbal band for Communicator One alone, then the nonverbal band for Communicator One, then the verbal band for Communicator Two; and finally, the nonverbal band for Communicator Two. He suggests three to five coders or observers.

[15]R. Harrison, "Verbal-Nonverbal Interaction Analysis: The Substructure of an Interview," paper presented to the Association for Educational Journalism, Berkeley, California, 1969. Also see J. Frahm, "Verbal-Nonverbal Interaction Analysis: Exploring a New Methodology for Quantifying Dyadic Communication Systems," unpublished Ph.D. dissertation, Michigan State University, 1970.

Observing and Recording Nonverbal Behavior

Table 11.1

Code category	C_1 Verb	NonV	C_2 Verb	NonV	Description: (from doctor-patient example)
1	+	0	0	0	Communicator One (doctor) talking, not gesturing; Communicator Two (patient) silent, not gesturing.
2	+	+	0	0	Doctor talking, gesturing; patient silent, not moving.
3	+	0	0	+	Doctor talking, not gesturing; patient silent, but moving.
4	+	+	0	+	Doctor talking, gesturing; patient silent, but moving.
5	0	0	+	0	Doctor silent, not moving; patient talking, not moving.
6	0	0	+	+	Doctor silent, not moving; patient talking, moving.
7	0	+	+	0	Doctor silent, but moving; patient talking, not moving.
8	0	+	+	+	Doctor silent, but moving; patient talking and moving.
9	0	+	0	0	Doctor silent, but moving; patient silent and unmoving.
10	0	0	0	+	Doctor silent, not moving; patient silent, but moving.
11	0	+	0	+	Doctor silent, but moving; patient silent, but moving.
12	0	0	0	0	Silence, no movement by doctor or patient.
13	+	×	+	×	Both doctor and patient talking; includes all combinations of movement.

If we wanted to specify verbal behavior in more categories than Harrison has done, we would logically look to extant systems for observing and recording verbal behavior. A system developed by Bales[16] and later adapted and applied to classroom interaction by Flanders[17] is perhaps the most popular one available. The possibilities for a marriage of verbal and nonverbal systems, using interaction process analysis, are noted by Amidon.[18]

[16] R. Bales, *Interaction Process Analysis* (Cambridge, Mass.: Addison-Wesley, 1950).

[17] N. A. Flanders, *Interaction Analysis in the Classroom: A Manual for Observers* (Minneapolis: University of Minnesota, 1960). Also see P. Amidon, *Nonverbal Interaction Analysis* (Minneapolis: P. S. Amidon & Associates, 1971).

[18] E. J. Amidon, "Interaction Analysis," in P. Emert and W. D. Brooks (eds.), *Methods of Research in Communication* (Boston: Houghton Mifflin, 1970).

Observing and Recording Nonverbal Behavior

During this period the observer may detect nonverbal cues that will help him make accurate decisions in coding the verbal interaction [p. 378]. . . . Some of the limitations are [that] . . . the system is designed for use only when the student and teacher are engaged in verbal interaction; no record of nonverbal interaction is made (although the system could be adapted to other forms of human interaction, both verbal and nonverbal) [p. 397].

Since we are aware of the theoretical limitations of dividing behavior into verbal and nonverbal units, we can appreciate the arguments of those who suggest we can not even legitimately observe the two systems separately. Our coding of the verbal may be so influenced by the nonverbal that we are presuming to observe dichotomous systems which, in reality, do not exist.

In an effort to avoid some of the pitfalls of current notational systems, and to summarize or bring together some of the material in this book, the following categories for a "global analysis" are proposed. Obviously, this method is not designed for sophisticated research purposes; it is designed for students and others who want to acquire a general framework for looking at interpersonal transactions. It will give you a general feel for the judgments needed to observe an act of human communication. The number of questions within each category should act only as starters for observations. You will think of other important questions which have been omitted. Some of the questions included will probably seem very insignificant for interpreting some situations—and very important for others. You will also note that not all of the questions concern directly observable elements; some require inferences.

How might you use such a "global analysis"? First, it is recommended that you read all the questions in all the categories to give you a general perspective on the bases for observing communication events. Then you may wish to take one or two categories at a time to perfect observational skills in those particular areas—observing only those dimensions in several encounters and adding to the questions already suggested. After having worked with the separate categories for some time, try observing a communication event using all nine categories. Compare your observations with those of another observer and the two (or more) communicators if possible. The discussion of your observations may be more valuable than any notation system which might be proposed at this time.

Global Analysis: Initial Phase
(Recording First Impressions)

The Environment. Are there any environmental stimuli likely to affect this interaction? Is the temperature going to be a factor? How about the number of other people around the two interactants? How will these other

Observing and Recording Nonverbal Behavior

397

people influence what the two interactants may do—even if they do not say anything? Will the colors and general decor influence this interaction? How much space is available between and around the communicators? What architectural factors may influence what happens? Chairs (soft–hard)? Tables? Walls? Desks? Out of all the available places in the immediate environment, why might the interactants have chosen the exact place they did? Does it seem like a familiar environment for both parties? Do they appear to feel at home? What behavior can be expected in this environment?

The Participants. Will the sex of the participants likely affect the interaction? How? Will age have any influence on what happens? How about the status or authority relationships involved? How do the participants look? Is attractiveness going to be a factor? Will hair style or body size affect the interaction? How? What is the role of dress in this interaction? Does the participants' dress meet expectations for the environment and their roles and mutual expectations? Can any odors be detected? Are the participants aware of them? Are there any differences in education, occupation, or socioeconomic status which may affect the communication behavior? How? Does race or cultural background play any major part in interpersonal behavior in this situation? Will artifacts such as lipstick, glasses, and the like, affect participant reactions to any significant degree? What is the relationship of these two participants to one another? Do they have any previous experience with each other which will likely be influential here? Do they seem to like each other? Why? Do the participants enter this transaction with compatible goals or purposes? What information do the participants bring to this subject on this occasion?

As an observer, you must recognize that some of these initial observations and hypotheses may change as the interaction progresses—a woman may remove her glasses, a man may take off his ring, or attitudes may not be as similar as predicted. Observers should be prepared to note such changes.

Global Abalysis: Interaction Phase
(Recording Ongoing Verbal-Nonverbal Responses)
Touching Behavior. Is there any physical contact at all? If so, does it seem to be deliberate or accidental? Does this action seem to be motivated by some specific purpose—for example, reinforcing a point? If there is no contact, why? Did the situation call for contact or no contact? Was contact made only at special times during the interaction? How frequent was the contact? How long did it last? Who initiated the contact? What was the apparent effect on the person being touched?

Observing and Recording Nonverbal Behavior

398

Facial Expressions.   Do either or both communicators have a relatively consistent facial expression in this situation? Are they generally communicating one attitude or emotion with their facial expressions? Were there gross changes at certain points in the conversation? What might have accounted for such gross facial changes—verbal or nonverbal behavior? Were there times when one person's facial expression elicited a similar expression from the other person? Did you see any "micromomentary" or fleeting facial expressions which suggested attitudes contrary to those being expressed verbally? At what points did you notice expressions which would generally be described as frowning or sad, smiling and happy, angry, anxious, impatient, bored, puzzled, serious, or surprised? Did the facial expressions differ in intensity at various points in the transaction? Did the facial expression seem genuine? If so, why? If not, why not?

Eye Behavior.   Is there generally a lot of visual contact or not very much? Why? Does one person look away more than the other? Why? Do one or both participants seem to stare or extend eye contact beyond "normal" limits? Is there a pattern to the places a person looks when he or she does not look at the other person? If so, can you explain why this pattern may occur? Is there any excessive blinking by one or both parties? At what points is eye gaze most evident? Not evident? What effect does eye gaze or lack of it seem to have on the other participant?

Posture-Position.   Do both participants assume the same posture? Why? Are both standing? Sitting? If one is standing and one is sitting, how does this relate to their respective roles in this situation? Does the assumed posture seem to be relaxed or tense? Does this change during the course of interaction? If so, why? Are one or both participants leaning back? Leaning forward? What does this suggest? Are the participants facing head-on? At an acute angle? At an obtuse angle? Side by side? Have they arranged their bodies to block others from entering their conversation? What is the relative distance used for communicating—close, medium, far? Do leg and arm positions communicate impenetrability or coldness? Do leg positions suggest inclusion? Are one person's changes in posture matched by the other person? How long do the participants maintain a given posture? Why do they change?

Vocal Behavior.   Are both participants using the appropriate level of loudness for the situation? Does one person have an unusually soft or loud voice? What is the effect on the other person? Is talking rate a factor in this situation? How? Are there times when you perceive an incongruity between vocal cues and verbal statements? What is the effect on the other participant? Do one or both participants have fairly deep voices? Fairly high voices? Are

Observing and Recording Nonverbal Behavior

there periods of silence beyond normal pauses? Why? Do vocal cues such as laughing or groaning play a significant part? What about a quivering or quaking voice during periods of nervousness? Does vocal quality such as hoarseness seem to affect the total impression of one or both of the participants? Are there excessive nonfluencies? With what effect?

Physical Movement. What were the significant movements in the event? Did head nodding play a major part? How? How about hand gestures? Did one participant seem to be moving in on the other while the other moved back? Was there generally a lot of movement or not too much? Why? Did hand or finger movements play a part? How? Did hand or foot cues suggest clues to deception? How about foot tapping? Were there major changes in posture? How frequent were they? Did you observe any cues for terminating the conversation—for example, a participant looking at his or her watch; making motions to get up or move out the door, taking a deep breath, frequently looking around and out the window, and the like?

Verbal Behavior. Here we will ask about some familiar, typical types of verbal responses. Consider: (1) What was the general style of one or both participants? Can it be generally characterized in any one or two categories? (2) What specific kinds of remarks elicited what specific kinds of nonverbal behaviors? In other words, what seemed to be the effect of certain verbal responses on the initiator's nonverbal behavior and on the receiver's verbal and nonverbal responses? Response types: Disagreement about content? Agreement about content? Advice about feelings? Advice about action? Ambiguous responses? Interrupting responses? Personal attack? Defensive response? Evaluative response? Supportive response? Questions? Opinions? Tension release through jokes and the like? Tangential response? Irrelevant response? Expression of own feelings: Positive? Expression of own feelings: Negative? Interpretive response? Request for clarification of feelings? Request for clarification of content?

A final, but important, note. In the Preface to this book, we observed that a book devoted entirely to nonverbal communication might be considered misleading—that nonverbal systems should not be portrayed as separate processes, independent from verbal behavior. To overcome this danger, we have stressed the integral relationship between verbal and nonverbal systems whenever possible. But an equally misleading view of the nonverbal communication process may result from the organization of this book into seemingly separate categories of behavior. Even our "global analysis" reflects this apparent separation. We could not leave any discussion of these various categories without further noting that even within the nonverbal system, the dynamics cannot be ignored. Clearly, these categories are not discrete when

Observing and Recording Nonverbal Behavior

400

they are used for the observation and analysis of nonverbal behavior. Proximity, eye gaze, and forward lean, as we noted previously, are all closely related and interdependent if we are trying to make observations about intimacy, approval-seeking, or warmth. As you use the global analysis, you should keep in mind these relationships *between* categories as well as within categories.

There are numerous measurement techniques (many of which have been noted in previous chapters) which can be very helpful in nonverbal observations—for example, tape recordings, filtered tape recordings for vocal cue analysis, voice prints, mercury strain gauges for noting slight changes in facial musculature, and event recorders. Event recorders have a series of on-off switches which can be activated during the observation of an event and which will provide a graphic representation of the activity observed. They will provide information on how often a behavior occurred, how long it lasted, what behaviors co-occurred with it, and at what points in the interaction the behavior occurred. Since much of our nonverbal behavior is visible phenomena, the next section will focus on obtaining and using permanent visual recordings.

Working with Visual Records

There may be any number of reasons why you might want to obtain permanent visual records of the subject of your observations. Sometimes the action under scrutiny is so fleeting that you feel you'll miss part of the action the first time and want an opportunity to view it again and again—sometimes in slow motion; you may feel that you are missing important aspects of the action when you turn your eyes to your notation system for recording purposes; you may feel that your presence and note-taking would seriously affect the behavior of those being observed; you may want a visual record which can later be examined by others who are looking for different behaviors; you may want a visual record to facilitate coding procedures by several individuals simultaneously; you may want a method of obtaining intercoder reliability estimates without having all your coders "on site," and so forth.

Obviously, a film or video tape will provide us with the flow or "process perspective" of an event, but still photographs can also be used effectively.[19] Dynell Electronics Corporation is even reported to have developed a three-dimensional copying process called "solid photography." An object is photo-

---

[19] R. U. Akeret, *Photoanalysis: How to Interpret the Hidden Psychological Meaning of Personal and Public Photographs* (New York: Wyden, 1973); S. Milgram, "The Image-Freezing Machine," *Psychology Today* 10 (1977): 50–52, 54, 108; and H. Becker, "Photography and Sociology," *Studies in the Anthropology of Visual Communication* 5 (1974): 3–26.

graphed from all sides and each photograph has enough three-dimensional information so that the combined photographs can produce a life-like reproduction. Ekman and Friesen have developed a coding system for six emotions shown in the human face—happiness, anger, surprise, sadness, disgust, and fear.[20] Coding is broken down into three areas of the face: (1) the brows-forehead area, (2) the eyes-lids-bridge-of-the-nose area, and (3) the lower face—including cheek, nose, mouth, chin, jaw. Photographic examples from a wide spectrum of different types of subjects and verbal descriptions are used to train coders to recognize the various components of each emotion—a rather unique, but important method when dealing with visual stimuli. Ekman claims high levels of accuracy can be obtained from coders after only six hours of training. In short, here is a visual dictionary for identification of these six emotions—showing the range of possible facial configurations associated with each. When coders are confronted with brow movements associated with one emotion and mouth movements associated with another, they code this as a facial blend. Ekman and Friesen have also developed a method of describing any facial movement which is visually recorded based on an analysis of the facial anatomy and moving muscles.[21] This Facial Action Code is complex, but it is an important step toward scientifically describing the range of everyday facial behavior in a manner which can easily be replicated.

Perhaps the system which has the most potential for the future of kinesic analysis is the Visual Information Display and Retrieval system (VID-R) developed by Ekman and his colleagues.[22] This system uses films and video tapes to overcome the problems encountered when observers cannot continuously monitor an ongoing event. In addition, it is useful for analyses of events which will not occur again or situations in which units of measurement have not been thoroughly specified by previous research and films need to be viewed over and over.

The VID-R system was constructed to serve the following purposes: (1) To allow the observer(s) to view the video taped event at actual, slowed, or fast speed. At high-speed playback, a ninety-minute reel of video tape may be viewed in approximately six minutes. (2) To permit each frame of the tape to be coded, so any given frame or frames can be automatically recalled at any time by a computer hookup. This allows the observer to compare events previously viewed with events currently seen. (3) To facilitate assembly of similar, or

[20]P. Ekman and W. V. Friesen, *Unmasking the Face* (Englewood Cliffs, N.J.: Prentice-Hall, 1975).

[21]P. Ekman and W. V. Friesen, "Measuring Facial Movement." *Environmental Psychology and Nonverbal Behavior* 1 (1976): 56–75.

[22]P. Ekman, W. V. Friesen, and T. J. Taussig. "VID-R and SCAN: Tools and Methods in the Analysis of Facial Expression and Body Movement," in G. Gerbner, O. Holsti, K. Krippendorff, W. Paisley, and P. Stone (eds.), *Content Analysis* (New York: Wiley, 1969).

Observing and Recording Nonverbal Behavior

difficult to code, events without destroying the original record. The computer can be instructed to find the first frame in which a particular action occurs, to search for all similar events, and to record them, in succession, on a separate video tape. For instance, you may want to select out a particular hand movement used by an interviewee during a long interview; then you may want the computer to select out all the facial expressions associated with those hand movements. Then you can assemble a tape of only the events you are studying. (4) To store observer measurements or observations in a manner that allows automatic retrieval of the visual phenomena they refer to. (5) Potentially, to facilitate compilation of a systematic visual dictionary of kinesic variables with specific models of each action or event. Operators would have rapid, automated access for display of these visual definitions.

For all the promise which film and video tape offer to the observation of nonverbal behavior, they are not without problematic issues and potential sources of error. For many people, a permanent visual record—regardless of what is shown or how it is shown—has an almost unquestioned believability. The fact that events and actions can be "seen" seems to take precedence over any observer's secondhand report. For this reason, the following issues should be carefully considered.

First, and perhaps most basic, is the influence of a camera on the behavior of the observed. In laboratory settings, the camera can be hidden or, if this is not possible or desirable, you can assume that the initial anxiety of being filmed will dissipate after a few minutes when the subjects get used to the camera. This assumption should be checked, however, because people may get used to the camera at different rates, some may try to perform naturally, and some may never be comfortable in front of the camera. Eibl-Eibesfeldt reports an ingenious method of filming which attempts to overcome biases encountered when people know they are being filmed. Figure 11.2 shows a camera developed by P. Hass which has a prism built into the lens which permits filming to the side. Thus, the camera is pointed in one direction, but the event being filmed is at a right angle.

A second issue concerns how the action, event, or individual is filmed. We know, for instance, that camera angles can affect the meaning we attach to a situation—for example, a person can be made to look shorter by filming from a higher angle; a close-up may cause a given behavior to assume an exaggerated importance—like the familiar close-up of a person's hands seen in so many television newscasts; rapidly shifting from scene to scene may give an illusion of speed which does not accompany the actual event; and so on. In short, meanings can be in the movement patterns of the camera as well as movement patterns of those being filmed. A related problem concerns the self-editing or sampling process one uses while filming or video-taping. Viewing tapes is a long and arduous process, and sometimes careful sampling of the behaviors

Observing and Recording Nonverbal Behavior

Figure 11.2 Bolex Camera with Mirror Lens

under observation will prevent coders from experiencing fatigue during later viewing. Sometimes these samples are no longer than one minute in length. Again we can see the possible distorting effects on the interaction "process." Even if the interaction samples are representative of the total interaction, we cannot account for what came before and after the sample used. Although this same argument could be applied to the use of complete interaction episodes, the use of episode segments or samples only magnifies the problem.

Sometimes video-taping or filming takes place in the laboratory setting rather than the field. A familiar technique in these situations is to "standardize" a confederate's behavior by instructing him or her to "remain neutral," "ask exactly the same questions," "do not look at the other person," and any number of other instructions designed to control the confederate's behavior. The rationale for this procedure is that if you know what one person is doing, you can increase the precision of your analyses about the causes of the subject's behavior. And, independent ratings of the confederate's behavior can be obtained to confirm the constancy of the behavior. But such designs must also consider how accurately they describe the process of interaction. If we video-tape or film only one participant in an interaction, it is difficult to make inferences about the dynamics of the process. Certainly no one would argue that a confederate's behavior was *exactly the same* in every situation, but without dual-channel recording, such changes cannot be fully accounted for. Furthermore, the constancy of behavior creates an "unreal" situation for the subject—a perception which may warrant unreal behavior on his or her part. How would you feel interacting with a person for five minutes who constantly stared at you? Ideally, then, we should (1) maintain a visual record of *both* interactants and (2) gather pretest data in a series of interviews without stringent control to determine the *range of possible behaviors* on the part of both per-

Observing and Recording Nonverbal Behavior

sons. This pretesting will not only provide guidelines for what type of confederate control is desired, but will also provide a rough guide to the limits of generalization for the obtained results.

After many hours of viewing visual materials, you sometimes get the uneasy feeling that you are observing and recording minute behaviors which may have relatively little real-life impact—if any at all. You wonder whether the interacting parties are cognizant of fleeting movements, which, only with the advantage of replays, you are able to observe. You are uncomfortable with the knowledge that video tapes or films represent something short of an accurate representation of what actually took place—and wish they did more. Somehow we need to obtain supplementary "natural state" feedback from interactants to determine which of the many behaviors we examine are attended to. Some may question the relevance of looking at micromomentary facial expressions, eyebrow flashes, and pupil dilation by asking the question: "Are such behaviors perceived everyday human interaction?" Even if the answer is no, this does not suggest that such research is unimportant or even irrelevant, but it raises the question of observational priorities for those concerned with understanding human communication. And, it reiterates the need to establish observational categories which are meaningful to human interaction.

There are many potential sources of error rooted in the viewing behavior of coders who examine visual records. If a coder is given a list of ten or twelve nonverbal behaviors to code which range from head movements to foot movements, it is inevitable that intercoder reliability will suffer. To correct for this, areas of observation can be broken down into smaller portions and coders can focus on that one area. In some cases, too much focus may cause an observer to miss important co-occurring behavior. We also have a tendency to follow a conversation like a Ping-Pong match—shifting our head from side to side as the speaking turns shift. If the observer is asked to focus on the behavior of one interactant, looking only at the talker will surely bias observations.

Finally, there are far too many problems concerning the technical use of video tape and film to detail here, but there are numerous (frightfully easy) ways to obtain poor quality video tape and film. Since sharp resolution of the picture is so critically important in the observation of nonverbal behavior, it is worth investigating seemingly mundane problems like the type and size of video tape or film, type of recorder and playback unit which will provide the best overall quality, and so on. For some of our research using video tape we have found it useful to get a medium-close full body shot and an extreme close-up of the face and head for each participant. The face and head shots can be superimposed in the corners of the screen which seem to contain the least important actions for the particular project. With a straight medium close-up, anything but gross head movements are extremely difficult to observe and code on most current equipment. This would greatly hinder, for instance, observations of gazing and nodding.

Observing and Recording Nonverbal Behavior

Summary

In this chapter we have reviewed some general principles of observing human communication behavior and some specific and formalized systems developed for this purpose. We started by examining the process of systematic observation itself—occasions for observation, ethical issues, and the various roles an observer can play relative to his or her field of observation. We tried to explore some of the characteristics of people who seemed to be insightful observers. One characteristic we pursued in some depth was an understanding of the process of human perception. "Good" observers, it was argued, would familiarize themselves with possible sources of observer distortion and would adapt accordingly. In this treatment of human perception we discussed how we sometimes project our own needs, desires, and expectations onto those we are observing, how we sometimes perceive only those things which will make sense to our own view of human behavior, how what we observe first may affect later observations—and vice versa, how the expressions of our observations can be a source of perceived bias, and how we must be careful to distinguish observed "facts" from inferences.

The major part of this chapter was devoted to a presentation of some notation systems and the categories of behavior observers have used. Hall's proxemic analysis, the kinesic categories for observation of Birdwhistell, Efron, Kendon, and Mehrabian were outlined. While such systems may be interesting from the point of view of what others are doing, most readers of this book require a less formalized system for the kind of observing they will be doing. Thus, we presented a nine-category "global analysis" system which can be used by anyone and which can significantly increase verbal and nonverbal sensitivity to social interaction. The global analysis gives just enough structure to guide initial observations and, it is hoped, will stimulate additional ideas which can be applied and adapted to almost any encounter.

The last section dealt with various aspects of visual records. We suggested several advantages in obtaining such records but cautioned against possible pitfalls. It was noted that the methods of filming can inject meaning into the visual documents which may bias interpretations of them. Finally, we offered some suggestions regarding what to film and how to view these visual records.

SELECTED BIBLIOGRAPHY

Akeret, R. U. *Photoanalysis: How to Interpret the Hidden Psychological Meaning of Personal and Public Photographs*. New York: Wyden, 1973.

Amidon, E. J. "Interaction Analysis." In P. Emmert and W. D. Brooks (eds.), *Methods of Research in Communication*. Boston: Houghton Mifflin, 1970.

Observing and Recording Nonverbal Behavior

Amidon, P. *Nonverbal Interaction Analysis*. Minneapolis: P. S. Amidon & Associates, 1971.

Anderson, R. D., Struthers, J. A., and James, H. H. "Development of a Verbal and Nonverbal Observation Instrument." Paper presented to the American Educational Research Association, Minneapolis, 1970.

Argyle, M., and Williams, M. "Observer or Observed? A Reversible Perspective in Person Perception." *Sociometry* 32 (1969): 396–412.

Ayres, J. "Observer Judgments of Audience Members' Attitudes." *Western Speech* 39 (1975): 40–50.

Axinn, G., and Axinn, N. "The Indigenous Observer, Diary Keeping: A Methodological Note." *Human Organization* 14 (1969): 78–86.

Babchuk, N. "The Role of the Researcher as Participant Observer and Participant-as-Observer in the Field Situation." *Human Organization* 21 (1962): 225–230.

Bales, R. *Interaction Process Analysis*. Reading, Mass.: Addison-Wesley, 1950.

Barker, L. L., and Collins, N. B. "Nonverbal and Kinesic Research." In P. Emmert and W. D. Brooks (eds.), *Methods of Research in Communication*. Boston: Houghton Mifflin, 1970.

Becker, H. "Photography and Sociology." *Studies in the Anthropology of Visual Communication* 5 (1974): 3–26.

Birdwhistell, R. L. *Kinesics and Context*. Philadelphia: University of Pennsylvania Press, 1970.

Bower, K. S. "Situationalism in Psychology: An Analysis and Critique." *Psychological Review* 80 (1973) 307–336.

Brandt, R. M. *Studying Behavior in Natural Settings*. New York: Holt, Rinehart and Winston, 1972.

Brannigan, C. R., and Humphries, D. A. "Human Non-verbal Behavior: A Means of Communication." In N. Blurton-Jones (ed.), *Ethological Studies of Infant Behavior*. Cambridge: Cambridge University Press, 1971.

Buehler, R. E., and Richmond, J. F. "Interpersonal Communication Behavior Analysis: A Research Method." *Journal of Communication* 13 (1963): 146–155.

Collier, J. *Visual Anthropology: Photography as a Research Method*. New York: Holt, Rinehart and Winston, 1967.

Condon, W. S. "Method of Microanalysis of Sound Film of Behavior," *Behavior Research Methods and Instrumentation* 2 (1970): 51–54.

Condon, W. S., and Ogston, W. D. "Sound Film Analysis of Normal and Pathological Behavior Patterns." *Journal of Nervous and Mental Disease* 143 (1966): 338–346.

Cranach, M. von, and Ellgring, J. H. "Problems in the Recognition of Gaze Direction." In M. von Cranach and I. Vine (eds.), *Social Communication and Movement*. New York: Academic Press, 1973.

Dierssen, G., Lorenc, M., and Spitalerl, R. M. "A New Method for Graphic Study of Human Movements." *Neurology* 2 (1961): 610–618.

Duncan, S. "Nonverbal Communication." *Psychological Bulletin* 72 (1969): 118–137.

Duncan, S., and Fiske, D. W. *Face-To-Face Interaction: Research, Methods, and Theory.* Hillsdale, N.J.: Lawrence Erlbaum Associates, 1977.

Efron, D. *Gesture, Race and Culture.* The Hague: Mouton, 1972.

Ekman, P. "A Methodological Discussion of Nonverbal Bahavior." *Journal of Psychology* 53 (1957): 141–149.

Ekman, P., and Friesen, W. V. "A Tool for the Analysis of Motion Picture Film or Video Tape." *American Psychologist* 24 (1969): 240–243.

Ekman, P., and Friesen, W. V. "Measuring Facial Movement." *Environmental Psychology and Nonverbal Behavior* 1 (1976): 56–75.

Ekman, P., Friesen, W. V., and Taussig, T. "VID-R and SCAN: Tools and Methods in the Analysis of Facial Expression and Body Movement." In G. Gerbner, O. Holsti, K. Krippendorff, W. Paisley, and P. Stone (eds.), *Content Analysis.* New York: Wiley, 1969.

Ekman, P., Friesen, W. V., and Tomkins, S. S. "Facial Affect Scoring Technique: A First Validity Study." *Semiotica* 3 (1971): 37–58.

Filstead, W. J. (ed.). *Qualitative Methodology.* Chicago: Markham Publishing Co., 1970.

Frahm, J. "Verbal-Nonverbal Interaction Analysis: Exploring a New Methodology for Quantifying Dyadic Communication Systems." Ph.D. dissertation, Michigan State University, 1970.

Frey, S., and Cranach, M. von. "A Method for the Assessment of Body Movement Variability." In M. von Cranach and I. Vine (eds.), *Social Communication and Movement.* New York: Academic Press, 1973.

Gardiner, J. C. "A Synthesis of Experimental Studies of Speech Communication Feedback." *Journal of Communication* 21 (1971): 17–35.

Goffman, E. *Frame Analysis.* New York: Harper and Row, 1974.

Grant, B. M., and Hennings, D. G. *The Teacher Moves: An Analysis of Nonverbal Activity.* New York: Columbia Teachers College Press, 1971.

Haggard, E. A., and Issacs, K. S. "Micromomentary Facial Expressions as Indicators of Ego Mechanisms in Psychotherapy." In L. A. Gottschalk and A. H. Auerbach (eds.), *Methods of Research in Psychotherapy.* New York: Appleton-Century-Crofts, 1966.

Hall, E. T. "A System for the Notation of Proxemic Behavior." *American Anthropologist* 65 (1963): 1003–1026.

Hall, E. T. *Handbook of Proxemic Research.* Washington: Society for the Anthropology of Visual Communication, 1974.

Hastorf, A. H., Schneider, D. J., and Polefka, J. *Person Perception.* Reading, Mass.: Addison-Wesley, 1970.

Observing and Recording Nonverbal Behavior

Hutchinson, A. *Labanotation: The System of Analyzing and Recording Movement.* New York: Theatre Arts Books, 1970.

Ing, D. "Proxemics Simulation: A Validation Study of Observer Error." Unpublished Ph.D. dissertation, University of Oregon, 1974.

Jones, E. E., and Davis, K. E. "From Acts to Dispositions: The Attribution Process in Person Perception." In L. Berkowitz (ed.), *Advances in Experimental Social Psychology,* Vol. 2. New York: Academic Press, 1965.

Jones, E. E., and Nisbett, R. E. "The Actor and the Observer: Divergent Perceptions of the Causes of Behavior." In E. E. Jones et al. (eds.), *Attribution: Perceiving the Causes of Behavior.* Norristown, N.J.: General Learning Press, 1972.

Jones, F. P., and Hanson, J. A. "Time-Space Pattern in a Gross Body Movement." *Perceptual and Motor Skills* 12 (1961): 35–41.

Jones, F. P., and Nara, M. "Interrupted Light Photography to Record the Effect of Changes in the Poise of the Head upon Patterns of Movement and Posture in Man." *Journal of Psychology* 40 (1955): 125–131.

Jones, F. P., O'Connell, D. N., and Hanson, J. A. "Color-Coded Multiple Image Photography for Studying Related Rates of Movement." *Journal of Psychology* 45 (1958): 247–251.

Kelley, H. H. "The Processes of Causal Attribution." *American Psychologist* 28 (1973): 107–128.

Kendon, A. "Some Theoretical and Methodological Aspects of the Use of Film in the Study of Social Interaction." In G. P. Ginsburg (ed.), *Emerging Strategies in Social Psychological Research.* New York: Wiley, in press.

Kendon, A., and Ex, J. "Progress Report of an Investigation into Aspects of the Structure and Function of the Social Performance in Two-Person Encounters." Cited in M. Argyle, *Social Interaction.* New York: Atherton, 1969. Pp. 102; 123–126; 463.

Lofland, J. *Analyzing Social Settings.* Belmont, Calif.: Wadsworth, 1971.

Mehrabian, A. "Methods and Designs: Some Referents and Measures of Nonverbal Behavior." *Behavior Research Methods and Instrumentation* 1 (1969): 203–207.

Milgram, S. "The Image-Freezing Machine." *Psychology Today* 10 (1977): 50, 52, 54, 108.

Newtson, D. "Attribution and the Unit of Perception of Ongoing Behavior." *Journal of Personality and Social Psychology* 28 (1973): 28–38.

Olson, J. N., Barefoot, J. C., and Strickland, L. H. "What the Shadow Knows: Person Perception in a Surveillance Situation." *Journal of Personality and Social Psychology* 34 (1976): 583–589.

Paisley, W. "Identifying the Unknown Communicator in Painting and Music: The Significance of Minor Encoding Habits." *Journal of Communication* 14 (1964): 219–237.

Pittenger, R. E., Hockett, C. F., and Danehy, J. J. *The First Five Minutes*. Ithaca, N.Y.: Martineau, 1960.

Reiss, A. J. "Systematic Observation of Natural Social Phenomena." In H. L. Costner (ed.), *Sociological Methodology*. San Francisco: Jossey-Bass, 1971.

Sainesbury, P. A. "A Method of Recording Spontaneous Movements by Time–Sampling Motion Pictures." *Journal of Mental Science* 100 (1954): 742–748.

Scheflen, A. E. "Natural History Method in Psychotherapy: Communicational Research." In L. A. Gottschalk and A. H. Auerbach (eds.), *Methods of Research in Psychotherapy*. New York: Appleton-Century-Crofts, 1966.

Scheflen, A. E., Kendon, A., and Schaeffer, J. "A Comparison of Videotape and Moving Picture Film in Research in Human Communication." In M. M. Berger (ed.), *Videotape Techniques in Psychiatric Training and Treatment*. New York: R. Brunner, Inc., 1970.

Shannon, A. "Facial Expression of Emotion: Recognition Patterns in Schizophrenics and Depressives." *Proceedings: 1971 ANA Research Conference*. New York: American Nurses' Association, 1971.

Smith, R. L., McPhail, C., and Pickens, R. G. "Reactivity to Systematic Observation with Film: A Field Experiment." *Sociometry* 38 (1975).

Speier, M. *How to Observe Face-to-Face Communication: A Sociological Introduction*. Pacific Palisades, Calif.: Goodyear Publishing Co., 1973.

Targiuri, R. "Person Perception." In G. Lindzey and E. Aronson (eds.), *The Handbook of Social Psychology*, Vol. 3. Reading, Mass.: Addison-Wesley, 1969.

Taylor, S. E., and Koivumaki, J. H. "The Perception of Self and Others: Acquaintanceship, Affect, and Actor-Observer Differences." *Journal of Personality and Social Psychology* 33 (1976): 403–408.

Trager, G. L. "Paralanguage: A First Approximation." *Studies in Linguistics* 13 (1958): 1–12.

Wachtel, P. L. "An Approach to the Study of Body Language in Psychotherapy." *Psychotherapy* 4 (1967): 97–100.

Watson, O. M., and Graves, T. D. "Quantitative Research in Proxemic Behavior." *American Anthropologist* 68 (1966): 971–985.

Webb, E. J., Campbell, D. T., Schwartz, R. D., and Sechrest, L. *Unobtrusive Measures*. Chicago: Rand McNally, 1966.

Weick, K. E. "Systematic Observational Methods." In G. Lindzey and E. Aronson (eds.), *Handbook of Social Psychology* (2nd edition), Vol 2. Reading, Mass.: Addison-Wesley, 1968. Pp. 357–451.

Whiteside, T. C. D., Graybill, A., and Niven, J. I. "Visual Illusions of Movement." *Brain* 88 (1965): 193–211.

Zelditch, M. "Some Methodological Problems of Field Studies." *American Journal of Sociology* 67 (1962): 566–576.

12 The Ability to Send and Receive Nonverbal Signals

Americans are characteristically illiterate in the area of gesture language.
W. LA BARRE

As we noted in the first chapter of this book, the subject of non-verbal communication has received a great deal of attention in the last decade. Elementary, secondary, and college students are exposed to entire courses devoted to an understanding of nonverbal behavior; adults can purchase any number of books and pamphlets at local newsstands which, with varying degrees of fidelity, introduce readers to this fascinating world without words. Thus, it is reasonable to assume that contemporary Americans are not non-verbally "illiterate." However, as we look around, we readily note that there are some people who seem to be more sensitive to nonverbal cues than others; some people seem more proficient at expressing their feelings and attitudes nonverbally. And, it is eminently clear that the ability to send and receive these nonverbal cues accurately, like verbal cues, is essential for developing social competence—whether it is in the office, the courtroom, the barroom, the bedroom, or whether we want to effectively bridge gaps in social class and/or culture. If we accept the premise that one's ability to communicate nonverbal messages is important and that some are more effective than others, we might legitimately ask: How did these people become effective? and Can the same ability be developed in others?

While the foregoing questions seem simple enough, there are many related questions which add to the complexity of the issue and prohibit any easy, uncomplicated answer. First, are we talking about sending ability or receiving ability? If you are proficient at sending, does this automatically mean you will also be a sensitive decoder of nonverbal cues? Immediately, then, we are faced with the question of whether we are talking about a single skill or several separate skills. This issue is inherent in most of the following questions too—even though the singular form of the word *ability* is used throughout. Second, are we talking about an ability which manifests itself with a particular channel (face, space, voice, touch) or an ability related to various combinations of channels—for example, facial plus vocal cues? Third, are we talking about an ability which applies to all nonverbal messages or just specific types—for example, messages for specific emotions (angry, sad), messages for general affect (pleasant, unpleasant), or attitudinal messages (dominant, submissive)? Fourth, are we talking about an ability for which there are common standards for judging success? For instance, are we looking for similarities between the intended message sent and the message understood by the receiver? Are we comparing one's performance against norms developed from others? Or are we applying different standards for different age and cultural groups? Fifth, can we measure this ability by one or many methods—physiological, verbal, paper-and-pencil methods, nonverbal response forms, self reports, and the like. Sixth, are we talking about an ability which transcends specific situations or one which applies to many situations—public vs. private situations? posed vs. spontaneous situations? meeting a course requirement vs. defending yourself in court? And finally, are we talking about an ability which transcends different communication partners? That is, will we manifest a similar level of competence in interactions with superiors, subordinates, peers, intimates, strangers?

The preceding is an almost staggering list of questions and the answers, as we might expect from a relatively new field of study, are limited. With any area of study, the researchers first tackle questions related to the nature of the phenomena; then, training and skill development programs can be established and grounded on these findings. Before we report studies which have tried to answer some of these specific questions surrounding one's ability to communicate nonverbally, we will briefly look at some conventional methods of developing social skills—with a special concern for nonverbal skill development.

Methods for Developing Nonverbal Skills

Most of the ability we now have in sending and receiving nonverbal signals is derived from "on-the-job training"—with the job, in this case, referring to the process of daily living. In short, we learn (not always consciously) nonverbal skills by imitating and modeling ourselves after others and by adapting our responses to the coaching, feedback, and advice of others. This feedback is not necessarily "about" our behavior but often takes the form of a response to our behavior. Feedback, then, may refer to a person who says, "Well, you don't *look* happy" or, without making such a statement, your partner may just respond to you as a person who isn't happy. Through feedback we increase our awareness of ourselves *and others*—for example, "Can't you see I don't like you!" We not only learn what behaviors to enact, but how they are performed, with whom, when, where, and with what consequences. Naturally, some of us have more and better "helpers" than others; some of us seek help more than others. You can practice nonverbal sending and receiving frequently, but without regular, accurate feedback, you may not improve your ability.

Although our primary focus has been on interpersonal feedback, we also know that audience feedback to public speakers can also alter nonverbal behavior if it is perceived. Speaker fluency, utterance rate, length of speaking, voice loudness, stage fright, eye gaze and movement may all be affected by perceived positive or negative audience feedback.[1] One study suggests that the sex of the person observing is not as crucial a variable in accurately perceiving nonverbal audience feedback as the sex of the audience members.[2] Female audience members' attitudes were more often judged accurately than males'. The question of sex differences in sending and receiving ability will be examined in more detail later in this chapter.

So, one source of developing your nonverbal skills resides in the feedback you receive from others and your sensitivity and receptivity to it. Ironically, some feedback will be in the form of subtle nonverbal cues—the very thing you are trying to learn. Nevertheless, situations which provide you with an opportunity for feedback and interpersonal "coaching" will certainly be preferred over situations where feedback is minimal, coaching is inhibited, and your receptivity to feedback is low.

Another popular method for teaching any social skill is through role-playing. Usually a situation is presented and the learner attempts to behave in a manner which would approximate his or her behavior if this situation actually occurred. In Stanislavsky's method of teaching acting, for instance, students may improvise various kinds of walks—walking impatiently, walking to pass time, walking to annoy people living in an apartment below you, and so on. L. A. Longfellow's game "Body Talk: A Game of Feeling and Expression" is a

[1]J. C. Gardiner, "A Synthesis of Experimental Studies of Speech Communication Feedback," *Journal of Communication* 21 (1971): 17–35.

[2]H. J. Ayres, "A Baseline Study of Nonverbal Feedback: Observers' Judgments of Audience Members' Attitudes," unpublished Ph.D. dissertation, University of Utah, 1970.

The Ability to Send and Receive Nonverbal Signals

modified role-playing experience.[3] Players try to communicate various emotions listed on cards using either the hand, the head, or the whole body and a condition called "interpersonal" which allows the player to use another person and sounds—but not words. Accuracy in communicating feelings such as love, hate, loneliness, hope, anger, shyness, and the like, and accuracy in interpreting the communications of others enables you to "win" the game—and I suppose, theoretically improve your nonverbal skills. But, we don't know. Role-playing and other exercises which make the learner an active participant are familiar fare in sensitivity groups and body-awareness workshops.[4] Some even contend that participants in such groups make great gains in their sensitivity to their own and others' nonverbal behavior. Objective data is difficult to obtain, but some people undoubtedly learn much from such experiences. Most of the evidence for the effectiveness of these workshops, however, is derived from testimony given by the participants. Thus, we must wonder about those participants who chose not to testify; and of those who testified, how much of their self-perceived learning was due to the reduction of cognitive dissonance?—that is, how much of the positive evaluations about role-playing a mother comforting a child, touching others, baring your body to strangers, and the like, is due to a need to justify the time, effort, and psychological output expended?

Various media have also been used in nonverbal skill development. Several well-known scholars in nonverbal behavior have found videotaped playbacks to be useful in developing nonverbal awareness—Birdwhistell, Scheflen, Ekman. Ekman, in a relatively short six-hour training program, has been able to train nurses to accurately identify micromomentary facial expressions. Jecker, Maccoby, and Breitrose claim success in improving the accuracy with which teachers could judge student "understanding" from short films.[5] The training consisted of four sessions of approximately two hours each during which the attention of the trainees was focused on the gestures and facial expressions which accompanied "understanding." Teachers were tested on one series of films prior to the course, trained with another set of films, and posttested with still a third set of films. Control groups receiving no training did not improve in their recognition of these cues. Davitz found that accuracy in identifying emotions from tape-recorded speeches with "neutral" content could be improved by training.

[3]*Psychology Today* 4 (1970): 45–54.

[4]Some of these exercises are found in J. W. Pfeiffer and J. E. Jones, *A Handbook of Structured Experiences for Human Relations Training* (Iowa City, Iowa: University Associates, 1969–1970); Vol. 1, pp. 109–111; Vol. 2, pp. 102–104. Participative exercises as well as audiovisual learning aids are found in M. Wiemann and M. L. Knapp, *Instructor's Guide to Nonverbal Communication in Human Interaction* (New York: Holt, Rinehart and Winston, 1978).

[5]J. D. Jecker, N. Maccoby and H. S. Breitrose, "Improving Accuracy in Interpreting Nonverbal Cues of Comprehension," *Psychology in the Schools* 2 (1965): 239–244.

The Ability to Send and Receive Nonverbal Signals

Michael Argyle has reported a method of developing nonverbal skills which approaches the "global analysis" reported in Chapter 11.[6] Groups of two to five people interact in front of a larger group. Different group members are asked to record only one aspect of verbal and nonverbal behavior—for example, eye gaze, length and number of utterances, interruptions and pauses, facial expressions, and the like. The data from each observer is then assembled, and the whole interaction process is discussed. Field observations could also provide a broader experiential base—for example, using Sommer's schema as a basis for examining seating and spatial patterns in the local library. (Chapter 4).

Finally, some educators and trainers argue for the value of lectures and reading assignments. Certainly the development of any social skill is somewhat mediated by the amount of knowledge obtained in these ways. However, it is difficult to teach people about nonverbal behavior by spoken and written words alone. Secondly, it is difficult to learn any social skill without practice at the skill itself. P. Ekman and W. V. Friesen's *Unmasking the Face* is an attempt to minimize these problems.[7] The book contains many photographs of facial expressions which serve as models for various expressions of emotion—including blends. Test photos are provided for analyzing one's skill at decoding various expressions. In addition, specific methods for analyzing one's encoding ability are also given. Readers are given detailed instructions for making visual records of their own expressions, for obtaining reactions from people who view the photos, for interpreting these reactions from others, and for correcting any errors in encoding.

It should be obvious by this time that there have been few attempts to scientifically measure the degree of improvement derived from various training methods designed to develop nonverbal skills. It is difficult to say what works and what doesn't. Of course, training programs have a variety of goals. Some may wish to refine a very specific movement or expression; others may want to work on larger, coordinated clusters of behavior. And, it is reasonable to assume that different training methods may be necessary for optimum learning of different nonverbal signals—that is, can we develop skills in vocal behavior in the same manner as emblems or proxemics? For now, we must rely on generalities. Ultimately, the development of your nonverbal skills will depend on the following: (1) *Motivation*. The more you desire to learn nonverbal skills, the greater your chances of doing so. Often this will develop when you feel such skills will help improve the nature of your career or personal life. (2) *Attitude*. People enter learning situations with productive or unproductive attitudes—for example, "I *can* do this" vs. "I can't do this" or "This will be fun" vs. "This will be tedious." You may be highly motivated, but unproductive attitudes toward the learning situation will inevitably lessen the learning outcome. (3) *Knowl-*

---

[6]M. Argyle, *Social Interaction* (New York: Atherton, 1969), p. 415.
[7]Englewood Cliffs, N.J.: Prentice-Hall, 1975.

The Ability to Send and Receive Nonverbal Signals

edge. The development or refinement of any skill is partly dependent on an understanding of the nature of that skill. True, we seem to unconsciously obtain a lot of nonverbal knowledge from watching others as we develop. Some of this knowledge we have is only known to ourselves when we hear or read about it from another source. This "consciousness-raising" may be an important ingredient in making future nonverbal adaptations. (4) *Experience.* Skills cannot be learned in isolation. With the proper guidance and useful feedback, practice will assist you in developing nonverbal skills. The greater the variety of one's experiences, the greater the opportunities for increased learning. Any given experience may provide useful information for future skill development even if you are ineffective in that particular situation.

Students frequently ask me whether all these attempts to learn about and develop skills in nonverbal communication won't have negative consequences. They wonder whether we'll know "too much" about others for our own good, whether those who have this information might use it to manipulate others for self-serving ends. Consider a parallel case in the area of study known as "persuasion." We could also be fearful of learning too much, and we've seen how some people have tried to control and manipulate others without regard for their welfare, as in brainwashing. Unfortunately, there are people with misguided intentions found in any area of study. However, we've been studying persuasion for over two thousand years and it does not appear that anyone has become so sophisticated that he or she invariably succeeds in persuading anyone in any situation. Furthermore, it is the nature of human adaptation to change behavior when it becomes unproductive. If people who know more about nonverbal behavior are using it "against" others, I suspect it won't be long before we see attempts to expose these activities and, if that doesn't stop it, behavioral changes will follow.

With this overview of some common methods and some general prerequisites for nonverbal skill development, we will now turn to another approach to the same issue. This approach seeks to understand the characteristics of people who are effective or ineffective senders and receivers of nonverbal signals. Most of the research relevant to nonverbal skills has been conducted within this framework.

Profiles of Nonverbal Senders and Receivers

There are a variety of methods used to test a person's nonverbal abilities. For encoding or sending ability, the person is usually asked to record a sentence or series of letters while expressing different emotional/attitudinal states. For facial encoding, the person is asked to facially express a series of

The Ability to Send and Receive Nonverbal Signals

emotional and/or attitudinal states. Buck shows a series of "emotionally loaded" color slides to his subjects which are categorized as scenic, sexual, maternal, unpleasant, and unusual.[8] Facial reactions to the slides can then be assessed. In this case, then, "senders" probably differ in the degree of conscious intent from senders who are asked to portray a particular expression. We will discuss this issue of posed vs. spontaneous behavior later in this chapter. Decoding or receiving ability is usually assessed by asking people to identify the emotional or attitudinal state expressed by another person—either "live" or on film, video tape, photograph, or audio recording. Social psychologist Robert Rosenthal and his associates have developed what is perhaps the most comprehensive method for testing nonverbal decoding ability, which he calls the Profile of Nonverbal Sensitivity (PONS).[9] The PONS test is a forty-five-minute black and white sound film. It contains 220 numbered auditory and visual segments which viewers are asked to respond to. Each segment is a two-second excerpt from a scene portrayed by an American woman. There are five scenes which portray a positive-dominant affect or attitude—for example, "admiring a baby"; five which portray positive-submissive behavior, such as "being interviewed for a job"; five which portray negative-dominant, such as "angry at someone for making a mess"; and five which portray negative-submissive—for example "showing someone that your feelings have been hurt." Each scene is presented to viewers in eleven different ways:

Face only
Body only (neck to knees)
Face plus body
Electronically filtered speech only*
Randomized splicing of speech only*
Face plus electronically filtered speech
Face plus randomized splicing of speech
Body plus electronically filtered speech
Body plus randomized splicing of speech
Face and body plus electronically filtered speech
Face and body plus randomized splicing of speech

Thus, a receiver or viewer obtains a score for particular channels and combinations of channels in addition to a total score. The test has been administered to

[8]R. Buck, R. E. Miller, and W. F. Caul, "Sex, Personality and Physiological Variables in the Communication of Affect via Facial Expression," *Journal of Personality and Social Psychology* 30 (1974): 587–596.

[9]R. Rosenthal, D. Archer, M. R. DiMatteo, J. H. Koivumaki, and P. L. Rogers, "Measuring Sensitivity to Nonverbal Communication: The PONS Test," Unpublished manuscript, Harvard University, 1975.

*See Chapter 10 for descriptions of these techniques.

The Ability to Send and Receive Nonverbal Signals

several thousand people of different ages, occupations, and nationalities. For this reason, we will use the results of the PONS test as the primary basis for answering our questions about decoding abilities: (1) What are the characteristics of people who are skilled at receiving nonverbal signals? and (2) what factors affect the accuracy with which people receive nonverbal signals?

Characteristics of Skilled Nonverbal Receivers. Perhaps the most consistent finding, from PONS and other research efforts, is that females tend to score higher than males. This is true from grade school up through the middle twenties. Rosenthal examined forty-three independent studies of adults and children and found females to have an advantage in judging ability in thirty-three of them. Although some studies show no differences between male and female nonverbal receiving ability, rarely do males, as a group, score higher.

Age has also been studied and generally shows a gradually increasing skill at decoding nonverbal cues from kindergarten until it levels off between ages twenty and thirty. Older age groups have not been tested. Independent studies of the ability to accurately decode vocal cues[10] and facial expressions[11] support the PONS results. Typically, younger children will score better on tests of vocal discriminations than on visual ones.

In two studies, the race of the receiver did not provide any particular advantage or disadvantage in accurately judging facial expressions.[12] The results from several groups of students who took the PONS test tend to refute the notion that intelligence or academic ability characterizes effective nonverbal receivers. Neither I.Q., SAT (Scholastic Aptitude Test) scores, class rank, nor scores on vocabulary tests had much relationship to this nonverbal ability. Thus, you may do well in school, where most criteria for success are based on verbal ability, but this doesn't mean you will also be able to accurately interpret nonverbal signals.

People who do well on the PONS test also seem to have the following personality profile: better adjusted, more interpersonally democratic and encouraging, less dogmatic, and more extroverted. In addition, skilled nonverbal receivers were judged more popular and interpersonally sensitive by others, such as acquaintances, clients, spouses, and supervisors. Snyder would probably include what he calls "self-monitoring" as a characteristic of accurate

---

[10]L. Dimitrovsky, "The Ability to Identify the Emotional Meaning of Vocal Expressions at Successive Age Levels," in J. R. Davitz (ed.), *The Communication of Emotional Meaning* (New York: McGraw-Hill, 1964).

[11]G. S. Gates, "A Test for Ability to Interpret Facial Expressions," *Psychological Bulletin* 22 (1925): 120; and M. L. Hamilton, "Imitative Behavior and Expressive Ability in Facial Expressions of Emotions," *Developmental Psychology* 8 (1973): 138.

[12]Gates, ibid.; and R. Eiland and D. Richardson, "The Influence of Race, Sex and Age on Judgments of Emotion Portrayed in Photographs," *Communication Monographs* 3 (1976): 167–175.

The Ability to Send and Receive Nonverbal Signals

decoders of nonverbal information in both face and voice.[13] Self-monitors are sensitive to and exert strong control over their own behavior, but they are also sensitive to the behaviors of others—using these cues as guidelines for monitoring their own self-presentation.

Certain occupational groups also tend to have better scores on the PONS decoding experience. In order, the top three groups tested so far include actors, students studying nonverbal behavior, and students studying visual arts. Buck's research on the interpretation of facial expressions found students who were fine arts majors and business majors to be better receivers than science majors—that is, students in biology, chemistry, math, and physics.[14] Business executives who took the PONS test didn't seem to show the same expertise that Buck's business majors did. Business executives and teachers showed significantly less ability than clinical psychologists and college students, who were significantly lower than the top three groups previously mentioned. Don't forget that these are group scores. Individual teachers, supervisors, and clinicians who were rated excellent at their job also did well on the PONS instrument. Finally, it seems that parents (particularly mothers) of preverbal children have more nonverbal receiving sensitivity than married nonparents.

The PONS has also been administered to people from over twenty different nations. As might be expected, people from countries most similar to the United States in language and culture (modernization, widespread use of communications media) scored highest. Some of the scores from foreign nations were high enough, however, to suggest a multicultural component. In a related venture, word-free voice samples of Cree Indians and white, English-speaking Canadian residents were also judged along ethnic and cultural lines.[15] Each group was more accurate in perceiving the emotional content in the voice samples made by members of their own group. As we've stated in earlier chapters, some cultures use and pay more attention to certain types of nonverbal behavior and would naturally be expected to show more proficiency in those areas than a culture which de-emphasized a particular behavior or channel of communication.

Although a vast amount of research suggests that similarity rather than dissimilarity is the key to selecting friends and romantic partners, Rosenthal and his colleagues found what seems to be an interesting exception. Romantic partners were more similar on their PONS scores to randomly selected peers

[13]M. Snyder, "Self-Monitoring of Expressive Behavior," *Journal of Personality and Social Psychology* 30 (1974): 526–537.

[14]R. Buck, "A Test of Nonverbal Receiving Ability: Preliminary Studies," *Human Communication Research* 2 (1976): 162–171.

[15]D. C. Albas, K. W. McCluskey, and C. A. Albas, "Perception of the Emotional Content of Speech: A Comparison of Two Canadian Groups," *Journal of Cross Cultural Psychology* 7 (1976): 481–490.

The Ability to Send and Receive Nonverbal Signals

than they were to each other! And, the more dissimilarity in nonverbal sensitivity, the greater the level of reciprocal verbal disclosures, suggesting that effectiveness in the verbal modality may be used to offset a lack of proficiency in the nonverbal mode. Some people argue that differences of this type are related to the dependency shown in the relationship, with the more dependent member showing more sensitivity because he or she has the most to gain. Although this finding is intriguing, we don't know how much of a difference will affect the relationship's stability. Most authors have predicted an increased reliance on nonverbal cues and an increased proficiency of reading them with a specific other person in a long-term, intimate relationship.[16]

There is also some indication that people can improve their scores in receiving ability on the PONS with practice. And one study suggests that physiological arousal may be advantageous for judging emotions in the faces of others.[17] Passive receivers, then, seem to be less effective than those who get actively involved in the task.

Like any skill, nonverbal decoding ability is affected by any number of factors. Some of these factors reside within the characteristics of people which reveal differences between groups of people. Some of the factors which affect one's skill reside within the person being judged or the situation where the judging takes place. The following review considers only those factors which have been examined by researchers using PONS or other tests and does not pretend to detail all the potential sources of variations in one's accuracy in identifying nonverbal signals.

Factors Affecting Nonverbal Receiving Accuracy. You may think that the particular channels (face, voice, and the like) that are tested will make a difference in a person's nonverbal receiving accuracy. Indeed, several studies do show that emotions and attitudes of liking/disliking are more accurately perceived in the face than in the voice. And, although you may be better able to recognize many emotions and attitudes if you get both audio and visual cues, some messages may be more effectively communicated in one mode than another—for example, vocal cues may be more effective for communicating anxiety and seductiveness than other individual communication channels.[18] Furthermore, it seems that if you are accurate in recognizing facial signals, you will also be accurate in perceiving vocal ones. This does not deny the possibility that some people may have a preference for and rely more heavily on a particular channel. Beldoch's work extended beyond the traditional facial/

[16]M. L. Knapp, *Social Intercourse: From Greeting to Goodbye* (Boston: Allyn & Bacon, 1978).

[17]J. T. Lanzetta and R. E. Kleck, "Encoding and Decoding of Nonverbal Affect in Humans," *Journal of Personality and Social Psychology* 16 (1970): 12–19.

[18]K. L. Burns and E. G. Beier, "Significance of Vocal and Visual Channels in the Decoding of Emotional Meaning," *Journal of Communication* 23 (1973): 118–130.

The Ability to Send and Receive Nonverbal Signals

vocal dichotomy.[19] He obtained word-free tape recordings of twelve emotions, asked musicians to write and record short musical renditions of the same twelve emotions, and, finally, asked artists to create abstract art which they felt captured the emotions under consideration. The results support the idea that one's ability to accurately decode feelings in one medium may carry over to other media. Similarly, accuracy may vary according to whether expressions are posed (usually higher) or spontaneous, but if you do well in decoding one, you'll probably do well in the other.[20] Some preliminary work with a still-photo version of the original PONS indicates the possibility that a person skilled in one may be skilled in the other. It is clear that some emotional and attitudinal states are more difficult to judge than others. Negative nonverbal messages, some argue, may even be more readily conveyed than positive ones. Gubar says that if you (as a judge) have had prior experience in the expression-inducing situation, your accuracy will supersede those who have not had such experiences.[21] Thus, we find variations in accuracy attributable to the channel of communication and the type of message, but we also find several indications of individual consistency across conditions.

Although Eiland and Richardson found that differences in the sex, age, and race of the person expressing a facial emotion would significantly affect judgments of accuracy, this is not a consistent finding.[22]

We might also speculate, as did the PONS researchers, that the amount of time a receiver was exposed to a nonverbal signal would affect his or her accuracy in identification. The PONS materials were presented to people with the exposure time varied—for example, 1/24 of a second, 3/24 of a second, and so on. While accuracy did increase as exposure time increased, these differences are probably minimal when exposure times reach higher levels. There are some people, it seems, who achieve high levels of accuracy with minimal exposure time. They perceive and process this nonverbal information very quickly. It is even speculated that these persons may "see too much" and have less satisfying interpersonal relationships because of it.

Now that we have examined decoding abilities, we can turn to our next two questions—focusing on encoding or sending ability: (1) What are the charac-

---

[19]M. Beldoch, "Sensitivity to Expression of Emotional Meaning in Three Modes of Communication," in J. R. Davitz (ed.), *The Communication of Emotional Meaning* (New York: McGraw-Hill, 1964).

[20]M. Zuckerman, J. A. Hall, R. S. DeFrank, and R. Rosenthal, "Encoding and Decoding of Spontaneous and Posed Facial Expressions," *Journal of Personality and Social Psychology* 34 (1977): 966–977.

[21]G. Guber, "Recognition of Human Facial Expressions Judged Live in a Laboratory Setting," *Journal of Personality and Social Psychology* 4 (1966): 108–111.

[22]R. Eiland and D. Richardson, "The Influence of Race, Sex and Age on Judgments of Emotion Portrayed in Photographs," *Communication Monographs* 43 (1976): 167–175.

The Ability to Send and Receive Nonverbal Signals

teristics of people who are skilled at sending nonverbal signals? and (2) what factors affect the accuracy with which people send nonverbal signals?

Characteristics of Skilled Nonverbal Senders. Although we do not have the wide-ranging results for encoding patterns which the PONS test gave us for decoding, some trends seem evident. For instance, females also seem to manifest greater encoding skills than males.[23] This sex-related difference in sending ability has not been found with children between four and six years old.[24]

Some personality characteristics have also been associated with accurate senders of nonverbal information. Like receivers, high "self-monitors" are better able to send emotional information through facial and vocal channels.[25] "Internalizers" are poorer stimuli for others to judge than "externalizers."[26] Internalizers are people who tend to repress emotional reactions—to "keep feelings inside." Buck's personality profile for young children shows many of the same characteristics we reviewed earlier for decoders.[27] Children who were effective senders were extroverted, outgoing, active, popular, and somewhat bossy and impulsive. Ineffective senders tended to play alone, were introverted, passive, shy, controlled, and rated as cooperative.

Two studies suggest lower physiological arousal tends to be associated with more accurate nonverbal sending ability.[28]

There have been studies which have addressed the question of what factors will affect nonverbal sending ability, but like the studies of sender characteristics, they are few in number.

Factors Affecting Nonverbal Sending Ability. In a study which obtained both spontaneous and posed expressions from the same people, we learn that accuracy in sending transcends the question of intent.[29] That is, if a person's spontaneous facial expression to pleasant stimuli ("The Carol Burnett Show") and unpleasant stimuli (gory accident scene) was clearly expressed and interpreted, the same person would show skill in performing posed expressions. We also know that the type of message (positive/negative; dominant/submissive;

[23]Buck et al., "Sex, Personality and Physiological Variables . . ."; and S. Zaidel and A. Mehrabian, "The Ability to Communicate and Infer Positive and Negative Attitudes Facially and Vocally," *Journal of Experimental Research in Personality* 3 (1969): 233–241.

[24]R. Buck, "Nonverbal Communication of Affect in Children," *Journal of Personality and Social Psychology* 31 (1975): 644–653.

[25]Snyder, "Self-Monitoring of Expressive Behavior."

[26]R. Buck, V. Savin, R. Miller, and W. Caul, "Communication of Affect Through Facial Expressions in Humans," *Journal of Personality and Social Psychology* 23 (1972): 362–371.

[27]Buck, "Nonverbal Communication of Affect in Children."

[28]Lanzetta and Kleck, "Encoding and Decoding of Verbal Affect in Humans"; and Buck et al., "Sex, Personality and Physiological Variables . . .".

[29]Zuckerman et al., "Encoding and Decoding of Spontaneous and Posed Facial Expressions."

The Ability to Send and Receive Nonverbal Signals

type of emotion) will affect one's accuracy in sending, with the more extreme emotional experiences often being more accurate.

At this point, we are ready to address the final question for this chapter: Are skilled encoders also skilled decoders and vice versa?

The Relationship Between Sending and Receiving Skills. As far back as 1945, Knower reported evidence which suggested that effective senders of facial and vocal expressions of emotions were also effective receivers.[30] Since then, several other studies have reported a similar conclusion. Levy, for instance, found a strong relationship between one's ability to send vocal emotional signals, to interpret vocal signals of others, and to interpret his or her own vocal cues.[31] These researchers, then, hypothesize a "general communication ability." This means that, although there are separate skills involved in sending and receiving, there also seems to be a general ability which overlaps these separate skills. In other words, effective senders are often effective receivers and vice versa.

There have also been researchers who have found no relationship between sending and receiving ability with nonverbal signals. The study by Lanzetta and Kleck is frequently cited as support for this position because a negative relationship between sending and receiving ability was found—that is, people who were accurate senders were poor receivers and vice versa.[32] College-age males were video-taped as they responded to a series of red and green lights. The red light signaled the advent of a shock. These subjects and others were then asked to discriminate between shock and no-shock trials by viewing the video-taped reactions.

Zuckerman and his associates tried to sort through the studies which supported and denied a relationship between encoding and decoding abilities with nonverbal cues.[33] Their own study of facial and vocal emotions and their analysis of other studies support a general communication ability which is superimposed with abilities related to specific emotions. It seems that studies which do not find sending and receiving skills interrelated tend to measure a single emotion and are more apt to deal with spontaneous expressions. It boils down to this: If a person is skilled at sending, the same person is probably also skilled at receiving (and vice versa), but for any given emotion the person may show very different levels of expertise.

[30]F. H. Knower, "Studies in the Symposium of Voice and Action: V. The Use of Behavioral and Tonal Symbols as Tests of Speaking Achievement," *Journal of Applied Psychology* 29 (1945): 229–235.

[31]P. K. Levy, "The Ability to Express and Perceive Vocal Communication of Feelings," in J. R. Davitz (ed.), *The Communication of Emotional Meaning* (New York: McGraw-Hill, 1964).

[32]Lanzetta and Kleck, "Encoding and Decoding of Verbal Affect in Humans."

[33]M. Zuckerman, M. S. Lipets, J. H. Koivumaki, and R. Rosenthal, "Encoding and Decoding Nonverbal Cues of Emotion," *Journal of Personality and Social Psychology* 32 (1975): 1068–1076.

We should also remember that even though we may demonstrate accuracy in sending and receiving, our receiving skills may be higher than our sending skills. Odom and Lemond speculated that the production of facial expressions, for instance, may never attain the same level of accuracy we have in interpreting facial expressions of emotion.[34] This idea was an outgrowth of their analysis of sending and receiving skills of kindergarten and fifth-grade children. Six of the eight emotions tested with these children showed differences in sending and receiving ability—with sending ability lower.

Summary

This chapter dealt with nonverbal skills—how to develop them and characteristics of people who have such skills. This is an area which is just beginning to receive scientific exploration, and few firm conclusions are forthcoming. We seem to have a pretty good grasp of various methods for developing social skills in general, but specific procedures for developing specific nonverbal skills have received little attention. The first part of this chapter reviewed training methods such as feedback, modeling, coaching, role-playing, sensitivity groups, films and video tapes, observational experiences, lectures and readings. At present, we can only say that nonverbal skill development will accrue with a strong desire or motivation to improve, with positive and productive attitudes toward the learning situation, with an adequate understanding of the knowledge related to nonverbal behavior, and with guided experience and practice in a variety of situations.

The second half of this chapter examined people and conditions associated with effectiveness in nonverbal sending and receiving. Most of the research in this area has focused on questions of decoding or receiving ability. The most comprehensive and widely tested instrument was developed by Robert Rosenthal and his colleagues at Harvard University and is called the Profile of Nonverbal Sensitivity (PONS). The results of this eleven-channel test and other research probes provided the following information about nonverbal receiving skills: (1) As a group, females generally tend to be better decoders than males; (2) decoding skills tend to increase up to the mid-twenties; (3) there seems to be a minimal relationship between intelligence and other verbal measures and nonverbal decoding ability; (4) the personalities of effective decoders seem to reflect extroversion, popularity, self-monitoring and judgments of interpersonal effectiveness by others; (5) actors, students of nonverbal behavior, and students

---

[34]R. D. Odom and C. M. Lemond, "Developmental Differences in the Perception and Production of Facial Expressions," *Child Development* 43 (1972): 359–369.

The Ability to Send and Receive Nonverbal Signals

in visual arts tend to score well on tests of nonverbal decoding ability, but anyone from any occupational group who is rated excellent on his or her job can be expected to do well at nonverbal decoding; (6) tests using facial, body, and vocal stimuli from American subjects tend to elicit the highest scores from cultures most similar to America, but accuracy scores do suggest the possibility of a multicultural component in decoding nonverbal behavior; (7) physiological arousal and practice also seem to improve one's decoding ability. We also discussed how one's accuracy in decoding may vary due to the channel in which the information was presented, whether the expressions were posed or spontaneous, what characteristics the stimulus person had, and how long the behavior was seen or heard. In spite of these possible variations, some evidence suggests that if you are proficient at decoding one channel, you will be proficient in others, and if you are proficient at decoding posed expressions you will be proficient at decoding spontaneous ones.

Our discussion of sending or encoding skills was abbreviated because little empirical work has focused on sending ability. In the little work done so far, we find (1) females are also skilled senders; (2) skilled senders are also extroverted, popular, monitor their own behavior carefully, do not internalize their emotions, and show decreased physiological arousal. Again, if you can send accurate spontaneous expressions there is an indication that you will also accurately send posed expressions—and vice versa.

Generally, "good" encoders are also "good" decoders and vice versa. But for any given emotion a person may show very different sending and receiving abilities. Thus, some have proposed that there is a general communication ability which is superimposed with specific abilities tied to particular message classes.

SELECTED BIBLIOGRAPHY

Albas, D. C., McCluskey, K. W., and Albas, C. A. "Perception of the Emotional Content of Speech: A Comparison of Two Canadian Groups." *Journal of Cross Cultural Psychology* 7 (1976): 481–490.

Beckman, D. R. "Fifth Language Arts: Nonverbal Communication." *Elementary English* 40 (1963): 191–193.

Beier, E. G. "Nonverbal Communication: How We Send Emotional Messages." *Psychology Today* (1974): 53, 55–56.

Beldoch, M. "Sensitivity to Expression of Emotional Meaning in Three Modes of Communication." In J. R. Davitz (ed.), *The Communication of Emotional Meaning* (New York: McGraw-Hill), 1964.

Brooks, W. D., and Strong, J. W. "An Investigation of Improvement in Bodily

Action as a Result of the Basic Course in Speech." *Southern Speech Journal* 33 (1969): 9–15.

Buck, R. "A Test of Nonverbal Receiving Ability: Preliminary Studies." *Human Communication Research* 2 (1976): 162–171.

Buck, R. "Nonverbal Communication of Affect in Children." *Journal of Personality and Social Psychology* 31 (1975): 644–653.

Buck, R. Miller, R. E., and Caul, W. F. "Sex, Personality and Physiological Variables in the Communication of Affect via Facial Expression." *Journal of Personality and Social Psychology* 30 (1974): 587–596.

Buck, R., Savin, V., Miller, R., and Caul, W. "Communication of Affect Through Facial Expressions in Humans." *Journal of Personality and Social Psychology* 23 (1972): 362–371.

Burns, K. L., and Beier, E. G. "Significance of Vocal and Visual Channels in the Decoding of Emotional Meaning." *Journal of Communication* 23 (1973): 118–130.

Collett, P. "Training Englishmen in the Non-verbal Behaviour of Arabs: An Experiment in Intercultural Communication." *International Journal of Psychology* 6 (1971): 209–215.

Davitz, J. R. "Personality, Perceptual, and Cognitive Correlates of Emotional Sensitivity." In J. R. Davitz (ed.), *The Communication of Emotional Meaning.* (New York: McGraw-Hill), 1964.

Davitz, J. R. (ed.), *The Communication of Emotional Meaning.* (New York: McGraw-Hill), 1964.

Dimitrovsky, L. "The Ability to Identify the Emotional Meaning of Vocal Expressions at Successive Age Levels." In J. R. Davitz (ed.), *The Communication of Emotional Meaning.* (New York: McGraw-Hill), 1964.

Eiland, R., and Richardson, D. "The Influence of Race, Sex and Age on Judgments of Emotion Portrayed in Photographs." *Communication Monographs* 43 (1976): 167–175.

Ekman, P., and Friesen, W. V. *Unmasking the Face* (Englewood Cliffs, N.J.: Prentice-Hall), 1975.

Ekman, P., Friesen, W. V., and Ellsworth, P. *Emotion in the Human Face* (Elmsford, N.Y.: Pergamon Press), 1972.

Frijda, N. H. "Recognition of Emotion," In L. Berkowitz (ed.), *Advances in Experimental Social Psychology*, Vol. 4. (New York: Academic Press), 1969.

Gates, G. S. "A Test for Ability to Interpret Facial Expressions." *Psychological Bulletin* 22 (1925): 120.

Gates, G. S. "The Role of the Auditory Element in the Interpretation of Emotions." *Psychological Bulletin* 24 (1927): 175.

Gitter, G., Mostofsky, D., and Quincy, A. "Race and Sex Differences in the Child's Perception of Emotion." *Child Development* 42 (1971): 2071–2075.

The Ability to Send and Receive Nonverbal Signals

426

Guilford, J. P. "An Experiment in Learning to Read Facial Expressions." *Journal of Abnormal Social Psychology* 24 (1929): 191–202.

Hall, J. A., Rosenthal, R., Archer, D., DiMatteo, M. R., and Rogers, P. L. "The Profile of Nonverbal Sensitivity: Toward Understanding the Role of Nonverbal Communication Accuracy in Interpersonal Interaction." *Human Nature* (in press).

Hamilton, M. L. "Imitative Behavior and Expressive Ability in Facial Expressions of Emotions." *Developmental Psychology* 8 (1973): 138.

Hoffman, M. "The Effects of Training on the Judgment of Non-verbal Behavior." Unpublished Ph.D. dissertation, Harvard University, 1964.

Jecker, J. D., Maccoby, N., and Breitrose, H. S. "Improving Accuracy in Interpreting Nonverbal Cues of Comprehension." *Psychology in the Schools* 2 (1965): 239–244.

Kellogg, W. N., and Eagleson, B. M. "The Growth of Social Perception in Different Racial Groups." *Journal of Educational Psychology* 22 (1931): 374–375.

Kier, R. J. and Harter, S. "Children's Ability to Order Facial and Non Facial Continua as a Function of MA, CA, and I.Q." *Journal of Genetic Psychology* 120 (1972): 241–251.

Knower, F. H. "Studies in the Symposium of Voice and Action: V. The Use of Behavioral and Tonal Symbols as Tests of Speaking Achievement." *Journal of Applied Psychology* 29 (1945): 229–235.

Lanzetta, J. T., and Kleck, R. E. "Encoding and Decoding of Nonverbal Affect in Humans." *Journal of Personality and Social Psychology* 16 (1970): 12–19.

Levitt, E. A. "The Relationship Between Abilities to Express Emotional Meanings Vocally and Facially." In J. R. Davitz (ed.), *The Communication of Emotional Meaning* (New York: McGraw-Hill, 1964.

Levy, P. K. "The Ability to Express and Perceive Vocal Communication of Feelings." In J. R. Davitz (ed.), *The Communication of Emotional Meaning* (New York: McGraw-Hill), 1964.

McKnight, P. C. "Micro-teaching in Teacher Training: A Review of Research." *Research in Education* 6 (1971): 24–38.

Mehrabian, A. "Styles and Abilities in Implicit Communication." In A. Mehrabian, *Nonverbal Communication* (Chicago: Aldine-Atherton), 1972. Pp. 133–146.

Odom, R. D., and Lemond, C. M. "Developmental Differences in the Perception and Production of Facial Expressions." *Child Development* 43 (1972): 359–369.

Osgood, C. E. "Dimensionality of the Semantic Space for Communication via Facial Expression." *Scandinavian Journal of Psychology* 7 (1966): 1–30.

Patterson, M. L. "Stability of Nonverbal Immediacy Behaviors." *Journal of Experimental Social Psychology* 9 (1973): 97–109.

Pfeiffer, J. W., and Jones, J. E. *A Handbook of Structured Experiences for*

The Ability to Send and Receive Nonverbal Signals

Human Relations Training (Iowa City, Iowa: University Associates Press), 1969–1970. Vol. 1, Pp. 109–111; Vol. 2, Pp. 102–104.

Rosenthal, R., Archer, D., DiMatteo, M. R., Koivumaki, J., Rogers, P. "Body Talk and Tone of Voice; The Language Without Words." *Psychology Today* 8 (1974): 64–68.

Rosenthal, R., Archer, D., DiMatteo, M. R., Koivumaki, J. H., and Rogers, P. L. "Measuring Sensitivity to Nonverbal Communication: The PONS Test." Unpublished manuscript, Harvard University, 1975.

Shapiro, J. G. "Responsivity to Facial and Linguistic Cues." *Journal of Communication* 18 (1968): 11–17.

Snortum, J., and Ellenhorn, L. "Predicting and Measuring the Psychological Impact of Nonverbal Encounter Techniques." *International Journal of Group Psychotherapy* 24 (1974): 217–228.

Snyder, M. "Self-Monitoring of Expressive Behavior." *Journal of Personality and Social Psychology* 30 (1974): 526–537.

Thompson, D. F., and Meltzer, L. "Communication of Emotional Intent by Facial Expression." *Journal of Abnormal and Social Psychology* 68 (1964): 129–135.

Zaidel, S., and Mehrabian, A. "The Ability to Communicate and Infer Positive and Negative Attitudes Facially and Vocally." *Journal of Experimental Research in Personality* 3 (1969): 233–241.

Zuckerman, M., DeFrank, R. S., Hall, J. A., and Rosenthal, R. "Accuracy of Nonverbal Communication as a Determinant of Experimenter Expectancy Effects." Unpublished manuscript, University of Rochester, 1977.

Zuckerman, M., Hall, J. A., DeFrank, R. S., and Rosenthal, R. "Encoding and Decoding of Spontaneous and Posed Facial Expressions." *Journal of Personality and Social Psychology* 34 (1977): 966–977.

Zuckerman, M., Lipets, M. S., Koivumaki, J. H., and Rosenthal, R. "Encoding and Decoding Nonverbal Cues of Emotion." *Journal of Personality and Social Psychology* 32 (1975): 1068–1076.

Author Index

This index refers the reader only to those authors cited in the text itself. Additional references to these authors and others not cited here can be found in the bibliographies at the end of each chapter.

Bourhis, R. Y., 337
Bowyer, M. D., 337
Bradford, A., 334
Bradford, G., 334
Brandt, J. F., 337
Brannigan, C. R., 266
Breitrose, H. S., 414
Breitrose, M. 33
Brislin, R. W., 158
Brody, E. B., 169
Brommel, B. J., 352
Brooks, W. D., 396
Broughton, A., 302
Broune, V. T., 337
Brown, B. L., 324
Brown, W., 96
Bruneau, T. J., 360
Buck, J., 334
Buck, R., 283, 417, 419, 422
Buehler, R. E., 26
Bugental, D. E., 22, 23
Burgoon, J. K., 124–125
Burns, K. L., 420
Burns, T., 130
Bustos, A. A., 299, 303
Byrne, D., 158, 159

Cahnman, W. J., 166
Calhoun, J. B., 120–121
Campbell, D. T., 379
Campbell, R., 161
Carr, S. J., 99
Caul, W. F., 283, 417, 422
Cavan, S., 103
Cavior, N., 67
Cervenka, E., 202–203
Chaikin, A. L., 35
Channing, H., 166
Chapple, E. D., 358
Charlesworth, W. R., 50, 72
Chase, J., 266
Cheek, F. E., 98
Chevalier-Skolnikoff, S., 52, 56, 57, 58
Choresh, N., 69
Christian, J. J., 120
Christy, L., 284
Clay, V. S., 245
Clement, R., 334
Clifford, M. M., 156
Cline, M., 282
Clore, G. L., 225, 226
Cohen, A. A., 16
Collins, M., 105
Compton, N., 181–182
Condon, W. S., 71, 208–209
Conger, J. C., 160

Conklin, F., 351
Connolly, P. R., 127
Cook, K. V., 70
Cook, M., 29, 133, 136, 137, 138, 139, 296, 335, 354
Coombs, R. H., 157
Cooper, J., 357
Cortes, J. B., 162, 163
Cranach, M. von, 297
Cross, J., 67
Cross, J. F., 67
Curtis, J. F., 330

Dabbs, J. M., 99
Dance, F. E. X., 3, 4
Danehy, J. J., 387
Darwin, C., 27, 74, 380
Davis, D. E., 120
Davis, F., 169, 208, 228, 257–258
Davis, M., 338
Davis, P. B., 339
Davitz, J. R., 28, 341, 343, 345, 414
Davitz, L., 341, 343
Day, M. E., 299
Deabler, H. L., 97
Dean, J., 124, 303
DeFrank, R. S., 283, 421
DeMente, B., 264
Dennis, H. S., 229
Derlega, V. J., 35
Deutsch, M., 105
Diehl, C. F., 350
DiMatteo, M. R., 417
Dimitrovsky, L., 72, 418
Dion, K. K., 67
Dittmann, A. T., 28, 65, 201, 202, 209–210, 219–220
Donecki, P. R., 67
Dornbusch, S., 68
Dosey, M., 129
Draper, P., 123
Drew, C. J., 104
Dukes, W. F., 264
Duncan, S., Jr., 25, 214, 353
Dunhame, R., 283
Dunlap, K., 279, 280

Efran, J. S., 302
Efran, M. G., 156
Efron, D., 27, 202, 220, 390
Eibl-Eibesfeldt, I., 44, 48, 49, 50, 51, 53, 58, 59, 403
Eiland, R., 283, 418, 421
Ekman, P., 6, 10, 13, 15, 17, 21, 24, 27, 28, 29, 31, 45, 62–64, 203, 218, 220, 227, 229, 231, 232, 265, 267, 268, 269, 270, 271,

277, 281, 282, 284, 286, 300, 384, 385, 390, 402, 414
Eldridge, C., 302
Ellgring, J. H., 297
Ellis, D. S., 340
Ellsworth, P., 29, 277, 296
Emmert, P., 396
Erickson, D., 337
Erickson, F., 127
Ex, J., 393
Exline, R. V., 26, 28, 302, 305, 307

Faloultah, E., 155
Fast, J., 28
Fay, P., 338, 339
Fenster, A., 72
Ferber, A., 211–212
Ferris, S. R., 323
Ferror, D., 334
Festinger, L., 105
Fillenbaum, S., 335
Finando, S. J., 118
Finkelstein, J. C., 35
Fisher, J. D., 242
Fisher, M. J., 357
Fiske, D. W., 214
Fitzgerald, H. E., 68
Flanders, N. A., 396
Fode, K., 34
Ford, B., 71
Forston, R. F., 126
Fox, M. N., 22
Frahm, J., 395
Frank, L. K., 28, 245
Frankel, H., 333
Freedman, D. G., 175
Freedman, N., 219, 253–254
Freud, S., 229
Friedman, R. J., 13
Friedrich, G. W., 17, 26, 211
Friesen, W. V., 6, 10, 13, 17, 24, 28, 29, 31, 45, 64, 203, 218, 229, 230, 232, 265, 267, 268, 269, 271, 277, 284, 300, 384, 385, 402, 415

Gadpaille, W. J., 159
Galle, O. R., 122
Gardiner, J. C., 217, 413
Gardner, R. C., 335
Gates, G. S., 72, 418
Gatti, F. M., 162, 163
Gellert, E., 68
Gerbner, G., 402
Gianette, R. M., 22
Gibbins, K., 181
Gilat, Y., 69

Giles, H., 337
Gilliland, A. R., 305–306
Glasgow, G. M., 350
Glass, D. C., 98
Goffman, E., 115, 116, 211, 228, 257, 380
Goldman-Eisler, F., 26, 28, 355, 356, 357
Goldstein, A. M., 72
Goldstein, K., 99
Golomb, C., 67
Goodman, N., 68
Goranson, R. E., 91
Gorman, W., 168
Gottschalk, L. A., 270, 378
Gove, W. R., 122
Grant, B. M., 387
Graves, T. D., 126
Gray, D., 26
Greenacre, P., 294
Griffin, J. H., 169
Griffitt, W., 91
Guardo, C. J., 69
Guber, G., 421
Gumpert, P., 307

Haase, R. F., 227
Hackney, H., 217
Haggard, E. A., 270
Hall, E. T., 11, 27, 30, 69, 94, 114,123–124, 130, 170–171, 387, 389, 390
Hall, J. A., 283, 421
Hamid, P. N., 185
Hamilton, M. L., 418
Hanneman, G. H., 11
Hanley, T. D., 334
Hare, A., 132
Harlow, H. F., 246
Harms, L. S., 340
Harper, L., 70
Harris, R. M., 127, 248, 268, 326
Harrison, R., 16, 26, 29, 31, 284, 395
Hart, C. J., 165
Hart, R. J., 324
Hart, R. P., 17, 26, 212, 229
Harvey, L. A., 338
Hastorf, A., 68
Hawkins, G. J., 351, 352
Hayes, A. S., 326
Hays, E. R., 310
Haythorn, W. W., 116
Hearn, G., 302
Hecker, M. H. L., 327
Heinberg, P., 332
Henley, N. M., 229, 247–248, 306
Hennings, D. G., 387
Herman, J., 283
Heslin, R., 244, 247, 250, 255, 256, 259

Hess, E. H., 28, 29, 309–311, 313–314
Hewes, G. W., 220, 221
Hewgill, M. A., 352
Hickey, C. B., 307
Hockett, C. F., 387
Hodgson, R. C., 335
Hoffman, G. E., 245
Hoffman, S. P., 219
Hollien, H., 339
Holmes, Sherlock, 152
Holsti, O., 402
Hooff, J. A. R. A. M. von, 52
Hook, L., 132
Horai, J., 155
Houck, J. E., 324
Hoult, R., 177–178
Howard, L. R., 67
Howells, L. T., 132
Hughes, K. R., 337
Humphries, D. A., 266
Huntington, E., 92
Hutchinson, A., 387
Hutt, C., 70

Iliffe, A. M., 161
Ingham, R., 297
Irwin, T. K., 91
Isaacs, F. S., 270
Itkin, S., 225, 226
Izard, C. E., 21, 284, 302

Jacobson, L., 33
Jaffe, J., 299
James, J. W., 118
Janisse, M. P., 310
Jecker, J., 33, 414
Jensen, J. V., 360
Johnson, H. G., 203
Johnson, P. A., 68
Johnson, V. E., 246
Jones, J. E., 412
Jones, S., 69, 125, 127
Jourard, S. M., 168, 248, 252

Karabenick, S. A., 68
Kartus, S., 248
Kaswan, J. W., 22, 23
Katz, M. M., 13
Kees, W., 12, 28, 30, 83, 102
Keller, H., 244
Kelley, J., 180
Kendon, A., 28, 127, 209, 211–212, 248, 268, 297, 326, 393
Kenkel, W. F., 157
Kennedy, R., 105
Kessler, J. B., 156
Key, M. R., 127, 248, 268, 326

Kibler, R. J., 350
King, D. 91
King, M. G., 118, 129
Kirman, J. W., 258
Kleck, R., 128, 303, 304, 305, 420, 422, 423
Kleinke, C. L., 299, 303
Klinger, H. N., 350
Klopfer, P. H., 115
Klubeck, S., 132
Knapp, H., 376
Knapp, J. R., 68
Knapp, M. L., 16, 17, 25, 26, 87, 139–140, 212, 214, 229, 353, 414, 420
Knower, F. H., 423
Knowles, E. S., 119, 120
Koivumaki, J. H., 29, 343, 417, 423
Koneya, W., 86
Korn, S. J., 68
Kotsch, W. E., 284
Kotulak, R., 5
Kramer, E., 330–331, 342
Krasher, L., 358
Kreutzer, M. A., 50, 72
Krippendorff, K. 402
Krivonos, P. D., 25, 212
Krout, M., 219
Kulka, R. A., 156
Kumin, L., 66, 202

La Barre, W., 411
Lack, D., 45
Ladefoged, P., 329
Laffal, J., 325
LaFrance, M., 214, 298
Lalljee, M., 354, 356
Lamb, P. F., 154
Lambert, W., 333, 335
Lane, A. B., 281
Lane, H. L., 71
Lanzetta, J. T., 420, 422, 423
Larson, C. E., 139, 140
Larson, C. U., 126
Lass, N. J., 337, 338
Laughery, K. R., 281
Lavrakas, P. J., 160
Lawick-Goodall, J. van, 53
Lazar, M., 66, 202
Lazarus, W., 296
Lee, D., 93
LeFevre, R., 226
Lefkowitz, M., 179
Leipold, W. E., 127
Lemond, C. M., 422
Lenneberg, E., 46
Lerner, R. M., 68
Levin, H., 71

Author Index

432

Author Index

433

Pitcairn, T. K., 44, 48, 58, 60
Pittenger, R. E., 387
Plax, T. G., 182, 310
Polt, J. M., 309
Poyatos, F., 326
Prebor, L. D., 337
Prigge, D. Y., 334
Proctor, R. L., 104

Quitkin, F., 219

Ray, C., 248
Redding, W. C., 167
Reece, M., 26, 224–225
Reed, J. A. P., 184
Reeves, D. L., 245
Reeves, K., 158
Reich, A. R., 330
Rhead, C. C., 105
Rheingold, H. L., 70
Rice, B., 310
Richardson, D., 283, 418, 421
Richardson, S. A., 68
Richman, P., 325
Richmond, J. F., 26
Ricketts, A. F., 73
Rifkin, A., 219
Robin, G. L., 324
Rochester, S. R., 354
Rogers, P. L., 342, 417
Rohe, W., 122
Rohmann, L., 158
Rose, E., 33
Rosenfeld, H., 129, 227
Rosenfeld, L. B., 182, 248
Rosenthal, R., 28, 33, 34, 35, 283, 342, 343,
    417, 418, 419, 421, 423, 424
Ross, H., 100
Rubin, J. E., 252
Rubin, Z., 303
Rubinstein, S., 303
Ruesch, J., 12, 28, 30, 83, 102
Russo, N., 119, 132
Rytting, M., 242

Sachs, J., 337
Sainesbury, P., 219
Saks, M. J., 31
Salitz, R., 204–205
Sander, L. W., 71, 209
Sanders, K. M., 70
Sapir, E., 196
Saslow, G., 358
Satz, P. H., 350
Savin, V., 422
Savitsky, J. C., 284, 285

Saxe, L., 159
Sayles, L. R., 358
Schachter, S., 105
Scheflen, A. E., 28, 29, 36, 209, 215, 225, 226,
    378, 414
Scherer, K. R., 35, 229, 342, 343, 347
Schiffrin, D., 212
Schlien, J. M., 309
Schlosberg, H., 96
Schuette, D., 26
Schulz, R., 128
Schulze, G., 326
Schwartz, J., 178
Schwartz, R. D., 379
Scott, M. B., 117
Seaford, H. W., 268
Sebeok, T. A., 326
Sechrest, L., 379
Secord, P. F., 168, 264, 280
Seltzer, A. L., 309
Sereno, K. K., 351, 352
Shakespeare, W., 263, 322
Shamo, G. W., 334
Shapira, A., 69
Shapiro, J. G., 22, 283
Sheldon, W. H., 27, 163
Sheppard, W. C., 71
Shontz, F. C., 168
Shroeder, C., 68
Shulman, G. M., 17, 26, 212
Shuter, R., 126, 258
Siegel, B., 165
Sigler, E., 35
Silverman, I., 71
Sim, M. E., 285
Singer, J. E., 98, 154
Singh, B. N., 158
Skinner, B. F., 106, 107
Smith, A. J., 255
Smith, W. J., 266
Smythe, M. J., 414
Snortum, J. R., 69
Snyder, J., 335
Snyder, M., 344, 418–419
Solender, E., 156
Solender, E. K., 156
Solomon, D., 22
Sommer, R., 28, 84, 85, 86, 100, 101, 119,
    124, 126, 127, 133, 135–136, 415
Sontag, S., 157
Spitz, R. A., 68
Sroufe, L. A., 73
Staffieri, J. R., 68
Staneski, R. A., 299, 303
Star, S. A., 180
Starkweather, J. A., 341, 342

Author Index

434

Subject Index

Subject Index

437

Leave-taking, 212–213
Leakage, 231
Lighting, behavior and, 99
Linguistic-kinesic analogy, 197–202
Listener responses, 65

Machiavellianism, 154–155, 184, 306, 307, 308
Markers, 210, 215
Mesomorphs, 67–68, 163–166
Microkinesics, 198
Morphemes, 200
Movable objects, communication behavior and, 99–101, 116
Multicultural studies, 58–64, 126–127, 133–136, 257–258, 308–309, 419
Music, behavior and, 98

Natural environment, 89–93
Nature-nurture issue, 44–46
Noise, behavior and, 98
Nonpersons, 93, 251
Nonverbal behavior, 3, 4
  classifying, 12–20, 27
  control over, 29
  developmental perspectives, 44–76
  observation of, 376–406
  primary sources of, 45
  primary uses of, 21–26
  recording, 376–406
Nonverbal information processing, 4–5, 11, 23
Nonverbal signals, ability to send and receive, 411–425
Nonverbal skills, 411–425
  development of, 412–416
  relationship between sending and receiving, 423

Object-adaptors, 17–18
Object language, 12
Objects, movable, communication behavior and, 99–101, 116
Observation of nonverbal behavior, 376–406
Olfactory communication, 169–171, 389
Ontogeny, 45, 65–75
Origins (nonverbal behavior), 44–75
Overpopulation, 120–123

Parakinesic phenomena, 198
Paralanguage, 18–19, 28
  ingredients of, 326–327
Paralinguistic phenomena, 198
Pauses, 355–357
  placement of, 355–356
  reasons for, 357
  types of, 356–357

People, as part of the environment, 93–94
Perceptions, 87–89
  fallibility of, 381–384
Personal characteristics, judgments of, by vocal cues, 336–340
Personal space, 69–70, 114–141
Personality characteristics, 131, 139
Personality judgments, clothes and, 180–185, 305–306, 418, 422
  face and, 263–264
  vocal cues and, 330–336
Persuasion, body, 224
  eyes, 307
  height, 167–168
  vocal cues and, 351–353
Phones, 199
Phylogeny, 45, 47–64
Physical appearance, communication and, 67–68, 152–187
Physical behavior, human communication and, 196–233
Physical characteristics, nonverbal communication and, 18
Politics, televised, nonverbal communication and, 31–33
Posture, 12, 24, 119, 202, 388, 399
Prekinesics, 198
Prevalence of nonverbal communication, 30–31
Primates, nonhuman, nonverbal communication and, 51–58
Privacy, perceptions of, 88
Profile of Nonverbal Sensitivity (PONS), 417–421
Proxemic analysis, 387–390
Proxemics, 19, 27, 69–70, 114–141
Pipillometrics, 29

Race, 105, 126–127, 168–169, 245, 283, 336–337, 418
Receivers of nonverbal signals, ability of, 411–425
Recording of nonverbal behavior, 376–406
Regulating, nonverbal behavior and, 24–26
Regulators, 16–17, 46, 211–218, 265–266, 298–300
Repetition, nonverbal communication and, 21
Research, behavioral, nonverbal communication and, 34–35
Role-playing, 413

Sanpaku, 296
Seating behavior, 131–139
Self-adaptors, 17
Self-description test, 162–163
Self-image, 168

Subject Index